Imperfect Competition and International Trade

MIT Press Readings in Economics
edited by Benjamin Friedman and Lawrence Summers

New Keynesian Economics, 2 vols., edited by N. Gregory Mankiw and David Romer, 1991

Imperfect Competition and International Trade, edited by Gene M. Grossman, 1992

Imperfect Competition and International Trade

edited by Gene M. Grossman

The MIT Press
Cambridge, Massachusetts
London, England

This book was set in Times Roman by Asco Trade Typesetting Ltd., Hong Kong, and was printed and bound in the United States of America.

Library of Congress Cataloging-in-Publication Data

Imperfect competition and international trade / edited by Gene M. Grossman.
p. cm.—(MIT Press readings in economics)
Includes bibliographical references and index.
ISBN 0-262-07140-1 (hc).—ISBN 0-262-57093-9 (pbk.)
1. Competition, Imperfect. 2. International trade. 3. Oligopolies. I. Grossman, Gene M.
II. Series.
HB238.I47 1992
382—dc20 91-44394
CIP

Contents

Contributors

Richard E. Baldwin
Graduate Institute of International Studies, Geneva

Shmuel Ben-Zvi
Tel Aviv University

James A. Brander
University of British Columbia

Avinash K. Dixit
Princeton University

Jonathan Eaton
Boston University

Wilfred J. Ethier
University of Pennsylvania

Gene M. Grossman
Princeton University

Elhanan Helpman
Tel Aviv University

Kala Krishna
Tufts University

Paul R. Krugman
Massachusetts Institute of Technology

James R. Markusen
University of Colorado

Victor Norman
Norwegian School of Economics and Business Administration

Luis A. Rivera-Batiz
University of California at San Diego

Paul M. Romer
University of California at Berkeley

Barbara J. Spencer
University of British Columbia

Anthony J. Venables
University of Southampton

Series Foreword

Economics, like many scientific disciplines, combines deductions from axiomatic principles and inference from empirical observations. Rigorous, logical thinking about the consequences that follow from specified sets of circumstances constitutes the backbone of the subject. But because the primary object of most economic thinking is to gain an understanding of a particular set of circumstances—those characterizing, in whole or in part, the world in which real men and women live, and work, and consume the fruits of their labors—observations of that world provide a way to distinguish which sets of circumstances and consequences (in economists' common parlance, which "models") merit investigation and perhaps even application. To a large extent, progress in the field has historically reflected just this combination of axiomatic deduction and empirical inference. Visible changes in the economic environment suggest new sets of conditions to be analyzed. The resulting model delivers specific implications. Whether those implications do or do not jibe with observed economic phenomena steers researchers either to build on the underlying model—to extend or refine it, or apply it to more specialized situations—or to search for a new model potentially more consistent with observed reality. And so, thinking in economics continues to evolve.

One result of this continuing evolution is that the study of economics, especially at the graduate level, is problematic. What economists "know" depends on when they are supposed to know it. Although the basic principles governing economic behavior presumably have not changed, economic thinking in many subfields of the discipline now differs markedly from what it was in 1970 or 1950 or 1930. (And by 2010 it will almost surely be different than it is today.) No student of economics is well advised to study only developments of the most recent few years, be they conceptual or practical. But especially for those who are learning economics with the hope of advancing the discipline by their own research, it is essential to know where the frontier of the subject lies and what lies on it. Because of the continual and often rapid evolution of thinking that results from the ongoing interaction between axiomatic reasoning and empirical observation, that frontier is, in important ways, a moving target. By the time new advances are fully integrated into textbooks and treatises, their day on the frontier is past. For this reason the student preparing to do economic research must rely to a great extent on new thinking and new findings not yet digested into secondary sources. The MIT Press Readings in Economics series is designed to help students and other potential researchers come rapidly to the frontier by providing carefully selected collections of readings in areas in which rapid progress has recently been made.

This volume edited by Gene M. Grossman brings together the major papers in the large and expanding literature on international trade in the presence of imperfect competition. It has long been recognized that a large part of international trade cannot be credibly explained by differences in national patterns of comparative advantage. Many countries both import and export products in the same narrow industrial classification, counter to the prediction of classical trade theory that nations will specialize in industries where they have a comparative advantage. But systematic work on theories of international trade that can account for the actual pattern of trade is a relatively recent development. It has required analytic tools, many first forged in the context of industrial organization studies, for working with markets in which producers enjoy economies of scale and do not take prices as given. The papers in this volume show just how powerful these tools are for studying both the determinants and the consequences of international trade. Any economist concerned with understanding trade patterns or with making policy recommendations directed at altering them will have to consider their insights.

Benjamin M. Friedman
Lawrence H. Summers

Acknowledgments

I am grateful to Jim Brander, Avinash Dixit, Elhanan Helpman, and Paul Krugman for their comments on the selection of papers for this volume, and to Tracey Bartzak for her help in assembling and preparing the materials. Thanks go also to Jim Laity and Kristen Willard who assisted with the proofreading of the manuscript.

Imperfect Competition and International Trade

Introduction

Gene M. Grossman

The theory of international trade has been much enriched in recent years by studies that dispense with the traditional assumption of perfect competition. The orthodox trade theory of a decade ago, which had perfect competition as one of its linchpin assumptions, did a fine job of explaining why countries distinguished by technological and resource endowments exchange goods produced in different sectors. But it was hard pressed to explain why so much of international trade takes place between similarly endowed countries and why these countries import and export goods emanating from the same industry. The orthodox theory could explain why factors might migrate across international borders, but not why direct foreign investment occurs with firms residing in one country acquiring ownership and control of productive facilities located elsewhere. And it could explain how technological advantages give rise to particular patterns of specialization and trade, but not why the technological differences might develop in the first place. Recent work on trade that incorporates various forms of imperfect competition can provide explanations for the high volume of intraindustry trade, for the existence of multinational corporations, and for the emergence of international technology gaps.

The explorations of trade with imperfect competition also have deepened our understanding of the costs and benefits of trade policies. The orthodox theory of a decade ago saw export subsidies as unambiguously harmful, and improvements in the terms of trade as the only first-best justification for import protection. It drew on the powerful theorems of welfare economics to deny any national-interest role for interventionist trade policies, except as second-best palliatives for market failures due to externalities and price rigidities. The recent research has recognized that generalizations about policy are harder to come by in an environment where prices deviate from marginal costs. On one hand, free international trade can serve a valuable disciplining function in tempering the noncompetitive practices of firms with monopoly power. On the other hand, national governments may find a strategic motivation for intervening in support of local firms engaged in (imperfect) global competition with foreign rivals. To put it differently, imperfect competition enhances the potential gains from free trade but at the same time adds to the list of possible exceptions to the rule.

In this book I have collected nineteen papers that contain many of the central messages of the recent literature on trade with imperfect competition. The papers address a variety of issues including the causes of international trade, the static and dynamic determinants of the pattern of trade, the raison d'être of multinational corporations, and the positive and normative implications of trade policy. Of course, it has not been possible to include all of the interesting papers in this area in a volume of reasonable length, and so I have been forced to omit many valuable and seminal contributions. I have chosen to try to "cover the field" rather than to provide a historical accounting for the origins of various ideas. Thus, I have selected later papers where they cover more succinctly the lessons contained in earlier contributions and I have left out several papers that clearly were critical to the early development of thinking in this area. Hopefully, I can give credit where credit is due in the remainder of this introductory chapter, which attempts a brief survey of the terrain.[1]

Antecedents

The issues treated in the recent literature are not new. Ohlin (1924) and Graham (1923) recognized that increasing returns to scale can explain the emergence of large-scale production units and thus international specialization and trade in manufactured products. Balassa (1966) and Grubel and Lloyd (1975) documented the large volume of intraindustry trade in similar products, while Balassa (1967) and Kravis (1971) argued that the growth of postwar trade could not be explained without reference to scale economies and imperfect competition. Melvin and Warne (1973) incorporated a monopoly sector into a traditional general equilibrium model of trade and explored the issue of gains from trade. In the trade policy literature, Bhagwati (1965) realized that import restrictions would affect market conduct by protected monopolists, and Corden (1967) studied the welfare effects of import tariffs and subsidies in the presence of a monopolistic local producer. Finally, Hymer (1960) and Caves (1971) argued forcefully that direct foreign investment is a manifestation of the existence of specific assets, which inevitably confer monopoly power on their owners.

These valuable insights were slow to take hold in the trade literature largely because researchers in the field lacked the tools necessary to formalize and refine the ideas in tractable mathematical models. All of this changed in the mid-1970s, when microeconomic theorists developed a variety of simple and useful models of alternative market structures. It did not take long for the approach to monopolistic competition developed by Lancaster (1975), Spence (1976), Dixit and Stiglitz (1977), and Salop (1979) to find application in models of intraindustry trade in differentiated products. Similarly, investigations of the strategic role of trade policy in oligopolistic settings drew heavily on the analysis of two-stage games developed by Selten (1965), and especially on its application to the problems of commitment and entry deterrence by Spence (1977, 1979) and Dixit (1980). Modelers of multinational corporations have borrowed from work in the industrial organization literature on vertical integration (Williamson 1971; Porter and Spence 1977; Grossman and Hart 1986), while Judd's 1985 extension of the Dixit-Stiglitz model to incorporate explicit dynamics has been indispensable to several recent studies of innovation and trade.

Oligopoly

The earliest work on international oligopolistic competition was driven by the observation that much trade is conducted by large corporations with significant market power, and that when these firms are located in different countries they often penetrate one another's local markets. Brander (1981) showed that two competitors producing identical products will invade each other's market if transport costs are not too great and if the firms behave as Cournot competitors (taking rival's deliveries as given) in each market separately. Thus, "cross-hauling" or two-way trade can arise as a natural outgrowth of oligopolistic competition under certain assumptions about market conduct. Brander and Krugman (chapter 1) extended the original Brander contribution by establishing that a trade equilibrium with cross-hauling exists for arbitrary forms of market demand. They also emphasized the importance of the segmented-markets assumption: two-way trade occurs when firms perceive the markets in each country as distinct and so separately allocate quantities to each one.

Ben-Zvi and Helpman (chapter 2) and Venables (1990) have questioned whether it is plausible that firms make independent decisions regarding their shipments to geographically separated markets, without there being any connection between these decisions.[2] They studied equilibria in which firms install capacity that can be used to serve any market in the world, and then subsequently allocate their output among the various markets in the light of demand conditions and transportation costs. Ben-Zvi and Helpman included a third stage in their model of multimarket competition wherein firms set (possibly different) prices in the separate markets. The advantage of their approach is that it gives rise to cross-country price differentials that are consistent with the assumptions about transport costs, and so the equilibrium is not characterized by unexploited (and unexplained) arbitrage opportunities. The approach yields conclusions that are, however, in stark contrast with those for segmented markets: with positive transport costs, cross-hauling of identical goods never takes place.

Markusen (chapter 3) went even further than Ben-Zvi and Helpman and Venables in his modeling of the connectedness of national markets. He treated the world as a single integrated market, where producers choose an aggregate output level and then let arbitragers determine the cross-country allocation of sales.[3] One interesting implication of this assumption is that if countries are identical in size and factor endowments, and if they have access to the same technologies, then there are gains from trade even though no goods actually cross national boundaries in the free trade equilibrium. Competition between the producers in the imperfectly competitive sector of each economy leads to an expansion of sectoral output relative to the sum of the monopoly outputs in the autarky equilibrium. This procompetitive effect of (potential) trade moves the national consumption points closer to their efficient levels, just as in Caves's 1974 discussion of the gains that result from exposing a domestic monopolist to (perfect) foreign competition.

When oligopolistic firms located in different countries compete in segmented markets, national trade policies can affect the nature and outcome of their competition. For example, Krugman (chapter 4) studied tariffs that protect a duopolist in its local market when that firm competes with a foreign rival both at home and abroad. He considered several scenarios with static or dynamic economies of scale. With increasing returns to scale, a tariff that causes the local producer to expand its output for the home market may lower the firm's marginal cost of production. If so, the firm becomes a more effective competitor in the foreign market as well. In other words, import protection can serve to promote exports.

Itoh and Ono (1982), Harris (1985) and Krishna (chapter 5) have studied the effects of quantitative restrictions (QRs) such as import quotas and voluntary export restraints on the oligopolistic interaction between a home firm and a foreign firm. The first two of these papers take the home firm to be a Stackelberg leader, while Krishna makes the perhaps more natural assumption that neither firm is able to commit to a price before the other.[4] When the home firm is a Stackelberg leader, the foreign follower will never set a price that causes demand for its product to exceed the level allowed by the QR. But with simultaneous price setting, demand conditions for some price combinations may call for more imports than are permitted, and so a rationing rule must be introduced for these cases. Krishna supposes that individuals with the greatest willingness to pay ultimately acquire the imports at a price that clears the domestic market. With this assumption of efficient rationing, there does not exist any Nash equilibrium in pure pricing strategies, so she studied the mixed strategy equilibrium that always does exist.

In both the Stackelberg and Nash settings, QRs have very different effects than do tariffs on the outcome of oligopolistic competition. As Bhagwati (1965) first noted for the case of a domestic monopolist facing a competitive foreign fringe, QRs limit the response of foreign rivals to noncompetitive actions by the local producer. As a result, the QR enables the home firm to exploit its market power with relative impunity. The QR may work as a "facilitating device," allowing the home and foreign firms to achieve a relatively collusive outcome that would not be sustainable in the absence of the trade barrier. QRs that do not restrict trade far below the free trade level yield profit gains to both the home and the foreign firms.[5] Of course, it is domestic consumers who pay the price.

The effects of trade policies on oligopolistic firms' ability to sustain collusion have been further analyzed by Davidson (1984), Rotemberg and Saloner (1989) and Lambson and Richardson (1987). These authors all studied repeated oligopoly games where cooperative behavior is supported by credible threats to punish aggressive deviations. Trade policies alter not only the profitability of cooperating, but also the potential gain from cheating, and so these policies affect the set of outcomes that can be supported as subgame perfect equilibria under specified punishment schemes. Davidson considered a situation with fixed and arbitrary numbers of home and foreign firms, and he showed that a small tariff enlarges the set of sustainable outcomes while a large tariff reduces the prospects for collusive behavior. Both Rotemberg and Saloner and Lambson and Richardson demonstrated that a QR may support a more competitive equilibrium than might a tariff in this context, because domestic firms have a greater temptation to cheat on a highly collusive cartel when a QR is in place, and so cartels that would be stable with tariff protection may not be so under a quota.[6]

Strategic Trade Policy

I have thus far discussed the positive effects of trade policies in a variety of oligopoly situations. Much of the interesting work in recent years has concerned the normative implications of policy in such settings. An early and important insight was provided by Katrak (1977) and Svedberg (1979), who showed in the context of an example with linear demand that a tariff could be used to extract rents from a foreign monopolist. Brander and Spencer (chapter 6) extended this result to general demands, establishing that a small tariff levied against a good supplied by a foreign monopolist improves domestic welfare, provided that the marginal revenue curve is steeper than the demand curve at the free trade equilibrium point. Tariffs also can be used to extract rents when a foreign monopolist facing potential competition from domestic firms prices in such a way as to deter entry; see Brander and Spencer (1981).

The second major insight in this area concerns the potential use of trade policies for "profit shifting." In an oligopoly situation, firms earn excess profits that form a part of total national surplus. If government policy can be used to increase the share of industry profits that accrues to domestic firms, there can be a national welfare gain. The simplest setting to consider is one where a single foreign and a single domestic firm engage in Cournot (quantity) competition in a segmented, third-country market. Brander and Spencer (1985) proved that, if the home government is the only one actively using policy, an export subsidy raises home welfare when the firms' reaction curves slope downward.[7] The subsidy lends credibility to an aggressive output choice by the home firm, and so the foreign firm responds by ceding market share and profits. Tariffs can play a similar, strategic role when a foreign and a domestic firm behave as quantity setters in the home market (chapter 6), while R&D subsidies serve to shift profits in a two-stage rivalry when a research competition precedes the production stage (Spencer and Brander 1983).

Subsequent studies have refined and qualified the Brander-Spencer argument for export subsidies and import tariffs in support of domestic oligopolistic competitors. Dixit (1984) and Eaton and Grossman (chapter 7) showed that the case for an export subsidy (when competition takes place in a third-country market) weakens as the number of domestic participants in the industry grows. At some critical number of domestic firms, the optimal subsidy becomes zero, and of course when the number of domestic firms grows large, the orthodox terms-of-trade argument indicates an optimal export tax. Eaton and Grossman also explored the connection between the form of oligopolistic competition and the nature of the optimal trade policy.[8] When a single home firm and a foreign firm compete as Bertrand (price) setters in a third-country export market (and the foreign firm's reaction curve is upward sloping), an export tax rather than an export subsidy raises domestic welfare.[9] The tax makes credible the home firm's promise not to undercut the price of its foreign rival and so allows the two firms to sustain a high degree of collusion.[10] Dixit and Grossman (1986) made the further point that several domestic oligopolies often compete for a common resource that may be available in relatively inelastic supply. In the event, even if all oligopolists participate in Cournot competitions, a trade policy designed to shift profits to domestic firms in one particular industry may be socially harmful, because it will raise factor costs for other domestic oligopolists and so disadvantage them in their respective industry competitions.

Several authors have dealt with issues of entry and exit in the context of the design of optimal trade policies for oligopolies. Dixit and Kyle (1985) argued that trade policies can be used strategically to deter or promote entry. As an example of their analysis, consider an industry in which a foreign firm has already borne the sunk cost of entry. Suppose a domestic rival contemplates entry but cannot cover its fixed cost in duopolistic competition with the foreign incumbent. Then the home country will benefit from an import prohibition as long as the domestic firm earns positive profits as a monopolist and its marginal cost is not too much greater than that of the foreign firm. The welfare benefit of the protectionist policy is readily seen from the fact that consumer surplus is not much affected by the switch from one monopolist to another, but producer surplus increases from zero when the policy-induced entry occurs.

Horstmann and Markusen (1986) and Venables (1985) studied oligopoly settings in which free entry drives the profits of the marginal entrant to zero. Horstmann and Markusen supposed that the home and foreign markets are integrated, in the sense described above (i.e., each firm chooses an aggregate output level, and its goods command the same price no matter where in the world they are sold). In this case, export subsidies and import tariffs that advantage domestic firms in the global competition induce inefficient entry at home. Any profits that are shifted strategically to domestic firms are dissipated in the cost of entry, and national welfare typically falls. By contrast, Venables found that import tariffs raise home welfare when national markets are segmented and intermarket transport costs are positive. In this case, an expansion in the number of active domestic firms at the expense of the number of foreign firms benefits domestic consumers, because the home firms avoid the extra cost of transporting goods to the local market. These results and others are nicely synthesized in a paper by Markusen and Venables (chapter 8).

Having established that certain types of trade interventions are beneficial in some circumstances but not in others, researchers found it essential to identify the empirically relevant cases. To date, empirical work in this area is still in its infancy, although a number of industries have been examined in order to see what types of outcomes may be possible. The predominant method that has been used in these studies has been that of a "calibrated equilibrium." This procedure calls for the researcher to posit a particular model of an industry by specifying the mode of conduct, the extent of market integration, the possibilities for entry or exit, and so on. He or she then inserts what data and parameters are readily available into the model. Finally, unavailable data and parameters are generated by the researcher so that the equilibrium solution of the model matches the observed outcome for some base year.

In their study of the semiconductor market, Baldwin and Krugman (chapter 10) found that there is great scope in that industry for government policy to alter the structure of competition, but less scope for strategic policies to generate national welfare gains. Dixit (chapter 9) concluded similarly that the welfare gains from strategic trade policy are modest in the automobile industry, except when the social value of the government revenue generated by tariffs is large or when much of the payment to automobile workers is viewed as rent rather than as an opportunity cost. Baldwin and Krugman (1988) found that strategic subsidies to Airbus in support of their development of wide-bodied jet aircraft may have raised aggregate European welfare somewhat, but this finding stems more from the gain in consumer surplus that resulted from earlier product introduction than it does from any shifting of excess profits.

Greater support for the potential benefits of strategic trade interventions emerges from Baldwin and Flam's 1989 analysis of the world market for 30 to 40-seat commuter aircraft. Smith and Venables (1988, 1991), on the other hand, found substantial gains to Europe from further liberalization of its internal trade in a variety of oligopolistic industries, and particularly in the car market. Several recent calibration studies are included in a volume edited by Smith and Krugman (forthcoming).

Monopolistic Competition

Economies of scale give rise to gains from specialization that potentially can explain the widespread practice of intraindustry trade. If the products in an industry are differentiated and each is manufactured with increasing returns to scale, then a country may specialize in producing a subset of varieties for home consumption and export, while importing those varieties that are not supplied domestically. But economies of scale at the firm level are inconsistent with perfect competition, because firms that price at marginal cost suffer losses when average cost exceeds marginal cost.

The problem of specifying a market structure consistent with scale economies that are internal to firms delayed for many years the formal modeling of trade based on increasing returns to scale (see Krugman 1990, introduction). The breakthrough came in the late 1970s, when Krugman (1979a) and Lancaster (1979) independently developed models of trade in differentiated products by adopting the Chamberlinian notion of monopolistic competition. Krugman used the Dixit-Stiglitz specification of household preferences that reflect individuals' desire for variety in consumption. Lancaster, by contrast, introduced consumer heterogeneity, with individuals distinguished by their most preferred set of product characteristics. Differentiated products exist on the market in this formulation to serve households with different tastes. In both cases, increasing returns in production limit the extent of diversity that the market can provide. Gainful trade takes place between similarly endowed countries, because trade expands the size of the market and so enables a greater variety of goods to be produced.

The earliest models by Krugman and Lancaster had a single tradable goods sector and identical countries. Krugman (chapter 11) allowed countries to differ in their taste patterns and made transportation costly. This elaboration generates a "home market effect" in the spirit of Linder (1961), whereby countries develop competitive advantage in the goods that are highly demanded at home. Meanwhile, Dixit and Norman (chapter 12), Lancaster (1980), Helpman (chapter 13), and Krugman (1981) introduced a second output sector and cross-country differences in factor endowments (or, in the case of Lancaster, sectoral productivities). These extensions enabled an integration of traditional trade theory and the new ideas about product differentiation, as the extended models predict that trade based on comparative advantage and trade based on scale economies will take place side by side. It is noteworthy that these authors reached similar conclusions, even though Krugman and Dixit and Norman followed the love-of-variety approach whereas Lancaster and Helpman pursued the ideal-variety specification. In both formulations, the pattern of interindustry trade is dictated by countries' relative factor endowments and sectors' relative factor intensities, just as in the Heckscher-Ohlin model with perfect competition, while the volume of intraindustry trade depends upon the extent of scale economies and the similarity in the sizes of the two countries. When trade arises primarily from considerations of comparative advantage, as for example when countries differ greatly in the composition of their factor endowments, then a conflict exists in the attitudes of differently endowed individuals toward trade. However, in exchange between similar countries, where most specialization is due to scale economies, all factor owners may share in the gains from trade (Krugman 1981).

Ethier (chapter 14) showed that intraindustry trade can arise not only because aggregate household demands exhibit a preference for diversity, but also because firms realize productivity gains from increasing specialization of their production processes. He constructed a model of trade in differentiated intermediate goods that has proved useful in some recent extensions of trade and growth theory to include endogenous innovation. An important implication of Ethier's work is that, when there are increasing returns at the firm level in the production of intermediates, and when these goods are priced above marginal cost, the aggregate production function for the industry that assembles the components has the same form as it would if there were an external economy in the production of the final good. Moreover, international trade serves to propagate this production externality worldwide.[11] Ethier also established results on the relationship between intraindustry and interindustry trade and on the distributional implications of trade that reinforced those of Helpman, Dixit and Norman, Lancaster, and Krugman.

Several authors have investigated the role of trade policy in settings with monopolistic competition. Venables (1982) studied a small economy that imports an exogenously determined number of differentiated varieties at a fixed price. He assumed that the small country's monopolistically competitive sector cannot profitably export.[12] Tariffs can increase welfare in this setting by influencing the number of domestically produced brands. Tariffs also can be used to counteract the consumption distortion arising from the markup pricing of domestic goods (Flam and Helpman 1987; Gros 1987). Gros observed that even a very small country will want to set a positive optimal tariff for this purpose, because the relative price of imports compared to domestically produced goods falls short of their relative opportunity cost in the free trade equilibrium. Since the small country is the unique world supplier of its differentiated export products, it will be able to influence its terms of trade. If the small country's market is segmented from world markets, the country can further use the tariff to extract monopoly rents from foreign producers (Jones and Takemori 1989).

Multinational Corporations

The extent of multinational activity and the importance of multinational corporations in the conduct of world trade have been rising steadily through time. Trade theory based on perfect competition could not fully explain this development. A theory of multinational investment ought to explain not only why a firm would prefer to locate some of its activities offshore, but also why the firm would be able to compete with locally owned establishments in performing these activities despite the evident disadvantages that derive from relative unfamiliarity with local customs, business practices, etc. Traditional models of direct foreign investment seen as a movement in capital could explain the locational advantage for the multinational but not the competitive advantage vis-à-vis locally owned firms.

Theories of trade with scale economies and imperfect competition can provide the missing links. A firm may own a product-specific asset that gives it a competitive advantage in producing a particular good over foreign or domestic rivals. This asset might be the know-how to manufacture a particular differentiated product, for example. By dint of its ownership of this asset, the firm can overcome its competitive disadvantage vis-à-vis local producers in the foreign market. But the product-specific asset is likely to confer market power on its owner, and so this explanation for multinational activity is not consistent with the assumption that markets are perfectly competitive.

Markusen (1984) and Helpman (1984b) were the first to construct general equilibrium models with multinational corporations based on this type of reasoning. In Markusen's work, the advantage to the multinational firm from operating plants in two locations stems from an assumed property of the production technology, namely the existence of multiplant economies.[13] Markusen argued that activities such as R&D, advertising, marketing, and distribution are nonrival or "joint" inputs for the firm inasmuch as they can be provided in one place to support varying amounts of production and sales in several locations. The multinationals that he studied engage in manufacturing activities in each of two countries but perform their "corporate" activities only in the home country. Helpman similarly distinguished what he called "headquarter services"—activities such as management, marketing, and product-specific R&D—and ordinary manufacturing activities. The former must take place in the home country of a firm, but the latter can take place anywhere in the world. Helpman's multinationals have only one manufacturing operation, which is geographically separated from the firms' headquarters. The firms in his model locate their production facilities offshore in order to take advantage of the lower labor costs there.

In a follow-up paper, Helpman (chapter 15) elaborated his model in order to allow for vertical as well as horizontal integration of firms. What results is a monopolistically competitive theory of trade in differentiated products in which firms with production facilities in more than one country trade intermediate components, finished goods, and invisibles (headquarter services). The theory predicts a large volume of intrafirm trade, in accordance with the observed data.

A firm owning a specific asset that generates a competitive advantage, and that sees a locational advantage from manufacturing abroad, still could choose to allow a foreign producer to undertake the manufacturing by licensing the use of its proprietary asset. Both Markusen and Helpman took for granted the firm's decision to internalize its international transactions in preference to dealing at arm's length. Ethier (chapter 16) endogenized the firm's internalization decision. The incentive to internalize stems from the asymmetries of information that may exist across corporate boundaries and from the difficulties that are associated with the writing of state-contingent contracts. According to the theory espoused by Ethier, the integrated multinational will be better able to respond efficiently in its manufacturing operations to contingencies that arise from the activities of its research or marketing branches than would a foreign licensee dealing at arm's length with the domestic firm in accordance with the provisions of some prespecified contract. His model predicts two-way direct foreign investment between similarly endowed countries, and an increasing extent of multinational activity and intraindustry trade as countries' factor endowment bundles become more alike.

Technology and Trade

Technology has played a central role in trade theory. Some theories have exploited an assumption of identical technologies in all countries to link trade patterns to other distinguishing features of the economies, such as their factor endowments. Others have focused on the existence of cross-country differences in technical know-how as an explanation for trade. But the conventional theories cannot predict what patterns of technology differences are likely to emerge across countries, nor can they provide convincing justification for the assumption of identical technologies. Due to the static nature of the notion of comparative advantage that underlies much of traditional thinking about trade, the theory has been of little use in analyzing the evolution of trade patterns over time.

The traditional approaches also have had little to say about the effects of trade and trade policy on the dynamic performance of economies. When combined with a neoclassical model of growth, the theory generates an irrelevance result: long-run growth in an open economy proceeds at a rate that is independent of its trade policies or the nature of its international economic relations.

The models of trade with imperfect competition point the way to endogenizing the technology factor. Firms will devote resources to research and development if they can earn a sufficient return on their investments. While there can be no incentive for R&D in a perfectly competitive world in which all producers have immediate and costless access to any new technologies, firms may be willing to spend on industrial research when governments protect intellectual property rights and tolerate limited expression of market power. Moreover, the up-front nature of R&D investments and the fact that knowledge once generated can be used in many applications simultaneously lend credence to the belief that scale economies characterize many modern production processes and thus that these economies play a major part in explaining the incentives for specialization and trade.

Grossman and Helpman (chapter 17) have extended the two-sector model of intraindustry and interindustry trade with monopolistic competition to allow for explicit dynamics stemming from investments in technology. They assumed that differentiated products must be developed in a research lab before they can be manufactured and marketed. The monopoly profits that firms earn when they exploit their unique ability to produce some variety provide the incentive for engaging in R&D. Grossman and Helpman replaced the Chamberlinian assumption of free entry into production and zero profits with one of free entry into R&D and normal returns in that activity. They then showed that many of the predictions of the static models apply to the long run of a dynamic world economy. In particular, their model predicts the coexistence of intraindustry and interindustry trade, with the pattern of the latter determined by the compositions of countries' resource endowments.

The initial Grossman-Helpman model predicts, however, that firms will cease their R&D efforts in the long run. The returns to product development fall as the number of available varieties expands, while the resource costs of R&D do not change over time. As a result, the incentive to introduce new brands shrinks and ultimately disappears. But, as Romer (1990) has suggested, innovation need not peter out in the long run if advances in the state of knowledge enable R&D to be conducted more productively with the accumulation of experience. He described a process of endogenous innovation whereby investments in new blueprints generate spillover contributions to a public stock of knowledge capital, which in turn serves as a public input into subsequent research. Grossman and Helpman (1991c, ch. 7) have borrowed Romer's formulation of technological externalities, assumed that the spillovers extend across international borders, and proved that the long-run pattern of trade is determined in this context by national factor endowments.[14] Grossman and Helpman (1991e) and Grossman (chapter 19) have established similar results for an economy in which firms devote their R&D efforts to improving the quality of a fixed set of goods rather than to expanding the variety of available products.

The assumption that technological spillovers are global in scope is critical to extending the conventional wisdom linking patterns of specialization to national resource endowments alone. When there are technological spillovers that benefit only firms and researchers operating in a geographically concentrated region, new forces come into play in the determination of the trade pattern. Krugman (1987b) was the first to argue that increasing returns arising from local external economies could generate cumulative advantages, so that history would play a role in explaining the evolution of the trade pattern. A country with an initial advantage in some activity can widen its lead as a consequence of the benefits of learning by doing (see also Young 1991). Grossman and Helpman (1991c, ch. 8) suggested that the external benefits from learning by doing might be generated by research activities rather than production activities, and examined a model of endogenous product development. They too found that history matters, along with country size, in the determination of dynamic comparative advantage.

The approach that combines imperfect competition in product markets and technological spillovers in industrial research enables a fresh look at the relationship between trade and growth. Rivera-Batiz and Romer (chapter 18) described two reasons why international integration promotes growth. Cross-border spillovers of technical knowledge improve research productivity in each location and the expansion of the world resource base that attends international integration implies a larger scale of world research activity. Grossman and Helpman (1991f) argued that the extent of international spillovers of technology might be related to the amount of trade contact between two economies, so that trade would further contribute to growth by promoting the international transmission of knowledge. But Feenstra (1990) has established that trade can be detrimental to growth in a small country whose innovators compete with a larger research sector abroad in a setting where spillovers in the research process are only national in reach. All of these results are synthesized by Grossman and Helpman (1991c, ch. 9) who also explain the connection between intersectoral specialization due to comparative advantage and the growth rate in an economy that has a relative paucity of the resources used intensively in the knowledge-generating sectors.

Once a link can be drawn between the economic environment and the growth rate, it becomes possible to explore the growth effects of trade policies and of other policies that might be implemented in an open economy. Grossman and Helpman (1990; 1991c, ch. 10) and Grossman (chapter 19) have studied the growth effects of import tariffs, export subsidies, and technology policies. Subsidies to R&D typically stimulate innovation and growth in the country that undertakes the policy, but slow innovation and growth in its trade partners. The world growth rate often rises, but may fail to do so if innovation is encouraged by a country with comparative disadvantage in undertaking R&D. Protectionist trade policies, on the other hand, promote manufacturing activities at the expense of R&D, thereby impeding innovation in the policy-active country.[15] The effect on world growth depends upon whether the protectionist country has comparative advantage or disadvantage in conducting research. If protectionist policies are invoked by all countries concurrently, then growth rates typically will fall worldwide (Rivera-Batiz and Romer 1991).

The recent focus on technological change as a driving force behind international specialization has allowed light to be shed on the trade relations between the industrialized "North" and the less developed "South." Krugman (1979b) developed a model of (exogenous) innovation in the North and (exogenous) imitation by the South to formalize some of the ideas in Vernon's 1966 theory of the product life cycle. He used his model to study the links between rates of innovation and imitation and the relative wage rates in the two regions. Grossman and Helpman (1991a) endogenized the technological change in Krugman's model, by making both innovation and imitation the result of profit-seeking investments by forward-looking entrepreneurs.[16] They derived the feedbacks between the two learning processes and showed that faster imitation in the South need not diminish the incentives for innovation in the North. They also reexamined the link between the rates of imitation and innovation and relative regional wage rates, and showed that some of Krugman's conclusions rely on his assumption that technological change occurs exogenously and costlessly.

Conclusion

The introduction of imperfect competition into formal modeling of international trade has increased the consonance between theory and reality and expanded the range of policy questions that the theory can address. Trade theory now can explain why similar countries will engage in trade and why that trade may not generate such distributional conflicts as commonly arise when exchange takes place between countries at different levels of development. It can account for the cross-hauling of very similar goods produced by large corporations in different countries. And it can contribute to our understanding of the motivation that governments see for aiding their national firms in international competition. We are now able to construct models that incorporate multinational corporations as key players in the conduct of international trade and that make technological progress the outgrowth of investment decisions by profit-seeking entrepreneurs. There can be no doubt that the theory is richer and more complete than it was a decade ago.

The next step surely must be a careful testing of the new theories. Empirical work has lagged in this area to the point where skeptics question whether the approach has testable implications.[17] But just as the theoretical developments were delayed by the absence of appropriate tools, so the empirical implementation has been awaiting developments in the "new empirical industrial organization" (see Bresnahan 1989). I expect (or at least hope) that it won't be too long now before it is time for someone to collect a book of quantitative articles on imperfect competition and international trade.

Notes

I am grateful to Avinash Dixit and Elhanan Helpman for their comments on an earlier draft of this introductory chapter and to the National Science Foundation for financial support.

1. The literature on trade and imperfect competition does not suffer from a lack of surveys. More comprehensive overviews of parts or all of the subject matter covered by this book may be found in Baldwin (1992), Dixit (1987), Helpman (1984a, 1990), Helpman and Krugman (1985, 1989), Krugman (1987a, 1989), Richardson (1989), and Venables and Smith (1986).

2. In the industrial organization literature, Bulow, Geanakoplos, and Klemperer (1985) and Bernheim and Whinston (1990) studied multimarket interactions between oligopolistic competitors. Bulow, Geanakoplos, and Klemperer focus on interactions between markets that arise because firms have nonconstant marginal costs, while Bernheim and Whinston consider whether simultaneous competition between a pair of firms in several markets enhances the possibility that the firms can sustain an equilibrium with tacit collusion.

3. The Ben-Zvi and Helpman equilibrium converges on this integrated-markets equilibrium when cross-market transport costs approach zero.

4. See also Buffie and Spiller (1986) who study the positive effects of small reductions in the level of a quota in a conjectural variations model with free entry and exit.

5. Krishna and Itoh (1988) show that the opposite result is possible when trade is restricted by a domestic content requirement: policy intervention may cause the foreign firm to react more aggressively to price increases by the home firm, and so the equilibrium may support less collusion and yield both firms lower profits than under free trade.

6. This somewhat implausible result is an example of what Shapiro (1989) terms the "topsy-turvy principle" of infinitely repeated games: anything that makes more competitive behavior feasible or credible actually supports greater collusion, because the threat of reversion to the competitive outcome becomes a more compelling deterrent to those who would contemplate deviant actions. The usefulness of all of the results for infinitely repeated games surely is limited by the multiplicity of equilibria that exist in these situations and by the theory's inability to select among potential outcomes.

7. The subsidy remains an optimal policy for an individual government when both governments engage in strategic intervention, although welfare levels in the resulting noncooperative equilibrium may be lower than under free trade.

8. Cheng (1988) extended the Eaton-Grossman analysis to allow for the simultaneous use of two policy instruments in cases where a home and a foreign firm compete in the domestic market.

9. The Eaton-Grossman analysis assumes, as do Brander and Spencer, that the government sets its policy instrument prior to the competition between the producing firms, and that the government can commit itself to a particular level of policy for the duration of the competition. Different conclusions emerge when the policy level is chosen after the firms have set their prices; see Carmichael (1987), Gruenspecht (1988), and Neary (1991).

10. The home firm's profits may not rise, because this firm must pay the tax on its export sales. But the sum of tax revenue and domestic profits will rise with the introduction of a small export tax.

11. Ethier thereby provided the microfoundations for the assumption of international returns to scale that he exploited in his 1979 article.

12. The analysis in Flam and Helpman (1987) is similar, except that these authors relax the assumption of no exporting by the monopolistically competitive sector.

13. In Markusen (1984), the single multinational in the model chooses to produce in both locations rather than concentrating production in a single location, because this firm is sufficiently large in relation to the two national economies that factor prices in the two countries would diverge were the firm to concentrate its manufacturing operations. Horstmann and Markusen (1987) introduced an alternative motivation for maintaining several distinct manufacturing plants: when transport costs or trade barriers segment markets, direct foreign investments can be used to preempt entry by local firms.

14. If resources such as human capital are themselves accumulated, then dynamic comparative advantage derives from the factors that determine the incentives to accumulate; see Grossman and Helpman (1991c, ch. 5).

15. Grossman and Helpman (1991b) examined the welfare implications of trade and technology policies for a small country that innovates by developing new varieties of a nontraded intermediate input. Feenstra and Judd (1982) examined similar issues, but in a static model of trade in differentiated products.

16. Jensen and Thursby (1986, 1987) had made earlier attempts to accomplish the same thing. But unlike Grossman and Helpman, who posited a competitive research environment in the North and a competitive imitative activity in the South, these authors assumed that all R&D is carried out by a single, northern monopolist, and that the rate of technology transfer is set by a national welfare maximizing southern government. Segerstrom, Anant, and Dinopoulos (1990) developed a model of the product cycle based on continuing quality improvements, which is also the approach pursued in Grossman and Helpman (1991d).

17. There are, of course, a few exceptions to this rule. For example, Loertscher and Wolter (1980) examined a cross section of countries for a single year and found that differences in per capita income correlate negatively with the share of bilateral trade that is intraindustry, as the theory would predict if per capita income were a perfect proxy for capital-to-labor ratios. Helpman (1987) confirmed this finding for an extended data set and showed that the relative importance of intraindustry trade has been rising as the industrial countries have grown more similar. Wickham and Thompson (1989) studied how the level of multinational activity impinges upon the relationship between factor endowment differences and the share of intraindustry trade in the bilateral trade flows of twenty-seven countries. More recently, Levinsohn (1988, 1991) has used econometric methods to investigate the effects of taxes and tariffs on equilibrium outcomes in imperfectly competitive industries.

References

Balassa, Bela. 1966. Tariff reductions and trade in manufactures. *American Economic Review* 56:466–473.

Balassa, Bela. 1967. *Trade Liberalization among Industrial Countries: Objectives and Alternatives.* New York: McGraw-Hill.

Baldwin, Richard E., and Harry Flam. 1989. Strategic trade policy in the market for 30–40 seat commuter aircraft. *Weltwirtschaftliches Archiv* 125:484–500.

Baldwin, Richard E., and Paul R. Krugman. 1988. Industrial policy and international competition in wide-bodied jet aircraft. In Robert E. Baldwin (ed.), *Trade Policy Issues and Empirical Analysis.* Chicago: University of Chicago Press for the National Bureau of Economic Research.

Baldwin, Robert E. 1992. Are economists' traditional trade policy views still valid? *Journal of Economic Literature* 30: forthcoming.

Bernheim, B. Douglas, and Michael D. Whinston. 1990. Multimarket contact and collusive behavior. *Rand Journal of Economics* 21:1–26.

Bhagwati, Jagdish N. 1965. On the equivalence of tariffs and quotas. In R. E. Baldwin et al. (eds.), *Trade, Growth and the Balance of Payments: Essays in Honor of Gottfried Haberler.* Chicago: Rand McNally.

Brander, James A. 1981. Intra-industry trade in identical commodities. *Journal of International Economics* 11:1–14.

Brander, James A., and Barbara J. Spencer. 1981. Tariffs and the extraction of foreign monopoly rents under potential entry. *Canadian Journal of Economics* 14:371–389.

Brander, James A., and Barbara J. Spencer. 1985. Export subsidies and international market share rivalry. *Journal of International Economics* 18:83–100.

Bresnahan, Timothy F. 1989. Empirical studies of industries with market power. In R. Schmalensee and R. Willig (eds.), *Handbook of Industrial Organization*, vol. 2. Amsterdam: North-Holland.

Buffie, Edward F., and Pablo T. Spiller. 1986. Trade liberalization in oligopolistic industries. *Journal of International Economics* 20:65–82.

Bulow, Jeremy, John Geanakoplos, and Paul Klemperer. 1985. Multimarket oligopoly: Strategic substitutes and complements. *Journal of Political Economy* 93:488–511.

Carmichael, Calum. 1987. The control of export credit subsidies and its welfare consequences. *Journal of International Economics* 23:1–20.

Caves, Richard E. 1971. International corporations: The industrial economics of foreign investment. *Economica* 38:1–27.

Caves, Richard E. 1974. International trade, international investment, and imperfect markets. *Special Papers in International Economics*, no. 10. Princeton: International Finance Section, Princeton University.

Cheng, Leonard K. 1988. Assisting domestic industries under international oligopoly: The relevance of the nature of competition to optimal policies. *American Economic Review* 78:55–68.

Corden, W. Max. 1967. Monopoly, tariffs and subsidies. *Economica* 34:50–58.

Davidson, Carl. 1984. Cartel stability and trade policy. *Journal of International Economics* 17:219–237.

Dixit, Avinash K. 1980. The role of investment in entry deterrence. *Economic Journal* 90:95–106.

Dixit, Avinash K. 1984. International trade policy for oligopolistic industries. *Economic Journal* 94:(supplement) 233–249.

Dixit, Avinash K. 1987. Strategic aspects of trade policy. In T. F. Bewley (ed.), *Advances in Economic Theory, Fifth World Congress.* Cambridge: Cambridge University Press.

Dixit, Avinash K., and Gene M. Grossman. 1986. Targeted export promotion with several oligopolistic industries. *Journal of International Economics* 21:23–49.

Dixit, Avinash K., and Albert S. Kyle. 1985. The use of protection and subsidies for entry promotion and deterrence. *American Economic Review* 75:139–152.

Dixit, Avinash K., and Joseph E. Stiglitz. 1977. Monopolistic competition and optimum product diversity. *American Economic Review* 67:297–308.

Ethier, Wilfred J. 1979. Internationally decreasing costs and world trade. *Journal of International Economics* 9:1–24.

Ethier, Wilfred J. 1982. Decreasing costs in international trade and Frank Graham's argument for protection. *Econometrica* 50:1243–1268.

Feenstra, Robert C. 1990. Trade and uneven growth. National Bureau of Economic Research, working paper no. 3276.

Feenstra, Robert C., and Kenneth L. Judd. 1982. Tariffs, technology transfer, and welfare. *Journal of Political Economy* 90:1142–1165.

Flam, Harry, and Elhanan Helpman. 1987. Industrial policy under monopolistic competition. *Journal of International Economics* 22:79–102.

Graham, Frank D. 1923. Some aspects of protection further considered. *Quarterly Journal of Economics* 37:199–227.

Gros, Daniel. 1987. A note on the optimal tariff, retaliation and the welfare loss from tariff wars in a framework with intra-industry trade. *Journal of International Economics* 23:357–367.

Grossman, Gene M., and Elhanan Helpman. 1990. Comparative advantage and long-run growth. *American Economic Review* 80:796–815.

Grossman, Gene M., and Elhanan Helpman. 1991a. Endogenous product cycles. *The Economic Journal* 101:1214–1229.

Grossman, Gene M., and Elhanan Helpman. 1991b. Growth and welfare in the small open economy. In E. Helpman and A. Razin (eds.), *International Trade and Trade Policy*. Cambridge, Mass.: MIT Press.

Grossman, Gene M., and Elhanan Helpman. 1991c. *Innovation and Growth in the Global Economy*. Cambridge, Mass.: MIT Press.

Grossman, Gene M., and Elhanan Helpman. 1991d. Quality ladders and product cycles. *Quarterly Journal of Economics* 106:557–586.

Grossman, Gene M., and Elhanan Helpman. 1991e. Quality ladders in the theory of growth. *Review of Economic Studies* 58:43–61.

Grossman, Gene M., and Elhanan Helpman. 1991f. Trade, knowledge spillovers, and growth. *European Economic Review* 35:517–526.

Grossman, Sanford, and Oliver Hart. 1986. The costs and benefits of ownership: A theory of vertical and lateral integration. *Journal of Political Economy* 94:691–719.

Grubel, Herbert G., and Peter J. Lloyd. 1975. *Intra-industry Trade: The Theory and Measurement of International Trade in Differentiated Products*. New York: John Wiley.

Gruenspecht, Howard K. 1988. Export subsidies for differentiated products. *Journal of International Economics* 24:331–344.

Harris, Richard G. 1985. Why voluntary restraints are voluntary. *Canadian Journal of Economics* 18:799–809.

Helpman, Elhanan. 1984a. Increasing returns, imperfect markets, and trade theory. In R. W. Jones and P. B. Kenen (eds.), *Handbook of International Economics*. Amsterdam: North-Holland.

Helpman, Elhanan. 1984b. A simple theory of trade with multinational corporations. *Journal of Political Economy* 92:451–472.

Helpman, Elhanan. 1987. Imperfect competition and international trade: Evidence from fourteen industrial countries. *Journal of the Japanese and International Economies* 1:62–81.

Helpman, Elhanan. 1990. Monopolistic competition in trade theory. *Special Papers in International Economics*, no. 16. Princeton: International Finance Section, Princeton University.

Helpman, Elhanan, and Paul R Krugman. 1985. *Market Structure and Foreign Trade*. Cambridge, Mass.: MIT Press.

Helpman, Elhanan, and Paul R. Krugman. 1989. *Trade Policy and Market Structure*. Cambridge, Mass.: MIT Press.

Horstmann, Ignatius J., and James R. Markusen. 1986. Up the average cost curve: Inefficient entry and the new protectionism. *Journal of International Economics* 20:225–247.

Horstmann, Ignatius J., and James R. Markusen. 1987. Strategic investments and the development of multinationals. *International Economic Review* 28:109–121.

Hymer, Stephen H. 1960. The international operations of national firms: A study of direct foreign investment. Ph.D. dissertation, Massachusetts Institute of Technology, Cambridge.

Itoh, Motoshige, and Yoshiyasu Ono. 1982. Tariffs, quotas and market structure. *Quarterly Journal of Economics* 96:295–305.

Jensen, Richard, and Marie Thursby. 1986. A strategic approach to the product life cycle. *Journal of International Economics* 21:269–284.

Jensen, Richard, and Marie Thursby. 1987. A decision-theoretic model of innovation, technology transfer and trade. *Review of Economic Studies* 54:631–648.

Jones, Ronald W., and Shumpei Takemori. 1989. Foreign monopoly and optimum tariffs for the small open economy. *European Economic Review* 33:1691–1707.

Judd, Kenneth L. 1985. On the performance of patents. *Econometrica* 53:567–586.

Katrak, Homi. 1977. Multinational monopolies and commercial policy. *Oxford Economic Papers* 29:283–291.

Kravis, Irving. 1971. The current case for import limitations. In Commission on International Trade and Investment Policy, *United States Economic Policy in an Interdependent World*. Washington, D.C.: Government Printing Office.

Krishna, Kala, and Motoshige Itoh. 1988. Content protection and oligopolistic interaction. *Review of Economic Studies* 55:107–125.

Krugman, Paul R. 1979a. Increasing returns, monopolistic competition and international trade. *Journal of International Economics* 9:469–479.

Krugman, Paul R. 1979b. A model of innovation, technology transfer, and the world distribution of income. *Journal of Political Economy* 87:253–266.

Krugman, Paul R. 1981. Intraindustry specialization and the gains from trade. *Journal of Political Economy* 89:959–973.

Krugman, Paul R. 1987a. Increasing returns and the theory of international trade. In T. F. Bewley (ed.), *Advances in Economic Theory, Fifth World Congress*. Cambridge: Cambridge University Press.

Krugman, Paul R. 1987b. The narrow moving band, the Dutch disease, and the competitive consequences of Mrs. Thatcher: Notes on trade in the presence of dynamic scale economies. *Journal of Development Economics* 27:41–55.

Krugman, Paul R. 1989. Industrial organization and international trade. In R. Schmalensee and R. Willig (eds.), *Handbook of Industrial Organization*, vol. 2. Amsterdam: North-Holland.

Krugman, Paul R. 1990. *Rethinking International Trade*. Cambridge, Mass.: MIT Press.

Lambson, Val, and J. David Richardson. 1987. Tacit collusion and voluntary restraint arrangements in the US auto market. Mimeo, University of Wisconsin-Madison.

Lancaster, Kelvin J. 1975. Socially optimal product differentiation. *American Economic Review* 65:567–585.

Lancaster, Kelvin J. 1979. *Variety, Equity and Efficiency*. New York: Columbia University Press.

Lancaster, Kelvin J. 1980. Intra-industry trade under perfect monopolistic competition. *Journal of International Economics* 10:151–175.

Levinsohn, James. 1988. Empirics of taxes on differentiated products: The case of tariffs in the U.S. automobile industry. In R. E. Baldwin (ed.), *Trade Policy Issues and Empirical Analysis*. Chicago: University of Chicago Press for the National Bureau of Economic Research.

Levinsohn, James. 1991. Testing the imports-as-market-discipline hypothesis. National Bureau of Economic Research, working paper no. 3657.

Linder, Stefan B. 1961. *An Essay on Trade and Transformation*. New York: John Wiley.

Loertscher, Rudolf, and Frank Wolter. 1980. Determinants of intra-industry trade: Among countries and across industries. *Weltwirtschaftliches Archiv* 8:280–293.

Markusen, James R. 1984. Multinationals, multi-plant economies, and the gains from trade. *Journal of International Economics* 16:205–226.

Melvin, James R., and Robert D. Warne. 1973. Monopoly and the theory of international trade. *Journal of International Economics* 3:117–134.

Neary, J. Peter. 1991. Export subsidies and price competition. In E. Helpman and A. Razin (eds.), *International Trade and Trade Policy*. Cambridge, Mass.: MIT Press.

Ohlin, Bertil. 1924. *Handelns Teori*. Stockholm: AB Nordiska Bokhandeln. Published in English in H. Flam and J. Flanders (eds.), *Heckscher-Ohlin Trade Theory*. Cambridge, Mass.: MIT Press, 1991.

Porter, Michael E., and A. Michael Spence. 1977. Vertical integration and differentiated inputs. Harvard Institute for Economic Research, discussion paper no. 576.

Richardson, J. David. 1989. Empirical research on trade liberalization with imperfect competition: A survey. *OECD Economic Studies* 12:7–50.

Rivera-Batiz, Luis, and Paul M. Romer. 1991. International trade and endogenous technological change. *European Economic Review* 35:971–1001.

Romer, Paul M. 1990. Endogenous technological change. *Journal of Political Economy* 98:S71–S102.

Rotemberg, Julio, and Garth Saloner. 1989. Tariffs vs. quotas with implicit collusion. *Canadian Journal of Economics* 22:237–244.

Salop, Steven C. 1979. Monopolistic competition with outside goods. *Bell Journal of Economics* 10:141–156.

Segerstrom, Paul S., Anant, T. C. A., and Dinopoulos, Elias. 1990. A Schumpeterian model of product life cycle. *American Economic Review* 80:1077–1092.

Selten, Reinhard. 1965. Spieltheoretische Behandlung eines Oligopolmodells mit Nachfragetragheit. *Zeitschrift fur die gesamte Staatswissenschaft* 23:301–324.

Shapiro, Carl. 1989. Theories of oligopoly behavior. In R. Schmalensee and R. Willig (eds.), *Handbook of Industrial Organization*, vol. 1. Amsterdam: North-Holland.

Smith, Alasdair, and Paul R. Krugman. Forthcoming. *Empirical Studies of Strategic Trade Policies*. Chicago: University of Chicago Press.

Smith, Alasdair, and Anthony J. Venables. 1988. Completing the internal market in the European Community. *European Economic Review* 32:1501–1525.

Smith, Alasdair, and Anthony J. Venables. 1991. Counting the costs of voluntary export restrictions in the European car market. In E. Helpman and A. Razin (eds.), *International Trade and Trade Policy*. Cambridge, Mass.: MIT Press.

Spence, A. Michael. 1976. Product selection, fixed costs, and monopolistic competition. *Review of Economic Studies* 43:217–236.

Spence, A. Michael. 1977. Entry, capacity, investment and oligopolistic pricing. *Bell Journal of Economics* 8:534–544.

Spence, A. Michael. 1979. Investment strategy and growth in a new market. *Bell Journal of Economics* 10:1–19.

Spencer, Barbara J., and James A. Brander. 1983. International R&D rivalry and industrial strategy. *Review of Economic Studies* 50:702–722.

Svedberg, Peter. 1979. Optimal tariff policy on imports from multinationals. *Economic Record* 55:64–67.

Venables, Anthony J. 1982. Optimal tariffs for trade in monopolistically competitive commodities. *Journal of International Economics* 12:225–242.

Venables, Anthony J. 1985. Trade and trade policy with imperfect competition: The case of identical products and free entry. *Journal of International Economics* 19:1–20.

Venables, Anthony J. 1990. International capacity choice and national market games. *Journal of International Economics* 29:23–42.

Venables, Anthony J., and Alasdair Smith. 1986. Trade and industrial policy under imperfect competition. *Economic Policy* 1:622–672.

Vernon, Raymond. 1966. International investment and international trade in the product cycle. *Quarterly Journal of Economics* 80:190–207.

Wickham, Elizabeth D., and Henry Thompson. 1989. An empirical analysis of intraindustry trade and multinational firms. In P. M. K. Tharaken and J. Kol (eds.), *Intraindustry Trade: Theory, Evidence and Extensions*. New York: Macmillan.

Williamson, Oliver. 1971. The vertical integration of production: Market failure considerations. *American Economic Review* 61:112–123.

Young, Alwyn. 1991. Learning by doing and the dynamic effects of international trade. *Quarterly Journal of Economics* 106:369–406.

I OLIGOPOLY

1 A "Reciprocal Dumping" Model of International Trade

James A. Brander and Paul R. Krugman

1 Introduction

The phenomenon of "dumping" in international trade can be explained by the standard theory of monopolistic price discrimination.[1] If a profit-maximizing firm believes it faces a higher elasticity of demand abroad than at home, and it is able to discriminate between foreign and domestic markets, then it will charge a lower price abroad than at home. Such an explanation seems to rely on "accidental" differences in country demands. In this paper, however, we show how dumping arises for systematic reasons associated with oligopolistic behavior.

Brander (1981) develops a model in which the rivalry of oligopolistic firms serves as an independent cause of international trade and leads to two-way trade in identical products.[2] In this paper we build on Brander (1981) to argue that the oligopolistic rivalry between firms naturally gives rise to "reciprocal dumping": each firm dumps into other firms' home markets.

We generalize Brander (1981) in that reciprocal dumping is shown to be robust to a fairly general specification of firms' behavior and market demand. The crucial element is what Helpman (1982) refers to as a "segmented markets" perception: each firm perceives each country as a separate market and makes distinct quantity decisions for each.

Reciprocal dumping is rather striking in that there is pure waste in the form of unnecessary transport costs.[3] Without free entry, welfare may improve as trade opens up and reciprocal dumping occurs, but it is also possible that welfare may decline. One wonders, therefore, if such a model might not provide a rationale for trade restriction. With free entry, the contrary seems to be true. We derive the fairly strong result that with free entry both before and after trade, the opening of trade (and the resultant reciprocal dumping) is definitely welfare improving for the Cournot case. The pro-competitive effect of having more firms and a larger overall market dominates the loss due to transport costs in this second-best imperfectly competitive world.

Section 2 develops a simple model of Cournot duopoly and trade that shows how reciprocal dumping can occur, and presents the associated welfare analysis. Section 3 describes the free-entry zero-profit equilibrium and derives the result that trade is welfare improving in this case. Section 4 contains concluding remarks.

2 The Basic Model

Assume there are two identical countries, one "domestic" and one "foreign," and that each country has one firm producing commodity Z. There are transport costs incurred in exporting goods from one country to the other. The main idea is that each firm

Originally published in the *Journal of International Economics* 15 (November 1983): 313–323.

regards each country as a separate market and therefore chooses the profit-maximizing quantity for each country separately. Each firm has a Cournot perception: it assumes the other firm will hold output fixed in each country.

The domestic firm produces output x for domestic consumption and output x^* for foreign consumption. Marginal cost is a constant, c, and transport costs of the "iceberg" type imply that the marginal cost of export is c/g, where $0 \leqq g \leqq 1$. Similarly, the foreign firm produces output y for export to the domestic country and output y^* for its own market, and faces a symmetric cost structure. Using p and p^* to denote domestic and foreign price, domestic and foreign profits can be written, respectively, as:

$$\pi = xp(Z) + x^*p^*(Z^*) - c\left(x + \frac{x^*}{g}\right) - F, \tag{1}$$

$$\pi^* = yp(Z) + y^*p^*(Z^*) - c\left(\frac{y}{g} + y^*\right) - F^*, \tag{2}$$

where asterisks generally denote variables associated with the foreign country and F denotes fixed costs. A little inspection reveals that the profit-maximizing choice of x is independent of x^* and similarly for y and y^*: each country can be considered separately.[4] By symmetry we need consider only the domestic country.

Each firm maximizes profit with respect to own output, which yields the first-order conditions:

$$\pi_x = xp' + p - c = 0 \tag{3}$$

$$\pi_y^* = yp' + p - \frac{c}{g} = 0, \tag{4}$$

where primes or subscripts denote derivatives. These are "best-reply" functions in implicit form. Their solution is the trade equilibrium. Using the variable σ to denote y/Z, the foreign share in the domestic market, and letting $\varepsilon = -p/Zp'$, the elasticity of domestic demand, these implicit best-reply functions can be rewritten as:

$$p = \frac{c\varepsilon}{\varepsilon + \sigma - 1}, \tag{3'}$$

$$p = \frac{c\varepsilon}{g(\varepsilon - \sigma)}. \tag{4'}$$

Equations (3′) and (4′) are two equations that can be solved for p and σ. The solutions are:

$$p = \frac{c\varepsilon(1 + g)}{g(2\varepsilon - 1)}, \tag{5}$$

$$\sigma = \frac{\varepsilon(g - 1) + 1}{1 + g}. \tag{6}$$

These solutions are an equilibrium only if second-order conditions are satisfied:

$$\pi_{xx} = xp'' + 2p' < 0, \tag{7a}$$

$$\pi^*_{yy} = yp'' + 2p' < 0. \tag{7b}$$

We also impose the following conditions:

$$\pi_{xy} = xp'' + p' < 0, \tag{8a}$$

$$\pi^*_{yx} = yp'' + p' < 0. \tag{8b}$$

Conditions (8) mean that own marginal revenue declines when the other firm increases its output, which seems a very reasonable requirement. They are equivalent to reaction functions (or best-reply functions) being downward sloping. They imply stability and, if they hold globally, uniqueness of the equilibrium. It is not inconceivable that (8) might be violated by possible demand structures, but such cases would have to be considered unusual. In any case, pathological examples of noncooperative models are well understood (see, for example, Seade 1980 and Friedman 1977) and we have nothing new to say about such problems here. Accordingly we assume (7) and (8) are satisfied.[5]

Positive solutions to (5) and (6) imply that two-way trade arises in this context. A positive solution will arise if $\varepsilon < 1/(1 - g)$ at the equilibrium since this implies that price exceeds the marginal cost of exports ($p > c/g$) and that $\sigma > 0$. Subject to this condition, and given (7) and (8), a unique stable two-way trade equilibrium holds for arbitrary demand. (Brander 1981 considered the case of linear demand only.) It can be easily shown[6] that, at equilibrium, each firm has a smaller market share of its export market than of its domestic market. Therefore, perceived marginal revenue is higher in the export market. The effective marginal cost of delivering an exported unit is higher than for a unit of domestic sales, because of transport costs, but this is consistent with the higher marginal revenue. Thus, perceived marginal revenue can equal marginal cost in both markets at positive output levels. This is true for firms in both countries, which thus gives rise to two-way trade. Moreover, each firm has a smaller markup over cost in its export market than at home: the f.o.b. price for exports is below the domestic price, and therefore there is reciprocal dumping.

The case of constant elasticity demand, $p = AZ^{-1/\varepsilon}$, is a useful special case that is illustrated in figure 1. For profit maximization by the domestic firm (condition (3)), p is decreasing in σ, while condition (4′) for the foreign firm has price increasing in σ. The intercepts on the price axis are, respectively, $c\varepsilon/(\varepsilon - 1)$ and c/g. Thus, provided $c\varepsilon/(\varepsilon - 1) > c/g$ [or $\varepsilon < 1/(1 - g)$] the intersection must be at a positive foreign market share. This condition has a natural economic interpretation, since $c\varepsilon/(\varepsilon - 1)$ is the price that would prevail if there were no trade, while c/g is the marginal cost of exports. What the condition says is that reciprocal dumping will occur if monopoly markups in its absence were to exceed transport costs.

Clearly, the reciprocal dumping solution is not Pareto efficient. Some monopoly distortion persists even after trade, and there are socially pointless transportation costs incurred in cross-hauling. What is less clear is whether, given a second-best world

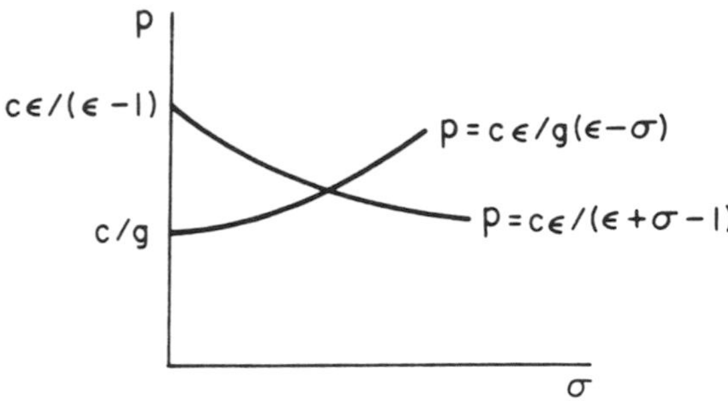

Figure 1

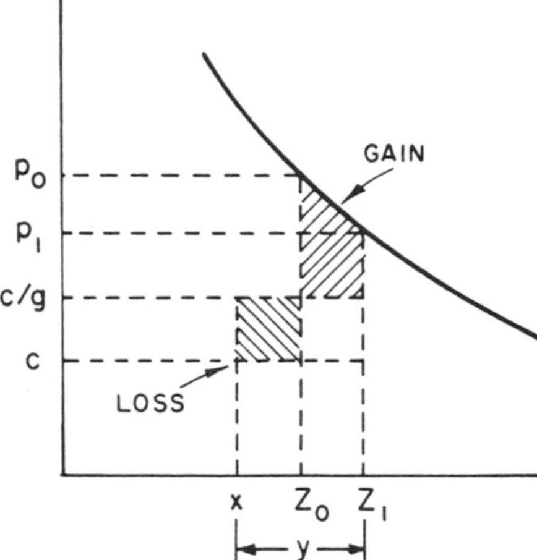

Figure 2

of imperfect competition, free trade is superior to autarky. This is a question with an uncertain answer, because there are two effects. On the one hand, allowing trade in this model leads to waste in transport, tending to reduce welfare. On the other hand, international competition leads to lower prices, reducing the monopoly distortion.

If demand is assumed to arise from a utility function that can be approximated by the form $U = u(Z) + K$, where K represents consumption of a numeraire competitive good, then the welfare effects of trade can be measured by standard surplus measures.

Figure 2 illustrates the point that there are conflicting effects on welfare. In the figure Z_0 is the pretrade output of the monopolized good, p_0 is the pretrade price, and c is marginal cost. After trade, consumption rises to Z_1 and price falls to p_1. But output for domestic consumption falls to x, with imports y. As the figure shows, there is a gain from the "consumption creation" $Z_1 - Z_0$, but a loss from the "production diversion" $Z_0 - x$.

There are two special cases in which the welfare effect is clear. First, if transport costs are negligible, cross-hauling, though pointless, is also costless and the pro-competitive effect insures that there will be gains from trade.

At the other extreme, if transport costs are just at the prohibitive level, then decline slightly so that trade takes place, such trade is welfare reducing. This is easily shown as follows. Overall welfare is given by

$$W = 2[u(Z) - cZ - ty] - F - F^*, \tag{9}$$

where we now use t to denote per unit transport costs instead of the iceberg notation. The 2 arises because there are two symmetric countries. A slight change in t alters welfare as indicated:

$$\frac{dW}{dt} = 2\left[(p - c)\frac{dZ}{dt} - t\frac{dy}{dt} - y\right]. \tag{10}$$

Starting at the prohibitive level, $p = c + t$ and $y = 0$; therefore since

$$\frac{dZ}{dt} = \frac{dx}{dt} + \frac{dy}{dt},$$

equation (10) reduces to

$$\frac{dW}{dt} = 2(p - c)\frac{dx}{dt} = 2t\frac{dx}{dt} > 0. \tag{11}$$

A slight fall in transport costs tends to make x fall[7] (as imports y come in) implying that dW/dt is positive. Therefore, a slight fall in t from the prohibitive level would reduce welfare. The intuition runs along the following lines. A decrease in transport costs has three effects. First, costs fall for the current level of imports, which is a gain. Second, consumption rises; so, for each extra unit consumed, there is a net gain equal to price minus the marginal cost of imports. Finally, there is a loss due to the replacement of domestic production with high cost imports. For near prohibitive levels of transport costs the first two effects are negligible, leaving only the loss.

3 Welfare Effects under Free Entry

The Cournot duopoly model of section 2 is quite specific. However, the existence result is robust to a wide variety of generalizations. One important generalization is to the free-entry case. Moreover, this case has strong welfare properties. Maintaining the assumptions and notation of section 2, except that there will now be n firms in each country in equilibrium, the after-trade price and foreign market share ny/Z, are given by

$$p = \frac{c\varepsilon n(1 + g)}{g(2n\varepsilon - 1)}, \tag{12}$$

$$\sigma = \frac{n\varepsilon(g - 1) + 1}{1 + g}, \tag{13}$$

where n is the number of firms that sets profits equal to zero for each firm i.

We now prove that, under free entry, trade improves welfare. Consider a pretrade free-entry equilibrium.[8] In the domestic industry each firm maximizes profit so that the following first-order condition is satisfied.

$$x_i p' + p - c = 0. \tag{14}$$

Also each firm earns zero profit:

$$\pi_i = x_i p - c x_i - F = 0. \tag{15}$$

After trade opens price changes, and the direction of price movement determines whether consumer surplus rises or falls, and therefore determines the direction of welfare movement since profits remain at zero by free entry. If price falls, welfare rises. The main step in the argument, then, is that price must fall with the opening of trade.

This is most easily seen by contradiction. From (14), $x_i = -(p - c)/p'$, so

$$\frac{dx_i}{dp} = \frac{-p' + (p - c)p''\, dZ/dp}{(p')^2} \tag{16}$$

$$= -\frac{p' + x_i p''}{(p')^2} \tag{17}$$

since $dZ/dp = 1/p'$ and $(p - c) = -p'x_i$. But (17) is strictly positive by (8), which means that x_i must rise if p rises. Also, x_i must stay constant if p remains constant, so as to satisfy (14). However, profits are now given by

$$\pi_i = (p - c)x_i - F + \left(p^* - \frac{c}{g}\right)x_i^*. \tag{18}$$

If price and quantity both rise or remain constant, then $(p - c)x_i - F$ is non negative by (15), and $(p^* - c/g)x_i^*$ is strictly positive since $p^* > c/g$ if trade is to take place. Therefore, π_i must be strictly positive, which is a contradiction. Price must fall and welfare must rise.

The structural source of welfare improvement is that firms move down their average cost curves. Although x_i falls, $x_i + x_i^*$ must exceed the original production levels and average cost must fall. Profits remain at zero and consumer surplus rises.

4 Concluding Remarks

This paper has shown that oligopolistic interaction between firms can cause trade in the absence of any of the usual motivations for trade; neither cost differences nor economies of scale are necessary. The model provides possible explanations for two phenomena not well explained by standard neoclassical trade theory: intraindustry trade and dumping. We refer to such trade as "reciprocal dumping." The welfare effects of such trade are interesting. If firms earn positive profits, the opening of trade will increase welfare if transport costs are low. On the other hand, if transport costs are high, opening trade may actually cause welfare to decline because the procompetitive effect is dominated by the increased waste due to transport costs. However, in the free-entry Cournot model, opening trade certainly increases welfare.

Reciprocal dumping is much more general than the Cournot model. One direction of generalization (either with or without free entry) is to a generalized conjectural variation model, of which the Cournot model is a special case. The essential element of the conjectural variation model is that each firm has a nonzero expectation concerning the response of other firms to its own output. Letting λ denote the expected change in industry output as own output changes, so that $\lambda = 1$ is the Cournot case, and letting foreign and domestic numbers of firms be n^* and n, respectively, yields $\sigma = (nn^*\varepsilon(g - 1) + n^*\lambda)/\lambda(n^* + ng)$ for the case of symmetric linear conjectural variations. This is positive for some range of transport costs. As long as $\lambda > 0$, so that firms believe that their behavior can affect price, the possibility of reciprocal dumping arises.[9] In general, the conjectures need not be symmetric and, for that matter, they need not be linear. An easily developed special case is the Stackelberg leader-follower model in which each firm is, for example, a leader in its home market and a follower abroad.[10]

If price is the strategy variable, reciprocal dumping does not arise in the homogeneous product case. However, a slight amount of product differentiation will restore the reciprocal dumping result, in which case the intraindustry trade motives described here augment the usual product differentiation motives for intraindustry trade. The important element is just that firms have a segmented markets perception. Given this perception, the possibility of the kind of two-way trade described here is relatively robust.

Finally, we should briefly note another application of our basic analysis. Throughout this paper we have assumed that firms must produce in their home country. Given the assumed equality of production costs, however, firms clearly have an incentive to save transport costs by producing near the markets, if they can. But if we allow them to do this, each firm will produce in both countries—and we will have moved from a model of reciprocal dumping in trade to a model of two-way direct foreign investment.

Notes

We would like to thank an anonymous referee for very helpful comments. J. Brander wishes to gratefully acknowledge financial support from a Social Sciences and Humanities Research Council of Canada postdoctoral fellowship.

1. For an exposition of dumping as monopolistic price discrimination, see Caves and Jones (1977, pp. 152–154).

2. Two-way trade in similar (but not necessarily identical) products is often referred to as intraindustry trade. Standard references on the importance of intraindustry trade are Balassa (1966) and Grubel and Lloyd (1975). Alternative explanatory models include Krugman (1979) and Lancaster (1980).

3. The "basing point" pricing literature of the 1930s and 1940s was concerned largely with the waste due to cross-hauling in spatial markets. Of special interest is a paper by Smithies (1942) that contains a model of spatial imperfect competition in which cross-hauling arises. It is a short step to extend this model to an international setting. Smithies' model differs from ours in that he takes price as the strategy variable, but the basic insight that imperfect competition can cause cross-hauling is central to both.

4. This separation is a very convenient simplification that arises from the assumption of constant marginal cost. It is not essential to the results.

5. Conditions (7) and (8) taken together imply, if they hold globally, that $\pi_{xx}\pi^*_{yy} - \pi_{xy}\pi^*_{yx} > 0$ globally, which in turn implies that reaction functions cross only once and that they do so such that the equilibrium is stable. Allowing violation of (8) and the possibility of multiple equilibria clearly does not upset the result that a two-way trade equilibrium exists. It would, however, complicate welfare analysis in the usual way: one could not be sure which equilibrium would obtain so welfare comparisons of different regimes would usually be ambiguous.

6. Expression (3) implies that $\varepsilon > (1 - \sigma)$, while (4) implies that $\varepsilon > \sigma$. Adding these it follows that $\varepsilon > 1/2$ at equilibrium. It is then clear from (6) that $\sigma < 1/2$ if $g < 1$. ($\sigma = 1/2$ if $g = 1$.)

7. The fact that x does fall is easily shown by totally differentiating (3) and (4), and using (7) and (8).

8. Demonstrating existence and uniqueness of free-entry Cournot equilibrium is a general problem to which we have nothing to add. Clearly, there may be "integer" problems in small-numbers cases. The interested reader might consult Friedman (1977) and the references cited there.

9. If $\lambda = 0$, the first-order conditions become $p = c$ for domestic firms and $p = c/g$ for foreigners. Clearly, these cannot both hold. There is a corner solution at $p = c$ and $\sigma = 0$ where the Kuhn-Tucker condition $y(p - c/g) = 0$ holds. Ignoring the lower bound at $y = 0$ leads to the nonsense result that foreign firms would want to produce negative output in the domestic market, which is why the expression for σ approaches $-\infty$ as λ approaches 0. σ should of course be bounded below at 0.

10. Brander and Spencer (1981) examine the implications for tariff policy of a market structure in which the foreign firm is an entry-deterring or potentially Stackelberg leader in both markets.

References

Balassa, Bela. 1966. Tariff reductions and trade in manufactures. *American Economic Review* 56:466–473.

Brander, James A. 1981. Intra-industry trade in identical commodities. *Journal of International Economics* 11:1–14.

Brander, James A. and Barbara J. Spencer. 1981. Tariffs and the extraction of foreign monopoly rents under potential entry. *Canadian Journal of Economics* 14:371–389.

Caves, Richard and Ronald W. Jones. 1977. *World Trade and Payments*, 2d ed. Boston: Little Brown.

Ethier, Wilfred. 1982. Dumping. *Journal of Political Economy* 90:487–506.

Friedman, James W. 1977. *Oligopoly and the Theory of Games*. Amsterdam: North-Holland.

Grubel, Herbert and Peter Lloyd. 1975. *Intra-industry Trade*. New York: Wiley.

Helpman, Elhanan. 1982. Increasing returns, imperfect markets, and trade theory. Discussion Paper, Tel Aviv University.

Krugman, Paul. 1979. Increasing returns, monopolistic competition and international trade. *Journal of International Economics* 9:469–479.

Lancaster, Kelvin. 1980. Intra-industry trade under perfect monopolistic competition. *Journal of International Economics* 10:151–175.

Seade, Jesus. 1980. On the effects of entry. *Econometrica* 48:479–489.

Smithies, Arthur. 1942. Aspects of the basing-point system. *American Economic Review* 32:705–726.

2 Oligopoly in Segmented Markets

Shmuel Ben-Zvi and Elhanan Helpman

1 Introduction

The theory of oligopoly has focused on single markets. There exist, however, many interesting circumstances in which oligopolistic firms interact in several markets, with international trade forming a prime example.[1] Whenever there exist identifiable markets, there often also exist specific costs of servicing them. These costs may differ across firms. Cities provide an example of identifiable markets. Firms located in different cities do not face the same transport costs to a particular market. In the context of international trade, firms located in one country find it cheaper to service the domestic market than to export to other countries. These costs are affected by many factors, including trade policies such as tariffs and export subsidies. All such costs generate some degree of market segmentation and introduce room for market-specific sales decisions rather than overall production decisions. Even in the absence of market-related servicing costs, market segmentation may also arise for institutional reasons, such as the availability of strategic moves under various forms of conduct.

These considerations raise a fundamental question: What is a suitable description of such markets? Namely, how do oligopolistic firms behave when faced with segmented markets, and what are the consequences of this behavior? This is a broad question that cannot possibly be answered in the framework of a single article. A complete answer requires treatment of products with different characteristics, various forms of conduct, entry considerations, and the like. In this paper we deal with a limited problem concerning homogeneous products. We propose a new approach and examine its implications. We argue that our approach is more appealing than the existing alternative, both in principle and because it yields more sensible results.[2]

A detailed motivation and justification of our formulation is provided in the next section. In section 3 we describe the formal model. Then, in section 4 we characterize its solution and discuss economic implications. This is followed by the development of an example in section 5. Concluding comments are provided in section 6.

2 Motivation

In order to justify our formulation of oligopolistic competition in segmented markets, we first describe the accepted formulation. We rely on an explicit example in order to bring out as clearly as possible some of its features. Consider therefore a homogeneous product that is traded in two separate markets, identified by $i = 1, 2$. The demand functions are $x_i = A_i - p_i$, where x_i represents quantity and p_i price. There exist two firms, each one located in a different market. Both have the same unit production costs $c < A_i$ for $i = 1, 2$; zero transport costs to the local market; and transport costs $t < (A_i - c)/2, i = 1, 2$, to the other market. What is a reasonable structure of competition between these firms?

The accepted formulation assumes that each firm j chooses a sales vector $x^j = (x_1^j, x_2^j)$, where x_i^j represents sales of j in market i, taking as given the sales vector of its rival. The outcome is identified with a Nash equilibrium of this game. This is suggested to be a natural extension of Cournot competition to a multimarket setting (see Brander 1981 and the monopoly-duopoly case in Bulow, Geanakoplos, and Klemperer 1985). It is easy to show that the unique equilibrium of this game is $x_i^j = (A_i - c - 2t)/3$ for $i \neq j$; $x_i^i = (A_i - c + t)/3$ for $i = 1, 2$; and $p_i = (A_i + 2c + t)/3$ for $i = 1, 2$.

In this example every firm sells in both markets despite the existence of cross-market transport costs. In the context of international trade it implies wasteful intraindustry (two-way trade) in identical products. Clearly, every firm would have had a higher profit level if it was restricted to sell only in its own market. Given the postulated conduct, however, no firm can credibly precommit to stay away from its rival's market. When transport costs t approach zero, the limit of this equilibrium allocation implies equal sharing of *each* market. It follows that even in the absence of transport costs, the distinction of sales in different markets remains meaningful due to strategic considerations.

It is apparent from this example that in the absence of transport costs, prices differ across markets whenever the intercepts of the demand functions differ. In the event, there exist arbitrage opportunities. One needs therefore to exclude cross-market resale possibilities on some external grounds in order to sustain this equilibrium. It is, however, difficult to find a good justification for this exclusion in the absence of transport costs or other impediments to trade.

This model yields results that differ greatly from other international trade models. Some of them, such as the result on intraindustry trade, do not change when the model is extended to allow for economies of scale in production and free entry of firms. In the latter case a country also has an incentive to impose a tariff. The tariff improves its terms of trade to an extent that outweighs the negative welfare effect caused by additional entry (see Venables 1985). It has also been used to derive an argument about import protection as export promotion (see Krugman 1984).

Evidently, the accepted model of multiple-market oligopolies has strong and unusual implications. It seems therefore desirable to examine its reasonableness in view of accepted ways of thinking about Cournot competition, in particular in view of the fact that price competition seems to be more prevalent (see Scherer 1980, p. 152). For this reason Bertrand price competition is often regarded to better approximate reality. Nevertheless, the Cournot paradigm has been resurrected by Kreps and Scheinkman (1983), who have shown that it describes the outcome of a two-stage game in which firms choose capacities in the first stage and compete in prices in the second. This interpretation is appealing because it separates price from quantity decisions in a reasonable way. Firms have first to build up capacity. Later on, when precommitted to a capacity level, they still have the flexibility to set prices. Naturally, the choice of capacity in the first stage anticipates the outcome of the second-stage game (the solution is subgame perfect). An important distinction between price and quantity is that a firm can precommit to a capacity level but cannot precommit to a price.

In view of this description one could ask how reasonable is the accepted formulation of segmented markets. The answer is not transparent and requires a careful analysis. What our discussion reveals, however, is that following the lead of Kreps and Scheinkman (1983), there exists a natural way to approach this problem. Let firms choose productive capacity in the first stage. This capacity can be used to serve either market. In the next stage they choose selling prices for different markets. Given that markets are distinguishable, a firm can set a different price for each market, at least in principle. Its ability to discriminate depends, however, on how markets operate. After setting prices, firms can allocate sales across markets in the most desirable way. The last stage does not exist in the Kreps-Scheinkman formulation, which deals with a single market, but it plays an essential role in a multimarket setting. A comparison of this approach to the accepted formulation reveals a major difference: here prices are set before the allocation of sales, while in the accepted formulation sales are allocated before the determination of prices. It follows that the accepted approach is suitable for situations in which, say, shipments of goods are committed to destinations before the arrival of concrete orders, while our formulation is suitable to situations in which firms set prices first, receive orders later, and ship commodities afterward. We believe that our formulation better describes the majority of transactions.

In the following section we formalize this idea. Then we ask: What are the properties of equilibria that result from the proposed three-stage game, and how do they compare to equilibria in the accepted formulation? The answers prove to be striking. For one thing, two-way trade in identical products is not an equilibrium outcome in our formulation whenever cross-market unit sales costs (e.g., transport costs) are higher (on average) than in local markets. In addition, cross-market price differentials are bounded by differentials in unit sales costs, and they vanish when the difference in unit sales costs vanishes. It follows that there exist no cross-market arbitrage opportunities. Moreover, in the absence of differences in unit sales costs the equilibria collapse to Cournot equilibria in a single integrated market. This result provides a firm basis to a class of models of international trade that was developed in Helpman and Krugman (1985, ch. 5).

3 The Model

Consider two markets, indexed by $i = 1, 2$. One firm is located in each market; firm j is located in market j. The firms compete in three stages. In the first stage they choose capacities $\bar{x}^j$; in the second stage they choose prices $p^j = (p_1^j, p_2^j)$, where p_i^j describes the price charged by firm j in market i; and in the third stage they choose sales $x^j = (x_1^j, x_2^j)$, where x_i^j describes sales of firm j in market i. There exists a capacity buildup cost that we need not specify now. The unit profit vector of firm j, exclusive of capacity buildup costs, equals $\pi^j = (p_1^j - t_1^j - c^j, p_2^j - t_2^j - c^j)$, where c^j represents unit manufacturing costs and t_i^j represents the unit sales cost in market

i. The latter may result from transport costs, tariffs, export subsidies, sales taxes, and the like. Our typical case consists of $t_k^j > t_j^j$, $k \neq j$. Namely, it is cheaper to sell in one's own market than in the rival's market. This is necessarily the case when there exist no taxes and transport costs to the rival's market are higher. In the context of international trade this inequality is reinforced by the existence of tariffs. On the other hand, export subsidies can reverse it. For these reasons we do not impose a priori restrictions on sales costs.

We denote by $D_i(p_i)$ the demand function in market i, where p_i represents the consumer price. The demand functions are continuous and decreasing. In what follows we use the efficient rationing rule (see [P1] below). Before stating it formally, however, we provide for it a rationale that is based on an interesting economic structure. Assume that in each market there exists a large number of competitive retailers who buy goods from the producers, sell them to final users, and operate with zero costs. We assume at this stage that neither retailers nor final users can resell commodities in the other market. We will show, however, that this assumption is not needed in the most interesting cases. Since the retailers operate with zero costs, the market-clearing price p_i is determined by $D_i(p_i) = x_i^1 + x_i^2$. Whenever the prevailing market i clearing price exceeds producer j's requested price (i.e., $p_i > p_i^j$), retailers are willing to buy additional units from this producer. If the prevailing market i clearing price falls short of producer j's requested price (i.e., $p_i < p_i^j$), retailers refuse to buy goods from this producer. And if $p_i^1 = p_i^2 \leq p_i$, retailers are indifferent as to from whom to buy. We assume that in the last case retailers send half the orders to each one of them. If a producer does not satisfy the placed orders, the orders are rechanneled to the other producer. It is easy to see that this procedure produces the efficient rationing rule: If a firm, say, firm 1, charges a lower price in market i (i.e., $p_i^1 < p_i^2$), it can supply as much as it chooses up to $D_i(p_i^1)$. If it chooses not to supply all this quantity, the second firm can choose to supply up to $D_i(p_i^2) - x_i^1$, provided this expression is nonnegative. When both firms charge the same price, firm j is free to choose sales up to the limit $\max[D_i(p_i^j)/2, D_i(p_i^j) - x_i^k]$.

All the above information is known to all players. We identify the outcome of oligopolistic interaction with the subgame perfect equilibrium of this three-stage game. In order to derive properties of such equilibria, we work backward in the usual way, starting with the last stage.

Sales Game

In the third stage the capacity vector $\bar{x} = (\bar{x}^1, \bar{x}^2)$ and the price vector $p = (p^1, p^2)$ are given. They impose restrictions on feasible sales. The decision problem of firm j can be represented by

$$\max_{x^j} \pi^j \cdot x^j$$

$$\text{s.t.} \quad x_1^j + x_2^j \leq \bar{x}^j, \tag{P1}$$

$$x_i^j \leq \begin{cases} D_i(p_i^j) & \text{for } p_i^j < p_i^k, \\ \max\left[\dfrac{D_i(p_i^j)}{2}, D_i(p_i^j) - x_i^k\right] & \text{for } p_i^j = p_i^k, \qquad i = 1, 2. \\ \max[0, D_i(p_i^j) - x_i^k] & \text{for } p_i^j > p_i^k. \end{cases}$$

This is a linear programming problem whose constraints are described in figure 1 (except that some of the adjacent points, such as A and B, can coincide). It is clear from the figure that given positive unit profit levels, the solution is at point B when unit profits are higher in market 2 and at C when unit profits are higher in market 1. When unit profits equal each other the solution set consists of the entire line segment $\overline{BC}$. It follows that whenever the constraints are as described in the figure and the rival increases sales in market i, the firm responds either by not changing its sales in market i or by redirecting sales to the other market. A third possibility arises when points B and C coincide below the full capacity line (the downward-sloping line). Then the firm responds by cutting back sales in market i without changing sales in the other market. Finally, observe that the quantity response of the firm is one for one with the expansion of the rival. These explanations clarify the nature of the sales game. We now proceed to describe its solution.

Let $X(p, \overline{x})$ be the set of (x^1, x^2) that constitute a pure strategy Nash equilibrium of the sales game. This set may contain more than one element. For this reason it is useful to focus on a particular solution, a focal point, if there exists one with particularly appealing properties. In our context it is natural to assume that whenever there exists

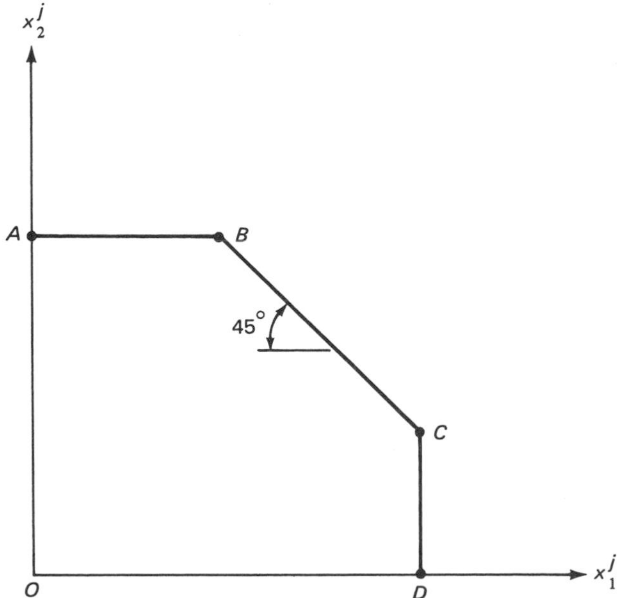

Figure 1

a single Pareto-optimal Nash equilibrium, this equilibrium constitutes the solution. We will show this to be indeed the case. For this purpose we define:

DEFINITION (x^1, x^2) is an *agreeable sales allocation* if $(x^1, x^2) \in X(p, \bar{x})$ and $\pi^j \cdot x^j \geq \pi^j \cdot \tilde{x}^j$, for $j = 1, 2$ and all $(\tilde{x}^1, \tilde{x}^2) \in X(p, \bar{x})$.

DEFINITION $\Pi_S(p, \bar{x}) = (\pi^1 \cdot x^1, \pi^2 \cdot x^2)$ is an *agreeable payoff* of the sales game if (x^1, x^2) is an agreeable sales allocation for $(p, \bar{x})$.

Remark: It is clear from these definitions that if there exist more than one agreeable sales allocation all of them have the same agreeable payoff. Hence, whenever there exists an agreeable sales allocation, $\Pi_S(p, \bar{x})$ is a vector function.

PROPOSITION 1 For every $(p, \bar{x})$ there exists an agreeable sales allocation. (The proof of this proposition is provided in the appendix.)

Price Game

In the second stage the firms take as given capacity levels (that were chosen in the first stage) and choose prices. Prices are chosen in anticipation of the third stage. We are interested in subgame perfect equilibria. Since in the third stage there is a unique agreeable payoff $\Pi_S(p, \bar{x}) = [\Pi_S^1(p, \bar{x}), \Pi_S^2(p, \bar{x})]$, firm j solves in the second stage:

$$\max_{p^j} \Pi_S^j(p, \bar{x}), \qquad j = 1, 2,$$

and the Nash equilibrium of this price game constitutes the solution to the second stage.

We know from Kreps and Scheinkman (1983) that in the single-market case there may not exist a pure strategy equilibrium to the price game. This happens when capacities are in some sense too large. Capacities, which are chosen in the first stage, cannot be arbitrary, and their level is determined, among other things, by the costs of their buildup (see Tirole 1988, ch. 5). In our multiple market setup this issue becomes somewhat more complicated. We proceed by assuming that the parameters of the problem ensure existence of a subgame perfect pure strategy equilibrium for the three-stage game. It follows that the relevant set of capacities for the price game is the set of capacities that are a component of the overall equilibrium. This assumption avoids explicit treatment of the existence issue and enables us to concentrate on the characterization of equilibria, which is our main concern.

Capacity Game

In the general case there does not exist a single Nash equilibrium or focal point to the price game (see the example in section 5). For this reason, when firms choose capacity, they have to form expectations on the outcome of the second stage for every capacity choice. Fortunately, most economic characteristics of the resulting equilibria that we wish to emphasize depend only on the last two stages of the game. Therefore they do not depend on the structure of expectations in the first stage and apply to all subgame perfect equilibria.

4 Economic Implications

We now discuss economic properties of the resulting equilibria. We base our analysis mainly on the last two stages of the game. For this reason most of the discussion is conducted for given capacity levels, which are suppressed unless needed explicitly. The first result, which we prove in the appendix, establishes a relationship between consumer and producer prices.

PROPOSITION 2 If (p^1, p^2, x^1, x^2) is an equilibrium of the last two stages (i.e., prices are a Nash equilibrium of the price game, and sales are an agreeable sales allocation for these prices) such that $x_i^j > 0$, then $p_i^j = p_i$, where p_i represents the consumer price in market i.

That is, if a firm sells in a market, it charges the consumer price. In this case the retailers make zero profits. In addition, when both firms sell in a market, they charge the same price.

Next we establish that whenever average unit sales costs are higher in a rival's market than in the domestic market, at most one firm sells in its rival's market.

PROPOSITION 3 If (p^1, p^2, x^1, x^2) is an equilibrium of the last two stages and $t_2^1 + t_1^2 > t_1^1 + t_2^2$, then either $x_2^1 = 0$ or $x_1^2 = 0$.

Proof: The proof is by contradiction. Suppose, to the contrary, that $(x_2^1, x_1^2) > 0$. This, we argue, implies

(i) $p_2^1 - t_2^1 \geq p_1^2 - t_1^1$, and

(ii) $p_1^2 - t_1^2 \geq p_2^1 - t_2^2$.

First we prove (i). Suppose, to the contrary, that

(a) $p_2^1 - t_2^1 < p_1^2 - t_1^1$.

Then, in the second stage firm 1 can choose $p_1'^1 = p_1^2 - \varepsilon$, $\varepsilon > 0$, and gain a price advantage over firm 2 in market 1. For ε sufficiently small its unit profit $\pi_1'^1 = p_1^1 - t_1^1 - c^1$ exceeds the unit profit in market 2 (which has not changed). Given its price advantage in market 1 and its preference for sales in this market, the solution to the sales game yields (see [P1])

(b′) $x_1'^1 = \min[\bar{x}^1, D(p_1'^1)]$,

which is larger, we argue, than its sales in market 1 in the original agreeable sales allocation; that is, $x_1'^1 > x_1^1$. This can be seen as follows. From proposition 2 we know that when both firms sell in a market they charge the same price. Therefore $D_1(p_1'^1) \geq$

$D_1(p_1^2) \geq x_1^1 + x_1^2$. Using this inequality and the capacity constraint $\bar{x}^1 \geq x_1^1 + x_2^1$, condition (b′) yields

(b) $x_1'^1 \geq x_1^1 + \min(x_1'^2, x_2^1) > x_1^1$.

The next thing to note is that total sales of firm 1 do not decline as a result of the price reduction in market 1; that is,

(c) $x_1'^1 + x_2'^1 \geq x_1^1 + x_2^1$.

This we show as follows. From (P1) we know that in response to an increase in sales by firm 1 in market 1 of, say, Δ, firm 2 does not increase its sales in market 2 by more than Δ. Moreover, we know that the upper limit on sales that firm 1 faces in market 2 does not decline by more than the increase in sales in this market by firm 2. Therefore

$$x_1'^1 - x_1^1 \geq x_2^2 - x_2'^2 \geq x_2^1 - x_2'^1,$$

which proves (c).

Now, using condition (c), the change in the agreeable payoff to firm 1 as a result of the proposed price reduction satisfies

$$\Delta\Pi_s^1 = (\pi_1'^1 x_1'^1 + \pi_2'^1 x_2'^1) - (\pi_1^1 x_1^1 + \pi_2^1 x_2^1) \geq x_1'^1(\pi_1'^1 - \pi_2^1) + x_1^1(\pi_1^1 - \pi_2^1).$$

The first term on the far right-hand side is strictly positive for sufficiently small ε. Therefore, when $x_1^1 = 0$, the entire expression on the far right-hand side is positive. On the other hand, when $x_1^1 > 0$, we know from proposition 2 that both firms charge the same price in market 1. It follows that in this case $\pi_1^1 = \pi_1'^1 + \varepsilon$, which together with (b) implies

$$\Delta\Pi_s^1 \geq \min(x_1'^2, x_2^1)(\pi_1'^1 - \pi_2^1) - \varepsilon x_1^1.$$

The right-hand side is positive for ε sufficiently small because the first term on the right-hand side does not approach zero as ε goes to zero (see [a] and the construction of $p_1'^1$). This shows that when $(x_2'^1, x_1^2) \geq 0$ and (a) holds, firm 1 can choose prices in the second stage that increase its agreeable payoff. Hence, (a) cannot hold in equilibrium and (i) is satisfied. A symmetrical argument implies that (ii) holds.

Finally, combining (i) and (ii), we obtain $t_1^1 + t_2^2 \geq t_2^1 + t_1^2$, which contradicts the proposition's supposition. It follows that whenever average unit sales costs are lower in the firms' own markets, at least one of them does not service the rival's market. □

This proposition has important implications. Note that under normal circumstances a firm's unit sales costs are higher in a rival's market than in the local market because transport costs are higher. The proposition implies that in these circumstances we will not observe cross-hauling of identical products. This conclusion differs from the implication of the accepted formulation in which cross-hauling of identical products is an equilibrium phenomenon. Another implication is that when both firms sell positive quantities and both markets are served, each firm sells a positive quantity in its own market.

As far as international trade is concerned, proposition 3 implies that oligopolistic competition in segmented markets per se cannot explain intraindustry trade. In addition, the existence of tariffs, which increase unit sales costs of foreign rivals, reinforces the lack of intraindustry trade. Export subsidies reduce a firm's unit sales costs to a rival's market. Nevertheless, the proposition implies that even in their presence (in both countries or in the country that would be importing the product under free trade) there exists no intraindustry trade whenever international transport costs and tariffs are sufficiently high. Naturally, it is possible to produce examples of two-way exports with sufficiently high export subsidies. But the latter type of two-way trade is not specific to oligopolistic market structures; it can also arise in competitive environments.

Our next proposition establishes bounds on cross-market price differentials.

PROPOSITION 4 If (p^1, p^2, x^1, x^2) is an equilibrium of the last two stages and

(a) average cross-market unit sales costs are higher than average local market unit sales costs: $t_2^1 + t_1^2 > t_1^1 + t_2^2$;

(b) both markets are active: $D_i(p_i) > 0$ for $i = 1, 2$;

(c) both firms are active: $x_1^j + x_2^j > 0$ for $j = 1, 2$; then

(d) $t_1^1 - t_2^1 \leq p_1 - p_2 \leq t_1^2 - t_2^2$.

Proof: First, observe that the conditions of this proposition satisfy the conditions of proposition 3. Therefore we conclude that either $x_2^1 = 0$ or $x_1^2 = 0$. This conclusion together with suppositions (b) and (c) imply $(x_1^1, x_2^2) > 0$. The latter implies

(i) $p_1^1 - t_1^1 \geq p_2^2 - t_2^1$, and

(ii) $p_2^2 - t_2^2 \geq p_1^1 - t_1^2$.

The proof of conditions (i) and (ii) proceeds in the same way as does the proof of the similar conditions (i) and (ii) in proposition 3 (all we have done is replace the indices of the markets). By proposition 2, $p_1^1 = p_1$ and $p_2^2 = p_2$. These together with (i) and (ii) prove the postulated bounds on cross-market price differentials. □

The proposition identifies bounds on possible equilibrium price differences whenever both firms are active and both markets are served. For concreteness consider the realistic case in which unit sales costs are nonnegative (i.e., subsidies to sales in the rival's market are not too large). Then the bounds imply

$$p_1 + t_2^1 \geq p_2 + t_1^1 \geq p_2 \quad \text{and} \quad p_2 + t_1^2 \geq p_1 + t_2^2 \geq p_1.$$

It follows that whenever retailers and other agents face cross-market transport costs that are no lower than those of the firms, there do not exist arbitrage opportunities across markets.

Some observations on this proposition are in order; we state them without proof in order to save space. First, when the inequality in (a) is reversed (i.e., average unit sales costs across markets are lower than average unit sales costs in local markets), then there exists a similar inequality to (d) with an appropriate switch of market indices. Hence, the conclusion that there do not exist profitable arbitrage opportunities remains valid. Next, if market 1 is not active, the right-hand side inequality in (d) still applies, and if market 2 is not active the left-hand side inequality still applies. In these cases arbitrage opportunities do not exist either. Obviously, if one firm is not active the other is a monopoly facing a threat of entry. In this case (d) does not apply. For example, if unit manufacturing costs of one firm are sufficiently high and the other has zero unit sales costs, it may nevertheless choose to price discriminate across markets. In that case there exist arbitrage opportunities and our no-resale assumption gains significance.

Next, observe that when cross-market transport costs are the same in both directions, say, t, while local transport costs are zero, we obtain

$$|p_1 - p_2| \leq t.$$

Namely, the absolute value of the price differential is bounded above by the cross-market transport cost. Therefore, when transport costs go to zero, the price differential vanishes.

PROPOSITION 5 If both markets are served, both firms are active, and unit sales costs equal zero, then $p_1 = p_2$.

Proof: First observe that it follows from the preceding discussion that the price differential can be made as small as desirable by a choice of sufficiently small unit sales costs. What prevents this argument from being directly applied to the limiting case of zero unit sales costs is the fact that when unit sales costs equal zero, supposition (a) of proposition 4 does not apply. For this reason we provide a direct proof of proposition 5.

Suppose, to the contrary, that prices differ across markets. For concreteness let $p_1 < p_2$. In this case there must exist a firm, say, firm j, that serves market 1 and is not the sole supplier of market 2 (from the fact that both markets are served and both firms are active). This firm can charge a price $p_2 - \varepsilon$, $\varepsilon > 0$, in market 2 and gain a price advantage over its rival who charges p_2 (from proposition 2). It is easy to see that this generates an increase in profits for firm j. □

This result also differs from the accepted formulation. Here the absence of transport costs leads to equal prices in both markets, independently of demand and cost structures. In the accepted formulation they may differ. The introduction of price competition brings about price integration across markets despite the existence of an a priori identification of separate markets. In fact, we prove the following stronger result:

PROPOSITION 6 When unit sales costs equal zero and there exist positive costs to build up capacity, the equilibria of the three-stage game coincide with the equilibria of a one-shot Cournot game in a single market facing the demand function $D(p) = D_1(p) + D_2(p)$.

Proof: Assume that there exists a pure strategy equilibrium to the three-stage game. Then, given the supposition that capacity buildup costs are positive, an active firm makes positive profits in the last two stages that are at least as high as the capacity costs. In the absence of sales costs this implies that an active firm charges a price that exceeds its marginal manufacturing costs c^j. In addition, from proposition 2, both firms charge the same price in every market that they share, and from proposition 5, there exists no price differential across markets. In the event, an active firm sells its entire capacity, for otherwise it gains by slightly reducing its price. Consequently, in every equilibrium of the last two stages,

(i) $D(p) = \bar{x}^1 + \bar{x}^2$.

Hence, there exists a unique equilibrium to the price game. Now, the first-stage game is conducted under constraint (i). Therefore it is a one-shot Cournot game. □

This proposition demonstrates that the identification of a priori separate markets does not necessarily imply market segmentation; whenever sales costs are nil, the outcome is the same as in a Cournot equilibrium of a single integrated market. Our model provides a foundation for the treatment of oligopolistic firms in a multi-market setup in the manner proposed in the first four sections of Helpman and Krugman (1985, ch. 5).

5 Example

In this section we present an example with linear demand functions whose purpose is to demonstrate some concrete equilibria and the possibility of multiple equilibria. We show, in particular, that an equilibrium with trade can coexist with an equilibrium without trade. The demand functions are

$$D_i(p_i) = 1 - p_i. \tag{1}$$

Marginal manufacturing costs equal zero; that is, $c^j = 0$, $j = 1, 2$. Transportation costs equal zero in local markets:

$$0 \le t_2^1 = t_1^2 = t < \tfrac{1}{2} \quad \text{and} \quad t_1^1 = t_2^2 = 0. \tag{2}$$

Capacities are fixed and the same for both firms:

$$0 < \bar{x}^j = \bar{x} \le \tfrac{1}{2}, \qquad j = 1, 2. \tag{3}$$

This specification focuses on the last two stages of the game: the choice of prices and sales allocations. Observe that proposition 3 implies that there are only two possible types of equilibria: type N, in which there is no trade and every firm sells only in its own market, and type T, in which there is trade and one firm sells also in its rival's market. First we establish that in both types of equilibria capacity is not underutilized.

CLAIM 1 Both firms sell all their capacity.

Proof: Suppose, to the contrary, that firm 1 sells less than all of its capacity. We show that in this case it can increase its equilibrium profit level. First, observe that proposition 3 implies that firm 1 sells in market 1. Consider the following two possibilities: (a) only firm 1 serves market 1; (b) both firms serve market 1. In the former case firm 1 will be better off reducing price in market 1 and selling more, because with sales smaller than $\frac{1}{2}$, marginal revenue is positive in market 1. In the latter case both charge the same price in market 1, which equals the consumer price (see proposition 2). An infinitesimal price reduction by firm 1 in this market enables it to increase sales by a finite amount, thereby raising profits. The same arguments apply to firm 2 and market 2. □

CLAIM 2 There exists a type N equilibrium.

Proof: We prove existence by construction. Let

(i) $x_j^j = \bar{x}^j = \bar{x}$ for all j and $x_i^j = 0$ for $i \neq j$;

(ii) $p_i^j = p_j = 1 - \bar{x}$ for all i, j.

We argue that (ii) represents equilibrium prices and (i) is the unique agreeable allocation corresponding to these prices. The second part of the argument is covered by case 9 (H) in the appendix. In order to prove the first part, observe that there are eight possibilities for a firm, say, 1, to deviate from the prices given in (ii), which we summarize in table 1:

Table 1

	$p_1'^1 > p_1$	$p_1'^1 = p_1$	$p_1'^1 < p_1$
$p_2'^1 > p_2$	*A*	*B*	*C*
$p_2'^1 = p_2$	*D*		*E*
$p_2'^1 < p_2$	*F*	*G*	*H*

Deviation *A* reduces sales in market 1 and does not increase sales in market 2. Since marginal revenue is positive (due to [3]), it reduces profits. Deviations *B* and *G* do not change the agreeable allocation and do not change profits. Deviation *C* does not change the agreeable allocation and reduces profits. Deviations *E* and *H* lead to lower unit profits and reduce profits. It therefore remains to deal with *D* and *F*. We only give the argument for *F*, which corresponds to case 9 (B) in the appendix, where it is shown that the agreeable allocation satisfies (see [A1] and [A2]):

$$x_1^1 = \min(\bar{x}, \max[0, 1 - p_1'^1 - x_1^2]), \tag{4a}$$

$$x_2^1 = \min[\bar{x} - x_1^1, 1 - p_2'^1], \tag{4b}$$

$$x_2^2 = \min(\bar{x}, \max[0, \bar{x} - x_2^1]), \tag{5a}$$

$$x_1^2 = \min[\bar{x} - x_2^2, \bar{x}]. \tag{5b}$$

The last two equations imply $x_1^2 = x_2^1$ while (4b) implies $x_2^1 = \bar{x} - x_1^1$. Together they imply $x_1^2 = \bar{x} - x_1^1$. Substituting this result into (4a) yields $x_1^1 = 0$. Hence, $x_2^2 = 0$ as well and $x_1^2 = x_2^1 = \bar{x}$. The conclusion is that deviation F leads each firm to sell all its capacity in the rival's market. This reduces firm 1's profits. □

CLAIM 3 There exists no type T equilibrium for $\bar{x} \leq t$.

Proof: Suppose, to the contrary, that a type T equilibrium exists. Let firm 1 be selling in market 2. Then the agreeable allocation is $x_2^1 > 0$, $x_1^1 = \bar{x} - x_2^1$, $x_1^2 = 0$ and $x_2^2 = \bar{x}$, and prices are $p_1^1 = p_1 = 1 - \bar{x} + x_2^1$, $p_2^j = p_2 = 1 - \bar{x} - x_2^1$ for all j. We do not specify p_1^2. Now suppose that firm 1 reduces its price in market 1 by $\varepsilon > 0$ and increases its price in market 2 by the same ε. In the new agreeable allocation, firm 1 loses ε sales in market 2 and gains ε sales in market 1. For ε sufficiently small its net increase in profits per unit price change is given by the difference in marginal revenues $\Delta\Pi = MR_1 - MR_2$, which is given by (the inverse demand function in market 1 is $1 - x_1^1$ and in market 2 it equals $1 - t - \bar{x} - x_2^1$):

$$\Delta\Pi = (1 - 2x_1^1) - (1 - t - \bar{x} - 2x_2^1) = (t - \bar{x}) + 4x_2^1. \tag{6}$$

In deriving the second equality, we used the fact that $x_1^1 + x_2^1 = \bar{x}$. It is now clear that for $\bar{x} \leq t$ firm 1 gains from the proposed price deviation. It follows that the proposed prices and agreeable allocation are not an equilibrium. □

CLAIM 4 There exists a type T equilibrium for $\bar{x} > t > 0$.

Proof: We prove it by construction. Let

(i) $0 < x_2^1 \leq \min\left[\frac{t}{2}, \frac{\bar{x} - t}{4}, 1 - 2\bar{x}\right];$

(ii) $x_1^1 = \bar{x} - x_2^1;$

(iii) $x_1^2 = 0;\ x_2^2 = \bar{x};$

(iv) $p_1^1 = p_1^2 = p_1 = 1 - \bar{x} + x_2^1;$

(v) $p_2^1 = p_2^2 = p_2 = 1 - \bar{x} - x_2^1.$

One verifies by inspection that (i)–(iii) is an agreeable allocation for the prices given in (iv)–(v) (see case 9 [D] in the appendix). In order to prove that this is an equilibrium, it is necessary to inspect all possible price deviations by firms 1 and 2 and verify that they do not increase profits of the deviating firm. In order to save space, we consider only two interesting deviations, one for each firm. First, consider the possibility that firm 1 reduces price in market 1 and increases price in market 2, with the price reduction being equal to the price increase. The change in profits per unit price change as a result of a small change equals $\Delta\Pi$ as given in (6). Clearly, (i) implies $\Delta\Pi < 0$, so this deviation is not profitable. Next, consider the possibility that firm 2 increases price in markets 1 and 2. The change in its revenue takes place along the demand curve $1 - x_2^1 - x_2^2$, which has a marginal revenue (evaluated at the initial point) of $1 - x_2^1 - 2\bar{x}$. This marginal revenue is nonnegative under (i), and therefore this price change does not increase profits. Other price deviations can be similarly analyzed. □

Claims 2 through 4 show that the capacity interval $[0, \frac{1}{2}]$ can be divided into two subsets, $N \equiv [0, t]$ and $T \equiv (t, \frac{1}{2}]$, such that on N there exists a unique equilibrium in which there is no trade and on T there exists a continuum of equilibria with the trade volume being anywhere between zero and the right-hand side of (i) in the proof of claim 4 (trade is, however, unidirectional). In order to compare these equilibria with the equilibria that obtain under the accepted formulation, observe that with fixed identical capacities in the interval $[0, \frac{1}{2}]$ the accepted formulation yields the following unique equilibrium sales:

$$x_i^j = \max\left[0, \frac{\bar{x} - t}{2}\right],$$

$$x_j^j = \bar{x} - x_i^j;\ i \neq j.$$

It follows that on N both solution concepts yield the same equilibrium. On T, however, the accepted formulation yields two-way trade, while our formulation yields an equilibrium without trade as well as a continuum of equilibria with one-way trade. Naturally, due to symmetry, either firm 1 or firm 2 can be selling in the rival's market. In our case the volume of trade does not exceed $(\bar{x} - t)/4$, while in the accepted formulation it equals $(\bar{x} - t)$. Hence, in our case the volume of trade is at most a quarter of the volume of trade in the accepted formulation.

Next, observe that the measure of the set of equilibria at a point in T can be represented by the upper bound on x_2^1 (or x_1^2). As transportation costs t decline toward zero, this measure also declines toward zero. Evidently, the extent of multiplicity of equilibria is bounded by transport costs whenever they are sufficiently small. In the limit, when $t = 0$, only type N equilibria exist. For $t = 0$ proposition 5 ensures that even when capacities are not the same, equilibrium prices are the same in both markets. Moreover, proposition 6 ensures that if we were to endogenize capacity choice, then for $t = 0$ the resulting unique equilibrium would have been the Cournot outcome in a single integrated market.

There are two interesting points concerning type T equilibria (with positive transportation costs). First, the firm that sells in both markets charges a lower price in the rival's market. Since it also incurs transportation costs to the rival's market, its unit profit differential is even larger than the price differential. In the context of international trade this price structure represents dumping under some common definitions. Observe, however, that the diversified firm cannot gain from a shift of sales from the rival's market to its own, despite the unit profit differential. The reason is that a comparison of marginal revenues across markets makes this shift unprofitable on T. Second, note that the diversified firm makes higher profits than the firm that sells only in its own market. This is seen as follows. Let the diversified firm reduce price in its own market to the level that enables it to sell the entire capacity in this market, and let it raise price in the other market. Then the resulting agreeable allocation enables it to sell all its output in its own market at a price that exceeds the price charged by the rival in the rival's market. Its profits under this allocation, which are the profits obtained in the corresponding type N equilibrium, are higher than the rival's, but smaller than in the original type T equilibrium. Therefore in a trading equilibrium the exporting firm has higher profits than in a nontrade equilibrium, and the nonexporting firm has lower profits than in a nontrade equilibrium.

6 Conclusions

Our solution to the problem of oligopolists that interact in several markets has a number of appealing features. First, the structure of the game seems to resemble actual trading practices. Second, in the resulting equilibrium there do not exist unexploited arbitrage opportunities. Third, there is no wasteful two-way trade in identical products. Fourth, market segmentation is possible only when cross-market unit sales costs are positive. When these costs approach zero, the equilibrium approaches the Cournot outcome for a single integrated market.

In deriving these results, we have used the efficient rationing rule. In addition, we have provided a new justification for its use in terms of an institutional structure that assigns a role to competitive retailers. We believe that our main results remain valid for other institutional structures that generate different rationing rules. For our purpose these rules need only ensure the existence of an agreeable allocation and consumer prices that are equal in equilibrium to the prices charged by active firms (propositions 1 and 2).

The proposed framework can be applied to a number of problems. For example, it is possible to interpret our markets as submarkets for differentiated products. In this case unit sales costs can be interpreted as the additional costs that a firm has to bear in order to adjust a unit of the basic product to the specified variety. The model can also be extended to spatial problems. Under this interpretation a choice of location in physical or characteristics space involves choosing a trade-off among different unit sales costs. The model can be applied to the analysis of trade structure and trade policy when each market is interpreted to be a different country. In general, it is possible to deal with short-run effects, for which the capacity levels are fixed, and with long-run effects that take account of capacity adjustments.

A final application concerns the formation of multinational corporations. The accepted formulation of the game in segmented markets assumes that firms can precommit quantities to particular markets. This, we have argued, is unreasonable when discussing arm's-length trade with production concentrated in a single location. Under these circumstances a firm can precommit total output (via a capacity buildup) but not its distribution across markets. It is, however, possible to think about foreign direct investment as a precommitment to quantities at particular locations (although in the third stage, after the choice of prices, it is necessary to decide how to allocate outputs across markets). It might, for example, be more expensive to build two plants, each one in a different market, than a single plant with their joint capacity. Nevertheless, the strategic value of these separate plants—that derives from the fact that they change the conditions of the subsequent stages of the game—may make it worthwhile to incur the additional costs. These considerations can be developed into a strategic theory of multinational corporations.

Appendix

In what follows we provide a joint proof of propositions 1 and 2 for the case $(\pi^1, \pi^2) \gg 0$. The arguments do not change much when some unit profit levels are nonpositive. Our proof outlines a method for constructing equilibria. In order to prove the second proposition, it is sufficient to prove

PROPOSITION 2′ Let (x^1, x^2) be an agreeable sales allocation for $(p, \bar{x})$, such that $x_i^j > 0$ and $p_i^j < p_i$ for some j. Then there exists a firm k that can raise its agreeable payoff by deviating from p^k.

For the purpose of the proposition it is sufficient to consider cases in which a firm's price is below the consumer price; if it is above the consumer price, retailers do not buy from this firm and its sales are zero, thereby violating the supposition of proposition 2 that requires positive sales.

We have already shown that (P1) is a linear programming problem whose constraints are described in figure 1. Recall that when the firm has a higher unit profit in market 1 it chooses point C, because it desires to sell as much as possible in the market with the higher unit profits. The residual capacity is sold in the other market (if possible). If unit profits are the same in both markets, it cares only about total sales and is therefore indifferent between all points along the line segment $\overline{BC}$. In many of the situations to be discussed it proves useful to consider a particular market in isolation. The next lemma provides conditions under which this is possible and establishes the uniqueness of equilibrium sales in the isolated market. The proof of the lemma is by construction, which helps us to understand subsequent arguments.

LEMMA If for every j, (i) $\pi_k^j < \pi_i^j$, or (ii) an equilibrium value of x_k^j is known,

(a) then there exist unique values of sales in market i that are part of the equilibrium sales vector;

(b) and if the solution implies that $x_i^j > 0$ and $p_i^j < p_i$, then (x_i^1, x_i^2) are also equilibrium sales when p_i^j is replaced with $p_i'^j = p_i^j + \varepsilon$, for $\varepsilon > 0$ sufficiently small.

Proof: The known limit of firm j's sales in market i is denoted by y_i^j and it is defined by

$$y_i^j = \begin{cases} \bar{x}^j - x_k^j & \text{for } x_k^j \text{ known,} \\ \bar{x}^j & \text{otherwise.} \end{cases}$$

Hence, if sales in market k are known the limit on sales in market i is given by residual capacity, and if sales in market k are not known (but under the conditions of the lemma profit margins are higher in market i) the limit on sales in market i is given by capacity. In both cases each firm would like to sell as much as possible, up to its sales limit, in market i. If one of the firms, say, firm 1, has a strictly lower price in market i, then in the third-stage equilibrium $x_i^1 = \min[y_i^1, D_i(p_i^1)]$ and $x_i^2 = \min(y_i^2, \max[0, D_i(p_i^2) - x_i^1])$ (because firm 1, which has the lower price, is free to sell in market i as much as it wishes under the demand constraint). This proves part (a) for the case of unequal prices.

To prove part (b), first consider firm 1. If its price is lower than the consumer price, $x_i^1 = y_i^1$. Neither this solution nor the sales of firm 2 change when firm 1 slightly raises its price. Next, consider firm 2. If its price is below the consumer price, $x_i^1 = y_i^1$ and $x_i^2 = y_i^2$. This solution does not change either when firm 2 slightly raises its price.

Next, consider the case in which both firms charge the same price in market i, say, p_i. If for one of them, say, firm 1, $y_i^1 < D_i(p_i)/2$, then in equilibrium $x_i^1 = y_i^1$ and $x_i^2 = \min[y_i^2, D_i(p_i) - y_i^1]$. If, on the other hand, the known limits on sales in market i are larger than half the demand for both firms, each one supplies half the demand. This proves part (a) for the equal price case. To prove part (b), note that $p_i^1 = p_i^2 < p_i$ implies $x_i^1 = y_i^1$ and $x_i^2 = y_i^2$. Clearly, this solution does not change when one of the firms slightly raises its price. It is also clear from this proof that the equilibrium in market i corresponds to the efficient rationing rule in a single market (see Tirole 1987, ch. 5). □

Now, in order to prove the propositions, we have to deal with nine cases that are described in table A1. The columns describe firm 1's possibilities of unit profit differentials across markets, while the rows describe these possibilities for firm 2. It is clear from the table that a proof of case 9 also covers case 1; a proof of case 2 also covers 4, 6, and 8; and a proof of 3 also covers 7. In fact, it will become clear from the proof of 9 that it applies to all even cases. Hence, we proceed to prove the propositions for cases 3, 5, and 9.

Table A1

	$\pi_1^1 < \pi_2^1$	$\pi_1^1 = \pi_2^1$	$\pi_1^1 > \pi_2^1$
$\pi_2^2 < \pi_1^2$	1	2	3
$\pi_2^2 = \pi_1^2$	4	5	6
$\pi_2^2 > \pi_1^2$	7	8	9

Proof of Case 3: In this case both firms have higher unit profits in market 1. Hence, we can apply part (a) of the lemma to establish unique equilibrium sales levels in market 1. Using these quantities we can again use part (a) of the lemma to establish unique sales levels in market 2. These sales levels constitute the unique agreeable sales allocation. This completes the proof of proposition 1. In this case part (b) of the lemma is applicable, which proves proposition 2′.

Proof of Case 9: Table A2 presents a subdivision of this case on the basis of whoever charges a lower price in each market; columns represent price advantages in market 1 while rows represent price advantages in market 2. In all these cases firm j has a higher unit profit level in market j (the critical distinction is that each firm has a higher unit profit level in a different market). The resulting nine possibilities are grouped into four categories. In category A at least one firm has a price advantage (lower price) in the market in which it prefers to sell (i.e., in which it has a higher unit profit level). In B every firm has a price advantage in the less preferred market. In C one firm has a price advantage in the less preferred market, while there is no price difference in the other market. Finally, in D there are no price advantages in either market. We now proceed to prove the propositions for each category.

Subcase A: Without loss of generality, consider the case in which firm 1 has a price advantage in market 1 (the first column). Since it also prefers to sell in market 1, it will use the price advantage to sell there as much as possible. Hence, $x_1^1 = \min[\bar{x}^1, D_1(p_1^1)]$. Now consider market 2. Firm 2 prefers to sell there, and firm 1's sales in market 1 are known. Hence, we may apply part (a) of the lemma to obtain the unique equilibrium sales in market 2. Having obtained these sales we may now compute the sales of firm 2 in market 1 as $x_1^2 = \min(\bar{x}^2 - x_2^2, \max[0, D_1(p_1^2) - x_1^1])$. This proves the first proposition. In order to prove the second proposition, consider first market 1, in which firm 1 has a price advantage. Since in this case $x_1^1 = \min[\bar{x}^1, D_1(p_1^1)]$, then if its price is lower than the consumer price, $x_1^1 = \bar{x}^1 < D_1(p_1^1)$. In this case it can slightly raise its price and still be able to sell its entire capacity in this market without affecting other components of the agreeable sales allocation. The result is higher profits. Next, consider market 2. We have used part (a) of the lemma to prove uniqueness of the equilibrium allocation. Part (b) can now be used to prove the second proposition.

Table A2

	$p_1^1 < p_1^2$	$p_1^1 = p_1^2$	$p_1^1 > p_1^2$
$p_2^2 < p_2^1$	A	A	A
$p_2^2 = p_2^1$	A	D	C
$p_2^2 > p_2^1$	A	C	B

Subcase B: In this case each firm has a price advantage in the market in which it earns lower unit profits. Hence, as is clear from (P1), its sales in the market with the higher unit profit—in which it wants to sell as much as possible—are constrained by either its capacity or by residual demand. Therefore in the solution to (P1) for firm 1

$$x_1^1 = \min(\bar{x}^1, \max[0, D_1(p_1^1) - x_1^2]). \tag{A1}$$

Naturally, the firm wants to sell the residual capacity in market 2, but it may face there insufficient demand. Hence, in the solution to (P1)

$$x_2^1 = \min[\bar{x}^1 - x_1^1, D_2(p_2^1)], \tag{A2}$$

where x_1^1 is taken from (A1). It is now clear from (A1) and (A2) that the firm's best response in each market depends on x_1^2 but not on x_2^2. We will characterize equilibria by considering the best response functions $x_2^1 = R^1(x_1^2)$ and $x_1^2 = R^2(x_2^1)$ (the derivation of the best response function for the second firm follows the same steps as the derivation of the best response function for firm 1). There exist only two types of response functions that are implicit in (A1) and (A2); they are described by reaction curves in the two panels of figure 2. Type I reaction curve arises when $D_1(p_1^1) \geq \bar{x}^1$ and type II arises when $D_1(p_1^1) \leq \bar{x}^1$. The two types coincide when demand equals capacity.

It is evident from the shapes of these curves that when both firms' reaction curves are combined in the same figure they intersect only once, unless one curve is of type I and the other of type II. In the latter case there also exists a single intersection, unless $\bar{x}^1 + \bar{x}^2 = D_1(p_1^1) + D_2(p_2^2)$. When this condition is met the reaction curves coincide on the upward-sloping portion, as demonstrated in figure 3. In this case there exists a

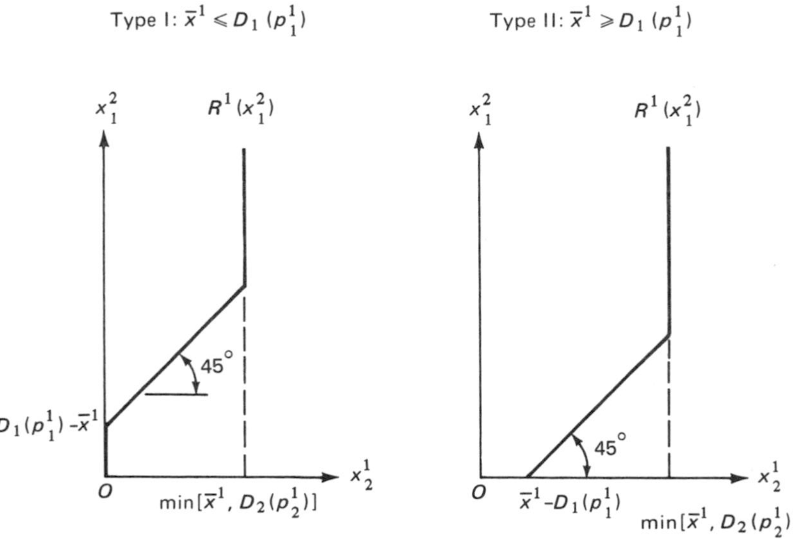

Figure 2

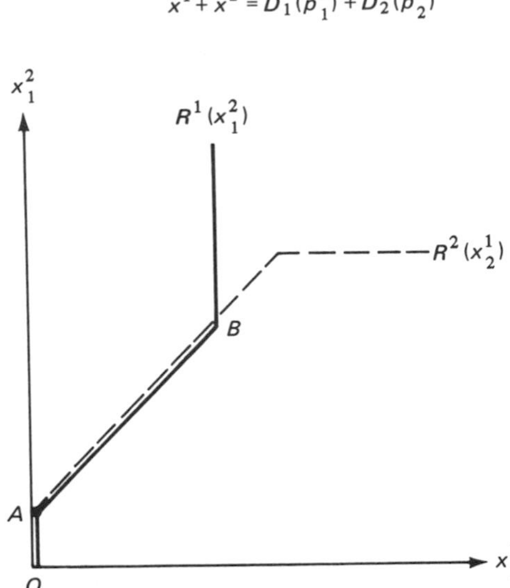

Figure 3

continuum of Nash equilibria to the sales game. However, the closer an equilibrium point is to the origin, the higher the profit level of every firm (because by moving toward the origin firms swap sales from a market with lower unit profits to one with higher unit profits). Hence, there exists a unique agreeable sales allocation (point A in the figure). This completes the proof of the first proposition.

In order to prove the second proposition, we first consider the case in which $\bar{x}^1 + \bar{x}^2 \neq D_1(p_1^1) + D_2(p_2^2)$. We have shown that in this case there exists a unique equilibrium of the sales game. It is straightforward to observe that (i) if both firms sell in a market and one has a lower price, the equilibrium does not change when the lower price firm raises its price slightly; and (ii) if a firm sells in a market and its price is lower than the consumer price, a slight increase in its price does not change equilibrium sales. Next, consider the case $\bar{x}^1 + \bar{x}^2 = D_1(p_1^1) + D_2(p_2^2)$. If in addition $\bar{x}^1 = D_1(p_1^1)$, the unique agreeable sales allocation is $x_i^i = \bar{x}^i$, and therefore also $p_i^i = p_i$ for $i = 1, 2$. In this case the conditions of the proposition are not satisfied. When $\bar{x}^1 \neq D_1(p_1^1)$, there exists a firm, say, firm 2, for whom $\bar{x}^2 > D_2(p_2^2)$. From figure 3, which describes this case, one can see that (i) $x_2^2 = D_2(p_2^2)$, $x_2^1 = 0$, and therefore $p_2^2 = p_2$, so the suppositions of the proposition are not satisfied by market 2, and (ii) $x_1^2 > 0$ and $p_1^1 = p_1 > p_1^2$, a case in which point A is the agreeable sales allocation (this point does not change when firm 2 slightly raises its price and, therefore, its profits).

Subcase C: First consider the market in which no firm has a price advantage. Clearly, if the firm that has a higher unit profit in this market has a capacity level that falls short of half of demand, it will sell all its capacity in this market. It is then straightforward to calculate the resulting unique equilibrium allocation. In addition, in these circumstances there is no market in which both sell and in which one has a price advantage. This covers both propositions for this case.

Next, consider the case in which the firm that has a higher unit profit in the market with equal prices, say, firm 1, has a capacity level that exceeds half of demand. Clearly, it will supply at least half the demand. Define therefore its pseudocapacity to be $\bar{\mathbf{x}}'^1 = \bar{x}^1 - D_1(p_1^1)/2$ and the pseudodemand in market 1 to be half the original demand. Using these pseudoquantities in conjunction with the remaining original data, we can redefine the problem giving firm 2 a price advantage in market 1. This brings us to case *B*, and its arguments can now be applied to prove both propositions.

Subcase D: If there exists a firm with a capacity that is less than half of demand in the market in which it has a higher unit profit, apply the first half of the argument in *C*. If not, apply the argument in the second half of *C*, defining pseudocapacities for both firms.

Proof of Case 5: In this case a firm cares only about its total sales; their division across markets does not affect profits. However, constraints on sales in particular markets depend on prices. For this reason it is possible to categorize the relevant subcases on the basis of price advantages in different markets, as we have done in case 9. This classification is presented in table A3. Instead of discussing each category, we demonstrate the arguments for *F* and *H* only.

Subcase F: Here one firm has a price advantage in both markets, say, firm 1. Hence, if aggregate demand $D_1(p_1^1) + D_2(p_2^1)$ falls short of its capacity, it supplies both markets and firm 2 sells nothing. This is the unique equilibrium, and it does not satisfy the conditions of proposition 2′. If, on the other hand, the above aggregate demand exceeds its capacity, it sells its entire capacity and firm 2 picks up the residual demand. Since firm 1 is indifferent about which market it sells in, the agreeable sales allocation is achieved when sales of firm 2 are maximized subject to the constraint that firm 1 sells its entire capacity. This problem has a unique solution, which proves the first proposition.

Table A3

	$p_1^1 < p_1^2$	$p_1^1 = p_1^2$	$p_1^1 > p_1^2$
$p_2^2 < p_2^1$	*E*	*G*	*F*
$p_2^2 = p_2^1$	*G*	*H*	*G*
$p_2^2 > p_2^1$	*F*	*G*	*E*

To prove the second proposition, observe that as long as firm 1 has a price advantage in both markets and aggregate demand (evaluated at its prices) exceeds its capacity, it is able to sell the entire capacity. Hence, a slight price increase in a market in which its price is lower than the consumer price does not eliminate its price advantage and raises its profits. If, on the other hand, aggregate demand is lower or equal to its capacity, it sells the demanded quantities, and the consumer price in each market is equal to its price. In this case the suppositions of the proposition are not satisfied; neither are they satisfied for firm 2, which has a price higher than the consumer price and no sales.

Subcase H: In this case both firms are indifferent about sales in alternative markets (they care only about total sales), and none of them has a price advantage in either market. Therefore, if there exists a firm whose capacity is smaller or equal to $[D_1(p_1^j) + D_2(p_2^j)]/2$, it sells its entire capacity and the other firm picks up the residual demand up to its own capacity level. Since they are indifferent as to which market they are serving, there typically exists a continuum of agreeable sales allocations, all yielding the same agreeable payoff. If the capacity of every firm is larger than half of aggregate demand, each firm supplies half of every market. This is the unique Nash equilibrium and the agreeable allocation. As far as the second proposition is concerned, observe that if the firms' price in a market is below the consumer price, both sell their entire capacity. Let a firm slightly raise its prices in both markets. This shifts us to subcase *F*, but it is quite clear that for sufficiently small price increases it is able to sell its entire capacity after the price increase and thereby increase profits. This proves the second proposition. □

Notes

This paper was written when both authors were visiting MIT. We wish to thank Motti Perry and Jean Tirole for helpful comments.

1. International trade theory has been concerned with this phenomenon for a number of years (see, for example, Brander 1981 and Helpman and Krugman 1985, ch. 5). But multiple market interactions have also been addressed in the industrial organization literature (see Bulow, Geanakoplos, and Klemperer 1985).

2. Venables (1990) is concerned with a similar issue. His approach differs, however, from ours.

References

Brander, J. A. 1981. Intra-industry trade in identical commodities. *Journal of International Economics* 11:1–14.

Bulow, J., J. Geanakoplos, and P. Klemperer. 1985. Multimarket oligopoly: Strategic substitutes and complements. *Journal of Political Economy* 93:488–511.

Helpman, E., and P. R. Krugman. 1985. *Market Structure and Foreign Trade*. Cambridge, Mass.: MIT Press.

Kreps, D., and J. Scheinkman. 1983. Quantity precommitment and Bertrand competition yield Cournot outcomes. *Bell Journal of Economics* 12:326–337.

Krugman, P. R. 1984. Import protection as export promotion: International competition in the presence of oligopoly and economies of scale. In Kierzkowski, H. (ed.), *Monopolistic Competition and International Trade*. Oxford: Oxford University Press.

Scherer, F. M. 1980. *Industrial Market Structure and Economic Performance*, 2d ed. Chicago: Rand McNally.

Tirole, J. 1988. *The Theory of Industrial Organization.* Cambridge, Mass.: MIT Press.

Venables, A. J. 1985. Trade and trade policy with imperfect competition: The case of identical products and free entry. *Journal of International Economics* 19:1–19.

Venables, A. J. 1990. International capacity choice and national market games. *Journal of International Economics* 29:23–42.

3 Trade and the Gains from Trade with Imperfect Competition

James R. Markusen

1 Introduction

It is probably fair to say that international trade economists have long recognized the importance of imperfect competition and increasing returns to scale in determining both the direction of and gains from trade. Both of these factors are given important roles by such distinguished economists as Graham (1923), Ohlin (1933), and Kindleberger (1969). Much more recently, trade theorists have begun to construct formal models of imperfect competition and increasing returns to scale in order to sort out the precise circumstances under which the propositions of earlier writers are or are not valid.

The role of IRS as a determinant of trade has, for example, been recently examined by Melvin (1969), Ethier (1979), Krugman (1979), and Markusen and Melvin (1981). Among other things, these authors show that increasing returns imply that there will often exist gains from trade even if two countries are absolutely identical in all respects. More specifically, trade under conditions of increasing returns may permit cost savings through increased specialization even though there does not exist any natural pattern of comparative advantage.

Considerably less well-developed is a growing literature on general equilibrium and trade under conditions of imperfect competition. Negishi (1961) and Krugman (1979) adopt monopolistic competition models in which firms with decreasing average cost produce differentiated goods. Krugman points out that trade will allow the production of more types of goods, resulting in gains from trade even for two identical economies. Melvin and Warne (1973) consider the case of pure monopoly, and derive necessary and sufficient conditions for the existence of monopoly equilibrium. Melvin and Warne also discuss the question of gains from trade, but are able to derive very few firm results. They discuss the possibility of one or even both countries losing from trade, but do not prove that any of these situations can or cannot occur. Finally, Fishelson and Hillman (1979) and Auquier and Caves (1979) consider commercial policy questions from the point of view of a single country when one or more domestic industries are monopolized. None of these authors has, however, dealt with the problem of oligopolistic interdependence and the relationship between the trading (duopoly) and autarky (pure monopoly) equilibria.

The purpose of this paper is to offer a number of extensions to the basic theory for the case of monopoly/duopoly. The paper will, in particular, extend and in some cases reverse several propositions put forward by Melvin and Warne. In order to accomplish this purpose, section 2 develops a two-good, two-factor, two-country model in which the production of one good is monopolized in both countries (i.e., the same sector is monopolized in each country). The monopolist in each country is assumed to behave in a Cournot-Nash fashion when trade takes place.

Originally published in the *Journal of International Economics* 11 (November 1981): 531–551.

The first contribution of the paper is to formalize and prove a proposition that has existed for many years in the trade-policy literature: there can exist gains from trade due to the reduction of domestic monopoly power. To the best of my knowledge, there does not exist a formal two-country treatment of this problem. More specifically, it is demonstrated that if two countries are identical in all respects, there will in fact exist bilateral gains from trade given the Cournot-Nash assumption. Interestingly, trade will not occur when both identical economies are open unless there are increasing returns in production. The presence of potential competition, however, implies that the two Cournot duopolists will each produce more than in the absence of trade possibilities, thus leading to an improvement in welfare. Imperfect competition can therefore lead to gains from trade for two identical economies. This finding is similar to and indeed complementary to the point made by Melvin (1969) and Krugman (1979) about gains from trade under conditions of increasing returns.

When countries differ in size, and when there are constant returns to scale in production, it is demonstrated that the Cournot-Nash equilibrium involves the large country importing the monopolized good. With constant returns, total world real income is always increased by trade, a finding that Melvin and Warne (1973) were not able to prove. The distribution of gains will, however, be unequal if country sizes are unequal. The small country will always be an absolute and a relative gainer, while the large country may in fact lose relative to autarky.[1] A sufficient condition for the large country to gain is that trade lead to an expansion in the domestic production of the monopolized good. One final result for the different-country-size, constant-returns case is that trade may make relative factor prices more unequal in the two countries relative to autarky.[2]

The final section of the paper considers briefly the more complicated case of increasing returns in the production of the monopolized good. With increasing returns to scale, the large country has a cost advantage in producing and exporting the monopolized good. This cost-side condition thus tends to work in the opposite direction to the demand-side condition just mentioned. This unfortunately leaves us with a Cournot-Nash equilibrium in which both the direction of trade and the distribution of gains from trade are indeterminant. Trade is still guaranteed to increase total world real income, however, provided that the production set of each country is convex.

At a general level, this paper thus concludes that the conventional wisdom regarding the procompetitive aspects of trade is only partly correct. While trade generally increases world real income, it is not guaranteed to increase the real income of each trading country.[3]

2 Cournot-Nash Equilibrium: The Constant-Returns-to-Scale Case

Two countries (country L and country S) produce and trade two goods (X and Y) from factors in fixed and inelastic supply. Superscripts l and s will denote country L and country S, respectively. In each country, X is produced by a monopolist who owns no factors of production while Y is produced competitively. The monopolist, in other words, only owns "property rights" to the production of X. p will denote the price of X in terms of $Y(p = p_x/p_y)$.

In order to focus on the output market distortion, we will assume that factor markets are competitive. Thus, the monopolist views himself as being able to influence the price of X but not the prices of factors of production. This could occur, for example, if X is a small percentage of national output. Adding the assumption of monopsony power (Herberg and Kemp 1971; Feenstra 1980; McCulloch and Yellen 1980; Markusen and Robson 1980) would significantly complicate the analysis via distortions in the production frontier but would not, in my opinion, add to or alter the results in any substantial way.

Given this factor-market assumption, we have of course the standard result that production will be efficient and that it will take place at a point on the efficient production frontier. This production frontier, or production possibility curve, will be specified as follows:

$$\begin{aligned} &Y^i = F^i(X^i), \qquad F^{i'}(X^i) < 0, \qquad i = l, s, \\ &-F^{i'} = \frac{MC_x^i}{MC_y^i} = MRT^i, \qquad i = l, s, \end{aligned} \tag{1}$$

where MC_x and MC_y are respectively the marginal costs of X and Y and MRT is the marginal rate of transformation, defined to be positive. Throughout this section we will assume constant returns to scale and differing factor intensities between goods such that $F'' < 0$; that is, the production possibility curve is concave (the production set is convex). A second very useful result that follows from constant returns is that the MRT depends only on the output ratio X^i/Y^i if two countries have identical relative factor endowments. Thus, if X and Y are produced from capital and labor (K and L), for example, we have the following result:

$$\frac{\bar{K}^l}{\bar{L}^l} = \frac{\bar{K}^s}{\bar{L}^s} \quad \text{implies} \quad F^{l'} = F^{s'} \Leftrightarrow \frac{X^l}{Y^l} = \frac{X^s}{Y^s}, \tag{2}$$

where $\bar{K}^i$ and $\bar{L}^i$ are country i's total endowments of capital and labor, respectively. Throughout the paper we will assume that endowment ratios are equal so as to "neutralize" the Heckscher-Ohlin basis for trade.

On the demand side of the model, it is assumed that all consumers, including the two duopolists, have identical and homothetic utility functions. Second, it is assumed that the duopolists maximize profits in their roles as producers, rather than maximize the utility of their consumption bundles (see Markusen 1981).

Under these assumptions, the equilibrium condition for a closed economy (i.e., the autarky equilibrium condition) follows from Markusen:

$$MRT = p\left(1 - \frac{1}{\eta_x}\right) < p = MRS, \tag{3}$$

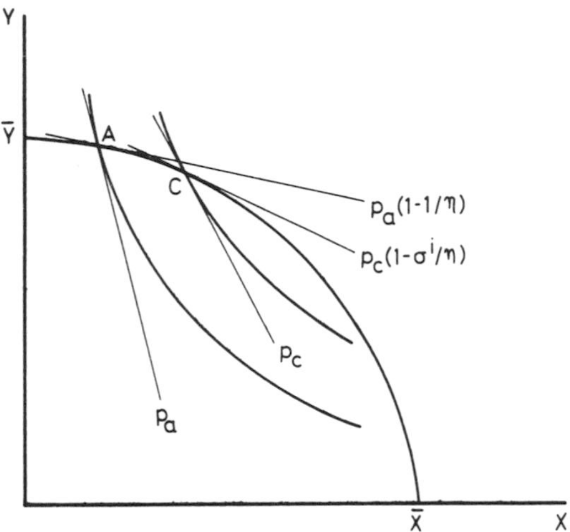

Figure 1

where η is the elasticity of demand for X and MRS is the consumer's marginal rate of substitution. Such an equilibrium is shown in figure 1 by point A, where $MRT < MRS$.

Little more can be said without making more specific assumptions about the utility functions. The reason for this is that the properties of η_x depend entirely on the properties of the preference functions. Thus, for the remainder of the paper we will assume that community preferences in each country can be represented by a CES utility function of the following form:

$$U = (aX^{-\beta} + bY^{-\beta})^{-1/\beta}, \qquad -1 < \beta < \infty,$$
$$\gamma = \frac{1}{1+\beta}. \tag{4}$$

Values of β less than zero correspond to elasticities of substitution greater than 1, and vice versa.

Denoting community income in terms of Y as I, (4) can be maximized subject to I to yield a demand function for X:

$$X = \frac{I}{p[1 + (b/a)^{1/(\beta+1)}p^{-\beta/(\beta+1)}]} = \frac{I}{p(1 + \alpha^{\gamma}p^{-\beta\gamma})}, \tag{5}$$

where $\alpha = (b/a)$ and $I = pX + Y$.

Elsewhere (Markusen 1981) I have demonstrated that with homothetic demand it is immaterial whether the monopolist views total income as fixed or variable. Demand elasticities depend only on relative outputs and not on income. Denoting the monopolist's costs in terms of Y as $C(X)$, we can therefore represent each monopolist's closed economy problem as follows:

$$\max pX - C(X)$$
$$\text{s.t.} \qquad X = \frac{\bar{I}}{p(1 + \alpha^{\gamma} p^{-\beta\gamma})}. \tag{6}$$

Equation (5) can be rearranged as follows:

$$Xp(1 + \alpha^{\gamma} p^{-\beta\gamma}) = X(p + \alpha^{\gamma} p^{1-\beta\gamma}) = \bar{I}. \tag{7}$$

Differentiating with respect to p and X gives us

$$X(1 + \alpha^{\gamma}(1 - \beta\gamma)p^{-\beta\gamma})\frac{dp}{dX} + (p + \alpha^{\gamma} p^{1-\beta\gamma}) = 0. \tag{8}$$

We can then solve for dp/dX and multiply through by X/p to get the elasticity of demand:

$$\frac{1}{\eta_x} = -\frac{X}{p}\frac{dp}{dX} = \frac{(1 + \alpha^{\gamma} p^{-\beta\gamma})}{(1 + \alpha^{\gamma}(1 - \beta\gamma)p^{-\beta\gamma})} < 1, \qquad \text{iff} \begin{cases} \beta < 0, \\ \gamma > 1. \end{cases} \tag{9}$$

As noted in (9), values of $1/\eta_x$ less than 1 only exist if the elasticity of substitution exceeds 1. Thus, it is clear from (9) that a solution to (3) exists only for values of γ greater than 1. This result was derived by Melvin and Warne (1973) and requires us to restrict the range of functions under consideration to those having $\gamma > 1 (\beta < 0)$. Proof of the existence and uniqueness of a solution for all values of β between -1 and 0 is straightforward and analyzed in detail by Melvin and Warne and by Markusen. It is sufficient for our purposes to note that $1/\eta_x$ increases monotonically with the ratio of X to Y (X/Y) in consumption given the restriction that $\beta < 0$. Since p (the consumer price ratio) decreases monotonically with X/Y, this in turn implies that $p(1 - 1/\eta_x)$ falls monotonically with X/Y. $p(1 - 1/\eta_x)$ approaches infinity as X/Y approaches zero (i.e., as we approach the Y-axis end of the production frontier) and approaches zero as X/Y approaches infinity.

Given these results, the autarky equilibria are very simply given as follows:

$$p^i\left(1 - \frac{1}{\eta_x^i}\right) = -F^{i\prime}(X^i), \qquad i = l, s, \tag{10}$$

since $C'(X) = F^{i\prime}(X^i)$ in the absence of factor market distortions. What I wish to emphasize here is that if (a) there are constant returns and identical relative factor endowments in the two countries such that equation (2) holds, and if (b) all consumers have identical and homothetic tastes as assumed above, then the solution to (10) is the same for each country. In autarky the two countries would have identical price ratios.

According to classical trade theory, identical autarky price ratios generally preclude gains from trade. This is not the case in the present formulation. Suppose that we open the two economies to trade, and that the monopolist in each country behaves in a Cournot-Nash fashion. More specifically, each monopolist behaves as though his rival's output is fixed and unresponsive. Algebraically, the monopolist in country L, for example, confronts the following problem:

$$\max pX^l - C^l(X^l)$$
$$\text{s.t.} \qquad X^l + \overline{X}^s = \frac{\bar{I}^l + \bar{I}^S}{p(1 + \alpha^\gamma p^{-\beta\gamma})}. \tag{11}$$

p now denotes the world price of X in terms of Y and $\overline{X}^s$ denotes the Cournot-Nash assumption that X^s is assumed fixed. The elasticity of total world demand is now given by

$$\frac{1}{\eta_x} = -\frac{(X^l + X^s)}{p}\frac{dp}{dX} = \frac{1 + \alpha^\gamma p^{-\beta\gamma}}{1 + \alpha^\gamma(1 - \beta\gamma)p^{-\beta\gamma}}. \tag{12}$$

Multiplying (12) through by $X^l/(X^l + X^s)$ gives the elasticity of demand as viewed by the monopolist in country L:

$$\frac{\sigma^l}{\eta_x} = -\frac{X^l dp}{p\,dX} = \frac{1 + \alpha^\gamma p^{-\beta\gamma}}{1 + \alpha^\gamma(1 - \beta\gamma)p^{-\beta\gamma}} \cdot \frac{X^l}{X^l + X^s}$$
$$\sigma^l = \frac{X^l}{X^l + X^s}. \tag{13}$$

σ^l is thus country L's market share of total world production of X.[4] The equilibrium conditions for Cournot equilibrium that correspond to the autarky conditions given in (10) are as follows:

$$p^i\left(1 - \frac{\sigma^i}{\eta_x}\right) = -F^{i'}(X^i), \qquad i = l, s. \tag{14}$$

Presuming that there are no tariffs or transport costs that would make prices unequal between countries, equation (14) implies a very simple relationship:

$$\sigma^l > \sigma^s \Leftrightarrow -F^{l'}(X^l) < -F^{s'}(X^s). \tag{15}$$

Given constant returns and identical endowment ratios as assumed in equation (2), we also have

$$\sigma^l > \sigma^S \Leftrightarrow -F^{l'}(X^l) < -F^{s'}(X^s) \Leftrightarrow \frac{X^l}{Y^l} < \frac{X^s}{Y^s}. \tag{16}$$

Consider first the case where both countries are of identical size such that both of their identical production frontiers are represented by $\overline{YX}$ in figure 1. In this special case the opening of the two economies to trade will not actually cause trade, but will lead to an expansion in the production of X in each country, as shown by the movement from A to C in figure 1.

This result can be demonstrated using equations (14) and (16). Note first from (14) that point A in figure 1 can no longer be an equilibrium. With the opening of trade,

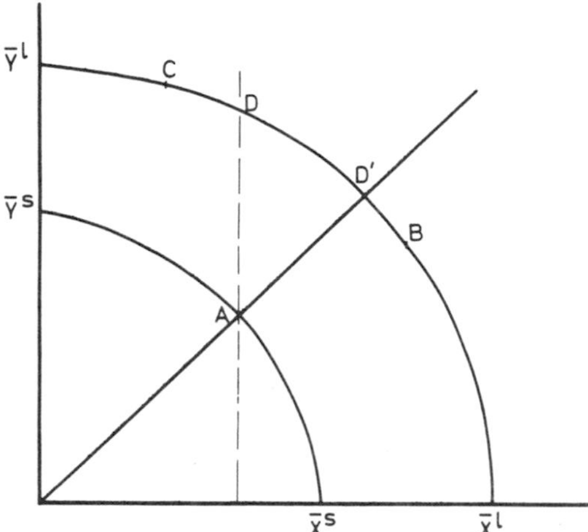

Figure 2

σ^i falls from one to one-half, thus giving the monopolist in each country the incentive to expand production. Suppose at the new equilibrium, X^l exceeds X^s. This implies that $\sigma^l > \sigma^s$ but also that $X^l/Y^l > X^s/Y^s$ by virtue of the fact that the two countries are identical. This violates equation (16), however. A similar argument shows that X^s cannot exceed X^l, and thus it must be the case that $X^s = X^l$. Equation (14) in turn assures us that the open economy equilibrium must be to the right of A in figure 1, at a point like C. This Cournot equilibrium involves no trade (consumer prices are equalized without trade) but does involve an unambiguous gain in welfare relative to autarky.

Differences in country size can be analyzed with the help of figure 2, where $\overline{Y}^l\overline{X}^l$ and $\overline{Y}^s\overline{X}^s$ are the production frontiers of countries L and S, respectively. Once again, we continue to assume that relative factor endowment ratios are equal such that equation (2) holds. Suppose that point A in figure 2 is the open-economy Cournot equilibrium for country S. Point B in figure 2 cannot be the corresponding equilibrium for country L because a comparison of A and B shows that $\sigma^l > \sigma^s$ but $-F^{l'}(X^l) > -F^{s'}(X^s)$, which violates equation (16). Similarly, point C in figure 2 cannot be the equilibrium for country L since $\sigma^l < \sigma^s$ and $-F^{l'}(X^l) < -F^{s'}(X^s)$ which also violates (16). The equilibrium for country L which corresponds to A, must lie strictly within the segment DD' in figure 2. The large country will continue to enjoy a larger market share ($\sigma^l > \sigma^s$) but will produce a lower ratio of X/Y than will be produced by country S ($X^l/Y^l < X^s/Y^s$).

This result, together with the assumption of identical homothetic demand between countries, implies that the large country will import X in Cournot equilibrium. Such a situation is shown in figure 3, where A^l and A^s are the autarky equilibria of L and S, respectively. Given constant returns, the autarky price ratios are equal regardless of size. The trading equilibrium involves country L producing slightly more X than

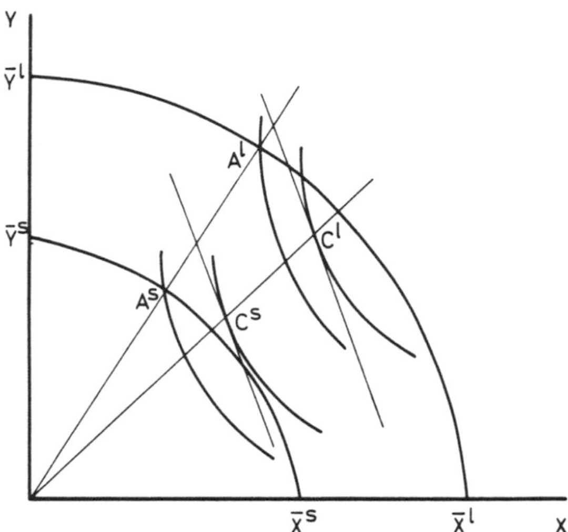

Figure 3

country S, but also importing X to reach a final consumption bundle at C^l. C^s shows the corresponding consumption bundle for country S.

With differences in country sizes, trade thus equalizes prices, but not marginal rates of transformation $(-F^{l'}(X^l) < -F^{s'}(X^s))$. One interesting consequence of this fact in the present model is that trade makes factor prices in the two countries unequal. With constant returns and Heckscher-Ohlin production technology, it is well known that factor prices depend only on marginal rates of transformation. In the absence of trade, our assumptions imply equal MRT and thus equal relative factor prices. Trade leaves the MRT lower in country L and thus makes relative factor prices unequal. By the Stolper-Samuelson relation, the price of the factor used intensively in the production of the monopolized good will be relatively high in the small country.

3 The Gains from Trade

The preceding analysis does not demonstrate that trade increases the income of both countries or even total world real income when countries are of different size. These topics form the subject matter of the present section.

Given that production frontiers are concave, it follows that the free trade production bundle, evaluated at the price ratio *tangent* to the production frontier, is at least as valuable as the autarky production bundle at that same price ratio. From (14) above, this price ratio is $p(1 - \sigma^i/\eta_x)$ in country i. Let subscripts f and a denote free trade and autarky quantities, respectively, and let C_x^i and C_y^i denote consumption quantities of X and Y in country i. The condition on the value of the production bundle can then be written as

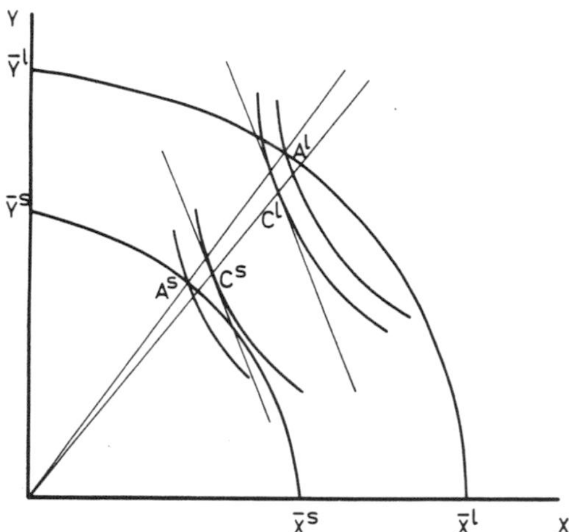

Figure 4

$$Y_f^i + p_f\left(1 - \frac{\sigma^i}{\eta_x}\right)X_f^i \geqq Y_a^i + p_f\left(1 - \frac{\sigma^i}{\eta_x}\right)X_a^i, \qquad i = l, s.$$
$$Y_a^i = C_{ay}^i, \quad X_a^i = C_{ax}^i, \quad Y_f^i + p_f X_f^i = C_{fy}^i + p_f C_{fx}^i. \tag{17}$$

The second line of (17) indicates that each economy must satisfy a balance of payments constraint when trading and that in autarky, supply must equal demand for each commodity. Substituting these constraints into the first equation of (17) we have

$$[C_{fy}^i + p_f C_{fx}^i] \geqq [C_{ay}^i + p_f C_{ax}^i] + p_f\left(\frac{\sigma^i}{\eta_x}\right)(X_f^i - X_a^i). \tag{18}$$

Equation (18) states that the free trade consumption bundle will be "revealed preferred" to the autarky consumption bundle if (but not only if) the free trade production of the monopolized good exceeds the autarky production ($X_f^i > X_a^i$).

As will be demonstrated below, figures 3 and 4 show two of the three possible outcomes given constant returns to scale. In all cases, trade increases the production of X in country S, and hence S always gains from trade.

Country L may gain as shown in figure 3 or may lose when trade decreases the production of X, as shown in figure 4. The third possibility (not shown) is that country L may experience an increase in welfare despite a decrease in the output of X.

The change in total world real income can be analyzed by simply summing the two equations in (18). This shows that a sufficient condition for trade to increase total world real income is that free trade production of X exceed autarky production $(X_f^l + X_f^s) > (X_a^l + X_a^s)$. Such an increase will in fact always occur given constant returns to scale.

These results can be demonstrated by constructing reaction functions for countries L and S as in figures 5 and 6. In each diagram point A gives the autarky production levels. The 45° line aa' through point A gives all production points yielding the same total world output as A. It follows from the preceding paragraph that any trading equilibrium above aa' yields a total world real income in excess of world income at the autarky equilibria. Any point to the northeast of A implies gains from trade for both countries.

ll' and ss' in figures 5 and 6 are the Cournot reaction curves of countries L and S, respectively. These curves give the duopolist's optimal output of X given the current output of the other duopolist. Consider first the point l' that gives L's optimal output of X when $X^s = 0$. l' must lie between X_a^l and a', as shown in figure 5 and 6. With S specialized in the production of Y ($Y^s = \overline{Y}^s$) the monopolist would not continue to produce X_a^l since marginal revenue would exceed autarky marginal revenue at that autarky output level ($X_a^l/(\overline{Y}^s + Y_a^l) < X_a^l/Y_a^l$). The monopolist would not, on the other hand, produce at or to the right of a' in figures 5 and 6. At a', marginal cost will be higher (concavity of the production frontier) and marginal revenue will be lower than in autarky. This latter effect occurs because with the world production of X unchanged ($X_f^l = X_a^l + X_a^s$) the world production of Y must be lower. This is due to the inefficiency introduced by having the two countries producing at different MRT.

A second property of ll' in figures 5 and 6 is that it must pass to the right of A. With trade at A, η_x and MC_x are the same as in the absence of trade, but marginal revenue must be higher due to L's lower market share. Thus, L should expand production given $X^s = X_a^s$.

A similar argument will show that s lies between a and X_a^s in figures 5 and 6, and that ss' must pass above point A.

The slopes of ll' and ss' can be found by using the first-order condition for the monopolist in each country. Denoting profit as π^i, these are given by

$$\frac{d\pi^l}{dX^l} = p + X^l \frac{dp}{dX^l} - C^{l'}(X^l) = 0, \tag{19}$$

$$\frac{d\pi^s}{dX^s} = p + X^s \frac{dp}{dX^s} - C^{s'}(X^s) = 0. \tag{20}$$

Differentiation of (19) and (20) gives us the following:

$$d\left(\frac{d\pi^l}{dX^l}\right) = 2\frac{dp}{dX^l}dX^l + \frac{dp}{dX^s}dX^s + X^l\frac{d^2p}{dX^{l2}}dX^l + X^l\frac{d^2p}{dX^l dX^s}dX^s - C^{l''}(X^l)dX^l = 0, \tag{21}$$

$$d\left(\frac{d\pi^s}{dX^s}\right) = 2\frac{dp}{dX^s}dX^s + \frac{dp}{dX^l}dX^l + X^s\frac{d^2p}{dX^{s2}}dX^s + X^s\frac{d^2p}{dX^l dX^s}dX^l - C^{s''}(X^s)dX^s = 0, \tag{22}$$

All first derivatives of p with respect to X^l and X^s are equal, as are all second derivatives since p is a function of the sum of X^l and X^s. Dropping the superscripts, the signs of the derivatives in (21) and (22) are given as follows:

$$\frac{dp}{dX^i} = \frac{dp}{dX} < 0, \quad \frac{d^2p}{dX^i dX^j} = \frac{d^2p}{dX^2}, \quad \left[2\frac{dp}{dX} + X^i \frac{d^2p}{dX^2}\right] < 0. \tag{23}$$

The signs in (23) follow from earlier restrictions guaranteeing diminishing marginal revenue. $C^{i''} > 0$ in (21) and (22) by virtue of increasing marginal cost (concavity of the production frontier).

Equations (21) and (22) give us the slopes of the reaction curves for L and S, respectively:

$$\left[\frac{dX^s}{dX^l}\right]^l = -\frac{[2(dp/dX) + X^l(d^2p/dX^2)] - C^{l''}(X^l)}{[(dp/dX) + X^l(d^2p/dX^2)]} \quad \text{(slope of } ll'\text{)}, \tag{24}$$

$$\left[\frac{dX^s}{dX^l}\right]^s = -\frac{[(dp/dX) + X^s(d^2p/dX^2)]}{[2(dp/dX) + X^s(d^2p/dX^2)] - C^{s''}(X^s)} \quad \text{(slope of } ss'\text{)}. \tag{25}$$

Combining (24) and (25) with (23), we have

$$\left[\frac{dX^s}{dX^l}\right]^l < -1, \quad -1 < \left[\frac{dX^s}{dX^l}\right]^s < 0. \tag{26}$$

Equation (26) notes that ll' must be everywhere steeper than aa' (the 45° line) in figures 5 and 6, and notes that ss' must be everywhere flatter than aa'. These two results, combined with the facts that ll' passes to the right of A, and ss' passes above

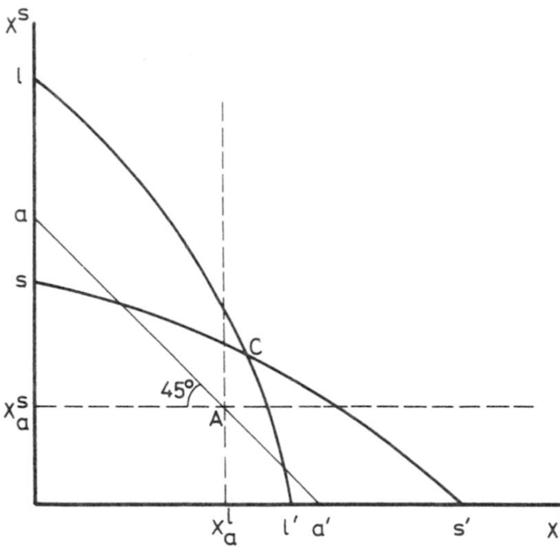

Figure 5

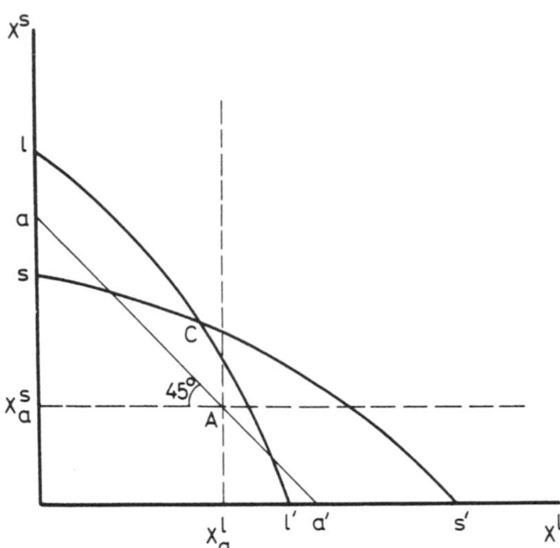

Figure 6

A, are sufficient to guarantee that ll' and ss' intersect exactly once and that this intersection occurs above aa', as shown in figures 5 and 6 (point C). It follows in turn from equation (18) that world real income must be higher at the Cournot equilibrium than in autarky.

Previous results allow us to place one additional restriction on C. It follows from the discussion of figure 2 and from earlier assumptions underlying that analysis (e.g., constant returns), that country L must have a lower relative market share in Cournot equilibrium than it had in autarky, implying that $(X^l_f/X^s_f) < (X^l_a/X^s_a)$. It then follows that point C in figures 5 and 6 must lie above a ray from the origin through point A. Combined with the result of the previous paragraph, this ensures us that $X^s_f > X^s_a$ and thus that country S unambiguously gains from trade (eq. [18]).

Two situations can occur with respect to country L. $X^l_f > X^l_a$, as in figure 5, or $X^l_f < X^l_a$, as in figure 6. In the former case, country L unambiguously gains. In the latter case, country L may gain or may lose (fig. 6). As noted earlier, such a finding is quite consistent with the general theory of distortions and welfare (Bhagwati and Ramaswami 1963; Bhagwati 1971). Trade in the presence of domestic distortions is not guaranteed to increase welfare relative to autarky.

Before moving on, I should note that James Brander and an anonymous referee have pointed out that these results relating to differences in country size depend on the assumption of only a single producer of X in each country. If the number of producers in a country were proportional to the size of the country, then the symmetric solution with no trade and bilateral gains would reemerge.[5] I am, however, especially interested in the single producer case for two reasons. First, I am interested in exploring the robustness of the notion that trade is procompetitive. The present model is valuable insofar as it demonstrates where the conventional wisdom can break down. Second, I am interested in imperfect competition in the context of increasing returns to scale since the two phenomena are probably closely related at an empirical level. If average cost is everywhere downward sloping (as per most industrial organization studies) and factors are perfectly mobile within a country, then the "natural monopoly" (single producer) outcome seems fairly reasonable.

4 Increasing Returns to Scale

One motivation for assuming monopoly in the production of X is that there are increasing returns to scale in the X industry. I held off introducing this assumption, however, in order that we could clearly distinguish effects due to monopoly power per se from those due to a combination of increasing returns and monopoly power. In this section I will show that many, but not all, of the results derived in the previous two sections continue to hold with increasing returns. Throughout this section we will continue to assume identical relative factor endowments in order to avoid the complications of Heckscher-Ohlin effects.

Previous papers have shown that increasing returns introduces two complications. First, the production frontier may be convex (the production set may be nonconvex) (Herberg and Kemp 1969; Melvin 1969; Chipman 1970). This result always occurs if, for example, there are no differences in factor intensities between industries such that the constant returns production frontier is linear.[6] Second, the MRT in the large country will be less than the MRT in the small country at any given output ratio X/Y, given increasing returns in X and constant returns in Y (Markusen and Melvin 1981). In terms of figure 2, the MRT will be less at D' than at A.

When two countries are absolutely identical in all respects, as in figure 1, the second complication is obviously irrelevant. Nonconvexity of the production set is also irrelevant for the question of the existence of equilibrium (Markusen 1981). There will continue to exist a Cournot-Nash equilibrium in which each country produces an identical bundle characterized by $X_f^i > X_a^i$, such that the welfare of each country is improved as in figure 1. This equilibrium may, however, be unstable, and may lead to production at an alternative equilibrium in which one or both countries is specialized. An analysis of this stability question is temporarily postponed.

Consider now the case in which countries are of different size, but in which returns to scale are insufficiently strong to cause nonconvexities in the production set. In this situation most of the properties of the reaction curves derived in the preceding section remain valid. The reason is that concavity of the production frontier continues to imply that the general-equilibrium marginal cost of X in terms of Y is an increasing function of X ($C''(X) > 0$). It follows from the arguments of the preceding section that (a) l' in figures 5 and 6 continues to lie between X_a^l and a', (b) the slope of ll' is everywhere less than -1 (eq. [24]), and (c) ll' passes to the right of A. Similar comments apply to ss'. It thus remains true that ll' and ss' intersect at a unique point above aa' in figures 5 and 6, and that trade necessarily increases total world real income.

The one property of the constant returns case that does not continue to hold is that given in equation (16). With increasing returns, size matters as noted above. Thus (16) must now be amended as follows:

$$\sigma^l > \sigma^s \Leftrightarrow -F^{l'}(X^l) < -F^{s'}(X^s)$$
$$\frac{X^l}{Y^l} \lesseqq \frac{X^s}{Y^s} \Rightarrow -F^{l'}(X^l) < -F^{s'}(X^s). \tag{27}$$

The second line of (27) is no longer an "if and only if" relation. With the MRT in L flatter along any ray from the origin, it is now possible that $\sigma^l > \sigma^s$ and $(X^l/Y^l > X^s/Y^s)$. Owing to cost advantage in the production of X, it can now be the case that country L exports X in Cournot equilibrium. This is not an inevitable outcome, but it becomes more likely the higher the degree of returns to scale. This result implies that country S can now lose from trade when it is the importer of X (eq. [18]). In terms of figures 5 and 6, Cournot equilibrium may now lie below X_a^s. The result of the previous section must be weakened somewhat to state that trade necessarily increases total world real income, but may lead to a deterioration in welfare for the country importing X.

Consider now the case where increasing returns dominate differences in factor intensities such that $C'' < 0$ (the production frontier is convex). This implies that l' must lie to the right of a' in figures 5 and 6. At a', MC for L is lower than at X_a^l and marginal revenue is higher than in autarky. This latter effect occurs since with total production of X the same as in autarky, the total production of Y must be greater than in autarky due to decreasing costs (see Melvin 1969). $(X_f/Y_f) < (X_a/Y_a)$ implies higher marginal revenue, as noted earlier. Thus, l' lies to the right of a' and s lies above a by a similar argument.

It remains true in the present case that ll' must pass to the right of A and that ss' must pass above A, as in figures 5 and 6. At A, the lower market share of each duopolist relative to his autarky share of l gives each an incentive to expand output holding the other duopolist's output constant.

The principal problem lies in the fact that the sign restrictions given in (26) may no longer be valid. Second-order conditions imply that both reaction curves continue to be downward sloping, but the fact that $C'' < 0$ may mean that one or both of the restrictions in (26) no longer holds. In particular, we have

$$C^{l''} < 0, \qquad |C^{l''}| > \left|\frac{dp}{dX}\right| \Rightarrow -1 < \left[\frac{dX^s}{dX^l}\right]^l < 0, \tag{28}$$

$$C^{s''} < 0, \qquad |C^{s''}| > \left|\frac{dp}{dX}\right| \Rightarrow \left[\frac{dX^s}{dX^l}\right]^s < -1. \tag{29}$$

Note from (28) and (29) that $C^{i''} < 0$ is a necessary but not a sufficient condition for the restriction on i's reaction function in (26) to be invalid.

It is probably apparent from (28) and (29) that all sorts of outcomes are possible, and I do not particularly want to get into a taxonomy of these possiblities. Perhaps, therefore, I can simply indicate what the important results are.

First, if both sign restrictions in (26) remain everywhere valid in spite of convex production frontiers, then ll' and ss' continue to cross above aa' in figures 5 and 6. However, this does not guarantee that trade increases world real income since equation (17) is no longer valid (Kemp 1969). In fact, the signs of (17) and (18) are reversed if both countries remain diversified in production. Diversification is ensured by (26) and by the fact that ll' passes to the right of A and ss' passes above A. From Kemp, (18) becomes

$$[C^i_{fy} + p_f C^i_{fx}] \leqq [C^i_{ay} + p_f C^i_{ax}] + p_f \left(\frac{\sigma^i}{\eta_x}\right)(X^i_f - X^i_a). \tag{30}$$

Equation (30) implies that expansion of world output of X is now a necessary but not a sufficient condition for trade to increase world real income.[7] Similarly, expansion in the domestic production of X is now a necessary condition for countries to gain individually.[8] The country that imports X is now definitely a loser.

Second, consider the case in which both sign restrictions in (26) are everywhere violated (i.e., [28] and [29] hold). Since it remains true that ll' passes to the right of A and ss' passes above A, it follows that ll' and ss' now cross in the opposite direction to that indicated in figures 5 and 6. Indeed, we can depict two of many possible cases by simply switching the labels ll' and ss' in figures 5 and 6. ll' and ss' may intersect either inside or outside of aa' or may not intersect at all. The important point, however, is that any interior intersection is unstable given that ll' and ss' must cross in this manner (i.e., ll' flatter than ss'). At a point on ll' to the right of C, for example, S will reduce output, followed by an increase by L, followed by a further decrease by S, and so forth, until point l' is reached.

l' and s will be stable equilibria in which the total production of X exceeds total autarky production (recall l' lies to the right of a' and s lies above a in this case). Either stable equilibrium involves an increase in total world real income relative to autarky. To show this, first consider point a', which is Pareto superior to point A in figures 5 and 6. At a', total production of X equals that at A, but total production of Y is greater than at A due to decreasing costs. But although a' is Pareto superior to A, it is not Pareto optimal since $p > MR > MC$. Any increase in X^l above a' increases welfare up to the point where $p = MC$. l' stops short of the equality, but is nevertheless Pareto superior to a', and thus to A. Similar comments apply to point s in figures 5 and 6. Thus, either stable equilibrium involves an increase in world real income relative to autarky. Once again, however, one of the countries may lose.[9] Interested readers are referred to Kemp (1969), Melvin (1969), or Markusen and Melvin (1981) for a more complete discussion of trading equilibria with nonconvex production sets.

5 Summary and Conclusions

The purposes of this paper were to show how imperfect competition can form a basis for trade, and to show the distribution of gains (or losses) from trade under this assumption. A two-good, two-country model was constructed in which the production of one good was monopolized in each country (i.e., the same good was monopolized in each country). Under the assumption of Cournot-Nash behavior, it was demonstrated that trade will lead to a bilateral welfare improvement when countries are identical in all respects. Trade doubles the size of the market relative to autarky and doubles the number of producers. If each duopolist continued to produce his autarky output, he would now find that perceived marginal revenue is greater than marginal cost. Thus, trade leads each duopolist to increase his output, resulting in bilateral welfare improvements. This finding is similar to the findings of Melvin (1969) and Krugman (1979), who note that increasing returns to scale may imply gains from trade even if countries are identical in all respects.

With constant returns to scale in production, but countries differing in size, it was shown that Cournot-Nash equilibrium will involve the large country importing the monopolized good. World real income will definitely increase with trade as will the real income of the smaller country. The monopolist in the large country may however reduce production relative to autarky, which could possibly result in negative gains from trade for the large country. As noted, this result is sensitive to the assumption that there is only a single producer of the monopolized good in each country. If the number of producers was proportional to the size of the country, then the solution would be symmetric with bilateral gains from trade assured.

A second interesting result in the unequal-size case is that trade makes factor prices unequal between countries. With constant returns and identical relative factor endowments, factor prices are equalized in autarky. At the Cournot-Nash equilibrium the price of the factor used intensively in the monopolized good is relatively high in the small country. This has a further implication not discussed in the paper: factor mobility will lead to an inflow (outflow) of the factor used intensively in the production of each country's export (import) good. Factor mobility could thus lead to an increase in the volume of trade that is contrary to the usual Heckscher-Ohlin case in which trade in goods and factors are substitutes.

With "weakly" increasing returns (i.e., the production frontier is concave), it remains true that trade must increase world real income relative to autarky. However, the large country will now have a cost advantage in the production of the monopolized good that works in the opposite direction to the country-size effect just mentioned. The result is that the direction of trade is indeterminate in the general case. The country that does export the monopolized good in Cournot-Nash equilibrium will always gain while the importer may or may not gain, as in the constant returns case.

A complication introduced by "strongly" increasing returns (i.e., the production frontier is convex) is that total world real income can fall with trade, provided that both countries are diversified in production at the Cournot-Nash equilibrium. In this situation, expansion in the domestic production of the monopolized good becomes a necessary rather than a sufficient condition for the country to gain from trade. This finding is similar to a result by Kemp (1969) for the case of externality-induced convexity of the production frontier.

A final result was to show that with strongly increasing returns, the Cournot-Nash equilibrium, with both countries diversified, may be unstable. Alternative stable equilibria in which only one country produces the monopolized good necessarily involve an increase in total world real income relative to autarky, but do not necessarily involve gains for both countries.

Overall, these findings suggest that the conventional wisdom regarding the pro-competitive aspects of trade is only partly correct. While trade generally increases world real income, it need not increase the income of both countries. Individual gains are closely related to the expansion in production of the monopolized good. If trade leads to a contraction in production, it may simply be acting to drive the country further away from its welfare-maximizing production bundle.

Notes

This paper was presented at the Workshop on "Production and Trade in a World with Internationally Mobile Factors of Production" financed by the Bank of Sweden Bicentenary Foundation, and held at the Institute for International Economic Studies, University of Stockholm, August 4–15, 1980. The author would like to thank participants in that workshop for helpful comments and suggestions. Thanks are also due to James Brander, John McMillan, and an anonymous referee.

1. Kindleberger (1969) makes a similar point in discussing foreign investment flows rather than trade flows. Direct foreign investment may have a very important impact on a small country's welfare via reducing the market power of domestic monopolies.

2. Markusen and Melvin (1981) note a similar result in the presence of increasing returns to scale: reductions in tariffs or transport costs between countries may make factor prices more unequal. As will be pointed out below, these results relating to differences in country size are subject to the assumption that there is only a single monopoly producer in each country.

3. This conclusion is of course quite consistent with the theory of distortions as developed by Bhagwati and Ramaswami (1963) and Bhagwati (1971). Among other things, this theory notes that gains from trade are not guaranteed in the presence of domestic distortions (e.g., domestic monopoly power).

4. σ^l is sometimes known as country L's "conjectural variation." For behavioral assumptions other than the Cournot assumption used here, conjectural variations are not in general equal to market shares.

5. Such a model would run into analytical problems insofar as the number of producers is a discrete variable, whereas the size of a country is a continuous variable. Nevertheless, if for example country L was exactly twice the size of country S and the former had two producers, then the solution to (14) would be symmetric. The market share for each producer in L would equal σ^s such that the left-hand side of (14) was the same for all three producers. The total output of X in L would be exactly double the output of X in S. This would in turn imply equal MRT in the two countries by virtue of constant returns and L being exactly twice as large as S. Output expansion and gains from trade would be assured for both countries.

6. The production frontier may contain both concave and convex segments (Herberg and Kemp 1969; Markusen and Melvin 1981). Indeed, the only robust result is that the frontier must be locally convex in the neighborhood of zero production of the IRS good. In what follows, we shall assume that the production frontier is either everywhere convex or everywhere concave over the relevant region.

7. The reader can see this result by constructing a simple diagram with a convex production frontier. Draw a tangent to any point on the production frontier (call it point A) and a line with the same slope as the

original tangent through any other point (call it point B). At the price ratio given by the tangent to A, the value of income at A is clearly lower than the value of income at B. The opposite relation between A and B occurs if the production frontier is concave. Hence (18) and (30) have opposite signs.

8. When countries are identical in all respects such that no trade takes place at the Cournot equilibrium, expansion in the domestic production of X remains a sufficient condition for an improvement in domestic welfare. The reader can see this by constructing a diagram as in the previous footnote, and by constructing the equilibria points A and C in figure 1 on the new diagram. It will be apparent that welfare at C (the trading equilibrium) will be higher than at A (the autarky equilibrium) even though production at C evaluated at the price ratio tangent to C ($p_f(1 - \sigma^i/\eta_x)$) is less than the value of production at A at that same price ratio.

9. Instability of the diversified equilibrium can also occur when both countries are of identical size. In this case, any of the equilibria, C, l' or s, are Pareto superior to A, and l' and s are in turn Pareto superior to C from the point of view of the world as a whole.

References

Auquier, A., and Richard E. Caves. 1979. Monopolistic export industries, trade taxes, and optimal competition policy. *Economic Journal* 89:559–581.

Bhagwati, Jagdish. 1971. The generalized theory of distortions and welfare. In Bhagwati et al., *Trade, the Balance of Payments and Growth: Essays in Honor of Charles P. Kindleberger*. Amsterdam: North-Holland.

Bhagwati, Jagdish, and V. K. Ramaswami. 1963. Domestic distortion, tariff, and the theory of optimum subsidy. *Journal of Political Economy* 71:44–50.

Chipman, John. 1970. External economies of scale and competitive equilibrium. *Quarterly Journal of Economics* 84:347–363.

Ethier, Wilfred. 1979. Internationally decreasing costs and world trade. *Journal of International Economics* 9:1–24.

Feenstra, R. C. 1980. Monopsony distortions in an open economy: A theoretical analysis. *Journal of International Economics* 10:213–236.

Fishelson, Gideon, and A. L. Hillman. 1979. Domestic monopoly and redundant tariff protection. *Journal of International Economics* 9:47–56.

Graham, Frank. 1923. Some aspects of protection further considered. *Quarterly Journal of Economics* 37:199–227.

Herberg, Horst, and Murray C. Kemp. 1969. Some implications of variable returns to scale. *Canadian Journal of Economics* 3:403–415.

Herberg, Horst, and Murray C. Kemp. 1971. Factor market distortions, the shape of the locus of competitive outputs, and the relation between product prices and equilibrium prices. In Bhagwati et al., *Trade, the Balance of Payments and Growth: Essays in Honor of Charles P. Kindleberger*, 22–48. Amsterdam: North-Holland.

Kemp, Murray C. 1969. *The Pure Theory of International Trade and Investment*, 154–179. New York: Prentice-Hall.

Kindleberger, Charles P. 1969. *American Business Abroad*, 1–36. New Haven: Yale University Press. Reprinted in R. E. Baldwin and J. D. Richardson (eds.), *International Trade and Finance*, 267–284. Boston: Little Brown, 1974.

Krugman, Paul. 1979. Increasing returns, monopolistic competition, and international trade. *Journal of International Economics* 9:469–480.

McCulloch, R., and J. L. Yellen. 1980. Factor market monopsony and the allocation of resources. *Journal of International Economics* 10:237–248.

Markusen, James R. 1981. Simple general equilibrium with a monopolized sector: A comparison of alternate specifications. University of Western Ontario Working Paper.

Markusen, James R., and James Melvin. 1981. Trade, factor prices, and the gains from trade with increasing returns to scale. *Canadian Journal of Economics* 14:450–469.

Markusen, James R., and Arthur Robson. 1980. Simple general equilibrium and trade with a monopsonized sector. *Canadian Journal of Economics* 13:668–682.

Melvin, James R. 1969. Increasing returns to scale as a determinant of trade. *Canadian Journal of Economics* 3:389–402.

Melvin, James R., and Robert Warne. 1973. Monopoly and the theory of international trade. *Journal of International Economics* 3:117–134.

Negishi, Takashi. 1961. Monopolistic competition and general equilibrium. *Review of Economics and Statistics* 28:196–201.

Ohlin, Bertil. 1933. *Interregional and International Trade*. Cambridge, Mass.: Harvard University Press.

4 Import Protection as Export Promotion: International Competition in the Presence of Oligopoly and Economies of Scale

Paul R. Krugman

1 Introduction

When businessmen try to explain the success of Japanese firms in export markets, they often mention the advantage of a protected home market. Firms with a secure home market, the argument runs, have a number of advantages: they are assured of the economies of large-scale production, of selling enough over time to move down the learning curve, of earning enough to recover the costs of R&D. While charging high prices in the domestic market, they can "incrementally price" and flood foreign markets with low-cost products.

No doubt the argument that import protection is export promotion is often a self-serving position of those who would like protection themselves. Still, there is an undeniable persuasiveness to the argument. Yet it is an argument that economists schooled in standard trade theory tend to find incomprehensible. In a world of perfect competition and constant returns to scale, protecting a product can never cause it to be exported. It may cause some other good that is complementary in production to be exported—but this is hardly what the businessmen seem to have in mind.

The purpose of this paper is to show that there is a class of models in which the businessman's view of import protection as export promotion makes sense. There are two basic ingredients in these models. First, markets are both oligopolistic and segmented: Firms are aware that their actions affect the price they receive and are able to charge different prices in different markets. As Brander (1981) has shown, and as Brander and Krugman (1981) elaborated, models of this type allow countries to be both importers and exporters within an industry, because firms will engage in "reciprocal dumping" into each others' home markets.

The second ingredient is some kind of economies of scale. These may take several forms. The simplest would be static economies of scale, namely, a declining marginal cost curve. It is also possible, however, for more subtle forms of scale economies to produce the same results: for example, dynamic scale economies of the "learning curve" type or competition in R&D. As the paper will stress, the end result is very similar. It is the distinction between increasing and decreasing costs, not the distinction between statics and dynamics, that usually sets the views of practical men and trade theorists apart.

In each case the basic story of protection as promotion remains the same. By giving a domestic firm a privileged position in one market, a country gives it an advantage in scale over foreign rivals. This scale advantage translates into lower marginal costs and higher market share even in unprotected markets.

The paper is in six sections. Section 2 presents the basic, static model of competition, and section 3 shows how protectionism can promote expansion in all markets. Section

Originally published in *Monopolistic Competition and International Trade*, ed. H. Kierzkowski (Oxford University Press, 1984).

4 develops an alternative model where there are no static economies of scale, but where R&D plays a similar role. In section 5 neither of these effects operates, but learning by doing is shown to produce similar effects. Finally, section 6 summarizes the results and suggests some conclusions.

2 Model I: Static Economies of Scale

There are two firms, home and foreign. Each firm produces a single product, which it sells in a number of markets in competition with the other firm. The firms' products may but need not be perfect substitutes. The segmented markets in which they compete may be divided by transport costs, border taxes, or type of purchaser; they may include markets in each firm's home country and also markets in third countries.

I will adopt an abbreviated way of representing demand conditions in the different markets; following Spencer and Brander (1982), I will skip the writing of demand functions and go directly to the revenue functions of the firms. In market i ($i = 1, \ldots, r$) the revenue function of the home firm is

$$R_i = R_i(x_i, x_i^*), \tag{1}$$

where x_i, x_i^* are deliveries to the ith market by the home and foreign firms, respectively. Similarly, the foreign firm's revenue function is

$$R_i^* = R_i^*(x_i, x_i^*). \tag{2}$$

I will assume that each firm's marginal revenue is decreasing in the other firm's output:

$$\frac{\partial^2 R_i}{\partial x_i \partial x_i^*} < 0, \tag{3}$$

$$\frac{\partial^2 R_i^*}{\partial x_i^* \partial x_i} < 0. \tag{4}$$

Another condition will also be assumed:

$$\Delta = \frac{\partial^2 R_i}{\partial x_i^2} \cdot \frac{\partial^2 R_i^*}{\partial x_i^{*2}} - \frac{\partial^2 R_i}{\partial x_i \partial x_i^*} \frac{\partial^2 R_i^*}{\partial x_i \partial x_i^*} > 0. \tag{5}$$

The usefulness of this condition will become obvious below; it amounts to saying that "own" effects on marginal revenue are greater than "cross" effects.

On the cost side, each firm will face both production costs and transport costs: thus total costs for each firm will be

$$TC = \sum t_i x_i + C(\sum x_i), \tag{6}$$

$$TC^* = \sum t_i^* x_i^* + C^*(\sum x_i^*), \tag{7}$$

where we assume declining marginal cost of production: C'', $C^{*\prime\prime} < 0$. Notice that transport costs need not be the same for the two firms. For the home firm's domestic market, presumably $t_i < t_i^*$; for the foreign firm's domestic market, we expect $t_i^* < t_i$; there may also be third country markets to which either may have lower transport cost.

How do these firms compete? Each firm must choose a vector of deliveries, that is, it must choose x_i or x_i^* for each market. The simplest assumption to make about competition is that each firm takes the other firm's deliveries as given in each market. The result is a multimarket Cournot model, where the firms' decision problems are

$$\max_{\{x_i\}} \Pi = \sum R_i(x_i, x_i^*) - \sum t_i x_i - C(\sum x_i), \tag{8}$$

$$\max_{\{x_i^*\}} \Pi^* = \sum R_i^*(x_i, x_i^*) - \sum t_i^* x_i^* - C^*(\sum x_i^*). \tag{9}$$

The first-order conditions that determine equilibrium are

$$\frac{\partial R_i}{\partial x_i} - t_i - \mu = 0, \qquad i = 1, \ldots, n, \tag{10}$$

$$\frac{\partial R_i^*}{\partial x_i^*} - t_i^* - \mu^* = 0, \qquad i = 1, \ldots, n, \tag{11}$$

where μ, μ^* are marginal production costs. In each market, firms set their marginal revenue equal to marginal cost.

To interpret this equilibrium, it is useful to think in terms of an imaginary iterative process by which we might compute the solution. Specifying this process is purely an expositional device, with no implications for the outcome, but it does help to make clear the underlying logic of the model.

Suppose, then, that we use the following procedure. We begin by making a guess about the firms' marginal cost and play a Cournot game in each market on the basis of that guess. We then sum the chosen levels of deliveries to get total output and compute the implied marginal cost. This estimate of marginal cost is then used for a second round and so on until convergence. The stages of this computation can be represented by the geometric apparatus presented in figures 1, 2, and 3.

Figure 1 shows the competition in a representative market for given estimates of marginal cost μ, μ^*. The curves FF and F^*F^* are the reaction functions of the domestic and foreign firm, respectively. Their slopes are

$$\frac{-\partial^2 R_i/\partial x_i^2}{\partial^2 R_i/\partial x_i \partial x_i^*} \quad \text{and} \quad \frac{-\partial^2 R_i^*/\partial x_i \partial x_i^*}{\partial^2 R_i^*/\partial x_i^{*2}},$$

both negative by (3) and (4) whereas by (5), FF is steeper than F^*F^*.

Suppose that we reduce μ, the home firm's estimate of marginal cost. The result will be to push FF out, as shown in the diagram; x_i will rise and x_i^* will fall. This will happen in *each* market in which the firms compete, so that total output of the home firm will rise and total output of the foreign firm will fall.

Figure 2 illustrates the next step. On one hand, the lower the firm's estimate of marginal cost, the larger its output. On the other hand, the larger the output, the lower

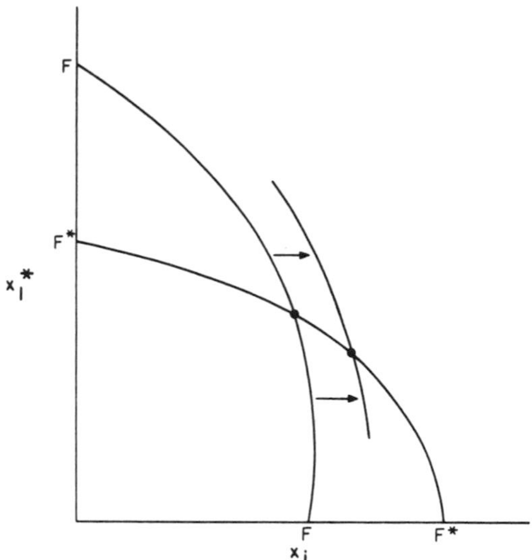

Figure 1

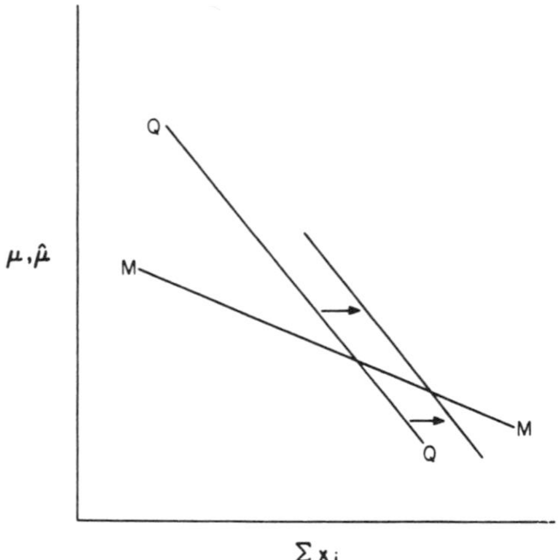

Figure 2

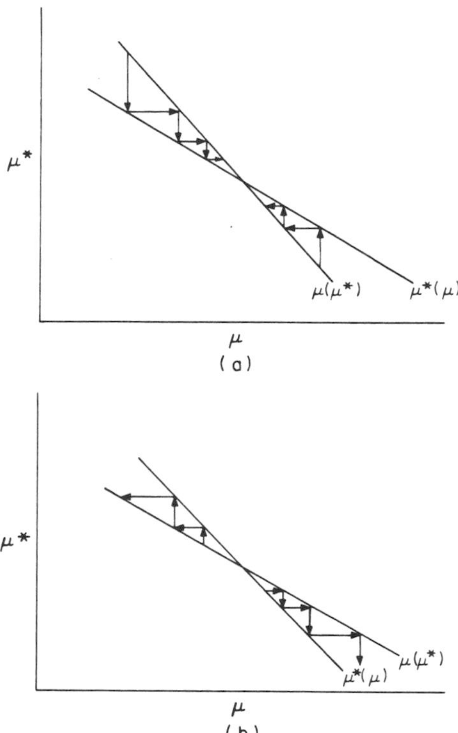

Figure 3

its actual marginal cost. These relationships are indicated by the curves QQ and MM. The equilibrium for the firm—conditional on the *other* firm's estimate of marginal cost—is where MM and QQ cross. As drawn, QQ is steeper than MM; this will be true if marginal costs do not fall too steeply, and we will assume that this is the case.

Suppose now that the foreign firm were to raise its estimated marginal cost, μ^*. This would imply a leftward shift of F^*F^* in each market. For a given μ, output of the home firm would rise, that is, the QQ curve shifts right. The end result is that domestic marginal cost is decreasing in foreign marginal cost, and vice versa. This takes us to the final step in determining equilibrium illustrated in figure 3.

Domestic marginal cost is decreasing in foreign, foreign marginal cost is decreasing in domestic; an equilibrium is where the schedules $\mu(\mu^*)$ and $\mu^*(\mu)$ cross. The curve $\mu(\mu^*)$ may cut $\mu^*(\mu)$ from above, as in figure 3a, or from below, as in figure 3b. A simple stability analysis suggests that the latter situation will "almost never" be observed. Suppose that the two firms revise their estimates of marginal cost alternately; then the dynamics will be those indicated by the arrows. If $\mu(\mu^*)$ is steeper than $\mu^*(\mu)$, that is, if "own" effects are again stronger than "cross" effects at this higher level, equilibrium is stable. If $\mu^*(\mu)$ is steeper, the equilibrium is unstable.

It is possible and even important that there may exist no stable equilibrium except where one firm or the other ceases production. For the rest of this chapter, however, we will assume that there is a unique stable equilibrium where both firms produce at positive levels.

We have now described the determination of equilibrium in this model. The essential feature is the circular causation from output to marginal cost to output. Our next step is to show how this circularity makes import protection an export promotion device.

3 Effects of Protection

Suppose that the home government excludes the foreign firm from some market previously open to it. This market might be the whole domestic market or it might be some piece, say procurement by government-owned firms. For simplicity we consider a complete exclusion of foreign product, although a quota or tariff would have much the same result.

To find the effects of this, we first hold μ constant. The effect under this assumption is solely to raise x_i and lower x_i^* in the newly protected market. This in turn, however, affects marginal cost; in terms of figure 2, the home firm's QQ curve shifts right, the corresponding foreign curve shifts left. That is, for a given level of foreign marginal cost, domestic cost falls; for a given level of domestic marginal cost, foreign cost rises. The curve $\mu(\mu^*)$ shifts left, $\mu^*(\mu)$ shifts right; as figure 4 shows, the result (assuming stability) is a fall in μ, a rise in μ^*.

It only remains to complete the circle. This is done in figure 5, which shows a representative market other than the protected one. The change in marginal cost causes FF to shift out, F^*F^* to shift in; x_j rises, x_j^* falls. *Protecting the domestic firm in one market increases domestic sales and lowers foreign sales in all markets.*

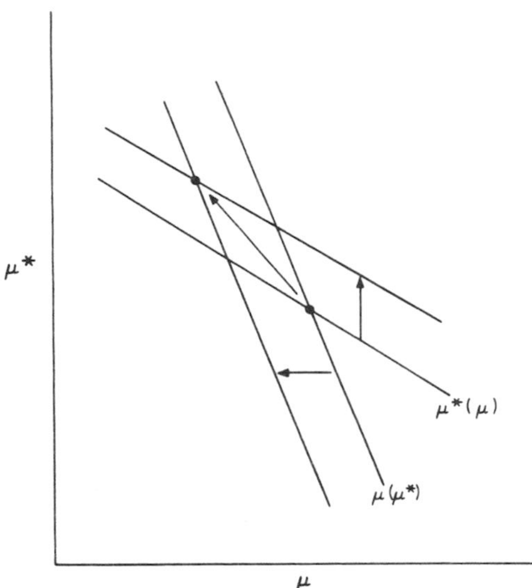

Figure 4

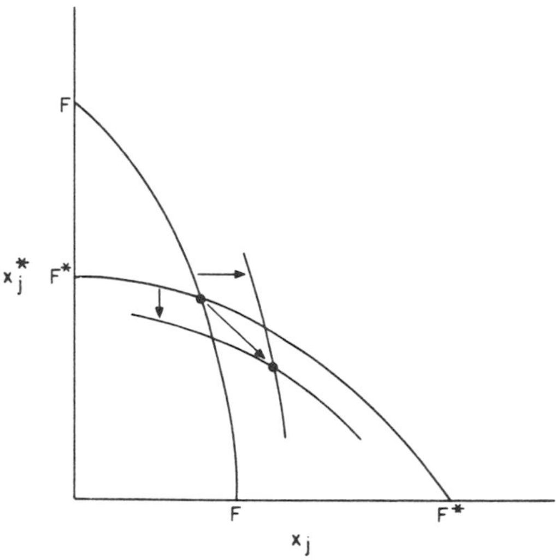

Figure 5

This is the businessman's view, and it should be clear why it is confirmed. There is a positive feedback from output to marginal cost to output. By protecting one market the government gives the domestic firm greater economies of scale, while reducing those of its foreign competitor. Thus decreasing costs are at the heart of the story.

Economists tend, however, to be skeptical of the importance of decreasing costs, at least for large industrial countries. Businessmen see more of a role for scale economies than economists do, but the empirical appeal of the protection-as-promotion argument lies in more subtle forms of decreasing cost. These are the dynamic economies of scale involved in the learning curve and in R&D. What I will do in the rest of this paper is show that these dynamic economies basically have the same implications as static decreasing cost, and that the protection-as-promotion argument remains valid.

4 Model II: Competition in R&D

In this section I assume that marginal costs are constant. Firms can, however, reduce their production costs by prior investment in R&D. This turns out to have effects very similar to those of static declining marginal cost.

There are again two firms, competing in a number of markets; demand looks the same as in model I. Costs, however, look somewhat different. Marginal production cost is independent of the level of output but decreasing in the amount of investment each firm does in R&D.

$$\mu = \mu(N), \tag{12}$$

$$\mu^* = \mu^*(N^*), \tag{13}$$

where

$$\frac{\partial \mu}{\partial N}, \ \frac{\partial \mu^*}{\partial N^*} < 0,$$

$$\frac{\partial^2 \mu}{\partial N^2}, \ \frac{\partial^2 \mu^*}{\partial N^{*2}} < 0.$$

Profits of each firm are revenue, less production and transport costs, and also less R&D expense:

$$\Pi = \sum_i R_i(x_i, x_i^*) - \sum_i t_i x_i - \mu(N) \cdot \sum_i x_i - N, \tag{14}$$

$$\Pi^* = \sum_i R_i^*(x_i^*, x_i) - \sum_i t_i^* x_i^* - \mu^*(N^*) \cdot \sum_i x_i^* - N^*. \tag{15}$$

In determining the outcome of a model like this, there is a question of the appropriate equilibrium concept. The issue is whether firms will adopt "open-loop" strategies, taking the other firm's deliveries as given, or will make sophisticated "closed-loop" calculations that take into account the effect of their own R&D decision on the other firm's subsequent actions. The issue has been repeatedly discussed; Spence (1981) is a recent example. I will opt for simplicity and use the open-loop concept. This also has the advantage of making the parallel between R&D and static scale economies very transparent.

The first-order conditions for the home firm are

$$\frac{\partial R_i}{\partial x_i} - t_i - \mu = 0, \tag{16}$$

$$\frac{\partial \mu}{\partial N} \cdot \sum_i x_i = 1, \tag{17}$$

where we neglect for simplicity the possibility of zero deliveries to some markets.

The important point to notice is that investment in R&D has an effect on profits that is proportional to expected sales. This is a form of increasing returns and is the key to this model.

As in model I, it is useful to think of calculating the equilibrium position iteratively. We first choose levels of R&D expenditure, use the implied marginal cost to compute outputs, recompute the optimal R&D using this, and so on to convergence. The crucial links are illustrated in figures 6 and 7. In figure 6 we show the determination of N given N^*. The higher is N, the lower will be marginal production cost, and thus the higher will be output; the curve QQ captures this relationship. On the other hand, the larger the output the greater the marginal profitability of R&D, so N is increasing in output along MM. As in figure 2, QQ is assumed steeper than MM.

If the foreign firm were to increase its own R&D, the effect would be to lower its marginal cost and reduce domestic output for any given N. Thus QQ would shift left

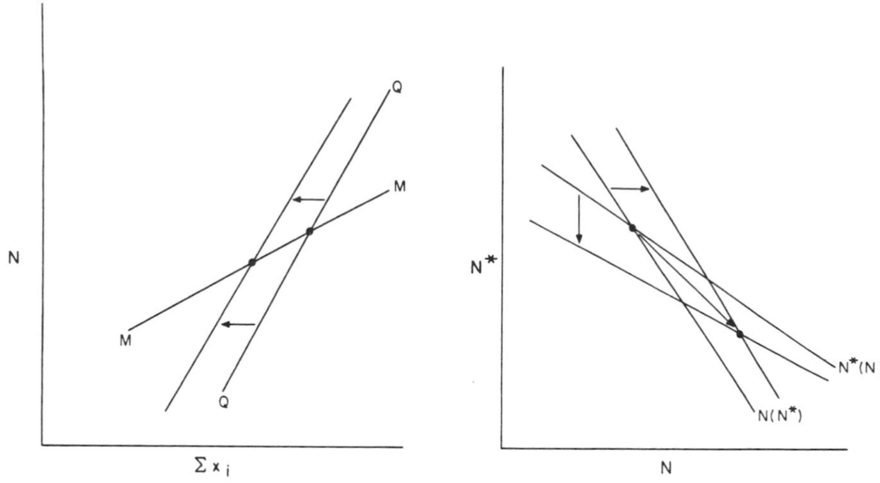

Figure 6

Figure 7

and N fall. The result is that N is decreasing in N^* and vice versa; in figure 7 we show the "stable" or "own effects dominating" case that we assume to prevail.

The effect of reserving some market for the domestic firm is now obvious. At given N and N^* domestic output rises and foreign output falls. The QQ curve shifts out, its foreign counterpart shifts in. Thus $N(N^*)$ shifts right, $N^*(N)$ shifts down; N rises, N^* falls. Reduced marginal production costs for the home firm and higher marginal production costs for the foreign firm mean increased domestic sales in all markets.

The point here is that protection, by increasing the home firm's sales and reducing those of its foreign competitor, increases the incentive for domestic R&D at foreign expense. This in turn translates into a shift in relative production costs that leads to increased domestic sales even in unprotected markets. Even though there are no static scale economies, the result is exactly the same as in model I.

5 Model III: The Learning Curve

In this final model we consider yet another form of economies of scale. In this version there are neither static economies of scale nor explicit investment in R&D; instead, the increasing returns take a dynamic form: higher output now reduces the costs of production later. These learning-by-doing economies turn out to yield results very similar to those in the other models.

The model is a generalized version of one developed by Spence (1981). Again there are two firms, home and foreign. They compete in a number of markets, but now they compete over time as well as space. In each market the revenues of the two firms are

$$R_i = R_i(x_i, x_i^*), \qquad i = 1, \ldots, n, \tag{18}$$

$$R_i^* = R_i^*(x_i^*, x_i), \qquad i = 1, \ldots, n \tag{19}$$

where x_i, x_i^* now represent rates of delivery per unit time; otherwise they have the same properties we have been assuming all along.

On the cost side, each firm faces constant transport costs t_i, t_i^* to each market. At a point in time, production costs are characterized by constant marginal costs μ, μ^*. These marginal costs are, however, dependent on previous output. Let $Q = \sum x_i$, the home firm's rate of output at a point in time; the home firm's cumulative output to time t is then

$$K(t) = \int_0^t Q\,dz. \tag{20}$$

The learning curve assumption is that marginal costs are a decreasing function of cumulative output to date:

$$\mu = \mu(K). \tag{21}$$

Now consider the firms' maximization problems. Following Spence, we will make the extremely useful assumption that firms maximize cumulative profits over a fixed horizon T *with no discounting*. Thus the home firm takes as its objective to maximize

$$\Pi = \int_0^T \left\{ \sum_i \left[R_i(x_i, x_i^*) - t_i x_i - \mu(K) x_i \right] \right\} dt. \tag{22}$$

What does the optimum solution look like? By selling another unit in market i, the firm gains two things: the direct marginal revenue, and the indirect cost saving on future production costs. On the other hand, it incurs the direct costs of transportation and production. Thus the first-order condition at a point in time is

$$\frac{\partial R_i}{\partial x_i} - t_i - \mu - \int_t^T \frac{\partial \mu}{\partial K} \cdot Q\,dz = 0. \tag{23}$$

If the left-hand side of (23) is zero at each point in time, it must also be constant over time. So we can differentiate with respect to time to get

$$\frac{d}{dt}\left[\frac{\partial R}{\partial x_i} - \frac{d}{dt}\mu + \frac{\partial \mu}{\partial K} \cdot Q\right] = \frac{d}{dt}\frac{\partial R}{\partial x_i} - \frac{\partial \mu}{\partial K} \cdot Q + \frac{\partial \mu}{\partial K} \cdot Q$$
$$= \frac{d}{dt}\frac{\partial R}{\partial x_i} = 0. \tag{24}$$

The economic implication of this, as Spence points out, is that the firm sets output on the basis of a constant shadow marginal cost. The level of the shadow marginal cost is determined by the terminal condition: at time T, when the firm no longer considers the effect of current output on future cost, the shadow and actual marginal costs converge.

Again we can imagine an iterative procedure for calculating equilibrium. We can make a guess at the firms' terminal marginal costs μ_T, μ_T^*; find the cumulative output

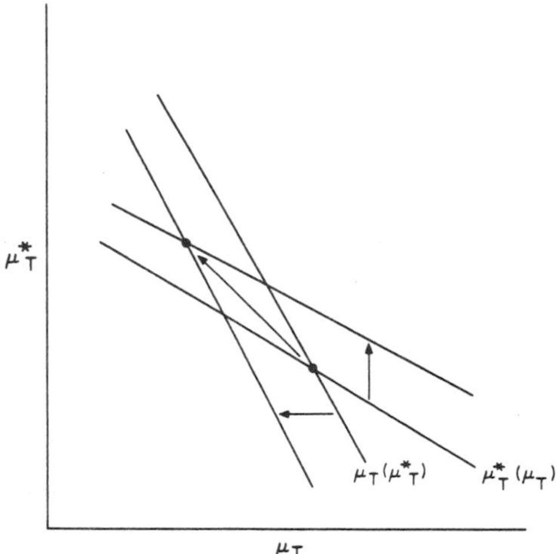

Figure 8

that results from these guesses, and the corresponding terminal marginal cost; and repeat the process. Without going into detail, it should be obvious that the result will be the same as in our first model. Each firm's terminal marginal cost will be decreasing in the other's; equilibrium is illustrated in figure 8, where we assume once again that "own" effects predominate over "cross" effects, so that $\mu_T(\mu_T^*)$ is steeper than $\mu_T^*(\mu_T)$.

The effect of protection is now exactly parallel to its effect in the case of static scale economies. Excluding the foreign firm from some market increases the cumulative output of the domestic firm and reduces the cumulative output of the foreign firm for given μ_T, μ_T^*. The result is that $\mu_T(\mu_T^*)$ shifts left, $\mu_T^*(\mu_T)$ shifts up; μ_T falls, μ_T^* rises. This in turn means that x_i rises and x_i^* falls in all markets, whether they were directly protected or not.

6 Summary and Conclusions

The idea that a protected domestic market gives firms a base for successful exporting is one of those heterodox arguments, common in discussions of international trade, that are incomprehensible in terms of standard models yet seem persuasive to practical men. This paper has developed some simple models that make sense of the argument for protection-as-promotion. To get heterodox conclusions, one needs heterodox assumptions: these models assume oligopoly instead of perfect competition, decreasing costs instead of constant returns. Interestingly, however, the economies of scale need not be simple static production economies but can take fairly subtle dynamic forms.

What is the moral of this paper? Certainly not that the United States should protect its manufacturers as a general strategy. For one thing, the paper contains no welfare analysis. The reason for this is that it is extremely complex. We are comparing second-best situations in any case; and if markets like the ones portrayed here are prevalent, we will not be able to use the standard tools of consumer and producer surplus.

Also, the difference between the conclusions of this paper and standard conclusions is one based on differences in assumptions; which view is more nearly true is an empirical matter. Showing that heterodox ideas are self-consistent does not show that they are right.

The moral of the paper, then, is a much more modest one: the things we are talking about here can be modeled. And it is important that we try. It may be that free trade and laissez-faire are good policies, and that most interventionist suggestions are self-serving, fallacious, or both. But the arguments of trade theorists will remain unpersuasive unless their models begin to contain at least some of the features of the world that practical men accuse them of neglecting.

References

Brander, J. A. 1981. Intra-industry trade in identical commodities. *Journal of International Economics* 11:1–14.

Brander, J. A., and P. R. Krugman. 1981. A reciprocal dumping model of international trade. M.I.T., mimeo.

Spence, A. M. 1981. The learning curve and competition. *Bell Journal of Economics* 12:49–70.

Spencer, B. J., and J. A. Brander. 1982. International R&D rivalry and industrial strategy. Boston College, mimeo.

5 Trade Restrictions as Facilitating Practices

Kala Krishna

1 Introduction

The analysis of trade restrictions has focused on their effects in the polar cases of monopoly and competition and hence has neglected their possible effects on the *nature* of strategic interaction between firms. Interactions between firms are crucial in oligopolistic situations, and when the nature of interaction between firms is affected, the consequences of "slight" restrictions are profound.

The effects of such restrictions depend on whether goods produced are substitutes or complements for each other and on the timing of moves by players. When firms compete in prices, move simultaneously, and produce substitute goods, such restraints alter the nature of the interaction between firms in a collusive direction and thereby raise the equilibrium prices and profits of all firms.[1] In this case trade restrictions impose on firms the collusion they themselves were unable to achieve—that is, they act as facilitating practices. VERs affect the market, not because they are set at restrictive levels, but because they impede the ability of firms to compete effectively when the goods are substitutes. The increase in foreign profits due to a VER is shown to make it unlikely for a VER to raise domestic welfare. In addition, tariffs are shown to be fundamentally nonequivalent to quotas as quotas affect the nature of strategic interaction between firms, while tariffs do not. This is the analogue in oligopolistic markets of Bhagwati's[2] famous result for the case of domestic monopoly.

In contrast to this, when goods are complements, so that an increase in the other product's price *reduces* instead of *raising* demand, a VER at the free trade level has no effect and a tariff is equivalent to a VER, except possibly in its revenue effects.

The work of Harris (1985) contains an analysis of VERs in a duopoly model much like mine. However, his approach and results differ from mine. Harris considers a different game from the one I consider, and only analyzes the case where goods are substitutes. Harris assumes that the imposition of a VER forces the foreign firm to price so that demand for its product does not exceed the level of the VER. He ensures this by assuming that the VER makes the domestic firm into a Stackelberg leader that gives it Stackelberg leadership profits associated with a first mover advantage. In contrast, I make no such assumption. Firms are assumed to move simultaneously both before and after the VER is imposed. I show that for a particular rationing rule, the domestic firm obtains the profits of a Stackelberg leader in the new game with a VER when goods are substitutes. This need not be the case with a different rationing rule. When goods are complements, a VER at the free trade level has no effect on equilibrium.

There has also been a good deal of work on the effects of VERs in other market structures, and with other strategic variables. Duopoly models are used in most cases.

Originally published in the *Journal of International Economics* 26 (May 1989): 251–270.

Itoh and Ono (1982) analyze Stackelberg leadership models and show that tariffs are not equivalent to quotas in these models. They also discuss the Bertrand model in Itoh and Ono (1984) but they assume that excess demand for one product has no effect on the demand for the other—a rather odd assumption since this lies at the heart of a VER's effects. Repeated game models have also been used to analyze VERs and tariffs. See, for example, Davidson (1984) and Rottemberg and Saloner (1986). However, the usual problems in such games arise, namely that they have too many equilibria.

In contrast to this, static models yield testable predictions. In a computable partial equilibrium model, such as that of Dixit (1986), the model predicts that the imposition of a VER at the free trade level would change the degree of competition as measured by the conjectural variations term in his calibrated model. As this is not the focus of Dixit's paper, further work focused on this question is required for a more precise estimate of the effects of a VER on competition in an industry.

In oligopolistic markets trade restrictions of many kinds can have effects of different kinds on the "game" played between firms. These effects can differ depending upon a variety of factors such as the form of the restriction, demand conditions, technology and the specification of out-of-equilibrium payoffs. For this reason it is vital to carefully specify how the payoffs are altered by the presence of restrictions since this provides a rich framework for the analysis of their effects.

In the next section I specify the model. In section 3 I analyze the effects of a VER when goods are substitutes or complements. In section 4 I compare tariffs and quotas. Section 5 concludes with a discussion of policy implications and directions for future research.

2 The Model

The simplest model that permits me to show how a trade restriction can affect oligopolistic interaction is used. There are assumed to be two firms, one home and one foreign, who produce differentiated products that are substitutes or complements for each other, and compete in prices in the domestic product market.[3] The equilibrium concept is that of Nash equilibrium.

Let P be the price of the home product, and p that of the foreign one. Similarly let $Q(p, P)$, $q(p, P)$ and $C(Q)$, $c(q)$ be the demand and cost functions facing the home and foreign firms, respectively. Thus,

$$\Pi(p, P) = PQ(p, P) - C(Q(p, P))$$

and

$$\pi(p, P) = pq(p, P) - c(q(p, \mathrm{P}))$$

are their profit functions.

For any given P, denote the profit-maximizing price p that the foreign firm can charge by $b(P)$; $B(p)$ is defined analogously. These constitute the best responses on the

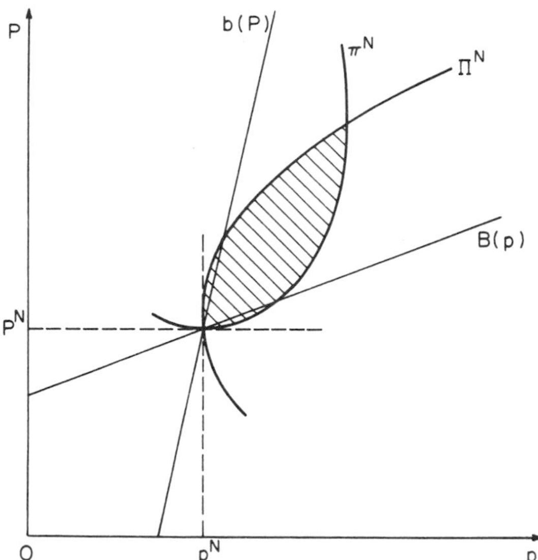

Figure 1

part of a firm to any price set by its competitor. By definition, the Nash equilibrium is given by the point (p^N, P^N) that satisfies both $b(P) = p$ and $B(p) = P$.

I assume that a unique stable Nash equilibrium exists.[4] In particular, I assume that profit functions are strictly concave in their own price alone,[5] that is, that upper contour sets are convex. The cases illustrated are such that best response functions are upward sloping when goods are substitutes, and downward sloping when goods are complements. However, as will become clear, this last assumption is not crucial.[6]

Figure 1 illustrates the equilibrium when goods are substitutes. $b(P)$ is the level of p such that the highest iso-profit contour for the foreign firm is reached, given the domestic price P. Hence, iso-profit contours of the foreign firm are horizontal along $b(P)$. Similarly, the domestic firm's iso-profit contours are vertical along $B(p)$. Profits increase in the competitor's price when goods are substitutes, which defines the direction in which higher profit contours are reached. $b(P)$ is steeper than $B(p)$ to ensure stability. The equilibrium is at the intersection of $B(p)$ and $b(P)$ denoted by the point (p^N, P^N) in figure 1. The corresponding profit levels are given by π^N and Π^N. If goods were complements, profits would decrease with an increase in the competitor's price, as in figure 5 below which depicts this case.

3 The Effects of a VER

In order to specify how a VER affects the equilibrium, it is necessary to examine how it alters the best responses of both firms. As these depend on how their profit functions are affected, we must first carefully examine this aspect of a VER. I will first show what happens when goods are substitutes for one another.

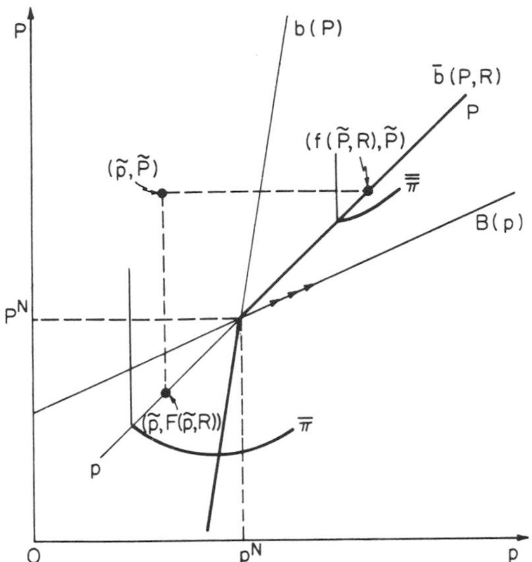

Figure 2

An import restraint at the level R will be just binding at prices (p, P) if $R = q(p, P)$. This relationship implicitly defines the foreign price $p = f(P, R)$ just required to maintain imports at R for a given P. This price is depicted in figure 2 by the line Pp when R is set at the free trade level of imports. Hence, it goes through $(p^{\mathrm{N}}, P^{\mathrm{N}})$. At points in figure 2 to the left of pP, the foreign price, p, is less than $f(P, R)$ and the import restraint is binding. Imports are not constrained at points to the right of pP.

Above pP, where the VER is binding, the foreign firm's iso-profit contours in the presence of a VER are thus vertical lines because its profits are independent of the domestic firm's price in this region as the VER is binding. Below pP, they are unaffected by the existence of a VER. The iso-profit contours are kinked along pP as shown by the two iso-profit contours $\bar{\pi}$ and $\bar{\bar{\pi}}$ in figure 2.

If the profit-maximizing foreign price $b(P)$ in the absence of a VER is to the left of pP, then the import restraint is binding at $b(P)$ and it follows that $f(P, R)$ (as illustrated by pP in fig. 2) is the foreign firm's best response under constraint R. In essence, for any given P, it pays the foreign firm to increase price above $b(P)$ to the point where the VER is just binding. If $b(P)$ is to the right of pP, then the VER is not binding at $b(P)$ and the best response function is unchanged. This is illustrated in figure 2, where the dark line $\bar{b}(P, R)$ represents the best response function of the foreign firm with the VER. Hence,

$$\begin{aligned}\bar{b}(P, R) &= f(P, R), \qquad \text{if } f(P, R) \geqq b(P) \text{ or } P \geqq P^{\mathrm{N}}, \\ &= b(P), \qquad \text{if } f(P, R) \leqq b(P) \text{ or } P \leqq P^{\mathrm{N}}.\end{aligned}$$

We now turn to how the domestic firm's profits are altered by a VER on the foreign firm. If prices lie above the line pP, then the demand for the foreign firm's product exceeds the level of the VER. Hence, at these prices, some consumers of the foreign product would be rationed. This would affect the demand for the *domestic* firm's product. A natural way of specifying the relationship between rationing in one market and its spillover effects in another is to allow costless arbitrage. This provides one rationing rule; many others are possible and the effects of a VER depend on the rationing rule used.

If the firms charge prices such that the demand for the foreign good exceeds R, there is room for arbitrage profits to be made. Assume that if demand exceeds R, it is as if the entire stock of the foreign good is thrown on the market for what it will bring. Consumers lucky enough to get the foreign good at the price charged make profits by selling the good at a price that clears the market. As the income effects of such transactions are assumed away, the effect on the domestic firm's demand is *exactly* what it would have been if the foreign firm *actually* charged the price that cleared the market, namely $f(P, R)$. Notice that when prices are such that the VER binds on the foreign firm, the domestic firm's demand depends *only* on its own price and is given by $Q(f(P, R), P)$.

This is illustrated in figure 2. If the domestic firm charges the price $\tilde{P}$ and the foreign one charges the price $\tilde{p}$, demand for the foreign product exceeds R. Consumers fortunate enough to get the foreign good sell it for what the market will fetch, $f(\tilde{P}, R)$. Thus, if prices charged are $\tilde{P}$ and $\tilde{p}$, the foreign price that enters the domestic firm's demand function is $f(\tilde{P}, R)$ and not $\tilde{p}$. Also, no matter what price the foreign firm charges, the domestic one can make the constraint bind on it by raising the price of the domestic good above the pP line. For any price p charged by the foreign firm, and VER at level R, define $F(p, R)$ as the price of the domestic product that makes demand for the foreign good equal R. Note that $P = F(p, R)$ is also illustrated by pP since $F(\cdot)$ is the inverse of $f(\cdot)$. Also notice that the constraint binds on the foreign firm if $P \geqq F(p, R)$ and does not if $P \leqq F(p, R)$. Hence, the profit function for the domestic firm, $\bar{\Pi}(p, P, R)$, is now

$$\begin{aligned} \bar{\Pi}(p, P, R) &= \Pi(p, P), && \text{if } P \leqq F(p, R), \\ &= \Pi(f(P, R), P), && \text{if } P \geqq F(p, R). \end{aligned}$$

Notice that at $P = F(p, R)$ a switch in the profit function occurs, and at this point the slope of $\bar{\Pi}$ is greater to the right of $F(p, R)$ than to its left. This creates a non-concavity in $\bar{\Pi}$.

The next question is: How is the best response function of the domestic firm affected by this change in its profit function. Let $(p^{\mathrm{H}}, P^{\mathrm{H}})$ be the point where the iso-profit curve of the domestic firm is tangent to pP so that P^{H} maximizes $\Pi(f(P, R), P)$. Let $(\hat{p}, P^{\mathrm{L}})$ be the point where this iso-profit contour intersects $B(p)$—as illustrated in figure 3.

Essentially, the firm has to choose whether to make the VER bind on the foreign firm or not. If $p > \hat{p}$, the domestic firm can obtain the profits at $B(p)$ by choosing not to make the VER bind. Since these profits exceed the maximum that it can obtain by making the VER bind, namely V, it will choose to charge $B(p)$ in this case. If $p < \hat{p}$, it can obtain V by choosing to charge P^{H} and making the VER bind. It is optimal for it to charge P^{H} since if it chooses not to make the VER bind, it can at most obtain the profits along $B(p)$ that are less than V when $p < \hat{p}$. If $p = \hat{p}$, it is indifferent between $B(\hat{p})$ and P^{H} as they both yield profits of V. Hence, the best response of the domestic firm to any price charged by its competitor is given by

$$\begin{aligned} \bar{B}(p,R) &= P^{\mathrm{H}}, \qquad \text{if } p \leqq \hat{p}, \\ &= B(p), \qquad \text{if } p \geqq \hat{p}. \end{aligned}$$

If foreign prices are high, domestic demand is high and it is not worthwhile for the domestic firm to make the VER bind on its competitor. If foreign prices are low, domestic demand is low if the VER is not made to bind and it is worthwhile to make it bind. Note that $\bar{B}(p,R)$ is discontinuous and takes on two values at $p = \hat{p}$. Also note that $\bar{B}(p,R)$ does *not* intersect $\bar{b}(P,R)$. Thus, there is no equilibrium in pure strategies.

THEOREM 1 Assume that the line pP is steeper than $B(p)$[7] and that a unique maximum exists to $\Pi(f(P,R),P)$, which is attained at $P = P^{\mathrm{H}}$. If R is set at or close to the free trade level, there is no equilibrium in pure strategies.

Proof: Follows from figure 3. □

The nonexistence of pure strategy equilibria can be understood by noting that a quantitative restriction acts like a capacity constraint on the foreign firm. The nonexistence of a Bertrand-Nash equilibrium in pure strategies in the presence of capacity constraints has been known since Edgeworth's classic criticism of Bertrand.[8] Of course, mixed strategy equilibria can be shown to exist under very general conditions.[9] However, the mere existence of a mixed strategy equilibrium does not yield any

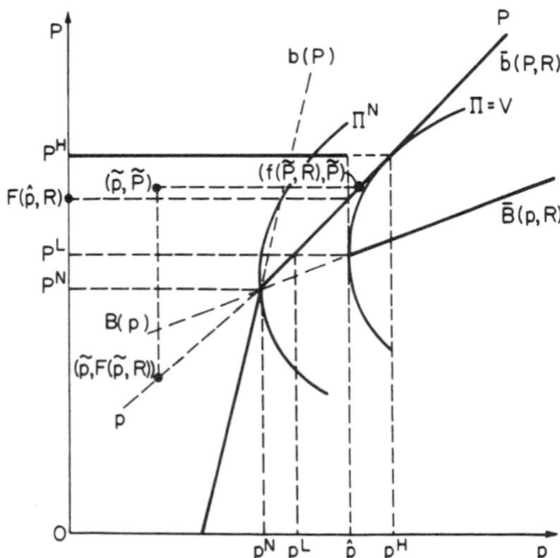

Figure 3

information about the effects of a VER. The form of the mixed strategy equilibrium needs to be characterized in order to get such information. We turn to this next.

Before we begin, notice that the domestic firm's profit function is nonconcave in its own price so that it may be in its interest to randomize its prices. However, the foreign firm's profit function remains concave in the price—*even* if the domestic firm chooses to use a mixed strategy since its profit function is concave and a convex combination of concave functions remains concave. Thus, it is *never* in the interest of the foreign firm to use a mixed strategy, and the foreign firm will always choose to charge only one price. If the foreign firm charges only one price, the domestic firm will only randomize if $p = \hat{p}$. In this case, it would randomize over P^{H}, P^{L}—which give it equal profit. These strategies are a natural candidate for the equilibrium.

THEOREM 2 The unique mixed strategy equilibrium consists of the foreign firm charging $\hat{p}$, and the domestic one randomizing over P^{H}, P^{L}—charging P^{H} with probability α, and P^{L} with probability $1 - \alpha$.

Proof: If the foreign firm charges $\hat{p}$ the domestic firm is indifferent between charging P^{H} or P^{L}, or randomizing over them, namely, charging P^{H} with probability α and P^{L} with probability $1 - \alpha$. If we could show that there exists an α between 0 and 1 such that the foreign firm's best response to this strategy of the domestic firm is to charge $\hat{p}$, the proof would be complete. That such an α exists can be seen by referring to figure 4. In figure 4, p^{H} and p^{L} are (as in fig. 3) defined as being equal to $\bar{b}(P^{\mathrm{H}}, R)$ and $\bar{b}(P^{\mathrm{L}}, R)$, respectively.

The profit function that the foreign firm maximizes when the domestic firm randomizes across P^{H} and P^{L} in the above manner is $\bar{\pi}(p, \alpha, R)$. It is a convex combination of $\bar{\pi}(p, P^{\mathrm{L}}, R)$ and $\bar{\pi}(p, P^{\mathrm{H}}, R)$. $\bar{\pi}(p, P, R)$ denotes profits of the foreign firm given prices and the level of restriction. These are depicted in figure 4. Hence,

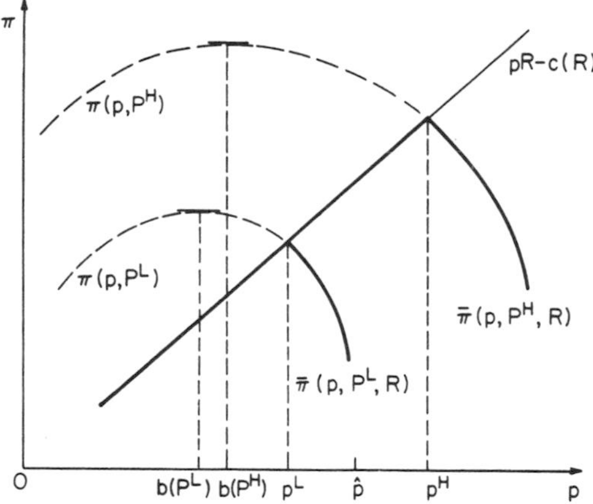

Figure 4

$$\begin{aligned}\bar{\pi}(p,\alpha,R) &= pR - c(R), && \text{if } p \leqq p^{L},\\ &= \alpha(pR - c(R)) + (1-\alpha)\pi(p,P^{L}), && \text{if } p^{L} \leqq p \leqq p^{H},\\ &= \alpha\pi(p,P^{H}) + (1-\alpha)\pi(p,P^{L}), && \text{if } p \geqq p^{H}.\end{aligned}$$

Note that if p is less than p^{L}, the restriction binds on the foreign firm irrespective of whether the domestic firm charges P^{H} or P^{L}. Thus, both profit functions take on the value $pR - c(R)$, and so does a convex combination of them. If p lies between p^{L} and p^{H}, the restriction binds only if the domestic firm charges P^{H}, so that the profit function for the foreign firm takes on a value given by a convex combination of $pR - c(R)$ and $\pi(p, P^{L})$. If $p > p^{H}$, then the restriction does not bind when *either* P^{H} or P^{L} are charged so that profits are just a convex combination of the unrestricted profit functions.

Notice that $p^{L} < \hat{p} < p^{H}$. In this region, the foreign firm's profits are a convex combination of $pR - c(R)$, which is increasing in p, and $\pi(p, P^{L})$, which is decreasing in p in this region. Thus, for all p's between p^{L} and p^{H} there exists an α such that the slope of the foreign firm's profit function at p is zero. As this is true for all p's between p^{L} and p^{H}, it is true for $\hat{p}$. Although figures 3 and 4 are drawn so that pP is flatter than $b(P)$, arguments similar to those above work even when pP is steeper than $b(P)$.

If the domestic firm is randomizing according to this α, and the foreign firm is charging $\hat{p}$, both are doing the best they can given what the other is doing, and this is a Nash equilibrium. Uniqueness of the equilibrium follows from the fact that it is not in the foreign firm's interest to randomize, and that the domestic firm wants to randomize only when the foreign firm is charging $\hat{p}$. □

With Theorem 2 in hand, it is possible to analyze the *effects* of a VER.

THEOREM 3 With substitute goods, the imposition of a VER at or close to the free trade levels raises both firms' prices and profits in equilibrium. In fact, the domestic firm attains the level of profits of a Stackelberg leader. As both prices rise, domestic output may rise or fall.

Proof: Notice that a VER at the free trade level raises the expected profits of the domestic firm from Π^{N} to V. Note that V is the level of profits that would have accrued to the domestic firm if the foreign firm's reaction function was given by $f(P, R)$ and the domestic firm was the Stackelberg leader.

The expected profits of the foreign firm also rise. Whether the domestic firm charges P^{H} or P^{L}, the foreign firm could charge p^{N} and sell R. This would give it free trade profits. As it prefers to charge $\hat{p}$ over p^{N}, its profits must rise due to the VER. Notice that P^{H}, P^{L}, and $\hat{p}$ are above their free trade levels. It is easy to construct examples to show that domestic output can rise or fall. □

Notice that the profits of the foreign firm in the equilibrium are less than the profits of a Stackelberg follower, namely, the profits of selling R at price p^{H}. When the home firm charges P^{H}, the foreign one can sell only R but charges $\hat{p}$, which is less than p^{H}, the price of a Stackelberg follower. When the home firm charges P^{L}, and the foreign

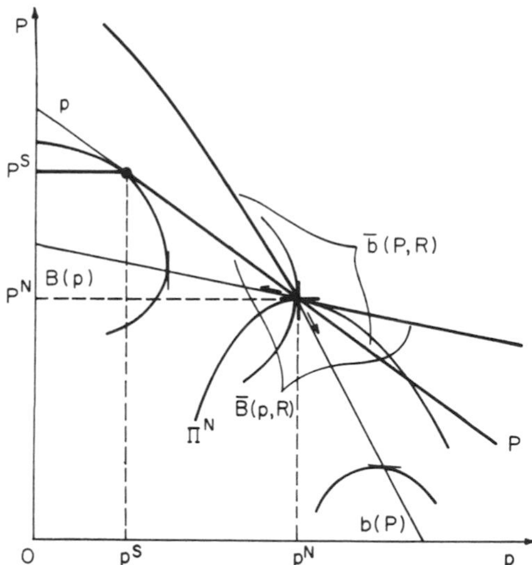

Figure 5

firm $\hat{p}$, demand for the foreign good is less than R. In both cases the foreign firm makes less than Stackelberg follower profits, so that its equilibrium profits are also below this level.

We now turn to the effects of a VER when goods are complements. As before, b and B are the best response functions of the firms and their intersection gives the Nash equilibrium prices (p^N, P^N). When goods are complements,[10] the analogue of the pP line is downward sloping. This is because an increase in P *reduces* demand for the complementary foreign good and a decrease in p is needed to keep demand for it at R. Moreover, the VER is binding when P is low, since reducing P raises the demand for the foreign good. The VER thus binds only below the pP line in figure 5. Since the goods are complements, profits increase along the respective best response functions as the other price falls, as shown by the arrows in figure 5. As before, we consider a VER at the free trade level so that pP passes through (p^N, P^N).

What is the effect of the VER on the best response function? First look at the foreign firm's best response function. If P lies above P^N, the foreign firm would, in the absence of the VER, like to charge the price $b(P)$, which is greater than that along pP, so that the VER has no effect on its best response function in this region. If P is below P^N, the foreign firm would, in the absence of the VER, wish to charge a price below that along pP and sell more than R. However, since it is constrained to sell no more than R it is better off raising its price to that along pP. This gives its best response function with a VER to be $\bar{b}(P, R)$, as depicted in figure 5. Notice that the foreign best response function is altered for *low* prices of the domestic firm as this is when foreign demand is high given that goods are complements.

Now consider the domestic firm's best response function. If $p > p^N$, then, in the absence of a VER, the firm would wish to charge $B(p)$. By reducing its price below $B(p)$

but above pP it can only reduce its profit since the VER does not bind here and $B(p)$ is its best response function in its absence. By reducing P below the pP line it could make the VER bind on the foreign firm, cause its output to be rationed, and raise its effective price on the market. However, this would only hurt the domestic firm since the goods are complements. Thus, for p above p^N, the domestic firm will wish to charge $B(p)$.

If $p < p^N$, the domestic firm will never wish to charge a price above pP where the VER is not binding because pP lies above $B(p)$ in this region. If the domestic firm charges a price below pP, it obtains the profits given by $\Pi(f(P, R), P)$. From figure 5 it can be seen that these are maximized by charging $F(p, R)$ when $p \geqq p^s$ and P^s when $p \leqq p^s$, where (p^s, P^s) is the point of tangency between the domestic iso-profit contour and the pP line. This defines $\bar{B}(p, R)$, the domestic best response function with a VER, which is depicted in figure 5. Thus (p^N, P^N) remains an equilibrium with a VER at the free trade level. This gives us Theorem 4.

THEOREM 4 With complementary goods, a VER at the free trade level has no effect. □

When goods are substitutes, the assumption made by Harris gives the same level of profits in equilibrium to the domestic firm as this model when the given rationing rule is used. But the profits to the foreign firm are below those in Harris's model of a Stackelberg follower, although they also rise. However, this is but one of the many rationing rules that could be used, and the effect of a VER depends on which rationing rule is most appropriate for the model in question.

The reason for using the rationing rule specified here is that it can be used without a specific underlying model of how market demand is generated. How this rationing rule compares to other rationing rules depends on the underlying model of market demand. Locational models of horizontal product differentiation à la Lancaster (1979), or of vertical product differentiation à la Gabszewicz and Thisse (1979), can easily be used for this purpose. While the extent to which the VER affects the equilibrium in any such model is, of course, sensitive to the form of the rationing rule, the manner in which it does so is not. In general, the effects of a VER tend to be small if the rationing rule allocates the rationed product to those consumers who would substitute the unrationed product for the rationed one, and large if it allocates it to consumers who would not substitute in this manner. Thus, the rationing rule used here generates large effects if consumers with a high willingness to pay for the foreign good are the ones who would not substitute between products, and small effects if consumers with a high willingness to pay are the ones who tend to substitute between the products. However, to the extent that all consumers are willing to substitute between products at some set of prices, the kinds of effects discussed here will exist.

It is worthwhile at this point to try to understand intuitively why VERs have such different effects depending on whether the goods are complements or substitutes for one another. In order to do so, one needs to understand intuitively how the game itself can change due to a VER. The essence of the argument that the game itself changes due to a VER can be understood by realizing that there are three effects of any restriction in oligopolistic markets. I call these the C, M, and I effects. The C effect is the only one that operates in competitive environments. In a competitive framework, any form of protection works by altering the market demand and/or supply functions whenever the constraint is binding. If the constraint is set so that it is just binding at the free trade levels, it will not alter the demand and/or supply functions at equilibrium so that the free trade equilibrium must remain an equilibrium. In other words, restrictions affect equilibrium in competitive markets only by being restrictive.

In the case of domestic monopoly and foreign competition, even restrictions that would not have produced any effect under competitive conditions have significant effects. These arise because such restrictions alter demand and/or supply conditions at points other than the unconstrained equilibrium point. Hence, they can affect the monopolist's choice. In this manner, restrictions can have significant effects by their sheer presence. This point was made in Bhagwati (1965). I call this the M effect, and it operates in addition to any C effect.

In a duopoly model, not only do the effects present in the monopoly case exist, but because *each* agent is affected in the manner the monopolist was in the previous paragraph, the actions of *all* agents can change. As the outcome depends on all agents interacting, an additional effect arises, which is called the I effect. Although the M effects of protection at free trade levels cannot but benefit domestic producers, the I effects can be harmful if they work against the M effects.[11] C effects are local effects, M effects and I effects are global effects like those of a change in regime. Therefore, they are likely to be very important.

In the analysis of VERs with substitute goods, the imposition of a VER on the foreign firm makes the domestic firm's demand function less elastic for price increases, since a price increase makes the VER bind on the foreign firm and makes it profitable for the domestic firm to raise the price at the free trade equilibrium. This is the M effect à la Bhagwati. The increase in the domestic firm's price makes the constraint bind on the foreign firm since the goods are substitutes and makes it optimal for the foreign firm to also raise its price since it is effectively supply constrained. This is the essence of the I effect.

Both effects raise domestic profits. Since foreign prices rise, as long as foreign supply is not constrained to be too much less than the free trade level, foreign profits must also rise. This is basically how VERs facilitate collusion with substitute goods.

With complementary goods, the imposition of a VER on the foreign firm makes the domestic firm's demand function less elastic for price decreases, since a price decrease makes the VER bind on the foreign firm. However, it is not profitable for the domestic firm to reduce its price and so there is no M effect and therefore no I effect of a VER. For this reason, a VER at the free trade level has no effect with complementary goods. These effects of a VER are shown to be why tariffs and quotas are fundamentally nonequivalent with substitutes produced and why they are equivalent when complements are produced.

It is useful to consider what the effects of a VER might have been had there been *no* effect of a ration in the market for the foreign product on the demand for the domestic one. This assumption is termed that of "no spillovers" in demand. This case should be thought of as a benchmark as it isolates the restrictive or C effect of a VER from the M and I effects. Even with this assumption, a VER close to the free trade level can be shown to raise both firms' profits when goods are substitutes.

THEOREM 5 If goods are substitutes, best response functions are upward sloping, there are no spillovers in demand, and the equilibrium is stable in the presence of a VER, then a VER set at the free trade level has no effect, while one set slightly below the free trade level must raise both firms' profits and prices.

Proof: The reason is very simple and is illustrated using figures 1 and 2.

Note that the assumption of "no spillovers" means that the domestic firm's profit function, and hence its best response function, is unaffected by the presence of a VER on the foreign firm. Thus, the VER only makes the foreign firm's best response function into $\bar{b}(P, R)$, as discussed earlier. Hence, a VER *at* the free trade level will have no effect on the equilibrium. This no-spillovers case is the only one considered in Itoh and Ono (1984). In order for the equilibrium to be *stable* it is necessary for the line pP to be steeper than $B(p)$—and this assumption is made in this section as well.

Now consider the effect of lowering the VER slightly. This moves the line pP to the right in figure 2. As pP is steeper than $B(p)$, the equilibrium given by the intersection of $B(p)$ and $\bar{b}(P, R)$ moves up along $B(p)$ in the direction of the arrows in figure 2. This must lie in the shaded area in figure 1, which is precisely the region of greater profits for both firms. Also, as $B(p)$ is upward sloping, prices must rise as well. □

4 The Effects of Tariffs and Quotas

The analysis of the previous section allows us to compare the effects of a VER or quota with those of an import equivalent tariff when goods are substitutes. It is shown that in this case: (1) prices under a tariff are lower than those under the VER set at the post-tariff import levels; (2) the profits of the domestic firm are also higher under the VER than under the tariff; (3) if the VER is set close to the free trade level of output, it will be preferred by the foreign firm to no restrictions. In addition, the foreign firm would prefer the VER to the tariff, even if the tariff revenues were returned to it as a lump sum.

A tariff, when costs are positive, moves the foreign firm's reaction function to the right, as in figure 6.[12] The analysis comparing a VER to an equivalent tariff is similar to that comparing a VER at the Nash equilibrium level to the equilibrium in the absence of any restriction, and the arguments made previously can be applied. To substantiate the first point, compare the level of domestic prices under a quantitative restriction set at the level of imports induced by a tariff, and under the tariff. The former are greater than the latter. This is shown in figure 6. $b(P, t)$ is the best response

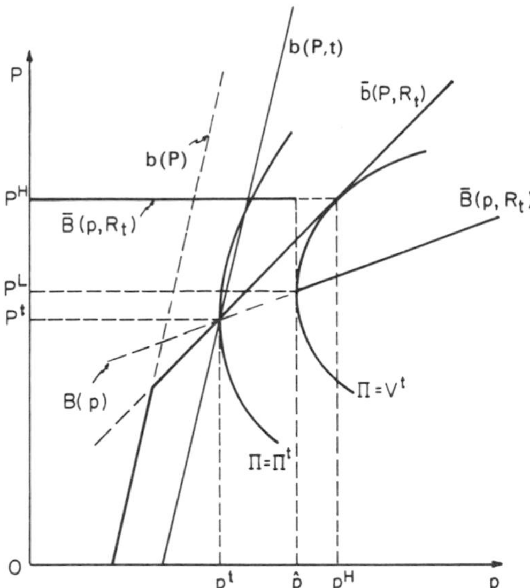

Figure 6

function of the foreign firm with the tariff, and R_t is the level of imports with the tariff. $\bar{b}(P, R_t)$ and $\bar{B}(p, R_t)$ are the best responses of the foreign and domestic firms, respectively, in the presence of a VER at the level of imports prevailing under the tariff at rate t. The notation used in figure 6 corresponds to that previously introduced for examining the effect of a VER. Both P^{L} and P^{H} are above P^{t}, the price of the home good with the tariff. Also, $\hat{p}$ is greater than p^{t}, the price of the foreign good with the tariff. Thus, prices are greater under the VER than under the equivalent import tariff.

It is also easy to see that the domestic firm's profits are higher under the VER than under the tariff, as V^{t} is greater than Π^{t}.

The foreign firm's profits must rise due to a VER as long as the VER is not too severe. As shown previously, the profits of the foreign firm must rise if the restriction is set at the free trade level. As its profits are strictly greater with a VER at the free trade level, continuity arguments show that they should remain so when R_t is close to the free trade output level.

In addition, even if revenues of the tariff were returned to the firm as a lump-sum transfer, the foreign firm would prefer a VER to a tariff. This is due to the equilibrium profits of the foreign firm with the VER being greater than its profits if the domestic firm randomized between P^{H} and P^{L} as given, and it charged p^{t}. This is because it could have charged p^{t}, but chose not to. If it had charged p^{t}, it would have earned $p^{t}R_t$ which is exactly the *total price paid* by consumers in the tariff regime, or what the foreign firm would get if tariff revenues were returned to it in a lump sum.

It is obvious that had we assumed that there were no "spillovers in demand," then a tariff and a quota at the level of imports generated by the tariff would lead to the same level of domestic prices. Tariffs and quotas would be equivalent. However, this is *not* true in general with substitute goods. Also, since no M and I effects exist with complementary goods, tariffs and quotas are equivalent for small tariffs and complementary goods.

Bhagwati (1965) pointed out that tariffs and quotas are not equivalent in the presence of monopoly elements. This section extended his results to duopolistic markets. Itoh and Ono (1984) claim that tariffs and quotas are equivalent with price competition and substitute goods, but consider *only* the case of no spillovers in demand, which is an extreme assumption.

5 Policy Implications and Conclusions

Voluntary export restraints have been shown to raise prices *and* profits of *both* the domestic and foreign firm since they have effects like those of a regime change when goods are substitutes for one another. When goods are complements for one another, there are no regime change effects and VERs at the free trade level have no effect on the equilibrium and therefore have no effect on welfare.

An argument which might be made *for* VERs with substitute goods is that while a VER lowers consumer welfare by raising prices, it also raises the profits of domestic producers. If the gain in national welfare because of the latter outweighed the loss due to the former, national welfare would rise. In this event, VERs would be in the national interest despite being far from the first-best policy. (See Brander and Spencer 1985 and Dixit 1987 for a discussion of such profit-shifting effects.)

Notice, however, that as a VER causes *both* firms' profits to rise, there is no profit *shifting* from foreign to domestic firms. Thus, the increase in the domestic firm's profits occurs solely at the expense of domestic consumers, who also pay for the increase in the foreign firm's profits. Hence, one would *expect* national welfare to *fall* due to the absence of any profit-shifting effects of a VER, so VERs would *not* be in the national interest. A possible exception arises if the market for the domestic product is more distorted than that for the foreign product and *domestic* output rises due to the VER. In this event the loss in welfare due to the decrease in imports and increase in foreign profits *could* be more than compensated for by the increase in domestic output. Of course, if domestic output fell due to a VER, welfare would have to fall as well. A fall in domestic output is sufficient, but not necessary for the national welfare to fall due to a VER. Another sufficient condition for national welfare to fall due to a VER is that *world* welfare *falls* when both prices rise and that a VER raises all prices. A more formal analysis of the welfare effects may be found in Krishna (1985).

Another argument made in favor of VERs is that they create employment (or prevent unemployment), which is desirable in itself. However, it is easy to construct examples where employment falls due to a VER.

A third argument made in favor of VERs is a more sophisticated one. It adapts the old infant industry arguments to a mature economy. The argument is that a mature economy subjected to unexpected shocks (like the oil crisis) needs time to adapt its products (cars) and increase the competitiveness of its products relative to (Japanese) imports. VERs are a temporary measure to buy that time. However, VERs raise domestic profits, which is likely to make unions more aggressive in their demands, making it harder for domestic products to compete effectively in the future.

An import-equivalent export tax imposed by the exporting nation would not have the severe anticompetitive effects associated with a VER. In addition, prices and foreign profits would be lower. However, it is clear from an examination of history that trade restrictions tend to be self-perpetuating. For this reason, it is essential to link any restriction to increases in the efficiency of domestic producers so that the restrictions would ultimately be removed. It is in the interest of domestic producers to lobby for quantitative restraints over tax policies that are import equivalent, because of the anticompetitive nature of the former. For this reason, such proposals should be viewed with some suspicion.

Finally, as trade restrictions in oligopolistic industries may have unexpected effects, special care should be taken in formulating policy for such industries.

Notes

I am grateful to the Sloan Foundation and to Princeton University for financial support and to Avinash Dixit, Gene Grossman, and Vijay Krishna for helpful discussions. An earlier version of this paper appeared as Discussion Paper in Economics no. 55, Woodrow Wilson School of Public and International Affairs, Princeton University, October 1983; a later version appeared as NBER Working Paper no. 1546, January 1985. Since this paper was written, independent work by R. Harris on the same subject has been published in the Canadian Journal of Economics, November 1985.

1. Whether or not the nature of interaction is affected by a trade restriction depends on how competitively firms behave and the form of the restriction. A restriction on market shares when firms compete in quantities has a similar effect to a restriction on output when firms compete on prices, and both affect the nature of interaction between firms. The importance of the strategic variable for policy is also brought out in Eaton and Grossman (1986).

2. See Bhagwati (1965).

3. If goods are produced at constant marginal and average costs, and there is no possibility of profitable resale in between markets, firms may compete in other markets as well. I will also assume that a numeraire good exists and, hence, that there are no income effects.

4. For conditions sufficient to ensure this, see Friedman (1981).

5. This ensures continuity of the functions B and b. Reasonable demand functions may lead to nonconcave profit functions, as in Roberts and Sonnenschien (1977).

6. It is well understood that best response functions could be either upward or downward sloping with price competition. Examples of this can be found in Krishna and Itoh (1988) and Bulow, Geanakoplos, and Klemperer (1985).

7. If pP was flatter than $B(p)$ no maximum to $\Pi(f(P, R), P)$ would exist given our assumptions about profits increasing in the competitor's price, as demonstrated by the following argument. If $p > p^N$ were the price charged by the foreign firm, the domestic firm would be able to ensure itself $\Pi(f(B(p), R), B(p))$ by charging $B(p)$. However, as $B(p)$ lies above pP, in this region it can certainly get more by raising its price, even if the scarcity price of the foreign good remained at $f(B(p), R)$. In addition, as the scarcity price of the foreign good rises as well, profits rise even more. As this argument can be repeated, no maximum to the above profit function can exist.

8. See Fellner (1960, pp. 77–86) for an excellent discussion.

9. If the strategy sets (the prices that can be charged) are assumed to be nonempty and compact, existence is ensured by Glicksburg's theorem as profit functions remain continuous despite the VER. See Dasgupta and Maskin (1986).

10. A good example might be a VER on an intermediate input that is imported and that is complementary in demand to an input produced at home.

11. The I and M effects may work in opposite directions when other restrictions such as content protection are considered. This is shown in Krishna and Itoh (1988), where the form of the content protection and demand and supply conditions in the production of the final good determine when domestic profits rise or fall.

12. If costs were zero, the presence of a tariff would not affect the reaction function of firm 1, as the profit function facing the foreign firm with a tariff would be a monotonic transformation of the profit function in the absence of one. If a tariff at rate t is imposed, the revenue of the foreign firm, when it sets a *market* price of p, is $(1-t)pq(p,P)$. Its profits are denoted by $\pi(p,P,t)$, which is equal to $p(1-t)q(p,P) - c(q(p,P))$. Maximizing this with respect to p gives the first-order condition:

$$\pi_1(p,P,t) = 0.$$

Totally differentiating the first-order conditions gives

$$\pi_{11}\,dp + \pi_{12}\,dP + \pi_{13}\,dt = 0.$$

Therefore, the change in p and P as t changes when the other price is fixed is given by

$$\frac{dp}{dt} = \frac{-\pi_{13}}{\pi_{11}} \quad \text{and} \quad \frac{dP}{dt} = \frac{-\pi_{13}}{\pi_{12}}.$$

As

$$\pi_{13} = -\frac{c'q_1}{(1-t)} > 0, \quad \pi_{11} < 0, \quad \pi_{12} > 0,$$

the reaction function of the foreign firm moves to the right, as in figure 6.

References

Bhagwati, J. 1965. On the equivalence of tariffs and quotas. In R. E. Baldwin et al. (eds.), *Trade, Growth and the Balance of Payments: Essays in Honor of Gottfried Haberler*, 53–67. Chicago: Rand McNally.

Brander, J., and B. Spencer. 1985. Export subsidies and international market share rivalry. *Journal of International Economics* 18:83–100.

Bulow, J., J. Geanakoplos, and P. Klemperer. 1985. Multimarket oligopoly. *Journal of Political Economy* 93:485–511.

Dasgupta, P., and E. Maskin. 1986. The existence of equilibrium in discontinuous economic games, I: Theory. *Review of Economic Studies* 53:1–26.

Davidson, C. 1984. Cartel stability and tariff policy. *Journal of International Economics* 17:219–237.

Dixit, A. 1986. Optimal trade and industrial policy for the U.S. automotive industry. Mimeo.

Dixit, A. 1987. Strategic aspects of trade theory. In T. Bewley (ed.), *Advances in Economic Theory: Fifth World Congress*. New York: Cambridge University Press.

Eaton, J., and G. Grossman. 1986. Optimal trade and industrial policy under oligopoly. *Quarterly Journal of Economics* 101:383–406.

Fellner, W. 1960. *Competition Among the Few*. New York: Augustus M. Kelly.

Friedman, J. 1981. Oligopoly theory. In K. Arrow and M. Intriligator (eds.), *The Handbook of Mathematical Economics*, vol. 2, 501–505. New York: North-Holland.

Gabszewicz, J., and J. Thisse. 1979. Price competition, quality and income disparities. *Journal of Economic Theory* 20:340–359.

Harris, R. 1985. Why voluntary export restraints are 'voluntary'. *Canadian Journal of Economics* 18:799–809.

Itoh, M., and Y. Ono. 1982. Tariffs, quotas, and market structure. *Quarterly Journal of Economics* 97:295–305.

Itoh, M., and Y. Ono. 1984. Tariffs vs. quotas under duopoly of heterogeneous goods. *Journal of International Economics* 17:359–374.

Krishna, K. 1985. Trade restrictions as facilitating practices. National Bureau of Economic Research, working paper no. 1546.

Krishna, K. and M. Itoh. 1988. Content protection and oligopolistic interactions. *Review of Economic Studies* 55:107–125.

Lancaster, K. 1979. *Variety, Equity and Efficiency*. New York: Columbia University Press.

Roberts, J., and H. Sonnenschein. 1977. On the foundations of the theory of monopolistic competition. *Econometrica* 45:101–113.

Rottemberg, J., and G. Saloner. 1986. Quotas and the stability of implicit collusion. National Bureau of Economic Research, working paper no. 1948.

II STRATEGIC TRADE POLICY

6 Tariff Protection and Imperfect Competition

James A. Brander and Barbara J. Spencer

1 Introduction

Experience with tariff negotiations yields the observation that most countries favor trade liberalization in principle but are reluctant to undertake unilateral reduction of trade barriers. In return for reducing tariffs or quotas countries usually require compensation in the form of being allowed freer access to foreign markets. Thus, most recent trade liberalization has been multilateral in character rather than unilateral.

Many explanations of such behavior could be advanced. Perhaps domestic political considerations make multilateral trade liberalization more feasible than unilateral liberalization, or perhaps most countries are large enough to pursue "monopoly tariff" (or "optimal tariff") policies. In this paper a rather simple contributing explanation, based on imperfect competition, is put forward. If imperfect competition is an important characteristic of some international markets, then firms in these markets may earn pure profits. Protection can shift some of this profit from foreign to domestic firms, and in addition, tariffs can transfer foreign rents to the domestic treasury in the form of tariff revenue. There is some cost in that markets are further distorted, but it is clear that, from a purely domestic point of view, protection is likely to be an attractive policy. A noncooperative international equilibrium will involve such tariffs. Simply shifting profit from one firm to another or from a firm to a government treasury is not beneficial to the world at large, so, from an international perspective, only the costs of protection remain. One country may benefit from protection, but the resulting losses to other countries usually more than offset this gain. Thus imperfect competition gives rise to beggar-thy-neighbor incentives for protective policies. The natural solution to this dilemma is through multilateral negotiation and trade liberalization, but unilateral tariff or quota reduction would not be expected.

This profit-shifting motive for protection suggests that a domestic firm would always favor protection of its industry, regardless of whether the industry happened to be capital- or labor-intensive. If the industry involved were large, there might be factor price effects, but they would be small compared to the transfers of rent. Furthermore, if labor were also imperfectly competitive and could extract a portion of the extra rents accruing to the firm, labor in the industry would also favor protection.

The idea that imperfect competition might call for policy intervention has of course been recognized in the "distortions" literature. (See, in particular, Bhagwati, Ramaswami, and Srinivasan 1969 and Bhagwati 1971.) Corden (1974) points out some second-best policy incentives that might arise under imperfect competition. Also the idea of using domestic policy to enhance the monopoly power of imperfectly competitive domestic firms has been considered. (See Basevi 1970, Frenkel 1971, and Auquier

Originally published in *Monopolistic Competition and International Trade*, ed. H. Kierzkowski (Oxford University Press, 1984).

and Caves 1979.) The setting in this paper, however, is quite different, as the central issue concerns shifting rent.

The possible use of protection to shift rents from imperfectly competitive foreign firms to domestic firms appears to have been largely ignored, which is surprising in view of the simplicity of the argument and its correspondence with actual perceptions in the business community. Katrak (1977) and Svedberg (1979) point out, using linear examples, that a tariff can be used to extract rent from a foreign monopoly, and De Meza (1979) suggests price controls. These papers do not, however, consider the role of domestic firms. Brander and Spencer (1981) consider the effects of a tariff in the case in which potential domestic entrants may be deterred from entering by a foreign monopolist.

Once it is recognized that both foreign and domestic firms are important, the question arises as to how firms interact with one another. There are many competing models of imperfect competition and the details of the analysis change according to which model is chosen. In this paper we first consider the case of simple foreign monopoly and then examine the simplest oligopoly model: Cournot duopoly with one foreign firm and one domestic firm. Even this simple Cournot model raises some interesting possibilities. From a purely positive perspective, intraindustry trade will normally arise, even if the firms produce identical products (as in Brander 1981). On the normative side, a tariff will usually raise domestic welfare, although it is just possible that a subsidy could be the optimum policy.

We are also interested in the interaction between countries. What happens if other countries unilaterally set tariffs in response to the initial "profit-shifting" tariff. We characterize the noncooperative tariff equilibrium and contrast it with the cooperative equilibrium that would arise if countries could bargain and make binding agreements so as to maximize world welfare.

2 Foreign Monopoly and the Tariff

The point that a tariff can be used to extract rent from foreign firms so as to increase domestic welfare can be made most simply in the case of foreign monopoly. The development in this section follows Brander and Spencer (1984). Taking the view that any one industry is small compared to the entire economy, we assume that domestic demand arises from a utility function that can be approximated by the form

$$U = u(X) + m, \tag{1}$$

where X is consumption of the good under consideration. In this section we use a partial equilibrium analysis so m is interpreted as expenditure on other goods. In later sections we embed the model in a simple general equilibrium framework where m is interpreted as consumption of a competitively produced numeraire good. Use of this utility function for both positive and normative analysis abstracts from a number of theoretical difficulties, including income effects, aggregation problems, and second-best problems induced by other distortions in the economy, and consequently allows us to focus on the pure rent-shifting incentives.

Since this utility function implies the marginal utility of income equals 1, inverse demand is just the derivative of u:

$$p = u'(X), \tag{2}$$

where p represents price. Also $u(X) - pX$ is equal to consumer surplus from X and is a consistent measure of the benefit to domestic consumers from consuming good X. Therefore, with tariff t, the net domestic gain, G, from imports of good X is

$$G(t) = u(X) - pX + tX. \tag{3}$$

Imports X depend on t, and the relationship $X = X(t)$ is determined by the behavior of the foreign monopolist. Domestic welfare is maximized when G_t ($\equiv dG/dt$) is equal to zero.

$$G_t = u'(X)X_t - Xp_t - pX_t + tX_t + X = 0, \tag{4}$$

where $p_t = p'X_t$. Using (2) and letting $\mu = -tX_t/X$, the elasticity of imports with respect to the tariff, (4) implies

$$G_t = -X(p_t + \mu - 1) = 0. \tag{5}$$

The effect of the tariff on price and the tariff elasticity of imports must sum to one. If the government placed no weight on consumer welfare and wished only to maximize tariff revenue, the condition would be $\mu = 1$. Equation (5) arises when tariff revenue and consumer surplus are given equal weight in the domestic objective function.

A useful rearrangement of (4) is

$$\hat{t} = \frac{X(p_t - 1)}{X_t}, \tag{6}$$

where $\hat{t}$ is the optimum tariff. Equation (6) indicates that $\hat{t}$ is positive if $p_t < 1$, that is, if an increase in the tariff causes price to rise by less than the tariff. On the other hand if $\hat{t}$ is negative a subsidy is appropriate. This arises if $p_t > 1$ so that an increase in the subsidy causes price to fall by more than the subsidy.

The comparative static effects p_t and X_t are therefore important in characterizing the optimal tariff. These are obtained by examination of the foreign firm's profit maximization problem. Letting V be variable profit from the domestic market for the foreign firm and using k to denote (constant) marginal cost (including transport costs) we have

$$V(X) = Xp(X) - kX - tX. \tag{7}$$

The first- and second-order conditions are

$$V_X = Xp' + p - (k + t) = 0, \tag{8}$$

$$V_{XX} = Xp'' + 2p' < 0. \tag{9}$$

The comparative-static effect X_t can be determined by differentiating $V_X = 0$ with respect to X and t which yields

$$X_t = \frac{1}{V_{XX}} < 0. \tag{10}$$

X_t can be seen to depend on the relative convexity of demand. The appropriate measure of relative convexity is denoted by a variable R where

$$R = \frac{Xp''}{p'}. \tag{11}$$

From (11) and (9), $V_{XX} = p'(2 + R)$ so from (10) and $p_t = p'X_t$ we have,

$$p_t = \frac{1}{R + 2}. \tag{12}$$

Therefore p_t exceeds, equals, or falls short of one as R is less than, equals, or exceeds -1. We can also write (6) as

$$\hat{t} = -p'X(R + 1), \tag{13}$$

which leads to the following proposition.

PROPOSITION 1 The optimum tariff is negative, zero, or positive as R is less than, equals, or exceeds minus one.

If R is less than minus one, the marginal revenue curve is less steeply sloped than demand. Therefore a decline in marginal cost due to a subsidy will cause price to fall by more than the subsidy and increase net domestic welfare. An example of a case in which a subsidy is optimal occurs if demand has constant elasticity. Denoting the constant elasticity by $\varepsilon = -p/p'X$ yields $R = -1 - 1/\varepsilon$ so $R < -1$ and $\hat{t} < 0$. Katrak (1977) and Svedberg (1979) consider the linear case. With linear demand $R = 0$ and $\hat{t}$ is positive. If one takes the view that demand is not likely to be highly convex, then it follows that positive tariffs will generally improve domestic welfare when the sole source of supply is an imperfectly competitive foreign industry.

3 Domestic and Foreign Firms

The main focus of this paper concerns the case in which there are both domestic and foreign firms. At this stage we also wish to make a few comments concerning embedding the industry of interest in a simple general equilibrium setting. Utility is assumed to arise from $U = u(X) + m^c$, where m^c is consumption of a competitively produced numeraire good, m, that can be produced in either the domestic country or the foreign country. Since the price of m is normalized to equal 1, domestic profit and government revenue are just added to $u(X)$ to obtain the domestic benefit function. (One extra dollar of profit or tariff revenue is used to buy one unit of m, which produces one extra unit of utility.)

$$G(t) = u(X) - pX + tx + \pi, \tag{14}$$

where π is the profit of the domestic firm (which is assumed to be owned by domestic residents). Output in the domestic economy is produced using a single factor, which we refer to as labor, and good m has production function

$$L_m = m^p, \tag{15}$$

where L is the amount of labor used in the production of m and m^p is the amount of m produced domestically (which may differ from m^c, the amount of m consumed domestically).

There is a single domestic firm producing good X. Its production is denoted by y, so that the total amount of X consumed domestically is $x + y$ where x is domestic sales by the foreign firm. The domestic production function for y is, in implicit form,

$$L_y = F + cy, \tag{16}$$

where F and c are measured in units of labor. Labor is supplied inelastically to the domestic economy in amount L so that $L_y + L_m = L$. The value of marginal product of labor in the competitive sector is one so the wage rate is one. The cost of producing y is then just $F + cy$ so the domestic firm has profit function

$$\pi = yp(X) - cy - F, \tag{17}$$

where F and c now represent dollar values. The variable c becomes marginal cost and F becomes fixed cost.

The foreign economy is similar, so the foreign firm has variable profit V from the domestic market where

$$V(x, y; t) = xp(X) - kx - tx, \tag{18}$$

where k is its (constant) marginal cost and t is the tariff.

This simple general equilibrium setting is, of course, equivalent to a partial equilibrium model in which profit functions (17) and (18) are specified directly. The point being made is that a partial equilibrium model can always be given the general equilibrium interpretation presented here. The essential question is not whether a model is partial or general equilibrium, but whether the industry in question is large enough to give rise to income effects, cross-substitution effects in demand, and factor price effects. We have assumed that it is not so as to focus on the issue of central interest here: the rent-shifting aspect of a tariff under imperfect competition.

Maximizing G with respect to t yields first-order condition

$$G_t = -Xp_t + tx_t + x + (p - c)y_t + yp_t = 0, \tag{19}$$

where subscripts denote derivatives. Rearrangement and substituting $\mu = -tx_t/x$ yields

$$G_t = -x(p_t - 1 + \mu) + (p - c)y_t = 0. \tag{20}$$

The first term captures the change in consumer surplus and the change in tariff revenue arising from a change in imports from the foreign firm. Since $(p - c)y_t = \pi_t - yp_t$, the second term reflects the change in domestic profit and consumer surplus arising from the change in the price of the domestic output. More directly the second term is the marginal surplus, $p - c$, from domestic production times the change in domestic output. Solving (from [20]) for the optimal tariff, $\hat{t}$, yields

$$\hat{t} = -\frac{(1 - p_t)x + (p - c)y_t}{x_t}. \tag{21}$$

Comparison of expressions (6) and (21) is illustrative. With both domestic and foreign firms the optimal tariff is related to the effect of a tariff on domestic firms in addition to its effect on the foreign firm. The nature of the interaction between the two firms becomes important. Most reasonable representations of this interaction have the property that $y_t > 0$ and $x_t < 0$: a higher tariff decreases imports and increases sales of the domestic firm.

As before, the condition $p_t < 1$ is sufficient to insure that the optimum tariff is positive. However, even if $p_t > 1$ the optimum tariff may still be positive because the term $(p - c)y_t$ is positive.

PROPOSITION 2 With both domestic and foreign firms, $p_t < 1$ is sufficient but not necessary for the optimal profit-shifting tariff to be positive. In particular (from [21]), a positive tariff is optimal if

$$p_t < 1 + \frac{(p - c)y_t}{x}. \tag{22}$$

Proposition 2 is no surprise. In addition to capturing tariff revenue a domestic tariff now has the added feature that profits are shifted to the domestic firm.

An illustrative special case is the case in which the market rivalry between the two firms is resolved as a Cournot duopoly. In this case the domestic firm maximizes profit (given by equation [17]) with respect to its own output yielding first-order condition

$$\pi_y \equiv yp' + p - c = 0. \tag{23}$$

The first-order condition associated with the profit maximization problem faced by the foreign firm is (from [18])

$$V_x \equiv xp' + p - k - t = 0. \tag{24}$$

Equations (23) and (24) are the reaction functions of the two firms in implicit form. Each shows the "best-reply" output for the firm, given whatever level of output the other firm happens to be producing. The Cournot equilibrium occurs when both (23) and (24) are satisfied: neither firm can improve its profit given the output level of its rival.

Second-order conditions require $\pi_{yy} < 0$ and $V_{xx} < 0$. In addition, only stable equilibria are of interest. Stability can be insured by that rather weak requirement that each firm's perceived marginal revenue declines when the output of its rival rises. This means $\pi_{yx} < 0$ and $V_{xy} < 0$ and also implies that

$$D = \pi_{yy} V_{xx} - \pi_{yx} V_{xy} > 0. \tag{25}$$

(Equation [25] is necessary for stability but does not imply $\pi_{yx} < 0$ and $V_{xy} < 0$. Therefore stability is possible even if $\pi_{yx} > 0$ and $V_{xy} > 0$. This unusual possibility is not something we wish to examine here.)

It is then an easy comparative static exercise to show that y_t is positive and x_t is negative. Totally differentiating (23) and (24) with respect to y, x, and t yields comparative static matrix equation

$$\begin{bmatrix} \pi_{yy} & \pi_{yx} \\ V_{xy} & V_{xx} \end{bmatrix} \begin{bmatrix} y_t \\ x_t \end{bmatrix} = \begin{bmatrix} 0 \\ 1 \end{bmatrix}. \tag{26}$$

Then

$$y_t = -\frac{\pi_{yx}}{D}, \tag{27}$$

$$x_t = \frac{\pi_{yy}}{D}. \tag{28}$$

Since π_{yx} ($\equiv yp'' + p'$) is negative and D is positive, y_t must be positive. Also with $\pi_{yy} < 0$ and $D > 0$, it follows that x_t is negative: an increase in the tariff increases output of the domestic firm and reduces imports. Furthermore, total domestic consumption tends to fall as the tariff is increased:

$$X_t = y_t + x_t = \frac{\pi_{yy} - \pi_{yx}}{D} = \frac{p'}{D} < 0. \tag{29}$$

PROPOSITION 3 A tariff reduces domestic consumption.

The main point of this section is that, even though a tariff reduces domestic consumption, a country would normally perceive an incentive to impose a tariff since gains to domestic firms and increases in government revenue would more than offset losses to consumers.

4 Two Countries

In considering a two-country world one important consideration is whether markets are unified or segmented (using the terminology of Helpman 1982). Segmented markets arise when firms treat different countries as different markets in that they choose their strategy variables (in this case quantity) for each market separately. The segmented markets assumption corresponds to our perception of the way in which many firms operate: Toyota makes distinct decisions concerning how many cars to produce for domestic consumption and how many to export to the United States; it does not bring its entire output to market in Tokyo and rely on arbitrage to distribute it throughout the world.

With segmented markets, imperfect competition gives rise to intraindustry trade. The causes and consequences of this type of intraindustry trade are described in Brander (1981) and Brander and Krugman (1983). The analytical point can be made by noting that the noncooperative solution to the profit-maximizing problem faced by the firms involves intraindustry trade. Assuming that both countries charge tariffs and using asterisks to denote variables associated with the foreign country, the domestic firm's total profit is

$$\pi = yp(X) + y^*p^*(X^*) - cy - c^*y^* - t^*y^* - F \tag{30}$$

and the profit of the foreign firm is

$$\pi^* = xp(X) + x^*p^*(X^*) - kx - k^*x^* - tx - F^*. \tag{31}$$

The coefficients c^* and k include transportation costs so $c^* > c$ and $k^* < k$. In any case, the first-order conditions are

$$\begin{aligned} &\pi_y = 0, \\ &\pi^*_x = 0, \\ &\pi_{y^*} = 0, \\ &\pi^*_{x^*} = 0. \end{aligned} \tag{32}$$

The first two equations, $\pi_y = 0$ and $\pi^*_x = 0$ are independent of x^* and y^* and their solution for the Cournot model is as presented in the previous section. Similarly $\pi_{y^*} = 0$ and $\pi^*_{x^*} = 0$ give rise to an equilibrium in the foreign country with both firms selling. Because of transportation costs, each firm will have a larger share of its home market than of its export market, but both firms will operate in both markets. Since firms set perceived marginal revenue equal to marginal cost in each market, and perceived marginal revenue is higher for the firm with the small market share, that firm can absorb transport costs and still find it profitable to be in the market. Helpman (1982) observes that the crucial element in firms' perceptions concerns market segmentation. Instead of perceiving only a single world market demand, each firm perceives distinct country-specific demands.

Our main focus here is on tariff policy. The domestic tariff t influences the market equilibrium in the domestic market and the foreign tariff t^* affects the foreign market. Each of these tariffs has an impact on the profits of both firms and therefore on the net welfare of both countries.

$$G = G(t; t^*) = u(X) - pX + tx + \pi, \quad (33)$$

$$G^* = G^*(t^*; t) = u^*(X^*) - p^*X^* + t^*y^* + \pi^*. \quad (34)$$

Once again the "best-reply" functions are defined by the first-order conditions:

$$\frac{dG}{dt} = 0, \qquad \frac{dG^*}{dt^*} = 0. \quad (35)$$

If the profit functions are as written in expressions (30) and (31) the term "best-reply" is rather misleading because the optimum tariff t is independent of t^*: what happens in the foreign market has no effect on the domestic market (and vice versa). If, however, marginal cost were not constant the two markets would interact and the tariff chosen by one country would depend on the tariff chosen by the other. Expression (35) is two equations in the two variables t and t^* whose solution characterizes the noncooperative tariff equilibrium. This equilibrium is to be compared with the cooperative or world welfare-maximizing tariff levels.

The total world welfare is $G + G^*$. Since any one country's tariff revenue is a cost to the foreign firm, tariff revenue is irrelevant to world welfare. It is however possible that a positive tariff could increase welfare if transport costs were high. With constant marginal costs the domestic tariff does not affect sales x^* and y^* in the foreign country, so the total effect of a change in the domestic tariff on world welfare $G_t + G_t^* = G_t + V_t$ where V is the variable profit from the exports of the foreign firm. From (20),

$$G_t = -x(p_t - 1 + \mu) + (p - c)y_t,$$

and from (5),

$$V_t = \frac{\partial V}{\partial x}x_t + \frac{\partial V}{\partial y}y_t + \frac{\partial V}{\partial t} = 0 + xp'y_t - x$$

(assuming Cournot behavior). Adding these and using $\mu = -tx_t/x$ and $p_t = p'(y_t + x_t)$ yields

$$G_t + V_t = -xp'x_t + tx_t + (p - c)y_t.$$

Then noting that the first-order condition for profit maximization by the foreign firm implies $p + xp' = t + k$, the change in world welfare is

$$G_t + V_t = (p - k)x_t + (p - c)y_t. \quad (36)$$

Expression (36) requires very little interpretation. The effect of a change in the tariff on world welfare is just the marginal net benefit associated with x times the change in x plus the marginal net benefit of y times the change in y. Using the Cournot example developed in section 3, we have $x_t < 0$ and $y_t > 0$. Since $p - k$ and $p - c$ are both positive, the two terms in (36) work in opposite directions. If k and c were roughly equal, x and y would also be roughly equal. Expressions (27), (28), and (29) then imply that y_t would be smaller in absolute value than x_t so $G_t + V_t$ would clearly be negative. However, if there are large transport costs k will exceed c and $G_t + V_t$ may be positive. The net benefit would be made possible by replacing high-cost foreign production with low-cost domestic production.

PROPOSITION 4 If foreign marginal cost (including transport costs) is less than or equal to domestic marginal cost, an increase in the domestic tariff decreases world welfare.

From the international point of view higher tariffs have the effect of reducing intraindustry trade. This may be beneficial if there are high transport costs and, as a consequence, substantial waste. If transport costs are low, however, the procompetitive effect of intraindustry trade offsets the waste due to transport costs and tariffs are inefficient. Tariffs are particularly undesirable if the domestic industry is "weak" in the sense of having higher costs. Yet this is precisely the case in which unilateral pressures for tariffs are usually strongest.

Now we consider whether the noncooperative solution involves a higher level of tariffs than the world welfare-maximizing solution. The world welfare-maximizing tariff requires that $G_t + V_t = 0$. Since $G_t = 0$ at the noncooperatively chosen tariff but $V_t \neq 0$ the noncooperative solution does not maximize world welfare. Since $V_t = xp'y_t - x < 0$, world welfare would increase if the tariff were reduced from the noncooperative or unilaterally chosen level.

PROPOSITION 5 The world welfare maximum may involve positive tariffs, but the noncooperatively chosen tariffs exceed the world welfare-maximizing tariffs.

The important point is that the noncooperative solution is generally inferior to the cooperative solution. Although each country perceives a unilateral incentive to impose a tariff, normally each would be better off if they could agree to have lower tariffs, hence the incentive for multilateral tariff reduction.

5 Concluding Remarks

An important aspect of world trade is that there is substantial trade in similar but not identical products. The greater variety of consumption made possible by international trade becomes an important source of gains from trade in addition to any procompetitive effects of trade. Several authors have analyzed such trade including Krugman (1979, 1980, 1981), Lancaster (1980), Helpman (1981), and Eaton and Kierzkowski (1984). Lancaster (1984) examines protection in such a context. The point we wish to make here is that the framework of this paper can be easily extended to include product variety and gives rise to a different treatment of variety than the other papers just mentioned. If the output of the foreign firm sells for p and p^* in the domestic and foreign countries respectively, while the (slightly different) domestic output sells at prices q and q^*, then profit functions become

$$\pi = yq(x, y) + y^*q^*(x^*, y^*) - cy - (c^* + t^*)y^* - F, \tag{37}$$

$$\pi^* = xp(x, y) + x^*p^*(x^*, y^*) - (k + t)x - k^*x^* - F^*. \tag{38}$$

As before, a noncooperative equilibrium where $\pi_y = 0$, $\pi_{y^*} = 0$, $\pi^*_x = 0$, and $\pi^*_{x^*} = 0$ will normally involve intraindustry trade. As before, optimum tariffs can be calculated and similar results as for the homogeneous case follow. An economically interesting set of questions arises concerning how the degree of substitutability affects the extent of intraindustry trade and the structure of optimum tariffs, but serious analysis of these issues is beyond the scope of the present paper. The fact remains, however, that the central points of this paper are robust to the introduction of product differentiation.

The world described in the paper is one in which the rivalry of imperfectly competitive firms serves as an independent cause of international trade. In such a world firms tend to invade one another's home markets, which gives rise to intraindustry trade, even in homogeneous products. Yet such trade tends to be welfare-improving because of its procompetitive effects. Only if transport costs are high will such trade be welfare reducing.

The main objective of the paper is to use this imperfectly competitive setting to present a simple explanation of why a country might impose tariffs on foreign firms but be in favor of multilateral trade liberalization. The distinction is just the difference between a noncooperative solution and a cooperative one.

We have used a simple Cournot model to demonstrate the main points. Similar insights would emerge in the more sophisticated, imperfectly competitive environments described by Krugman (1984) and Shaked and Sutton (1984) since the nature of tariff incentives is based chiefly on the presence of pure profits. The principal role of the tariff is to shift profit from foreign firms to domestic firms and to the domestic treasury. Naturally each country would be reluctant to reduce such rent-generating tariffs but might be persuaded to do so if domestically owned firms were to be allowed freer access to profitable markets.

We do not, of course, wish to suggest that policymakers singlemindedly pursue welfare-maximizing policies of the sort described here, nor that policymakers have access to all the relevant information required to formulate such policy. However, we would argue that if simple welfare-improving policies are available, some kind of incentive will be perceived, however imperfectly, by policy authorities.

Finally, it should be emphasized that our arguments should not be taken as support for using tariffs. The highly tariff-ridden world economy that would result from each country maximizing domestic welfare taking the policies of other countries as given would be a poor outcome. Our analysis is meant to contribute to an understanding of the motives that might underlie tariff policy and provides support for the multilateral approach to trade liberalization.

Note

J. A. Brander would like to acknowledge gratefully the support of the SSHRCC post-doctoral fellowship 456-81-3455.

References

Auquier, A., and R. Caves. 1979. Monopolistic export industries, trade, taxes and optimal competition policy. *Economic Journal* 89:559–581.

Basevi, G. 1970. Domestic demand and the ability to export. *Journal of Political Economy* 18:330–337.

Bhagwati, J. 1971. The generalized theory of distortions and welfare. In J. Bhagwati et al. (eds.), *Trade, Growth and the Balance of Payments: Essays in Honor of Gottfried Haberler*. Chicago and Amsterdam: Rand-McNally and North-Holland.

Bhagwati, J., V. Ramaswami, and T. N. Srinivasan. 1969. Domestic distortions, tariffs and the theory of optimum subsidy: Some further results. *Journal of Political Economy* 77:1005–1010.

Brander, J. 1981. Intra-industry trade in identical commodities. *Journal of International Economics* 11:1–14.

Brander, J., and P. Krugman. 1983. A reciprocal dumping model of international trade. *Journal of International Economics* 15:313–323.

Brander, J., and B. Spencer. 1981. Tariffs and the extraction of foreign monopoly rents under potential entry. *Canadian Journal of Economics* 14:371–389.

Brander, J., and B. Spencer. 1984. Trade warfare: Tariffs and cartels. *Journal of International Economics* 16:227–242.

Corden, W. M. 1974. *Trade Policy and Economic Welfare*. London: Oxford University Press.

De Meza, D. 1979. Commercial policy towards multinational monopolies—Reservations on Katrak. *Oxford Economic Papers* 31:334–337.

Eaton, J., and H. Kierzkowski. 1984. Oligopolistic competition, product variety, and international trade. In H. Kierzkowski (ed.), *Monopolistic Competition and International Trade*. Oxford: Oxford University Press.

Frenkel, J. 1971. On domestic demand and ability to export. *Journal of Political Economy* 79:668–672.

Helpman, E. 1981. International trade in the presence of product differentiation, economies of scale and monopolistic competition: A Chamberlin-Heckscher-Ohlin approach. *Journal of International Economics* 11:305–340.

Helpman, E. 1982, Increasing returns, imperfect markets and trade theory, discussion paper no. 18–82, Foerder Institute for Economic Research, Tel Aviv University.

Katrak, H. 1977. Multinational monopolies and commercial policy. *Oxford Economic Papers* 29:283–291.

Krugman, P. 1979. Increasing returns, monopolistic competition, and international trade. *Journal of International Economics* 9:469–479.

Krugman, P. 1980. Scale economies, product differentiation and the pattern of trade. *American Economic Review* 70:950–959.

Krugman, P. 1981. Intra-industry specialization and the gains from trade. *Journal of Political Economy* 89:959–973.

Krugman, P. 1984. Import protection as export promotion: International competition in the presence of oligopoly and economies of scale. In H. Kierzkowski (ed.), *Monopolistic Competition and International Trade*. Oxford: Oxford University Press.

Lancaster, K. 1980. Intra-industry trade under perfect monopolistic competition. *Journal of International Economics* 10:151–175.

Lancaster, K. 1984. Protection and product differentiation. In. H. Kierzkowski, *Monopolistic Competition and International Trade*. Oxford: Oxford University Press.

Shaked, A., and J. Sutton. 1984. Natural oligopolies and international trade. In H. Kierzkowski, *Monopolistic Competition and International Trade*. Oxford: Oxford University Press.

Svedberg, P. 1979. Optimal tariff policy on imports from multinationals. *Economic Record* 55:64–67.

7 Optimal Trade and Industrial Policy under Oligopoly

Jonathan Eaton and Gene M. Grossman

1 Introduction

Implicit in many arguments for interventionist trade or industrial policy that have been advanced recently in popular debate appears to be an assumption that international markets are oligopolistic. It can be argued that international competition among firms in many industries is in fact imperfectly competitive, either because the number of firms is few, because products are differentiated, or because governments themselves have cartelized the national firms engaged in competition. They may do so implicitly through tax policy or explicitly through marketing arrangements.

Government policies that affect the competitiveness of their firms in international markets, as well as the welfare of their consumers, involve not only traditional trade policy (trade taxes and subsidies) but policies that affect other aspects of firms' costs, such as output taxes and subsidies. We refer to intervention of this sort as industrial policy.

Until recently, the theory of commercial policy has considered the implications of intervention only under conditions of perfect competition or, more rarely, pure monopoly. As a consequence, this literature cannot respond to many of the arguments that have been advanced recently in favor of activist government policies. Our purpose in this paper is to extend the theory of nationally optimal policy to situations in which individual firms exercise market power in world markets.

The primary implications of oligopoly for the design of trade policy are (1) that economic profits are not driven to zero, and (2) that a price equal to marginal cost does not generally obtain. The first of these means that government policies that shift the industry equilibrium to the advantage of domestic firms may be socially beneficial from a national perspective. The second feature of oligopolistic competition suggests that trade policy may be a substitute for antitrust policy if policies can be devised that shrink the wedge between opportunity cost in production and marginal valuation to consumers.

A number of recent papers have focused on the profit-shifting motive for trade policy under oligopoly. Brander and Spencer (1985) develop a model in which one home firm and one foreign firm produce perfectly substitutable goods and compete in a third-country market. They consider a Cournot-Nash equilibrium and find that if the home country's government can credibly precommit itself to pursue a particular trade policy before firms make production decisions (and if demand is not very convex), then an export subsidy is optimal.[1] Dixit (1984) has extended the Brander-Spencer result to cases with more than two firms and established that an export subsidy in a Cournot oligopoly equilibrium is optimal so long as the number of domestic firms is not too large. Finally, Krugman (1984) shows that under increasing

Originally published in the *Quarterly Journal of Economics* 101 (May 1986): 383–406.

returns to scale, protection of a local firm in one market (e.g., by an import tariff) can shift the equilibrium to the firm's advantage in other markets by lowering its marginal cost of production.

These papers all provide examples in which interventionist trade policy can raise national welfare in imperfectly competitive environments. Yet each makes special assumptions about the form of oligopolistic competition, the substitutability of the goods produced, and the markets in which the goods are sold. It is difficult to extract general principles for trade policy from this analysis. Our purpose here is to provide an integrative treatment of the welfare effects of trade and industrial policy under oligopoly and to characterize the form that optimal intervention takes under a variety of assumptions about the number of firms, their assumptions about rivals' responses to their actions, the substitutability of their products, and the countries where their products are sold.

The paper is organized as follows. In the next section we consider a general conjectural variations model of a duopoly in which a single home firm competes with a foreign firm either in the foreign firm's local market or in a third-country market. We find that the sign of the optimal trade or industrial policy (whether a tax or subsidy is optimal) depends on the relationship between the home firm's conjectural variation and the actual equilibrium reactions of the foreign firm. We note the form that optimal policy takes in Cournot and Bertrand equilibria and in what Bresnahan (1981) and Perry (1982) have called a "consistent" conjectures equilibrium.

We extend these results to incorporate the interaction between the policies of the home government and an activist foreign government in section 3. Here we consider optimal intervention in a two-stage game in which governments achieve a Nash equilibrium in policies prior to the time that firms engage in product-market competition. In section 4 we further extend the analysis by allowing for oligopoly with arbitrary numbers of firms in each country.

The analysis in sections 2, 3, and 4 assumes a constant, exogenous number of firms. In section 5 we discuss briefly how our results would be modified if firms can enter or exit in response to government policies. Finally, in section 6 we return to the duopoly case and introduce domestic consumption for the first time. This allows us to consider the potential role for trade policy as a (partial) substitute for antitrust policy.

The main findings of the paper are summarized in a concluding section.

2 Optimal Trade Policy and the Role of Conjectural Variations: The Case of Duopoly

In this and subsequent sections we characterize optimal government policy in the presence of oligopolistic competition among domestic and foreign firms in international markets. Each firm produces a single product that may be a perfect or imperfect substitute for the output of its rivals. We specify competition among firms in terms of output quantities with arbitrary conjectural variations.[2] The domestic government can tax (or subsidize) the output of domestic firms, tax (or subsidize) the exports of these firms, and tax (or subsidize) the imports from the foreign rivals of domestic firms. Its objective is to maximize national welfare.

The government acts as a Stackelberg leader vis-à-vis both domestic and foreign firms in setting tax (subsidy) rates.[3] Thus, firms set outputs taking tax and subsidy rates as given. In other words, the government can precommit itself to a specific policy intervention that will not be altered even if it is suboptimal ex post, once firms' outputs are determined. At first we assume the absence of government policy in other countries. We also treat the number of firms as given. The implications of relaxing these assumptions are discussed below.

In this section we consider optimal government policy when oligopolistic competition takes its simplest possible form: a single domestic firm competes with a single foreign firm in a foreign market. In the absence of domestic consumption, government trade policy (export taxes and subsidies) is equivalent to government industrial policy (output taxes and subsidies). We assume that the government places equal weight on the home firm's profit and government tax revenue in evaluating social welfare. Its objective is therefore one of maximizing national product.

Denote the output (and exports) of the home firm by x and let $c(x)$ be its total production cost; $c'(x) > 0$. Uppercase letters denote corresponding magnitudes for the foreign firm, with $C'(X) > 0$. Pretax revenues of the home and foreign firms are given by the functions $r(x, X)$ and $R(x, X)$, respectively. These satisfy the conditions that

$$r_2(x, X) \equiv \frac{\partial r(x, X)}{\partial X} \leq 0,$$

$$R_1(x, X) \equiv \frac{\partial R(x, X)}{\partial x} \leq 0,$$

namely, that an increase in the output of the competing product lowers the total revenue of each firm. They are implied by the assumption that the products are substitutes in consumption.[4] Total after-tax profits of the home and foreign firms are given by

$$\pi = (1 - t)r(x, X) - c(x)$$

and

$$\Pi = R(x, X) - C(X),$$

respectively. Here t denotes the ad valorem output (or export) tax.[5] The domestic firm's conjecture about the foreign firm's output response to changes in its own output is given by the parameter γ. The foreign firm's corresponding conjectural variation is Γ.

The Nash equilibrium quantities, given the level of home country policy intervention, are determined by the first-order conditions:

$$(1-t)[r_1(x,X)+\gamma r_2(x,X)]-c'(x)=0, \tag{1}$$

$$R_2(x,X)+\Gamma R_1(x,X)-C'(X)=0. \tag{2}$$

We assume that the second-order conditions for profit maximization and the conditions for stability of the industry equilibrium are satisfied. We now demonstrate

THEOREM 1 A positive (negative) output or export tax can yield higher national welfare than laissez-faire ($t=0$) if the home firm conjectures a foreign change in output in response to an increase in its own output that is smaller (larger) than the actual response.

Proof National product generated by the home firm is given by w, where

$$\begin{aligned} w &= (1-t)r(x,X)-c(x)+tr(x,X) \\ &= r(x,X)-c(x). \end{aligned} \tag{3}$$

The change in welfare resulting from a small change in the tax (or subsidy) rate t is

$$\frac{dw}{dt}=[r_1(x,X)-c'(x)]\frac{dx}{dt}+r_2(x,X)\frac{dX}{dt}. \tag{4}$$

Substituting the first-order condition (1) into (4), we obtain[6]

$$\frac{dw}{dt}=\left[-\gamma r_2-\frac{tc'}{1-t}\right]\left(\frac{dx}{dt}\right)+r_2\left(\frac{dX}{dt}\right). \tag{5}$$

Expression (2) implicitly defines the output of the foreign firm X as a function of domestic output x. Denote this function $\Psi(x)$. The tax rate t does not appear directly as an argument of this function, since t does not appear in expression (2). Therefore, $dX/dt=\Psi'(x)(dx/dt)$. Define $g\equiv(dX/dt)/(dx/dt)=\Psi'(x)$. The term g measures the slope of the foreign firm's reaction curve, that is, its *actual* reaction to exogenous changes in x. A first-order condition for maximizing national welfare obtains when $dw/dt=0$,[7] or, incorporating the definition of g into equation (5),

$$-r_2(g-\gamma)=\frac{tc'}{1-t}. \tag{6}$$

Since $r_2<0$, the left-hand and right-hand sides of expression (6) are of the same sign if $1>t>0$ and $g>\gamma$, or $t<0$ and $g<\gamma$. The term $g-\gamma$ is the difference between the actual response of X to a change in x (i.e., $\Psi'(x)$) and the home firm's conjectural variation. When $g>\gamma$, a tax can yield more income than laissez-faire, conversely when $g<\gamma$. □

An intuitive explanation of this result is as follows. Government policy is implemented before the two firms choose their outputs, which they do simultaneously. Intervention consequently allows the domestic firm to achieve the outcome that would obtain if it were able to act as a Stackelberg leader with respect to its competitor. If $g > \gamma$, then the equilibrium output absent policy involves more domestic output than at the Stackelberg point because the home firm cannot or does not fully account for the foreign firm's reaction to an increase in its own quantity in choosing its output level. Conversely, if $g < \gamma$, the home firm's output more than fully reflects the extent of actual reaction by the rival. The sign of the optimal policy is determined accordingly.

We now turn to some specific conjectural variations that are commonly assumed in models of oligopolistic competition.

Cournot Conjectures

Under Cournot behavior, each firm conjectures that when it changes its output the other firm will hold its output fixed. Thus, $\gamma = \Gamma = 0$ in this case, and (6) becomes

$$-gr_2 = \frac{tc'}{1-t}. \tag{7}$$

Totally differentiating the equilibrium conditions (1) and (2) to solve for g, we may write this expression as

$$\frac{r_2 R_{21}}{R_{22} - C''} = \frac{tc'}{1-t}. \tag{8}$$

The second-order condition for the foreign firm's profit maximization ensures that the left-hand side of this expression has the sign of R_{21}. Letting t^* denote the optimal export tax (or subsidy, if negative), we have established

PROPOSITION 1 In a Cournot duopoly with no home consumption,

$\operatorname{sgn} t^* = \operatorname{sgn} R_{21}$.

Proposition 1 restates the Brander and Spencer (1985) argument for an export subsidy: this policy raises domestic welfare in a Cournot equilibrium by transferring industry profit to the domestic firm. This point is illustrated in figure 1. In the figure, representative iso-profit loci for the home firm are depicted in output space by u^0, u^c, and u^*. Lower curves correspond to higher levels of profit. The Cournot reaction function for the home firm *rr* connects the maxima of the iso-profit loci. The direction of its slope is given by the sign of r_{12}. The foreign firm's reaction curve *RR* is found similarly, and its slope is determined by the sign of R_{21}. Linear demand necessarily implies that $r_{12} < 0$ and $R_{21} < 0$, and many, but not all, specifications of demand imply this sign as well.

The Cournot equilibrium is at point *C*, where the home firm earns a profit corresponding to u^c. Note that among the points along *RR*, u^c does not provide the highest level of profit to the home firm and therefore does not yield the highest possible level of home country welfare. Rather, maximum profit corresponds to u^*, which would be the equilibrium if the home firm could credibly precommit its output level and thus

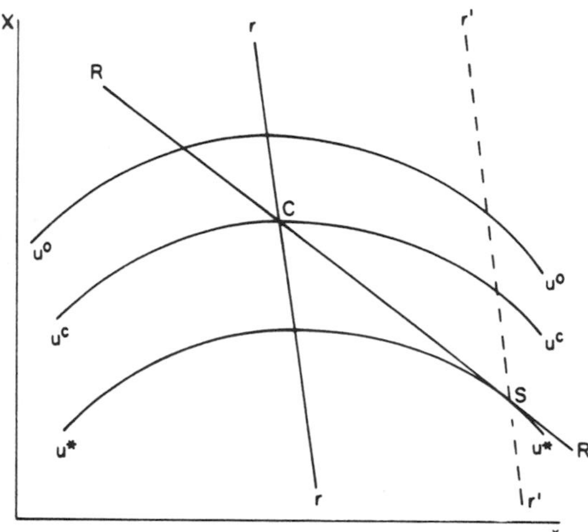

Figure 1
Optimal policy with Cournot competition

act as a Stackelberg leader. Lacking this ability, the home country could nonetheless achieve the outcome at u^* in a Nash equilibrium if the home government were to implement a trade policy that shifted the home firm's reaction locus to intersect RR at S. This is the optimal profit-shifting trade policy; it involves an export subsidy under the Cournot assumptions provided that RR is downward sloping (i.e., $R_{21} < 0$). A downward- (upward-) sloping foreign reaction curve implies a level of output in the Cournot equilibrium that is less (greater) than that at the point of Stackelberg leadership: thus, the sign of the optimal trade policy in this case.[8]

Note that the optimal export subsidy with Cournot competition benefits the home firm (and country) at the expense of the foreign firm. Indeed, the equilibrium with one country pursuing its optimal policy involves smaller (net-of-subsidy) profits for the two firms together than in the laissez-faire equilibrium. Consumers of the product benefit from lower prices when the subsidy is in place, and the net effect on world welfare is positive, since policy pushes prices toward their competitive levels.

Bertrand Conjectures

In a Bertrand equilibrium each firm conjectures that its rival will hold its price fixed in response to any changes in its own price. Define the *direct* demand functions for the output of the home and foreign firms as $d(p, P)$ and $D(p, P)$, respectively. The total profits of the two firms are

$$\pi(p, P) = (1 - t)pd(p, P) - c(d(p, P))$$

and

$$\Pi(p, P) = PD(p, P) - C(D(p, P)).$$

Each firm sets its price to maximize its profit, taking the other firm's price as constant. First-order conditions for a maximum imply that

$$\pi_1 = (1 - t)(d + pd_1) - c'd_1 = 0, \tag{9a}$$

$$\Pi_2 = D + (P - C')D_2 = 0. \tag{9b}$$

The actual and conjectured price responses can be translated into quantity responses by totally differentiating the demand functions to obtain

$$\begin{bmatrix} dx \\ dX \end{bmatrix} = \begin{bmatrix} d_1 & d_2 \\ D_1 & D_2 \end{bmatrix} \cdot \begin{bmatrix} dp \\ dP \end{bmatrix}.$$

The Bertrand conjecture on the part of the home firm implies a conjectured quantity response given by

$$\gamma = \left.\frac{dX/dp}{dx/dp}\right|_{dP=0} = \frac{D_1}{d_1}. \tag{10}$$

The actual response is

$$g = \frac{dX/dp}{dx/dp} = \frac{D_1 - D_2\Pi_{21}/\Pi_{22}}{d_1 - d_2\Pi_{21}/\Pi_{22}}.$$

It is straightforward to show, using the conditions for stability of the industry equilibrium, that the term $g - \gamma$ is positive if and only if $\Pi_{21} > 0$ (the foreign firm responds to a price cut by cutting its price). Applying theorem 1, we conclude

PROPOSITION 2 In a Bertrand duopoly with no home consumption,

$\operatorname{sgn} t^* = \operatorname{sgn} \Pi_{21}$.

If the two products are substitutes (i.e., $d_2 > 0$ and $D_1 > 0$) and returns to scale are nonincreasing ($c'' \geq 0$, $C'' \geq 0$), then $\Pi_{21} > 0$ *unless* an increase in its rival's price has a significantly negative effect on the *slope* of the demand curve facing the home firm. In the special cases of either perfect substitutes or linear demands, this sign necessarily obtains. Presumption regarding the sign of the optimal trade intervention when duopolistic behavior is Bertrand is consequently the opposite of that in the Cournot case; that is, an export *tax* is generally required.

Figure 2 illustrates this result. Representative iso-profit loci of the home firm (in price space) are shown as u^0, u^b, and u^*. Higher curves now correspond to higher profit. The Bertrand reaction curves are depicted by *rr* for the home firm and *RR* for the foreign firm, and the directions of their slopes correspond to the signs of π_{12} and Π_{21}, respectively.

The Bertrand equilibrium absent policy intervention is the intersection of the two curves, at point *B*. Here the home firm earns a profit corresponding to u^b. Given *RR*, a higher profit could be attained at point *S*, where the home firm charges a higher price

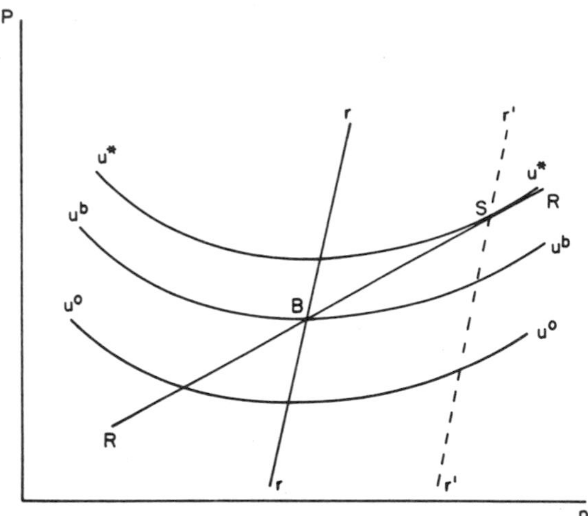

Figure 2
Optimal policy with Bertrand competition

than at B. However, unless the home firm can precommit to the higher price or act as a Stackelberg leader, point S is not achievable under laissez-faire. An appropriate output or export tax shifts the home reaction curve to $r'r'$, whence the Nash equilibrium in the resulting product-market competition yields the superior welfare outcome.[9] Notice that the Bertrand equilibrium for the case in which the foreign reaction curve is upward sloping in price space involves a lower domestic price and therefore a higher domestic output than at the Stackelberg leadership point. This is in contrast to the Cournot outcome and accounts for the qualitative difference in the policy conclusions.[10]

Another contrast with the Cournot outcome is that implementation of the optimal policy by the home government raises profits of the foreign firm. It does so by alleviating oligopolistic rivalry. Of course, the tax affects consumers adversely, and world welfare falls as the equilibrium becomes less competitive.

Consistent Conjectures

The final special case we consider is one in which the home firm's conjecture about its rival's response is "consistent," as is the case if the home firm is a Stackelberg leader vis-à-vis its foreign rival or in a "consistent conjectures equilibrium." This second concept, as defined and analyzed by Bresnahan (1981) and Perry (1982) among others, is an equilibrium in which each firm's conjectural variation is equal to the actual equilibrium responses of its rivals that would result if that firm actually were to change its output by a small amount at the equilibrium point.

The slope of the foreign reaction curve in our model is given by g. Thus, the home firm's conjectures about its rival's response are consistent in the sense of Bresnahan

(1981) and Perry (1982) if $\gamma = g$. The following proposition follows immediately from expression (6):[11]

PROPOSITION 3 In a duopoly with consistent conjectures on the part of the home firm and no home consumption, $t^* = 0$.

The optimality of free trade with consistent conjectures on the part of the home firm emerges because there exists no shift of the home firm's reaction curve that can transfer industry profit to that firm, given the response of its rival.

The duopoly example with no home consumption highlights the profit-shifting motive for trade policy intervention in an imperfectly competitive industry. Under optimal intervention the government uses its first-mover advantage to shift its national firm's reaction function so that it intersects the foreign firm's curve at a point of tangency between the latter curve and a (laissez-faire) iso-profit locus of the home firm. The direction of this shift, and thus the qualitative nature of the optimal policy, depends in general on the sign of the deviation of the home firm's conjectural variation from the slope of the foreign firm's reaction curve.

We now extend the basic result to allow for a foreign policy response, multifirm oligopoly, endogenous market structure, and domestic consumption.

3 Foreign Policy Response

In the analysis up to this point, we have assumed that the foreign rival's government pursues a laissez-faire policy. Imagine now a two-stage game with both governments active in which the governments first arrive at a Nash equilibrium in policy parameters and then duopolistic competition between the firms takes place. For simplicity, we assume no consumption in the rival's country as well. All consumption is elsewhere.

Denoting the foreign ad valorem output or export tax rate as T, the foreign firm's first-order condition for profit maximization, equation (2), becomes

$$(1 - T)[R_2(x, X) - \Gamma R_1(x, X)] - C'(X) = 0. \tag{2'}$$

A Nash equilibrium in policies is a pair of tax-subsidy rates (t, T) such that t maximizes w, given T, and T maximizes $W \equiv R(x, X) - C'(X)$, given t, where equations (1) and (2′) determine x and X.

For T < 1, the presence of a foreign tax does not affect the *qualitative* results of the previous section. Theorem 1 is unaffected. For Cournot competition equation (8) is replaced by

$$\frac{r_2(1 - T)R_{21}}{(1 - T)R_{22} - C''} = \frac{tc'}{1 - t}, \tag{8'}$$

so that the sign of t^* remains that of R_{21}. For Bertrand competition the profit of the foreign firm may be written as

$$\Pi(p,P) = (1 - T)PD(p,P) - C(D(p,P)).$$

Appropriate substitution into the previous analysis implies that proposition 2 is unaffected as well. Similarly, proposition 3 remains. Consequently, the *direction* of the optimal policy is unaffected by the possible presence of a foreign export tax or subsidy.

A parallel analysis determines the level of T that maximizes W given t. The following results are immediate.

Under Cournot competition between substitutes with $r_{12} < 0$ and $R_{21} < 0$, the perfect Nash equilibrium is for both governments to subsidize exports. Government interventions together move the product-market equilibrium away from the joint-profit-maximizing outcome toward the competitive equilibrium. Graphically, in terms of figure 1, both reaction loci shift outward. Both countries will typically benefit from a mutual agreement to desist from attempts to shift profit homeward via export subsidization. The effect on consumers and on world welfare of such an agreement is, of course, the opposite.

Under Bertrand competition with $\pi_{12} > 0$ and $\Pi_{21} > 0$, the perfect Nash equilibrium is for both governments to tax exports. Intervention moves the equilibrium toward the joint-profit-maximizing point away from the competitive equilibrium. In terms of figure 2 both reaction curves shift out. The exporters gain, consumers lose, and world welfare declines.

Finally, if both firms' conjectures are consistent, the perfect Nash equilibrium is laissez-faire.

4 Optimal Trade Policy: The Case of Multifirm Oligopoly and Consistent Conjectures

In this section we extend our analysis to situations of oligopoly, by allowing for the presence of n home firms and m foreign firms in the industry. For analytical convenience we confine our attention to configurations that are *symmetric*, in the sense that (1) each firm, home or foreign, has the same cost function, (2) the revenue functions of any two firms i and j (home or foreign) are identical, except that the arguments x^i and x^j are interchanged, and (3) any two firms producing at the same output level hold the same conjectures about the effect of changes in their own outputs on those of each of their rivals (including each other).

We assume that the conjectures held by all home firms are consistent. We take this as our benchmark case in order that we may isolate the new implications for trade policy that are introduced when the market structure is oligopolistic rather than duopolistic. When conjectures are other than consistent, the optimal trade policy will incorporate an element of the profit-shifting motive, as discussed in section 2, in addition to the terms-of-trade motive that is the focus of our attention in the present section. We also continue to assume that there is no home consumption of the outputs of the oligopolistic industry. This assumption, too, is dictated by our desire to isolate and discuss a single motive for trade policy at a time. Our basic result is stated in

PROPOSITION 4 In a symmetric, oligopolistic equilibrium with n home firms and m foreign firms and no home consumption, if the domestic firms' conjectures are consistent, then the optimal production or export tax is zero if $n = 1$ and positive if $n > 1$.

Proof See appendix A.

The result can be understood intuitively by noting that when home firms' conjectures about the responses of foreign firms are consistent, the profit-shifting motive for government intervention is not present. What remains is the standard terms-of-trade argument for export policy. Whenever there is more than a single home country firm and these firms do not collude perfectly, each home firm imposes a pecuniary externality on other domestic firms when it raises its output. Private incentives lead to socially excessive outputs, since home income includes all home firm profits. The government can enforce the cooperative equilibrium in which the home firms act as a group to maximize the home country's total profit by taxing exports or sales. The externality does not arise when there is only one home firm; consequently, free trade is optimal in that case.

Once we depart from the assumption of consistent conjectures, the profit-shifting and the terms-of-trade motives for trade policy intervention can be present simultaneously. Thus, Dixit (1984) finds that for a linear, Cournot, homogeneous-product oligopoly an export subsidy is optimal if the number of domestic firms is not "too large." In this case, the two motives for intervention identified here work in opposition. The two can also be reinforcing, as would generally occur when each of several domestic firms holds Bertrand conjectures.

5 Endogenous Entry and Exit

The analysis up to this point has assumed a fixed, exogenous number of firms. This assumption is reasonable if entry costs are large relative to the effect of policies on total profit or if other government policies determined the number of firms. Otherwise, trade and industrial policy is likely to affect the total number of firms in an industry, both domestically and abroad. A thorough treatment of optimal policies with endogenous market structure lies beyond the scope of this paper. Instead, we discuss how endogenous entry and exit would modify some of our previous results.[12]

The first point to make is that allowing for free entry and exit does not necessarily eliminate the profit-shifting motive for trade or industrial policy. All firms may earn positive profits in a free-entry equilibrium if fixed costs are relatively large compared with market size. Then, despite positive returns to firms present in the market, an additional firm could not enter profitably. Alternatively, heterogeneity among firms could imply zero profit for the marginal entrant but positive profits for inframarginal participants. In either of these cases an incentive remains for governments to use policy to shift profits toward domestic participants in the industry. Only if firms are homogeneous and the market can accommodate a large number of them, so that profits of all firms are identically zero, does the profit-shifting motive for trade or industrial policy vanish.

Two new issues are relevant for the formulation of optimal trade and industrial policy when market structure is endogenous. The first arises because policy alters the total number of firms active in an industry in equilibrium. If governments set their policy parameters before firms choose whether or not to incur their fixed costs of entry, or if firms anticipate policies that will be invoked after entry costs are borne, then export or production subsidies will encourage more firms to be active. This entry can raise industry average cost and cause the addition to national product deriving from profit-shifting to be (more than) dissipated in increased entry fees (see Horstmann and Markusen 1984). Then, a tax on exports or production that discourages entry may be called for even when a subsidy would be optimal given an exogenous market structure.

Second, trade and industrial policy alters the relative numbers of domestic and foreign firms. A subsidy to exports or production in the home country causes foreign firms to exit as domestic firms enter. When residual profits exist, the replacement of foreign firms by domestic ones raises national product. Dixit and Kyle (1985) analyze the potential role for trade policy in deterring foreign entry or encouraging domestic entry.[13] In their analysis, a subsidy can be optimal even if it entails no profit shifting among a *given* set of firms.

6 Trade and Industrial Policy When Goods Are Consumed Domestically

Thus far we have ruled out domestic consumption of the outputs of the oligopolistic industry under consideration. This has allowed us to focus on the profit-shifting and terms-of-trade motives for trade policy. However, by making this assumption, we have neglected a third way in which interventionist trade or industrial policy might yield welfare gains when markets are imperfectly competitive. Since oligopolistic markets are generally characterized by a difference between the price and the marginal cost of a product, there is a potential second-best role for trade and industrial policy (in the absence of first-best antitrust policy) to reduce this distortion.

When domestic consumption is positive, production taxes or subsidies and export taxes or subsidies are no longer identical. In this section we shall consider the welfare effects of both types of policies in the duopoly model of section 2 recognizing that if we were to allow for the existence of more than one domestic firm, the national-market-power motive for taxation of output or exports would also be present. In addition, in order to focus on the considerations for trade and industrial policy introduced by the presence of domestic consumption, we shall continue to use the consistent-conjectures duopoly model as our benchmark case.

To make our point as simply as possible, we assume that the duopolistic competitors produce a single, homogeneous good. We also assume perfect arbitrage with zero transport costs, so that under a production tax or subsidy consumers at home and abroad face the same price for the product. Thus, we consider the case of an integrated world market, where the potential second-best role for trade policy as a substitute for domestic antitrust policy is greatest.[14]

Production Tax or Subsidy

Let $p(x+X)$ be the inverse world demand function, and let home country direct demand be $h(p)$. The corresponding foreign demand is $H(p)$. If a production tax at rate t is imposed, the profit of the domestic firm is $\pi = (1-t)p(x+X)x - c(x)$. Consumer surplus at home is $\int_p^\infty h(q)\,dq$.[15] Domestic tax revenue is tpx. Summing these gives total home country welfare from producing, consuming, and taxing the product:

$$w = px - c + \int_p^\infty h(q)\,dq.$$

The change in home welfare resulting from a small change in the output tax is

$$\frac{dw}{dt} = (p + xp' - c')\frac{dx}{dt} + xp'\frac{dX}{dt} - h\frac{dp}{dt}.$$

Upon substitution of the first-order condition for the home firm's profit maximization, this becomes

$$\frac{dw}{dt} = \{xp'(g-\gamma) + t[p + xp'(1+\gamma)]\}\frac{dx}{dt} - h\frac{dp}{dt}. \tag{12}$$

Evaluating (12) at $t = 0$, and imposing the condition that conjectures are consistent ($g = \gamma$), we find that $dw/dt = -h\,dp/dt$. The choice between a production tax and a production subsidy hinges on which policy lowers the price faced by domestic consumers, thereby reducing the consumption distortion associated with imperfect competition.

It is easy to calculate $dp/dt = p'(x+X)(dx+dX)/dt$. Applying Cramer's rule to the total differentials of the two firms' first-order conditions, we have

$$\frac{d(x+X)}{dt} = \frac{c'}{\Delta}[(C'-p)X - C''], \tag{13}$$

where Δ is the determinant of the 2×2 Jacobian matrix and is assumed to be positive for stability. If foreign marginal cost is increasing ($C'' > 0$), then $p > C'$, and the right-hand side of (13) is unambiguously negative. A production subsidy raises world output and hence lowers world price. Alternatively, if marginal costs at home and abroad are constant ($c'' = 0$ and $C'' = 0$), then the consistent conjectures equilibrium is the Bertrand equilibrium (see Bresnahan 1981), so that $p = C'$ and $d(x+X)/dt = 0$. In this case the optimal industrial policy is laissez-faire.

PROPOSITION 5 In a homogeneous product duopoly with consistent conjectures and nonzero domestic consumption, (i) if $c'' = 0$ and $C'' = 0$, then $t^* = 0$; and (ii) if $C'' > 0$, then $t^* < 0$.

Trade Tax or Subsidy

Finally, we consider the welfare effects of a small export tax or import subsidy at rate τ.[16] Under this policy domestic consumers pay a price $p(1-\tau)$ for the good, and home government revenue is $p\tau(x-h)$. The world inverse demand function is now written as $p(x+X,\tau)$, where $p_1 = 1/\{H'(p) + (1-\tau)h'[p(1-\tau)]\}$ and $p_2 = ph'[p(1-\tau)]p_1$. Proceeding as before, we find that

$$\left.\frac{dw}{d\tau}\right|_{\tau=0} = hp_1\frac{d(x+X)}{d\tau} + p_2(x-h).$$

In this case, however, it is no longer possible to sign unambiguously the effect of a small trade tax or subsidy on total world output. In addition, there is a second term that now enters the expression for $dw/d\tau$, which at $\tau = 0$ is unambiguously positive or negative depending upon whether the home country is a net exporter or importer of the product. Given total output, an export tax raises the world price of an export good, while an import tariff lowers the world price of an import good. This standard terms-of-trade effect provides a further motive for an export tax or import tariff, just as it does when the market is competitive.

To recapitulate the arguments of this subsection, a trade policy of either sign may raise domestic welfare in a duopolistic market with domestic consumption. When conjectures are consistent, any profit-shifting motive for policy intervention is absent. What remains is a standard terms-of-trade motive on the consumption side, and what might be termed a "consumption-distortion motive," arising from the gap between price and marginal cost. The former always indicates an export tax or import tariff, while the latter may favor either a tax or a subsidy, depending on the precise forms of the demand and cost functions.

7 Conclusions

We have analyzed the welfare effects of trade policy and industrial policy (production taxes and subsidies) for a range of specifications of an oligopolistic industry. A number of general propositions for optimal policy emerge. First, either trade policy or industrial policy may raise domestic welfare if oligopolistic profits can be shifted to home-country firms. Policies that achieve this profit shifting can work only if the government is able to set its policy in advance of firms' production decisions, and if government policy commitments are credible. Furthermore, in the duopoly case, profits can be shifted only if firms' conjectural variations differ from the true equilibrium responses that would result if they were to alter their output levels. The choice between a tax and a subsidy in this case depends on whether the home firm's output in the laissez-faire equilibrium exceeds or falls short of the level that would emerge under "consistent" or Stackelberg conjectures.

Second, whenever there is more than one domestic firm, competition among them is detrimental to home-country social welfare. In other words, there exists a pecuniary externality when each domestic firm does not take into account the effect of its own actions on the profits of other domestic competitors. A production or export tax will lead domestic firms to restrict their outputs, shifting them closer to the level that would result with collusion. In this familiar way a production or export tax enables the home country to exploit its monopoly power in trade fully.

These propositions are unaffected by extension of the analysis to cases in which optimal interventions are set simultaneously by two policy-active governments. But allowing for endogenous entry and exit introduces two new considerations. First, policy-induced entry (exit) could raise (lower) the average cost of production. When subsidies engender profit shifting, the gain in national income can be dissipated in additional entry fees. Second, policy alters the relative numbers of domestic and foreign firms in an oligopolistic industry. In the presence of residual profits there is a potential role for trade or industrial policy that serves to deter foreign entry or promote domestic entry.

Finally, when there is domestic consumption of the output of the oligopolistic industry, there are two further motives for policy intervention. First, consumers' marginal valuation of the product will generally differ from domestic marginal cost of production due to the collective exertion of monopoly power by firms in the industry. A welfare-improving policy for this reason should increase domestic consumption. When industrial policy is used, a production subsidy will achieve this result, whereas the appropriate trade policy instrument may be either an export (or import) tax or an export (or import) subsidy. Second, there is the usual externality caused by the multiplicity of small domestic consumers, who do not take into account the effect of their demands on world prices. Industrial policy cannot be used to overcome this externality, but if the country is a net exporter (importer), an export (import) tax will have a favorable impact on the country's terms of trade. The formulation of optimal trade or industrial policy in general requires the weighting of these various influences.

Appendix A: Proof of Proposition 4

The profit of the representative home firm i is

$$\pi^i = (1 - t)r_i(x^1, \ldots, x^n, X^{n+1}, \ldots, X^{n+m}) - c(x^i),$$

where the t denotes the output or export tax imposed on domestic firms. A typical foreign firm earns

$$\Pi^j = R_j(x^1, \ldots, x^n, X^{n+1}, \ldots, X^{n+m}) - C(X^j).$$

(A foreign policy may be allowed for by defining R^j to be after-tax revenue.) The first-order conditions for profit maximization are

$$(1 - t)r_i^i - c^{i\prime} + (1 - t)\sum_{\substack{j=1 \\ j \neq i}}^{n+m} r_j^i \gamma^{ij} = 0, \qquad i = 1, \ldots, n; \tag{A1a}$$

$$R_i^i - C^{i\prime} + \sum_{\substack{j=1 \\ j \neq i}}^{n+m} R_j^i \Gamma^{ij} = 0, \qquad i = n+1, \ldots, n+m, \tag{A1b}$$

where γ^{ij} (Γ^{ij}) is the conjecture by the home (foreign) firm i about the output response by firm j, for $j \neq i, j = 1, \ldots, n+m$. Home-country national product deriving from this industry is

$$w = \sum_{i=1}^{n} (r^i - c^i). \tag{A2}$$

Differentiating (A2) with respect to t at $t = 0$, and imposing the condition of symmetry of the initial (free trade) equilibrium gives

$$\left.\frac{dw}{dt}\right|_{t=0} = nr_2^1 \left[(n-1)(1-\gamma)\frac{dx^i}{dt} + m\frac{dX^j}{dt} - m\gamma\frac{dx^i}{dt} \right], \tag{A3}$$

where $\gamma = \gamma^{ij}$ for all $j \neq i, i = 1, \ldots, n+m$.

Next we differentiate the first-order conditions (A1a) and (A1b) and again impose symmetry (i.e., $dx^i = dx^k$ for $i, k = 1, \ldots, n$ and $dX^j = dX^l$ for $j, l = n+1, \ldots, n+m$) to derive

$$\begin{bmatrix} \alpha + (n-1)\beta & m\beta \\ n\beta & \alpha + (m-1)\beta \end{bmatrix} \begin{bmatrix} dx^i \\ dX^j \end{bmatrix} = \begin{bmatrix} \lambda dt \\ 0 \end{bmatrix}, \tag{A4}$$

where

$$\alpha \equiv r_{ii}^i - c^{i\prime} + (n+m-1)r_{ij}^i\gamma,$$

$$\beta \equiv r_{ij}^i + r_{jj}^i\gamma + (n+m-2)r_{jk}^i\gamma,$$

$$\gamma \equiv r_t^i + (n+m-1)r_j^i\gamma.$$

Note that the free trade equilibrium has symmetry not only among home firms but also between home and foreign firms, so that about this point $r_i^i = R_j^j$ and similarly for other derivatives. Using this fact and solving (A4) gives

$$\frac{dx^i}{dt} = \frac{[\alpha + (m-1)\beta]\lambda}{(\alpha - \beta)[\alpha + (n+m-1)\beta]} \tag{A5a}$$

and

$$\frac{dX^j}{dt} = \frac{-n\beta\lambda}{(\alpha - \beta)[(\alpha + (n+m-1)\beta)]}. \tag{A5b}$$

The value of γ determined by imposing the condition that conjectures be consistent is found by perturbing the equilibrium in (A1a) and (A1b) by an exogenous shift in the output of one firm, for instance, x^1, and solving for the full equilibrium response $dx^i/dx^1, i \neq 1$ (see the discussion in Perry 1982, especially n. 7). Doing so, we find that

$$\gamma = -\beta/[\alpha + (n + m - 1)\beta]. \tag{A6}$$

Finally, we substitute (A5a), (A5b), and (A6) into (A3) and perform some straightforward algebraic manipulations, which yield

$$\left.\frac{dw}{dt}\right|_{t=0} = \frac{n(n-1)r_2^1\lambda}{\alpha + (n + m - 2)\beta}. \tag{A7}$$

The denominator of (A7) must be negative for stability of the industry equilibrium (Seade 1980). From the first-order condition (A1a), $\lambda = c^{i\prime}/(1 - t) > 0$. The sign of expression (A7) is consequently opposite to that of r_2^1 if $n > 1$, that is, positive for goods that are substitutes. For $n = 1$, the expression is zero. □

Notes

Financial support for this research was provided by the National Science Foundation under grants SES 8207643 and PRA 8211940 and by the International Labor Affairs Bureau, U. S. Department of Labor, under contract J9K 30006. We are grateful to Jim Brander, Avinash Dixit, James Mirrlees, Barbara Spencer, and Larry Summers for helpful discussions and comments.

1. Spencer and Brander (1983) study a two-stage game in which a capacity or R&D investment is made at a stage prior to production. In such a setting, export subsidies and R&D subsidies are each welfare improving if implemented separately, but an optimal policy package involves an export subsidy and an R&D tax. Brander and Spencer (1984) extend the basic argument for intervention to situations in which duopolistic competition takes place in the home market. In such cases an import tariff often is beneficial.

2. We recognize the serious limitation of the conjectural variations framework in its attempt to collapse the outcome of what is actually a dynamic process into a static formulation. While there exist extensive-form representations of Cournot and Bertrand competition, such is not the case for other conjectural assumptions, including that of "consistent conjectures" introduced below. Nevertheless, characterizing the equilibrium in terms of conjectural variations does provide a parsimonious representation of alternative assumptions of firm interaction that includes Cournot and Bertrand equilibria as special cases. In addition, this approach highlights the source of the potential benefit from policy intervention, namely, the deviation between conjectured and actual responses.

Ideally, oligopolistic behavior would be modeled as a truly dynamic, multistage game. Since the development of such models remains, as of now, at a fairly nascent stage, and since existing work on optimal trade policy under oligopoly has been formulated in terms of static models, we choose to pursue the simpler conjectural variations approach.

Note that, within the class of static, conjectural variations models, restricting attention to those involving output rivalry entails no loss of generality. Kamien and Schwartz (1983) demonstrate that any conjectural variations equilibrium (CVE) in quantities has a corresponding CVE in prices.

3. Analysis of government policy in international markets typically is based on this assumption. See, e.g., Spencer and Brander (1983). It may be justified by specifying the political process of establishing policy as time-consuming and costly or by endowing the government with a reputation for adhering to announced policy.

4. The case of complementary goods can be analyzed similarly. When the two goods are complements ($r_2 > 0$), some of the results reported here (e.g., Theorem 1) are reversed.

5. For concreteness, we consider the case of ad valorem taxes and subsidies. Our results would not be affected by the introduction of *specific* taxes and subsidies, as the reader may verify.

6. We henceforth drop the arguments of the revenue and cost functions and their partial derivatives whenever no confusion is created by doing so. The revenue functions and their partial derivatives are understood to be evaluated at the equilibrium value of (x, X), while the cost functions and their derivatives are evaluated at x or X, whichever is appropriate.

7. The second-order condition for a maximum is satisfied locally as long as (1) the home firm's first- and second-order conditions for profit maximization are satisfied, and (2) the foreign firm's actual response to a change in x does not differ substantially from the response conjectured by the home firm.

8. If products are complements ($r_2 > 0$), the presumption is also in favor of an export subsidy, since in this case most specifications of demand, including the linear, imply that $R_{21} > 0$: the rival expands output when the domestic firm does, to the benefit of the home firm. The home firm consequently produces less, in Cournot competition, than it would as a Stackelberg leader.

9. When products are complements, $D_2 < 0$. The presumption then is that $\Pi_{21} < 0$: a price increase by the home firm engenders a price cut by its competitor. So, in this case as well, an export tax is optimal. Such a tax causes the foreign firm to lower its price, increasing the home firm's revenue

10. Our findings for the cases of Cournot and Bertrand competition can be stated concisely using the phraseology suggested by Bulow, Geanakoplos, and Klemperer (1985). They introduce the terms "strategic substitutes" and "strategic complements" to denote situations where "more aggressive" behavior on the part of one firm respectively lowers and raises the "marginal profitability" of similar moves by its rival. The classification of goods as strategic substitutes or complements can be made only after the designation of a specific strategy variable, which then gives meaning to the term "more aggressive." For Cournot and Bertrand competition, in which quantity and price are the strategy variables, respectively, their classification hinges on the slope of the reaction curves in the relevant strategy spaces. Accordingly, our propositions 1 and 2 could be rephrased as follows: *for Cournot and Bertrand competition among (ordinary) substitutes, optimal policy involves subsidizing exports if the goods are strategy substitutes and taxing exports otherwise.* If the goods instead are (ordinary) complements, then the opposite correspondence between strategic substitutes and complements and optimal policy obtains.

11. The second-order condition for a social optimum is satisfied at the free-trade equilibrium if the product-market equilibrium is stable.

12. Horstmann and Markusen (1984) and Venables (1985) analyze the effects of trade policy with free entry for the case of Cournot competition. The first authors assume, as we do in section 6 below, that world markets are integrated. The second assumes segmented national markets. Both assume large numbers of homogeneous firms, so that all firms' profits are zero.

13. In Venables (1985) the simultaneous exit of foreign firms and entry of an equal number of domestic firms is beneficial because national markets are segmented and transport costs are present. For a given total number of firms, consumer prices at home are lower the greater is the relative number of domestic participants.

14. If world markets are segmented, as has been assumed in a number of the previous studies of trade policy under conditions of oligopoly (e.g., Dixit 1984 and Krugman 1984), then trade policy can act as a second-best substitute for domestic antitrust policy only to the extent that marginal cost is not constant, so that the quantities supplied by an oligopolist to the various markets are interdependent.

15. We assume that this integral is bounded.

16. One consequence of our assumption that world markets are integrated is that at most one firm will export. Two-way trade of the sort discussed by Brander (1981) will not emerge as an equilibrium outcome. Thus, our trade policy tool τ, which combines a production tax and a consumption subsidy at equal rates, corresponds to an export tax or an import subsidy, depending on the direction of net industry trade.

References

Brander, J. A. 1981. Intra-industry trade in identical commodities. *Journal of International Economics* 11:1–14.

Brander, J. A. and B. J. Spencer. 1984. Tariff protection and imperfect competition. In H. Kierzkowski (ed.), *Monopolistic Competition in International Trade*, 194–206. Oxford: Oxford University Press.

Brander, J. A. and B. J. Spencer. 1985. Export subsidies and international market share rivalry. *Journal of International Economics* 18:83–100.

Bresnahan, T. F. 1981. Duopoly models with consistent conjectures. *American Economic Review* 71:934–945.

Bulow, J. I., J. D. Geanakoplos, and P. D. Klemperer. 1985. Multimarket oligopoly: Strategic substitutes and complements. *Journal of Political Economy* 93:488–511.

Dixit, A. K. 1984. International trade policy for oligopolistic industries. *Economic Journal Conference Papers* 94:1–16.

Dixit, A. K., and A. S. Kyle. 1985. The use of protection and subsidies for entry promotion and deterrence. *American Economic Review* 75:139–152.

Horstmann, I., and J. R. Markusen. 1984. Up the average cost curve: Inefficient entry and the new protectionism. Mimeograph.

Kamien, M. I., and N. L. Schwartz. 1983. Conjectural variations. *Canadian Journal of Economics* 16:191–211.

Krugman, P. R. 1984. Import protection as export promotion: International competition in the presence of oligopoly and economies of scale. In H. Kierzkowski (ed.), *Monopolistic Competition in International Trade*, 180–193. Oxford: Oxford University Press.

Perry, M. K. 1982. Oligopoly and consistent conjectural variations. *Bell Journal of Economics* 13:197–205.

Seade, J. K. 1980. On the effects of entry. *Econometrica* 48:479–489.

Spencer, B. J., and J. A. Brander. 1983. International R&D rivalry and industrial strategy. *Review of Economic Studies* 50:702–722.

Venables, A. J. 1985. Trade and trade policy with imperfect competition: The case of identical products and free entry. *Journal of International Economics* 19:1–20.

8 Trade Policy with Increasing Returns and Imperfect Competition: Contradictory Results from Competing Assumptions

James R. Markusen and Anthony J. Venables

1 Introduction

The subfield of trade policy under conditions of imperfect competition and increasing returns to scale has reached a certain maturity, at least as measured by the number of published articles on the topic. But this does not seem to imply that we have a clear and complete understanding of either the positive or normative implications of these twin assumptions. Different papers produce a bewildering variety of policy conclusions; the contents of the various contributions do not, in other words, aggregate into a coherent "model" in the sense we get from factor proportions theory.

An example of this can be provided by the various results in the literature on export subsidies. If firms produce at price in excess of marginal cost, then there is a possibility that welfare may be raised by using export subsidies to expand the output of domestic firms. This argument has been extensively analyzed for oligopolistic industries (Krugman 1984, Brander and Spencer 1985, Dixit 1984, Eaton and Grossman 1986). If the assumption that there is a fixed number of firms is replaced by free entry, then the export subsidy will attract new firms into the industry, and so may not expand the output of individual firms or change their average costs. Recent papers by Horstmann and Markusen (1986) and Venables (1985) demonstrate that the role of export subsidies then depends crucially on whether international markets are segmented or integrated. In the former case firms can set sales in domestic and foreign markets independently, creating the possibility that the price of a product may be different in the two markets. In the latter case firms can control only their total world sales, and the allocation of this quantity between countries occurs so as to equalize product prices in all markets.

This example suggests that policy conclusions depend on industry structure assumptions (oligopoly [no entry] versus free entry) and market structure assumptions (segmentation versus integration). The purpose of this paper is to provide a single model from which to draw the four possible cases generated by combining the industry structure and the market structure assumptions. Our primary aim is to use the model to generate comparisons between results already in the literature. In addition, we obtain some new results concerning policy with oligopoly and integrated markets and concerning the role of transport costs in the case of free entry and segmented markets.

In order to accomplish this purpose in a relatively transparent way, we need to sacrifice generality in other directions. We have done this with a vengeance by making the following assumptions: (1) demand curves are linear, (2) only specific taxes and subsidies are considered, (3) marginal costs are constant, and (4) conjectures are Cournot. While many of the above-mentioned papers use these assumptions in any case, it is nevertheless true that the results generated by the four models are not robust

Originally published in the *Journal of International Economics* 24 (May 1988): 299–316.

with respect to variations in these assumptions. Many results can, for example, turn on whether or not conjectures are Cournot (Eaton and Grossman 1986). But the purpose of this paper is to offer a meaningful comparison of models, not to examine in detail any single case. We thus feel that the sacrifice of generality is worthwhile, but urge those not familiar with the literature to remember that the policy implications of any particular model may not be robust.

2 Equilibrium

Each economy has a single factor of production; the domestic economy's share of the world endowment of this factor is denoted l, and that of the foreign economy is denoted l^* ($l + l^* = 1$). This factor may be used to produce a tradable composite commodity under perfect competition and constant returns to scale. Units are chosen such that the factor of production and the composite may be taken as numeraire. In addition, each country contains firms from an imperfectly competitive industry. We assume that all firms from this industry in a particular country produce an identical product but permit national product differentiation; the products produced by domestic and foreign firms will be denoted X and Y, respectively. Asterisks denote foreign quantities so, for example, X^* is the total amount of X sold in the foreign market and X is the total sold in the domestic market. Lowercase $x(x^*)$ and $y(y^*)$ denote the outputs per firm sold to the domestic (foreign) market. n_x and n_y are the numbers of firms in the X and Y industries so $X = n_x x$ and $X^* = n_x x^*$, etc. The same notational convention is employed on prices, so $p_x(p_x^*)$ and $p_y(p_y^*)$ denote the consumer prices of X and Y in the domestic (foreign) economy. Domestic demands for the outputs of the imperfectly competitive industry take the linear form

$$n_x x = X = l\{a - p_x - b(p_x - p_y)\}, \tag{1}$$

$$n_y y = Y = l\{a - p_y - b(p_y - p_x)\}, \tag{2}$$

and foreign demands are

$$n_x x^* = X^* = l^*\{a - p_x^* - b(p_x^* - p_y^*)\}, \tag{3}$$

$$n_y y^* = Y^* = l^*\{a - p_y^* - b(p_y^* - p_x^*)\}. \tag{4}$$

These demand functions are symmetric across both countries and products. That is to say, within each country demand functions for X and Y are the same, and for each product demand is the same in both countries, except for the terms l and l^*, which scale demand to the size of the countries' endowments. The parameter b may be interpreted as a measure of closeness of substitution between output produced in each country; as $b \to \infty$, the products become perfect substitutes.

The unit revenue that a firm receives from sales is the consumer price, net of any taxes (t), or transport costs (s). We consider only specific taxes, so that producer prices (q) may be defined as

$$q_x = p_x - t_x, \qquad q_x^* = p_x^* - t_x^* - s_x^*, \tag{5}$$

$$q_y = p_y - t_y - s_y, \quad q_y^* = p_y^* - t_y^*. \tag{6}$$

t_y and t_x^* may represent either import tariffs or export taxes, depending on which government receives the revenue. Firms in the imperfectly competitive industry produce with a fixed cost F_x (F_y) and a constant marginal cost c_x (c_y). The profits of a single representative firm in the domestic economy, r_x, are

$$r_x = (q_x - c_x)x + (q_x^* - c_x)x^* - F_x. \tag{7}$$

Consider first this firm's supply decision under the hypothesis of segmented markets. The firm can then independently vary producer prices in each country, q_x and q_x^* (and hence consumer prices p_x and p_x^*). With Cournot behavior the firm conjectures that if it changes q_x the sales of all other firms are unchanged. In order to hold Y constant this implies (from demand eq. [2] together with $dp_x = dq_x$ from [5]), that p_y changes to satisfy

$$(1 + b)\,dp_y = b\,dq_x.$$

Given this price change and the fact that the sales of other domestic firms are constant, the slope of the firm's perceived demand curve for domestic sales is, from the demand curve (1),

$$\frac{dX}{dq_x} = \frac{dx}{dq_x} = -\frac{l(2b + 1)}{b + 1} = -lB, \tag{8}$$

where B is defined as $B = (2b + 1)/(b + 1)$. Analogous reasoning establishes that the slope of the firm's perceived demand curve for foreign sales, dx^*/dq_x^*, is

$$\frac{dx^*}{dq_x^*} = -\frac{l^*(2b + 1)}{b + 1} = -l^*B. \tag{9}$$

Using (8) and (9) in (7), the first-order conditions for profit maximization are

$$\begin{aligned} \frac{dr_x}{dq_x} &= x - (q_x - c_x)lB = 0, \\ \frac{dr_x}{dq_x^*} &= x^* - (q_x^* - c_x)l^*B = 0. \end{aligned} \tag{10}$$

Equivalent first-order conditions for a foreign firm are

$$\begin{aligned} \frac{dr_y}{dq_y} &= y - (q_y - c_y)lB = 0, \\ \frac{dr_y}{dq_y^*} &= y^* - (q_y^* - c_y)l^*B = 0. \end{aligned} \tag{11}$$

Equations (10) and (11) give the sales of a firm from each country in each market as a function of the relevant producer price. Using these equations in the definition of profits we can obtain the maximized value of profits as a function of producer prices. That is, using (10) in (7),

$$r_x = lB(q_x - c_x)^2 + l^*B(q_x^* - c_x)^2 - F_x, \tag{12}$$

and, for a foreign firm,

$$r_y = lB(q_y - c_y)^2 + l^*B(q_y^* - c_y)^2 - F_y. \tag{13}$$

Equilibrium with segmented markets is now characterized as follows. Equilibrium prices, conditional on the number of firms, n_x and n_y, can be found by equating demand (eqs. [1]–[4]) and supply (eqs. [10] and [11]) for each product in each market. Domestic producer prices are then implicitly defined by

$$\begin{aligned} q_x\{n_xB + b + 1\} - q_yb - n_xc_xB &= a - (1 + b)t_x + b(t_y + s_y), \\ q_y\{n_yB + b + 1\} - q_xb - n_yc_yB &= a - (1 + b)(t_y + s_y) + bt_x, \end{aligned} \tag{14}$$

and foreign producer prices by

$$\begin{aligned} q_x^*\{n_xB + b + 1\} - q_y^*b - n_xc_xB &= a - (1 + b)(t_x^* + s_x^*) + bt_y^*, \\ q_y^*\{n_yB + b + 1\} - q_x^*b - n_yc_yB &= a - (1 + b)t_y^* + b(t_x^* + s_x^*). \end{aligned} \tag{15}$$

With free entry n_x and n_y become endogenous, and the two industry equilibrium conditions of zero profits must hold, that is, (12) and (13) are set equal to zero.

In the case where markets are integrated, firms can no longer vary prices in each market independently. Arbitrage ensures the equality of producer prices for each product:

$$q_x = q_x^*, \quad q_y = q_y^*. \tag{16}$$

Furthermore, Cournot behavior now implies that each firm takes the total output of other firms as constant, although the allocation of this output between markets may change. Suppose that a firm changes q_x (and q_x^*). In order to hold $Y + Y^*$ constant we have (adding [2] and [4] and using [5], [6], and [16])

$$(1 + b)\,dp_y = (1 + b)\,dp_y^* = b\,dq_x = b\,dq_x^*.$$

Adding demand functions (l) and (3) and holding other firms' output of X constant, the perceived slope of a domestic firm's world demand function is

$$\frac{d(X + X^*)}{dq_x} = \frac{d(x + x^*)}{dq_x} = -\frac{2b + 1}{b + 1} = -B. \tag{17}$$

Choosing q_x $(= q_x^*)$ to maximize profits therefore gives the first-order condition

$$\frac{dr_x}{dq_x} = x + x^* - B(q_x - c_x) = 0. \tag{18}$$

Foreign firms' choice of q_y $(= q_y^*)$ gives

$$\frac{dr_y}{dq_y} = y + y^* - B(q_y - c_y) = 0. \tag{19}$$

Equations (18) and (19) give each firm's world sales as a function of the producer price that is common to both markets. Since $(q_x - c_x) = (q_x^* - c_x)$ we may use these equations in equation (7) to give maximized profits as

$$r_x = B(q_x - c_x)^2 - F_x, \tag{20}$$

$$r_y = B(q_y - c_y)^2 - F_y. \tag{21}$$

The integrated market equilibrium may now be obtained as follows. Given price equations (5), (6), and (16) there are only two independent producer prices. Equating supply ([18] and [19]) with world demand ([1] plus [3], and [2] plus [4]), the producer prices of domestic and foreign output are implicitly defined by

$$\begin{aligned} &q_x\{n_xB + b + 1\} - q_yb - n_xc_xB \\ &\qquad = a - (1 + b)\{lt_x + l^*(t_x^* + s_x^*)\} + b\{l(t_y + s_y) + l^*t_y^*\}, \\ &q_y\{n_yB + b + 1\} - q_xb - n_yc_yB \\ &\qquad = a - (1 + b)\{l(t_y + s_y) + l^*t_y^*\} + b\{lt_x + l^*(t_x^* + s_x^*)\}. \end{aligned} \tag{22}$$

With free entry, n_x and n_y are endogenous, and we have additionally equations (20) and (21) set equal to zero.

In order to evaluate policy changes we need a welfare indicator. Welfare of consumers in the domestic economy is given by the indirect utility function

$$V(p_x, p_y, I), \quad I = l + n_xr_x + G. \tag{23}$$

Income (I) is composed of wage income (l), domestic firms' profits, n_xr_x, and domestic government revenue, G. Let the parameters g_y and g_x^* take on the value of 1 for a trade tax or subsidy instrument employed by the domestic government, and 0 for a foreign instrument. G is then

$$G = g_yt_yY + g_x^*t_x^*X^* + t_xX. \tag{24}$$

Consider instituting small taxes or subsidies. Differentiating (23) and (24), normalizing the marginal utility of income at unity, and using Roy's Identity (so $dV/dp_x = -X$, $dV/dp_y = -Y$) gives in the neighborhood of zero taxes

$$dV = -X\,dp_x - Y\,dp_y + r_x\,dn_x + n_x\,dr_x + g_yY\,dt_y + g_x^*X^*\,dt_x^* + X\,dt_x. \tag{25}$$

It will be convenient to express the welfare change in terms of changes in tax instruments and producer prices. From (5) and (6) we have

$$dp_x = dq_x + dt_x, \quad dp_y = dq_y + dt_y. \tag{26}$$

The term $r_x dn_x$ is equal to zero, since, if there is free entry, $r_x = 0$, and if there is no entry, $dn_x = 0$. dr_x can be obtained from (12) and (10) as

$$\begin{aligned} dr_x &= 2Bl(q_x - c_x)\,dq_x + 2Bl^*(q_x^* - c_x)\,dq_x^* \\ &= 2x\,dq_x + 2x^*\,dq_x^*. \end{aligned} \tag{27}$$

With $q_x = q_x^*$ this equation also holds for integrated markets, as can be checked from equation (18). Substituting (26) and (27) into equation (25) we obtain

$$dV = X\,dq_x - Y\,dq_y + 2X^*\,dq_x^* + g_x^* X^*\,dt_x^* + (g_y - 1)Y\,dt_y. \tag{28}$$

Equation (28) will be used to evaluate the welfare effects of small policy changes. Note that it is completely general with respect to segmented versus integrated markets and free entry versus no entry (but would be modified by ad valorem taxes).

The welfare change described in (28) may be interpreted in terms of the effects of policy on domestic distortions and on the terms of trade. Notice that, from equation (10), the change in a firm's supply with respect to a price change is

$$x\,dq_x = (q_x - c_x)\,dx, \quad x^*\,dq_x^* = (q_x^* - c_x)\,dx^*. \tag{29}$$

Differential (28) may now be decomposed into three terms.

(a) Firm expansion effect:

$$X\,dq_x + X^*\,dq_x^* = n_x\{(q_x - c_x)\,dx + (q_x^* - c_x)\,dx^*\}.$$

(b) Import terms of trade effect:

$$-Y\{dq_y - (1 - g_y)\,dt_y\}.$$

(c) Export terms of trade effect:

$$X^*(dq_x^* + g_x^*\,dt_x^*).$$

The firm expansion effect arises from the fact that, with prices in excess of marginal cost, a small expansion in firm output generates a welfare gain. The second and third terms measure terms of trade improvements due to changes in the import price of good Y and the export price of X, respectively.

3 Policy with Integrated Markets

First we shall analyze the effects of policy under the integrated markets hypothesis and with the number of firms in each country held constant. In order to find the effects of policy on producer prices the equilibrium conditions (22) may be differentiated to give, in matrix form,

$$Q\,dq = T[L\,dt + L^*\,dt^*]. \tag{30}$$

Lowercase symbols denote vectors, with first element for the X industry, and second for the Y industry, so $dq = [dq_x, dq_y]'$, $dt = [dt_x, dt_y]'$, etc. The matrices L and L^* are diagonal matrices with diagonal elements l and l^*, respectively, and Q and T are defined as follows:

$$Q = \begin{bmatrix} n_x B + b + 1 & -b \\ -b & n_y B + b + 1 \end{bmatrix}, \quad T = \begin{bmatrix} -(1+b) & b \\ b & -(1+b) \end{bmatrix}.$$

Equation (30) may be inverted to give

$$dq = dq^* = Q^{-1}T[L\,dt + L^*\,dt^*], \tag{31}$$

where

$$Q^{-1}T = \begin{bmatrix} -(1+b)(1+n_y) & bn_y \\ bn_x & -(1+b)(1+n_x) \end{bmatrix} \frac{1}{D}, \tag{32}$$

and $D = (1+b)(1+n_x+n_y) + n_x n_y B > 0$.

From equations (31) and (32) we see that the effect of policy on producer prices is a weighted average of policy changes in the two countries, where the weights are country size. From the sign pattern of the matrix $Q^{-1}T$, taxation of good x reduces the producer price of good x, but, since elements of $Q^{-1}T$ have absolute value less than unity, raises the consumer price in the country in which the tax is imposed. We also see that taxation of good x raises the producer price of good y; this is because expenditure is switched to good y, and, with linear demand curves, this additional expenditure raises monopoly power and producers' price-cost margins. To investigate the effect of policy on welfare, consider first a tax on domestic imports, $dt_y > 0$. Using the price changes derived from equation (31) in the welfare indicator, equation (28), gives

$$\frac{dV}{dt_y} = X\left(\frac{dq_x}{dt_y}\right) - Y\left(\frac{dq_y}{dt_y}\right) + 2X^*\left(\frac{dq_x^*}{dt_y}\right) + (g_y - 1)Y$$

$$= \frac{(X + 2X^*)bn_y l + Y(1+b)(1+n_x)l + DY(g_y - 1)}{D}. \tag{33}$$

The implications of equation (33) are summarized in proposition 1A.

PROPOSITION 1A (Fixed number of firms: integrated markets). (i) An import tariff ($dt_y > 0$, $g_y = 1$) raises domestic welfare. (ii) A foreign export tax ($dt_y > 0$, $g_y = 0$) has an ambiguous effect on domestic welfare.

The welfare change of proposition 1A comes from three sources. First, the tax raises the domestic consumer price of good y but decreases the producer price; the effects of this on the import terms of trade therefore depends on which government receives the revenue from the tax. Second, the tax increases the price and output of the domestic good x, thereby raising domestic welfare both by an improvement in the export terms of trade and by a firm expansion effect. The consequences of taxing domestic exports are described in equation (34) and proposition 1B:

$$\frac{dV}{dt_x^*} = X\left(\frac{dq_x}{dt_x^*}\right) - Y\left(\frac{dq_y}{dt_x^*}\right) + 2X^*\left(\frac{dq_x^*}{dt_x^*}\right) + g_x^* X^*$$

$$= \frac{-(X + 2X^*)(1 + b)(1 + n_y)l^* - Ybn_x l^* + DX^* g_x^*}{D}. \tag{34}$$

PROPOSITION 1B (Fixed number of firms: integrated markets). (i) A foreign import tariff ($dt_x^* > 0$, $g_x^* = 0$) reduces domestic welfare. (ii) An export tax ($dt_x^* > 0$, $g_x^* = 1$) has an ambiguous effect on domestic welfare.

This proposition may be applied to analysis of an export subsidy, $dt_x^* < 0$. A subsidy to domestic exports raises the producer price of good X. This has a beneficial firm expansion effect, but its effect on the domestic export terms of trade depends on which government pays the subsidy. In addition, the export subsidy reduces the price of good Y, so improving the import terms of trade. The net effect is that a subsidy paid by the foreign government certainly raises domestic welfare; if the subsidy is paid by the domestic government, its welfare effect is ambiguous but is more likely to be positive the smaller the number of firms and the smaller b is; both these factors raise the degree of monopolistic distortion.

We may also comment on the effect of reciprocal import tariffs or export taxes on world welfare. A measure of this may be obtained by assuming symmetry of the two economies and adding together the effects of foreign and domestic tax instruments on domestic welfare. Symmetry implies that $l = l^* = \frac{1}{2}$, $n_x = n_y$ and $X^* = Y$; in order to divide revenue equally between countries, let $g_y = 1$ and $g_x^* = 0$. Adding (33) and (34) then gives

$$\frac{dV}{dt_y} + \frac{dV}{dt_x^*} = \frac{-(1 + b + n)(X + Y)}{2D}. \tag{35}$$

We see that world welfare is unambiguously raised by small trade subsidies.

How are these results modified if we permit free entry while retaining integrated markets? This case has been analyzed by Horstmann and Markusen (1986) and is particularly transparent in the present model, where n_x and n_y are now endogenous, and zero profit conditions hold; these conditions are (eqs. [20] and [21])

$$B(q_x - c_x)^2 = F_x, \quad B(q_y - c_y)^2 = F_y. \tag{36}$$

Producer prices are therefore independent of the policies being analyzed. Welfare changes come immediately from (28):

$$\frac{dV}{dt_y} = (g_y - 1)Y, \quad \frac{dV}{dt_x^*} = g_x^* X^*, \tag{37}$$

giving propositions 2A and 2B.

PROPOSITION 2A (Free entry: integrated markets). (i) An import tariff ($dt_y > 0, g_y = 1$) has no effect on domestic welfare. (ii) A foreign export tax ($dt_y > 0$, $g_y = 0$) reduces domestic welfare.

PROPOSITION 2B (Free entry: integrated markets). (i) A foreign import tariff ($dt_x^* > 0$, $g_x^* = 0$) has no effect on domestic welfare. (ii) An export tax ($dt_x^* > 0$, $g_x^* = 1$) raises domestic welfare.

Propositions 2A and 2B derive their simplicity from the fact that producer prices are fixed. Policy changes lead only to entry and exit, at unchanged firm scale and producer price. Elasticities of supply are therefore infinite, although demand elasticities are finite. It follows from this that optimal import tariffs are zero (proposition 2A[i]) but that export taxes may be used to effect a transfer from foreign citizens to the domestic government (proposition 2B[ii]). From the point of view of world welfare, free trade is optimal.

4 Policy with Segmented Markets

With segmented markets firms can choose their sales in each national market independently. In order to find the effect of policy on producer prices equilibrium conditions (14) and (15) may be differentiated to give

$$Q\,dq + N\,dn = T\,dt, \quad Q\,dq^* + N^*\,dn = T\,dt^*, \tag{38}$$

where the matrices Q and T are as before, and N and N^* are defined by

$$N = \begin{bmatrix} B(q_x - c_x) & 0 \\ 0 & B(q_y - c_y) \end{bmatrix} = \begin{bmatrix} \frac{x}{l} & 0 \\ 0 & \frac{y}{l} \end{bmatrix},$$

$$N^* = \begin{bmatrix} B(q_x^* - c_x) & 0 \\ 0 & B(q_y^* - c_y) \end{bmatrix} = \begin{bmatrix} \frac{x^*}{l^*} & 0 \\ 0 & \frac{y^*}{l^*} \end{bmatrix}.$$

Consider first the case in which the number of firms is constant, $dn = 0$. The effect of policy is then

$$dq = Q^{-1}T\,dt, \quad dq^* = Q^{-1}T\,dt^*. \tag{39}$$

Comparing this with policy under the integrated market hypothesis (eqs. [31] and [32]), we see that the matrix $Q^{-1}T$ enters as before. However, the vector dq of producer price changes in the domestic country now depends only on taxes on domestic consumption, rather than being a weighted average of tax changes in both countries. A domestic tax on a good no longer has an effect on foreign prices but has

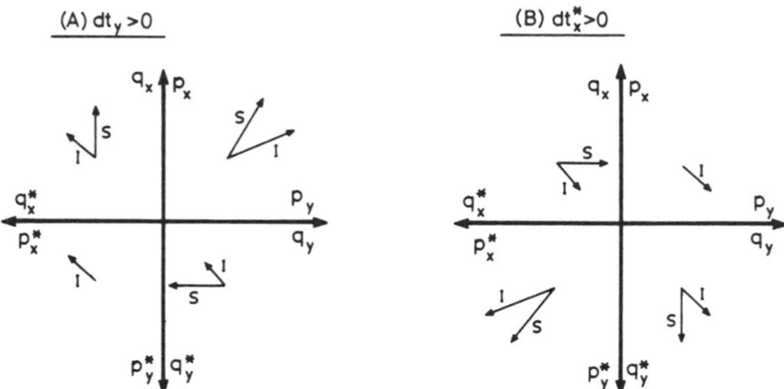

Figure 1
Price changes with fixed number of firms: segmented markets (*S*), and integrated markets (*I*)

a larger effect on domestic producer prices. This is illustrated in figure 1, which illustrates price changes associated with an import tariff (panel [A]) and export tax (panel [B]) for both the segmented (*S*) and integrated (*I*) equilibria.

The welfare effects of policy under the hypotheses of segmented markets and a fixed number of firms have been analyzed by Dixit (1984) (with the restriction that foreign and domestic goods are perfect substitutes) among others. For purposes of comparison we provide a brief statement of the effects of import and export taxes. A small tax on domestic imports, $dt_y > 0$, changes q_x and q_y (see fig. 1) and generates domestic welfare change:

$$\frac{dV}{dt_y} = X\left(\frac{dq_x}{dt_y}\right) - Y\left(\frac{dq_y}{dt_y}\right) + (g_y - 1)Y$$

$$= \frac{Xbn_y + Y(1 + b)(1 + n_x) + YD(g_y - 1)}{D}. \qquad (40)$$

PROPOSITION 3A (Fixed numbers of firms: segmented markets). (i) An import tariff ($dt_y > 0$, $g_y = 1$) raises domestic welfare. (ii) A foreign export tax ($dt_y > 0$, $g_y = 0$) has an ambiguous effect on domestic welfare.

A tax on domestic exports ($dt_x^* > 0$) leaves producer prices in the domestic market unchanged and so has welfare effect

$$\frac{dV}{dt_x^*} = 2X^*\left(\frac{dq_x^*}{dt_x^*}\right) + g_x^* X^*$$

$$= \frac{-2X^*(1 + b)(1 + n_y) + DX^* g_x^*}{D}. \qquad (41)$$

PROPOSITION 3B (Fixed numbers of firms: segmented markets). (i) A foreign import tariff ($dt_x^* > 0$, $g_x^* = 0$) reduces domestic welfare. (ii) An export tax ($dt_x^* > 0$, $g_x^* = 1$) has an ambiguous effect on domestic welfare.

Assuming symmetry of the two economies and adding together equations (40) and (41) gives the effect of reciprocal import tariffs or export taxes on world welfare as

$$\frac{dV}{dt_y} + \frac{dV}{dt_x^*} = \frac{Xbn - Y(1 + b)(1 + n)}{D}. \tag{42}$$

Quantitative comparison of the welfare effects of policy under segmented and integrated markets clearly depends on the volume of trade in the two equilibria (see, e.g., equations [33] and [40]); detailed comparison of a central case is undertaken in section 5. Qualitatively the difference is that, with segmented markets, an import tariff (export tax) no longer has an export terms-of-trade effect (import terms-of-trade effect). As noted above, price changes occur only in the country where policy is implemented.

We may now turn to policy with segmented markets and free entry of firms. dn may now be nonzero but can be eliminated from (38) to give the change in producer prices as a function of tax changes as

$$N^{-1}[Q\,dq - T\,dt] = N^{*-1}[Q\,dq^* - T\,dt^*]. \tag{43}$$

Industry equilibrium requires that maximized profits are zero. Differentiating equations (12) and (13) and using the matrices N and N^*, changes in producer prices must satisfy

$$\frac{dr}{2} = LN\,dq + L^*N^*\,dq^* = 0. \tag{44}$$

Using equations (44) and (43) we obtain the change in producer prices as a function of tax policy as

$$[Q + NN^{*-1}QN^{*-1}NL^{*-1}L]\,dq = T\,dt - NN^{*-1}T\,dt^*$$

and

$$[Q + N^*N^{-1}QN^{-1}N^*L^{-1}L^*]\,dq^* = T\,dt^* - N^*N^{-1}T\,dt. \tag{45}$$

The effects of tax policy on producer prices may be obtained from equation (45) in a straightforward, though laborious, manner; we consider only the case when the two economies are symmetric, so $L = L^*$ and $N = N^*$. Define m as the ratio of a firm's sales in its home market to its sales in its export market, that is, $m = x/x^* = y^*/y$ (and with symmetry, $m = X/X^* = Y^*/Y$); $m = 1$ if transport costs are zero and it is strictly increasing in transport costs. We then have

$$\frac{dq_x}{dt_y} = -\frac{1}{m}\cdot\frac{dq_x^*}{dt_y} = \frac{dq_y^*}{dt_x^*} = -\frac{1}{m}\cdot\frac{dq_y}{dt_x^*} = \frac{b\{nB(m^2 + 1) - (b + 1)(m^2 - 1)\}}{E}, \tag{46}$$

$$\frac{dq_x}{dt_x^*} = -\frac{1}{m}\cdot\frac{dq_x^*}{dt_x^*} = \frac{dq_y^*}{dt_y} = -\frac{1}{m}\cdot\frac{dq_y}{dt_y} = \frac{m\{(n + 1)(2b + 1)(m^2 + 1) + b^2(m^2 - 1)\}}{E}, \tag{47}$$

where $E = BD(m^2 + 1)^2 + b^2(m^2 - 1)^2 > 0$.

Several remarks may be made about these equations. First, because of symmetry the effect of a change in t_y on q_x is the same as the effect of a change in t_x^* on q_y^*, and so on. Second, each policy changes the price of a particular good with opposite sign in each market; producer price changes must be of opposite sign if zero profits are to be maintained. Third, the effects of a trade tax on good x on producer prices of x are unambiguous (similarly for y), as given by equation (47). However, the effect of a trade tax on y on the producer prices of good x is ambiguous (and similarly, trade tax on x on price of good y). From equation (46)

$$\frac{dq_x}{dt_y} > 0, \quad \frac{dq_x^*}{dt_y} < 0 \Leftrightarrow nB(m^2 + 1) > (b + 1)(m^2 - 1), \tag{A}$$

$$\frac{dq_x}{dt_y} > 0, \quad \frac{dq_x^*}{dt_y} > 0 \Leftrightarrow nB(m^2 + 1) < (b + 1)(m^2 - 1). \tag{B}$$

In case (B), an import tariff reduces the price of the domestic substitute. In order to understand this ambiguity it is instructive to consider two polar cases. The first is that in which transport costs are zero, so $m = 1$; inequality (A) therefore applies. The second is the case in which goods x and y are perfect substitutes, so $b \to \infty$, and inequality (B) holds. Now consider the effect of a domestic import tariff. This is a tax on foreign firms, so there must be entry and exit such that there is an increase in some weighted average of the consumer price of good y in each market, but not of good x; this is necessary to maintain zero profits. These price changes can take two forms. One is an increase in the price of good y relative to good x in each market; the other is an increase in the price of both y and x in a market where y has a large share, and a fall in the price of both y and x in a market where y has a small share. In general both of these effects occur. However, if transport costs are zero and market shares are equal ($m = 1$), then adjustment is entirely through the first route; if x and y are close substitutes, ($b \to \infty$), then relative prices within each country do not change, and adjustment is through the second route. The import tariff then causes the exit of foreign firms, thereby raising prices in the foreign market, attracting entry of domestic firms, and leading to a reduction in prices in the domestic market. This ambiguity means that general welfare results cannot be obtained for this case. However, we briefly report the welfare effects of policy for our two polar cases. When $m = 1$, inspection of equations (46) and (47) gives the effect of an import tariff as

$$\begin{aligned}\frac{dV}{dt_y} &= X\left(\frac{dq_x}{dt_y}\right) - Y\left(\frac{dq_y}{dt_y}\right) + 2X^*\left(\frac{dq_x^*}{dt_y}\right) + (g_y - 1)Y \\ &= \frac{Y\{(n + b + 1)/2 + (g_y - 1)D\}}{D}.\end{aligned} \tag{48}$$

PROPOSITION 4A (Free entry: segmented markets: zero transport costs: symmetric economies). (i) An import tariff ($dt_y > 0$, $g_y = 1$) raises domestic welfare. (ii) A foreign export tax ($dt_y > 0$, $g_y = 0$) reduces domestic welfare.

The effect of an export tax is

$$\frac{dV}{dt_x^*} = X\left(\frac{dq_x}{dt_x^*}\right) - Y\left(\frac{dq_y}{dt_x^*}\right) + 2X^*\left(\frac{dq_x^*}{dt_x^*}\right) + X^*g_x^*$$

$$= \frac{X^*\{-(n+b+1)/2 + g_x^*D\}}{D}. \tag{49}$$

PROPOSITION 4B (Free entry: segmented markets: zero transport costs: symmetric economies). (i) A foreign import tariff ($dt_x^* > 0$, $g_x^* = 0$) reduces domestic welfare. (ii) An export tax ($dt_x^* > 0$, $g_x^* = 1$) increases domestic welfare.

The second polar case is that in which transport costs are positive, and X and Y are perfect substitutes, $b \to \infty$. This is the case analyzed by Venables (1985). In the present model we obtain the effect of an import tariff as

$$\frac{dV}{dt_y} = X\left(\frac{dq_x}{dt_y}\right) - Y\left(\frac{dq_y}{dt_y}\right) + 2X^*\left(\frac{dq_x^*}{dt_y}\right) + (g_y - 1)Y$$

$$= \frac{X+Y}{m^2-1} + g_yY. \tag{50}$$

PROPOSITION 5A (Free entry: segmented markets: perfect substitutes: symmetric economies). (i) An import tariff ($dt_y > 0$, $g_y = 1$) raises domestic welfare. (ii) A foreign export tax ($dt_y > 0$, $g_y = 0$) raises domestic welfare.

The welfare effect of an export tax is

$$\frac{dV}{dt_x^*} = X\left(\frac{dq_x}{dt_x^*}\right) - Y\left(\frac{dq_y}{dt_x^*}\right) + 2X^*\left(\frac{dq_x^*}{dt_x^*}\right) + X^*g_x^*$$

$$= -(X+Y)\frac{m}{m^2-1} + g_x^*X^*. \tag{51}$$

PROPOSITION 5B (Free entry: segmented markets: perfect substitutes: symmetric economies). (i) A foreign import tariff ($dt_x^* > 0$, $g_x^* = 0$) reduces domestic welfare. (ii) An export tax ($dt_x^* > 0$, $g_x^* = 1$) reduces domestic welfare.

Propositions 5A and 5B differ from propositions 4A and 4B in that they establish that domestic welfare is raised by a small import tariff or export subsidy, regardless of whether the revenue implications of these policies fall on the domestic or the foreign government.

5 Summary and Conclusions

The purpose of this paper was to establish a common analytical framework within which competing models of trade with scale economies and imperfect competition could be compared. The idea was that this common framework would help us to better understand why different assumptions generate conflicting results. These assumptions were, on the one hand, integrated versus segmented markets and, on the other hand, free entry versus oligopoly (no entry). We were able to do this using the assumptions of linear demand, constant marginal cost, Cournot behavior, and specific taxes and subsidies. The effects of tariffs and export subsidies in each of the four models are summarized in propositions 1–5. Do any broad conclusions emerge? Cross-model comparisons can be made by comparing the welfare differentials that immediately precede each proposition. If we impose additional assumptions that limit still further the generality of the model, then some clear comparisons are possible.

Additional Assumptions

(1) The two economies are symmetric, that is, are the same size and have the same costs. (2) The number of firms under oligopoly is less than or equal to the number at the free entry equilibrium. (3) There are no transport costs. (4) In the case of free entry with segmented markets, the commodities are not perfect substitutes.

Assumptions 3 and 4 mean that propositions 5A and 5B of the text are excluded from the comparisons below. Assumption 3 also ensures that, in the absence of policy, the segmented and integrated market equilibria coincide. Assumptions 1 and 2 permit analytical comparisons among remaining cases, and are sufficient, but not necessary, for all the results which follow; assumption 2 will of course be satisfied unless firms make losses in the oligopoly cases. Our first comparison is between the segmented and integrated market hypotheses (propositions 1 and 2 compared to 3 and 4).

Result 1 Segmented markets imply that a small import tariff or export subsidy improves welfare more (or reduces it less) than if markets are integrated. This result is independent of the free entry/oligopoly assumption.

The intuition behind this result is that with segmented markets, the effect of a policy is concentrated on the market in question. Thus, an import tariff has a greater terms-of-trade effect with segmented markets than with integrated markets.

Let subscripts I = integrated, S = segmented, E = free entry, and N = no entry (oligopoly). Given the symmetry assumptions, we can subtract (33) from (40) to show that an import tariff is more effective under segmented markets than under integrated markets when oligopoly is the market structure:

$$\left(\frac{dV}{dt_y}\right)_{\mathrm{S,N}} - \left(\frac{dV}{dt_y}\right)_{\mathrm{I,N}} = \frac{Y(n_y + b + 1)}{2D} > 0. \tag{52}$$

For free entry, the import tariff is similarly more effective under segmentation ([48] minus [37]):

$$\left(\frac{dV}{dt_y}\right)_{\mathrm{S,E}} - \left(\frac{dV}{dt_y}\right)_{\mathrm{I,E}} = \frac{Y(n_y + b + 1)}{2D} > 0. \tag{53}$$

The other findings in result 1 are easily established in a similar fashion.

Result 2 Oligopoly implies that a small import tariff or export subsidy improves welfare more (or reduces it less) than if there is free entry. This result is independent of the segmentation/integration assumption.

Result 2 compares propositions 1 and 3 with 2 and 4. The intuition behind the result is that, under oligopoly, these policies have a fairly strong firm expansion effect that tends to improve welfare. With free entry, however, part of the industry expansion is in terms of new firms with a correspondingly smaller expansion in the outputs of existing firms.

We can subtract (48) from (40) to show that an import tariff under oligopoly is more effective than under free entry when markets are segmented:

$$\left(\frac{dV}{dt_y}\right)_{\mathrm{S,N}} - \left(\frac{dV}{dt_y}\right)_{\mathrm{S,E}} = \frac{2Xbn_y + Y(n_x + b + 1)/2}{D} > 0. \tag{54}$$

Similarly, we can subtract (37) from (33) to obtain a similar result when markets are integrated (note $l = \frac{1}{2}$, $X = X^*$, etc.):

$$\left(\frac{dV}{dt_y}\right)_{\mathrm{I,N}} - \left(\frac{dV}{dt_y}\right)_{\mathrm{I,E}} = \frac{3Xbn_y + Y(1 + b)(1 + n_x)}{2D} > 0. \tag{55}$$

The other results are established in a similar fashion.

Result 3 Free entry implies that an export subsidy reduces welfare. This result is independent of the segmentation/integration assumption.

Result 3 comes from propositions 2B and 4B; both this result and result 2 require assumption 3. If transport costs are positive and goods are close substitutes, then under free entry and segmented markets, an export subsidy will raise welfare, as in proposition 5 of this paper.

Our last two results concern the effect of policy on world welfare.

Result 4 Oligopoly implies that reciprocal import tariffs or export taxes reduce world welfare. This result is independent of the segmentation/integration assumption.

This is not quite so obvious if we recall that this is a local result in the neighborhood of zero taxes. In a competitive model there would be no local effect. But with the price/cost distortion of oligopoly, the reduction in firm output accompanying the reduced trade does have the local effect of reducing welfare.

Result 5 Free entry implies that world welfare is maximized by zero trade taxes and subsidies. This result is independent of the segmentation/integration assumption.

Unlike the oligopoly case, free entry implies that reciprocal tariffs or subsidies have no beneficial firm scale effect. Thus, the consumption distortion implied by either taxes or subsidies is welfare reducing. We should emphasize one final time that these results are not robust with respect to key assumptions, as is clear from our analysis of free entry with segmented markets when products are perfect substitutes and transport costs are positive. Nevertheless, we hope that the results are helpful in allowing us to organize our thinking and in enabling us to understand the role of market structure and entry assumptions.

References

Brander, J. A., and B. J. Spencer. 1985. Export subsidies and international market share rivalry. *Journal of International Economics* 18:83–100.

Dixit, A. K. 1984. International trade policy for oligopolistic industries. *Economic Journal Conference Papers* 94:1–16.

Eaton, J., and G. M. Grossman. 1986. Optimal trade and industrial policy under oligopoly. *Quarterly Journal of Economics* 101:383–406.

Horstmann, I., and J. R. Markusen. 1986. Up the average cost curve: Inefficient entry and the new protectionism. *Journal of International Economics* 20:225–247.

Krugman, P. R. 1984. Import protection as export promotion: International competition in the presence of oligopoly and economies of scale. In H. Kierzkowski (ed.), *Monopolistic Competition and International Trade*. Oxford: Oxford University Press.

Venables, A. J. 1985. Trade and trade policy with imperfect competition: The case of identical products and free entry. *Journal of International Economics* 19:1–20.

9 Optimal Trade and Industrial Policies for the U.S. Automobile Industry

Avinash K. Dixit

The traditional prescription of laissez-faire in the matter of international competition has recently faced serious theoretical challenge. The main new argument in this attack is the recognition of imperfect competition. This gives rise to a familiar distortion as prices diverge from marginal costs. More important, in oligopolistic industries equilibria allow positive pure profits, or rents, and it is in a country's selfish interest to capture more of these profits to add to its real national income. The general idea is that, by committing itself to a suitable policy, the government can change the outcome of the oligopoly in the favorable direction. Depending on the precise model of industry structure and conduct, all manner of taxes and subsidies on imports, exports, and domestic production can be justified. Recent surveys of this literature include Grossman and Richardson (1985), Dixit (1987a), and Venables (1985).

These developments may be welcome to many economists and policy advocates who favor such activism for a variety of reasons, but in the absence of serious empirical tests, the scope and significance of the theoretical results must remain doubtful. My aim here is to initiate such empirical work by using the U.S. automobile market as a case study. Both the theory and the data are so poor that the results are no more than preliminary suggestions. But I hope the tentative answers as well as the evident shortcomings of the study will stimulate further work.

The auto industry is an obvious candidate for such an exercise. The U.S.-Japan rivalry in this market has been prominent in recent years. The number of firms is small enough to raise suspicion of oligopoly. There is also reason to believe that a significant portion of the wage bill is monopoly rent to labor. On the other side, autos are an important part of consumer expenditure, and their prices have substantial effects on U.S. consumer surplus. Balancing these considerations to determine the optimal trade and domestic tax and subsidy policies is an important policy question.

There have been several empirical studies of the U.S. auto industry and the effects of the recent "voluntary" export restraints (VERs). Prominent among these are Feenstra (1984, 1985), Tarr and Morkre (1984), and Crandall (1984). However, all these authors assume the industry to be perfectly competitive. Gomez-Ibanez, Leone, and O'Connell (1983) do allow imperfect competition but assume special behavior rules by the U.S. and the Japanese firms.[1] I adopt a more flexible model that allows the data to determine the extent of monopoly or competition in the market. This is important in view of the theoretical finding of Eaton and Grossman (1986) that the optimum policies are sensitive to the assumptions in this regard. Bresnahan (1981) has a much richer model with product quality differentiation, and it can be extended to allow a more flexible equilibrium concept and to conduct policy analyses, but the task is too ambitious for an exploratory study such as this one. Later I offer some conjectures about the effects of incorporating quality differentiation.

Originally published in *Empirical Methods for International Trade*, ed. R. Feenstra (MIT Press, 1988).

There is another respect in which my aims differ from those of the mentioned studies, which estimate the costs of the actual VERs to the U.S. economy. I am trying to see if some other policies, specifically import tariffs and domestic production subsidies, can be deployed to bring net economic benefit to the United States. I ignore the problems of retaliation, GATT sanctions, or other international political repercussions; therefore, my answers are intended to be an upper bound on the possible benefits.

I focus on the most interesting aspect of the auto market for U.S. policy, namely, the rivalry between U.S. and Japanese firms. For the most part I assume that U.S. and Japanese cars are imperfect substitutes for each other but perfect substitutes within each nationality. For computational simplicity I take the demand system to be linear and the marginal costs to be constants. I model oligopolistic behavior as a Nash equilibrium with conjectural variations (CVs). The coefficients representing these conjectures are treated as parameters that measure the degree of competition or collusion in market conduct. Their values are determined from the data; the procedure is the "calibration" familiar from computable general equilibrium models.

The CV model has some serious shortcomings; see Friedman (1983) for a discussion. Of course, one does not have to believe that firms actually entertain such conjectures. One can say that the actual prices and quantities are ones that would result if firms acted in the assumed manner, and the implied CV parameters are a simple and intuitive summary measure of market conduct. I examine the outcomes for different years in this spirit.

The years I choose are 1979, 1980, and 1983. The first two form the base cases for the subsequent examination of optimum policies for these same years. The third allows us to understand the collusive effect of the VERs by posing the following question: If the actual outcome with the VERs were to be replicated in a CV model without VERs, how collusive would the conduct have to be? We know from Krishna (1984) that, in a Bertrand duopoly of one U.S. firm and one Japanese firm, VERs can greatly increase the implied collusion. My exercise allows a rough test of a similar effect for the actual oligopoly. The year 1983 was chosen because it was the first complete year of the VERs free from the effect of a serious recession and the last year for which the data I need were relatively easily available.

The validity of studying the effects of changing policies is far more problematic, for reasons of the Lucas critique. If the conjectures are not true behavioral parameters, then their values can change as the policy changes. Krishna (1984) shows that such is in fact the case for VERs. With tariffs Davidson (1984) shows that problems arise in a dynamic context. But in my static model we have no clear reason to suspect a change in the CV parameters as tariffs change. In the absence of an alternative that is at the same time logically superior and practically as manageable, I use the CV model for policy analyses with tariffs. This is done for the last two years in which there were no VERs, namely, 1979 and 1980.

The years offer quite a contrast. In 1979 the market as a whole was relatively buoyant, and the demand for large cars was strong. In 1980 the market weakened, and there was a sharp shift of demand toward smaller cars. The performance of U.S. firms deteriorated, and Japanese import penetration grew. It would be interesting to see how this translates into differences in market conduct and in the scope for welfare-improving trade policies.

For each year the model is calibrated to reproduce the initial equilibrium where only the most favored nation (MFN) tariff applied to Japanese imports. The effects of alternative policies are then examined. Because the data on demand elasticities and marginal costs are poor and subject to error, sensitivity analysis over quite a wide range of parameters is also carried out.

One must be cautious in drawing conclusions from such a crude and preliminary analysis. With this warning the broad findings here are as follows. The market was much more competitive in 1980 than in 1979. The case for strategic trade and antitrust policies was therefore weaker in 1980.

The roles and the significance of such policies depend on the size of monopoly rents in U.S. labor costs. First, suppose that there is no rent component. For the central cases of parameter values the optimal tariffs are moderate (8%) in 1980 and larger (17%) in 1979. For the lower end of the range of marginal costs, corresponding to a greater degree of implicit collusion in the market, even higher tariff rates can be justified. But the aggregate economic gains to the United States are quite small even when the tariff rates are large. In the central case tariffs added only \$17 million to U.S. real income in 1980 and only \$80 million in 1979; in no case could they add more than \$230 million. It should also be stressed that I am neglecting the possibility of retaliation; therefore the figures for the gains from tariffs are overestimates, possibly grossly so. The role of domestic antitrust policies is more significant than that of tariffs; they can add over \$700 million to U.S. real income in some cases.

Next consider the opposite case, in which as much as half of U.S. labor cost is monopoly rent. Now in the central case the optimum tariff rates, when tariffs are the only available instrument, rise to 16% in 1980 and 24% in 1979. The additions to U.S. real income are \$111 million and \$185 million, respectively. However, subsidies or other domestic antitrust policies are the appropriate instrument to solve the problem. On their own they can add \$1.34 billion to U.S. real income in 1980 and \$1.94 billion in 1979. When they are available, the role of tariffs shrinks dramatically, to 5% in 1980 and 11% in 1979.

In section 1 I describe the model. In section 2 I discuss the data and the nature of the initial equilibrium. In section 3 I examine the implied optimal policies. The sensitivity of the results over the ranges of uncertainty in some parameter values and assumptions is examined in section 4. Section 5 offers some concluding remarks and suggestions for future work.

1 The Model

Let the subscripts 1 and 2 denote U.S. and Japanese cars, respectively. Other imports, mostly from Europe, are less important in comparison and are ignored. Denote prices by p_1 and p_2 and aggregate quantities by Q_1 and Q_2. The demand functions are assumed to be

$$Q_1 = A_1 - B_1 p_1 + K p_2, \tag{1}$$

$$Q_2 = A_2 + K p_1 - B_2 p_2. \tag{2}$$

All the parameters are positive, and $(B_1 B_2 - K^2) > 0$. The corresponding inverse demand functions are

$$p_1 = a_1 - b_1 Q_1 - k Q_2, \tag{3}$$

$$p_2 = a_2 - k Q_1 - b_2 Q_2. \tag{4}$$

Again, all the parameters are positive, as is $(b_1 b_2 - k^2)$. This demand system can be derived by maximizing, subject to the budget constraint

$$Q_0 + p_1 Q_1 + p_2 Q_2 = \text{income},$$

an aggregate utility function of the form

$$u = Q_0 + U(Q_1, Q_2),$$

where Q_0 is the aggregate consumption of a competitive numeraire good measured in real dollars and U is a quadratic subutility function for the automobile sector defined by

$$U(Q_1, Q_2) = a_1 Q_1 + a_2 Q_2 - \tfrac{1}{2}(b_1 Q_1^2 + b_2 Q_2^2 + 2k Q_1 Q_2). \tag{5}$$

Then the consumer surplus C is given by

$$C = U(Q_1, Q_2) - p_1 Q_1 - p_2 Q_2. \tag{6}$$

The marginal costs are assumed to be constants. The U.S. unit production cost is denoted by c_1, and the Japanese unit cost of production and transport to the U.S. market by c_2. Not all these costs need be resource costs; in particular, there may be monopoly rents to labor. Assuming fixed input coefficients and a constant fraction of each worker's compensation to be rent, we can use a composite parameter r_1 to measure the rent per U.S. car.[2]

Only the United States is assumed to be active in policy. It has two instruments, an import tariff t in U.S. dollars per Japanese car, and a home production subsidy of s in U.S. dollars per U.S. car. The effect of s is to reduce the private cost to U.S. firms and thereby bring the market price of U.S. cars closer to the true social marginal cost. This lowers the domestic distortion. However, we do not normally think of solving the problem of monopoly by subsidizing the monopolist. There are several reasons. First, there may be adverse distributional effects. Second, and more important, if the government does not have independent and accurate information about the firms' costs, there will be incentive effects as the firms overstate their costs or add managerial slack with impunity. If the government cannot police price-fixing conspiracies well, then firms in an industry will have additional gains from cartelization, namely, the larger subsidies that the government then offers to achieve a lower price. For all these reasons a subsidy as such may be poor policy. In my model it should be interpreted as an imperfect proxy for antitrust policy in its effect of price reduction. If there is U.S. labor monopoly rent, then production subsidies, by increasing the sales of U.S. cars, also raise the amount of such rent. This is another feature that makes a subsidy a desirable policy, but the remarks about the danger of exploitation of such policies by the monopolist apply with at least equal force to unionized labor.

If there were sizable exports of U.S. cars, we would have to distinguish a subsidy for home sales from a production subsidy. Fortunately for the analysis, this is not a significant issue.[3]

Now consider a typical U.S. firm. Denote its sales by q_1. Its profit[4] is $(p_1 - c_1 + s)q_1$. When q_1 is chosen to maximize this, we have the first-order condition

$$p_1 + c_1 + s + q_1 \frac{dp_1}{dq_1} = 0, \tag{7}$$

where the derivative represents the firm's belief about the effect on its price if it sells another unit, taking into account its conjectures about the output responses of other firms. One can split this conjecture into components corresponding to the separate responses of home and foreign firms, but that is not necessary for my purpose. If each firm assumes that the others hold their outputs constant, that is, if the oligopoly is conducted along Cournot lines, then $dp_1/dq_1 = -b_1$. If conduct is more competitive, that is, if each firm believes its price is more nearly constant with respect to its output variations, then dp_1/dq_1 is negative but numerically smaller. In the limiting case of perfect competition, each firm assumes $dp_1/dq_1 = 0$.

Suppose that there are n_1 U.S. firms. By aggregating the first-order conditions over them, we have

$$p_1 - c_1 + s - Q_1 V_1 = 0, \tag{8}$$

where V_1 is the aggregate version of the conjectural variation parameter. It equals b_1/n_1 in the case of Cournot conduct. It is numerically smaller if the oligopoly is more competitive than that, and 0 in the case of perfect competition.

The effects of the U.S. firms' conduct on the market outcome are thus channeled through the single parameter V_1. However, intuition about the conduct is better served by looking at the matter from a different angle The same market equilibrium would arise if there were $n_1^* = b_1/V_1$ U.S. firms (allowed to be noninteger for this purpose) behaving in a Cournot manner. Call n_1^* the Cournot-equivalent number of U.S. firms, and compare this with the actual number. If $n_1 < n_1^*$, then the actual conduct must be more competitive than Cournot; otherwise, less. An equivalent procedure is to find the equilibrium prices that would arise if the n_1 actual firms behaved in a Cournot fashion. If these prices exceed the observed prices, then the actual conduct must be more competitive than Cournot; otherwise, less. I carry out these tests for each of the years to be considered in the next section.

Similarly, for the Japanese firms we have

$$p_2 - c_2 - t - Q_2 V_2 = 0. \tag{9}$$

The parameter V_2 can be interpreted in the same way.

The conditions (8) and (9) can be solved together with the demand equations (3) and (4) to obtain the equilibrium prices and quantities for any given policy configuration of s and t. Then we can calculate the consumer surplus as indicated in equation (6). Total U.S. welfare W is obtained by adding the consumer surplus, the profits of U.S. firms, any monopoly rent to U.S. labor, and the revenues of the U.S. government. Therefore

$$W = C + (p_1 - c_1 + s)Q_1 + r_1 Q_1 + (tQ_2 - sQ_1). \tag{10}$$

Distributional considerations can be captured by giving the components different weights; I do not consider this complication here.

This completes the specification of the model and allows us to proceed to an examination of the optimal policies. Explicit expressions can be found, but they are not informative in this context. Therefore I omit them and consider only the numerical values for the particular cases at hand. Interested readers will find the algebraic details in a related theoretical paper (Dixit 1988).

There are four policy configurations that are of particular interest. The first is the status quo, with the MFN tariff of 2.9% applied to Japanese imports and no significant antitrust measures (or the proxy production subsidies) applied to U.S. producers. Call the resulting welfare W_0. Next suppose that the subsidy is kept at 0 but that the tariff is chosen optimally, and write the welfare level as W_t. Third, suppose that trade is free but that the domestic antitrust policy, here represented by s, is chosen optimally. Suppose this yields W_s. Finally, let both s and t be at their jointly optimal levels; let the resulting welfare level be W_{ts}.

Once we obtain these figures, we can answer some questions of interest about trade policy. The first is the simplest: Are the tariffs that emerge from such economic optimization large in relation to the policies that are now in effect? The second is, How large are the economic welfare gains that are available from the pursuit of optimal tariffs? Here we must consider two cases separately, one where a domestic production subsidy or antitrust policy is not available and the other where it is. In the first case the gain from using an optimal tariff over the status quo is $(W_t - W_0)$. In the second case the contribution of the optimal tariff over and above what is possible with the subsidy is given by $(W_{ts} - W_s)$.

In section 3 I carry out this program for 1979 and 1980 for ranges of cost and demand parameters suggested by the data. The next section sets the stage by examining the data sources and determining such ranges.

2 The Data and Market Conduct

Table 1 summarizes the information on prices, quantities, costs, and demand elasticities for 1979 and 1980, obtained from statistical sources and the research literature. Here I explain the sources and the procedures in some detail.

The prices and quantities are obtained from the *Summary of Trade and Tariff Information*, U.S. International Trade Commission Publication 841 (Washington, D.C.: International Trade Commission, June 1984). The prices are unit values, the U.S. ones being at the manufacturing level, and the Japanese ones at the cost-including-freight (CIF) import stage. The quantities for Japanese imports are straightforward. Those for U.S. cars were obtained as U.S. production minus exports plus imports from Canada. Other captive U.S. imports were not published here on a comparable basis and were ignored. Their numbers are small enough not to affect the results to any great degree.[5]

Costs raise difficult issues of measurement as well as of interpretation. The main question of interpretation is the contribution of capital costs to marginal costs. A

Table 1
Data and parameters

Parameter	1979	1980	1983
Quantities (millions)			
Q_1	8.341	6.581	7.020
Q_2	1.546	1.819	2.112
Prices (\$)			
p_1	5,951	6,407	7,494
p_2	4,000	4,130	5,239
Range of U.S. costs, c_1 **(\$)**			
Low	5,000	5,700	6,600
Central	5,400	6,100	7,000
High	5,600	6,300	7,300
Range of Japanese costs, c_2 **(\$)**			
Low	3,000	3,400	4,000
Central	3,400	3,800	4,400
High	3,600	4,000	4,600
Range of total market elasticity			
Low	0.75	0.75	0.75
Central	1.00	1.00	1.00
High	1.50	1.50	1.50
Range of elasticity of substitution			
Low	1.50	1.50	1.50
Central	2.00	2.00	2.00
High	3.00	3.00	3.00

Sources and calculations are explained in the text.

satisfactory treatment would require an intertemporal optimization problem. In years when the capacity constraint is binding, its shadow price will appear as a component of the marginal cost. This is quite difficult to do properly. It negates my year-by-year approach. Inflation and the complexities of the corporate income tax have to be handled. Finally, the data on capital and investment are hard to find and use at the required level of disaggregation. For all these reasons I have chosen to neglect capital costs altogether. The cost figures used (comprising labor and material costs) should then be thought of as a lower bound for the actual costs. The implied markups of the observed prices over these cost figures, and therefore the implied degree of monopoly in the market, should be thought of as an upper bound for the corresponding realities. The resulting role of trade policy is likewise an exaggeration. The extent of the bias will vary from one year to another; one would suspect capacity constraints to be more important, and therefore the bias to be greater, in 1979 than in 1980. All this should be kept in mind when interpreting the results in section 3.

Even labor and material costs are hard to measure and allocate accurately, and different sources give different answers. I have used findings from alternative approaches to establish the range for sensitivity analysis.

Three approaches were available for U.S. production costs. The first is based on the Census of Manufactures. The Industry Series publication MC82-I-37A (Washington, D.C.: Government Printing Office) gives annual ratios of payroll and material costs to the value of shipments for SIC category 3711 (motor vehicles and car bodies). One would ideally like to have the corresponding figures for category 37111 (passenger cars). However, nearly 70% of the value of shipments of motor vehicles and car bodies comes from passenger cars; therefore, the error should be tolerable. The ratios are as follows: 1979, 85%; 1980, 89%. Using the earlier figures for unit values, we get unit costs: 1979, $5,058; 1980, $5,702.

The second approach follows Abernathy, Clark, and Kantrow (1981). They estimate the total costs of production of a subcompact car in the United States in 1979 at $4,875, of which $1,485 comes from payroll costs, and $2,584 from component and material costs. (The two add up to $4,069, which is 85% of the total, in conformity with the Census of Manufactures figure.) They state that the average Ford car is the equivalent in cost of 1.38 subcompacts. If we assume the same for the U.S. industry as a whole, the cost figure for 1979 becomes $5,615.

To get the figure for 1980 by this method, I applied the 1980/1979 ratio of the automobile industry compensation rate change from unpublished Bureau of Labor Statistics data ($16.29/$13.68), and a 2% factor for productivity improvements (this is the cyclically corrected average annual rate for the period 1979 to 1983), to the payroll costs, and the 1980/1979 ratio of the U.S. wholesale price index from the International Monetary Fund's *International Financial Statistics* (100/87.6) to the component and materials costs. The resulting cost figure for 1980 was $6,423.

The third approach used profit figures from U.S. company reports, aggregated in the U.S. Department of Commerce publication *The U.S. Automobile Industry 1982* (Washington, D.C.: Government Printing Office, 1983). The totals from operations (not subtracting depreciation and amortization, in conformity with my neglect of capital costs) were as follows: 1979, $8.3 billion; 1980, $2.5 billion. If all of this is attributed to passenger cars, we can use the quantity figures from the U.S. ITC to get the operating profits per car: 1979, $980; 1980, $380. Subtracting these from the unit values, we have unit costs: 1979, $4,971; 1980, $6,027. These profits are overestimates because in reality some of the profit is attributable to other operations of the same companies. Therefore the cost figures are underestimates. This reinforces the bias already built in by the omission of capital costs.

The ranges in table 1, for example, $5,000–$5,600 for 1979, were chosen to span the three approaches. The central cases, for example, $5,400 in 1979, were chosen slightly above the mean of the range to make partial allowance for the downward biases discussed. Even then, I suspect that the figures at the upper ends of the ranges are the more likely ones.

The 1979 or 1980 range was converted to 1983 by using an index number procedure similar to that already outlined. However, the central case figures for these two years yielded over $7,300 for 1983. Because the unit value for that year is $7,494, the cost figure is quite inconsistent with the sharp recovery in the profitability of the U.S. auto industry in that year. To accommodate for this, I took $7,300 to be the top of the range, and $7,000 as the center.

A similar variety of methods was used to estimate the delivered unit costs of Japanese cars to the U.S. market. Abernathy, Clark, and Kantrow (1981) estimate the production cost advantage of a Japanese subcompact to be $1,670 in 1979. This stems entirely from a labor cost advantage, part of which is embodied in the cost of purchased components. Katz (1980) estimates a smaller figure of approximately $1,000, but Abernathy, Clark, and Kantrow claim that this neglects the contribution of purchased components. Toder (1978, p. 151) estimates the Japanese cost advantage to be 16.8%, which in 1979 translates into the still smaller figure of $819 for a subcompact. Bresnahan (1981) finds that, once we control for all relevant attributes, such as size and horsepower, the marginal costs of U.S. and Japanese autos are equal. Fuss and Waverman (1986) find little underlying technological advantage for Japan but find a significant cost advantage in 1980 because of differences in capacity utilization and exchange rate differences. A round figure average of all these approaches is $1,000.

We have two estimates of freight costs, $400 for 1979 (Katz 1980) and $650 for 1975 (Toder 1978, p. 153). Toder's estimate appears to have a firmer base in the schedules supplied by the Massport Authority, but freight to Boston from Japan probably greatly overstates the cost to the average U.S. market point. If we take $500 as a reasonable figure for 1979, the range of net delivered cost advantage for a Japanese subcompact becomes $500.

The subcompact equivalent of our 1979 range of U.S. unit costs is $3,600–$4,060. Subtracting the average Japanese advantage yields $3,100–$3,560. To reflect the greater uncertainty, I have taken a somewhat wider range of $3,000–$3,600, with the central case of $3,400. To obtain the corresponding figures for 1980 and 1983, I constructed an index based on changes in labor compensation (the manufacturing wages index from the IMF, *International Financial Statistics*), productivity (figure averaged from calculations for Toyota and Nissan in Cusumano 1985), material costs (IMF's WPI), exchange rate changes (IMF), and ocean freight costs (World Bank, *Commodity Trade and Price Trends*).

For demand Toder (1978) estimates a total market demand elasticity of about 1 and an elasticity of substitution between U.S. and Japanese cars of about 2. These seem to be the most cited figures in the literature and are used by others, for example, Tarr and Morkre (1984). I take them to be central values and use the ranges shown in table 1.

The parameters of the system of equations (1)—(4) can be calculated by using the actual prices and quantities and the assumed elasticities. This is the process of calibration. Consider the direct demand functions (1) and (2). There are five parameters to be determined. In any one year substitution of the actual prices and quantities give us two relations among them. Further work is based on the elasticity information.

Because U.S. and Japanese cars are being treated as imperfect substitutes, I interpret the total market elasticity as the effect of an equiproportionate rise in the price of the two on the corresponding (dual) quantity aggregate. Thus let

$$p_1 = P_{10}P, \quad p_2 = P_{20}P,$$

where P_{10}, P_{20} are the initial prices and P is the proportional change factor. The dual quantity index is

$$\begin{aligned} Q &= P_{10}Q_1 + P_{20}Q_2 \\ &= (P_{10}A_1 + P_{20}A_2) - (B_1P_{10}^2 + B_2P_{20}^2 - 2KP_{10}P_{20})P. \end{aligned}$$

The total market elasticity ε is then the elasticity of Q with respect to P, evaluated at the initial point $P = 1$. This gives us the third relation among the parameters.

The elasticity of substitution is defined as

$$\sigma = -\frac{d\log(Q_1/Q_2)}{d\log(p_1/p_2)}.$$

Substituting the assumed value of σ gives us a fourth relation. However, in general, equations (1) and (2) define Q_1/Q_2 as a function of the vector (p_1, p_2), not of the single ratio p_1/p_2. Explicitly, we have

$$\frac{Q_1}{Q_2} = \frac{A_1(1/p_2) - B_1(p_1/p_2) + K}{A_2(1/p_2) + K(p_1/p_2) - B_2}.$$

If this is to be a function of (p_1/p_2) alone, at least locally, then the partial derivative of the right-hand side with respect to $(1/p_2)$ at the initial equilibrium point should be 0. The condition for this turns out to be

$$P_{10}(A_1K + A_2B_1) = P_{20}(A_2K + A_1B_2).$$

This is the fifth relation that completes the required set.

Table 2
Demand parameters in the central case

Parameter	1979	1980	1983
Direct demand function			
A_1 (million)	16.590	12.722	14.040
A_2 (million)	3.236	3.986	4.224
B_1	1,555	1,160	1,099
B_2	762	884	736
K	240	259	232
Inverse demand function			
a_1	11,902	12,814	14,988
a_2	8,000	8,260	10,478
b_1 (10^{-4})	6.758	9.226	9.748
b_2 (10^{-4})	13.794	12.102	14.558
k (10^{-4})	2.132	2.701	3.083

Notation and calculations are explained in the text.

The values of the demand parameters are not directly informative, but for completeness I have shown in table 2 the sets for the central cases of elasticities for 1979, 1980, and 1983.

Economically more interesting information is to be had by computing the implied conduct. As explained in section 1, this can be done by comparing the actual prices with those that would prevail if the actual firms behaved in a Cournot manner or by comparing the Cournot-equivalent number of firms corresponding to the actual conduct with the actual numbers. Because actual U.S. firms are not identical, we need the right proxy for their number. This is as usual the number equivalent of the U.S. firms' Herfindahl index of concentration, but its value changes a great deal according to whether we take each U.S. company or each division to be the appropriate noncooperative profit-maximizing unit. In the absence of any clear reason to select one, I have shown the calculations on both bases.

The results for the central cases of costs and elasticities are given in table 3. We see that the conduct in 1980 was a lot more competitive than Cournot regardless of whether we use the company basis or the division basis for the United States. Using the division basis, we observe that the actual prices fall halfway between those that would arise under Cournot and Bertrand behavior. The outcome is a lot less competitive in 1979; if we use the division basis for the United States, then the Japanese firms are quite close to playing Cournot, and the U.S. divisions are closer to Cournot than to Bertrand. On the whole this confirms the impression that there was a greater degree of monopoly in the market and therefore a greater role for strategic trade policy in 1979 than in 1980.

The outcomes for 1983 show the extent of collusion that would have replicated the actual prices and quantities observed under the VERs. Recall that the result should give us an idea of whether the VERs make the conduct substantially more collusive. Here we find strong evidence of increased collusion on the part of the Japanese firms. When the U.S. firms are considered on a division basis, the Japanese firms are implicitly acting a little more collusive than Cournot. This degree of collusion exceeds the 1979 level by a little and the 1980 level by a lot. However, collusion by the U.S. firms does not appear to be greatly strengthened by the VERs. Perhaps their competition with one another is strong enough that the Japanese firms' restraint does not bring forth parallel restraint from U.S. firms. If this observation is borne out by further work, then it says that the presence of imperfect competition did not cause much additional harm from the VERs to U.S. consumers, or greater profit to U.S. firms, than that indicated by earlier studies based on perfect competition.

Before we can carry out the policy exercises, we need one more item of information, namely, the labor monopoly rent. This again poses serious problems of measurement and interpretation. Over this period, labor compensation in the U.S. auto industry was 65% above that in U.S. manufacturing as a whole (Munger 1985, table 3). If the difference is solely due to union monopoly, then the share of rent in auto labor compensation is about 40%. To the extent that there is human capital in auto labor relative to overall manufacturing labor, the rent component is less; to the extent that there is rent in all manufacturing labor, it is more. If we think that union power is

Table 3
Market conduct in the central case

Conduct indicator	1979	1980	1983
Number equivalents of Herfindahl indexes			
United States (company basis)	2.250	2.077	2.262
United States (division basis)	6.931	6.679	7.937
Japan	4.040	4.034	4.350
Cournot-equivalent firm numbers corresponding to actual prices			
United States	10.174	19.116	13.851
Japan	4.464	10.487	4.161
U.S. car prices in $			
If actual firms behave Cournot			
U.S. company basis	7,280	8,099	9,217
U.S. division basis	6,176	6,910	7,818
Actual conduct	5,951	6,407	7,494
Bertrand conduct	5,400	6,100	7,000
Japanese car prices in $			
If actual firms behave Cournot			
U.S. company basis	4,128	4,525	5,320
U.S. division basis	4,056	4,451	5,233
Actual conduct	4,000	4,130	5,239
Bertrand conduct	3,400	3,800	4,400

less important in the Japanese auto industry, the existence of a 30–35% premium for auto labor above average manufacturing labor in Japan supports the former view.

Some indirect evidence from another industry (trucking) comes from Rose (1985). She finds that deregulation led to a reduction of 30–50% in the union premium over nonunion wages.

All this is indirect and imprecise, but it seems that some recognition of the issue is important. I make two extreme assumptions that span the likely range of the effect. One is that there is no labor monopoly rent; the other is that it comprises half of the wage bill, amounting to $1,000 per car in 1979 and $1,200 in 1980.

3 Results

Now we can carry out the various policy comparisons discussed at the end of section 1. This is done for 1980 and 1979. Remember that because the CV model would be inappropriate for policy analyses under VERs, the year 1983 is not considered further.

My procedure is as follows. First I consider the optimum tariff and subsidy policies for the central cases of the parameter values for 1979 and 1980, and then I examine the sensitivity over the parameter ranges discussed. I consider the no-rent cases for both years first and the cases where labor monopoly rent is half of the wage bill immediately afterward.

Let us begin with table 4, which covers 1980 for the no-rent case and the central values of the other parameters. The last column shows the full optimum, where both a tariff and a subsidy are used optimally. The subsidy solves the domestic monopoly problem and makes the U.S. price equal to cost. Once this is done, the tariff has a

Table 4
Policy calculations for the central case, 1980

Variable	Unit	MFN tariff	Optimum tariff	Optimum subsidy	Optimum tariff and subsidy
t	$/car	100	298	0	211
s	$/car	0	0	372	325
p_1	$	6,407	6,409	6,053	6,100
p_2	$	4,130	4,309	4,030	4,222
Q_1	million	6.361	6.405	6.745	6.741
Q_2	million	1.993	1.835	1.990	1.832
Japan profit	$ billion	0.458	0.387	0.457	0.386
U.S. profit	$ billion	1.953	1.980	2.196	2.193
U.S. consumer surplus	$ billion	24.493	24.136	27.011	26.327
Tariff revenue	$ billion	0.199	0.546	0	0.387
Subsidy cost	$ billion	0	0	2.512	2.193
Total U.S. welfare	$ billion	26.645	26.662	26.696	26.714
Gain over MFN	$ million	0	17	51	69

relatively small role of profit shifting. The optimal tariff of \$211 per Japanese car means an ad valorem rate of 5.5%. This is nearly twice as large as the MFN tariff but still quite moderate when contrasted to historic rates or the ones often talked about in recent policy debates in the United States.

When a subsidy is not available, the tariff indirectly serves the function of reducing the domestic distortion: A higher tariff means greater sales of U.S. cars, which is a welfare gain because the price exceeds the marginal cost. At the same time, however, the analogous trade distortion is worsened. For a linear demand the former effect is the more important; Eaton and Grossman (1986) examine the general case. Of course the primary role of the tariff in this context is that of shifting the profits away from the Japanese firms. Now the optimum tariff rate is 7.8%, which is quite sizable. The decline in the volume of Japanese imports from 1.993 to 1.835 million is impressive, and in these terms the tariff is nearly as restrictive as the VERs were.

More important than tariff rates or import volumes are the dollar values of the economic gains to the United States. Table 4 shows these to be quite small. When a subsidy is not available, for example, the optimal tariff confers an aggregate gain of only \$17 million over the MFN tariff. As usual, there are much larger redistributions concealed behind the small aggregate. U.S. firms' profits go up by \$27 million, and U.S. government revenue by \$347 million, whereas U.S. consumer surplus goes down by \$357 million. Japanese firms' profits decline by \$71 million. Similarly, when a subsidy is available, using the tariff yields an additional aggregate welfare gain of only \$18 million, but there is a net swing in government revenue of over \$706 million.

When a subsidy to domestic production is the only available instrument, it has the direct role of reducing the domestic distortion as well as the indirect role of capturing foreign profits by squeezing their demand. We see that the two functions combine to yield an optimum subsidy that takes the domestic price a little below the marginal cost. The reason is a familiar one: For the first bit of subsidy beyond the point where $p_1 = c_1$, the domestic deadweight burden from driving price below marginal cost is of the second order, whereas the gain from profit capture is of the first order. The use of a subsidy alone produces an aggregate welfare gain over MFN trade of \$51 million. This is not much either, but it is quite a lot more than the contributions of the tariff. In this sense and recalling that the subsidy was intended as a modeling proxy for antitrust policy, it appears that for the U.S. auto industry in 1980, trade policy was less important than antitrust policy, and the absolute importance of either was not large.

In 1979 the market outcome was more monopolistic. This shows up in the policy results of table 5. The optimum tariff is 16.8% when a subsidy is not available and 12% when used in conjunction with an optimal subsidy. The import quantity reductions (down to 1.32 million) are large enough to make the U.S. industry's and labor unions' mouths water. However, the aggregate welfare gains are still quite small. When no subsidy is used, an optimal tariff yields \$80 million more than the MFN tariff. When an optimal subsidy is available, the further contribution of the tariff is only \$58 million. Once again, domestic antitrust policy on its own is considerably more impor-

Table 5
Policy calculations for the central case, 1979

Variable	Unit	MFN tariff	Optimum tariff	Optimum subsidy	Optimum tariff and subsidy
t	\$/car	100	570	0	408
s	\$/car	0	0	673	611
p_1	\$	5,951	5,957	5,339	5,400
p_2	\$	4,000	4,381	3,882	4,216
Q_1	million	8.295	8.378	9.218	9.204
Q_2	million	1.618	1.329	1.561	1.321
Japan profit	\$ billion	0.809	0.546	0.752	0.539
U.S. profit	\$ billion	4.571	4.663	5.645	5.627
U.S. consumer surplus	\$ billion	27.918	27.310	33.463	32.421
Tariff revenue	\$ billion	0.162	0.758	0	0.539
Subsidy cost	\$ billion	0	0	6.206	5.627
Total U.S. welfare	\$ billion	32.651	32.731	32.902	32.960
Gain over MFN	\$ million	0	80	251	309

tant: The optimum subsidy on its own yields a welfare gain of $251 million over MFN trade. However, even this figure is not impressive enough to make it a major policy issue. After all, it is only a little over a dollar per capita.

Let us turn to the corresponding calculations when half of U.S. labor compensation is monopoly rent. Tables 6 and 7 show the results for 1980 and 1979, respectively. The first point to note is the dramatic increase in the optimum tariff rates when they are the only available instruments. For 1980 the rate goes up from the 7.8% of table 4 to 15.8% in table 6; for 1979 we have 16.8% in table 5 and 23.8% in table 7. The additional cuts in the volume of imports are equally dramatic. In 1980 the introduction of rent considerations causes an additional cut of 255,000 in Japanese imports and an increase of 112,000 in the sales of U.S. cars; for 1979 the figures are 149,000 and 126,000, respectively.

The second point to note is the equally dramatic absence of any role for tariffs when optimum domestic subsidies are used. If anything, the tariff rates in the first-best columns are a little lower when rent is allowed than when it is not. This is because the high subsidies cut import competition so severely that there is little scope for tariffs to do anything more.

The theory of policy hierarchy under perfect competition tells us that a domestic distortion is best remedied by a domestic tax or subsidy policy that acts directly on that margin (Bhagwati 1971). There is no similar general theorem under imperfect competition, but the result works in the present instance. The labor market distortion is best met by a subsidy. In stipulating a constant rent per U.S. car, we have implicitly assumed fixed input coefficients. Therefore, a production subsidy serves the purpose. If capital-labor substitution were allowed, an employment subsidy would be better still.

Table 6
Policies with labor monopoly rent, 1980[a]

Variable	Unit	MFN tariff	Optimum tariff	Optimum subsidy	Optimum tariff and subsidy
t	\$/car	100	604	0	182
s	\$/car	0	0	1,632	1,592
p_1	\$	6,407	6,412	4,860	4,900
p_2	\$	4,130	4,588	3,997	4,163
Q_1	million	6.361	6.473	8.121	8.117
Q_2	million	1.993	1.590	1.710	1.574
Japan profit	\$ billion	0.458	0.293	0.337	0.285
U.S. profit	\$ billion	1.953	2.022	3.183	3.179
Labor monopoly rent	\$ billion	7.633	7.768	9.745	9.741
U.S. consumer surplus	\$ billion	24.493	23.638	35.942	35.343
Tariff revenue	\$ billion	0.199	0.961	0	0.286
Subsidy cost	\$ billion	0	0	13.254	12.921
Total U.S. welfare	\$ billion	34.278	34.389	35.615	35.629
Gain over MFN	\$ billion	0	0.111	1.337	1.351

a. Labor rent \$1,200/U.S. car, other parameters as in central case.

Table 7
Policies with labor monopoly rent, 1979[a]

Variable	Unit	MFN tariff	Optimum tariff	Optimum subsidy	Optimum tariff and subsidy
t	\$/car	100	812	0	358
s	\$/car	0	0	1,767	1,713
p_1	\$	5,951	5,959	4,347	4,400
p_2	\$	4,000	4,577	3,823	4,115
Q_1	million	8.295	8.421	10.749	10.735
Q_2	million	1.618	1.180	1.368	1.157
Japan profit	\$ billion	0.809	0.431	0.579	0.413
U.S. profit	\$ billion	4.571	4.710	7.673	7.655
Labor monopoly rent	\$ billion	8.295	8.421	10.748	10.735
U.S. consumer surplus	\$ billion	27.918	27.040	43.458	42.516
Tariff revenue	\$ billion	0.162	0.959	0	0.414
Subsidy cost	\$ billion	0	0	18.995	18.390
Total U.S. welfare	\$ billion	40.945	41.130	42.885	42.930
Gain over MFN	\$ billion	0	0.185	1.940	1.985

a. Labor rent \$1,000/U.S. car, other parameters as in central case.

We can get an idea of the quantitative significance of the second-best tariff policies in relation to the first-best. In 1980, with labor rent included, the optimal tariff alone increases U.S. welfare by $111 million. For the full first-best tariff policy, the figure is $1.351 billion. In 1979 the corresponding figures are $185 million and $1.985 billion, respectively. Thus the second-best policy captures only 8–9% of the welfare gain that is possible with first-best policies.

4 Sensitivity Analysis

I said before and would like to emphasize again that all these conclusions are preliminary and tentative. It would take a much more ambitious research project, with much better theory and data, to obtain reliable results. The best I can do at this point is to perform sensitivity analyses with the material available. In this section I report several such experiments, involving changes in the parameter values as well as in the model itself.

Let us begin with the cost and elasticity parameters. Their plausible ranges were examined earlier and are displayed in table 1. Now we can vary them over these ranges for the years 1979 and 1980 and find out the effects on the optimum tariff and subsidy policies and the implications for welfare gains.

Table 8 shows the effects of changing costs on the optimal tariffs in 1979 per Japanese car. Each pair of numbers corresponds to the indicated combination of U.S. and Japanese costs. The first number in each pair shows the optimal tariff when no subsidy is available, and the second number is the optimal tariff when an optimal subsidy is also used. For a given U.S. cost figure, the higher the Japanese cost, the lower the tariffs. For a given Japanese cost, higher U.S. costs correspond to lower tariffs when a subsidy is not used but higher ones when it is. In theory the formulas for the optimal tariffs involve the cost parameters c_i as well as the conjectures V_i. In the exercise conducted here a change in costs entails a recalibration of the model and therefore a change in the conjectures. The net result cannot be easily predicted by

Table 8
Sensitivity analysis for costs, 1979[a]

U.S. unit costs, c_1	Japanese unit costs, c_2 3,000	3,400	3,600
5,000	(918,648)	(654,388)	(508,245)
5,400	(841,677)	(570,408)	(420,259)
5,600	(798,691)	(524,418)	(371,266)

a. U.S. welfare comparisons:
(i) c_1 = \$5,000, c_2 = \$3,000.
Gain from optimum tariff over MFN tariff: $230 million.
Gain from optimum tariff and subsidy over optimum subsidy alone: $139 million.
(ii) c_1 = \$5,600, c_2 = \$3,600.
Gain from optimum tariff over MFN tariff: $27 million.
Gain from optimum tariff and subsidy over optimum subsidy alone: $25 million.

Table 9
Sensitivity analysis for costs, 1980[a]

U.S. unit costs, c_1	Japanese unit costs, c_2		
	3,400	3,800	4,000
5,700	(690,498)	(390,201)	(214,28)
6,100	(606,519)	(298,211)	(115,30)
6,300	(561,529)	(247,216)	(61,31)

a. U.S. welfare comparisons:
(i) $c_1 = \$5,700$, $c_2 = \$3,400$.
Gain from optimum tariff over MFN tariff: $145 million.
Gain from optimum tariff and subsidy over optimum subsidy alone: $98 million.
(ii) $c_1 = \$6,300$, $c_2 = \$4,000$.
Gain from optimum tariff over MFN tariff: $660,000.
Gain from optimum tariff and subsidy over optimum subsidy alone: $380,000.

intuition. But on the whole, higher costs are associated with more competitive conduct and thus with lower tariffs, as we can see by scanning the table from the upper left to the lower right.

The clearest conclusion from table 8 is that tariff rates are highly sensitive to costs. Therefore the design of good policies makes it essential to have accurate cost information. This is an important point to remember when we think about future research. Next, for the low end of the cost range and therefore at the high end of the range of implied degree of monopoly in the market, the tariff rates are very large, sometimes over 30%. However, even in the most extreme case the aggregate U.S. welfare gains from the use of tariffs are not large. In the case of the top left pair of numbers in table 8, the gain from an optimum tariff over the MFN tariff is $230 million, and the contribution of the tariff when the subsidy is also available is only $139 million. It should also be borne in mind that the cost figures I used are biased downward, and the lower ends of the ranges are not likely to be relevant.

The sensitivity of tariff rates to costs in 1980 is similar. Table 9 gives the details. The welfare gains are much smaller. At the upper end of the cost range, the gain of $660,000 from an optimum tariff when a subsidy is not available and of $380,000 when it is are really minuscule numbers.

Tables 10 and 11 show the sensitivity of the tariff rates to variations in the total and substitution demand elasticities in the two years. Two offsetting influences are at work. Inelastic demand on its own is conducive to greater market power. But, to be consistent with the observed prices and costs, an inelastic demand entails more competitive conduct. We see that the net effect of the two is quite small. This is fortunate, because the estimates of these elasticities are even less reliable than those of the costs.

The remaining sensitivity exercises involve changing some of the assumptions of the model. First, the policy analyses up to this point incorporated the standard partial equilibrium assumption that any subsidies were financed, or tax revenues were disbursed, by nondistorting means. This is clearly not the case. Although the deadweight loss associated with a marginal dollar of tax revenues is not known with any degree

Table 10
Sensitivity analysis for elasticities, 1979

Total demand elasticity	Elasticity of substitution 1.50	2.00	3.00
0.75	(590,425)	(612,402)	(624,364)
1.00	(537,432)	(570,408)	(593,370)
1.50	(445,445)	(497,421)	(539,381)

Table 11
Sensitivity analysis for elasticities, 1980

Total demand elasticity	Elasticity of substitution 1.50	2.00	3.00
0.75	(303,215)	(322,210)	(338,199)
1.00	(273,217)	(298,211)	(321,201)
1.50	(221,221)	(255,215)	(289,204)

of precision, it seems important to examine the effect of using a plausible nonzero figure. Hausman (1985) reports that, for some particular tax reform exercises, such as 10% and 30% income tax cuts for prime age males, the ratio of the deadweight loss to the tax revenue is 15–20%. I have used 20% as a plausible figure and calculated the effects on optimum policies in 1979. The policy packages being studied are therefore ones where the net revenues from taxes and subsidies in the auto industry are offset by changing the rest of the distorting tax system, leaving government expenditures on goods and services constant. The results are shown in table 12. They should be contrasted with those in table 5, where the deadweight loss effects were assumed absent.

We saw earlier that the other net welfare effects of tariff and subsidy policies were relatively small. It is therefore not surprising that they are overwhelmed by the reduction in the deadweight losses of the general tax system, made possible by the revenues available from auto industry taxation. The optimum tariff is much higher, going from \$570 per car in table 5 to \$791 in table 12. More dramatically, the optimum subsidy acting on its own changes from \$673 (12.6% of the price) to −\$357 (a *tax* of 5.6% of the price). This harms consumers and producers quite a lot, but the net revenue turnaround of nearly \$9 billion means a reduction in the deadweight burden of \$1.8 billion. In the final reckoning in table 12 the optimum tariff yields a gain over MFN trade of \$219 million, of which \$189 million is accounted for by the deadweight loss reduction. For the optimum domestic tax the deadweight loss reduction gives \$551 million, which more than offsets losses to consumers and producers, leaving a net of \$97 million. When tariffs and domestic taxes are jointly optimized,[6] there is less intraindustry substitution and therefore less deadweight loss in auto consumption. The revenue aspects therefore become even more important, and both tariffs and

Table 12
Effect of existing distortions in the tax system[a]

Variable	Unit	MFN tariff	Optimum tariff	Optimum subsidy	Optimum tariff and subsidy
t	\$/car	100	791	0	922
s	\$/car	0	0	−354	−487
p_1	\$	5,951	5,959	6,271	6,402
p_2	\$	4,000	4,560	3,938	4,692
Q_1	million	8.295	8.417	7.782	7.759
Q_2	million	1.618	1.193	1.742	1.199
Japan profit	\$ billion	0.809	0.440	0.937	0.444
U.S. profit	\$ billion	4.571	4.706	4.023	3.999
U.S. consumer surplus	\$ billion	27.918	27.062	25.448	23.319
Tariff revenue	\$ billion	0.162	0.944	0	1.105
Subsidy cost	\$ billion	0	0	−2.757	−3.779
Reduction in DWB	\$ billion	0.032	0.189	0.551	0.977
Total U.S. welfare	\$ billion	32.682	32.901	32.779	33.179
Gain over MFN	\$ million	0	219	97	497

a. Ratio of deadweight burden to tax revenue is .2; other parameters are as in the central case for 1979. Negative subsidies are domestic taxes, and the corresponding "costs" are revenues.

domestic taxes are high. The effect of the reduction in the deadweight loss of the general tax system is nearly \$1 billion, of which only half is left as net gain after the costs to auto consumers and producers are subtracted.

The conclusion from this exercise is that existing distortions in the tax system have a powerful influence on the optimal policies for an industry, and the usual neglect of such effects in partial equilibrium analysis is a poor practice.

5 Concluding Comments

I am painfully aware of the many shortcomings of this work. Greater disaggregation would bring out further margins of substitution, leading to higher figures for the costs of monopoly or other inefficiencies.[7] For example, Bresnahan (1981) finds substantially greater costs of imperfect competition (over \$7 billion), in contrast to my few hundred million difference between the status quo and the first-best policy. Second, it would be a great improvement to have the demand parameters estimated by systematic econometrics, instead of calibrating them using each year's prices and quantities and outside estimates of elasticities. Third, capital costs need to be handled better in both the theory and the empirical work. Fourth, conjectural variations are not a good basis for the theory of oligopoly, and a better, workable alternative should be sought. Finally, the functional forms (linear demand and constant marginal cost) should be improved. As I have said repeatedly, this exercise is intended as no more than a tentative exploration into the empiricism of trade policy under oligopoly. The various exercises on the data and the numerous tables of results are merely what becomes of back-of-the-envelope calculations in the age of the personal computer. I am working on some of the extensions just mentioned and hope that others will be stimulated to do better.

Notes

I am grateful to Robert Feenstra for his help with ideas and data throughout this research. Timothy Bresnahan, Robert Crandall, John Kwoka, Nancy Rose, and my discussant, Jonathan Eaton, also gave helpful comments. The research was supported by the National Science Foundation under grant SES-8509536.

A shorter paper based on some of this work is Dixit (1987b).

1. They assume that the Japanese firms are collusive profit-maximizing Stackelberg leaders and that the U.S. firms' reaction functions are one of three rules of thumb that can hold either price or quantity constant or make equal percentage changes in the two.

2. The assumption that r_1 is constant raises the specter of the Lucas critique once again. Jonathan Eaton, in his comment, suggests a better model that holds promise for future work.

3. In 1981 the United States exported about 469,000 cars to Canada and imported about 564,000 from that country. This is best seen as a production rationalization arrangement. All other U.S. exports of complete cars amounted to only 66,000 units, most of them large luxury cars sold to oil-producing countries. U.S. exports of chassis and components are similarly concentrated in its trade with Canada (World Motor Vehicles Data and U.S. ITC).

4. This omits costs that are fixed for the purpose of the production decision being considered here. However, the question of how to apply this criterion in practice is a difficult one. More on this point later.

5. In an earlier paper (Dixit 1987b) reporting on a part of this work, quantities from World Motor Vehicles Data were used. There are nonnegligible differences, largely because the ITC figures include specialty vehicles and figures for Puerto Rico. I have shifted to ITC data partly to conform to the usage of Feenstra (1985) and of Tarr and Morkre (1984) and partly as a sensitivity test. Although figures for the profits, welfare, etc., under each policy regime change with the quantities, the rates of optimum tariffs and subsidies and the figures for the welfare gains are almost unchanged.

6. This is no longer the first-best policy because there is the preexisting distortion of the general tax system.

7. I have performed an experiment distinguishing U.S. large cars from U.S. and Japanese small cars, where the latter are assumed to be perfect substitutes in demand. Then the optimum subsidies (or antitrust policies) are substantial because of the monopoly power in the U.S. large-car market. Optimum tariffs are at smaller levels than they were in table 5, though they lead to greater reductions in the quantity of imports (because of the perfect substitution between domestic small cars and imports). The rapid reduction in import volume makes the tariff a poor instrument for capturing profits away from the Japanese.

References

Abernathy, W. J., K. B. Clark, and A. M. Kantrow. 1981. The new industrial competition. *Harvard Business Review* 59:68–82.

Bhagwati, J. N. 1971. The generalized theory of distortions and welfare. In *Trade, Balance of Payments and Growth: Papers in International Economics in Honor of Charles P. Kindleberger*, J. N. Bhagwati, R. A. Mundell, R. W. Jones, and J. Vanek (eds.), 69–90. Amsterdam: North-Holland.

Bresnahan, T. F. 1981. Departures from marginal-cost pricing in the American automobile industry: Estimates for 1977–1978. *Journal of Econometrics* 127:201–227.

Crandall, R. W. 1984. Import quotas and the automobile industry: The costs of protectionism. *The Brookings Review* 2:8–16.

Cusumano, M. A. 1985. *The Japanese Automobile Industry*. Cambridge, Mass.: Harvard University Press.

Davidson, C. 1984. Cartel stability and tariff policy. *Journal of International Economics* 17:219–237.

Dixit, A. 1987a. Strategic aspects of trade policy. In *Advances in Economic Theory*, T. Bewley (ed.), 329–362. Cambridge: Cambridge University Press.

Dixit, A. 1987b. Tariffs and subsidies under oligopoly: The case of the U.S. automobile industry. In *Protection and Competition in International Trade*, H. Kierzkowski (ed.), 112–127. Oxford: Basil Blackwell.

Dixit, A. 1988. Anti-dumping and countervailing duties under oligopoly. *European Economic Review* 32:55–68.

Eaton, J., and G. M. Grossman. 1986. Optimal trade and industrial policy under oligopoly. *Quarterly Journal of Economics* 101:383–406.

Feenstra, R. C. 1984. Voluntary export restraint in U.S. autos, 1980–81: Quality, employment and welfare effects. In *The Structure and Evolution of Recent US Trade Policy*, R. E. Baldwin and A. O. Krueger (eds.), 35–59. Chicago: University of Chicago Press and National Bureau of Economic Research.

Feenstra, R. C. 1985. Automobile prices and protection: The U.S.-Japan trade restraint. *Journal of Policy Modelling* 7:49–68.

Friedman, J. W. 1983. *Oligopoly Theory*. Cambridge: Cambridge University Press.

Fuss, M., and L. Waverman. 1986. The extent and sources of cost and efficiency differences between U.S. and Japanese automobile producers. National Bureau of Economic Research working paper no. 1849.

Gomez-Ibanez, J. A., R. A. Leone, and S. A. O'Connell. 1983. Restraining auto imports: Does anyone win? *Journal of Policy Analysis and Management* 2:196–219.

Grossman, G. M., and J. D. Richardson. 1985. Strategic trade policy: A survey of issues and early analysis. *Special Papers in International Economics*, no. 15. Princeton: International Finance Section, Princeton University.

Hausman, J. A. 1985. Taxes and labor supply. In *Handbook of Public Economics*, vol. 1, A. J. Auerbach and M. Feldstein (eds.), 213–263. Amsterdam: North-Holland.

Katz, A. 1980. Statement before hearings of the subcommittee on trade of the House Ways and Means Committee. World auto trade: Current trends and structural problems. Serial 96–78. Washington, D.C.: Government Printing Office.

Krishna, K. 1984. Trade restrictions as facilitating practices. Discussion paper 1119. Cambridge, Mass.: Harvard Institute of Economic Research, Harvard University.

Munger, M. C. 1985. A time-series investigation into factors influencing U.S. auto assembly employment. Bureau of Economics Staff Report. Washington, D.C.: Federal Trade Commission.

Rose, N. L. 1985. Union wage gains under regulation: Evidence from the trucking industry. Working paper 1683–85. Cambridge, Mass.: Sloan School of Management, Massachusetts Institute of Technology.

Tarr, D. G., and M. E. Morkre. 1984. Aggregate costs to the United States of tariffs and quotas on imports. Bureau of Economics Staff Report. Washington, D.C.: Federal Trade Commission.

Toder, E. J., with N. S. Cardell and E. Burton. 1978. *Trade Policy and the U.S. Automobile Industry*. New York: Praeger.

Venables, A. J. 1985. International trade and industrial policy and imperfect competition: A survey. Discussion paper 74. London: Centre for Economic Policy Research.

10 Market Access and International Competition: A Simulation Study of 16K Random Access Memories

Richard E. Baldwin and Paul R. Krugman

The technology by which complex circuits can be etched and printed onto tiny silicon chips is a remarkable one. Until the late 1970s it was also a technology clearly dominated by the United States. Thus it was a rude shock when Japanese competition became a serious challenge to established U.S. firms and when Japan actually came to dominate the manufacture of one important kind of chip, the random access memory (RAM). More perhaps than any other event, Japan's breakthrough in RAMs has raised doubts about whether the traditional American reliance on laissez-faire toward the commercialization of technology is going to remain viable.

There are two main questions raised by shifting advantage in semiconductor production. One is whether it matters who produces semiconductors in general or RAMs in particular. That is, does the production of RAMs yield important country-specific external economies? This is, of course, the $64K question. It is also an extremely difficult question to answer. Externalities are inherently hard to measure, because by definition they do not leave any trace in market transactions. Ultimately the discussion of industrial policy will have to come to grips with the assessment of externalities, but for the time being we will shy away from that task.

Here, we instead focus on the other question. This is where the source of the shift in advantage lies. Did Japan simply acquire a comparative advantage through natural causes, or was government targeting the key factor?

Although strong views can be found on both sides, this is also not an easy question to answer. On one side, Japanese policy did not involve large subsidies. The tools of policy were instead encouragement with modest government support of a joint research venture, the Very Large Scale Integration (VLSI) project, and tacit encouragement of a closure of domestic markets to imports. Given that Japan became a large-scale exporter of chips, a conventional economic analysis would suggest that government policy could not have mattered much.

Semiconductor manufacture, however, is not an industry in which conventional economic analysis can be expected to be a good guide. It is an extraordinarily dynamic industry, where technological change reduced the real price of a unit of computing capacity by 99% from 1974 to 1984. This technological change did not fall as manna from heaven; it was largely endogenous, the result of R&D and learning by doing. As a result, competition was marked by dynamic economies of scale that led to a fairly concentrated industry, at least within the RAM market. So semiconductor manufacture is a dynamic oligopoly rather than the static competitive market to which conventional analysis applies.

It is possible to show that in a dynamic oligopoly the policies followed by Japan could in principle have made a large difference. In particular, a protected domestic market can serve as a springboard for exports (Krugman 1984). The question, how-

Originally published in *Empirical Methods for International Trade*, ed. R. Feenstra (MIT Press, 1988).

ever, is how important this effect has been. If the Japanese market had been as open as U.S. firms would have liked, would this have radically altered the story, or would it have made only a small difference? There is no way to answer this question without a quantitative model of the competitive process.

Our purpose here is to provide a preliminary assessment of the importance of market access in one important episode in the history of semiconductor competition. This is the case of the 16K RAM, the chip for which Japan first became a significant exporter. Our question is whether the alleged closure of the Japanese market could have been decisive in allowing Japan to sell not only at home but also in world markets. The method of analysis is the development of a simulation model, derived from recent theoretical work and "calibrated" to actual data. The technique is in the same spirit as the study on the auto industry by Dixit (chapter 9).

Obviously we are interested in the actual results of this analysis. As we will see, the analysis suggests that privileged access to the domestic market was in fact decisive in giving Japanese firms the ability to compete in the world market. The analysis also suggests, however, that this "success" was actually a net loss to the Japanese economy. Finally, the attempt to construct a simulation model here raises many difficult issues, to such an extent that the results must be treated quite cautiously.

The modeling endeavor has a secondary purpose, however, that might be more important than the first. This is to conduct a trial run of the application of new trade theories to real data. It is our view that RAMs are a uniquely rewarding subject for such a trial run. On one hand, the product is well defined: RAMs are a commodity, in the sense that RAMs from different firms are near-perfect substitutes and can in fact be mixed in the same device. Indeed, successive generations of RAMs are still good substitutes—a 16K RAM is pretty close in its use to four 4K RAMs, and so on. On the other hand, the dynamic factors that new theory emphasizes are present in RAMs to an almost incredible degree. The pace of technological change in RAMs is so rapid that other factors can be neglected, in much the same way that nonmonetary factors can be neglected in studying hyperinflation.

In section 1 we provide background on the industry. In section 2 we develop the theoretical model underlying the simulation. In section 3 we explain how the model was "calibrated" to the data. We describe and discuss simulations of the industry under alternative policies in section 4, and we describe the results of some sensitivity analysis in section 5. Finally, we conclude with a discussion of the significance of the results and directions for further research.

1 The Random Access Memory Market

Technology and the Growth of the Industry

So-called dynamic random access memories are a particular general-purpose kind of semiconductor chip. What a RAM does is to store information in digital form in such a way as to allow that information to be altered (hence "dynamic") and read in any desired order (hence "random access"). The technique of production for 16K RAMs involved the etching of circuits on silicon chips by a combination of photographic techniques and chemical baths, followed by baking. The advantage of this method of manufacture, in addition to the microscopic scale on which components are fabricated, is that in effect thousands of electronic devices are manufactured together, all in a single step. The disadvantage, if there is one, is that the process is sensitive. If a chip is to work, everything—temperature, timing, density of solutions, vibration levels, dust—must be precisely controlled.

The sensitivity of the manufacturing process gives rise to a distinctive form of learning by doing. Suppose that a semiconductor chip has been designed and the manufacturing process worked out. Even so, when production begins, the yield of usable chips will ordinarily be low. That is, chips will be produced, but most of them—often 95%—will not work because in some subtle way the conditions for production were not quite right. Thus the manufacturing process is in large part a matter of experimenting with details over time. As the details are worked out, the yield rises sharply. Even at the end, however, many chips still fail to work.

Technological progress in the manufacture of chips has had a more or less regular rhythm in which fundamental improvements alternate with learning by doing within a given framework. In the case of RAMs the fundamental innovations have involved packing ever more components onto a chip through the use of more sophisticated methods of etching the circuits. Given the binary nature of everything in this industry, each such leap forward has involved doubling the previous density; because chips are two-dimensional, each such doubling of density quadruples the number of components. Thus the successive generations of RAMs have been the 4K (4×2^{10}), the 16K, the 64K, and the 256K. Basically a 16K chip does four times as much as a 4K and, given time, costs not much more to produce, so the succession of generations creates a true product cycle in which each generation becomes more or less thoroughly replaced by the next.

Table 1 shows how the successive generations of RAMs have entered the market and how the price has fallen. To interpret the data, bear in mind that one unit of each RAM generation is roughly equivalent to four units of the previous generation. The pattern of product cycles then becomes clear. The effective output of 16K RAMs was already larger than that of 4K RAMs in 1978, and the effective price was clearly lower by 1979. The 16K RAM was in its turn overtaken in output in 1981, in price in 1982. As of the time of this writing, the 64K has not yet been overtaken by 256K RAMs. Missing from the table, as well, is a collapse in RAM prices during 1985, to levels as little as a tenth of those of a year earlier.

From an economist's point of view, the most important question about a technology is not how it works but how it is handled by a market system. This boils down largely to the questions of appropriability and externality. Can the firm that develops a technological improvement keep others from imitating it long enough to reap the rewards of its cleverness? Do others gain from a firm's innovations (other than from its improved product or reduced prices)? When we examine international competition,

Table 1
Prices and total sales of RAMs by generation

Factor	1974	1975	1976	1977	1978	1979	1980	1981	1982	1983	1984
Average price (dollars)											
4K	17.0	6.24	4.35	2.65	1.82	1.92	1.94	1.76	1.62	2.72	3.00
16K			46.4	18.6	8.53	6.03	4.77	2.06	1.24	1.05	0.90
64K					150	110	46.3	11.0	5.42	3.86	3.16
256K									150	47.7	19.9
Total shipments (million units)											
4K	.6	5.3	28	57	77	70	31	13	5	2	2
16K			.1	2	21	70	183	216	263	239	121
64K							13	104	371	853	
256K										2	44
Rate of growth of 16K RAM output					2.35	1.20	0.96	0.17	0.20		

Source: Dataquest.

we also want to know whether external benefits, to the extent that they are generated, are national or international in scope.

From the nature of what is being learned, there seem to be clear differences between the two kinds of technological progress in the semiconductor industry. When a new generation of chips is introduced, the knowledge involved seems to be of a kind that is relatively hard to maintain as private property. Basic techniques of manufacture are hard to keep secret and in any case respond to current trends in science and "meta-technology." Thus everyone knew in the late 1970s that a 64K RAM was possible and roughly how it was going to be done. Furthermore, even the details of chip design are essentially impossible to disguise: Firms can and do make and enlarge photographs of rivals' chips to see how their circuits are laid out. Also, the ability of firms to learn from each other is not noticeably restricted by national boundaries.

The details of manufacture, as learned over time in the process of gaining experience, are by contrast highly appropriable. The facts learned pertain to highly specific circumstances and are indeed sometimes plant- as well as firm-specific. Unlike the design of the chips, the details of production are not evident in the final product. Thus the knowledge gained from learning by doing in this case is a model of a technology that poses few appropriability problems.

It seems, then, that the basic innovations involved in passing from one generation to the next in RAMs are relatively hard to appropriate, whereas those involved in getting the technology to work *within* a generation are relatively easy to appropriate. This observation is the basis of the key untrue assumption that we make in implementing our simulation analysis. We treat product cycles—the displacement of one generation by the next, better one—as completely exogenous. This allows us to focus entirely on the competition within the cycle, in which technological progress takes place by learning. It also allows us to put time bounds on this competition: A single product cycle becomes the natural unit of analysis.

Like any convenient assumption, this one does violence to reality. It is at least possible that the assumptions we make are in fact missing the key point of competition in this industry. For now, however, let us make our simplification and leave the critical discussion to section 6.

Market Structure and Trade Policy

Some fourteen firms produced 16K random access memories for the commercial market from 1977 to 1983. Table 2 shows the average shares of these firms in world production during the period. Taken as a whole, the industry was not exceptionally concentrated, though far from competitive: The Herfindahl index for all firms, taking the average over the period, was only 0.099. This overstates the effective degree of competition, however, for two main reasons. First, some of the firms producing small quantities were probably producing specialized products in short production runs and thus were really not producing the same commodity as the rest. Second, there was, as we will see shortly, a good deal of market segmentation between the United States and Japan, so that each market was substantially more oligopolized than the figures

Table 2
Competitors in the 16K RAM market

Firm	Share of world production, 1977–1983
AMD	5.4
Eurotech	1.5
Fairchild	1.6
Fujitsu	9.5
Hitachi	6.4
Intel	2.4
Mitsubishi	1.2
Mostek	15.3
Motorola	5.4
National	10.6
NEC	15.2
Siemens	3.1
ITT	5.7
TI	12.5
Toshiba	3.6

Source: Dataquest.

suggest. Nonetheless, when we create a stylized version of the market for simulation purposes, we will want to make sure that the degree of competition is roughly consistent with this data. As it turns out, we will develop a model in which the baseline case contains six symmetric U.S. firms and three symmetric Japanese firms, which does not seem too far off.

Another feature of the semiconductor industry's market structure is not shown in the table. This is the contrast between the nature of the U.S. firms and their Japanese rivals. The major U.S. chip manufacturers shown here are primarily chip producers. (There is also "captive" U.S. production by such firms as IBM and AT&T, but, during the period we are considering, little of this production found its way to the open or "merchant" market.) The Japanese firms, by contrast, are also substantial consumers of chips in their other operations. The Japanese firms are not, however, vertically integrated in the usual sense. Each buys most of its chips from other firms and in turn sells most of its chip output to outside customers. There have been repeated accusations, however, that the major suppliers and buyers of Japanese semiconductor production—who are the same firms—collude to form a closed market and exclude foreign sources.

The claim that the Japanese market is effectively closed rests on this difference in market structure. U.S. firms argued that the "buy Japanese" policy of the major firms was tacitly and perhaps even explicitly encouraged by the government, so that even in the absence of any formal tariffs or quotas Japan was able to use a strategy of infant-industry protection to establish itself. It is beyond our ability to assess such claims or to determine how important the government of Japan, as opposed to its

Table 3
Average market shares by country of origin[a]

Market	Source	
	US	Japan
United States	91.2	8.8
Japan	13.7	86.3
Rest of world	56.0	44.0

Source: Author estimates, using tables 2.8, 2.12, and 2.13 from Finan and Amundsen (1985); and Dataquest.
a. We assume that the pattern of consumption for RAMs is the same as for all integrated circuits.

social structure, was in closing the market to foreigners. There is, however, circumstantial evidence of a less than open market. The evidence is that of market shares. Consider table 3 (the entries should be treated as estimates). We see that U.S. firms dominated both their own home market and third-country markets, primarily in Europe. Yet they had a small share in Japan, probably again in specialized types of RAMs rather than in the basic commodity product. Transport costs for RAMs are small; they are, as we have stressed, commoditylike in their interchangeability. So the disparity in market shares suggests that some form of market closure was in fact happening.

Here is where economic analysis comes in. We know that, in an industry characterized by strong learning effects, as we have argued is the case here, protection of the home market can have a kind of multiplier effect. Privileged access to one market can give firms the assurance of moving further down their learning curves and thus can encourage them to price aggressively in other markets as well. Our next task is to develop a simulation model that can be used to ask how important this effect could have been in the case of RAMs.

2 A Theoretical Model of Competition in RAMs

The Yield Curve Model of Production

Consider a firm that at the start of a product cycle commits some amount of resources to production. We define one unit of capacity as the resources needed to produce one "batch" per unit of time. Let K be the capacity in which a firm invests.

Now we suppose that production takes the form of "batches": Each period, one unit of capacity can be used to engrave and bake one batch of semiconductor chips. Thus the firm produces batches at a constant rate K throughout the cycle, and the total number of batches produced after t periods has passed is Kt.

In semiconductor production, however, much of a batch of chips will not work. The yield of usable chips per batch rises with experience. We assume specifically that the yield of usable chips per batch $y(t)$ is a function of the total number of batches that a firm has made so far, Kt, according to the functional form

$$y(t) = [Kt]^{\theta}. \qquad (1)$$

Obviously the functional form (1) cannot be right for the whole range. It implies that the yield of usable chips per batch rises without limit as experience accumulates. In fact, the yield cannot exceed the total number of chips in a batch, so something like a logistic would seem more reasonable. The functional form here is, however, a tremendous help in keeping the problem manageable. So long as the product cycle remains short, it may not be too bad an approximation.

The total number of chips produced by a firm per unit time will then be

$$x(t) = Ky(t) = K^{1+\theta}t^{\theta}. \tag{2}$$

Now it is immediately and gratifyingly obvious that equation (2) behaves much as if there were ordinary increasing returns to scale. Time enters in a way that is multiplicatively separable from capacity, so that the rate of growth of output is in fact independent of the size of the firm. Although we started with a dynamic formulation, the advantages of greater experience show up as the fact that the exponent on K is larger than 1, just as if the economies of scale were static and productivity growth were exogenous.

It is also possible to show the analogy between this formulation and the conventional learning curve. In learning-curve models it is usual to compare current average cost with cumulative experience. Although costs are all sunk in the yield-curve model, current cost as measured would presumably be proportional to the capacity K. Thus current average cost would be measured as proportional to $K/x(t)$. At the same time, cumulative output to date can be found by integrating equation (2). Let $X(t)$ be cumulative output to time t, and let $C(t)$ be the measured average cost of production $cK/x(t)$, where c is the annualized cost of a unit of capacity. Then we have

$$X(t) = (Kt)^{1+\theta}/(1 + \theta),$$

$$C(t) = c(Kt)^{-\theta}$$

$$= c[X(t)(1 + \theta)]^{-\theta/(1+\theta)}.$$

If we were to think of this as a conventional learning curve, then $\theta/(1 + \theta)$ would be the slope of that learning curve.

The close parallels between our formulation and both static economies of scale and the learning curve are helpful. Usually studies of technological change in semiconductors have been framed in terms of learning curves; what we can do is reinterpret the results of those studies in terms of a yield curve, transforming estimates of the learning-curve elasticity to derive estimates of θ. At the same time, the parallel with static economies of scale suggests a solution technique for our model, when it is fully specified: Collapse our model into an equivalent static model, and solve that model instead. We need to specify the demand side to show that in fact such a procedure is valid, but this will in the end be the technique we use.

A final point about the assumed technology: The reason for assuming the yield-curve model instead of the learning-curve model is that it implies growing output over the product cycle. Can we say anything more than this? The answer is that the specific formulation adopted here implies also that output grows at a declining rate. By taking logs and differentiating equation (2), we find that the rate of growth of output will decline according to the relationship

$$\frac{dx(t)}{dt}\frac{1}{x(t)} = \frac{\theta}{t}. \tag{3}$$

The prediction of a declining rate of growth in output over the product cycle is borne out, except for a slight reversal at one point, by the data in table 1.

Demand and Trade

Turning now to the demand side, we suppose that there are two markets, the United States and Japan. We denote Japanese variables with an asterisk and leave U.S. variables unstarred. In each market there is a constant elasticity demand curve for output, which we write in inverse form as

$$P = AQ^{-\alpha}, \tag{4}$$

$$P^* = A^*(Q^*)^{-\alpha}. \tag{5}$$

We thus assume that the elasticity of demand, $1/\alpha$, is the same in both markets.

Firms are assumed to be located in one market or the other and to be able to ship to the other market only by incurring an additional transport cost. Transport costs will be of the "iceberg" variety, with only a fraction $1/(1 + d)$ of any quantity shipped arriving.

The problem of firms has two parts. First, they must decide on a capacity level. This fixes the path of their output through the product cycle. Second, at each point in time they must decide how much to sell in each market. Let us for the moment take the capacity choice as given and focus only on the determination of the division of output.

This choice can be analyzed as follows (the essence of this analysis is the same as that in the purely static models presented by Brander 1981 and Brander and Krugman 1983). Each firm will want to allocate its current output between markets so that the marginal revenue, net of transport cost of shipping to the two markets, is the same. Consider the case of a U.S. firm. The marginal revenue (MR) it receives from shipping an additional unit to the U.S. market is

$$MR_U = P(1 - \alpha S_U V_U), \tag{6}$$

where S_U is the share of the firm in the U.S. market; we will define V_U in a moment. Its marginal revenue from selling in the Japanese market is

$$MR_J = \frac{P^*(1 - \alpha S_J V_J)}{1 + d}, \tag{7}$$

where S_J is the share of the firm in the Japanese market.

The two terms V_U and V_J—and their counterparts V_{U^*} and V_{J^*} in the decision problem of a Japanese firm—are conjectural variations. They measure the extent to which a firm expects a one-unit increase in its own deliveries to a market to increase *total* deliveries to that market and thus to depress the price. In the simplest case of Cournot competition, we would have all four conjectural variations equal to 1.

The use of a conjectural variations approach in modeling oligopoly is not a favored one. Many authors have pointed out the shaky logical foundations of the approach, and to use it in an empirical application adds an uncomfortable element of "ad-hockery." We introduce these terms now because we have found that we need them; indeed, as soon as we discuss entry, it will become immediately apparent that, to reconcile the industry's structure with its technology, we must abandon the hypothesis of Cournot competition. Whether there are alternatives to the conjectural variations approach is a question we return to in section 6.

Suppose that we suppress our doubts and accept the conjectural variations approach. Then we can notice the following point. Suppose that, for some P, P^*, S_U, and S_J, the first-order condition $MR_U = MR_J$ is satisfied. Then the condition will continue to be satisfied with the same S_U and S_J even for different prices, so long as P/P^* remains the same.

What this means is that, if all firms grow at the same rate, so that it is feasible for them to maintain constant market shares, and if prices fall at the same rate in both markets, the optimal behavior will in fact be to maintain constancy of market shares. Fortunately, our assumptions on the yield curve ensure that all firms will indeed grow at the same rate. Furthermore, if firms continue to divide their output in the same proportions between the two markets, the fact that all firms grow at the same rate and that the elasticity of demand is assumed constant ensures that prices in the two markets will indeed fall at the same rate. So we have demonstrated that, given the initial capacity decisions of the firms, the subsequent equilibrium in the product cycle is a sort of balanced growth in which market shares do not change but output steadily rises and prices steadily fall.

We note finally that, in principle, this equilibrium may be one in which there is two-way trade in the same product. Firms with a small market share (or a low conjectural variation) in the foreign market may choose to "dump" goods in that market, even though the price net of transport and tariff costs is less than at home. Because this may be true of firms in each country, the result can be two-way trade based on reciprocal dumping.

So far we have discussed equilibrium given the number of firms and their capacity choices; our final steps are to consider capacity choice and entry.

Capacity Choice

Following Spence (1981), we assume that the product cycle is short enough that firms do not worry about discounting. Thus the objective of a U.S. firm is to maximize

$$W = \int_0^T \left[Pz(t) + \frac{P^*z^*(t)}{1+d} \right] dt - cK \tag{8}$$

subject to the constraint

$$z(t) + z^*(t) = K^{1+\theta}t^{\theta} \qquad \text{for all } t,$$

where T is the length of the product cycle, $z(t)$ and $z^*(t)$ are deliveries to the U.S. and Japanese markets, respectively, and c is the cost of a unit of capacity.

This maximization problem may be simplified by noting that we have already seen that marginal revenue will be the same for deliveries to the two markets. Thus we can evaluate the returns from a marginal increase in K by assuming that the whole of that increase is allocated to the U.S. market. The first-order condition then becomes

$$(1+\theta)\int_0^T P(t)(1-\alpha S_U V_U)(Kt)^{\theta}\,dt = c. \tag{9}$$

We can rewrite this first-order condition in a revealing form. First, to simplify notation, let us choose units so that the length of the product cycle T is equal to 1. Also, we note that, given the output path (3) and the elasticity of demand, we have

$$P(t) = P(T)(t/T)^{-\alpha\theta}.$$

By substituting and integrating, we find

$$\left(\frac{1+\theta}{(1-\alpha)\theta+1}\right)P(T)(1-\alpha S_U V_U) = cK^{-\theta},$$

or

$$P(1-\alpha S_U V_U) = MC_U, \tag{10}$$

where P is the average price received by the firm over the product cycle; thus the whole left-hand term is the average marginal revenue over the cycle. The term on the right-hand side can be shown to equal the marginal cost of producing one more unit of total cycle output. Thus we see that our problem can be expressed in a form that is effectively the same as one where economies of scale are purely static. Something that looks like marginal revenue is set equal to something that looks like marginal cost.

This means that we can solve for equilibrium by collapsing the problem into an equivalent static problem. Given the balanced growth character of the equilibrium, there is a one-to-one relationship between total deliveries to each market and the average price, which continues to take a constant elasticity form

$$P = AQ^{-\alpha}. \tag{11}$$

And we can write an average cost function for cumulative output, which takes the form

$$C = C_U X^{-\theta/(1+\theta)}. \tag{12}$$

A model of the form of (10)–(12) may be solved using methods described in Brander and Krugman (1983) and Krugman (1986). For any given marginal costs we can solve for equilibrium prices and market shares. From prices we can determine total sales, and by using market shares, we can find output per firm. This output, however, implies a marginal cost. A full equilibrium is a fixed point where the marginal costs assumed at the beginning are the same as those implied at the end. In practice, such an equilibrium can easily be calculated using an iterative procedure. We make a guess at the marginal costs, solve for output, use this to recompute the marginal costs, and continue until convergence.

Once we have solved this collapsed problem, we can then solve for the implied capacity choices and the whole time path of output and prices.

Entry

Finally, we turn to the problem of entry. Here we assume that there are many potential entrants with the same costs and that all potential entrants have perfect foresight about the postentry equilibrium. An equilibrium with entry must then satisfy two criteria: It must yield nonnegative profits for all those firms that do enter, but any additional firm that might enter would face losses. If we could ignore integer constraints, this would imply a zero-profit equilibrium. In practice, this will not be quite the case. However, as we will see, our estimates of profits turn out to be quite small.

An important point about the relationship between entry and conjectural variations should be noted. This is that the conjectural variations must be high—that is, postentry firms had better not be too competitive—if there are strong increases in yield. To see this, consider a single market with elasticity of demand $1/\alpha$ and yield-curve parameter θ, where all firms are the same. Then the number of firms that can earn zero profits can be shown to be $\alpha(1 + \theta)V/\theta$, where V is the conjectural variation. For the estimates of α and θ that we will be using, this turns out to be $1.98V$. That is, with Cournot behavior only two firms could earn zero profits. Not surprisingly, in order to rationalize the existence of the six large U.S. firms that actually competed and that furthermore faced some foreign competition, we end up needing to postulate behavior a good deal less competitive than Cournot.

We have now described a theoretical model of competition in an industry that we hope captures some of the essentials of the random access memory market. Our next step is to try to make this model operational using realistic numbers.

3 Calibrating the Model

Our theoretical model of the random access memory market is recognizably one in which protection of the domestic market will in effect push a firm down its marginal cost curve and lead to a larger share of the export market as well. What we want to do, however, is to quantify this effect. To do this, we need to choose realistic parameter values. We take outside estimates for some of the parameters and then use data on the industry to calibrate the model to fix the remaining parameters.

Parameters from Outside Estimates

The parameters for which we took numbers directly from other sources were the elasticity of demand α, the elasticity of the yield curve θ, and the transport cost d.

Finan and Amundsen (1985) estimate demand elasticity at 1.8 for the U.S. market. In fact, we can confirm that this must be at least approximately right by comparing the fall in prices and the rise in quantity from 1978 to 1981, that is, over the period when 16K RAMs were the dominant memory chip. Prices fell by a logarithmic 142% over that period, whereas sales rose by 233%, 1.6 times as much, despite a recession and high interest rates that depressed investment. In general, it is apparent that the elasticity of demand for semiconductor memories must be more than 1 but not too much more, given that the price per bit has fallen 99% in real terms over the past decade. If demand were inelastic, the industry would have shrunk away; if it were very elastic, we would be having chips with everything by now.

The elasticity of the yield curve can, as we noted in our earlier discussion, be derived from the elasticity of the associated learning curve. Discussions of learning curves in general often offer numbers in the 0.2–0.3 range. An Office of Technology Assessment study (Office of Technology Assessment 1983) estimated the slope of the learning curve for semiconductors at 0.28. Converted to yield-curve form, this implies $\theta = 0.3889$.

Finally, there is general agreement that costs of transporting semiconductors internationally are low, as one would expect given the high ratio of value to weight or bulk. We follow Finan and Amundsen's 1985 estimate of $d = 0.05$.

Costs

The data in tables 2 and 3 show fourteen firms in three markets. If we were to try to represent the complete structure of the industry, we would need to specify fourteen cost functions and forty-two conjectural variations parameters. Instead, we have stylized the market in such a way as to need to specify only two cost parameters and four conjectural variations.

The less important step in this stylization is the consolidation of the U.S. and the rest of world (ROW) markets into a single market. This may be justified on the grounds that transport costs are small, and the crucial issue is the alleged closure of the Japanese market. Also, as our data suggest, the market share of U.S. firms in the U.S. and ROW markets is fairly similar.

The more important step is the representation of the U.S. and Japanese industries as a group of symmetric representative firms. There are many objections to this procedure. The essential problem is that the size distribution of firms presumably has some meaning, and to collapse it in this way means that we are neglecting potentially important aspects of reality. As with our other problematic assumptions, this should be viewed as a simplification that we hope is not crucial.

In table 2 we noted that there were nine firms with market shares over 5%: six U.S. and three Japanese. We represent the industry by treating it as if these were the only firms and as if all firms from each country were the same. Thus our model industry consists of six equal-cost U.S. firms, which share the entire U.S. market share, and three equal-cost Japanese firms, which do the same for Japan's market shares.

Table 4
Market shares and sales per firm

Market	Producer: United States	Japan
Sales (million units)		
United States and rest of world	69.3	32.2
Japan	5.0	62.3
Market shares		
United States and rest of world	13.5	6.3
Japan	2.3	28.6

Source: Table 3, Finan and Amundsen (1985); Dataquest.

We do not have direct data on costs. Instead, we attempt to infer costs by assuming that in the actual case firms earned precisely zero profits. As we know, because of integer constraints, this need not have been the case. It should have been close, however, and it allows us to use price and output data to infer costs.

First, we have data on prices. This data shows that from 1978 to 1983 the average price of a 16K RAM was identical in the two markets, at $1.47. There is reason to suspect this data, because the Japanese had been threatened with an antidumping action and the structure of the Japanese industry may have made it easy for effective prices to differ from those posted. Lacking any information on this, however, we will go with the official data.

Next, we use our stylized industry structure to calculate the *per firm* sales in each market. These are shown in the first part of table 4. Given this information, we can net out transport costs on foreign sales to calculate the average revenue (AR) of a representative firm of each type; that is,

$$AR = \frac{\int_0^T [P(t)z(t) + P^*(t)(z^*(t))/(1 + d)]\,dt}{\int_0^T [z(t) + z^*(t)]\,dt}$$

for a U.S. firm.

But the zero-profit assumption allows us to infer that average cost is equal to average revenue. This in turn implies both the level of marginal cost (MC) and the constant term in the average cost function:

$$MC_U = \frac{AR}{1 + \theta},$$

$$C_U = AR(X^{\theta/1+\theta}),$$

where X is cumulative output. When we solve these equations we find that

$$MC_U = 1.054, \quad MC_J = 1.040,$$

$$C_U = 3.524, \quad C_J = 3.733.$$

This says that U.S. firms would have had somewhat lower (about 6%) costs if they had had the same output as their Japanese rivals but that Japanese firms, thanks to larger scale, ended up with slightly lower marginal costs.

This result confirms what industry experts have claimed in a qualitative sense about the industry. Most estimates based on direct observation have given U.S. firms a larger inherent cost advantage—Finan and Amundsen (1985) suggests 10–15%. Given the roundabout nature of our method and the problems of some of our data, we would not quarrel with this.

One might wonder about the coincidence that costs in the two countries appear to be so close. Is there something about our method that forces this? The answer, we believe, is that this is a result of our method of selecting an industry to study. The 16K RAM was the first semiconductor for which Japan became an exporter on a large scale. Not surprisingly, it is a product for which costs were close. Had we done the 4K RAM, for which Japanese firms sold only to a protected domestic market, or the 64K RAM, for which they came to be the dominant producers, we would presumably have found quite different answers.

Conjectural Variations

Our next step is to calculate conjectural variations parameters. We begin with per firm market shares. These are shown in the second part of table 4.

We next note the relationship between average prices, market shares, and marginal cost:

$$(1 - \alpha S_U V_U) \int_0^T P(t)\,dt = MC_U$$

for U.S. firms in the U.S. market, and similarly for Japanese firms in the two markets. Note that we cannot use this method to estimate the conjectural variation for U.S. firms in the Japanese market. The reason is that the whole point of this study is the allegation that U.S. firms were constrained by implicit trade barriers from selling as much as they would have under free trade.

When we solve these equations for the conjectural variations, we find

$$V_U = 3.760, \quad V_{J*} = 1.828, \quad V_{U*} = 7.345.$$

What about the U.S. conjectural variation in the Japanese market? Here it is impossible to disentangle the effects of U.S. behavior and whatever implicit protection Japan imposed. This is a key point on which there seems to be nothing we can do except make an assumption. Our assumption is this: U.S. firms have the same conjectural variation in the Japanese market that they do at home. Thus we *assume*

$$V_J = V_U = 3.760.$$

This conjecture would lead to a substantially higher U.S. market share in Japan than we actually observe. The difference we attribute to protection. This protection can be

Table 5
Simulation results

Variable	Base case	Free trade	Trade war
Welfare			
United States	1,651.8	1,827.5	335.3
Japan	698.4	738.9	104.0
Consumer surplus			
United States	1,651.8	1822.5	335.3
Japan	698.4	738.9	104.0
Price			
United States	1.47	1.30	1.49
Japan	1.47	1.37	2.19
Profit			
United States	0	5	0
Japan	0	—	0
Import shares			
United States in Japan	.14	1.0	0.0
Japan in United States	.19	0.0	0.0
Number of firms			
United States	6	7	7
Japan	3	0	5

represented by an implicit tariff. The implicit tariff rate necessary to reproduce the actual market share is 0.2637.

There are two points to note about these results. First, we note that all three estimated conjectural variations are substantially more than 1; that is, the market is less competitive than Cournot. This is an inevitable consequence of the high degree of economies of scale that we have assumed, together with the zero-profit condition. Relatively uncompetitive behavior is needed to rationalize how many firms there are in the market. Second, Japanese firms seem to have been cautious about selling in the U.S. market. Is this number picking up concerns about U.S. trade policy, or is it simply an artifact of our model? In general, the conjectural variations are not too plausible; we consider in section 6 what this implies for our general approach.

We have now calibrated the model to the data. That is, when the model is simulated using our assumed parameters, it reproduces the actual prices, outputs, and market shares of the 16K RAM product cycle. We summarize this baseline case in table 5. Our next step is to ask how the results change under alternative policies.

4 Effects of Alternative Policies

We consider two alternative policies. The first is free trade, represented in our model by a removal of the implicit tariff on U.S. sales to Japan. The second is a trade war, in which both countries block imports. The effects of the two policies are shown next to the baseline case in table 5.

It is important to note the underlying assumptions behind these calculations. In each case all parameters are assumed constant, except for the implicit tariff on U.S. exports to Japan. In particular, the conjectural variations are assumed to remain unchanged. This is not a particularly satisfactory assumption, but, of course, if we allow these parameters to change, anything can happen.

To solve the model in each case, we followed a two-stage procedure. First, we took the initial number of firms and iterated on marginal cost to get the equilibrium. Then we searched across a grid of numbers of Japanese and U.S. firms to find an entry equilibrium.

Free Trade

Our first policy experiment goes to the heart of the debate over Japanese trade policy. We ask what would have happened if the Japanese market had been open. This is done by removing the implicit tariff on U.S. exports to Japan.

The results, reported in the second column of table 5, are quite striking. According to our model, in the absence of protection the Japanese firms that were net exporters in the baseline case do not even enter; only U.S. firms remain in the field. The reason is a sort of circular causation typical in models with scale economies. Japanese firms, deprived of their safe haven in the domestic market, would have smaller cumulative output even with constant marginal cost. The smaller output, however, means a higher marginal cost. This implies still smaller output, which implies still higher marginal cost, and so on. In the end, no Japanese firms find it profitable to enter.

The exit of the Japanese firms and the new access to the Japanese market produce an increase in the profits of the U.S. firms. It turns out that this increase allows an additional U.S. firm to enter. Increased competition, combined with larger output and hence lower marginal cost of the U.S. firms, leads to a fall in price in *both* markets.

The lower price means an increase in consumer surplus in both countries. In the United States this is supplemented with a small rise in profits. The result is a gain in welfare, measured as the sum of consumer and producer surplus, in both nations.

If we reverse the order in which we consider columns 2 and 3 of table 5, we can arrive at an evaluation of the effects of Japanese policy. According to our estimates, privileged access to the domestic market *was* crucial, not only in providing Japanese firms with domestic sales but in allowing them to get their marginal cost down to the point where they could successfully export. However, this result of protection was a Pyrrhic victory in welfare terms. It raised Japanese prices, hurting consumers, without generating compensating producer gains. The policy was thus not a successful beggar-my-neighbor one, or more accurately it beggared my neighbor only at the cost of beggaring myself as well.

Trade War

Although a Japanese policy of export promotion through home market protection does not seem to be desirable even in and of itself, it is easy to imagine that it could provoke retaliation. The fourth column of table 5 asks what would have happened if Japan and the United States had engaged in a "trade war" in 16K RAMs, with each blocking all imports from the other. (For the purposes of the simulation we achieved this by letting each country impose a 100% tariff.)

The result of this trade war is unfavorable for both countries. Firms are smaller and thus have higher marginal cost. Prices are therefore higher in both markets, though especially in the smaller Japanese market. Small profits do not compensate for the loss of consumer surplus, so welfare is reduced in both nations.

This trade war example makes a point that has been mentioned in some discussion of high-technology industries but needs further emphasis. Although the nonclassical aspects of these industries offer potential justifications for government intervention, they also tend to magnify the costs of protection and trade conflict. We have a case of two countries with similar inherent costs, that is, little comparative advantage. In a constant-returns, perfect-competition situation this would mean that a trade war would have few costs. In this case, however, protection leads to reduced competition and reduced scale, imposing substantial losses.

These results are clearly extremely striking. Furthermore, even though we do *not* find that Japan was successfully pursuing a beggar-thy-neighbor policy at U.S. expense, the implication for market shares is potentially politically explosive. Thus it is important to ask how sensitive the results are to changes in the assumed parameters.

5 Sensitivity Analysis

In calibrating the model, we used two sources of information. On one side we used actual data on the industry. Although these data are not ironclad, we did not experiment with how our conclusions might have changed if the data had looked different. Instead, we confined ourselves to analysis of the sensitivity of the results to the value of the parameters we took from outside sources. There are three of these: the elasticity of demand, the transport cost, and the elasticity of learning.

Conducting a sensitivity analysis with respect to these parameters is not simply a matter of rerunning a simulation with a different parameter. If we believe that, say, transport costs are actually twice as large as we assumed in the base case, we must also revise our estimates of the costs of U.S. and Japanese firms and of their conjectural variations. That is, we must recalibrate the entire model before resimulating. Our sensitivity analysis therefore involved a series of recalibrations for different values of the three outside parameters.

The results of these exercises are summarized in table 6. Recall that our baseline estimates were that the elasticity of learning $\phi = \theta/(1 + \theta) = 0.28$; the elasticity of demand $\varepsilon = 1.8$; and the transport cost $d = 0.05$. We have treated these as a central

Table 6
Sensitivity of key results to parameters

Parameter	Free trade, Japanese share in United States	Free trade, U.S. share in Japan	Welfare effect of protection
$\varepsilon = 1.8, d = 0.05$			
$\phi = 0.56$	0	1	−
$\phi = 0.28$[a]	0	1	−
$\phi = 0.14$	0	1	0
$\phi = 0.07$	0	1	+
$\phi = 0.28, d = 0.05$			
$\varepsilon = 1.4$	0	1	−
$\varepsilon = 1.8$[a]	0	1	−
$\varepsilon = 2.2$	0	1	−
$\varepsilon = 1.8, \phi = 0.28$			
$d = 0.2$	0	1	+
$d = 0.05$[a]	0	1	−
$d = 0.025$	0	1	−
Alternative implicit conjectural variation	0	1	−

a. Base case.

case and asked what happens when each of the parameters in turn is varied around the central case. For each recalibration/resimulation exercise we report three numbers: the free trade share of Japanese firms in the United States, the free trade share of U.S. firms in Japan, and the *sign* of the welfare effect of protection on Japan. In the central case, as we already noted, these entries are 0, 1, −: The Japanese industry would not have existed without protection, but nonetheless protection made Japan worse off. The question is whether some plausible variation in the parameters could either reduce the strong implication of the trade policies for market shares or make protection appear to be a successful predatory policy.

The first group of runs holds ε and d at their base levels and varies the elasticity of the learning curve, from twice its central value to only one-fourth as large. It appears that the strong result on market shares is highly robust to this parameter. Somewhat surprising, however, is that Japan might have gained from protection if dynamic scale economies had been fairly *low*. This runs opposite to our intuition, which is that unconventional trade policy answers depend on increasing returns being important. The explanation, as best we can understand it, is that our estimate of relative Japanese costs is inversely related to the degree of scale economies. Our calibration requires that Japanese marginal costs be slightly below those of U.S. firms; in our base case we find nonetheless that underlying Japanese costs are higher, with the greater length of Japanese production runs accounting for the difference. If scale economies are smaller, our calibration makes the underlying costs of Japan's firms closer to those of U.S. firms. When firms in the two countries have similar underlying costs, it then becomes possible for protection actually to lower prices in the protecting country, a point noted by Venables (1985). That is what seems to be happening.

The second group of runs holds $\phi = 0.28$ and varies the elasticity of demand. As we noted earlier, this is a parameter we are fairly sure of, and the model seems relatively insensitive within a plausible range.

The third group of runs holds ϕ and ε at their central values while varying d. Even implausibly high transport costs do not shake the strong result that Japan's industry would not have existed without protection. With sufficiently high transport costs, however, Japan is better off even with a high-cost domestic industry than importing, and protection actually lowers prices—the Venables effect again.

The last item in table 6 addresses one arbitrary assumption we made in our analysis. As we pointed out, it was not possible to disentangle the effects of protection and U.S. behavior in the Japanese market. In the base case we assumed that U.S. firms in the Japanese market would have the same conjectural variation as they did in their home market. Here we try assuming instead that they behave like Japanese firms in the Japanese market. The qualitative result is unchanged.

The results of the sensitivity analysis seem to indicate that we need not worry too much about the accuracy of the "outside" parameters. Although we varied these parameters over a wide range, we did not encounter any reversals of the market share result, and only in extreme and implausible cases did the welfare result change. Thus, if there is something wrong with the analysis, it is not in these parameters but in the more fundamental conception of the model.

6 Concluding Remarks

The results of our simulation analysis seem fairly clear. What we want to focus on here are the difficulties with the analysis and directions for further work.

The difficulties with the model as it stands are of two kinds. First, it is disturbing that we are forced to rely on conjectural variations to make the model track reality and still more disturbing that the conjectural variations are estimated to be such high numbers. Second, our characterization of the technology, although extremely convenient as a simplification, may simplify too much. As we will argue in a moment, these two difficulties may be related.

Conjectural Variations

Our reliance on conjectural variations, and the large value of these conjectures, is forced by two factors. First is the relatively large number of firms operating in the market. Second is the high learning-curve elasticity we have taken from other sources. These imply that firms can only be making nonnegative profits if they have conjectural variations well in excess of 1.

If this result is wrong, it must be because one of the parameters is mismeasured. One possibility would be that firms are in fact producing imperfect substitutes, so that the elasticity of demand faced by each firm is lower than our perfect-substitutes calculation indicates. This seems implausible, however, given what we know about the applications of RAMs. The alternative possibility is that the degree of scale economies is in some way overstated.

Now we know that, in fact, extremely rapid learning took place and, more important, was expected to take place in RAMs. This would seem to imply large dynamic scale economies. However, it is possible that the pace of learning was more a matter of time elapsed than of cumulative output. If this was the case, large firms would not have had as great an advantage over small firms as we have assumed. A reduction in our estimate of the effective degree of scale economies would in turn reduce the need to rely on conjectural variations to track the data. We should note, however, that the conventional wisdom of the industry is that cumulative output, not time alone, is the source of learning.

Even if the learning curve is as steep as we have assumed, the longer-term dynamics of technological change offer an alternative route by which effective scale economies could have been lower than we say. To see this, however, we need to turn to our second problem, the nature of technological competition.

Technological Competition

In order to simplify the analysis, we have assumed that the competition for each generation of semiconductor memories in effect stands in isolation. The techniques to construct a new size memory become available, and firms are off in a race to learn. This approach neglects three things. It neglects the R&D that is involved in the endogenous development of each generation, and it neglects two technological linkages that might be important. One is the link between successive generations of memories; the other is the link between memories and other semiconductor products.

The endogenous development of new generations, in and of itself, actually adds a further degree of dynamic scale economies. Firms invest in front-end R&D, which acts like a fixed cost. This should actually require still higher conjectural variations to justify the number of firms in the industry.

On the other side, technological linkages could help to explain why so many firms produced 16K RAMs. It has sometimes been asserted that you must produce 16K RAMs to be able to get into 64K RAMs, etc. (although Intel, for example, made a decision to skip a generation so as to leapfrog its competitors). It has also been asserted that firms producing other kinds of semiconductors need a base of volume production on which to hone their manufacturing skills and that commodity products such as memories are the only places they can do this. Either of these linkages could have the effect of making firms willing to accept direct losses in RAM production in order to generate intrafirm spillovers to current or future lines of business.

It should be pointed out, however, that these spillovers can explain the presence of a larger number of firms in RAM production only if they involve a *diminishing* marginal product to memory production. That is, they must take the form of gains that you get by having a foothold in the RAM sector but that do not require a dominant presence. Otherwise, the effect will simply be to make competition in RAMs more intense, with lower prices offsetting the extra incentive to participate.

But if the linkages take this form, they will reduce the degree of economies of scale relevant for competition. Firms will view the marginal cost of production as the actual cost less technological spillovers, but these spillovers will decline as output rises, leaving economic marginal cost less downward sloping than direct cost. Of course, if true marginal costs are less downward sloping than we have estimated, we have less need of conjectural variations to explain the number of firms.

What to Make of the Results

Our concluding remarks have been skeptical about some of the underlying structure of the model. It is at least possible that the data can be reinterpreted in a way that leads us to a substantially lower estimate of dynamic scale economies. If this were the case, the results of our simulation exercises would be much less striking. On the other hand, the view that, in such a dynamic industry as semiconductors, where U.S. firms were widely agreed to still have a cost advantage in the late 1970s, protection may have been the key to Japanese success is not implausible.

The final judgment, then, must be that this is a preliminary attempt, not the final word. We believe, however, that it has been useful. It is crucial that study of trade policy in dynamic industries go beyond the unsupported assertions that are so common and attempt quantification. We expect that the techniques for doing this will get much better than what we have managed here, but this is at least a first try.

References

Brander, J. A. 1981. Intra-industry trade in identical commodities. *Journal of International Economics* 11:1–14.

Brander, J. A., and P. R. Krugman. 1983. A 'reciprocal dumping' model of international trade. *Journal of International Economics* 15:313–321.

Finan, W., and C. Amundsen. 1985. An analysis of the effects of targeting on the competitiveness of the US semiconductor industry. Report prepared for the U.S. Trade Representative, unpublished.

Krugman, P. R. 1984. Import protection as export promotion. In *Monopolistic Competition and International Trade*, H. Kierzkowski (ed.), 180–193. Oxford: Oxford University Press.

Krugman, P. R. 1986. Market access and competition in high technology industries: A simulation exercise. Mimeo.

Office of Technology Assessment. 1983. *International Competitiveness in Electronics*. Washington, D.C.: Government Printing Office.

Spence. A. M 1981. The learning curve and competition. *Bell Journal of Economics* 12:49–70.

Venables, A. 1985. Trade and trade policy with imperfect competition: The case of identical products and free entry. *Journal of International Eonomics* 19:1–19.

III MONOPOLISTIC COMPETITION

11 Scale Economies, Product Differentiation, and the Pattern of Trade

Paul R. Krugman

For some time now there has been considerable skepticism about the ability of comparative cost theory to explain the actual pattern of international trade. Neither the extensive trade among the industrial countries, nor the prevalence in this trade of two-way exchanges of differentiated products, make much sense in terms of standard theory. As a result, many people have concluded that a new framework for analyzing trade is needed.[1] The main elements of such a framework—economies of scale, the possibility of product differentiation, and imperfect competition—have been discussed by such authors as Balassa (1967), Grubel (1967, 1970), and Kravis (1971), and have been "in the air" for many years. In this paper I present a simple formal analysis that incorporates these elements and show how it can be used to shed some light on some issues that cannot be handled in more conventional models. These include, in particular, the causes of trade between economies with similar factor endowments, and the role of a large domestic market in encouraging exports.

The basic model of this paper is one in which there are economies of scale in production and firms can costlessly differentiate their products. In this model, which is derived from recent work by Dixit and Stiglitz (1977), equilibrium takes the form of Chamberlinian monopolistic competition: each firm has some monopoly power, but entry drives monopoly profits to zero. When two imperfectly competitive economies of this kind are allowed to trade, increasing returns produce trade and gains from trade even if the economies have identical tastes, technology, and factor endowments. This basic model of trade is presented in section 1. It is closely related to a model I have developed elsewhere; in this paper a somewhat more restrictive formulation of demand is used to make the analysis in later sections easier.

The rest of the paper is concerned with two extensions of the basic model. In section 2, I examine the effect of transportation costs and show that countries with larger domestic markets will, other things equal, have higher wage rates. Section 3 then deals with "home market" effects on trade patterns. It provides a formal justification for the commonly made argument that countries will tend to export those goods for which they have relatively large domestic markets.

This paper makes no pretense of generality. The models presented rely on extremely restrictive assumptions about cost and utility. Nonetheless, it is to be hoped that the paper provides some useful insights into those aspects of international trade that simply cannot be treated in our usual models.

1 The Basic Model

Assumptions of the Model

There are assumed to be a large number of potential goods, all of which enter symmetrically into demand. Specifically, we assume that all individuals in the econ-

Originally published in the *American Economic Review* 70 (December 1980): 950–959.

omy have the same utility function,

$$U = \sum_i c_i^\theta, \qquad 0 < \theta < 1, \tag{1}$$

where c_i is consumption of the ith good. The number of goods actually produced, n, will be assumed to be large, although smaller than the potential range of products.[2]

There will be assumed to be only one factor of production, labor. All goods will be produced with the same cost function:

$$l_i = \alpha + \beta x_i, \qquad \alpha, \beta > 0, \qquad i = 1, \ldots, n, \tag{2}$$

where l_i is labor used in producing the ith good and x_i is output of the good. In other words, I assume a fixed cost and constant marginal cost. Average cost declines at all levels of output, although at a diminishing rate.

Output of each good must equal the sum of individual consumptions. If we can identify individuals with workers, output must equal consumption of a representative individual times the labor force:

$$x_i = Lc_i, \qquad i = 1, \ldots, n. \tag{3}$$

We also assume full employment, so that the total labor force must just be exhausted by labor used in production:

$$L = \sum_{i=1}^{n} (\alpha + \beta x_i). \tag{4}$$

Finally, we assume that firms maximize profits but that there is free entry and exit of firms, so that in equilibrium profits will always be zero.

Equilibrium in a Closed Economy

We can now proceed to analyze equilibrium in a closed economy described by the assumptions just laid out. The analysis proceeds in three stages. First I analyze consumer behavior to derive demand functions. Then profit-maximizing behavior by firms is derived, treating the number of firms as given. Finally, the assumption of free entry is used to determine the equilibrium number of firms.

The reason that a Chamberlinian approach is useful here is that, in spite of imperfect competition, the equilibrium of the model is determinate in all essential respects because the special nature of demand rules out strategic interdependence among firms. Because firms can costlessly differentiate their products, and all products enter symmetrically into demand, two firms will never want to produce the same product; each good will be produced by only one firm. At the same time, if the number of goods produced is large, the effect of the price of any one good on the demand for any other will be negligible. The result is that each firm can ignore the effect of its actions on other firms' behavior, eliminating the indeterminacies of oligopoly.

Consider, then, an individual maximizing (1) subject to a budget constraint. The first-order conditions from that maximum problem have the form

$$\theta c_i^{\theta-1} = \lambda p_i, \qquad i = 1, \ldots, n, \tag{5}$$

where p_i is the price of the ith good and λ is the shadow price on the budget constraint, that is, the marginal utility of income. Since all individuals are alike, (5) can be rearranged to show the demand curve for the ith good, which we have already argued is the demand curve facing the single firm producing that good:

$$p_i = \theta\lambda^{-1}\left(\frac{x_i}{L}\right)^{\theta-1}, \qquad i = 1, \ldots, n. \tag{6}$$

Provided that there are a large number of goods being produced, the pricing decision of any one firm will have a negligible effect on the marginal utility of income. In that case, (6) implies that each firm faces a demand curve with an elasticity of $1/(1-\theta)$, and the profit-maximizing price is therefore

$$p_i = \theta^{-1}\beta w, \qquad i = 1, \ldots, n, \tag{7}$$

where w is the wage rate, and prices and wages can be defined in terms of any (common!) unit. Note that since θ, β, and w are the same for all firms, prices are the same for all goods and we can adopt the shorthand $p = p_i$ for all i.

The price p is independent of output given the special assumptions about cost and utility (which is the reason for making these particular assumptions). To determine profitability, however, we need to look at output. Profits of the firm producing good i are

$$\pi_i = px_i - (\alpha + \beta x_i)w, \qquad i = 1, \ldots, n. \tag{8}$$

If profits are positive, new firms will enter, causing the marginal utility of income to rise and profits to fall until profits are driven to zero. In equilibrium, then, $\pi = 0$, implying for the output of a representative firm:

$$\begin{aligned} x_i &= \frac{\alpha}{p/w - \beta} \\ &= \frac{\alpha\theta}{\beta(1-\theta)}, \qquad i = 1, \ldots, n. \end{aligned} \tag{9}$$

Thus output per firm is determined by the zero-profit condition. Again, since α, β, and θ are the same for all firms we can use the shorthand $x = x_i$ for all i.

Finally, we can determine the number of goods produced by using the condition of full employment. From (4) and (9), we have

$$n = \frac{L}{\alpha + \beta x} = \frac{L(1-\theta)}{\alpha}. \tag{10}$$

Effects of Trade

Now suppose that two countries of the kind just analyzed open trade with one another at zero transportation cost. To make the point most clearly, suppose that the countries have the same tastes and technologies; since we are in a one-factor world there cannot be any differences in factor endowments. What will happen?

In this model there are none of the conventional reasons for trade, but there will nevertheless be both trade and gains from trade. Trade will occur because, in the presence of increasing returns, each good (i.e., each differentiated product) will be produced in only one country—for the same reasons that each good is produced by only one firm. Gains from trade will occur because the world economy will produce a greater diversity of goods than would either country alone, offering each individual a wider range of choice.

We can easily characterize the world economy's equilibrium. The symmetry of the situation ensures that the two countries will have the same wage rate, and that the price of any good produced in either country will be the same. The number of goods produced in each country can be determined from the full-employment condition

$$n = \frac{L(1-\theta)}{\alpha},$$
$$n^* = \frac{L^*(1-\theta)}{\alpha}, \tag{11}$$

where L^* is the labor force of the second country and n^* the number of goods produced there.

Individuals will still maximize the utility function (1), but they will now distribute their expenditure over both the n goods produced in the home country and the n^* goods produced in the foreign country. Because of the extended range of choice, welfare will increase even though the "real wage" w/p (i.e., the wage rate in terms of a representative good) remains unchanged. Also, the symmetry of the problem allows us to determine trade flows. It is apparent that individuals in the home country will spend a fraction $n^*/(n + n^*)$ of their income on foreign goods, while foreigners spend $n/(n + n^*)$ of their income on home country products. Thus the value of home country imports measured in wage units is $Ln^*/(n + n^*) = LL^*/(L + L^*)$. This equals the value of foreign country imports, confirming that with equal wage rates in the two countries we will have balance-of-payments equilibrium.

Notice, however, that while the *volume* of trade is determinate, the *direction* of trade—which country produces which goods—is not. This indeterminacy seems to be a general characteristic of models in which trade is a consequence of economies of scale. One of the convenient features of the models considered in this paper is that nothing important hinges on who produces what within a group of differentiated products. There is an indeterminacy, but it doesn't matter. This result might not hold up in less special models.

Finally, I should note a peculiar feature of the effects of trade in this model. Both before and after trade, equation (9) holds; that is, there is no effect of trade on the scale of production, and the gains from trade come solely through increased product diversity. This is an unsatisfactory result. In another paper I have developed a slightly different model in which trade leads to an increase in scale of production as well as an increase in diversity.[3] That model is, however, more difficult to work with, so that it seems worth sacrificing some realism to gain tractability here.

2 Transport Costs

In this section I extend the model to allow for some transportation costs. This is not in itself an especially interesting extension although the main result—that the larger country will, other things equal, have the higher wage rate—is somewhat surprising. The main purpose of the extension is, however, to lay the groundwork for the analysis of home market effects in the next section. (These effects can obviously occur only if there are transportation costs.) I begin by describing the behavior of individual agents, then analyze the equilibrium.

Individual Behavior

Consider a world consisting of two countries of the type analyzed in section 1, able to trade but only at a cost. Transportation costs will be assumed to be of the "iceberg" type, that is, only a fraction g of any good shipped arrives, with $1 - g$ lost in transit. This is a major simplifying assumption, as will be seen below.

An individual in the home country will have a choice over n products produced at home and n^* products produced abroad. The price of a domestic product will be the same as that received by the producer p. Foreign products, however, will cost more than the producer's price; if foreign firms charge p^*, home country consumers will have to pay the c.i.f. price $\hat{p}^* = p^*/g$. Similarly, foreign buyers of domestic products will pay $\hat{p} = p/g$.

Since the prices to consumers of goods of different countries will in general not be the same, consumption of each imported good will differ from consumption of each domestic good. Home country residents, for example, in maximizing utility will consume $(p/\hat{p}^*)^{1/(1-\theta)}$ units of a representative imported good for each unit of a representative domestic good they consume.

To determine world equilibrium, however, it is not enough to look at consumption; we must also take into account the quantities of goods used up in transit. If a domestic resident consumes one unit of a foreign good, his combined direct and indirect demand is for $1/g$ units. For determining total demand, then, we need to know the ratio of total demand by domestic residents for each foreign product to demand for each domestic product. Letting σ denote this ratio, and σ^* the corresponding ratio for the other country, we can show that

$$\sigma = \left(\frac{p}{p^*}\right)^{1/(1-\theta)} g^{\theta/(1-\theta)},$$
$$\sigma^* = \left(\frac{p}{p^*}\right)^{-1/(1-\theta)} g^{\theta/(1-\theta)}. \tag{12}$$

The overall demand pattern of each individual can then be derived from the requirement that his spending just equal his wage; that is, in the home country we must have $(np + \sigma n^*p^*)d = w$, where d is the consumption of a representative domestic good; and similarly in the foreign country.

This behavior of individuals can now be used to analyze the behavior of firms. The important point to notice is that the elasticity of *export* demand facing any given firm is $1/(1-\theta)$, which is the same as the elasticity of *domestic* demand. Thus transportation costs have no effect on firms' pricing policy, and the analysis of section 1 can be carried out as before, showing that transportation costs also have no effect on the number of firms or output per firm in either country.

Writing out these conditions again, we have

$$p = \frac{w\beta}{\theta}, \quad p^* = \frac{w^*\beta}{\theta},$$
$$n = \frac{L(1-\theta)}{\alpha}, \qquad n^* = \frac{L^*(1-\theta)}{\alpha}. \tag{13}$$

The only way in which introducing transportation costs modifies the results of section 1 is in allowing the possibility that wages may not be equal in the two countries; the number and size of firms are not affected. This strong result depends on the assumed form of the transport costs, which shows at the same time how useful and how special the assumed form is.

Determination of Equilibrium

The model we have been working with has a very strong structure—so strong that transport costs have no effect on either the numbers of goods produced in the countries, n and n^*, or on the prices relative to wages, p/w and p^*/w^*. The only variable that can be affected is the relative wage rate $w/w^* = \omega$, which no longer need be equal to one.

We can determine ω by looking at any one of three equivalent market-clearing conditions: (1) equality of demand and supply for home country labor, (2) equality of demand and supply for foreign country labor, and (3) balance-of-payments equilibrium. It will be easiest to work in terms of the balance of payments. If we combine (12) with the other equations of the model, it can be shown that the home country's balance of payments, measured in *wage units* of the *other* country, is

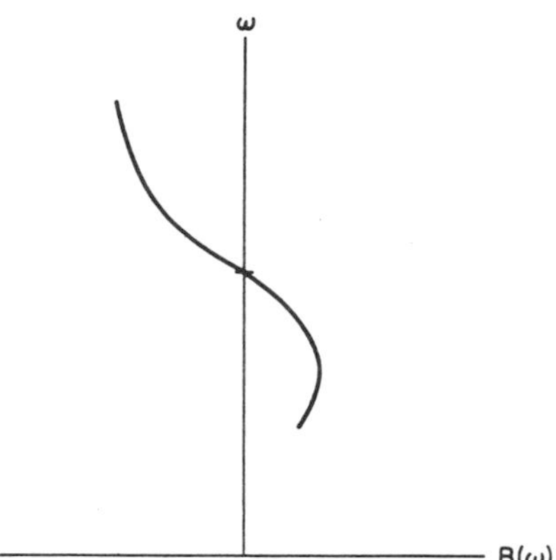

Figure 1

$$B = \frac{\sigma^* n\omega}{\sigma^* n + n^*} L^* - \frac{\sigma n^*}{n + \sigma n^*} \omega L$$
$$= \omega L L^* \left[\frac{\sigma^*}{\sigma^* L + L^*} - \frac{\sigma}{L + \sigma L^*} \right]. \tag{14}$$

Since σ and σ^* are both functions of $p/p^* = \omega$, the condition $B = 0$ can be used to determine the relative wage. The function $B(\omega)$ is illustrated in figure 1. The relative wage $\bar{\omega}$ is that relative wage at which the expression in brackets in (14) is zero, and at which trade is therefore balanced. Since σ is an increasing function of ω and σ^* a decreasing function of ω, $B(\omega)$ will be negative (positive) if and only if ω is greater (less) than $\bar{\omega}$, which shows that $\bar{\omega}$ is the unique equilibrium relative wage.

We can use this result to establish a simple proposition: *that the larger country, other things equal, will have the higher wage.* To see this, suppose that we were to compute $B(\omega)$ for $\omega = 1$. In that case we have $\sigma = \sigma^* < 1$. The expression for the balance of payments reduces to

$$B = LL^* \left[\frac{1}{\sigma L + L^*} - \frac{1}{L + \sigma L^*} \right]. \tag{14'}$$

But (14′) will be positive if $L > L^*$, negative if $L < L^*$. This means that the equilibrium relative wage ω must be greater than one if $L > L^*$, less than one if $L < L^*$.

This is an interesting result. In a world characterized by economies of scale, one would expect workers to be better off in larger economies, because of the larger size of the local market. In this model, however, there is a secondary benefit in the form of better terms of trade with workers in the rest of the world. This does, on reflection, make intuitive sense. If production costs were the same in both countries, it would always be more profitable to produce near the larger market, thus minimizing transportation costs. To keep labor employed in both countries, this advantage must be offset by a wage differential.

3 "Home Market" Effects on the Pattern of Trade

In a world characterized both by increasing returns and by transportation costs, there will obviously be an incentive to concentrate production of a good near its largest market, even if there is some demand for the good elsewhere. The reason is simply that by concentrating production in one place, one can realize the scale economies, while by locating near the larger market, one minimizes transportation costs. This point—which is more often emphasized in location theory than in trade theory—is the basis for the common argument that countries will tend to export those kinds of products for which they have relatively large domestic demand. Notice that this argument is wholly dependent on increasing returns; in a world of diminishing returns strong domestic demand for a good will tend to make it an import rather than an export. But the point does not come through clearly in models where increasing returns take the form of external economies (see Corden 1970). One of the main contributions of the approach developed in this paper is that by using this approach the home market effect can be given a simple formal justification.

I will begin by extending the basic closed economy model to one in which there are two industries (with many differentiated products within each industry). It will then be shown for a simple case that when two countries of this kind trade, each will be a net exporter in the industry for whose products it has the relatively larger demand. Finally, some extensions and generalizations will be discussed.

A Two-Industry Economy

As in section 1, we begin by analyzing a closed economy. Assume that there are two classes of products, *alpha* and *beta*, with many potential products within each class. A tilde will distinguish *beta* products from *alpha* products; for example, consumption of products in the first class will be represented as $c_1, \ldots, c_n$ while consumption of products in the second are $\tilde{c}_1, \ldots, \tilde{c}_n$.

Demand for the two classes of products will be assumed to arise from the presence of two groups in the population.[4] There will be one group with L members, which derives utility only from consumption of *alpha* products; and another group with $\tilde{L}$ members, deriving utility only from *beta* products. The utility functions of representative members of the two classes may by written

$$U = \sum_i c_i^\theta, \quad \tilde{U} = \sum_j \tilde{c}_j^\theta, \qquad 0 < \theta < 1. \tag{15}$$

For simplicity assume that not only the form of the utility function but the parameter θ is the same for both groups.

On the cost side, the two kinds of products will be assumed to have identical cost functions:

$$\begin{aligned} l_i &= \alpha + \beta x_i, \qquad i = 1, \ldots, n, \\ \tilde{l}_j &= \alpha + \beta \tilde{x}_j, \qquad j = 1, \ldots, \tilde{n}, \end{aligned} \tag{16}$$

where, l_i, $\tilde{l}_j$ are labor used in production on typical goods in each class, and x_i, $\tilde{x}_j$ are total outputs of the goods.

The demand conditions now depend on the population shares. By analogy with (3), we have

$$\begin{aligned} x_i &= Lc_i, \qquad i = 1, \ldots, n, \\ \tilde{x}_j &= \tilde{L}\tilde{c}_j, \qquad j = 1, \ldots, \tilde{n}. \end{aligned} \tag{17}$$

The full-employment condition, however, applies to the economy as a whole:

$$\sum_{i=1}^{n} l_i + \sum_{j=1}^{\tilde{n}} \tilde{l}_j = L + \tilde{L}. \tag{18}$$

Finally, we continue to assume free entry, driving profits to zero. Now it is immediately apparent that the economy described by equations (15)–(18) is very similar to the economy described in equations (1)–(4). The price and output of a representative good—of either class—and the total number of products $n + \tilde{n}$ are determined just as if all goods belonged to a single industry. The only modification we must make to the results of section 1 is that we must divide the total production into two industries. A simple way of doing this is to note that the sales of each industry must equal the income of the appropriate group in the population:

$$npx = wL, \quad \tilde{n}\tilde{p}\tilde{x} = \tilde{w}\tilde{L}. \tag{19}$$

But wages of the two groups must be equal, as must the prices and outputs of any products of either industry. So this reduces to the result $n/\tilde{n} = L/\tilde{L}$: the shares of the industries in the value of output equal the shares of the two demographic groups in the population.

This extended model clearly differs only trivially from the model developed in section 1 when the economy is taken to be closed. When two such economies are allowed to trade, however, the extension allows some interesting results.

Demand and the Trade Pattern: A Simple Case

We can begin by considering a particular case of trade between a pair of two-industry countries in which the role of the domestic market appears particularly clearly. Suppose that there are two countries of the type just described, and that they can trade with transport costs of the type analyzed in section 2.

In the home country, some fraction f of the population will be consumers of *alpha* products. The crucial simplification I will make is to assume that the other country is a *mirror image* of the home country. The labor forces will be assumed to be equal, so that

$$L + \tilde{L} = L^* + \tilde{L}^* = \bar{L}. \tag{20}$$

But in the foreign country the population shares will be reversed, so that we have

$$L = f\bar{L}, \quad L^* = (1 - f)\bar{L}. \tag{21}$$

If f is greater than one-half, then the home country has the larger domestic market for the *alpha* industry's products; and conversely. In this case there is a very simple home market proposition: *that the home country will be a net exporter of the first industry's products if* $f > 0.5$. This proposition turns out to be true.

The first step in showing this is to notice that this is a wholly symmetrical world, so that wage rates will be equal, as will the output and prices of all goods. (The case was constructed for that purpose.) It follows that the ratio of demand for each imported product to the demand for each domestic product is the same in both countries.

$$\sigma = \sigma^* = g^{\theta/(1-\theta)} < 1. \tag{22}$$

Next we want to determine the pattern of production. The expenditure on goods in an industry is the sum of domestic residents' and foreigners' expenditures on the goods, so we can write the expressions

$$\begin{aligned} npx &= \frac{n}{n + \sigma n^*} wL + \frac{\sigma n}{\sigma n + n^*} wL^*, \\ n^*px &= \frac{\sigma n^*}{n + \sigma n^*} wL + \frac{n^*}{\sigma n + n^*} wL^*, \end{aligned} \tag{23}$$

where the price p of each product and the output x are the same in the two countries. We can use (23) to determine the relative number of products produced in each country, n/n^*.

To see this, suppose *provisionally* that some products in the *alpha* industry are produced in both countries; namely, $n > 0$, $n^* > 0$. We can then divide the equations (23) through by n and n^*, respectively, and rearrange to get

$$\frac{L}{L^*} = \frac{n + \sigma n^*}{\sigma n + n^*}, \tag{24}$$

which can be rearranged to give

$$\frac{n}{n^*} = \frac{L/L^* - \sigma}{1 - \sigma L/L^*}. \tag{25}$$

Figure 2 shows the relationship (25). If $L/L^* = 1$, so does n/n^*; that is, if the demand patterns of the two countries are the same, their production patterns will also be the same, as we would expect. And as the relative size of either country's home market rises for *alpha* goods, so does its domestic production, as long as L/L^* lies in the range $\sigma < L/L^* > 1/\sigma$.

Outside that range, (25) appears to give absurd results. Recall, however, that the derivation of (24) was made on the provisional assumption that n and n^* were both nonzero. Clearly, if L/L^* lies outside the range from σ to $1/\sigma$, this assumption is not valid. What the figure suggests is that if L/L^* is less than σ, $n = 0$; the home country

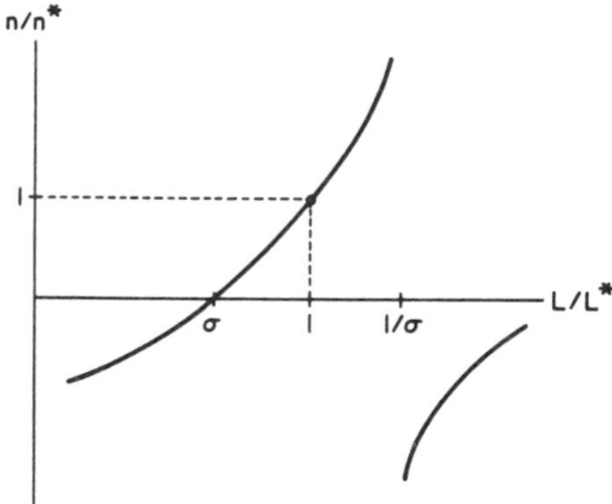

Figure 2

specializes entirely in *beta* products, producing no *alpha* products (while the foreign country produces only *alpha* products). Conversely, if L/L^* is greater than $1/\sigma$, $n^* = 0$, and we have the opposite pattern of specialization.

We can easily demonstrate that this solution is in fact an equilibrium. Suppose that the home country produced no *alpha* products, and that a firm attempted to start production of a single product. This firm's profit-maximizing f.o.b. price would be the same as that of the foreign firm's. But its sales would be less, in the ratio

$$\frac{\sigma^{-1}L + \sigma L^*}{L + L^*} < 1.$$

Thus such a firm could not compete.

This gives us our first result on the effect of the home market. It says that if the two countries have sufficiently dissimilar tastes each will specialize in the industry for which it has the larger home market. Obviously, also, each will be a net exporter of the class of goods in which it specializes. Thus the idea that the pattern of exports is determined by the home market is quite nicely confirmed.

We also get some illuminating results on the conditions under which specialization will be incomplete. Incomplete specialization and two-way trade within the two classes of products will occur if the relative size of the domestic markets for *alpha* goods lies in the range from σ to $1/\sigma$, where $\sigma = g^{\theta/(1-\theta)}$. But g measures transportation costs, while $\theta/(1-\theta)$ is, in equilibrium, the ratio of variable to fixed costs;[5] that is, it is an index of the importance of scale economies. So we have shown that the possibility of incomplete specialization is greater, the greater are transport costs and the less important are economies of scale.

A final result we can take from this special case concerns the pattern of trade when specialization is incomplete. In this case each country will both import and export products in *both* classes (though not the same products). But it remains true that, if one country has the larger home market for *alpha* producers, it will be a *net* exporter in the *alpha* class and a net importer in the other. To see this, note that we can write the home country's trade balance in *alpha* products as

$$B_\alpha = \frac{\sigma n}{\sigma n + n^*} wL^* - \frac{\sigma n^*}{n + \sigma n^*} wL$$

$$= wL^* \left[\frac{\sigma n}{\sigma n + n^*} - \frac{\sigma n^*}{n + \sigma n^*} \frac{L}{L^*} \right]$$

$$= \frac{\sigma w L^*}{\sigma n + n^*} [n - n^*], \tag{26}$$

where we used (24) to eliminate the relative labor supplies. This says that the sign of the trade balance depends on whether the number of *alpha* products produced in the home country is more or less than the number produced abroad. But we have already seen that n/n^* is an increasing function of L/L^* in the relevant range. So the country with the larger home market for the *alpha*-type products will be a net exporter of those goods, even if specialization is not complete.

Generalizations and Extensions

The analysis we have just gone through shows that there is some justification for the idea that countries export what they have home markets for. The results were arrived at, however, only for a special case designed to make matters as simple as possible. Our next question must be the extent to which these results generalize.

One way in which generalization might be pursued is by abandoning the "mirror image" assumption: we can let the countries have arbitrary populations and demand patterns, while retaining all the other assumptions of the model. It can be shown that in that case, although the derivations become more complicated, the basic home market result is unchanged. Each country will be a net exporter in the industry for whose goods it has a relatively larger demand. The difference is that wages will in general not be equal; in particular, smaller countries with absolutely smaller markets for both kinds of goods will have to compensate for this disadvantage with lower wages.

Another, perhaps more interesting, generalization would be to abandon the assumed symmetry between the industries. Again, we would like to be able to make sense of some arguments made by practical men. For example, is it true that large countries will have an advantage in the production and export of goods whose production is characterized by sizable economies of scale? This is an explanation that is sometimes given for the United States' position as an exporter of aircraft.

A general analysis of the effects of asymmetry between industries would run to too great a length. We can learn something, however, by considering another special case. Suppose that the *alpha* production is the same as in our last analysis, but that the production of *beta* goods is characterized by *constant* returns to scale and perfect competition. For simplicity, also assume that *beta* goods can be transported costlessly.

It is immediately apparent that in this case the possibility of trade in *beta* products will ensure that wage rates are equal. But this in turn means that we can apply the analysis above to the *alpha* industry. Whichever country has the larger market for the products of that industry will be a net exporter of *alpha* products and a net importer of *beta* products. In particular: if two countries have the same composition of demand, the larger country will be a net exporter of the products whose production involves economies of scale.

The analysis in this section has obviously been suggestive rather than conclusive. It relies heavily on very special assumptions and on the analysis of special cases. Nonetheless, the analysis does seem to confirm the idea that, in the presence of increasing returns, countries will tend to export the goods for which they have large domestic markets. And the implications for the pattern of trade are similar to those suggested by Linder (1961), Grubel (1970), and others.

Notes

1. A paper that points out the difficulties in explaining the actual pattern of world trade in a comparative cost framework is Hufbauer and Chilas (1974).

2. To be fully rigorous, we would have to use the concept of a continuum of potential products.

3. To get an increase in scale, we must assume that the demand facing each individual firm becomes more elastic as the number of firms increases, whereas in this model the elasticity of demand remains unchanged. Increasing elasticity of demand when the variety of products grows seems plausible, since the more finely differentiated are the products, the better substitutes they are likely to be for one another. Thus an increase in scale as well as diversity is probably the "normal" case. The constant elasticity case, however, is much easier to work with, which is my reason for using it in this paper.

4. An alternative would be to have all people alike, with a taste for both kinds of goods. The results are similar. In fact, if each industry receives a fixed share of expenditure, they will be identical.

5. One can see this by rearranging equation (9) to get $\beta x/\alpha = \theta/(1 - \theta)$.

References

Balassa, B. 1967. *Trade Liberalization Among Industrial* Countries. New York: McGraw-Hill.

Corden, W. M. 1970. A note on economies of scale, the size of the domestic market and the pattern of trade. In I. A. McDougall and R. H. Snape (eds.), *Studies in International Economics.* Amsterdam: North-Holland.

Dixit, A. and J. Stiglitz. 1977. Monopolistic competition and optimum product diversity. *American Economic Review* 67:297–308.

Grubel, H. 1967. Intra-industry specialization and the pattern of trade. *Canadian Journal of Economics* 33:374–388.

Grubel, H. 1970. The theory of intra-industry trade. In I. A. McDougall and R. H. Snape (eds.), *Studies in International Economics.* Amsterdam: North-Holland.

Hufbauer, G., and J. Chilas. 1974. Specialization by industrial countries: Extent and consequences. In H. Giersch (ed.), *The International Division of Labor.* Tübingen: J. C. B. Mohr.

Kravis, I. 1971. The current case for import limitations. In Commission on International Trade and Investment Policy, *United States Economic Policy in an Interdependent World.* Washington, D.C.: U.S. Government Printing Office.

Krugman, P. 1979. Increasing returns, monopolistic competition, and international trade. *Journal of International Economics* 9:469–480.

Linder, S. 1961. *An Essay on Trade and Transformation.* New York: John Wiley.

12 Product Differentiation and Intraindustry Trade

Avinash K. Dixit and Victor Norman

As we have demonstrated elsewhere, trade is merely a vehicle for market expansion. For analyzing the implications of this, we do not have to consider trade explicitly. For many purposes, however, we need explicit models of trade in the context of scale economies and imperfect competition. In particular, if we are to study the determinants of intraindustry trade, we must have explicit trade models. The same is true if we are to understand how trade based on scale economies interacts with trade based on comparative advantage. The model that follows is an example of an explicit theory of trade with product differentiation, economies of scale, and imperfect competition.

The model is based on Norman (1976) but has several similarities with Krugman (1978a, b). It attempts to explain trade within an industry consisting of close substitute products with similar technologies, as well as trade of the products of this industry for outputs of other industries. We relate the determinants of the two kinds of trade to the underlying reasons for trade and show how intraindustry trade can be explained by product differentiation while conventional explanations apply to interindustry trade. The basic model is kept extremely simple to allow explicit solutions that bring this aspect to the forefront. Some questions of generalizations are discussed at the end.

1 Demand

We simplify the demand side by using the stock assumption of international trade theory, namely, identical and homothetic preferences for all consumers in both countries. Then the aggregate commodity demands can be derived from a similar utility function. Two kinds of goods enter into the utility function. One, labeled 0, is a numeraire good intended to embody all goods other than the ones in the industry on which we wish to focus, the other kind being goods of that industry. These are assumed to be differentiated, so that the elasticity of substitution between any pair of them is finite. The product varieties are indexed 1, 2, ...; but we assume perfect symmetry so that it does not matter which label a particular product type bears. We take a special form of the utility function, where utility is Cobb-Douglas in the quantity of the numeraire good and a scalar measure of consumption of differentiated products, this scalar measure being a constant-elasticity-of-substitution function in the quantities of each product type.

As the total number of consumers in the two countries will be fixed, we can set world population at 1 without loss of generality. In that case, we do not have to distinguish between total and per capita quantities, so we let c_0 and c_k $(k = 1, 2, \ldots)$ denote the respective (total or per capita) quantities of the numeraire and the differentiated goods. The utility function is then

Originally published in *Theory of International Trade*, Avinash K. Dixit and Victor D. Norman (Cambridge University Press, 1980).

$$u = \left(\sum_k c_k^{\beta}\right)^{\alpha/\beta} c_0^{1-\alpha}, \tag{1}$$

where we can regard the term in parentheses as a measure of consumption of differentiated products. In order for the product varieties to be imperfect substitutes, we must have $\beta < 1$. On the other hand, we need $\beta > 0$ for the differentiated products to be good enough substitutes to warrant the label "product group": The elasticity of substitution between any pair of differentiated products is $1/(1 - \beta)$. Thus, if $\beta < 0$, the elasticity of substitution is less than unity. But given our Cobb-Douglas specification, the elasticity of substitution between differentiated goods and the numeraire good is unity, so if $\beta < 0$, the differentiated goods and the numeraire good are closer substitutes than are the differentiated goods among themselves. We therefore require $0 < \beta < 1$. In addition, we need $0 < \alpha < 1$ for our canonical representation of the utility function to be concave.

World demands can be found by maximizing the utility function subject to the budget constraint

$$c_0 + \sum_k p_k c_k = y, \tag{2}$$

where the p_k are prices, and y is the total of factor income and profits for the world. It is easy to find the inverse demand functions for the differentiated goods:

$$p_j = \frac{\alpha c_j^{\beta-1} y}{z}, \tag{3}$$

where

$$z = \sum_k c_k^{\beta}. \tag{4}$$

The demand for the numeraire is

$$c_0 = (1 - \alpha)y. \tag{5}$$

Note that these demand functions pertain to the world as a whole. Each country's quantities can be found by multiplying world demands by that country's share in world income.

2 Production

The numeraire good is produced under constant returns to scale in a perfectly competitive market. There are economies of scale in the production of the differentiated products, and the market structure is one of Chamberlinian monopolistic competition. Production functions are the same for all product varieties. The potential range of varieties is assumed to be so large that only a finite subset of the range is actually produced. The number of differentiated goods produced will therefore be determined by the entry condition for the industry. The two countries have identical technologies.

The numeraire good has a unit cost function $b(w)$ of factor prices. In principle, factor prices can be different in the two countries, although we shall investigate the possibility of their equalization through trade. Reverting to our home and foreign country notational convention, let w be the vector of factor prices in the home country and W that in the foreign country. We assume for the moment that both countries produce the numeraire good, so we have the zero-pure-profit conditions

$$b(w) = 1 = b(W). \tag{6}$$

As for the differentiated products, each product type has a total cost function $f(\cdot)\,h(\cdot)$, where f depends on factor prices and h on the output quantity. Thus the production functions are homothetic; in particular the factor proportions are independent of the output level. This is restrictive but has the merit of highlighting certain aspects of the question of factor price equalization and thereby providing the point of departure for further analyses. There are significant economies of scale, namely, $h(x)/x$ is decreasing over the relevant range of output levels x.

Production of each product variety in such an industry will be undertaken by only one producer, since a potential entrant can always do better by introducing a new product variety than by sharing in the production of an existing product type. We assume that the number of varieties produced is large enough to make oligopolistic interactions negligible, so that we have a monopolistically competitive industry. Each producer attempts to maximize profit given the inverse demand function facing him, and treating the outputs of others as fixed and world income as beyond his control. Entry occurs until the marginal firm is just breaking even; with symmetry this implies zero profit all around.

We can find the elasticity of the inverse demand function for the producer of good j from (3) and (4). From (3) we have

$$\frac{c_j}{p_j}\frac{\partial p_j}{\partial c_j} = (\beta - 1) - \frac{c_j}{z}\frac{\partial z}{\partial c_j}.$$

The second term here is the indirect effect, through total industry output, that an increase in the quantity of one product type has on the price of that variety. Using (4) we see that this effect is

$$\frac{c_j}{z}\frac{\partial z}{\partial c_j} = \beta\frac{c_j^\beta}{z} = \beta\frac{c_j^\beta}{\sum_k c_k^\beta}.$$

This is clearly inversely related to the total number of product varieties in existence; in fact, in a symmetric equilibrium, it is simply β times the inverse of the number of product varieties. Under our assumption of large numbers, therefore, this term will be negligible. The elasticity of inverse demand can then be approximated by $(1 - \beta)$ in absolute value, so the marginal revenue for the producer of product type j is βp_j. For profit maximization, this will be equated to marginal cost. In the home country, marginal cost is $f(w)h'(x_j)$, so if product type j is produced there, we shall have

$$\beta p_j = f(w)h'(x_j). \tag{7}$$

We shall consider only long-term equilibria, that is, equilibria in which no producer has incentives to enter or leave the industry. If the differentiated products are produced in the home country at all, this means that there must be zero pure profits in the industry, that is, the number of product types must be such that average revenue equals average cost:

$$p_j = \frac{f(w)h(x_j)}{x_j}. \tag{8}$$

Dividing (7) by (8), we find

$$\beta = \frac{x_j h'(x_j)}{h(x_j)}.$$

This must be true for all products j that are produced. In particular, it must hold regardless of factor prices, so long as differentiated products are produced at all in the country we are looking at. Provided the right-hand side is a monotonic function of x_j, the equation will have a unique solution. The implication is that all product varieties in existence will have the same output level, the common value of x being defined by

$$\beta = \frac{xh'(x)}{h(x)}. \tag{9}$$

This result depends crucially on homotheticity in production. The special form of the utility function is less important; for much more general functions, the left-hand side will be a function of x alone, which is all that matters. The convenience of the result lies in the fact that it allows us to concentrate on the number of products in the industry.

3 General Equilibrium

We assume that each country is active in the production of at least one variety from the industry. Then we have equations like (7) and (8) in each country for at least one j. Using (9), all these can be summarized into the following:

$$\beta p = f(w)h'(x) = f(W)h'(x), \tag{10}$$

$$px = f(w)h(x) = f(W)h(x). \tag{11}$$

Note that given (9), only one of (10) and (11) can be regarded as independent. Given (9) and (10), for example, we can derive (11).

Next we have the equilibrium conditions in the factor markets. We know that the cost-minimizing factor inputs are the derivatives of the appropriate cost functions with respect to factor prices. Let x_0 be the home production of the numeraire good and n the number of differentiated products produced in the home country; let X_0 and N be the corresponding entities for the foreign country. Strictly speaking, n and N must be integers, which causes problems attaining an exact balance in factor markets. The fact that we have assumed the total number of product types to be large [i.e., $(n + N)$ large] does not solve this problem. Nevertheless, we shall regard both n and N as real numbers. In places where the integer constraint matters, however, we shall point out how. With both as real numbers, we have the equilibrium conditions

$$x_0 b_w(w) + n f_w(w) h(x) = v, \tag{12}$$

$$X_0 b_w(W) + N f_w(W) h(x) = V, \tag{13}$$

where v and V are the vectors of factor endowments.

Finally, we require that the world output levels be compatible with equilibrium in the goods markets. Noting that world income is factor income alone, since profits vanish in a Chamberlinian equilibrium, total income is $(w \cdot v + W \cdot V)$. Substituting in (3) and (5), we have

$$p = \frac{\alpha(w \cdot v + W \cdot V)}{x(n + N)}, \tag{14}$$

$$x_0 + X_0 = (1 - \alpha)(w \cdot v + W \cdot V). \tag{15}$$

If m is the number of factors in each country, we have in (12)–(15) $(2m + 2)$ equations, of which one is redundant by Walras's law. To complete the determination of equilibrium, we append (6) and (9)–(11), which contribute five more independent equations, making $(2m + 6)$ in all. These suffice to determine the $(2m + 6)$ unknowns p, x, n, N, x_0, X_0, w, and W, subject to the usual caveats concerning existence and uniqueness.

It is instructive to regard the equilibrium formally in a different light. Let (9) fix x, and then think of the industry under consideration as producing just one good, namely, the number of products. This is produced at constant unit cost $\phi(w) = f(w)h(x)$ and sold competitively at price $\rho = px$. The equilibrium conditions then become

$$b(w) = 1 = b(W), \tag{16}$$

$$\phi(w) = \rho = \phi(W), \tag{17}$$

$$x_0 b_w(w) + n\phi_w(w) = v, \tag{18}$$

$$X_0 b_w(W) + N\phi_w(W) = V, \tag{19}$$

$$x_0 + X_0 = (1 - \alpha)(w \cdot v + W \cdot V), \tag{20}$$

$$n + N = \frac{\alpha(w \cdot v + W \cdot V)}{\rho}. \tag{21}$$

These are formally exactly like the conditions for a competitive equilibrium in a two-good economy with each good produced in both countries. We will have to be careful when it comes to assessing the welfare consequences of trade, since this shorthand description treats all product varieties essentially in an additive way, whereas they are in fact imperfect substitutes. But as far as descriptive aspects are concerned, this approach has some immediate implications. We begin with the most important of these, which leads to our drawing a distinction between interindustry and intraindustry trade.

4 Interindustry Trade

The model gives an account of the trade between the numeraire good and the aggregate quantity of differentiated goods. Further, given identical technologies and preferences in the two countries, the mechanism is exactly like that of the conventional factor-abundance model. For example, if the differentiated goods are more capital-intensive, the more capital-abundant country will have a comparative advantage in them. We can then establish the Rybczynski propositions concerning changes in the supplies of differentiated goods as a result of factor endowment changes and other comparative static results. This is left to the reader.

5 Intraindustry Trade

However, the important new feature of this model is intraindustry trade. Suppose the home country accounts for a fraction λ of world income. With homothetic preferences, it consumes a fraction λ of the world output of each good, $c_0 = \lambda(x_0 + X_0)$, and $c = \lambda x$ for each of the $(n + N)$ differentiated goods produced. Its production is x_0 for the numeraire good and x for each of n varieties of the differentiated goods. Without loss of generality, suppose that the home country is a net exporter of differentiated goods. Suppose it produces the first n of these by choice of labeling. Define $\sigma = n/(n + N)$, so σ is the home country's share in world production of differentiated products. For the home country, net imports of the numeraire are $c_0 - x_0 = \lambda X_0 - (1 - \lambda)x_0$. Its exports of varieties $1, 2, \ldots, n$ are $(1 - \lambda)x$ each, and its imports of varieties $(n + 1), \ldots$ $(n + N)$ are λx each. Total trade is balanced, that is,

$$\lambda X_0 - (1 - \lambda)x_0 = np(1 - \lambda)x - Np\lambda x.$$

Gross exports of differentiated goods are of value

$$npx(1 - \lambda) = (n + N)px\sigma(1 - \lambda),$$

while net exports of differentiated goods are

$$\begin{aligned} npx(1 - \lambda) - Npx\lambda &= (n + N)px\{\sigma(1 - \lambda) - (1 - \sigma)\lambda\} \\ &= (n + N)px(\sigma - \lambda). \end{aligned}$$

Remember that we have chosen labels so that the home country is a net exporter of these goods, that is, $\sigma > \lambda$. For the foreign country, gross exports of differentiated goods are similarly seen to be $(n + N)px(1 - \sigma)\lambda$. For the world as a whole, then, the value of gross trade T_G is

$$T_G = (n + N)px\{\sigma(1 - \lambda) + (1 - \sigma)\lambda\}, \tag{22}$$

and that of net trade, T_N, is

$$T_N = (n + N)px(\sigma - \lambda). \tag{23}$$

The difference is intraindustry trade T_I. Simplifying, we see

$$T_I = 2(n + N)px\lambda(1 - \sigma). \tag{24}$$

These expressions have some immediate implications for the pattern of trade. The simplest is a confirmation of our earlier observation that net trade (i.e., the net exchange of differentiated goods for the numeraire good) is explained by conventional comparative advantage. In the formula for net trade, this boils down to the fact that the share of the home country in the production of differentiated goods is larger than its share of world income. If the countries were identical, we would have $\lambda = \sigma = \frac{1}{2}$ and no net trade. More generally, if the two were scaled replicas of each other, we would have $\lambda = \sigma$ and no net trade.

Next, gross trade is not related to comparative advantage as such, but to a correlation between comparative advantage and country size. Fixing $(n + N)px$ and varying λ and σ in (22), we find that the expression in the brackets takes on its maximum value when $\lambda = 0$ and $\sigma = 1$, namely, when a small country has great comparative advantage in the production of differentiated goods.

Turning to intraindustry trade, we see from (24) that it will be more important when λ is large and when σ is small. Since we have $\sigma > \lambda$, this means that intraindustry trade will be at its height when each of these is nearly $\frac{1}{2}$. In other words, if the two countries are of a similar size and have no clear comparative advantage across industries, then we will see the predominant pattern of trade as one of intraindustry trade. Movements of factors, transmission of technology, and convergence of tastes are all shifts that are conducive to such a state of affairs.

It is possible to relate our model to the work of Grubel and Lloyd (1975) and express their ratio index of intraindustry trade in terms of our σ and λ. As that does not yield any further insights, we leave it as an exercise for the reader.

The assumption of symmetry between the differentiated goods has a further implication that the matter of which country produces which good can be settled in an arbitrary manner. The total volume of trade is determinate, but its pattern is not. These observations concerning intraindustry trade may be seen as a partial confirmation of the views of Linder (1961).

6 Factor-Price Equalization

Let us turn to the question of factor prices. We assumed an equilibrium where each country produced both kinds of goods. In the manner of conventional theory, we could then ask whether the price-equals-unit-cost conditions uniquely fix factor prices, that is, whether (16) and (17) must yield $w = W$ for given ρ. With two factors and no factor-intensity reversals, such would be the case. Better still, we could follow a general equilibrium approach, making endogenous the question of specialization and the determination of output prices. If there is an equilibrium with trade in goods but with equal factor prices, it must be an equilibrium of an integrated world with factors as well as goods traded. Conversely, given the factor prices $\hat{w}$ of such an integrated equilibrium, these will serve as equalized factor prices following trade in goods alone, provided the world outputs can be decomposed into feasible x_0, X_0, n, and N satisfying the separate factor-market equilibrium conditions (18) and (19) for the two countries. With two factors, we can examine this in a diagram. In figure 1, we show the unit factor input vectors $b_w(\hat{w})$ and $\phi_w(\hat{w})$ of the integrated equilibrium in directions OA_1 and OA_2. The lengths OC_1 and OC_2 mark off the amounts needed to produce the total outputs, $(x_0 + X_0)$ of the numeraire good and $(n + N)$ varieties of differentiated goods in amounts x each. The coordinates of O' relative to O give the total world factor endowments. Then we know that if the factor endowments of the home country measured relative to O (and simultaneously those of the foreign country relative to O') lie outside the parallelogram $OC_1O'C_2$, it will be impossible to achieve such a decomposition. Then our assumption of completely nonspecialized production will not be valid, and factor-price equalization will not occur. Inside the parallelogram, there is a slight new problem. Not all the points there are feasible, given the requirement that the number of differentiated goods must be an integer, and each must be produced in the fixed amount x. Therefore we mark off along OC_2 all integer multiples of $\phi_w(\hat{w})$, the factor requirement of each variety. The numeraire good being assumed perfectly

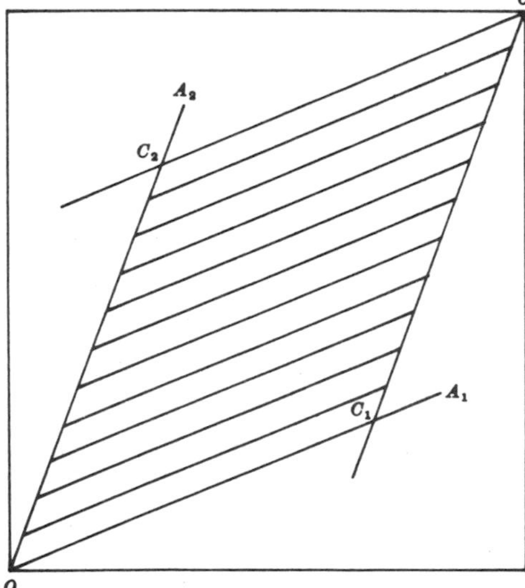

Figure 1

divisible, we draw from these points lines parallel to OA_1. For home factor endowments lying on any of this family of parallel lines, we can determine a part of the total world production to be undertaken at home while achieving exact clearing of factor markets. Within the parallelogram but off these lines, such exact equilibrium is not possible. However, so long as the number of products is large, any point in the parallelogram will be relatively close to one of the lines, and we will be justified in thinking of an approximate equilibrium with diversified production and factor-price equalization.

The generalization of these arguments to the case of m factors and $(n - 1)$ industries of differentiated goods is in principle clear. Insofar as the likelihood of factor-price equalization depends on the relative numbers of goods and factors, what is then at stake is the number of *industries* with differentiated products, and not the total distinguishable number of commodities. This may be of some interest to those who believe that there are "obviously" more goods than factors in the world.

7 Unequal Factor Proportions

As demonstrated, this result depends on the assumption that all product types in the industry have the same factor proportions. This may be a reasonable assumption for some industries, but one would like to know how robust the result is. To answer this question, consider an example where the differentiated goods are graded by relative factor intensities. Suppose for sake of clarity of exposition that there are two factors, and that the numeraire good is more factor-1 intensive than any of the differentiated goods. Form the box of world factor endowments as in figure 2. Let OA_1 be the direction of factor proportions of the numeraire good as usual, and let $O'A'_1$ be the

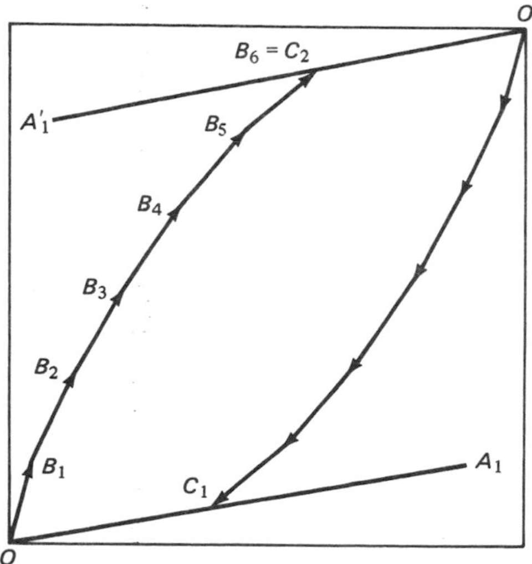

Figure 2

parallel direction from O'. Let OB_1 be the direction and magnitude of the factor requirements in the fully integrated equilibrium for the world production of the most factor-2 intensive differentiated goods. String at the end of this B_1B_2, the factor requirement for the next most factor-2 intensive type, and so on. Finally we reach $O'A'_1$, at the point we have been calling C_2. Proceeding symmetrically from O', we reach C_1 on OA_1. For consistency of the integrated equilibrium, OC_1 must be the factor requirement for the numeraire in that equilibrium. Arguing as before, and with the same proviso about approximations in factor-market equilibration made necessary by the indivisibilities in the production of differentiated goods, we can say that for factor endowments in the region $OC_1O'C_2O$, there will be diversified production and factor-price equalization, and that outside it, there will not be factor-price equalization.

The general point is that, although a variety of factor proportions across the differentiated goods brings with it a greater number of factor proportions vectors for spanning the home and foreign factor endowments, the output of each type is correspondingly smaller in the economy, and therefore we cannot be sure whether a greater area of the factor-endowment box will be compatible with factor-price equalization. Therefore, even a large number of product types with different factor proportions is no automatic guarantee of equal factor prices. We reached the same uncertain conclusion elsewhere when we increased the number of goods without classifying them into industries. With some differences caused by scale economies and imperfect competition, the present verdict is analogous.

8 Other Asymmetries

Having departed from the symmetry assumption of the formal model in one respect, we take this opportunity to say something about cases where differentiated goods do not enter preferences in a symmetric way. Precise models are difficult to specify, but some likely conclusions stand out. The asymmetry may pertain to product types or to countries. Consider first the case where goods can be ordered along a chain labeled 1, 2, 3, ... Preferences shift systematically along the chain, and goods farther apart are poorer substitutes than ones closer together in labels. The case most favorable to large intraindustry trade, as well as to a large shift in the pattern of production towards differentiated goods after the opening of trade, is the one where each country's preferences are strongest where its comparative cost advantage is weakest along the chain. In isolation, each country would not find it worthwhile to devote much of its resources to the production of relatively high cost and weakly desired differentiated goods. With the possibility of trade, each will be able to produce the types of differentiated goods desired by the other. On the other hand, if preferences match comparative cost advantage with respect to differentiated goods, there will be little intraindustry trade. There may be net trade of differentiated goods for the numeraire good depending on conventional comparative advantage.

The above discussion took the pattern of preferences over the spectrum of differentiated goods to be exogenous. But it could depend on income, thus giving rise to endogenous explanations of intraindustry trade. For example, suppose mass-produced varieties of goods are relatively capital intensive. On the other hand, a capital-abundant country has a higher real income per head of population, which is at the margin more heavily spent on the handcrafted varieties. This would be a case compatible with a large volume of intraindustry trade.

9 Gains from Intraindustry Trade

To conclude this discussion, we return to the symmetric case and examine the welfare aspects of trade. To concentrate on the new feature of intraindustry trade, it is best to consider the simple case where this is the only kind of trade. As we saw before, this occurs when each country is a scaled replica of the world. Suppose the home country has a fraction λ of the population and of each primary factor of production. We can determine the autarky equilibrium of the home country by methods similar to those employed at the beginning of the discussion. The output of each differentiated good will be governed by (7) and (8) and will therefore be the same, x, for all of them, and given by (9). Factor and output market conditions will then imply that the numeraire output, and the number of varieties produced, are each proportional to the size of the economy. When the two economies are allowed to trade, the output of each variety will remain unchanged, but the total numbers will increase. The gain from trade has its source here.

Suppose that the trading world would have $\hat{n}$ varieties of differentiated goods and an output $\hat{x}_0$ of the numeraire good. Recall that units are chosen so that world population equals 1. The consumption levels per capita are $\hat{x}_0$ for the numeraire good and x for each of the $\hat{n}$ differentiated goods. Substituting in (1), each consumer's utility is

$$\hat{u} = (\hat{n}x^{\beta})^{\alpha/\beta}\hat{x}_0^{1-\alpha}.$$

Now consider the countries in isolation. In the home country, there would be λ consumers, an amount $\lambda\hat{x}_0$ of the numeraire good, and $\lambda\hat{n}$ varieties of differentiated goods each in quantity x. Per capita consumption levels would be $\hat{x}_0$ for the numeraire good and x/λ for each of $\lambda\hat{n}$ varieties of differentiated goods. Therefore the utility of each home consumer under autarky would be

$$\begin{aligned} u &= \left[\lambda\hat{n}\left(\frac{x}{\lambda}\right)^{\beta}\right]^{\alpha/\beta}\hat{x}_0^{1-\alpha} \\ &= \lambda^{\alpha(1-\beta)/\beta}\hat{u}. \end{aligned}$$

Similarly, in the foreign country, utility of each consumer would be

$$U = (1-\lambda)^{\alpha(1-\beta)/\beta}\hat{u}.$$

Since $\beta < 1$, each of u and U is less than $\hat{u}$. We see the essential role played by product differentiation. Total consumption of differentiated products per capita is the same in autarky as under free trade—it is $\hat{n}x$ under free trade, and $(\lambda\hat{n})(x/\lambda) = \hat{n}x$ in autarky. The gain arises because the consumer gets a larger number of product varieties and a proportionally smaller amount of each variety; with convex preferences, the consumer prefers this.

References

Grubel, H. G., and Peter J. Lloyd. 1965. *Intra-industry Trade: The Theory and Measurement of International Trade in Differentiated Products.* New York: Wiley.

Krugman, P. 1978a. Increasing returns, monopolistic competition, and international trade. Mimeo, Yale University.

Krugman, P. 1978b. Scale economies, product differentiation, and the pattern of trade. Mimeo, Yale University.

Linder, S. B. 1961. *An Essay on Trade and Transformation.* New York: Wiley.

Norman, V. 1976. Product differentiation and international trade. Paper presented at the Summer Research Workshop, Warwick University.

13 International Trade in the Presence of Product Differentiation, Economies of Scale, and Monopolistic Competition: A Chamberlin-Heckscher-Ohlin Approach

Elhanan Helpman

1 Introduction

The interest in the effects of product differentiation, economies of scale, and monopolistic competition on international trade has existed for many years. Nevertheless, traditional theories of international trade have not been extended to incorporate these elements. With the growth in recent years of formal models of industrial organization, there now seem to exist more than ever before the conditions necessary for an integration of theories of industrial organization with theories of international trade.

Two recent studies—Krugman (1979) and Lancaster (1979, ch. 10)—that used a one-sector model began the new literature on the effects of product differentiation, monopolistic competition, and economies of scale on problems of international trade. Despite the fact that each one of them used a different approach to the specification of preferences, they reached the same broad conclusions regarding the nature of intraindustry trade and gains from specialization that are secured by taking advantage of economies of scale.

It is my purpose to provide in this paper an integration of the Heckscher-Ohlin approach to international trade with a Chamberlin-type approach to product differentiation, economies of scale, and monopolistic competition. In the present framework, the Heckscher-Ohlin approach is used to explain intersectoral trade while that of Chamberlin is used to explain intraindustry trade (see also Dixit and Norman 1980, ch. 9; Lancaster 1980; Krugman 1981). The theory that emerges from this study is a proper generalization of the Heckscher-Ohlin theory, and it yields interesting as well as useful results. For example, I provide a factor-price equalization theorem without requiring homotheticity of the production function in the differentiated product industry. Thus, it is shown that in the presence of monopolistic competition, we can predict the pattern of *intersectoral* trade from factor endowments even when the production function of the differentiated product, which exhibits economies of scale, is not homothetic. A capital-rich country will be a *net* exporter of the capital-intensive good while a labor-rich country will be a *net* exporter of the labor-intensive good. Differentiated products will be imported and exported by every country.

Secondly, it is shown that it is generally impossible to predict the pattern of trade from information about pretrade relative commodity prices or relative factor rewards. However, when differentiated products are produced with a homothetic production function and consumers spend fixed budget shares on each good (Cobb-Douglas utility functions), relative *factor* rewards can be used to predict the intersectoral pattern of trade. The country with the lower wage-rental ratio will be a net exporter of the labor-intensive good while the other country will be a net exporter of the capital-intensive good. But, even in this case relative *commodity* prices cannot be used

Originally published in the *Journal of International Economics* 11 (August 1981): 305–340.

to predict the intersectoral pattern of trade, because country size matters. Other things being equal, the larger country has a lower relative price of the good produced with economies of scale. Lancaster (1980) has termed this feature "false comparative advantage." In order to overcome the size bias, I develop an index that I call the scale-adjusted price, which can be used to predict the pattern of trade. Thus, the country with the lower scale-adjusted relative price of a good will be a net exporter of this good.

Third, I prove a general theorem on the composition of trade in terms of intersectoral versus intraindustry trade. The theorem says that within some well-defined limits a redistribution of factor endowments that enlarges the difference in capital-labor ratios available in each country reduces the *share* of intraindustry trade in the total volume of trade. The *volume* of trade is not related monotonically to the difference in capital-labor ratios, unless country *sizes* are kept constant. The volume of trade is declining as pure size differentials increase.

Fourth, based on this theorem, as well as on additional considerations, I propose two hypotheses concerning the relationship between the share of intraindustry trade and incomes per capita. The first hypothesis, which deals with a cross-section comparison, is that the bilateral share of intraindustry trade is negatively correlated with the absolute bilateral difference in incomes per capita. The second hypothesis, which deals with a time series comparison, is that the share of intraindustry trade in world trade is negatively correlated with the dispersion of the countries' incomes per capita. The first hypothesis finds support in a recent study by Loertscher and Wolter (1980); I am not aware of any studies that shed light on the second hypothesis.

Since the theory of consumer behavior that is used in this study is new and probably not widely known, sections 2 and 3 provide a detailed description of consumer behavior and the behavior of monopolists that use true demand functions for profit maximization. These sections build on Lancaster's recent important study (see Lancaster 1979). Here I wish only to point out that I have chosen to work with Lancaster's demand theory because it enables me to discuss monopolistic competition in terms that are commonly used in industrial organization, and I consider this to be an advantage. For example, in this model, a firm that produces a variety of a certain product chooses a specification and a price, knowing the demand curve that it faces. Its demand curve depends on its product's price, its specification, and also on the prices and product specifications of its closest competitors, namely, those whose varieties are closest to the firm's variety. If the firm increases its price, it loses customers and those who remain buy less; that is, its market share declines.

An equilibrium of a two-by-two closed economy is described in section 4. Then, in section 5, I discuss trading equilibria of a two-country world. There, I interpret well-known theorems from the Heckscher-Ohlin theory and prove the theorem on the relationship between the share of intraindustry trade and the difference in factor endowments. Then, in section 6, I consider the predictive power of pretrade commodity prices and factor rewards regarding the pattern of intersectoral trade. Finally, in section 7, I discuss some empirical implications of the theory.

2 Consumers

Assume that a typical consumer consumes two goods—a manufactured commodity and food. Food is a homogeneous product with a single specification; there is no more than one type of food. Manufactured goods, on the other hand, have many potential specifications so that there are many types (varieties) of the manufactured product. I assume that there is a continuum of types of the manufactured product that can be produced, and that there is a one-to-one correspondence between these types and points on a circumference of a circle. Thus point b_i in figure 1 represents a product of a particular type, and so do points b_{i-1} and b_{i+1}. Moreover, each product type has a corresponding point on the circumference of the circle in figure 1.[1]

It is now assumed that among all varieties of the manufactured good that can possibly be produced, each consumer has a most preferred type. The meaning of the most-preferred-type assumption is as follows: If the consumer is faced with the bundle of x units of manufactured goods and y units of food and he is free to choose the specification of the manufactured good of which he will receive x units, then, independent of the quantities x and y, he will always prefer a particular type, referred to as his "ideal" type. Observe that this assumption implies something about the units in which quantities of manufactured goods are measured. At this stage it is perhaps appropriate to mention an assumption that will be made about production in the next section, namely, that units in which quantities of manufactured goods are measured and technologies are such that the production function of manufactured goods is independent of specification. This means that if a given combination of factors of production produces, say, X units of goods of type b_i in figure 1, then the same combination of factors of production will produce X units of every other possible type of manufactured goods. This assumption is needed in order to assure the possibility of a symmet-

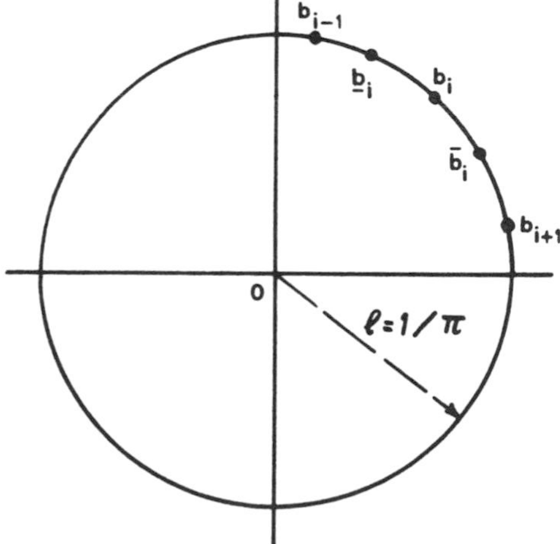

Figure 1

rical equilibrium. In cases in which one wants to give up symmetry, this assumption can be relaxed.

Now let $u(x, y)$ be a consumer's utility function that represents his preference ordering over food and quantities of *his* ideal manufactured good. For a complete representation of preferences we also have to specify preferences over food and other types of manufactured goods that are not the consumer's ideal type. This is done by assuming the existence of a function $h(v)$, defined for $0 \leqq v \leqq \pi l = 1$, where $l = 1/\pi$ is the radius of the circle in figure 1, such that the consumer is indifferent between x units of the ideal manufactured product and $h(v)x$ units of a good whose location on the circumference of the circle is at distance v (shortest arc distance) from the consumer's ideal manufactured product. The function $h(v)$ is called the compensation function and it is assumed to have the following properties:

$$h(0) = 1 \quad \text{and} \quad h(v) > 1 \qquad \text{for } v > 0, \tag{1a}$$

$$h'(0) = 0 \quad \text{and} \quad h'(v) > 0 \qquad \text{for } v > 0, \tag{1b}$$

$$h''(v) > 0 \qquad \text{for } v \geqq 0. \tag{1c}$$

Thus, the further away a product is located from the ideal product, the more of it is required to make the consumer indifferent between it and one unit of the ideal product. Also, due to (1c), the further away a product is located from the ideal product, the larger the required marginal compensation. A typical compensation function is presented in figure 2.

Let $x(v)$ denote the quantity of the manufactured product located at distance v from the consumer's ideal product that is being consumed by the consumer. Then, if he also consumes y units of food, his utility level is

$$u = u\left[\frac{x(v)}{h(v)}, y\right]. \tag{2}$$

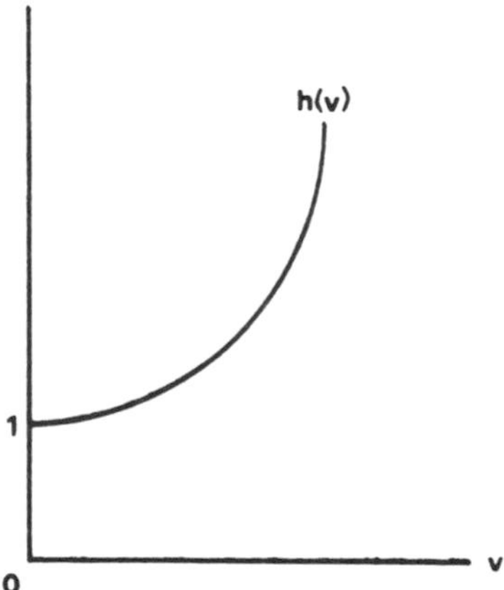

Figure 2

It is assumed that a consumer consumes only one type of manufactured good. In this case equation (2) provides a complete specification of his preferences. I assume that $u(\cdot)$ is increasing in each argument, strictly quasi-concave and homothetic.

In the present framework a consumer makes two decisions. The first decision concerns the variety of the manufactured good that he will consume. Among all the varieties available in the market, and taking account of the relative prices of the available varieties, the consumer chooses the product that fits him best. Then he makes the second decision, which is the allocation of his budget between food and the manufactured product that he has chosen to consume. The second decision is a standard decision in consumer theory. If he chooses to consume a variety that is located at a distance v from his ideal product, his demand functions will be (due to homotheticity of preferences):[2]

$$\frac{x(v)}{h(v)} = \alpha_x[p_x h(v), p_y]I, \tag{3a}$$

$$y = \alpha_y[p_x h(v), p_y]I, \tag{3b}$$

where p_x is the price of the manufactured good located at distance v from the consumer's ideal type, p_y is the price of food, I is the consumer's income and $\alpha_x(\cdot)$ and $\alpha_y(\cdot)$ are functions homogeneous of degree (-1), with the property $p_x h(v)\alpha_x[p_x h(v), p_y] + p_y\alpha_y[p_x h(v), p_y] \equiv 1$.

The interpretation of the demand functions in (3) is as follows. Suppose the consumer decides to purchase a variety of the manufactured product that is located at distance v from his ideal type, and whose price is p_x. Then, his *effective* price per unit of the ideal type is $p_x h(v)$, because in his welfare calculations $h(v)$ units of the available good are equivalent to one unit of the ideal type. Hence, the right-hand side of (3a) represents the demand for units of the ideal type and (3b) represents the demand for food, with $p_x h(v)$ standing for the price of a unit of the ideal type and p_y standing for the price of food. Since $\alpha_x(\cdot)I$ represents demand for units of the ideal type, we have—on the left-hand side of (3a)—$x(v)/h(v)$, which represents the quantity of the ideal type that is equivalent from the point of view of the consumer to $x(v)$ units of the product located at distance v from the ideal type. It is now clear which variety the consumer will choose to purchase—he will choose the variety that provides him with the lowest effective price of the ideal product.

So far I have discussed the properties of an isolated consumer. In order to analyze market behavior I also need to specify properties of the population of consumers. This will be done in the remaining part of this section.

It is assumed that there is a continuum of consumers and that all consumers have the same income and the same utility function. Since income is derived from ownership of factors of production, the assumption is really that all consumers have the same fraction of ownership of all factors of production. However, not all consumers have the same ideal type of the manufactured product. Preferences for the ideal type are assumed to be uniformly distributed on the circumference of the circle in figure 1.

This means that when L is the population size in a country, the density of consumers whose ideal type is b_i (see fig. 1) is $\xi = L/(2\pi l) = L/2$ in this country, with the same density applying to every point on the circumference of the circle. Thus, although equation (3) represents every consumer's demand function, the consumers' reference points in the form of ideal products are evenly distributed on the circumference of the circle. These assumptions assure symmetry in aggregate demand for varieties of manufactured products. The role of this symmetry will become clearer in later discussions.

3 Producers

I assume that food is produced by means of labor and capital with a usual twice-differentiable, increasing, linear homogeneous, strictly quasi-concave production function $Y = F_Y(L_Y, K_Y)$. This production function has associated with it the cost function

$$C_Y(w,r,Y) \equiv c_Y(w,r)Y, \tag{4}$$

where w is the wage rate, r is the capital rental rate, and $c_Y(w,r)$ is an increasing, concave, linear homogeneous function that represents marginal (=average) costs. This cost function yields demand functions

$$L_Y = a_{LY}(w,r)Y, \tag{5a}$$

$$K_Y = a_{KY}(w,r)Y, \tag{5b}$$

where $a_{LY}(w,r) = \partial c_Y(w,r)/\partial w$ is the labor-output ratio and $a_{KY}(w,r) = \partial c_Y(w,r)/\partial r$ is the capital-output ratio.

As usual, the food sector will produce a positive and finite output level only if the price of food equals marginal costs of production, and it will produce no food if the price of food falls short of its marginal costs of production. Thus, if the industry is to produce at a finite level, we require

$$p_y = c_Y(w,r). \tag{6}$$

Independently of whether the food industry produces or not, its profits are always zero.

Now consider the manufacturing sector. It is assumed that the production function of a single variety is $X = F_X(L_X, K_X)$, where L_X and K_X are labor and capital employed in the production of this variety. The production function applies to every variety represented by a point on the circumference of the circle in figure 1. It is assumed that at positive output levels $F_X(\cdot)$ is twice differentiable, increasing, strictly quasi-concave, and that it exhibits economies of scale at least for a range of output from zero to some upper limit $\overline{X}$, and that the economies of scale are declining as output increases.[3] Let $C_X(w,r,X)$ be the cost function associated with the production function $F_X(L_X, K_X)$. The inverse of the elasticity of the cost function with respect to output represents the usual measure of economies of scale (see Hanoch 1975). Thus, if $\theta(w,r,X)$ is our measure of economies of scale, we have

$$\theta(w,r,X) = \frac{C_X(w,r,X)}{C_{XX}(w,r,X)X}, \tag{7}$$

where $C_{XX}(\cdot)$ represents marginal costs of production. There are local economies of scale at the output level X if $\theta(w,r,X) > 1$, there are local diseconomies of scale if $\theta(w,r,X) < 1$, and there are local constant returns to scale if $\theta(w,r,X) = 1$. My assumptions on the structure of economies of scale imply[4]

$$\theta(w,r,X) > 1 \qquad \text{for} \qquad 0 < X < \overline{X} \leqq +\infty, \tag{8a}$$

$$\frac{\partial\theta(w,r,X)}{\partial X} < 0. \tag{8b}$$

The demand functions for factors of production are derivable from the cost function:

$$L_X(w,r,X) = \frac{\partial C_X(w,r,X)}{\partial w}, \tag{9a}$$

$$K_X(w,r,X) = \frac{\partial C_X(w,r,X)}{\partial r}. \tag{9b}$$

It remains to explain how a firm chooses its output level, the variety it produces and the price it charges. Due to the economies of scale in production of manufactured goods, generally not all possible types of products will be produced. My interest lies in equilibria in which only a finite number of varieties is produced. Consequently, the following discussion is limited to such situations.[5]

Suppose that the products identified by points b_{i-1} and b_{i+1} in figure 1 are produced and that they are offered for sale at prices p_{xi-1} and p_{xi+1}, respectively. Suppose also that no other variety on the segment connecting b_{i-1} and b_{i+1} is produced. Now take a firm that considers producing a variety that is located between b_{i-1} and b_{i+1} at, say, b_i. If it attracts any customers at all, the first to come will be those for whom b_i is the ideal product. This means that the price it charges cannot exceed the effective price for consumers whose ideal product is b_i when they have to buy either b_{i-1} or b_{i+1}. Hence, if the firm is to operate at a positive output level its price has to satisfy $p_{xi} \leqq \min[p_{xi-1}h(v_{i-1}), p_{xi+1}h(v_{i+1})]$, where v_{i-1} is the arc distance between b_{i-1} and b_i and v_{i+1} is the distance between b_i and b_{i+1}. We have thus identified a price at which the demand facing the firm is zero. Clearly, demand is also zero for every higher price.[6]

Now suppose that the price chosen by firm i is sufficiently low so that it attracts customers. Then, clearly, consumers whose ideal product lies within the vicinity of b_i are part of its customers. But we can determine precisely the market width of this firm. Among all consumers whose ideal product lies between b_i and b_{i+1}, consider the subset of those whose ideal product lies at arc distance smaller or equal to $\bar{d}_i$ from b_i, where $\bar{d}_i$ is implicitly defined by

$$p_{xi}h(\bar{d}_i) = p_{xi+1}h(v_{i+1} - \bar{d}_i). \tag{10}$$

Let $\bar{b}_i$ be at arc distance $\bar{d}_i$ from b_i. Then equation (10) says that a consumer whose ideal product is $\bar{b}_i$ is just indifferent between purchases of b_i and b_{i+1}, since his effective price is the same in both cases.[7] It is clear that all the consumers whose ideal product is between b_i and $\bar{b}_i$ will be attracted to the firm that produces product b_i.

Similarly, if $\underline{b}_i$ is at arc distance $\underline{d}_i$ from b_i and $\underline{d}_i$ is implicitly defined by

$$p_{xi}h(\underline{d}_i) = p_{xi-1}h(v_{i-1} - \underline{d}_i), \tag{11}$$

then all consumers whose ideal product is between b_i and $\underline{b}_i$ will also be the firm's customers. The logic behind (11) is similar to the logic behind (10).[8]

We have thus determined the market width of our firm. All consumers whose ideal product is between $\underline{b}_i$ and $\bar{b}_i$ become the firm's customers. These customers make up a share $(\underline{d}_i + \bar{d}_i)/2$ of potential buyers of manufactured products.

From (10) and (11), we can solve for $\underline{d}_i$ and $\bar{d}_i$ as functions of $p_{xi-1}, p_{xi+1}, p_{xi}, v_{i-1}$ and v_{i+1}. Of particular interest are the variables p_{xi}, v_{i-1} and v_{i+1}, which are decision variables of the firm; p_{xi} is its price while (v_{i-1}, v_{i+1}) determine the type of product produced by it. The firm can choose v_{i-1} and v_{i+1} subject to $v_{i-1} + v_{i+1} = 2D_i$, where $2D_i$ is the arc distance between b_{i-1} and b_{i+1}. Using this constraint, the solution to $\underline{d}_i$ and $\bar{d}_i$ can be represented as follows:

$$\bar{d}_i = \bar{\delta}(p_{xi}, v_{i-i}; p_{xi-1}, p_{xi+1}, D_i), \tag{12a}$$

$$\underline{d}_i = \underline{\delta}(p_{xi}, v_{i-i}; p_{xi-1}, p_{xi+1}, D_i). \tag{12b}$$

Implicit differentiation of (10) and (11) enables us to calculate the partial derivatives of the functions $\bar{\delta}(\cdot)$ and $\underline{\delta}(\cdot)$; these derivatives are calculated in the appendix. It is shown there that both $\bar{\delta}(\cdot)$ and $\underline{\delta}(\cdot)$ are declining with p_{xi}, and that $\bar{\delta}(\cdot)$ is decreasing with v_{i-1} while $\underline{\delta}(\cdot)$ is increasing with v_{i-1}.

Now, using (3) and (12), we can calculate the demand function facing the producer of variety b_i:

$$Q(p_{xi}, v_{i-1}; p_y, p_{xi-1}, p_{xi+1}, D_i, \xi I) = \xi I \left[\int_0^{\bar{\delta}(\cdot)} \alpha_x[p_{xi}h(v), p_y]h(v)\mathrm{d}v + \int_0^{\underline{\delta}(\cdot)} \alpha_x[p_{xi}h(v), p_y]h(v)\mathrm{d}v \right]. \tag{13}$$

This demand function depends on the price and variety chosen by the producer as well as on prices of competing goods—food and the closest varieties of manufactured products. An increase in the price of variety b_i affects demand through two channels. First, it reduces the number of customers who purchase the product through a reduction in $\bar{\delta}(\cdot)$ and $\underline{\delta}(\cdot)$ (see [A1] and [A4] in the Appendix).[9] Second, it reduces the quantity purchased by every remaining customer [since $\alpha_x(\cdot)$ is declining in its first argument]. Hence, the demand function $Q(\cdot)$ is downward sloping. Unlike a price change, a change in specification affects demand in two opposing directions. An increase in v_{i-1} changes only the number of customers who purchase the firm's product; there is no change in the quantity purchased by a customer who does not leave the firm. However, an increase in v_{i-1} causes a net loss of customers on one side of the market and a net gain of customers on the other side of the market (see [A2] and [A4] in the appendix).[10] For example, if the utility function is Cobb-Douglas, $u(x, y) = x^s y^{1-s}$, $0 < s < 1$, then (13) implies $Q(\cdot) = s\xi I[\underline{\delta}(\cdot) + \bar{\delta}(\cdot)]/p_{xi}$.

Now we have all the relevant information concerning the demand function faced by a typical producer of the manufactured product. The demand function specified in (13) is a *true* demand function that is assumed to be known to the producer. The producer of b_i is assumed to take as given the price of food and the actions taken by other producers of manufactured goods, and he is assumed to maximize profits. His profits are

$$\Pi_i = p_{xi}Q(p_{xi}, v_{i-1};\ldots) - C_X[w, r, Q(p_{xi}, v_{i-1};\ldots)]. \tag{14}$$

Hence, the first-order conditions for profit maximization are

$$p_{xi}\left[1 + \frac{1}{E(p_{xi}, v_{i-1};\ldots)}\right] = C_{XX}[w, r, Q(p_{xi}, v_{i-1};\ldots)], \tag{15}$$

$$[p_{xi} - C_{XX}[w, r, Q(p_{xi}, v_{i-1};\ldots)]]\frac{\partial Q(\cdot)}{\partial v_{i-1}} = 0, \tag{16}$$

where $E(\cdot)$ is the elasticity of $Q(\cdot)$ with respect to p_{xi}. Condition (15) is the standard condition for maximum profits of a monopolist, that is, marginal revenue equals marginal costs. Condition (16) is the condition for profit-maximizing product differentiation. As long as the product's price exceeds marginal costs of production, it pays to slightly change the variety produced so as to increase demand. However, since $E(\cdot) < 0$, (15) implies that the price does indeed exceed marginal costs. Therefore the profit-maximizing variety is such that slight changes in specification of the product do not change the quantity demanded. Formally, due to (15), equation (16) reads

$$\frac{\partial Q(\cdot)}{\partial v_{i-1}} = 0. \tag{17}$$

This completes the specification of the behavior of firms. We shall now discuss equilibria.[11]

4 Equilibrium in a Closed Economy

My discussion is limited to symmetrical equilibria. It is assumed that the varieties that are available in equilibrium are equally spaced on the circumference of the circle. This means that if, say, N varieties are consumed, the arc distance between any two adjacent varieties that are available is $D = 2/N$. And if n varieties are produced, then in a closed economy equilibrium requires

$$N = n. \tag{18}$$

Due to the symmetrical position of each producer of a manufactured product, each type of manufactured product sells in equilibrium for the same price p_x. This is seen from (10) and (11) by observing that the variety b_i is located at equal distance from its closest competitors if and only if $p_{xi-1} = p_{xi} = p_{xi+1} = p_x$. This implies that the equilibrium values of $\bar{\delta}(\cdot)$ and $\underline{\delta}(\cdot)$ are both $D/2 = 1/N$, while $v_{i-1} = D = 2/N$. Using this information to evaluate (13) at an equilibrium yields

$$Q(\cdot) = 2\xi I \int_0^{1/N} \alpha_x[p_x h(v), p_y] h(v) dv. \tag{19}$$

It is also shown in the appendix that at such an equilibrium $\partial\bar{\delta}(\cdot)/\partial v_{i-1} = -\frac{1}{2}$ and $\partial\underline{\delta}(\cdot)/\partial v_{i-1} = \frac{1}{2}$, and that this implies $\partial Q(\cdot)/\partial v_{i-1} = 0$. This means that the profit-maximizing product differentiation condition (17) is satisfied. It stems from the fact that in our symmetrical equilibrium a firm that tries to slightly alter the specification of its product loses (gains) at the "upper" end of its market the same number of customers that it gains (loses) at the "lower" end of its market, while at the same time the marginal consumers that are gained consume the same quantity of the product as the marginal consumers that are lost. Hence, slight changes in specification do not alter the quantity demanded.

Now, using (19) and (A11) in the Appendix we can calculate the elasticity of demand at an equilibrium point:

$$\begin{aligned}\tilde{E}(p_x, p_y, N) \equiv & \left[\int_0^{1/N} \alpha_x[p_x h(v), p_y] h(v) \mathrm{d}v\right]^{-1} \\ & \times \left\{p_x \int_0^{1/N} \alpha_{x1}[p_x h(v), p_y][h(v)]^2 \mathrm{d}v \right. \\ & \left. - \frac{1}{2h'(1/N)} \alpha_x\left[p_x h\left(\frac{1}{N}\right), p_y\right]\left[h\left(\frac{1}{N}\right)\right]^2\right\}.\end{aligned} \tag{20}$$

Since $\alpha_x(\cdot)$ is homogeneous of degree (-1), $\alpha_{x1} < 0$, and $\alpha_{x2} > 0$, it can be shown that $\tilde{E}(\cdot) < -1$, as required for the fulfillment of (15).

It is useful to define at this stage a new function that describes the degree of monopoly power faced by a producer of a manufactured product. The function $R(p_x, p_y, N)$ is defined as the equilibrium ratio of price (p_x) to marginal revenue. This is a standard measure of monopoly power; the larger this ratio, the larger the monopoly power:

$$R(p_x, p_y, N) \equiv \left[1 + \frac{1}{\tilde{E}(p_x, p_y, N)}\right]^{-1}. \tag{21}$$

The function $R(\cdot)$ obtains values larger or equal to one and it approaches one (no monopoly power) when the elasticity of demand approaches infinity. The elasticity of demand, on the other hand, approaches infinity when the compensation function $h(\cdot)$ flattens out, which means that all possible manufactured varieties become perfect substitutes in consumption. This is seen from (20) by evaluating it at $h'(1/N) \to 0$.

It is also interesting to note that the degree of monopoly power depends on the available number of differentiated products. One would expect the degree of monopoly power to decline as the number of products increases, because an increase in the number of products indicates in a sense "more" competition. This is indeed the case if the utility function is of the Cobb-Douglas type and the elasticity of $h(v)$ is increasing with v, but it cannot be shown in the general case, except when N is very large. Observe that due to (1b), $\tilde{E}(\cdot)$ approaches infinity and $R(\cdot)$ approaches one as N approaches infinity, which means that all monopoly power is lost when there are infinitely many varieties. This means that for sufficiently large N, the degree of monopoly power is declining with N. In what follows I *assume* that $R(\cdot)$ is declining with N.

It is assumed that in the long run there is free entry into industries and that labor and capital are mobile between both firms and sectors. As a result, every firm faces the same factor prices and free entry drives profits down to zero. Hence, in a long-run equilibrium the following zero-profit conditions have to be satisfied:

$$p_y = c_Y(w, r), \tag{22}$$

$$p_x X = C_X(w, r, X), \tag{23}$$

where X is the output level of a typical firm in the industry producing differentiated products.

A firm that produces X equates marginal revenue to marginal costs. Evaluating (15) at an equilibrium, this condition reads:

$$p_x\left[1 + \frac{1}{\tilde{E}(p_x, p_y, N)}\right] = C_{XX}(w, r, x).$$

Now combining it with (23), (21), and (7), we obtain

$$R(p_x, p_y, N) = \theta(w, r, X), \tag{24}$$

that is, the degree of monopoly power equals the degree of economies of scale.

Conditions (22)–(24) provide a complete specification of the long-run equilibrium conditions for firms. Given factor prices and the number of varieties available to consumers, they provide solutions for equilibrium commodity prices and the equilibrium output level of a firm in the manufacturing sector. The equilibrium output level of a firm in the food sector cannot be determined due to the existence of constant returns to scale in the production of food. It remains to specify the equilibrium conditions in the markets for goods and factors of production.

The demand functions for factors of production are described by equations (5) and (9). If we let Y represent total output of food, and we remember that there are n firms in the manufacturing sector, each one producing X units of the variety in which it specializes, we can write down the equilibrium conditions in factor markets as

$$a_{LY}(w, r)Y + L_X(w, r, X)n = L, \tag{25}$$

$$a_{KY}(w, r)Y + K_X(w, r, X)n = K, \tag{26}$$

where L is the country's total labor force (which equals its population 2ξ) and K is the country's capital stock. The left-hand side of (25) represents aggregate demand for labor. It is composed of labor demanded by the food sector and of labor demanded by the n firms in the manufacturing sector. The right-hand side of (25) represents labor supply. A similar interpretation applies to equation (26), which is the equilibrium condition in the capital market.

It remains to specify equilibrium conditions in commodity markets. Using (19), the equilibrium condition in the market for manufactured products can be written as

$$2\xi I \int_0^{1/N} \alpha_x[p_x h(v), p_y] h(v) \mathrm{d}v = X, \tag{27}$$

that is, the demand for a particular variety is equal to its supply. Now, the set of consumers who consume a particular variety of manufactured products also consumes Y/N units of food. Therefore, using (3b), the equilibrium condition in the market for food can be written as

$$2\xi I \int_0^{1/N} \alpha_y[p_x h(v), p_y] \mathrm{d}v = \frac{Y}{N}. \tag{28}$$

Finally, dividing (27) by (28), we obtain

$$\frac{\int_0^{1/N} \alpha_x[p_x h(v), p_y] h(v) \mathrm{d}v}{\int_0^{1/N} \alpha_y[p_x h(v), p_y] \mathrm{d}v} = \frac{X}{Y/N}. \tag{29}$$

The system of equilibrium conditions for the closed economy is represented by equations (18), (22)–(26), and (29). This system is homogeneous of degree zero in (p_x, p_y, w, r). It provides, therefore, a solution to X, Y, N, n, and three relative prices, say, p_x/p_y, w/p_y, and r/p_y.[12] I assume that in an equilibrium n is relatively large. This is needed for two reasons. First, there is the so-called integer problem. Strictly speaking n should be an integer, but there is nothing in the equilibrium conditions that ensures that n is an integer. However, if n is large enough, our equilibrium will be a good approximation to the true equilibrium in which n is an integer. Second, if n is small, say, 2, the concept of equilibrium that we have employed may not be appropriate. For these reasons I require n to be large. This outcome can be assured by appropriate assumptions on the degree of economies of scale in manufacturing. In particular, if the economies of scale are small enough, n will be large in equilibrium.

This completes the discussion of equilibrium in a closed economy. It is required as background to the main concern of this paper, namely, international trade, which is taken up in the next section.

5 International Trade in a Two-Country World

Consider a world that consists of two countries—a home country and a foreign country—both being of the type discussed in the previous sections. Assume that the technologies are identical across countries, which implies that cost functions are the same in every country. All consumers are assumed to have the same utility function $u(x, y)$ and the same compensation function $h(v)$. In every country the consumers are uniformly distributed on the circumference of the circle in figure 1 according to their ideal product. Countries may, however, differ in population size and stocks of capital. Hence, as in the familiar Heckscher-Ohlin model, countries differ only in factor endowments (population size equals labor endowment).

The foreign country's variables are denoted with asterisks while the home country's variables are denoted without asterisks. For example, L^* and K^* are used to denote the foreign country's labor force (population) and capital stock, while $\xi^* = L^*/2$ is used to denote the foreign country's population density. The letter N, on the other hand, is still used to denote the number of varieties of manufactured products that are available to consumers. In the presence of frictionless international trade, as is assumed here, all varieties that are produced in the world economy are available to consumers in every country; the location of production does not affect the availability of products to consumers.

Now consider an equilibrium in the world economy that has the following two properties:

1. No sectoral specialization, that is, every country produces food and manufactured products. Clearly, no single type of manufactured product will be produced in both countries for the same reason that no two firms in a country will produce the same variety; there is always specialization in the production of varieties. What is required here is that no country produces only food or only manufactured products.
2. Symmetry in the market for differentiated products, in the sense that every two adjacent varieties are equally spaced on the circumference of the circle. This implies that all varieties are sold at the same price.

If these two conditions are met, a *subset* of the equilibrium conditions for the world economy consists of country-specific variants of (22)–(26), which can be written as

$$p_y = c_Y(w, r), \tag{30}$$

$$p_x X = C_X(w, r, X), \tag{31}$$

$$R(p_x, p_y, N) = \theta(w, r, X), \tag{32}$$

$$a_{LY}(w, r)Y + L_X(w, r, X)n = L, \tag{33}$$

$$a_{KY}(w, r)Y + K_X(w, r, X)n = K, \tag{34}$$

$$p_y = c_Y(w^*, r^*), \tag{35}$$

$$p_x X^* = C_X(w^*, r^*, X^*), \tag{36}$$

$$R(p_x, p_y, N) = \theta(w^*, r^*, X^*), \tag{37}$$

$$a_{LY}(w^*, r^*)Y^* + L_X(w^*, r^*, X^*)n^* = L^*, \tag{38}$$

$$a_{KY}(w^*, r^*)Y^* + K_X(w^*, r^*, X^*)n^* = K^*. \tag{39}$$

Equations (30)–(34) constitute the home country's block of equilibrium conditions, while equations (35)–(39) constitute the foreign country's block of equilibrium conditions. A typical country-specific block describes, basically, the country's supply sector. Given the world price of food p_y, and the prices of competing manufactured products p_x, a country's producers equate marginal revenue to marginal costs and, due to entry competition, firms find themselves charging prices that equal average costs (in the food industry marginal revenue equals the price of food and marginal costs equal average costs). These conditions are described by the first three equations of a country-specific block. Given commodity prices, these three equations determine the country's factor prices and the output level of a typical firm in the manufacturing sector. If the mapping from (w, r, X) to (p_x, p_y, N), which is described by (30)–(32) and (35)–(37), is univalent, then both countries will have the same factor prices and the same level of output of a firm in the manufacturing sector. For example, if manufactured goods are produced with a homothetic production function, then univalence of the mapping is assured by the usual assumption of no factor intensity reversal.[13] I have thus proved the following:

PROPOSITION 1 If both countries have the same technologies as specified above, the univalence of mapping conditions is satisfied, in the trading equilibrium every country produces both food and manufactured products (i.e., no sectoral specialization), and all varieties of manufactured products are equally spaced (i.e., symmetrical equilibrium), then in the trading equilibrium factor prices are the same in both countries and the output level of a firm in the manufacturing sector is the same in both countries.

I have thus provided a generalization of the factor-price equalization theorem. Observe that in the context of differentiated products the factor-price equalization theorem is widened to include equalization of output levels of manufacturing firms and it does not require homotheticity in the production of differentiated products.

For the sake of concreteness, let us now assume that in equilibrium manufactured goods are relatively capital intensive.[14] Then, comparing (33)–(34) with (38)–(39) and taking account of proposition 1, we have immediately:

PROPOSITION 2 Suppose that the conditions of proposition 1 are satisfied and that manufactured products are relatively capital intensive. Then the country with the higher capital-labor ratio produces less food per capita and more varieties per capita than the country with the lower capital-labor ratio. If both countries have the same capital-labor ratio, they produce the same quantity of food per capita and the same number of manufactured products per capita.

Since in the present context manufacturing firms produce the same output level, independent of country association, the country that produces more varieties per capita produces also more manufactured goods per capita. It is, therefore, clear that proposition 2 is a version of the Rybczynski theorem. The particular feature introduced by the existence of differentiated products is that changes in factor endowments change the number of varieties produced, and therefore the number of firms, rather than output per firm.[15]

Since in the equilibrium I have been discussing every manufacturing firm produces the same output level, every manufacturing firm receives also the same share of customers. Hence, the remaining equilibrium conditions—which are worldwide conditions—can be expressed as (compare to [18] and [29]):

$$N = n + n^*, \tag{40}$$

$$\frac{\int_0^{1/N} \alpha_x[p_x h(v), p_y] h(v) \mathrm{d}v}{\int_0^{1/N} \alpha_y[p_x h(v), p_y] \mathrm{d}v} = \frac{X}{(Y + Y^*)/N} = \frac{X^*}{(Y + Y^*)/N}. \tag{41}$$

Condition (40) just says that the number of varieties available to consumers equals the number of varieties produced in the home country plus the number of varieties produced in the foreign country. The left-hand side of (41) represents the ratio of manufactured goods to food consumed by that part of the world population that is being served by a single manufacturing firm (remember that all consumers have the same functions $u(\cdot)$ and $h(\cdot)$). This has to equal the firm's output divided by the output of food that is being allocated to this population. But since this population is a typical segment of N identical segments, it gets $1/N$ of the world's output of food. In such a typical segment the ratio of home country residents to foreign country residents is $\xi/\xi^* = L/L^*$.

Equations (30)–(41) provide a complete representation of a symmetrical equilibrium. This system is homogeneous of degree zero in $(p_x, p_y, w, r, w^*, r^*)$. It provides a solution (whenever such a solution exists) to X, X^*, Y, Y^*, n, n^*, N, and the relative prices p_x/p_y, w/p_y, r/p_y, w^*/p_y, r^*/p_y.

Now what can we say about the pattern of trade? Clearly, as long as no country specializes in the production of food, there will always be intraindustry trade in manufactured products. This is so since the home country will import the n^* varieties produced in the foreign country while the foreign country will import the n varieties produced in the home country. Hence, the existence of intraindustry trade depends on differences in factor proportions only to the extent that differences in factor proportions lead to an equilibrium in which one country specializes in the production of food. However, the share of intraindustry trade in total trade does depend on differences in factor proportions.

It is clear that in a symmetrical equilibrium the ratio of manufactured goods to food in consumption is the same in every country. This is, of course, part of condition (41). But this means that the country that produces more food per capita in a trading equilibrium has to export food while the country that produces more varieties per capita has to be a *net* exporter of manufactured products. Combining this observation with proposition 2, we obtain

PROPOSITION 3 Suppose that the conditions of proposition 1 are satisfied and that independent of the scale of operation manufactured products are relatively capital intensive. Then, although both countries are exporters and importers of manufactured products, the country with the higher capital-labor ratio is a *net* exporter of manufactured goods and an importer of food, while the country with the lower capital-labor ratio is an exporter of food and a *net* importer of manufactured products. If both countries have the same capital-labor ratio, all trade is intraindustry trade and there is no intersectoral trade; that is, no food is exported or imported and *net* exports (imports) of manufactured products are zero in every country.

This proposition is, of course, a generalization of the Heckscher-Ohlin theorem. In the present context we use Heckscher-Ohlin to explain intersectoral trade while intraindustry trade is explained by the existence of economies of scale and differentiated products. We have seen that in the absence of a divergence in the capital-labor ratios with which countries are endowed, there will be only intraindustry trade while in the presence of such a divergence there will be both intraindustry and interindustry trade. Now I want to show that the larger the divergence in the capital-labor ratios with which countries are endowed, the smaller the share of intraindustry trade in world trade.

In order to discuss the relationship between intraindustry trade and factor proportion divergences, we need an index of the share of intraindustry trade in world trade. I will use the standard index (see Grubel and Lloyd 1975, p. 22). Assuming that the home country's capital-labor ratio is smaller or equal to the foreign country's capital-labor ratio (the home country exports food), this index translates in the present case into

$$Intra = 1 - \frac{p_y(Y - A_y) + p_x(n^*A_x - nA_x^*)}{p_y(Y - A_y) + p_x(nA_x^* + n^*A_x)}, \tag{42}$$

where A_y = aggregate consumption of food in the home country, A_x = aggregate consumption of a variety of manufactured goods in the home country, and A_x^* = aggregate consumption of a variety of manufactured goods in the foreign country. Remember that, due to the symmetry in our system, a country consumes the same quantity of each variety.

Due to the balance of trade (income) constraint, namely, exports equal imports, which translates in our case into

$$p_y(Y - A_y) + p_x nA_x^* = p_x n^* A_x,$$

we can write (42) as

$$Intra = \frac{n/A_x}{n^*/A_x^*}. \tag{43}$$

Observe that $0 \leq Intra \leq 1$, $n = 0$ implies $Intra = 0$, which is the case when there is only intersectoral trade, and $n^*A_x = nA_x^*$ implies $Intra = 1$, which is the case when all trade is intraindustry trade. Hence, *Intra* is a true share measure.

Now I want to argue that for a particular experiment *Intra* declines as the divergence between the foreign and the home country's capital-labor ratio increases. In this experiment we reallocate the world's labor and capital stock so that the capital-labor ratio employed in the foreign country increases while the capital-labor ratio employed in the home country declines, but only within the limits in which commodity prices and factor rewards do not change. These limits are imposed in order to preserve the economic size of the world. This leads to an increase in $(n^*/A_x^*)/(n/A_x)$, which can be seen as follows. Each country spends the same proportion of its income on manufactured products. Hence, $(n^*/A_x^*)/(n/A_x) = (n^*/AI^*)/(n/AI)$, where AI and AI^* represent aggregate income in the home and foreign country, respectively. However,

$$\frac{n^*}{AI^*} = \frac{n^*}{p_y Y^* + p_x X^* n^*} = \frac{1}{p_y Y^*/n^* + p_x X^*},$$

where X^* is output per firm in the manufacturing sector, and it is not affected by the reallocation of labor and capital because prices remain constant and therefore $n + n^* = N$ remains constant. Now, since the capital-labor ratio increases in the foreign country, Y^*/n^* declines (the Rybczynski effect), which implies an increase in n^*/AI^*. A similar argument shows that n/AI decreases. Hence, the ratio $(n^*/AI^*)/(n/AI)$ increases and *Intra* declines. We have thus proved:[16]

PROPOSITION 4 Assume that the world economy is in an equilibrium in which factor prices are equalized and the home country has a lower (or equal) capital-labor ratio than the foreign country. Then if we reallocate the world's labor and capital stock in a way that increases the foreign country's capital-labor ratio and reduces the home country's capital-labor ratio without disturbing commodity prices and factor rewards, then the share of intraindustry trade as measured by *Intra* will decline.

This proposition suggests that there exists a relationship between the composition of trade (in terms of intra- versus interindustry trade) and the dispersion of relative factor endowments. It suggests that endowment ratio similarity breeds intraindustry trade while dissimilarity breeds intersectoral trade. The insights of this proposition are used in section 7 to formulate two testable hypotheses.

We have thus seen that the share of intraindustry trade is a declining function of the absolute difference in the capital-labor ratios. Does there exist also a monotonic relationship between the difference in capital-labor ratios and the volume of trade? The answer is yes if the larger gap in relative factor endowments is obtained by a redistribution that does not change the relative size of countries, while the answer is no if the relative size changes.

In order to see these points, consider two trading countries with equalized factor prices, and with the home country being the labor-rich country (i.e., the home country exports food as food is the labor-intensive good). The volume of trade is $p_y(Y - A_y) + p_x(nA_x^* + n^*A_x)$. Let μ be the share of the home country in world income. Then $A_y = \mu(Y + Y^*)$, $A_x = \mu X$ and $A_x^* = (1 - \mu)X$. Using these relationships as well as (33), (34), (38), and (39) to solve for Y, Y^*, n, n^*, the volume of trade can be written as

$$V = \Delta^{-1}[p_y(1-\mu)(LK_X - KL_X) - p_y\mu(L^*K_X - K^*L_X) + p_x(1-\mu)(a_{LY}K - a_{KY}L)X + p_x\mu(a_{LY}K^* - a_{KY}L^*)X],$$

where a_{LY}, a_{KY}, L_X, K_X are the same in both countries and $\Delta = a_{LY}K_X - a_{KY}L_X > 0$.

Now suppose that we transfer labor from the foreign country to the home country and capital from the home country to the foreign so as to preserve each country's size in terms of its national income (a marginal reallocation does not change factor and commodity prices). Hence, $\mathrm{d}L = -\mathrm{d}L^*$, $\mathrm{d}K = -\mathrm{d}K^*$, $w\mathrm{d}L + r\mathrm{d}K = 0$, and $\mathrm{d}\mu = 0$. Using these conditions, a direct calculation shows $\mathrm{d}V = 2\Delta^{-1}p_y p_x \mu X \,\mathrm{d}L/r > 0$, which proves:

PROPOSITION 5 Assume that the world economy is in an equilibrium in which factor prices are equalized. Then if we reallocate the world's labor and capital stock in a way that increases the capital-labor ratio in the capital-rich country and reduces the capital-labor ratio in the capital-poor country, but preserves the relative size of each country and does not disturb commodity prices and factor rewards, the volume of trade will increase.

In order to see the relative size effect on the volume of trade, consider the case in which both countries have the same capital-labor ratio, namely, $L = \mu\bar{L}$, $K = \mu\bar{K}$, $L^* = (1-\mu)\bar{L}$ and $K^* = (1-\mu)\bar{K}$, where $\bar{L}$ and $\bar{K}$ are the world's labor force and capital stock, respectively. In this case all trade is intraindustry trade and $V = \Delta^{-1}2(a_{LY}\bar{K} - a_{KY}\bar{L})p_x X\mu(1-\mu)$. Since food is labor intensive, $(a_{LY}\bar{K} - a_{KY}\bar{L}) > 0$, and we see that V is increasing in μ when $\mu < \frac{1}{2}$ and that it is decreasing in μ when $\mu > \frac{1}{2}$. Hence, we have proved:

PROPOSITION 6 Assume that both countries have the same capital-labor ratio. Then a redistribution of resources that preserves each country's initial capital-labor ratio increases the volume of trade if it reduces the inequality in country size, and it reduces the volume of trade if it increases the inequality in country size. The volume of trade is largest when both countries are of equal size.

Let me conclude this section with a comparison of the present model with the familiar two-sector Heckscher-Ohlin model. I wish to argue that equations (30)–(39) provide a natural generalization of the production structure of the Heckscher-Ohlin model. In order to see this point, consider what happens when the manufacturing sector produces with constant returns to scale. In this case $C_X(w,r,X) = c_X(w,r)X$ and it is immediately obvious that equations (30)–(31) and (35)–(36) reduce to the Heckscher-Ohlin pricing equations. Since with constant returns to scale $L_X(w,r,X) = a_{LX}(w,r)X$ and $K_X(w,r,X) = a_{KX}(w,r)X$, equations (33)–(34) and (38)–(39) represent in this case the Heckscher-Ohlin equilibrium conditions in factor markets. However, with constant returns to scale in the production of X, the factor market equilibrium conditions depend on aggregate output of manufactured products, nX, and they do not depend on the number of firms in the industry. Thus, industry output is well determined, but not its composition in terms of the number of firms and output per firm.

It remains to consider the implication of constant returns to scale for (32) and (37). From (7), constant returns to scale imply $\theta(\cdot) \equiv 1$. Hence, in the present case (32) reads $R(p_x, p_y, N) = 1$. This can be satisfied in either one of two cases. First, when $h(v)$ is flat, which means that different types of manufactured products are perfect substitutes in consumption. This interpretation I believe to be closest in spirit to the common view of the Heckscher-Ohlin model. In this case any number of varieties can be produced; it is simply not relevant. Second, when $h(v)$ satisfies (1). In this case $R(p_x, p_y, N) = 1$ implies that N goes to infinity. This means that every consumer can purchase his own ideal product—due to the constant returns to scale in production, manufactured products are custom made! This interpretation is also consistent with the Heckscher-Ohlin model. Since every consumer is of measure zero, aggregate output of manufactured products is still well determined, even though there is a continuum of varieties produced. This interpretation seems to provide wider applicability to the standard model than had been recognized in the past.

6 Predicting the Intersectoral Pattern of Trade

In the traditional Heckscher-Ohlin model there are three predictors of the pattern of trade: (1) relative commodity prices, (2) relative factor rewards, and (3) relative factor endowments. It is well known that under the standard assumptions, which include the assumptions of no factor intensity reversal and identical homothetic preferences, all three predictors provide the same valid prediction of the pattern of trade. Thus, if the home country is relatively labor abundant, then in the pretrade equilibrium its relative price of the labor-intensive good and its wage-rental ratio are lower than in the capital-rich country, and all three predictors suggest that in the presence of international trade the home country will be an exporter of the labor-intensive good. In this section I investigate the extent to which relative commodity prices and relative factor rewards can provide valid predictions of the pattern of trade in the Chamberlin-Heckscher-Ohlin model.

The fact that relative factor endowments provide a valid prediction of the intersectoral pattern of trade was established in the previous section (see proposition 3). It was shown that the country with relatively more capital will be a net exporter of the capital-intensive good while the country with relatively more labor will be a net exporter of the labor-intensive good. This prediction is based on the assumption that one sector is more capital intensive than the other for all factor prices and *all* output levels of a single firm. The new element that appears here is the requirement that factor intensity reversal should not take place as a result of changes in the output level of a firm in the differentiated product industry. This requirement is relevant only when the production function of manufactured products is not homothetic, and I have allowed for nonhomothetic production functions. If manufactured products are produced with a homothetic production function, then employed factor proportions are scale independent and the absence of factor intensity reversals obtains the usual meaning.

What about relative commodity prices and relative factor rewards ? Relative commodity prices cannot provide a valid prediction of the pattern of trade because, due to the economies of scale, a country's size affects its pretrade relative commodity prices. Thus, the larger a country is, the better advantage it can take of the economies of scale, an advantage that is expected to translate into relatively lower prices of manufactured products. Hence, if we observe two countries in autarky that are identical except for size, we may expect the larger country to have a relatively lower price of manufactured goods. However, if trade opens, there will be *no* intersectoral trade between these countries—all trade will be intraindustry trade. It is therefore clear that in this case relative commodity prices cannot be used in the usual way to predict the pattern of trade.[17] This raises the following question: Is there a way to adjust prices for the scale effect so as to obtain *scale-adjusted* prices that provide a valid prediction of the pattern of trade? There is an interesting case in which this can be done: when (1) the utility function is Cobb-Douglas, and (2) manufactured goods are produced with a homothetic production function. In this case relative factor rewards also provide a valid prediction of the intersectoral pattern of trade. In what follows I discuss this case, including a description of the scale-adjusted prices in a form that is empirically measurable. Then I discuss the difficulties that exist in other cases.

Let the production function $F_X(L_X, K_X)$ be homothetic. Then its cost function can be written in the form

$$C_X(w,r,X) \equiv c_x(w,r)e(X). \tag{44}$$

In this case (7) implies

$$\theta(X) = \frac{e(X)}{e'(X)X}, \tag{45}$$

that is, the elasticity of scale is independent of factor prices. In addition, (9) implies

$$L_X(w,r,X) = a_{LZ}(w,r)e(X), \tag{46a}$$

$$K_X(w,r,X) = a_{KZ}(w,r)e(X), \tag{46b}$$

where $a_{LZ}(\cdot) \equiv \partial c_X(\cdot)/\partial w$ and $a_{KZ}(\cdot) \equiv \partial c_X(\cdot)/\partial r$. Observe that $a_{LZ}(\cdot)$ is not the labor-output ratio and $a_{KZ}(\cdot)$ is not the capital-output ratio. The labor-output ratio is $a_{LZ}(\cdot)e(X)/X$ while the capital-output ratio is $a_{KZ}(\cdot)e(X)/X$, and they depend not only on factor prices but also on the level of output. However, the capital-labor ratio does not depend on the output level.

Let the utility function be

$$u(x, y) = x^s y^{1-s}, \qquad 0 < s < 1. \tag{47}$$

Then

$$\alpha_x[p_x h(v), p_y] \equiv \frac{s}{p_x h(v)}, \tag{48a}$$

$$\alpha_y[p_x h(v), p_y] \equiv \frac{1-s}{p_y}, \tag{48b}$$

and

$$R(N) = 1 + 2\varepsilon_h\left(\frac{1}{N}\right), \tag{49}$$

where $\varepsilon_h(\cdot)$ is the elasticity of the function $h(\cdot)$.

Consider now the equilibrium of an isolated country in which $F_x(L_x, K_x)$ is homothetic and in which the utility function is Cobb-Douglas. Using (44)–(49), the equilibrium conditions (18), (22)–(26), and (29) can be written as

$$N = n, \tag{50}$$

$$p_y = c_y(w, r), \tag{51}$$

$$\frac{p_x X}{e(X)} = c_z(w, r), \tag{52}$$

$$R(n) = \theta(X), \tag{53}$$

$$a_{LY}(w, r)Y + a_{LZ}(w, r)e(X)n = L, \tag{54}$$

$$a_{KY}(w, r)Y + a_{KZ}(w, r)e(X)n = K, \tag{55}$$

$$\frac{nX}{Y} = \frac{s}{1-s}\frac{p_y}{p_x}. \tag{56}$$

Now define two auxiliary variables:

$$p_z \equiv \frac{p_x X}{e(X)}, \tag{57}$$

$$Z \equiv e(X)n. \tag{58}$$

Using (57)–(58) and food as numeraire (i.e., $p_y = 1$), the equilibrium conditions (50)–(56) can be written in the form

$$N = n, \tag{50'}$$

$$1 = c_Y(w, r), \tag{51'}$$

$$p_z = c_Z(w, r), \tag{52'}$$

$$R(n) = \theta(X), \tag{53'}$$

$$a_{LY}(w, r)Y + a_{LZ}(w, r)Z = L, \tag{54'}$$

$$a_{KY}(w,r)Y + a_{KZ}(w,r)Z = K, \tag{55'}$$

$$\frac{Z}{Y} = \frac{s}{1-s}\frac{1}{p_z}. \tag{56'}$$

Now observe that (51′)–(52′) and (54′)–(55′) represent a standard Heckscher-Ohlin production structure, with p_z being the relative price of Z. There exist, therefore, functions $\eta_w(p_z)$, $\eta_r(p_z)$, $\phi_Y(p_z, L, K)$, $\phi_z(p_z, L, K)$, such that in the absence of sectoral specialization:

$$w = \eta_w(p_z), \tag{59a}$$

$$r = \eta_r(p_z), \tag{59b}$$

$$Y = \phi_Y(p_z, L, K), \tag{60a}$$

$$Z = \phi_Z(p_z, L, K). \tag{60b}$$

The functions $\phi_y(\cdot)$ and $\phi_z(\cdot)$ are homogeneous of degree one in (L, K), $\phi_Y(\cdot)$ is decreasing in p_z, and $\phi_z(\cdot)$ is increasing in p_z. Now define

$$\phi(p_z, K/L) \equiv \frac{\phi_Z(p_z, 1, K/L)}{\phi_Y(p_z, 1, K/L)}. \tag{61}$$

The function $\phi(\cdot)$ is increasing in p_z, and due to (60),

$$\frac{Z}{Y} = \phi\left(p_z, \frac{K}{L}\right). \tag{62}$$

Assuming that manufactured products are capital intensive implies that $\phi(\cdot)$ is increasing in its second argument (Rybczynski) and that $\eta_w(\cdot)$ is decreasing and $\eta_r(\cdot)$ is increasing in p_z (Stolper-Samuelson).

For a given capital-labor ratio, K/L, I plot (56′) and (62) in figure 3 (this is similar to figure 7.2 in Caves and Jones 1977). The intersection between these two curves determines the equilibrium values of p_z and $\rho = Z/Y$, $\tilde{p}_z$ and $\tilde{\rho}$. Then, substituting $\tilde{p}_z$ into (59) and (60), we obtain equilibrium factor prices and output levels. Having done this, we use (58) and (53′) to calculate equilibrium values of X and n, and then, using (57), we calculate the equilibrium value of p_x. I will come back to these calculations later.

Now suppose that there are two identical countries, a home country and a foreign country, except that $L^* = \lambda L$, $K^* = \lambda K$, $\lambda \geqq 1$. Hence, both countries have the same factor proportions but the foreign country is possibly larger. I want to compare these countries' pretrade equilibria. Since they have the same factor proportions, the equilibrium values of p_z and ρ are the same in both countries (see figure 3). But this implies, via (59)–(60) and the homogeneity of degree one of the functions $\phi_Y(\cdot)$ and $\phi_Z(\cdot)$, that

$$\tilde{w}^* = \tilde{w}, \tag{63a}$$

$$\tilde{r}^* = \tilde{r}, \tag{63b}$$

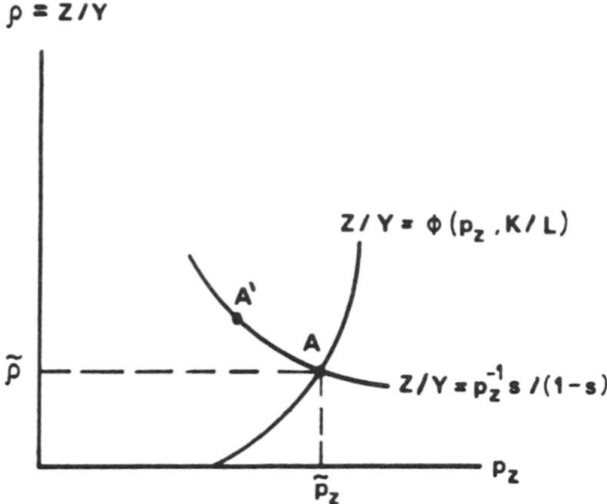

Figure 3

$$\tilde{Y}^* = \lambda \tilde{Y}, \tag{64a}$$

$$\tilde{Z}^* = \lambda \tilde{Z}, \tag{64b}$$

where "tildes" indicate equilibrium values. I have thus shown that factor rewards in terms of food are the same in both countries and that the foreign country produces λ times the amount of food and Z produced in the home country.

Now let us compare $(\tilde{n}, \tilde{X})$ with $(\tilde{n}^*, \tilde{X}^*)$. Equation (53′) implies that $(\tilde{n}, \tilde{X})$ and $(\tilde{n}^*, \tilde{X}^*)$ both lie on the upward-sloping curve in figure 4 that satisfies $R(n) = \theta(X)$, while (58) implies that $(\tilde{n}, \tilde{X})$ lies on the downward-sloping curve $e(X)n = \tilde{Z}$ and that $(\tilde{n}^*, \tilde{X}^*)$ lies on the downward-sloping curve $e(X)n = \tilde{Z}^*$. The curve $e(X)n = \tilde{Z}^*$ is vertically λ times higher than the curve $e(X)n = \tilde{Z}$, and it is drawn on the assumption $\lambda > 1$. Hence Q is the home country's equilibrium point, and Q^* is the foreign country's equilibrium point.

Finally, observe that due to the fact that $\tilde{p}_z^* = \tilde{p}_z$, $\tilde{X}^* > \tilde{X}$, and the elasticity of $e(\cdot)$ is smaller than one, (57) implies

$$\tilde{p}_x^* < \tilde{p}_x, \tag{65}$$

which means that the relative price of manufactured products is lower in the foreign country. We have thus seen that (1) factor prices in terms of food are the same in both countries; (2) the larger country produces more varieties, with a higher output per firm; and (3) the relative price of manufactured products is lower in the larger country.

In the pretrade equilibrium both countries have the same relative factor rewards and use therefore the same techniques of production. Since they also have the same factor proportions, the larger country employs in each sector more labor and capital in direct proportion to its relative size. This results in a proportionately higher output of food, and due to the economies of scale, a more than proportionately higher output of manufactured products, with the higher output of manufactured products being

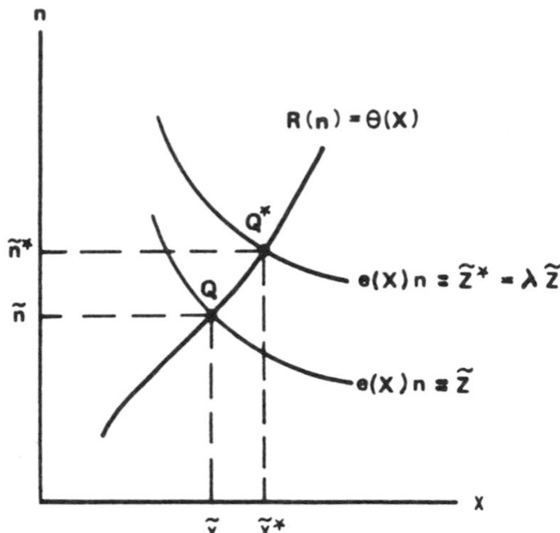

Figure 4

composed of more varieties and a higher output per firm. The relatively larger supply of manufactured products makes their relative price lower in the larger country.[18]

If we were to use pretrade relative commodity prices to predict the pattern of trade, we would predict that the large country will be a net exporter of manufactured products and an importer of food. However, it is clear from proposition 2 (as well as directly from the present context) that as a result of equal factor proportions all international trade will be intraindustry trade within the manufacturing sector, and that every country will produce its own consumption of food.[19] It is therefore clear that in the world I have been discussing, pretrade relative commodity prices do not serve as reliable predictors of the pattern of trade. Moreover, the very same economic factors that lead prior to trade to a relatively lower price of manufactured products in the larger country (when both countries have the same factor proportion), make the posttrade relative price of manufactured products lower than the relative price of manufactured products in either one of the countries prior to trade. This stems from the fact that the introduction of international trade combines both countries into an integrated economy. Hence, pretrade relative commodity prices do not provide the usual bounds on the posttrade relative commodity prices, for we have just seen that the posttrade relative price of manufactured goods will be outside (and to the left of) the bounds determined by pretrade relative prices of these goods. If countries have different factor proportions, the location of relative commodity prices in a trading equilibrium relative to the location of pretrade relative commodity prices depends on the above-mentioned scale effect and the usual Heckscher-Ohlin effect. Clearly, if factor proportions do not differ by much, the scale effect dominates.

How useful then are pretrade commodity prices in predicting the pattern of trade? Observe that the pretrade values of p_z do predict the intersectoral pattern of trade.

Suppose the foreign country has a higher capital-labor ratio. Then its equilibrium point in figure 3 is on a downward-sloping curve to the left of A, say, at A'. This is so because due to the fact that manufactured products are relatively capital intensive, the foreign country's upward-sloping curve will be above the upward-sloping curve of the home country (the Rybczynski effect). In this case the foreign country will have a lower p_z, which via (59) means a higher wage rate and a lower rental rate in terms of food. Hence, the country with the lower p_z will be a net exporter of manufactured products. But p_z can be considered to be the scale-adjusted relative price of manufactured products, which is the index we have been looking for.

The implication of all this is quite simple. Since $p_z = p_x X/e(X)$, then in order to predict the pattern of trade we need to know both pretrade relative commodity prices and the scale of operation of manufacturing firms in each country. In addition, we need to have an estimate of $e(X)$, which is a component of the cost function. This information can be used to calculate the scale-adjusted relative price of manufactured products in each country in order to predict the intersectoral pattern of trade.

Now let us consider the predictive power of factor rewards. We have seen that countries with identical factor proportions have the same factor rewards in terms of food. Hence, they have the same wage-rental ratio. In such cases the Heckscher-Ohlin prediction is that the opening of international trade will lead to no active trade. In the present context the opening of international trade leads to no active intersectoral trade, but it does lead to intraindustry trade. Since the Heckscher-Ohlin theory is concerned with intersectoral trade, it is fair to argue that its factor rewards oriented prediction of the pattern of trade remains valid if we can also show that in the presence of differences in factor proportions the capital-rich country has a higher wage-rental ratio in the pretrade equilibrium. In the case considered so far this relationship holds, as I have shown above. Hence, in the present case relative scale-adjusted commodity prices and relative factor rewards provide a valid prediction of the intersectoral pattern of trade.

What happens when preferences cannot be represented by a Cobb-Douglas utility function? In this case—even with homothetic production functions—factor rewards, as well as the simple index of scale-adjusted relative prices developed above, cannot be used to predict the pattern of trade. The reason for this difficulty stems from the fact that whenever the elasticity of substitution in consumption does not equal one (as it does in the Cobb-Douglas case), aggregate relative demand depends not only on relative commodity prices but also on the number of varieties available to consumers. For example, if the utility function is CES and the elasticity of substitution is larger than one, it can be shown that the relative demand for manufactured goods increases as the number of varieties increases, or alternatively that the share of income spent on food declines as the number of varieties increases. In addition, a nonunitary elasticity of substitution implies that $R(\cdot)$ depends on relative commodity prices in a rather complex way. As a result, the simple links that I have presented above break down. In this case size differences can lead to differences in relative factor rewards and scale-adjusted relative commodity prices as a result of differences in relative demands. The result is that the pattern of trade cannot be predicted from price information but only from information about relative factor endowments.

In order to see this point in a clear way, consider two countries, one of which has λ times more labor and capital than the other, with $\lambda > 1$. Suppose that in the pretrade equilibrium both countries have the same wage rate and rental rate in terms of food, which due to (52′) also means that they have the same scale-adjusted price p_z. In this case the large country produces λ times the food and Z produced by the small country. Preferences are assumed to differ from those of Cobb-Douglas. I will use superscript λ to denote equilibrium values of the large country, while variables without a superscript denote equilibrium values for the small country.

Comparing the equilibrium conditions of the two countries under the assumption of equal factor prices which result in an equal scale-adjusted price p_z, taking $p_y^\lambda = p_y$ (since food is used as numeraire), the following relations have to hold:

$$R(p_y, p_x^\lambda, n^\lambda) = \theta(X^\lambda), \tag{66}$$

$$e(X^\lambda)n^\lambda = \lambda Z, \tag{67}$$

$$\frac{p_x^\lambda X^\lambda}{e(x^\lambda)} = p_z. \tag{68}$$

Equation (66) is the same as condition (53′), except that now the degree of monopoly power depends also on prices. Equation (67) says that $Z^\lambda = \lambda Z$, which has to be satisfied if factor prices are equal, while (68) says that $p_z^\lambda = p_z$, which also has to be satisfied if factor prices are equal. Finally, consider the general demand equilibrium condition (29) which replaces (56) and (56′). Let the left-hand side of (29) be represented by the function $\rho(p_y, p_x, N)$, which is the relative demand for manufactured products. Then, using $N = n$, (29) reads

$$\rho(p_y, p_x, n) = \frac{nX}{Y} = \frac{Zp_z}{Y}\frac{1}{p_x}.$$

With equal factor prices, $p_z Z/Y$ is the same in both countries. Hence, demand equilibrium implies

$$p_x^\lambda \rho(p_y, p_x^\lambda, n^\lambda) = \frac{p_z Z}{Y} = p_x \rho(p_y, p_x, n). \tag{69}$$

Equality of factor prices is consistent with equilibrium if and only if there exist p_x^λ, n^λ, and X^λ that satisfy equations (66)–(69). We have four equations with three unknowns. Therefore a necessary condition for a solution to exist is either that at least two equations are dependent or that at least one equation is redundant. In the Cobb-Douglas case (69) is redundant because $p_x\rho(\cdot) \equiv s/(1-s)$, so I was able to use (66)–(68) to solve for p_x^λ, n^λ, X^λ. However, if the utility function is not Cobb-Douglas, equation (69) is not redundant, and there will, generally, not exist a solution to the above four-equation system. This means that under these circumstances relative factor prices and relative scale-adjusted commodity prices will not be the same in both countries. Since they have the same relative endowments, there will be no intersectoral trade when trade is opened, but by relying on relative factor rewards or relative scale-adjusted commodity prices one would wrongly predict the existence of intersectoral trade.

7 Some Empirical Implications

Now suppose that there are many countries and many commodity groups, but maintain the assumption that labor and capital are the only factors of production. A commodity group consists of different varieties of the same good: cars, TV sets, bicycles, etc. Some of these groups may consist of homogeneous products.

Using the results from Jones (1974), it is clear that with homothetic production functions in a trading equilibrium, countries with higher capital-labor ratios produce on average more capital-intensive goods. In particular, if we consider two countries whose factor prices are not equalized, then the capital-rich country will produce varieties from at least one commodity group such that the capital intensity of this group is higher than the capital intensity of *all* commodity groups being produced in the capital-poor country, or the capital-poor country produces varieties whose capital intensity is lower than the capital intensity of *all* commodity groups being produced in the capital-rich country.

If countries are far apart in their capital-labor ratios, they may happen to produce entirely different groups of commodities, making all bilateral trade interindustry trade. Intraindustry trade, on the other hand, will take place between countries with close factor proportions. Hence, intraindustry trade tends to be larger between countries with close factor proportions than between countries with far apart factor proportions. Since the higher the capital-labor ratio the higher is income per capita (in a cross-country comparison), this raises the hypothesis that a country's share of bilateral intraindustry trade is negatively correlated with the absolute bilateral difference in incomes per capita. Note that this has the flavor of the Linder hypothesis (see Linder 1961), but it is restricted to intraindustry trade and it stems from supply considerations, while the Linder hypothesis concerns total volumes of trade and it is based on the assumption that relative demands change with income per capita.

A negative correlation between the absolute difference in income per capita and the share of intraindustry trade in the bilateral volume of trade has been recently reported for the OECD countries in the early seventies. In a study of the determinants of intraindustry trade, Loertscher and Wolter (1980) explain an index of the share of intraindustry trade that is a variant of *Intra* that I employed in section 5. In their regression analysis they use absolute differences in incomes per capita as one of the explanatory variables, and they find a negative coefficient that differs from zero at the one percent significance level (see their table 2).

A second hypothesis, which is related to the previous one, can be formulated about the time series of the share of intraindustry trade in the world's volume of trade. The hypothesis is that this share is negatively correlated with a measure of dispersion of incomes per capita. For example, one could use the variance or the standard deviation of the distribution of incomes per capita across countries to test whether over time such a negative correlation exists, but I have not been able to find a study that provides a test of this hypothesis.

The present theory does not predict strong relationships between volumes of trade and similarity of incomes per capita. We have seen that a link of this type exists only for an appropriate experiment in which relative country *size* does not change (proposition 5), but I have also shown that changes in relative size have strong effects on the volume of trade. This explains, perhaps, the weak results that emerge from tests of the Linder hypothesis.

The present theory is consistent with the observed differential in the rates of growth of GNP and the volume of trade. In the post–World War II period, the volume of trade of the industrial countries grew at an average rate which was almost double the average growth rate of their GNP. The present model is indeed capable of producing a growth rate of the volume of trade which exceeds the rate of growth of GNP. Take, for example, the case of a homothetic production function in the manufacturing sector and Cobb-Douglas preferences (see section 6). Then, if labor and capital grow at a uniform rate that is the same in every country, GNP of each country also grows at this rate. The volume of trade in food grows at the general growth rate, but output and the volume of trade in manufactured products grows faster. Hence, the total volume of trade grows faster than GNP.

Appendix

The purpose of this appendix is to provide explicit calculations of terms that are used in the main body of the paper. Implicit differentiation of (10) and (11) yields the following partial derivatives of the functions $\bar{\delta}(\cdot)$ and $\underline{\delta}(\cdot)$ that are defined in (12):

$$\frac{\partial\bar{\delta}(\cdot)}{\partial p_{xi}} = \frac{-h[\bar{\delta}(\cdot)]}{p_{xi}h'[\bar{\delta}(\cdot)] + p_{xi+1}h'[2D_i - v_{i-1} - \bar{\delta}(\cdot)]} < 0, \tag{A1}$$

$$\frac{\partial\bar{\delta}(\cdot)}{\partial v_{i-1}} = \frac{-p_{xi+1}h'[2D_i - v_{i-1} - \bar{\delta}(\cdot)]}{p_{xi}h'[\bar{\delta}(\cdot)] + p_{xi+1}h'[2D_i - v_{i-1} - \bar{\delta}(\cdot)]} < 0, \tag{A2}$$

$$\frac{\partial\underline{\delta}(\cdot)}{\partial p_{xi}} = \frac{-h[\underline{\delta}(\cdot)]}{p_{xi}h'[\underline{\delta}(\cdot)] + p_{xi-1}h'[v_{i-1} - \underline{\delta}(\cdot)]} < 0, \tag{A3}$$

$$\frac{\partial\underline{\delta}(\cdot)}{\partial v_{i-1}} = \frac{p_{xi-1}h'[v_{i-1} - \underline{\delta}(\cdot)]}{p_{xi}h'[\underline{\delta}(\cdot)] + p_{xi-1}h'[v_{i-1} - \underline{\delta}(\cdot)]} > 0, \tag{A4}$$

while differentiation of (13) yields

$$\frac{\partial Q(\cdot)}{\partial p_{xi}} = \xi I \left\{ \int_0^{\bar{\delta}(\cdot)} \alpha_{x1}[p_{xi}h(v), p_y][h(v)]^2\, dv \right.$$
$$\left. + \int_0^{\underline{\delta}(\cdot)} \alpha_{x1}[p_{xi}h(v), p_y][h(v)]^2\, dv \right\}$$
$$+ \xi I \left\{ \alpha_x[p_{xi}h\{\bar{\delta}(\cdot)\}, p_y] h[\bar{\delta}(\cdot)] \frac{\partial \bar{\delta}(\cdot)}{\partial p_{xi}} \right.$$
$$\left. + \alpha_x[p_{xi}h\{\underline{\delta}(\cdot)\}, p_y] h[\underline{\delta}(\cdot)] \frac{\partial \underline{\delta}(\cdot)}{\partial p_{xi}} \right\}, \tag{A5}$$

$$\frac{\partial Q(\cdot)}{\partial v_{i-1}} = \xi I \left\{ \alpha_x[p_{xi}h\{\bar{\delta}(\cdot)\}, p_y] h[\bar{\delta}(\cdot)] \frac{\partial \bar{\delta}(\cdot)}{\partial v_{i-1}} \right.$$
$$\left. + \alpha_x[p_{xi}h\{\underline{\delta}(\cdot)\}, p_y] h[\underline{\delta}(\cdot)] \frac{\partial \underline{\delta}(\cdot)}{\partial v_{i-1}} \right\}. \tag{A6}$$

It is explained in section 4 that in equilibrium $p_{xi} = p_x$, $\bar{\delta}(\cdot) = \underline{\delta}(\cdot) = 1/N$ and $v_{i-1} = 2/N$. Using this information to evaluate (A1)–(A6) yields

$$\frac{\partial \bar{\delta}(\cdot)}{\partial p_{xi}} = \frac{-h(1/N)}{2p_x h'(1/N)}, \tag{A7}$$

$$\frac{\partial \bar{\delta}(\cdot)}{\partial v_{i-1}} = -\frac{1}{2}, \tag{A8}$$

$$\frac{\partial \underline{\delta}(\cdot)}{\partial p_{xi}} = \frac{-h(1/N)}{2p_x h'(1/N)}, \tag{A9}$$

$$\frac{\partial \underline{\delta}(\cdot)}{\partial v_{i-1}} = \frac{1}{2}, \tag{A10}$$

$$\frac{\partial Q(\cdot)}{\partial p_{xi}} = 2\xi I \int_0^{1/N} \alpha_{x1}[p_x h(v), p_y][h(v)]^2\, dv$$
$$- \frac{\xi I \alpha_x[p_x h(1/N), p_y][h(1/N)]^2}{p_x h'(1/N)}, \tag{A11}$$

$$\frac{\partial Q(\cdot)}{\partial v_{i-1}} = 0, \tag{A12}$$

where, in the calculations of (A11) and (A12), use has been made of (A7)–(A10).

Notes

This is a revised version of Seminar Paper No. 157, The Institute for International Economic Studies, University of Stockholm. I am grateful to Eitan Berglas, Ronald Jones, and Assaf Razin for helpful comments and discussions. Eitan Berglas was particularly helpful in the formulation of Proposition 4 while Ronald Jones was particularly helpful with parts of section 6. An earlier version of this paper was presented at the 1980 Warwick Summer Workshop, as well as at the Workshop on Production and Trade in a World of Internationally Mobile Factors of Production financed by the Bank of Sweden Tercentenary Foundation and held at the Institute for International Economic Studies, University of Stockholm. I am grateful to participants of these workshops for helpful discussions.

1. Lancaster (1979) prefers to work with product specifications that can be represented by a line instead of a circle. For many purposes the line specification is more appropriate but it is more convenient to work with the circle specification. Both specifications yield similar results if in the case of a line specification one is willing to make special assumptions about the behavior of the "edges" (see Lancaster 1979, ch. 6). The circle (loop) specification appears in Vickrey (1964, ch. 8). See also Salop (1979).

2. Formally the consumer's problem is max $u[x(v)/h(v), y]$ subject to $p_x x(v) + p_y y = I$. Define a new variable $x' = x(v)/h(v)$. Then, transforming variables, the original problem can be rewritten as max $u(x', y)$ subject to $p_x h(v)x' + p_y y = I$. This yields, due to the homotheticity of $u(\cdot)$, the demand functions $x' = \alpha_x[p_x h(v), p_y]I$, $y = \alpha_y[p_x h(v), p_y]I$, which imply (3). The function $\alpha_x(\cdot)$ is declining in its first argument and increasing in the second.

3. I do not assume homotheticity of $F_X(\cdot)$. Ohlin, for example, thought that in the presence of economies of scale the efficient techniques of production do depend on the level of output (see Ohlin 1933, p. 107).

4. An example of a cost function that satisfies these assumptions is

$$C_X(w, r, X) = \begin{cases} r + wX & \text{for } X > 0, \\ 0 & \text{for } X = 0. \end{cases}$$

5. If the cost function is linear in output, as in the example of note 4, then in *every* equilibrium only a finite number of varieties is produced.

6. This discussion, as well as what follows, is based on the assumption that firms cannot price-discriminate.

7. Equation (10) applies for p_{xi} such that $p_{xi} \leqq p_{xi+1}h(v_{i+1})$ and $p_{xi}h(v_{i+1}) \geqq p_{xi+1}$.

8. Equation (11) applies for p_{xi} such that $p_{xi} \leqq p_{xi-1}h(v_{i-1})$ and $p_{xi}h(v_{i-1}) \geqq p_{xi-1}$.

9. This effect is the main theme in Novshek and Sonnenschein (1979).

10. The demand function $Q(\cdot)$ is well defined for the set of parameters that satisfy the inequalities of notes 7 and 8. By a proper extension of the domain of $\bar{\delta}(\cdot)$ and $\underline{\delta}(\cdot)$, the domain of $Q(\cdot)$ can be extended. In any case, my discussion is limited to the domain specified in notes 7 and 8.

11. I have not discussed second-order conditions, but assume that they are satisfied.

12. I will always assume the existence of an equilibrium.

13. If $F_X(\cdot)$ is homothetic, then $C_X(\cdot)$ obtains the separable form $C_X(w, r, X) \equiv c_x(w, r)e(X)$, with $e'(X) > 0$. In this case $\theta(\cdot)$ is only a function of output and it does not depend on factor prices. Then (32) and (37) imply $X = X^*$. Equation (31) can now be written as $p_X X/e(X) = c_X(w, r)$, while (36) can be written as $p_X X/e(X) = c_X(w^*, r^*)$. Since $[\partial c_X(\cdot)/\partial r]/[\partial c_X(\cdot)/\partial w]$ represents the capital-labor ratio employed by the firm, the absence of factor-intensity reversals assures univalence of the mapping from (w, r) to $[p_X X/e(X), p_y]$ given by (30) and $p_X X/e(X) = c_X(w, r)$.

14. If homotheticity in the production of manufactured products is not assumed, relative factor intensities may depend on the output level of manufacturing firms. This is why I consider only relative factor intensities in equilibrium (this is a cross-section comparison). Alternatively, one may employ a strong notion of no factor-intensity reversal, requiring, say, the manufacturing sector to employ more capital per unit labor for *all* output levels.

15. This is similar to the result derived by Mayer (1976) in a model with price uncertainty.

16. Krugman (1981) provides a specific example of this proposition.

17. Lancaster (1980) calls this situation "false comparative advantage."

18. It is interesting to note that average welfare is higher in the larger country for two reasons: (1) income per capita in terms of food is the same, but income per capita in terms of manufactured products is higher, so that every consumer can afford to buy more manufactured products; and (2) there are more varieties produced, which means that more consumers find manufactured products that are closer to their ideal products. If the location of the equally spaced varieties that are produced is drawn from a uniform

distribution, the expected utility of a consumer in the larger country is higher than the expected utility of a consumer in the smaller country.

19. For this result there is no need to assume the absence of factor-intensity reversals.

References

Caves, R. E., and R. W. Jones. 1977. *World Trade and Payments: An Introduction*, 2nd ed. Boston: Little, Brown and Co.

Dixit, A. K., and V. Norman. 1980. *Theory of International Trade.* Cambridge: Cambridge University Press.

Grubel, H. G., and P. J. Lloyd. 1975. *Intra-Industry Trade: The Theory and Measurement of International Trade in Differentiated Products.* London: Macmillan.

Hanoch, G. 1975. The elasticity of scale and the shape of average costs. *American Economic Review* 65:492–497.

Jones, R. W. 1974. The small country in a many commodity world. *Australian Economic Papers*: 225–236. Reprinted in R. W. Jones, *International Trade: Essays in Theory.* Amsterdam: North-Holland, 1979.

Krugman, P. R. 1979. Increasing returns, monopolistic competition, and international trade. *Journal of International Economics* 9:469–479.

Krugman, P. R. 1981. Intraindustry specialization and the gains from trade. *Journal of Political Economy* 89:959–973.

Lancaster K. 1979. *Variety, Equity and Efficiency.* New York: Columbia University Press.

Lancaster, K. 1980. Intra-industry trade under perfect monopolistic competition. *Journal of International Economics* 10:151–175.

Linder, S. B. 1961. *An Essay on Trade and Transformation.* New York: John Wiley.

Loertscher, R., and F. Wolter. 1980. Determinants of intra-industry trade: Among countries and across industries. *Weltwirtschaftliches Archiv* 8:280–293.

Mayer, W. 1976. The Rybczynski, Stolper-Samuelson, and factor price equalization theorem under price uncertainty. *American Economic Review* 66:796–808.

Novshek, W., and H. Sonnenschein. 1979. Marginal consumers and neoclassical demand theory. *Journal of Political Economy* 87:1368–1376.

Ohlin, B. 1933. *Interregional and International Trade.* Cambridge, Mass.: Harvard University Press.

Salop, S. C. 1979. Monopolistic competition with outside goods. *Bell Journal of Economics* 10:141–156.

Vickrey, W. S. 1964. *Microstatics.* New York: Harcourt, Brace and World.

14 National and International Returns to Scale in the Modern Theory of International Trade

Wilfred J. Ethier

For over a quarter century, the Heckscher-Ohlin-Samuelson (H-O-S) trade model has thoroughly dominated work in the pure theory of international trade. Indeed this model is often identified as "the" modern theory of trade. But this dominance has always been rendered uneasy by a widespread suspicion that the salient facts of modern commerce are inconsistent with the theoretical structure. Two broad areas of suspicion may be identified.

The first, concerned with whether actual trade patterns and factor endowments are related as predicted by the theory, consists of the Leontief Paradox and the huge volume of work it stimulated. My interpretation of this literature is that the factor-endowments theory of trade fares reasonably well, but that its two-factor, two-commodity version is essentially an inadequate description of reality. I have on other occasions investigated the consequences of many goods and factors and do not wish to do so now. This paper will accordingly confine itself to a factor-endowments model with two primary factors and two final goods.

The second (by no means unrelated) area of suspicion centers on the stylized fact that the largest and fastest growing component of world trade since World War II has been the exchange of manufactures between the industrialized economies. By contrast, the H-O-S model, and neoclassical theory generally, sees little basis for trade between similar economies. Two manifestations of this point may be found in the empirical literature. The first, of relevance to international monetary problems, concerns departures from purchasing-power parity among the industrial countries even for fairly disaggregated indices of traded goods (see Kravis and Lipsey 1978). The second, a central concern of this paper, involves intraindustry trade.

Although two-way trade had long been observed, it first became of major concern when economists investigated the consequences of economic integration in Europe (see, for example, Verdoorn 1960; Balassa 1966) and noted a tendency, not towards increased specialization, but rather for all countries to simultaneously increase exports of most categories of manufactures. Indeed in some cases specialization actually declined. Subsequent work divorced the phenomenon of intraindustry trade from economic integration and exposed the pervasive expansion of such trade between all industrial countries and across most manufacturing sectors, irrespective of tariff barriers or their changes (Hesse 1974; Grubel and Lloyd 1975; Pagoulatos and Sorenson 1975; Caves 1981). Furthermore, this expansion does not appear to be a matter of transition between equilibria[1] (Caves 1981).

The most natural explanations of intraindustry trade, advanced by Gottfried Haberler (1936), are product heterogeneity within aggregates and border trade (and its seasonal analog). But accumulated empirical work (for example, Hesse 1974; Grubel and Lloyd 1975; Caves 1981) strongly suggests that these explanations are inade-

Originally published in the *American Economic Review* 72 (June 1982): 950–959.

quate.[2] Attention has accordingly shifted to product differentiation and economies of scale (in theory the two go together, as scale economies supply the limitation to the degree of differentiation).[3]

International trade theory does contain a sizable literature on increasing returns to scale (see, for example, Matthews 1950; Meade 1952; Kemp 1969), but this literature would not appear to offer much that is relevant to the phenomenon at issue. Indeed it has not on balance had great influence on trade theory generally. This is no doubt largely because increasing returns establish a strong presumption for complete specialization, multiple equilibria, and indeterminancy, conclusions that both vitiate the standard comparative statics methodology of trade theory and that also bear questionable relevance to the facts of contemporary trade. Furthermore, this theory has generally assumed that the economies of scale were external to the firm and appropriate at an aggregate level, assumptions that preclude much relevance to intraindustry trade. Empirical work has likewise encountered difficulty in coming to grips with scale economies, although many researchers have argued their importance (for example, Balassa 1961, 1967; Daly, Key, and Spence 1968; Owen 1976; Caves 1981), and some have found relevance to intraindustry trade.

Recently I pointed out (Ethier 1979a) that scale economies resulting from an increased division of labor rather than from, say, an increased plant size, depended at an aggregate level upon the size of the world market rather than upon geographical concentration of the industry, as supposed in the traditional theory. Such "international" returns to scale were shown to be free of the presumption of indeterminancy and multiple equilibria[4] characteristic of "national" returns to scale, to imply a theory of intraindustry trade in intermediate goods, and generally to lead to conclusions much more in accord with the stylized facts of modern trade.

The purpose of this paper is to argue that, in the context of international returns, the factor-endowments theory is consistent with, and indeed helps to explain, the stylized facts discussed above. In order to do this I shall construct a simple but detailed model yielding international returns to scale and employ this model to systematically explore the relations between such international returns, the traditional national returns to scale, and the modern (or factor endowments) theory of international trade. I have four broad messages: (1) International returns depend in an essential way on an interaction between the two types of scale economies, which is also an interaction of internal and external (to the firm) economies. (2) The basic theorems of the factor-endowments theory are essentially robust in the presence of such scale economies, in contrast to the conclusions of the traditional literature.[5] Nevertheless there are some important modifications. (3) Intraindustry trade, like interindustry trade, has a factor-endowments basis. However, such trade is basically *complementary* to international factor mobility. (4) Although the existence of internal scale economies and product differentiation are essential to the theory, the degree of such phenomena need not be an essential determinant of the degree of intraindustry trade.

Recently Krugman (1979, 1981), Dixit and Norman (1980), Helpman (1981), and Lawrence and Spiller (1980) have extended to an international context the Dixit-

Stiglitz formalization of Chamberlinian monopolistic competition; and Lancaster (1980) has also applied to international trade his product-characteristics approach to consumption theory. These authors are concerned with the same stylized facts that my earlier paper (Ethier 1979a) had been, and they reach some broadly analogous conclusions, although from entirely different theoretical starting points. The present paper is not concerned with the differentiated consumer goods that are their subject. However I do hope to treat the differentiated producer goods central to my own theory in such a way as to bring out the parallels between the approaches of these other authors and my earlier work on intraindustry trade (I cannot resist the temptation to point out that producers' goods are in fact much more prominent in trade than are consumers' goods).

1 National and International Scale Economies

Production

Capital and labor combine to produce wheat (W) and manufactures (M). Wheat is produced subject to constant returns to scale via a smooth production function of the familiar sort. Manufactures, on the other hand, are potentially subject to increasing returns to scale, and I suppose that the production function for M is separable in the sense that I can write $M = km$, where k is an index of scale economies and m an index of the scale of operations; m can be thought of as produced via a familiar smooth production function. Thus the endowment of capital and labor determines a transformation curve:

$$W = T(m). \tag{1}$$

The possibility of returns to scale in manufacturing arises, first, from exploitation of the division of labor, as in the hoary examples of Adam Smith's pin factory and the Swiss watch industry. Finished manufactures are costlessly assembled from intermediate manufactured components.[6] The number n of components that are actually produced will be endogenously determined, and, I assume, only a fraction of a large number of potentially producible intermediate goods.[7] I am not interested in issues that depend upon distinctions between potential intermediate goods, so I assume that they are all producible from capital and labor via identical production functions, and that all produced components contribute in totally symmetric fashion to the finished manufactures. Under these assumptions, all components that are actually produced will be produced in equal amounts, and I denote the output of each such component by x, so that the total number of produced components of all types is nx. Assume that the output of finished manufactures is given by

$$M = n^{\alpha-1}(nx) \tag{2}$$

for some parameter $\alpha > 1$. It will be convenient to adopt the following specific form of the production function (2), where x_i denotes the quantity of the ith component and β is a parameter, $1 > \beta > 0$.

$$M = n^{\alpha}\left[\sum_{i=1}^{n} \frac{x_i^{\beta}}{n}\right]^{1/\beta} \tag{2'}$$

With all the x_i equal to a common x, as will be the case in equilibrium, (2′) reduces to (2). A higher value of β indicates that components can be more easily substituted for each other in the assembly of finished manufactures. Thus lower values of β correspond to greater "product differentiation" within the manufacturing sector. (Note the analogy to the ways in which Dixit and Stiglitz 1977; Krugman 1979, 1981; Dixit and Norman 1980; and Helpman 1981 measure the utility obtained from a bundle of differentiated consumer goods.)

The gains from an increased division of labor would mandate the production of an infinitesimal amount of an infinite number of separate components if that were possible. I assume that indivisibilities in the production of components prevents this[8] (the division of labor is limited by the extent of the market). If the scale variable m is interpreted as an index of the number of bundles of factors devoted to manufacturing production, suppose that the number of such bundles required to produce x units of any component is $ax + b$, for some $a, b > 0$. Then

$$m = n(ax + b). \tag{3}$$

The technology of the model is formally summarized by equations (1), (2) (or (2′)), and (3), with the usual H-O-S model behind the transformation curve $T(m)$.

Note that there are two distinct sources of increasing returns to scale. The individual component production functions, $ax + b$, display what Balassa (1967, ch. 5) refers to as "economies of scale in the traditional sense," and which I term "national" returns. These involve considerations of minimal plant size and the like, and they require total production x to be geographically concentrated. I assume that these economies are internalized by firms, and I shall examine equilibria in which the total output of each produced component is provided by a single firm in a single location. (I shall sometimes refer casually to b in equation [3] as "fixed costs," but I will not assume that b is variable in the long run.)

The finished-manufactures production function (2), or (2′), displays constant returns to scale for a given value of n. But an expansion of the manufacturing sector arising from an increased number of components (a rise in n with constant x) displays increasing returns, since M rises in greater proportion than nx. These economies reflect not an increased plant size but rather a greater division of labor; they are what Balassa (1967, ch. 5) refers to as "horizontal specialization" or "vertical specialization" and were the subject of my earlier paper (Ethier 1979a), where they were called "international" returns to scale. Economies of this sort depend upon the size of the market for finished manufactures, and they do not require that all manufacturing output be concentrated at a single place. I assume that these economies are external to the individual firm. Components are assembled into finished manufactures by many competitive firms, each of which takes n as a parameter and consequently views itself as subject to constant returns to scale.

Autarkic Equilibrium

Consider a closed economy with the above technology. An individual producer of finished manufactures uses components, subject to (2′), with n as a parameter. If q_0 and q denote the prices, in terms of wheat, of some pair of produced components with outputs x_0 and x, then cost minimization by producers of M, subject to (2′), requires

$$x_0 = x\left(\frac{q}{q_0}\right)^{1/(1-\beta)} \tag{4}$$

If n is sufficiently large so that the producer of each component acts as though his behavior does not influence that of other component producers, condition (4) is the demand curve faced by the producer of x_0, for given q and x. This curve has an elasticity of $1/(1-\beta)$. The component-producer purchases the services of primary factors in competitive markets and therefore has a cost function given by $-T'(m)\cdot[ax_0 + b]$, where $T'(m)$ is exogenous to the individual firm. This firm will therefore equate marginal revenue and marginal cost, and maximize its profit, by charging the price

$$q_0 = -T'(m)\frac{a}{\beta}. \tag{5}$$

Because of the symmetry assumption, q_0 is the price of each component that is actually produced. The profit of each component-producing firm is $q_0x_0 + T'(m)[ax_0 + b]$. These profits will be driven to zero in equilibrium by the entry and exit of firms, that is, by variations in n, as each component is produced by only one firm. Thus, from equation (5),

$$x_0 = \frac{b\beta}{a(1-\beta)}. \tag{6}$$

Finally, the number n of components is given by equation (3), for any given m and for $x = x_0$.

$$n = (1-\beta)\frac{m}{b}. \tag{7}$$

Equations (5), (6), and (7) now imply the value of k for $M = km$:

$$k = \left[\left(\frac{1-\beta}{b}\right)^{\alpha-1}\frac{\beta}{\alpha}\right]m^{\alpha-1}. \tag{8}$$

The relative supply price P_S of M in terms of wheat is given by $P_SM = q_0nx$, or $P_Sn^{\alpha}x = q_0nx$, or $P_S = n^{1-\alpha}q_0$. Thus substitution yields the supply curve of M:

$$P_S = -\frac{T'(m)}{k}. \tag{9}$$

The supply curve is illustrated in figure 1. The term M_0 denotes the value of M when

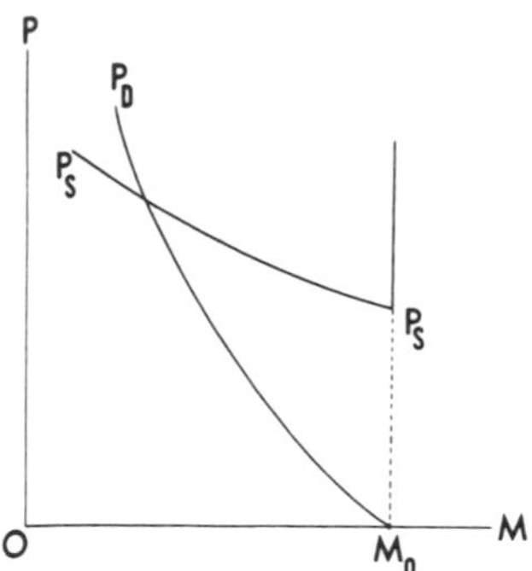

Figure 1

$T = 0$, and the curve P_S shows for each value of M the minimum price at which that quantity would be supplied (i.e., expression [9]). Note from (6) that x is independent of m. Thus a reallocation of resources from W to M involves an expansion of M production by an increase in n. The manufacturing sector thus displays increasing returns to scale, allowing a negatively sloped supply curve, as illustrated.

The picture of autarkic equilibrium is completed by a description of the demand for final goods. I assume that a constant fraction γ of income is always spent on manufactures. Each output combination M and W determines a demand price P_D that will clear commodity markets: $P_D M = \gamma[W + P_D M]$. Thus the demand curve can be written as

$$P_D = \left(\frac{\gamma}{1-\gamma}\right)\frac{T(m)}{km}. \tag{10}$$

The demand curve has a negative slope, as illustrated in figure 1, and it is easy to show that equations (9) and (10) imply that the demand curve intersects the supply curve from above. Thus in autarky the economy possesses a unique equilibrium that features production of both final goods.

International Equilibrium

Consider next free international trade between two economies—of the sort just described—identical in all respects other than factor endowments. Let m and m^* denote the scale of manufacturing operations at home and abroad (variables pertaining to the foreign country will be distinguished by an asterisk). In free trade equilibrium the total output of each component will be concentrated in a single country. Thus, if m and m^* are both positive, the two countries produce distinct collections of components. Equation (4) continues to represent the demand curve faced by each component producer (in either country), and the same argument as before establishes that (6) gives the output of each component actually produced somewhere. Then, if n_H and n_F denote the number of components produced at home and abroad, respectively, it follows as before that $n_H = (1-\beta)m/b$ and $n_F = (1-\beta)m^*/b$ so that $n = n_H + n_F$ is given by

$$n = \frac{(1-\beta)(m+m^*)}{b}, \tag{11}$$

and so, from (2), the world output of finished manufactures is

$$M + M^* = \left(\frac{\beta}{\alpha}\right)\left(\frac{1-\beta}{b}\right)^{\alpha-1}(m+m^*)^{\alpha}. \tag{12}$$

What determines m, m^*, and the relative prices? To answer this question I use the allocation-curve technique[9] developed in Ethier (1979a, 1982). For any m and m^*, the world demand price of finished manufactures in terms of wheat is given by

$$\begin{aligned} P_D &= \frac{\gamma}{1-\gamma}\frac{T(m)+S(m^*)}{M+M^*} \\ &= \frac{\gamma}{1-\gamma}\frac{a}{\beta}\left(\frac{b}{1-\beta}\right)^{\alpha-1}\frac{T(m)+S(m^*)}{(m+m^*)^{\alpha}}, \end{aligned} \tag{13}$$

where $S(m^*) = W^*$ denotes the foreign transformation curve. The home supply price P_S^H must be given by

$$P_S^H = -\left[\frac{(1-\beta)(m+m^*)}{b}\right]^{1-\alpha} T'(m)\frac{a}{\beta}. \tag{14}$$

Home-country equilibrium requires $P_D = P_S^H$, or, from equations (13) and (14),

$$\gamma[T(m)+S(m^*)] + (1-\gamma)(m+m^*)T'(m) = 0. \tag{15}$$

Equation (15) defines the "home allocation curve": the collection of m and m^* for which the home country is in equilibrium in the international economy. This relation is depicted as the HH' curve in each panel of figure 2. It is easily shown that the curve has a negative slope, that $P_D < P_S^H$ above the curve, and that $P_D > P_S^H$ below. In figure 2, m_0 and m_0^* denote the manufacturing scales if the home and foreign economies, respectively, specialize to manufactures, so the world is confined to the rectangle $0m_0Em_0^*$ in each panel, and that part of the graph of (15) lying outside this rectangle is irrelevant (it is easy to see that the graph of [15] cannot be completely excluded from the rectangle). If the home economy specializes, equilibrium is consistent with an excess of the relative demand price of the produced good over its relative supply price. Thus the home allocation curve also contains any part of $0m_0^*$ that lies above the intersection of $H'H$ with the vertical axis, and also any part of m_0E below its intersection with $H'H$.

Similarly, the foreign allocation curve, showing the m and m^* for which $P_D = P_S^F$, the foreign relative supply price, is given by

$$\gamma[T(m)+S(m^*)] + (1-\gamma)(m+m^*)S'(m^*) = 0. \tag{16}$$

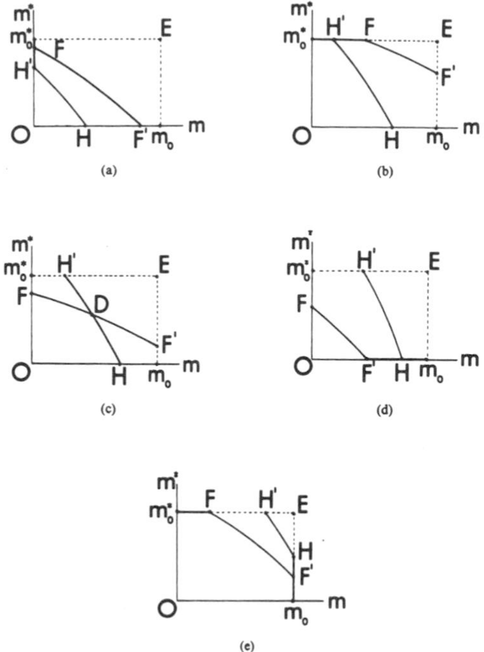

Figure 2

The graph of (16) is shown as FF' in each panel of figure 2. As illustrated, FF' must decline less steeply than $H'H$, reflecting the fact that each country's supply price is relatively more sensitive than the world demand price to that country's allocation of resources compared to the foreign allocation. Any part of m_0^*E lying below FF' and any part of $0m_0$ above FF' also constitute part of the foreign allocation curve.

International equilibrium requires each country to be individually in equilibrium in the world economy and is therefore determined by the intersection of the two allocation curves. Figure 2 depicts the five qualitatively distinct possibilities; equilibrium is shown by points F, H', D, H, and F' in panels (a)–(e), respectively (in addition there are the two boundary cases, featuring complete specialization in both countries, between cases [a] and [b] and between [d] and [e]). Evidently each case yields a unique international equilibrium.

The equilibrium values of m and m^* determine the relative price of finished manufactures in terms of wheat from equation (13) (or [14]). Then n is given by (11) and x by (6). The price of each component is as indicated by (5), or, if the home economy specializes to wheat, by the foreign analog.

Note that equation (12) can also be written $M + M^* = k(m + m^*)$ where $k = (\beta/a)[(1-\beta)/b]^{\alpha-1}(m + m^*)^{\alpha-1}$, thereby emphasizing that the extent of external scale economies depends on the size of the world market alone. If M and M^* denote the quantities of finished manufactures to which the respective countries obtain effective title as a result of their manufacturing activity (i.e., the most finished manufactures each country could consume without offering any wheat in exchange), then,

$$M = km,$$
$$M^* = km^*. \tag{17}$$

Note that M and M^* need not equal the quantities of finished manufactures actually assembled in each country. With assembly costless it can be divided in any way between the two countries. (If one of the components were an assembly process, $M + M^*$ would be all assembled in the country where that process happened to be located.)

2 The Modern Theory

Armed with a complete description of international equilibrium, this section inquires into the fate of the four central propositions supplied by the H-O-S model.[10] Henceforth manufacturing is assumed relatively capital intensive and wheat relatively labor intensive. Since inherent properties of the two factors do not figure in this paper, this pattern of factor intensities is in a formal sense only a definition. But the definition is not arbitrary: one intuitively associates a greater division of labor with significant use of capital. This could be introduced by letting manufacturing production explicitly take time, adding a positive interest rate, and allowing components to be producers' goods generally. It is straightforward to extend the main results of this paper to such a context by using the techniques in my article (Ethier 1979b), provided attention is restricted to steady states.

Factor-Price Equalization

Suppose that both countries operate both sectors, so that equilibrium is as in figure 2c. Then equations (15) and (16) hold, implying that $T'(m) = S'(m^*)$. Likewise, T' and S' are necessarily unequal if one or both countries specializes completely.[11] Now, with the assumption of identical technology, equality of T' and S' implies that domestically produced components sell at the same price as all foreign-produced components, from (14) and its foreign counterpart. Since T and S are generated by conventional H-O-S technologies, the standard factor-price equalization argument can now be employed to yield

PROPOSITION 1 *Factor-Price Equalization.* If both countries operate both sectors, and are not separated by a factor-intensity reversal, free trade implies factor-price equalization. A separating reversal, or (nonincipient) specialization in either country, precludes such equalization.

The Rybczynski Theorem

Note, first, that if domestic factor endowments are altered and $T'(m)$ is kept unchanged, the standard Rybczynski argument applies exactly: an increase in capital will cause a more than proportionate rise in m and a fall in W.

The next step is to relate the change in m to the production of individual components and finished manufactures. Expression (5) implies that constancy of $T'(m)$ is equivalent to constancy of the relative prices of components in terms of wheat. Then (6) implies that endowment changes cause *no* changes in the outputs of those components that are produced both before and after, while (7) reveals that the *number* of produced components varies in proportion to m. Thus:

PROPOSITION 2 *Rybczynski.* At constant relative component prices, an increase in the capital stock will absolutely reduce the production of wheat, have no effect on the outputs of all components initially produced, and increase the number of produced components in greater proportion than the rise in the capital stock itself.

Several features of this Rybczynski theorem deserve emphasis. First, despite the pervasive presence of economies of scale, the standard results are completely preserved at the interindustry level: changes in endowments produce magnified changes in the outputs of wheat and aggregate manufactures. Because all produced components sell at the same price and have equal outputs, aggregate component production can be measured by nx, which changes proportionally to n since the adjustment of manufacturing output occurs through variations in the *number* of components rather than in the *outputs* of individual components.

Second, at a disaggregated level, endowment changes produce magnified changes in the outputs of wheat and of those components that change status (and thereby experience infinite proportional output changes). The (zero) proportional output changes of the other components will be weighted averages of proportional endowment changes if and only if the latter are in opposite directions.

Note, third, that the present version of the Rybczynski theorem places no restrictions on the relative price of finished manufactures. Nor does it make any claims about the effective output M of these final goods. This is because international economies of scale influence the production of final manufactures independently of the internal, national economies associated with the production of individual components. The extent of the former depends upon patterns of production in both countries. Thus, in order to describe the effects of endowment changes in one country on that country's (effective) output of finished manufactures, the behavior of the rest of the world must be considered.

With relative component prices held fixed, m^* will be unchanged. Now equation (17) implies that the proportional change in M equals that in m plus that in k. With m^* constant, the proportional change in k equals that in m multiplied by $[(\alpha - 1)m/(m + m^*)]$. This is straightforward: an increase in m takes the form of an increased number of components and thereby raises M both directly and indirectly through the scale economies made possible by the increased division of labor. The latter *scale effect* depends upon the rate $\alpha - 1$ at which scale economies are realized, plus the extent to which an increase in m constitutes an increase in world manufacturing $m + m^*$. In any event, M changes in the same direction as m and in even greater proportion, so that the effect of economies of scale is to simply accentuate the standard results.

With constant component prices, changes in the scale of manufacturing activity must change the relative price of finished manufactures. Equation (14) reveals that this price falls in the proportion $(\alpha - 1)[m/(m + m^*)]\hat{m}$, where I use a circumflex to denote proportional change. This is the same scale effect as above, entering in for the same reason. The relative price of finished manufactures falls in the proportion that k rises; thus the *value* of finished manufactures, in terms of either wheat or components, rises in the same proportion as aggregate component output. This is a reflection of the external character of the relevant scale economies.

PROPOSITION 3 At constant relative component prices, an increase in capital increases the output of finished manufactures relative to that of components (and therefore to the capital stock) and also reduces the price of finished manufactures, so that the value of the output of finished manufactures rises in the same proportion as that of aggregate components.

It is natural to wonder how the Rybczynski theorem is affected when the relative price of finished manufactures in terms of wheat is held constant. The exercise is not in fact very interesting because of the international interdependence. For example, equation (14) reveals that any increase in m brought about by endowment changes must be accompanied by an increase in T' sufficient to leave $(m + m^*)^{1-\alpha}T'$ unchanged. Thus the relative price of components in terms of wheat rises, and the factor prices and techniques must change as well. Furthermore, if the rest of the world is not specialized to wheat, the equilibrium condition of equal component prices requires foreign changes in factor prices and techniques.

The Stolper-Samuelson Theorem

Expression (5) implies that the wheat price of components is linked to factor prices in essentially the same way as are commodity prices in the standard H-O-S model. Then the usual argument establishes the following:

$$\hat{P}_C = \theta_{km}\hat{r} + \theta_{Lm}\hat{w}, \tag{18}$$

$$\hat{P}_W = \theta_{kW}\hat{r} + \theta_{LW}\hat{w}. \tag{19}$$

In these equations P_C, P_W, r, and w denote the nominal prices of industrial components, wheat, capital, and labor, respectively (so that $q = P_C/P_W$). The θ_{kW} and θ_{LW} denote capital's and labor's distributive shares in the wheat industry and analogously for θ_{km} and θ_{Lm} in the components industry. The following is immediate from (18) and (19).

PROPOSITION 4 An increase in the price of wheat relative to the price of all components will raise the wage relative to the prices of both wheat and components and will reduce the rent relative to the prices of both wheat and components.

Industrial components are intermediate goods, and only wheat and finished manufactures are consumed. Thus proposition 4 says nothing about real factor rewards and so fails to come to grips with the essence of the Stolper-Samuelson theorem. The price P_M of finished manufactures is related to that of components by $P_M = n^{1-\alpha}P_C$, so that

$$\hat{P}_M = \hat{P}_C - (\alpha - 1)\hat{n}. \tag{20}$$

Now $\hat{n} = \hat{m}[m/(m + m^*)]$, and $\hat{m}$ can be related to $\hat{P}_M - \hat{P}_W$ by differentiation of (14) to obtain

$$(\hat{P}_M - \hat{P}_W) = \left[m\frac{T''}{T'} - (\alpha - 1)\frac{m}{m + m^*}\right]\hat{m}. \tag{21}$$

Substitution into (20) gives

$$(\hat{P}_M - \hat{P}_C) = Z(\hat{P}_M - \hat{P}_W), \tag{22}$$

where the elasticity of the *intraindustry* price structure P_M/P_C with respect to the *interindustry* price structure P_M/P_W is $Z = 1/\{1 - [mT''/T']/[(\alpha - 1)m/(m + m^*)]\}$.

Note first that, although Z may be of either sign, it can never fall between zero and unity. Thus variations in the intraindustry price structure are never damped versions of variations in the interindustry structure. This reflects the role of scale economies. A change in relative prices involves a reallocation of resources. If resources move into manufacturing, that is, if $\hat{m} > 0$, this will be associated with an increase in P_C/P_W to a degree dependent upon the curvature of the transformation curve. Since the cost of components contributes towards the cost of manufactures, this will also tend to be associated with a rise in P_M/P_W. This effect is simply the familiar H-O-S phenomenon, and I accordingly call it the *intersectoral price effect* of $\hat{m}$; it is reflected in the first term in the brackets in (21).

The variation in m will involve a variation in n rather than x, so individual firms will not experience internal scale economies. But the expansion of world manufacturing will induce external scale economies, and this *scale effect* will tend to reduce the cost of finished manufactures and will therefore work against the intersectoral effect. This scale effect, reflected in the second term in brackets in (21), is the same elasticity of k with respect to m encountered above. If the intersectoral effect dominates, P_M/P_W will therefore change in the same direction as, but to a lessor extent than, P_C/P_W, whereas a dominant scale effect[12] means that a rise in P_C/P_W actually reduces P_M/P_W.

PROPOSITION 5 If the scale effect dominates the intersectoral effect ($Z > 0$), changes in the intrasectoral price structure P_M/P_C are magnifications of changes in the intersectoral structure P_M/P_W. If the intersectoral effect dominates the scale effect ($Z < 0$), the two relative prices always change in opposite directions.

We are now in a position to relate factor rewards to final-goods prices. Substituting equation (22) into (18) and (19) gives

$$\hat{P}_M = \theta_{kW}\left[\frac{(\theta_{km}/\theta_{kW}) - Z}{1 - Z}\right]\hat{r} + \theta_{LW}\left[\frac{(\theta_{Lm}/\theta_{LW}) - Z}{1 - Z}\right]\hat{w}, \tag{23}$$

$$\hat{P}_W = \theta_{kW}\hat{r} + \theta_{LW}\hat{w}. \tag{19}$$

Note first that (19) is not affected, so that the proportional change in the price of wheat is still a weighted average of those in the two factor rewards. Second, the coefficients of $\hat{w}$ and $\hat{r}$ in (23) sum to unity, as in (18). With labor designated intensive to wheat, $\theta_{Lm} < \theta_{LW}$, so that the exclusion of Z from between zero and unity renders the coefficients of $\hat{w}$ in (23) positive. Thus that of $\hat{r}$ is less than unity. This is all that can be said without restrictions on technology.

If $Z < 0$, the coefficient of $\hat{r}$ in (23) is positive, so that $\hat{P}_M$ is a weighted average of $\hat{r}$ and $\hat{w}$. Furthermore, the coefficient of $\hat{r}$ in (23) exceeds that of $\hat{r}$ in (19), and the usual Stolper-Samuelson argument follows. If, on the other hand, $Z > 0$, then in fact $Z > 1$, so the coefficient of $\hat{r}$ in (23) is less than that in (19) and the standard results can not possibly hold.

PROPOSITION 6 *Stolper-Samuelson.* An increase in the price of manufactures relative to wheat raises the rent and lowers the wage relative to both final-goods prices, if and only if the intersectoral effect dominates the scale effect.

The reason for this result is straightforward. A dominant intersectoral effect ensures that a change in P_M/P_W produces a larger change, in the same direction, in P_C/P_W, to which proposition 4 can be applied to yield the standard result. A dominant scale effect precludes this result by causing P_C/P_W to change in the opposite direction. Note that propositions 5 and 6 together give a very simple test for the validity of the Stolper-Samuelson theorem: the intrasectoral price structure P_M/P_C and the intersectoral structure P_M/P_W should always change in opposite directions.

If Z exceeds unity it may or may not also exceed θ_{km}/θ_{kW}. If the scale effect is sufficiently dominant so that Z does exceed this latter term, the coefficient of $\hat{r}$ in equation (23) is again positive and $\hat{P}_M$ is a weighted average of $\hat{w}$ and $\hat{r}$. But the coefficient of $\hat{r}$ in (23) is less than that of $\hat{r}$ in (19). Thus the standard Stolper-Samuelson argument applies, but with the role of the factor-intensity pattern reversed, so that an "anti-Stolper-Samuelson" result follows.

PROPOSITION 7 An increase in the price of manufactures relative to wheat raises the wage and reduces the rent relative to both final-good prices, if and only if the scale effect dominates the intersectoral effect sufficiently so that $Z > \theta_{km}/\theta_{kW}$.

Finally, if Z lies between unity and θ_{km}/θ_{kW}, the coefficient of $\hat{r}$ in (23) is negative, and that of $\hat{w}$ in (23) exceeds that of $\hat{w}$ in (19). Thus any change in P_M/P_W causes w to rise relative to one final-good price and fall relative to the other, but the rental still behaves as above.

PROPOSITION 8 The relative price of manufactures and the real income of capital vary in the same or opposite directions according as the intersectoral and intrasectoral price structures vary in identical or opposite directions.

Note that a large scale effect tends to destroy the duality between the Stolper-Samuelson and Rybczynski theorems, since it works to reverse the former while leaving the latter unscathed.[13]

The Heckscher-Ohlin Theorem

Suppose that both countries produce both goods in international equilibrium, as in figure 2c. Then $T'(m) = S'(m^*)$, and proposition 3 implies that the output ratio M/W is higher in the country endowed with the higher capital-labor ratio. Since the two countries consume the two final goods in equal proportions, each country is a net exporter of the sector intensive to its relatively abundant factor.

Next suppose that at least one country specializes completely. As illustrated in figure 2, the home allocation curve is steeper than the foreign and, in this case, must lie either wholly outside or wholly inside the foreign. In the former case (fig. 2, panels [d] and [e]) the home country is a wheat importer and in the latter case (fig. 2, panels [a] and [b]) a wheat exporter. What distinguishes the two cases?

At point F', m and m^* satisfy equation (16). In the home country, from equations (13) and (14),

$$P_D - P_S^H = \frac{a}{\beta}\left(\frac{b}{1-\beta}\right)^{\alpha-1}(m+m^*)^{1-\alpha}\left[\frac{\gamma}{1-\gamma}\frac{T+S}{m+m^*} + T'\right].$$

Substitution of (16) into this expression reveals that, at F', $P_D - P_S^H$ has the same sign as $[T'(m) - S'(m^*)]$. Now, if F' falls in the interval $0m_0$, $m^* = 0$ and $0 < m \leq m_0$, whereas $0 \leq m^* < m_0^*$ and $m = m_0$ if F' lies in the interval m_0E. In either case, $T' - S'$ is necessarily negative if the foreign country is relatively capital abundant, provided that the two countries are not separated by a factor-intensity reversal. Then $P_D < P_S^H$ at F, which implies that F' lies above the home allocation curve. A similar argument applied to F reveals that the home allocation curve necessarily lies above the foreign when the home country is relatively capital abundant. Panels (a) and (b) of figure 2 accordingly illustrate home relative labor abundance, and panels (d) and (e) illustrate home capital abundance.

PROPOSITION 9 *Heckscher-Ohlin.* In international equilibrium, each country necessarily exports the good intensive in its relatively abundant factor, if the two countries are not separated by a factor-intensity reversal.

The quantity version of the Heckscher-Ohlin theorem remains intact. Clearly the price version cannot similarly escape unscathed: the scale effect can alter the relation between commodity and factor prices. Also section 1 showed that relative autarkic commodity prices depend upon national size as well as relative endowments. Since only the latter determine trade patterns, these patterns need not reflect autarkic price differences.

But in spite of all this, the price version does have a role to play, a role that depends on a distinction between intraindustry trade and interindustry trade. Basically, the pattern of free *interindustry* trade (the net exchange of manufactures for wheat) will correspond to what the pattern of relative factor prices in the two countries would be in the absence of such trade but with free *intraindustry* trade (the exchange of components). The latter in effect isolates the influence of internationally decreasing costs.

To see this, consider a *quasi-autarkic equilibrium* in which the two countries freely exchange industrial components, but in which there is no trade in wheat. That is, the home economy consumes $W = T(m)$ and $M = km$, where $k = \beta[(m + m^*)(1 - \beta)/b]^{\alpha-1}/a$, and analogously abroad. Such an equilibrium is as described in section 1 for each country, except that the two economies are linked by a common value of k dependent upon $m + m^*$. The equilibrium values of m and m^* are the solution to

$$\gamma T(m) - (1 - \gamma)T'(m)(m + m^*) = 0,$$

$$\gamma S(m^*) + (1 - \gamma)S'(m^*)(m + m^*) = 0.$$

In such an equilibrium, the home relative demand and supply prices are given by equations (10) and (9), and analogously abroad. If relative demand prices happen to be equal in the two countries, (10) implies $T(m)/m = S(m^*)/m^*$, since in quasi-autarkic equilibrium the countries share common values of k and n. Thus $T'(m)/m$ exceeds or falls short of $S'(m^*)/m^*$ according as the home country is relatively capital or labor abundant (in a physical sense). Or, in view of (9), the home relative supply price is less or greater than the foreign according as the home economy is relatively capital abundant or not. For demand price to equal supply price in each country, it is consequently necessary that the quasi-autarkic equilibrium relative price of manufactures be less in the relatively capital-abundant country. Proposition 9 then implies that the free trade exchange of wheat for manufactures is accurately predicted by comparative quasi-autarkic relative commodity prices.

Since in quasi autarky the two countries have distinct relative prices but common values of n and k, the logic of proposition 6 can be employed to compare the two national equilibria in the absence of a scale effect. This gives the present form of the price version of the Heckscher-Ohlin theorem.

PROPOSITION 10 *Quasi-autarky Theorem.* In the absence of a separating factor-intensity reversal, each country in free trade is a net exporter of the sector relatively intensive in that factor with the lower relative quasi-autarkic price in that country.

Note that the quasi-autarky theorem applies to a world such as that envisioned by Hufbauer and Chilas (1974), who stress that trade between industrial countries is largely intraindustry and involves much less interindustry specialization than does interregional trade within the United States. They see this as due in large part to the pattern of tariff reductions made since the war.

3 The Factor-Endowments Basis of Intraindustry Trade

The previous sections have established the continued relevance to *interindustry* trade of the basic Heckscher-Ohlin idea that trade is a substitute for international factor mobility. The present environment, for example, does no violence to the factor-price equalization theorem.

The purpose of this section is to establish that *intraindustry* trade likewise has a factor-endowments basis, but that such trade is *complementary* to international factor mobility. Thus a similarity of factor endowments between nations tends to promote such trade as it limits the scope for interindustrial exchange. This property is emerging as a central feature of models with intraindustry trade. The result was first deduced in Ethier (1979a) and subsequently appeared in the quite distinct work based on differentiated consumer goods.

The Complementarity Theorem

Recall the assumption that finished manufactures are costlessly assembled from bundles of all components. The above analysis established that if both countries produce manufactures, they specialize to distinct collections of components.

It will prove convenient, and consistent with both the balance of this paper and most empirical work, to measure intraindustry trade as what it would be if finished manufactures were assumed to be costlessly assembled where consumed, and if no component entered trade more than once, so that international trade in manufactures therefore consisted entirely of the shipment of components from their country of manufacture to where they are combined with other components and consumed. Then the home country's import M_C and export X_C of manufactures (components) must be

$$M_C = n_F x g, \quad X_C = n_H x(1 - g),$$

where g equals domestic national income as a fraction of world income (i.e., $(PM + W)/[P(M + M^*) + W + W^*]$). I shall use the relative index[14] employed by Hesse (1974), Grubel and Lloyd (1971), Caves (1981), and others: $\rho = 1 - |X_C - M_C|/(X_C + M_C)$. Then substitution yields

$$\begin{aligned} \rho &= \frac{2gn_F}{(1-g)n_H + gn_F} \qquad \text{if } n_H \geq gn, \\ &= \frac{2(1-g)n_H}{(1-g)n_H + gn_F} \qquad \textit{if } n_H \leq gn. \end{aligned} \tag{24}$$

Higher values of ρ indicate relatively more intraindustry trade; $\rho = 1$ if all manufacturing trade is intraindustry and $\rho = 0$ if it is all interindustry.

The complementarity between intraindustry trade and factor movements should now be apparent. Let h and h^* denote the capital-labor endowment ratios at home and abroad, and designate the home country as the capital-abundant one, so that $h > h^*$. Suppose that the two countries freely trade, with neither country specialized and with factor prices equalized. Suppose now that the factors are slightly "traded" between the two countries so as to reduce $h - h^*$ while leaving each country's income unchanged at the unchanged factor prices and commodity prices. Then n_H falls, n_F rises by the same amount, and g is unchanged. Now, since the home economy is relatively capital abundant, its share of the world output of components (n_H/n) must exceed its share of world income, g. Thus ρ equals the top expression in (24), which directly reveals that a relative-endowment-equalizing trade of factors must raise ρ.

PROPOSITION 11 *Complementarity Theorem.* If both countries initially produce both goods, and if there are no separating factor-intensity reversals, a small relative-endowment-equalizing trade of primary factors will increase ρ.

The basic complementarity property becomes most apparent upon the comparison of extreme cases. If the two countries' endowments differ sufficiently so that one country specializes to wheat, there is no intraindustry trade and all trade is interindustrial. If, on the other hand, $K = K^*$ and $L = L^*$, there is no basis at all for interindustry trade (each country will be self-sufficient in wheat), but intraindustry trade will be maximized since the two countries will produce distinct collections of an equal number of components.

Technological Structure and Intraindustry Trade

While the complementarity theorem establishes that intraindustry trade is sensitive to factor endowments, it is nonetheless clear that the existence of such trade is due to the assumptions about the technology of manufacturing production. Attention thus naturally focuses on the sensitivity of my measure of intraindustry trade to the technological parameters: a, b, and β.

Note, first, that these parameters do not influence the basic allocation of resources which, by proposition 9, is determined as described by the modern theory of international trade. The intersection of the allocation curves determines m and m^*, and these curves are invariant with respect to all three parameters. Attention therefore focuses on equations (6) and (7).

Consider the relative measure ρ. Changes in the technological parameters will not change g, because they produce offsetting changes on the volume and the relative price of finished manufactures, from (12) and (14). Substitution of (7) into the top line of (24) gives $\rho = 2gm^*/[(1 - g)m + gm^*]$. This immediately yields

PROPOSITION 12 The relative index of intraindustry trade is invariant with respect to the degree of product differentiation and the levels of fixed and marginal costs.

An increase in marginal costs, by reducing x with n_H and n_F constant, lowers both types of trade in proportion. An increase in product differention also reduces interindustry trade pari passu with intraindustry trade. This is surprising: with the existence of intraindustry trade dependent upon product differentiation, one might expect more differentiation to increase such trade. But the explanation is simple. From (7) the number of components does rise, but (6) reveals that the output of each falls in even greater proportion, because of fixed costs.

In sum, the technological parameters play a knife-edge role: their existence is crucial for the present theory, but changes in their values have few effects, or sometimes counterintuitive effects, upon intraindustry trade. Empirical investigations have so far produced mixed results (see Pagoulatos and Sorenson 1975; Caves 1981; and references cited therein).

Multilateral Trade

A brief consideration of this paper's implications for multilateral trade further illustrates the above discussion and also brings out some features that cannot arise at all in the two-country framework, but that reflect the stylized facts of modern trade.

The model used thus far is retained, except that many countries of the sort described above are allowed. Suppose that no factor-intensity reversal is displayed by the common technology. Let h_m and h_W denote the capital-labor ratios in the two sectors in countries that diversify production at the existing prices. Denote by h' the capital-labor ratio having the property that any country with an endowment $h > h'$ necessarily imports wheat, and any country with an endowment $h < h'$ necessarily exports wheat.[15] Assume $h_m > h' > h_W$. The various possibilities an individual country could experience are indicated in table 1.

The concerns of the complementarity theorem are best brought out in cases II, III, and IV where similarities of endowments (to each other and to the world as a whole) foster intraindustry trade while limiting interindustry trade. Cases I and V, on the other hand, illustrate behavior that cannot arise in a two-country context. Countries in case I engage in extensive intraindustry trade with the rest of the world (including other case I countries), by virtue of their specialization to manufacturing, despite the fact that their endowments are quite different from that of the rest of the world as a whole. Countries in case V, because they specialize to wheat, engage in no intraindustry trade at all with each other (or with anyone else), no matter how closely the factor endowments of these countries resemble each other. The relevance of all this to the stylized facts of contemporary trade should be clear.

Table 1
Possibilities in Multilateral Trade

Case	Endowment	Production	Intraindustry Trade	Interindustry Trade
I	$h \geq h_m$	specialized to m	with all other I, II, III, IV countries	imports W from IV and V
II	$h_m > h \geq h'$	diversified	with all other I, II, III, IV countries	imports some W from IV and V
III	$h = h'$	diversified	with all other I, II, III, IV countries	none
IV	$h' > h > h_W$	diversified	with all other I, II, III, IV countries	exports some W to I and II
V	$h_W \geq h$	specialized to W	none	exports W to I and II

4 Conclusion

This paper has developed a simple model of the interaction of national scale economies—internal to individual firms—with international returns to scale—external to firms—and with the modern, factor-endowments theory of international trade. The result furnishes a detailed microeconomic backdrop to my earlier paper (Ethier 1979a). In addition two conclusions emerge.

First, as formalized in the complementarity theorem, intraindustry trade in manufactures is complementary to international factor movements. Although the existence of such trade depends upon product differentiation and scale economies, these features play a knife-edge role and thereby leave the determination of the level of intraindustry trade largely to relative factor endowments. Second, the basic propositions of the modern theory of international trade remain, on the whole, essentially valid in the presence of scale economies, although some significant modifications do arise.

The second conclusion contrasts rather strongly with the traditional increasing-returns literature—thoroughly preoccupied with national returns to scale. The present treatment also gives national returns a prominent place. The indeterminancy and multiple equilibria characteristic of the standard analysis are still present (because national returns are still present), in terms of the location of production of individual components. But the sharp difference in my conclusions follows from the fact that, when national and international economies are allowed to interact, disturbances to equilibrium typically take the form of changes in the number of production units rather than in their size, so that the concerns of the traditional theory do not arise. Of course it is possible to chip away at this conclusion by relaxing some of my assumptions, especially those that components are symmetric and that internal scale economies arise solely from fixed costs. These assumptions reflect in simple form my views of what is relatively important, but they cannot be literally accurate.

My earlier paper (Ethier 1979a) argued that international increasing returns to scale are significant in the modern world economy. The present paper suggests that the conclusions of the earlier paper need not be altered even if national scale economies are also widespread and important. The resulting theory appears empirically relevant, with respect to both the stylized facts cited at the beginning of this article and also to recent studies—see Caves (1981) and Loertscher and Wolter (1980).

Notes

The research for this paper was supported by the National Science Foundation under grant no. SES-7925614. I have benefitted from seminars at the universities of Pennsylvania, Western Ontario, and Wisconsin, and Northwestern University. Richard Caves also supplied useful comments and suggestions.

1. See Hufbauer and Chilas (1974) for a contrasting argument that intraindustry trade is due to the GATT method of tariff reduction and to transitory responses with quasi-fixed factors of production. Finger (1975) also offers some contrasting evidence.

2. Grubel and Lloyd (1975), for example, found significant Australian intraindustry trade even at the seven-digit level. I do not mean to suggest that such trade indicates a violation of commodity arbitrage and could not be made to disappear completely in the face of relentless disaggregation. Indeed the theory to

follow will make use of product differentiation. Rather the point is that intraindustry trade appears significant even with sufficient disaggregation to remove relative cost differences between sectors as a likely determinant of such trade, so that the traditional theory, while not necessarily contradicted, fails to offer an explanation.

3. Theoretical discussions of intraindustry trade can be found in Grubel (1970), Gray (1973), Grubel and Lloyd (1975), and Davies (1977).

4. International scale economies actually "bury" these problems rather than eliminate them, as will become clear below.

5. In this respect the present paper complements recent work establishing the general validity of the basic H-O-S propositions. See Kemp (1976); Jones and Scheinkman (1977); Ethier (1974, 1979b); Chang, Ethier, and Kemp (1980).

6. One could instead interpret the intermediate goods as successive stages, Austrian fashion, or alternatively, allow some of the components to be assembly services, so that assembly is not costless. Either interpretation would leave the balance of this paper unscathed.

7. I ignore the difficulty of interpreting noninteger values of n.

8. This assumption was implicit in my earlier paper (Ethier 1979a) and explicit in Dixit and Stiglitz (1977) and in Krugman (1979).

9. The remainder of this section is rather terse as it closely follows Ethier (1979a), to which the reader is referred for more detail.

10. For a discussion of the basic H-O-S propositions see, for example, Caves and Jones (1977).

11. Except, of course, for the borderline case of "incipient diversification" in one country.

12. These conclusions can perhaps be made clearer by rewriting equation (22) as $(\hat{P}_C - \hat{P}_W) = (1 - Z)(\hat{P}_M - \hat{P}_W)$ and noting that Z cannot fall between zero and unity.

13. See Krugman (1981) for an interesting alternative treatment of income distribution in a model featuring relative factor-endowment differences and intraindustry trade in differentiated consumer goods.

14. Alternative measures are discussed in Grubel and Lloyd (1971).

15. If all countries diversify in production, h' equals the world capital-labor ratio.

References

Balassa, Bela. 1961. *The Theory of Economic Integration.* Homewood: Irwin.

Balassa, Bela. 1966. Tariff reduction and trade in manufactures among the industrial countries. *American Economic Review* 56:466–473.

Balassa, Bela. 1967. *Trade Liberalization among Industrial Countries.* New York: McGraw-Hill.

Caves, Richard. 1981. Intra-industry trade and market structure in the industrial countries. *Oxford Economic Papers* 33:203–233.

Caves, Richard, and Ronald W. Jones. 1977. *World Trade and Payments*, 2d ed. Boston: Little, Brown and Co.

Chang, Winston, Wilfred J. Ethier, and Murray C. Kemp. 1980. The theorems of international trade with joint production. *Journal of International Economics* 10:377–394.

Daly, Donald J., B. A. Key, and E. J. Spence. 1968. *Scale and Specialization in Canadian Manufacturing.* Staff study no. 21, Economic Council of Canada.

Davies, Robert. 1977. Two-way international trade: A comment. *Weltwirtschaftliches Archiv* 113:179–181.

Dixit, Avinash K., and Victor Norman. 1980. *Theory of International Trade.* Cambridge: Cambridge University Press.

Dixit, Avinash K., and Joseph Stiglitz. 1977. Monopolistic competition and optimum product diversity. *American Economic Review* 67:297–308.

Ethier, Wilfred J. 1974. Some of the theorems of international trade with many goods and factors. *Journal of International Economics* 4:199–206.

Ethier, Wilfred J. 1979a. Internationally decreasing costs and world trade. *Journal of International Economics* 9:1–24.

Ethier, Wilfred J. 1979b. The theorems of international trade in time-phased economies. *Journal of International Economics* 9:225–238.

Ethier, Wilfred J. 1982. Decreasing costs in international trade and Frank Graham's argument for protection. *Econometrica* 50:1243–1268.

Finger, J. Michael. 1975. Trade overlap and intraindustry trade. *Economic Inquiry* 13:581–589.

Gray, H. Peter. 1973. Two-way international trade in manufactures: A theoretical underpinning. *Weltwirtschaftliches Archiv* 109:19–29.

Grubel, Herbert G. 1970. The theory of intra-industry trade. In I. A. McDougall and R. H. Snape (eds.), *Studies in International Economics*. Amsterdam: North-Holland.

Grubel, Herbert G., and Peter J. Lloyd. 1971. The empirical measurement of intra-industry trade. *Economic Record* 47:494–517.

Grubel, Herbert G., and Peter J. Lloyd. 1975. *Intra-Industry Trade: The Theory and Measurement of International Trade in Differentiated Products*. London: Macmillan.

Haberler, Gottfried. 1936. *The Theory of International Trade, with its Applications to Commerical Policy*. London: W. Hodge.

Helpman, Elhanan. 1981. International trade in the presence of product differentiation, economies of scale and monopolistic competition. *Journal of International Economics* 11:305–340.

Hesse, Helmut. 1974. Hypotheses for the explanation of trade between industrial countries, 1953–1970. In H. Giersch (ed.), *The International Division of Labour: Problems and Perspectives*. Tübingen: J. C. B. Mohr.

Hufbauer, Gary C., and John C. Chilas. Specialization by industrial countries: Extent and consequences. In H. Giersch (ed.), *The International Division of Labour: Problems and Perspectives*. Tübingen: J. C. B. Mohr.

Jones, Ronald, and José A. Scheinkman. 1987. The relevance of the two-sector production model in trade theory. *Journal of Political Economy* 85:909–936.

Kemp, Murray C. 1969. *The Pure Theory of International Trade and Investment*. Englewood Cliffs: Prentice-Hall.

Kemp, Murray C. 1976. *Three Topics in the Theory of International Trade*. Amsterdam: North-Holland.

Kravis, Irving B., and Richard E. Lipsey. 1978. Price behavior in the light of balance of payments theories. *Journal of International Economics* 8:193–246.

Krugman, Paul. 1979. Increasing returns, monopolistic competition, and international trade. *Journal of International Economics* 9:469–480.

Krugman, Paul. 1981. Intraindustry specialization and the gains from trade. *Journal of Political Economy* 89:959–973.

Lancaster, Kelvin. 1980. Intraindustry trade under perfect monopolistic competition. *Journal of International Economics* 10:151–176.

Lawrence, Colin, and Pablo Spiller. 1980. Product diversity, economies of scale and international trade. Mimeo.

Loertscher, Rudolf, and Frank Wolter. 1980. Determinants of intra-industry trade. *Weltwirtschaftliches Archiv* 116:280–293.

Matthews, R. C. O. 1950. Reciprocal demand and increasing returns. *Review of Economic Studies* 17:149–158.

Meade, James E. 1952. *A Geometry of International Trade*. London: Allen and Unwin.

Owen, Nicholas. 1976. Scale economics in the EEC. *European Economic Review* 7:143–163.

Pagoulatos, Emilio, and Robert Sorenson. 1975. Two-way international trade: An econometric analysis. *Weltwirtschaftliches Archiv* 111:454–465.

Verdoorn, P. J. 1960. The intra-block trade of Benelux. In E. A. G. Robinson (ed.), *Economic Consequences of the Size of Nations*. London: Macmillan.

IV MULTINATIONAL CORPORATIONS

15 Multinational Corporations and Trade Structure

Elhanan Helpman

1 Introduction

The importance of multinational corporations in the conduct of foreign trade has been recognized for many years. Nevertheless, there exists no well-articulated theory that explains the conditions for their emergence and predicts under these conditions a structure of trade that comes close to observed trade patterns. I have developed in Helpman (1984) a theory that is designed to fill in this gap, and it is the purpose of this paper to extend it in order to make it better fit reality.

My earlier work builds on the standard theory of monopolistic competition in differentiated products in which every firm produces a single variety. The distinguishing feature of that study is the interpretation of the technology so as to allow for specialized inputs which service plants that are geographically separated from the location of the inputs' employment. In particular, those inputs can be located in one country and service plants located in other countries. Management and product-specific R&D are two examples of such inputs. Multinational corporations emerge in order to exploit cross-country differences in factor rewards. The result is a theory that describes conditions under which multinationals form and explains the structure of trade under these conditions. In particular, it shows how intersectoral, intraindustry, and intrafirm trade can coexist and how these trade components are related to differences in relative factor endowments.

However, due to the fact that all firms are single-product firms, a firm locates its manufacturing facility in the low-cost country, and in the absence of impediments to trade no firm has more than a single manufacturing facility. This is inconsistent with observed patterns of direct foreign investment; multinational corporations often have production facilities in several countries (see, e.g., U.S. Tariff Commission 1973, ch. 3). Moreover, in my earlier work all intrafirm trade consisted of trade in the services of the specialized inputs; namely, in headquarter services, while empirically a large part of intrafirm trade takes place in intermediate inputs (see Buckley and Pearce 1979). Hence, there is a need to extend the theory in order to take account of these missing features and in order to evaluate their contribution to the explanation of trade patterns. This task is undertaken in the following sections by incorporating the model of the horizontally and vertically integrated firm from Helpman (1983) into the theory of international trade and direct foreign investment in Helpman (1984). This combination leads to a theory of international trade in which horizontally and vertically integrated firms that have production facilities in more than one country trade in finished goods, intermediate inputs, and invisibles. The theory provides a prediction of trade patterns that seems to approximate reality reasonably well. The existence of integrated firms has a significant effect on the behavior of the volume of trade and the

Originally published in the *Review of Economic Studies* 52 (July 1985): 443–458.

share of intrafirm trade when compared with the results obtained for the single-product firm.

A brief presentation of the structure of production and the theory of the firm is given in section 2. Section 3 provides a description of equilibrium conditions in an integrated world economy. These conditions are then used in section 4 in order to derive trade patterns and in section 5 in order to analyze trade volumes and shares of intrafirm trade. A brief concluding section closes the paper.

2 The Structure of Production

Following a simplifying modeling strategy, it is assumed that there are two factors of production; input H, which can serve as a shared input, and homogeneous labor L. There exist also two final products; a homogeneous product Y, which is produced with H and L under constant returns to scale, and a differentiated manufactured product X, which is produced with H, L, and a middle product Z. All available technologies of production are common knowledge in the world economy.

The production function of the homogeneous product requires all inputs to be employed in the same location. Its unit cost function is $c_Y(w_L, w_H)$, where w_i is the reward to factor i. In a competitive equilibrium the homogeneous product is priced according to marginal (equals average) cost. Namely, taking Y to be the numeraire,

$$1 = c_Y(w_L, w_H). \tag{1}$$

Assume that there exists a continuum of varieties of the differentiated product X, which can be represented by points on the real line; every point represents a different variety of the product. Moreover, the closer two varieties are to each other on the line the better substitutes they are for each other in production in a sense to be described below. All consumers have the same preferences and all varieties are equally well substitutable for each other in consumption, with the elasticity of substitution $\sigma > 1$ being constant. This results in demand functions with a constant elasticity of demand σ that are the same for all varieties of the finished good (see Helpman 1983, sec. 2).[1]

The production of varieties of the differentiated product requires three components: (a) headquarter services, (b) labor, and (c) an intermediate input that is also a differentiated product. Headquarter services are proportional to the shared input employed for this purpose. A firm that hires the shared input has to adapt it at a cost to a certain variety, which will be referred to as the firm's *central* variety. Once adapted, the shared input can also serve the production of other varieties, but its efficiency declines the further away a variety is from the central variety and the more product lines it has to serve. This loss of efficiency is reflected in the need to employ more labor per unit output. In addition, the shared input can serve the production of intermediate inputs. I have explained in Helpman (1983) how the existence of the shared input generates economies of scope in the production of final goods, resulting in horizontally integrated firms in the sense that every firm in this industry finds it profitable to produce a spectrum of varieties of the finished product. The horizontal span of these firms is determined by profitability consideration.

It is assumed for simplicity that the production of every unit of the final differentiated product requires one unit of the middle product (intermediate input). The middle product is also differentiated and it can be represented by points on the real line. Choose a representation of the middle product that coincides with the representation of the finished good such that a point on the line represents a variety of the finished good and also the variety of the middle product that is best suited for its production. The meaning of a best-suited variety of the middle product is similar to the one described for the shared input; the further away the employed variety of the middle product is from the best-suited variety, the more labor per unit output has to be employed in the production of the finished good.

Intermediate inputs are produced by means of services of the shared input and labor. A firm that produces finished products can use its shared input to service the production of middle products. This is a reasonable assumption for manufactured goods that require similar technologies in the production of components and finally assembled products. This feature of production generates an incentive for vertical integration; an incentive that is strengthened when intermediate inputs are produced under increasing returns to scale that are not too strong, as is assumed in what follows. For with increasing returns to scale in the production of middle products, it is not profitable to provide best varieties of the middle product for all the varieties of the finished good that are produced. A firm that produces a spectrum of varieties of the finished good will use only a small number of varieties of the middle product (here the qualification that the returns to scale are not too strong is important). And if the horizontal span of firms is such that they do not overlap in product space in the sense that no variety is produced by more than one firm (which is the case in the equilibrium described below), then a bilateral monopoly situation would arise between an independent supplier and the user of the middle product if the latter chooses not to produce intermediate inputs for its own use. This market structure reinforces the rationale for vertical integration that was described above (see Williamson 1971; Porter and Spence 1977; Klein, Crawford, and Alchain 1978).

The above described reasoning provides the basis for the formal model of the firm, which will also be referred to as a corporation. The important point to notice is that this particular structure of the corporation stems from an endogenous decision of profit maximizers based on technology and market conditions. For simplicity it is assumed that the structure of returns to scale is such that every corporation finds it profitable to produce exactly *one* variety of the middle product (see Helpman 1983 for a discussion of considerations that are relevant for the profit-maximizing choice of the number of middle products).

It is clear that under the above described conditions a corporation in the differentiated product industry can be identified by its central variety, by its horizontal span, and by its middle products. In order to deal with multinational corporations it is assumed that the the shared input does not depend on the location of the product line.

I will consider the case in which entire product lines can be shifted to any desirable geographical location. It is also assumed for simplicity that the efficiency of headquarter services obtained from the shared input does not depend on the location of the product line. I will consider the possibility of geographical reallocation of lines that produce varieties of the finished good as well as middle products, although due to the fact that production of middle products that are used in many product lines requires general know-how that is available in the center, there seem to exist reasons to believe that it is less efficient to separate the production of middle products from the base than to do so with regard to finished goods.

Consider a firm that hires a quantity h of the shared input and adapts it to its central variety. The costs of hiring the shared input and the adaptation costs are fixed costs at the level of the firm. Apart from these there exist fixed costs that are specific to every product line including the intermediate input. Given h it is assumed that in order to produce in the range $(\delta, \delta + d\delta)$ the quantity $x(\omega)$ of varieties that are located at distance δ (on the real line) from the central variety the required quantity of direct labor use is represented by $l[x(\omega), h, \delta(\omega), m]\, d\delta$, where $\delta(\omega)$ is the distance of variety ω from the central variety, m is the measure of the set of varieties produced by the firm and $l(\cdot)$ is the inverse of a quasi-concave increasing returns-to-scale production function (i.e., increasing returns to scale in (l, h) holding (δ, m) constant). I will refer to m as the *number* of varieties produced by the firm. The labor requirement function $l(\cdot)$ is assumed to be increasing in output, decreasing in h, convex in (x, h), increasing in δ and nondecreasing in m. The last element describes possible congestability of the shared input. Labor requirement rises with the distance from the central variety. This represents the compensation needed for the loss of efficiency of the services of the shared input and in the current specification also the required compensation for the inappropriateness of the middle product, since both are most suitable for the production of the central variety. I also assume for simplicity that the labor requirement function has the following additively separable form:

$$l(x, h, \delta, m) \equiv g(x, h, m) + f(h, \delta, m). \tag{2}$$

Total costs of the firm consist of the fixed costs involved in hiring and adapting the shared input plus production costs of the intermediate input and of the finished good. Let $C^a(w_L, w_H, h)$ be a cost function, derived from a quasi-concave and increasing returns-to-scale production function that describes adaptation costs, where w_L is the wage rate and w_H is the reward to a raw unit of the shared input. Let Δ be the set of varieties produced by the firm with x_Δ standing for the description of the quantities of all varieties in Δ that are being produced, and let $m(\Delta)$ be the measure of Δ. Now assume that every variety of the middle product is produced under increasing returns to scale with the associated cost function $C^z(w_L, w_H, h, Z)$, where Z is the output level and $C^z(\cdot)$ is declining and convex in h. It is assumed that this cost function contains a fixed cost component that is an "atom." Since every unit of the finished good requires a unit of the intermediate input, we require

$$Z = \int_{\omega \in \Delta} x(\omega)\, d\delta(\omega).$$

Hence, the firm's cost function is

$$C[w_L, w_H, x_\Delta, m(\Delta)] \equiv \min_{h \geqq 0} \left\{ w_H h + C^a(w_L, w_H, h) + C^z \left[w_L, w_H, h, \int_{\omega \in \Delta} x(\omega)\, d\delta(\omega) \right] + w_L \int_{\omega \in \Delta} l[x(\omega), h, \delta(\omega), m(\Delta)]\, d\delta(\omega) \right\}. \tag{3}$$

This cost function contains all the above discussed components.

Given the assumption that $l(\cdot)$ is increasing in δ and the fact that the demand function for every variety is the same by assumption, it is clear that a firm that chooses to produce a subset of varieties in a range in which no other firm produces (as is the case in the equilibrium discussed below) finds it most profitable to produce a connected set Δ that is located symmetrically around the central variety. The reason is that for every set of output levels revenue is independent of the varieties that are being produced while costs are lowest when the set of varieties is chosen to be connected (except for a subset of measure zero) and symmetric around the central variety. For this reason we restrict the discussion to sets Δ that are connected and symmetric around the central variety. In this case it is appropriate to also call m the *horizontal span* of the firm, and the cost function for this type of Δ choice can be represented by

$$C(w_L, w_H, x_\Delta, m) \equiv \min_{h \geqq 0} \left\{ w_H h + C^a(w_L, w_H, h) + 2w_L \int_0^{m/2} l[x(\delta), h, \delta, m]\, d\delta + C^z[w_L, w_H, h, 2 \int_0^{m/2} x(\delta)\, d\delta] \right\}, \tag{4}$$

where $x(\delta)$ stands now for the output level of a variety located at distance δ from the central variety. This cost function exhibits ray economies of scale, and for sufficiently small m also economies of scope. The ray economies of scale mean that for a given horizontal span a proportional increase in the output level of all varieties within this span increases costs less than proportionately. The economies of scope mean that given m it is cheaper to produce the output levels x_Δ with a single firm (h adapted to a single variety) than with two or more firms (h adapted to two or more varieties). For details see Helpman (1983). This cost function is concave in factor rewards and its partial derivative with respect to a factor reward equals *total* employment of the factor of production. Thus, the partial derivative of costs with respect to the shared input equals h plus the quantity of H used in the adaptation process $(= \partial C^a(w_L, w_H, h)/\partial w_H)$, plus the quantity of H used in the production of the intermediate input $(= \partial C^z(w_L, w_H, Z)/\partial w_H)$.

It is assumed that firms engage in Chamberlinian monopolistic competition. Every firm chooses (Δ, p_Δ), where p_Δ is a description of the prices of all varieties in Δ, so as to maximize profits, taking as given the product mix and strategies of its competitors.[2] For every variety ω they believe to be facing the demand function (see Helpman 1983):

$$X(\omega) = k[p(\omega)]^{-\sigma}, \qquad \sigma > 1, \tag{5}$$

where $k \equiv E_X \int_{\omega' \in \Omega} [p(\omega')]^{-\sigma} d\omega'$, Ω is the set of varieties available, and E_X is total spending on X. The firm takes k to be independent of its actions. It is clear that under these circumstances a firm that seeks to maximize profits chooses a product mix that contains no varieties that are supplied by its rivals, unless it cannot choose a connected set Δ of the desired horizontal span that has this property due to the product space being "crowded" by other producers. However, since the set of potential varieties is the real line, then as long as there exists a finite number of firms, each one producing a finite number of varieties in a connected set, our firm can always find a desired finite size product set that does not overlap with the varieties produced by its rivals. This is the type of equilibria considered below.

Based on the above described assumptions a typical producer's problem can be described as the choice of m and $p(\delta)$ for $\delta \in [0, m/2)$ so as to maximize profits:

$$\pi = 2 \int_0^{m/2} p(\delta) x(\delta) \, d\delta - C(w_L, w_H, x_\Delta, m),$$

where the cost function is taken from (4) and the right-hand side of (5) is substituted for $x(\delta)$. This is a degenerate problem in the calculus of variations that can be solved by means of pointwise maximization. Now, using (2), and assuming an interior solution, one obtains the following first-order conditions:[3]

$$p(\delta)\left(1 - \frac{1}{\sigma}\right) = w_L g_x[x(\delta), h, m] + C_Z^z\left[w_L, w_H, h, 2 \int_0^{m/2} x(\delta') \, d\delta'\right] \quad \text{for } \delta \in \left[0, \frac{m}{2}\right) \tag{6}$$

$$p\left(\frac{m}{2}\right) x\left(\frac{m}{2}\right) \equiv w_L l\left[x\left(\frac{m}{2}\right), h, \frac{m}{2}, m\right] + w_L \int_0^{m/2} l_m[x(\delta), h, \delta, m] \, d\delta$$
$$+ C_Z^z\left[w_L, w_H, h, 2 \int_0^{m/2} x(\delta) \, d\delta\right] x\left(\frac{m}{2}\right), \tag{7}$$

where $g_x(\cdot) \equiv l_x(\cdot)$ is the partial derivative of $l(\cdot)$ with respect to output and $l_m(\cdot)$ is the partial derivative of $l(\cdot)$ with respect to the size of the horizontal span. The former represents marginal labor costs of an output expansion while the latter represents marginal costs associated with the loss of efficiency of the shared input that results from an expansion of the product range. The partial derivative of $C^z(\cdot)$ with respect to output is $C_Z^z(\cdot)$, and it represents marginal costs of the middle product. Condition (6) is the familiar marginal revenue equals marginal cost condition; it has to be satisfied for every product line. Here the marginal cost consists of direct plus indirect marginal costs. Condition (7) is the condition for an optimal horizontal span. The left-hand side represents marginal revenue from the extension of the product range on one side of the central variety. The right-hand side represents the marginal cost of this extension. This marginal cost has three components. The first one represents the direct labor costs involved in producing the marginal variety. The second represents the additional costs that are imposed on all product lines due to the congestability of the shared input. The third component represents the indirect costs that stem from the need to produce more intermediate inputs.

It follows from my assumptions that marginal costs of production on the right-hand side of (7) do not depend directly on δ (but only indirectly through the quantity $x(\delta)$). Therefore, since $x(\delta)$ is a declining function of $p(\delta)$ and $g_x(\cdot)$ is increasing in $x(\delta)$, (6) implies that $p(\delta)$ and $x(\delta)$ are the same for every $\delta \in [0, m/2)$; namely, $p(\delta) = p$ and $x(\delta) = x$ for $\delta \in [0, m/2)$. Since we know from this discussion that given (2) all varieties are equally priced in equilibrium and equal output levels of each one will be produced, it is useful to define a cost function for equal output levels by

$$C(w_L, w_H, x, m) \equiv \min_{h \geq 0} \left[w_H h + C^a(w_L, w_H, h) + C^z(w_L, w_H, h, mx) + w_L m g(x, h, m) + 2w_L \int_0^{m/2} f(h, \delta, m)\, d\delta \right], \tag{8}$$

where $C(\cdot)$ has the usual properties of a cost function with respect to (w_L, w_H, x). Using this cost function conditions (6) and (7) can be written as

$$p\left(1 - \frac{1}{\sigma}\right) = \frac{C_x(w_L, w_H, x, m)}{m}, \tag{6'}$$

$$px = C_m(w_L, w_H, x, m). \tag{7'}$$

This completes the description of a representative corporation in the differentiated product industry.

3 An Integrated World Economy

In order to study the nature of trade in regions of factor endowments in which factor-price equalization obtains it is useful to have as a benchmark the equilibrium of an integrated world economy. By an integrated world economy I mean an environment in which there is free and costless factor mobility across industries and geographical regions. We assume that production technologies are common knowledge and that preferences are homothetic and identical for all inhabitants of the world.

In an integrated economy, factor and commodity prices are the same everywhere. In the Y-sector, which is competitive, producers engage in marginal cost pricing. In the X-sector producers engage in Chamberlinian monopolistic competition, except that firms in this sector are horizontally and vertically integrated for the reasons described in the previous section. By Chamberlinian monopolistic competition I mean that every firm maximizes profits, taking as given prices and variety types that are produced by its competitors. Since our product space is represented by the real line and since it is optimal for a single corporation to produce a finite measure of varieties, every corporation chooses to produce a spectrum of varieties that does not overlap with varieties that are produced by its competitors. It is also assumed that there is free entry into industries and that, as a result, all producers make zero profits. The number of corporations in the differentiated product industry is large and treated as a continuous variable.

Adding to (1) and (6′)–(7′) the zero-profit condition and the factor market clearing conditions, we obtain the following set of conditions (using the cost function defined in [8]):

$$1 = c_Y(w_L, w_H) \tag{9}$$

$$p\left(1 - \frac{1}{\sigma}\right) = \frac{C_x(w_L, w_H, x, m)}{m} \tag{10}$$

$$px = C_m(w_L, w_H, x, m) \tag{11}$$

$$pxm = C(w_L, w_H, x, m) \tag{12}$$

$$a_{LY}(w_L, w_H)y + A_{LX}(w_L, w_H, x, m)n = \bar{L} \tag{13}$$

$$a_{HY}(w_L, w_H)y + A_{HX}(w_L, w_H, x, m)n = \bar{H}, \tag{14}$$

where $a_{iY}(w_L, w_H) \equiv \partial c_Y(w_L, w_H)/\partial w_i$, $i = L, H$; $A_{iX}(w_L, w_H, x, m) \equiv \partial C_X(w_L, w_H, x, m)/\partial w_i$, $i = L, H$; y is the output level of the homogeneous product; n is the number of firms in the differentiated product industry; and $(\bar{L}, \bar{H})$ are the endowments of labor and the shared input. Here condition (9) assures marginal cost pricing of the homogeneous product, (10) assures that for every variety of the differentiated product marginal revenue equals marginal cost, (11) assures that marginal revenue from an expansion of product range equals marginal costs of such an expansion, while (12) assures zero profits for every firm. The left-hand side of (13) represents demand for labor. It consists of labor demanded by the sector producing the homogeneous product, which equals labor demand per unit output $a_{LY}(\cdot)$ times the output level y, plus labor demanded by the differentiated product sector, which consists of labor demanded by a representative firm $A_{LX}(\cdot)$ times the number of firms in the industry. A similar interpretation applies to the shared-input market clearing condition (14). The number of varieties available to consumers equals nm; that is, the number of firms times the number of varieties produced by a representative firm.

In order to close the system we need to add an equilibrium condition in commodity markets. Since the preference ordering between the homogeneous product and the differentiated product is homothetic, it can be shown that the share of income spent on the homogeneous product $s_y(\cdot)$ depends only on relative prices and on the number of varieties available to consumers. Here, the commodity market clearing condition can be written as

$$y = s_Y(p, nm)(w_L\bar{L} + w_H\bar{H}). \tag{15}$$

Equations (9)–(15) represent an equilibrium system for a closed economy. They define implicitly equilibrium values for $(w_L, w_H, p, x, y, n, m)$. I assume for the remaining part of the discussion that in this equilibrium

$$\frac{A_{HX}}{A_{LX}} > \frac{a_{HY}}{a_{LY}},$$

namely that the differentiated product industry uses more H per worker than the homogeneous product industry.

4 Trade Patterns

It is shown in this section how the pattern of trade of a two-country world is related to differences in factor endowments, holding constant the resources of the world economy at the levels postulated in the previous section. This procedure identifies the dependence of trade patterns on two major factors: *relative* country size and differences in *relative* factor endowments. In particular, I am interested in identifying the link between these variables and (a) the economic rationale for the emergence of multinational corporations, (b) the intersectoral pattern of trade, (c) the intraindustry pattern of trade, and (d) the intrafirm pattern of trade.

Consider the box diagram in figure 1, which describes the feasible allocations of factor endowments between country 1 with the origin O_1, and country 2 with the origin O_2. We consider allocations that are above the diagonal O_1O_2 such that country 1 has more H per worker than country 2. In this figure the vectors O_1Q and O_2Q' describe the total (direct plus indirect) employment of resources by the differentiated product industry in the equilibrium of the integrated economy. Similarly, the vectors O_1Q' and O_2Q describe total employment of resources in the homogeneous product industry in this equilibrium. The vector O_1A describes total employment of labor and H by a representative corporation. Hence, the number of corporations is represented by the ratio $\overline{O_1Q}/\overline{O_1A}$. We may also use $\overline{O_1Q}$ to represent the output of X and use $\overline{O_1Q'}$ to represent the output of Y, where the output of X is defined to be mnx.

We begin by considering an allocation of factors of production that can be represented by a point in the set O_1QO_2, say point E. Using the standard parallelogram construction it is clear from figure 1 that in this case there exists an equilibrium with factor-price equalization in which factor prices, commodity prices, output levels, and techniques of production are the same as in the equilibrium of the integrated economy, with every corporation employing its inputs in a single country. Taking $\overline{O_1Q'}$ to represent total output y of the homogeneous good in the world economy, the allocation E implies that at an equilibrium with no multinational firms country 1 produces $\overline{O_1P_Y}$ units of the homogeneous good and its X-industry is occupied by $n_1 = \overline{O_1P_x}/\overline{O_1A}$ corporations, each one producing m varieties of the finished differentiated product and a single variety of the middle product for its own use. The industrial structure in country 2 can be described in a similar way. It is clear that in this case corporations have no incentive to become multinational.

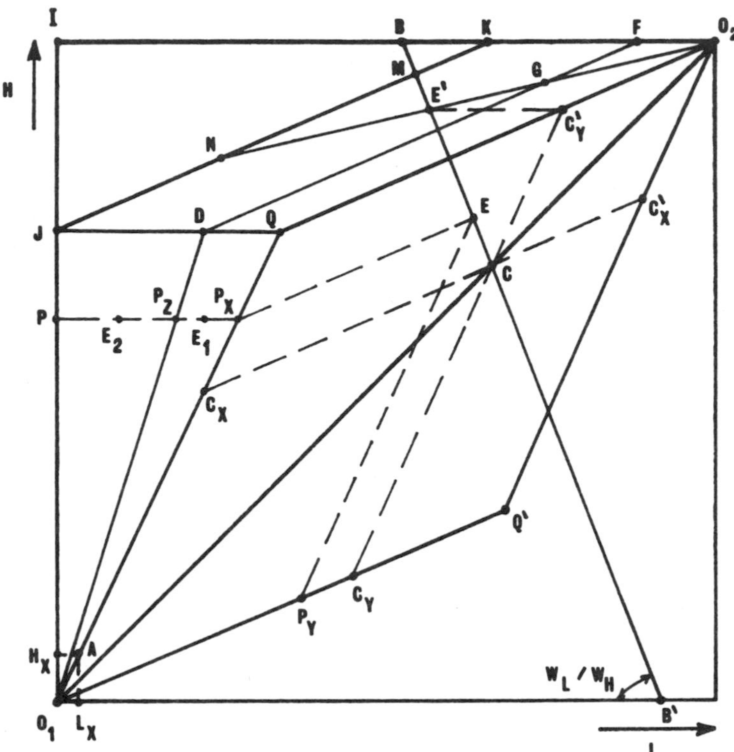

Figure 1

Since there are no pure profits in the system, the line BB' with slope w_L/w_H that is drawn through E describes the cross-country distribution of income that is associated with E. If we take $\overline{O_1 O_2}$ to represent the level of income in the world economy, then $\overline{O_1 C}$ represents the level of income in country 1 and $\overline{O_2 C}$ represents the level of income in country 2, where C is the intersection point of BB' with the diagonal. Since both countries spend the same budget shares on goods, we obtain a geometric representation of consumption levels by constructing a parallelogram between O_1 and C, namely, $O_1 C_X C C_Y$. Hence, $\overline{O_1 C_Y}$ describes consumption of the homogeneous product in country 1 and $\overline{O_1 C_X}$ describes consumption of the differentiated product. It is clear from the figure that country 1 consumes more Y-goods and fewer X-goods than it produces, implying that it imports the homogeneous product and it is a *net* exporter of finished differentiated products. At this equilibrium every country produces varieties of the finished manufactured good (mn_k varieties being produced in country k, where n_k is the equilibrium number of corporations in country k) and exports them to its trading partner. Hence, there is intersectoral trade with the relatively H-rich country importing the homogeneous product, and there is intraindustry trade in varieties of the differentiated product. At endowment points in the set $O_1 Q O_2$ there is no incentive for the formation of multinationals and there is, therefore, no intrafirm trade.

The important feature of the set O_1QO_2 is that at endowment points that belong to it every country can fully employ its resources with the techniques of production that are cost minimizing at the equilibrium factor prices of the integrated economy, with every firm operating in a single country. Clearly, every endowment allocation outside this set implies that factor-price equalization cannot obtain when every firm employs its inputs in a single country. In this case the wage rate is expected to be higher in country 1 and the reward to the common factor is expected to be higher in country 2. This means that at endowment points above O_1QO_2 corporations have an incentive to reallocate activities across national borders in order to exploit differences in factor prices. These reallocations eliminate cross-country differences in factor prices in some cases. Following the procedure used in Helpman (1984) it is assumed that corporations established subsidiaries abroad in a way that minimizes foreign labor employment. Moreover, since in the current model corporations are integrated both horizontally and vertically, it is assumed that the first activities to be shifted to subsidiaries are product lines of finished goods and that product lines of intermediate inputs are the last ones to be separated from the entrepreneurial unit (the corporation's base). The former assumption can be justified on the grounds that costs are increasing with the extent of foreign operation so that the corporation tries to minimize the extent of its foreign involvement. This is proxied by the minimization of foreign labor employment. The latter assumption can be justified by the observation that it is often more costly to separate the production of middle products from the center than finished product lines, because middle products require general know-how that is available in the center, but less so in subsidiaries. Although I do not consider explicitly the additional costs required in foreign operations, it is useful to interpret what follows as a description of the limit of a sequence of economies in which such costs exist and these costs converge to zero. There is conceptually no difficulty in analyzing the consequences of alternative assumptions, although no alternative is explored in this study.

First, identify in figure 1 point D on the horizontal line JQ as the point whose distance from J is equal to total labor employed in the production of middle products in the equilibrium of the integrated economy. Then draw a straight line connecting D with O_1. Assuming for the graphical analysis that no H is used in the adaptation process, for every point on O_1Q the line O_1D helps to identify labor employed in the production of middle products and labor employed in the production of differentiated finished goods. Thus, for example, when the country-1-based differentiated product industry employs resources O_1P_X, the figure indicates that the quantity of labor employed in the production of middle products is $\overline{PP_Z}$ and the quantity of labor employed directly in the production of finished products is $\overline{P_ZP_X}$. Now suppose that the endowment point is in the set O_1DQ, say at E_1. In this case the factor-price equalization equilibrium is sustained, but it requires country-1 firms to go multinational. In this equilibrium country 1 employs all its resources in the differentiated product industry that is occupied by $n_1 = \overline{O_1P_X}/\overline{O_1A}$ corporations. Country-1-based corporations have subsidiaries in country 2 in which they employ $\overline{E_1P_X}$ units of labor. Since

$\overline{E_1 P_X} < \overline{P_Z P_X}$, this means that the country-1-based multinationals can produce in their subsidiaries only finished goods, and given our assumption that product lines of finished goods are the first to be shifted to subsidiaries they indeed do so. The same argument can be made for every endowment allocation in the set $O_1 DQ$, implying the following pattern of trade:

1. The country that is relatively rich in the shared input specializes in the production of finished differentiated products and middle products. It imports the homogeneous good and varieties of the differentiated product. The latter are produced by its foreign subsidiaries and by corporations based in the relatively labor-rich country.
2. The country that is relatively rich in the shared input exports varieties of the differentiated finished product as well as middle products and headquarter services. These headquarter services are required by subsidiaries of its multinational corporations that operate in the relatively labor-rich country.

This is an elaborate pattern of trade that comes close to observed trade patterns. There is intersectoral, intraindustry, and intrafirm trade and the multiproduct firms have production facilities in both countries. Moreover, because every corporation in the X-industry produces m varieties of the finished product, then in a symmetrical equilibrium the multinational corporations produce some of these varieties at home and some of them abroad, while they choose to produce the middle products at home. The intrafirm trade of multinational corporations consists of trade in intermediate inputs and trade in invisibles, namely, headquarter services. The last trade component stems from the sharing of firm-specific assets by the subsidiaries and the center. There might also exist intrafirm trade in finished goods, in particular when marketing activities are tied to subsidiaries or to the center, but I will disregard this component of intrafirm trade in what follows.

At endowment points in the set $O_1 JD$ there is also factor-price equalization that is brought about by the emergence of multinational corporations. However, at these equilibria subsidiaries of country-1-based multinationals produce varieties of the finished good as well as intermediate inputs. Consider, for example, point E_2. Applying the minimum foreign employment rule implies that country-1-based multinationals employ $\overline{E_2 P_X}$ units of labor in foreign subsidiaries. This is more labor than required for direct use in the production of finished goods. Therefore $\overline{E_2 P_Z}$ units of foreign labor is employed by subsidiaries in order to produce middle products. Since the number of country-1-based corporations is $n_1 = \overline{O_1 P_X}/\overline{O_1 A}$ and entire product lines have to be allocated to subsidiaries, the number of varieties of the middle product that are produced by the subsidiaries in country 2 is $n_1 \overline{E_2 P_Z}/\overline{PP_Z}$. No finished X-products and no Y-goods are produced in country 1. Hence, in the set $O_1 JD$ we have the following trade pattern: *The relatively H-rich country imports the homogeneous product as well as all varieties of the finished manufactured good. It exports some varieties of the middle product and headquarter services.* One interesting feature of this trade pattern is that it does not exhibit intraindustry trade for sufficiently narrowly defined industries. By this I mean the following. If in the industrial classification finished differentiated products are classified to differ from the middle products that are used in their production, then under this classification there is no intraindustry trade in O_1JD. However, at existing levels of disaggregation of empirical data finished goods and middle products that are used in their production often appear in the same category, namely, electronics, chemicals, and wood products. Hence, from a practical point of view the above described trade pattern exhibits intraindustry trade. It also exhibits intrafirm trade in middle products as well as in headquarter services.

Factor-price equalization obtains also at endowment points that belong to O_2QJK. This can be seen as follows. Every point in this set has a shortest distance from O_2Q that does not exceed $\overline{JQ}$. Therefore, country-1-based multinationals that minimize subsidiary employment will enable country-2-based firms to employ resources that are proportional to O_2Q. Clearly, in this case country-2-based firms will produce only the homogeneous product while subsidiaries of country-1-based firms produce X-products and middle products.

The set O_2QJK is divided into four subsets by means of the lines DF and O_2N. Line DF is parallel to O_2Q and (similarly to O_1D) it separates endowment points at which subsidiaries of country-1-based multinationals produce only finished differentiated products (subset O_2QDF) from endowment points at which subsidiaries produce also differentiated middle products (subset $JKFD$). Line O_2N is designed to separate endowment points at which country 1 *imports* the homogeneous product (subset O_2QJN) from endowment points at which country 1 *exports* the homogeneous product (subset O_2NK).

The separating line O_2N is constructed as follows. Suppose that BB' describes the distribution of income across countries. This income distribution is achieved with all endowment points on CM and the relative income of country 1 that it represents is $\overline{O_1C}/\overline{O_2C}$. Constructing the parallelogram $O_2C'_XCC'_Y$ we obtain a representation of consumption levels in country 2; $\overline{O_2C'_Y}$ of the homogeneous product and $\overline{O_2C'_X}$ of the differentiated product. Now, draw a horizontal line through C'_Y and denote by E' its intersection point with BB'. Then, if our income distribution results from the endowment point E', the resulting equilibrium will be characterized by country-1-based multinational corporations that employ $\overline{E'C'_Y}$ units of labor in country 2, while country-2-based firms' employment vector is $O_2C'_Y$. Hence, country-2-based firms produce only the homogeneous product, and they produce precisely the quantity that is being consumed in country 2. Therefore in this case there is no trade in the homogeneous product.

Now, if the endowment point E' is moved on BB' towards C consumption levels are not changed while country 2 increases its output of the homogeneous product. On the other hand, if E' is moved towards M consumption does not change while country 2 reduces its output of the homogeneous product. This implies that at endowment points on $E'C$ country 2 exports the homogeneous product while at endowment points on $E'M$ country 2 imports the homogeneous product. Finally, drawing a straight line between O_2 and E' we obtain O_2N below which country 2 exports Y-goods and above which country 2 imports them. The following patterns of trade emerge in the four subsets of O_2QJK:

1. In O_2QDG the H-factor relatively rich country imports homogeneous goods and some varieties of the finished differentiated product, and it exports all varieties of the middle product and headquarter services.
2. In O_2GF the pattern of trade is as described in (1) except that the H-factor relatively rich country exports also the homogeneous good.
3. In $JNGD$ the H-factor relatively rich country imports the homogeneous good and all varieties of the finished differentiated product, and it exports some varieties of the middle product as well as headquarter services.
4. In $NKFG$ the pattern of trade is as described in (3) except that the H-factor relatively rich country exports also the homogeneous good.

5 Trade Volumes and Trade Shares

This section contains an analysis of the total volume of trade, the volume of intrafirm trade and the share of intrafirm trade, with an emphasis on novel features that arise from the existence of intermediate inputs. As far as the behavior of the total volume of trade is concerned, the detailed analysis in Helpman (1984, sec. 6) applies directly to the endowment allocation set in which middle products are produced only in parent firms (i.e., the set O_1DFO_2 in fig. 1). Thus, the main conclusion of that analysis that, controlling for relative country size, the volume of trade is larger the greater the difference in relative factor endowments, applies to the set O_1DFO_2 in figure 1. The interesting possibilities in the current context arise in the set O_1JKFD in which subsidiaries of country-1-based multinationals produce also middle products.

First consider the subset O_1DJ in which the labor relatively rich country exports all varieties of the finished differentiated product as well as the homogeneous product, neither one being produced in country 1. Since the volume of trade is defined as aggregate exports and trade is balanced, the volume of trade equals twice the exports of country 2; namely,

$$V = 2s_1(y + pxM) \qquad \text{for } E \in O_1JD, \tag{16}$$

where s_i is the share of country i in world income, y is world output of the homogeneous product, and $M = nm$ is the number of varieties of the differentiated finished product that are produced in the world economy. It is therefore clear that in this set reallocations of factor endowments that do not change relative country size (as measured by relative GNP) do not change the volume of trade. To be sure, such reallocations change the number of varieties produced in every country, resulting in changes in the volume of trade in middle products. However, changes in this component of the volume of trade are precisely offset by corresponding changes in the volume of invisibles trade. For example, a reallocation that increases the difference in relative factor endowments reduces the volume of trade in middle products and equally increases the volume of trade in headquarter services.

In *JNGD* country 1 imports all the varieties of the finished differentiated product and the homogeneous good, and the volume of trade is

$$V = 2(s_1 y - y_1 + s_1 pxM) \qquad \text{for } E \in JNGD, \tag{17}$$

where y_1 is output of the homogeneous good in country 1. Hence, controlling for relative country size, we see that reallocations that change the cross-country distribution of production of the homogeneous product change the volume of trade. In particular, it is evident from figure 1 that reallocations that widen the difference in relative factor endowments increase y_1 and reduce, therefore, the volume of trade. This results from the fact that such reallocations reduce the volume of trade in middle products while the volume of invisibles trade does not change. Since the volume of trade is constant on the subset *NKFG* (the proof is straightforward), we conclude that as long as the differences in relative factor endowments are not too large, an enlargement of these differences feeds trade (holding relative country size constant), but that for sufficiently large differences their widening depresses trade due to the decline in intrafirm trade.[4]

Now consider the behavior of the share of intrafirm trade. In the current model intrafirm trade consists of trade in headquarter services and middle products. Without dealing explicitly with the problem of transfer pricing, it seems safe—due to the existence of zero profits—to calculate the volume of intrafirm trade as the difference between the subsidiaries' total revenue and their labor costs. This procedure assumes that the difference between revenue and costs reflects payments for intermediate inputs and headquarter services. In the absence of zero profits this procedure is questionable, but it is accurate in the present context.[5] Hence, the volume of intrafirm trade is

$$V_{i-f} = px\mu - w_L L_f,$$

where μ is the number of varieties produced by subsidiaries and L_f is their labor employment (the calculations are restricted to the factor-price-equalization set). The quantity of labor L_f is the sum of two components: labor employed directly in the production of finished goods and labor employed in the production of middle products. Assuming that average direct labor employment per variety of the finished differentiated product is the same in subsidiaries as in the parent firm, we have

$$L_f = \frac{\mu A_{LX}^d}{m} + \eta A_{LZ},$$

where $A_{LX}^d = A_{LX} - A_{LZ}$ is direct labor employment by a representative corporation, $A_{LZ} \equiv \partial C^z(\cdot)/\partial w_L$ is the quantity of labor used in the production of a single variety of the middle product, and η is the number of middle products produced by subsidiaries. Hence,

$$V_{i-f} = \mu w_L m^{-1} A_{LX}^d - w_L L_Z \eta. \tag{18}$$

The analysis of the relationship between the share of intrafirm trade and differences in relative factor endowments that was presented in Helpman (1984) applies also to the current model for endowment allocations in sets in which middle products are produced only in the centers, because in these cases the centers provide the subsidiaries with *all* inputs apart from direct labor use in the production of finished goods. This means that in the set O_1DFO_2Q the share of intrafirm trade is larger the greater the difference in relative factor endowments, provided relative country size does not change. In the set O_1QO_2 there is no intrafirm trade.

In the set O_1JKFD all varieties of the finished differentiated product are produced by subsidiaries of country-1-based multinationals so that $\mu = M$ ($\equiv nm$) and it is constant, implying via (18) that the volume of intrafirm trade is larger the smaller the number of varieties of the middle product that are produced by subsidiaries. Now, given relative country size the total volume of trade is constant on the sets O_1JD and $NKFG$. Therefore, in these sets the share of intrafirm trade declines as the difference in relative factor endowments increases. This negative relationship stems from the fact that larger differences in relative factor endowments lead to a reallocation of activities within multinational corporations in a way that increases the self-sufficiency of subsidiaries, thereby reducing intrafirm trade.

Using (17) and (18) the share of intrafirm trade in the set $JNGD$ is calculated to be

$$S_{i-f} = \frac{w_L m^{-1} A^d_{LX} M - w_L A_{LZ}\eta}{2(s_1 y - y_1 + s_1 pxM)} \qquad \text{for } E \in JNGD. \tag{19}$$

However, $s_1 y - y_1 + s_1 pxM = m^{-1}A^d_{LX}M - w_L A_{LZ}\eta$, so that the share of intra-firm trade in the set $JNGD$ is constant and equal to one half.[6] The reason for this result is that in this set all exports of the country which is relatively rich in the shared input represent intra-firm trade.

We conclude from this section that the existence of horizontally and vertically integrated multinational corporations breaks the monotonic link between differences in relative factor endowments and the volume of trade on one hand, and the share of intrafirm trade on the other. The volume of trade and the share of intrafirm trade increase as the difference in relative factor endowments widens so long as this difference is not too large. But when the difference in relative factor endowments is sufficiently large, the shifting by multinational corporations of intermediate input product lines to subsidiaries can reduce the volume of trade and the share of intrafirm trade.

6 Concluding Comments

By extending the theory of multinational corporations to allow also for horizontal and vertical integration, I have developed in this paper a theory of international trade that predicts elaborate trade patterns whose components include intersectoral, intra-industry and intrafirm trade, with the volume of intrafirm trade consisting of trade in invisibles and intermediate inputs. This theory goes a long way towards explaining observed trade patterns by means of general equilibrium models, and it can shed light on international policy issues such as tariffs and corporate taxation. Further elaboration of the theory is required in order to deal with strategic behavior of small numbers of large corporations, with industrial dynamics, and with cross-country penetration; all real world issues with which the current study has not dealt.

Notes

This is a revised and combined version of HIER working papers number 961 and 969, which were written when I was a Visiting Professor in the Department of Economics at Harvard University. I wish to thank Richard Caves and Lars Svensson for comments on earlier drafts. I have also benefited from seminar discussions at Harvard University, Princeton University, University of Chicago, Tel-Aviv University, University of Rochester, University of Geneva, Stockholm University, Johns Hopkins University, and the University of Pennsylvania, and from comments of two referees.

1. The demand functions are $X(\omega) = k[p(\omega)]^{-\sigma}E_X$ for $\omega \in \Omega$ where $k \equiv \int_{\omega' \in \Omega}[p(\omega')]^{1-\sigma}\,d\omega'$, E_X is total spending on X-products, and Ω is the set of varieties available in the market. The assumption that all varieties are equally well substitutable for each other on the demand side is not essential for the main results of the paper, but it does significantly simplify the exposition. An alternative with which I have experimented is a locational representation of preferences, as, for example, in Lancaster (1979), without arriving at different conclusions.

2. In our case it does not matter whether firms use prices or output quantities as their strategic variables.

3. The profit maximization problem is usually not concave. The nonconcavity results from the choice of the horizontal span. It is, therefore, necessary to make sure in particular applications that there exists an interior solution.

4. This generalization applies only to cases in which the differences in relative country size are not "extreme"; namely, for relative sizes that can be represented by BB' lines that are not above G or below J.

5. The problem of choosing a method for the allocation of shared costs has received some attention in recent years (see, for example, Mirman and Tauman 1982). However, there does not seem to exist a universally applicable rule. See also Helpman (1984) for a discussion of possible confusions between profits and payments for invisible services.

6. The expression $s_1(y + pxM)$—which is GNP of country 1—in this set is equal to $y_1 + w_H n A_{HX} + (n - \eta) w_L A_{LZ}$, which upon rearranging implies

$$(w_H A_{HX} + w_L A_{LZ})n = (pxm - w_L A_{LX})n = w_L m^{-1} A^d_{LX} M$$

and

$$s_1 y - y_1 + s_1 pxM = w_L m^{-1} A^d_{LX} M - w_L A_{LZ}\eta.$$

References

Buckley, P. J., and R. D. Pearce. 1979. Overseas production and exporting by the world's largest enterprises: A study in sourcing policy. *Journal of International Business Studies* 10:9–20.

Helpman, E. 1983. The multiproduct firm: Horizontal and vertical integration. MIT, working paper no. 332.

Helpman, E. 1984. A simple theory of international trade with multinational corporations. *Journal of Political Economy* 92:451–471.

Klein, B., R. Crawford, and A. A. Alchain. 1978. Vertical integration, appropriable rents, and the competitive contracting process. *Journal of Law and Economics* 21:297–326.

Lancaster, K. 1979. *Variety, Equity, and Efficiency*. New York: Columbia University Press.

Mirman, L. J., and Y. Tauman. 1982. Demand compatible equitable cost sharing prices. *Mathematics of Operations Research* 7:40–56.

Porter, M. E., and A. M. Spence. 1977. Vertical integration and differential inputs. HIER, discussion paper no. 576, Harvard University.

Williamson, O. E. 1971. The vertical integration of production: Market failure considerations. *American Economic Review* 61:112–123.

16 The Multinational Firm

Wilfred J. Ethier

A particular framework of thought about foreign direct investment is now dominant. This framework suggests why multinational firms should exist at all in the face of presumed penalties for operating across national and cultural boundaries. It has three constituents. First, the firm should possess some *ownership* advantage, such as a patent or the ability to manage or organize some specific endeavor. Second, *locational* considerations, such as tariffs or comparative advantage, should mandate that the firm not concentrate all operations in one country and export to others. Finally, the *internalization* of international transactions must be preferable to the arm's-length use of markets. The firm, for example, should find it advantageous to conduct foreign manufacturing itself rather than to license a foreign firm to do it.

Internalization appears to be emerging as the Caesar of the OLI triumvirate. See, for example, McCulloch (1984, p. 5), Buckley and Casson (1976), Casson (1979), and Rugman (1980), who has gone so far as to assert (p. 370) that "the existing theories of FDI are really subcases of the theory of internalization."

I claim that, quite independently of how one reacts to all this, internalization should be the focus of theories of direct investment. Internalization is the only one of the three key elements not already incorporated into trade theory. Locational considerations are basic to the pure theory of international trade, and ownership advantages figure prominently in our recent theories of trade and imperfect competition. Internalization, by contrast, is one of our critical 'black boxes," always appealed to but never explained. The central task of any general equilibrium theory of the multinational corporation must be to elucidate the role of the internalization issue.

The OLI framework, or "eclectic theory," as John Dunning has dubbed it, has received an increasingly wide application.[1] Theoretical and empirical investigations of the multinational enterprise are very often conducted with reference to this framework,[2] and it is now standard stuff in undergraduate textbooks.[3] The literature on direct investment is truly gargantuan, and it has a commonly accepted framework for thought. Nevertheless, there has thus far been, with one notable exception, no attempt to supply a general equilibrium theory. The notable exception is the work of James Markusen and Elhanan Helpman on multinational enterprises generated by multi-plant scale economies.[4] These economies (or possession of the factors of production that enable the economies to be generated) are the basis for ownership advantages, and locational considerations are determined by relative factor endowments and technological parameters. That the exploitation of multiplant economies should be internalized is taken as a matter of course. Thus, this work falls squarely within the OLI framework.[5]

A general equilibrium theory is essential if we are to connect systematically direct investment to its fundamental determinants and if we are to understand the relation

Originally published in the *Quarterly Journal of Economics* 101 (November 1986): 805–834.

between standard international trade theory and the multinational firm. Two central outstanding issues well illustrate the need for such an understanding.

The first is the relation of direct investment to the relative factor abundance of countries. Conventional trade theory teaches us that differences in factor endowments induce international factor flows, but the larger part of actual direct investment is between countries with relatively similar factor endowments. Furthermore, two-way direct investment within industries is becoming increasingly prominent. (One cannot help but be reminded of how the uneasy relation between conventional theories and the relatively large volume of intraindustry trade between similar economies stimulated recent developments in trade theory.) The usual response to this puzzle is that direct investment concerns ownership and need not coincide at all with physical capital movements. Indeed the OLI framework does not address real capital flows. But such an answer is no answer at all. My intuition would have been that the considerations emphasized by the OLI framework—like the potential for physical factor movements—become more significant with larger differences in factor endowments. The latter certainly cause locational considerations to become more pronounced, and by making countries less alike can be expected to increase disparities in ownership advantages.[6] This intuition may be incorrect (and I shall in fact argue below that it is), but the OLI framework, when divorced from a general equilibrium theory, can take us no farther.

The second issue is the effect of direct investment on the incomes of the factors—labor in particular—employed at home by the multinational firm. This is in fact the preeminent source-country policy issue. But we completely lack the equipment to approach this question in the same way that international trade theory allows us to analyze the effects of commercial policy issues.

The present paper, like those of Markusen and Helpman, is concerned with general equilibrium theories. But whereas Markusen and Helpman each took internalization for granted, I wish to endogenize it. In the process I hope to shed some light on the two issues alluded to above. My conclusions differ dramatically from the implications of the Markusen-Helpman model. This establishes the potential importance of modeling internalization, regardless of how satisfactory my way of doing so might be.

1 Internalization and Information

Internalization is largely a matter of the international economics of information. That is, the critical consideration determining whether a particular international transaction should be internalized usually reduces to an analysis of the exchange of information between two agents. The argument is probably best advanced by explicit consideration of the more important examples.

Consider first the very large class of cases where the ownership advantage is itself the unique possession of some knowledge. The firm wishes to exploit this knowledge in a second, foreign market, by selling goods embodying the knowledge in that market or by importing from that country goods to be marketed at home. In either case the transaction can be done at arm's length: by selling the knowledge to a foreign collection of factors (or "firm"), or via internalization—by itself employing the foreign factors. The basic consideration working against the arm's-length alternative is the fact that in order to sell its information for its full value, the firm must convincingly indicate what it has to sell, thereby losing, at least in part, its monopoly advantage. Note that the critical feature of this class of examples is not the market imperfection represented by the monopoly position of the firm. Rather it is the problem of transacting in information.

As a second class of examples consider multiplant economies, as in the Markusen-Helpman model. Separate plants in different countries draw upon a "home office" utilizing a particular factor. In principle, the relation between the plants and the home office might be either arm's length or internalized. If the home office input is in effect knowledge (such as a research effort applicable to all the plants), this class of examples is a subset of the preceding one. So suppose that the input is something else, such as a coordinating function of some kind. This coordination could be done either at arm's length or internally: the home office and the plants would "do" the same thing in either case, with this behavior dictated alternatively by a contract or by centralized directives. But a contract that makes arm's-length behavior identical to internalized behavior becomes infeasible when the home office and plants must exchange a large volume of diverse information. This does not mean that internalization dominates; with much information to be processed decentralized decision making is likely to be attractive. The point is rather that the arm's-length and internalized industrial structures will no longer be identical but will confront the various agents with different sets of incentives.[7] Which structure is better will depend upon circumstances.

I do not claim that problems of information exchange are invariably central to direct investment, but only that this is sufficiently often the case to render it compelling that they occupy a central position in any general equilibrium theory. Further examples could be given, but those already cited include as special cases a good proportion of multinational activity and so suffice to make my point. What are the strategic implications for the construction of a general equilibrium theory of the multinational enterprise? The details of such a model must be colored, I should think, by the two aspects of information exchange that emerged in the above examples. That is, the public good nature of information, discussed with respect to the first class of examples,[8] and the size and diversity of information flows, central to the second.

The rest of this paper is devoted to a rudimentary model of international trade motivated by the discussion thus far. The purpose is to illustrate how the above issues should be reflected in the crude details of simple model construction. In particular, I wish the model to have a pair of parameters that I can associate with the two critical aspects of information exchange I have just identified. This will enable me to isolate the role played by these basic considerations.

2 The Rudimentary Model

The model contains two countries, two factors, and two goods. Both factors are nontraded. One of the goods, called wheat (W), is produced by the two factors, land (T) and labor (L). Land is specific to wheat production, so the second good, manufactures (M), uses only labor. Wheat production in the home country can be represented by $W = F(L_W, T)$, where F is a neoclassical production function and L_w denotes the amount of labor employed in the wheat sector. Foreign country variables will be distinguished by asterisks.

Manufactures are a collection of n differentiated goods, with n determined endogenously. Manufacturing involves three stages: research, upstream production, and downstream production. Upstream, each variant can be produced at a choice of quality levels, indexed by Q, $0 \leq Q \leq Q_1$. Labor is the only input into upstream production; the variable cost of production of one unit of a manufacture (of any variety) of quality Q is aQw, where a is a technological parameter and w denotes the wage rate in terms of wheat (so that $w = F_L(L_W, T)$). Q is the variable that will be used below to discuss the role of the size and diversity of information flows.[9]

The research activity helps determine the value of the parameter a. This latter can assume either of two values, $a_H > a_L$. The greater the volume R of resources devoted to research, the greater the probability $p(R)$ that $a = a_L$. I assume that $p' > 0$ and $p'' < 0$. Labor is the only input into research, so R is assumed measured in units of labor. The public good aspect of information will be associated with the variable R. Research furnishes the proprietary information that makes the firm's product unique (thereby providing the ownership advantage) and that helps to determine a (thereby linking this proprietary information to the uncertainty facing the firm).

The final stage is a downstream activity that is nontraded—the easiest way to model locational advantages. This also uses only labor as an input, with q units of labor required, in each country, for the downstream activity associated with one unit of a manufacture (of any variety or quality).

I assume that labor must be committed to research and to downstream production before the resolution of uncertainty about the value of a (that is, about the success of the research effort). Afterwards the quality of each variety can be chosen. Ex ante, all varieties are symmetric, although ex post they differ in the realized value of a and the chosen value of Q. In equilibrium the chosen research effort R will accordingly be the same for each chosen variety. If the number n of varieties is sufficiently large, the economywide average of a will be known ex ante to (approximately) equal $p(R)a_L + [1 - p(R)]a_H$, even if the value of a pertaining to any particular variety is not yet known. Thus, the equilibrium amount of labor devoted to research, manufacturing, and downstream production will be determined ex ante, for any value of n. This value must then be such as to clear factor markets.

Consumers in the two countries possess identical tastes. Furthermore, if a certain variety of manufactures is consumed at all, it is consumed in a fixed amount, independently of quality. Define units of measurement so that exactly one unit is consumed, worldwide, of each variety that is produced in equilibrium. Let μ denote the fraction of this unit consumed at home and $1 - \mu$ the fraction consumed abroad. Assume that μ is the same for each variety. Finally, I suppose that consumers regard a unit of any variety of manufactures of quality Q to be a perfect substitute for Q units of wheat. Thus, domestic consumers will consume μ units of a variety of quality Q if its price, in terms of wheat, is no greater than Q, and they will consume none otherwise. I make this assumption simply to divorce the present paper from issues involving the division of labor or the benefits of increased product differentiation. These issues have been treated in depth in the recent literature.[10]

Let me briefly summarize the rationale of my model. I have identified two key aspects of information exchange—its public good nature and the size and diversity of information flows—and have accordingly provided the model with two variables, R and Q, to serve as "pegs" on which, respectively, to hang these issues. In order for informational problems to be present at all, the model must have some intrinsic source of uncertainty (at least from the viewpoints of individual agents). This is provided here by what I call the "dispersion": $a_H - a_L$. In order to relate direct investment to standard trade theory, fundamental parameters of the latter must be included as well. This is represented here by relative factor endowments: $(L/T) - (L^*/T^*)$. The basic idea of the model, then, is that the fundamental determinants (the dispersion and relative factor endowments) should interact in the background while alternatives about industrial structure are related to the way the informational variables (R and Q) are treated.

I submit that this general structure is pretty much inevitable, given the goals of this paper, once my earlier arguments are accepted. In this sense my model is quite general. In two other ways it is not. The dimensionality is low, with each of the four basic elements represented by a single variable. But all our simple trade models have low dimensionality: this is what makes them simple. Less common is the linearity I have imposed on some basic functional forms, relating both to technology and to tastes.[11]

3 The Integrated Equilibrium

It will prove convenient to establish a point of reference by analyzing the model's solution when all stages for each variety are integrated within a single international firm. A single manufacturing firm, identified with a particular variety,[12] thus conducts research, upstream production, and downstream activity in both countries.

The Behavior of the Individual Firm

In order to allow the role of factor endowments to stand out in clear relief, I assume that the efficiency of labor in research relative to upstream production and to downstream production is the same at home as abroad. But the absolute productivities of the two nations' workers need not be the same, so let w^* denote the wage of an efficiency unit of foreign labor, that is, of that quantity of foreign labor that can do the same research (or other activity) that one unit of domestic labor can. It follows that, if $w \neq w^*$, all production and research will be conducted in the country with the lower wage, with such activities taking place in both countries only in the boundary case of international wage equalization. Consider first the case $w < w^*$.

Suppose for now that all firms are risk neutral. Let Q_L and Q_H denote the quality of goods delivered to home and foreign markets when $a = a_L$ and when $a = a_H$, respectively. The firm cannot influence the wage w, which will turn out to be state independent. Thus, the optimization problem confronted by the domestic manufacturer is to choose a combination (R, Q_L, Q_H) that maximizes expected profit:

$$p(R)Q_L(1 - a_L w) + [1 - p(R)]Q_H(1 - a_H w) - (wR + qw^0), \tag{1}$$

where $w^0 = \mu w + (1 - \mu)w^*$ and w^* denotes the foreign wage. The firm is here cognizant of the fact that Q is the highest price it will be able to charge for a unit of final output of quality Q.

The optimal strategy obviously depends upon the wages w and w^* faced by the firm. There are three distinct possibilities.

(*i*) $w > (1/a_L) > (1/a_H)$. In this case the firm must lose money if it operates, regardless of which state emerges. Consequently, it will not enter the market at all, that is, the solution to its problem is $R = Q_L = Q_H = 0$.

(*ii*) $(1/a_L) > (1/a_H) > w$. In this case the firm may or may not choose to enter, depending upon whether expected profit is nonnegative. If it does enter, it knows ex ante that it will pay to provide the highest feasible quality level, Q_1, regardless of which state is realized. The research effort R will be carried to the point where its marginal cost just equals the marginal expected cost reduction: $w = Q_1 p'(R)[(1 - a_L w) - (1 - a_H w)]$. Thus, if it enters, the solution to the firm's problem is $Q_L = Q_H = Q_1$ and $R = R_1$, where R_1 is the solution to

$$p'(R_1) = \frac{1}{Q_1(a_H - a_L)}. \tag{2}$$

Note that the wage rate has no influence on R_1. Since goods of the highest quality will be produced in both states, research affects only the chance of producing in the low-cost state rather than the high-cost one, and the difference in costs is strictly proportional to the wage, as is the cost of research.

(*iii*) $(1/a_L) > w > (1/a_H)$. Again, the firm may or may not enter. If it does, it knows that, should $a = a_H$, it will not in fact produce anything (or, rather, that it will produce goods of lowest quality 0 at variable cost 0), so that resources devoted to research and downstream production will be lost. If $a = a_L$, the firm will wish to provide the highest feasible quality Q_1. The research effort will be optimized when $w = Q_1 p'(R)(1 - a_L w)$. Thus, the optimal operation strategy is $Q_H = 0$, $Q_L = Q_1$, and $R = R_2(w)$, where $R_2(w)$ is the solution to

$$p'(R_2) = \frac{w}{Q_1(1 - a_L w)}. \tag{3}$$

(Note that $R_2(1/a_L) = 0$, $R_2(1/a_H) = R_1$, and $R_2' < 0$ when $w < 1/a_L$.) This strategy will be the chosen one if it yields nonnegative expected profit:

$$p(R_2)Q_1(1 - a_L w) - (wR_2 + w^0 q) \geq 0. \tag{4}$$

Otherwise the firm will not enter: $Q_L = Q_H = R = 0$. The reason that R_2 depends upon w, while R_1 does not, is that in this case the research effort determines the chance that the firm will choose to produce at all and thus increase its earnings by $1 - a_L w$, which is not proportional to the wage. This difference between cases (*ii*) and (*iii*) will turn out to be at the very center of the role of multinationals in this model.

In addition to the above three possibilities, there are two boundary cases. If $w = 1/a_L$, the firm has no chance to offset its fixed costs and so will not enter at all, just as in (*i*). If $w = 1/a_H$, the firm will be indifferent about what level of quality to provide whenever $a = a_H$. This is the only circumstance under which the firm could choose to do something other than provide the highest possible quality Q_1 or not produce at all.

Equilibrium in the Manufacturing Sector

There is free entry into manufacturing, and expected profits are driven to zero, or below if only wheat is produced in equilibrium. This means that, if $(1/a_L) > w > (1/a_H)$, expression (4) must hold with equality. When $w < (1/a_H)$, the zero-profit condition is

$$Q_1\{1 - w[p(R_1)a_L + (1 - p(R_1))a_H]\} - [wR_1 + w^0 q] = 0. \tag{5}$$

Thus, (4) and (5) determine the w and w^* consistent with manufacturing equilibrium [recall that $w^0 = \mu w + (1 - \mu)w^*$]. In figure 1 the Manufacturing Equilibrium schedule, labeled ME, shows for each value of w^* the corresponding equilibrium home wage w. The ME schedule is a straight line when $w < (1/a_H)$—reflecting the fact that (5) is a linear relation between w and w^*—but becomes steeper[13] as w exceeds $1/a_H$, since R_2 is a decreasing function of w in (4). Note that the nonlinear part of ME disappears if $p(R)$ is so responsive to increases in the research effort that $(p(R_1)/p'(R_1)) < R_1 + \mu q$.

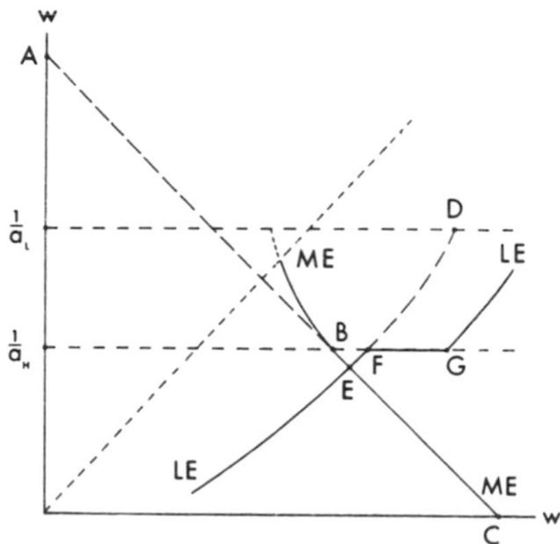

Figure 1

All this supposes that $w < w^*$, and so applies only to the part of figure 1 below the 45° line. But the opposite case of $w > w^*$ is easy to handle; simply reverse the roles of the two countries. Figure 2 shows both the home and foreign curves, labeled ME and ME^*, respectively, in representative cases, where (*a*) the dispersion $a_H - a_L$ is small, and where (*b*) the dispersion is large. It is easily shown, from (4), (5), and their foreign analogs, that ME must intersect ME^* from below, so that multiple intersections are not possible. As figure 2 makes clear, the single intersection will occur on the 45° line ($w = w^*$); this will be on the linear portions of ME and ME^* (that is, $w = w^* < 1/a_H$) if the dispersion is small and on the nonlinear portions ($w = w^* > 1/a_H$) if the dispersion is large.

Along a country's ME curve, profits in the manufacturing sector are zero; above, profits are negative, so research and production are not sustainable; below the curve, profits are positive and so not compatible with equilibrium. Thus, in figure 2 international equilibrium must take place on the outer envelope of the ME and ME^* curves, that is, along ACE in panel (a) and along $ABCDE$ in panel (b). Below point C all research and production takes place in the home country; above C it all takes place abroad.

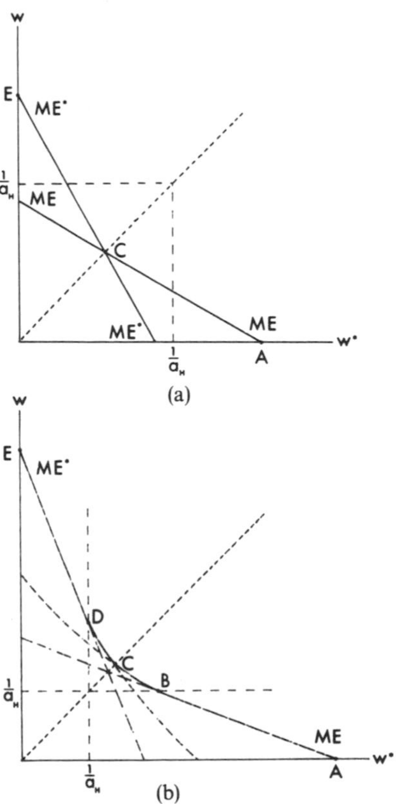

Figure 2

General Equilibrium

In full equilibrium[14] labor in each country must be paid the value of its marginal product in wheat, a traded good. This establishes a second relation between w and w^* and so closes the system. Labor-market equilibrium in the two countries is given, respectively, by

$$w = F_L(L_W, T)$$
$$= F_L(L - n[a(w)Q_1 + R(w) + \mu q] - n^*\mu q, T) \quad (6)$$

and

$$w^* = F_L^*(L_W^*, T^*)$$
$$= F_L^*(L^* - n(1-\mu)q - n^*[a(w^*)Q_1 + R(w^*) + (1-\mu)q], T^*), \quad (7)$$

where n denotes the number of firms with research and upstream production at home and n^* the number with such activities abroad. Here $a(w) = p(R_1)a_L + [1 - p(R_1)]a_H$ if $w < 1/a_H$, and $a(w) = p(R_2(w))a_L$ if $w > 1/a_H$. Also $R(w) = R_1$ if $w < 1/a_H$, and $R(w) = R_2(w)$ otherwise. Thus, $a(w)Q_1 n$ denotes the total employment of labor in manufacturing production and is known ex ante, even though the employment of labor in the production of each variety is not known. In addition, $n = 0$ whenever $w > w^*$, and $n^* = 0$ whenever $w < w^*$.

Thus, when $w < w^*$, equations (6) and (7) give two relations in the three variables w, w^*, and n; when $w > w^*$, the variables are w, w^*, and n^*; and when $w = w^*$, they are n, n^*, and w. Eliminating n gives the Labor Equilibrium schedule relating w and w^*.

This schedule is depicted as the *LE* line in figure 1, which, you will recall, depicts only cases where $w < w^*$. (To limit clutter, figure 2 does not also show the *LE* schedule.) This curve necessarily has a positive slope: a higher value of w^* requires a higher marginal product of labor in foreign wheat production and therefore less labor in that sector. This means that more labor is devoted to downstream production, which in turn means more manufactured goods, more domestic labor in the manufacturing sector, less labor in the wheat sector, and so a larger value of w. Note that the *LE* schedule is a step function, with a horizontal portion (depicted as *FG* in figure 1) when $w = 1/a_H$. This is because when $w = 1/a_H$, producers of manufactured goods for which $a = a_H$ are indifferent about which quality level to supply. Thus, a given manufacturing labor force can alternatively provide a larger number n of goods with less quality for those goods with $a = a_H$, or a smaller number of goods of greater quality. As we move from *F* to *G* in the figure, the quality level of those goods for which $a = a_H$ falls with n rising just enough so that L_W remains constant. But with downstream production costs independent of quality, the rise in n increases the size of the foreign downstream sector, thereby lowering L_W^* and so raising w^*.

Relations (6) and (7) determine a unique *LE* curve over all w and w^*. Suppose, for example, that for some value of w^* there is a corresponding $w > w^*$ that allows (6) and (7) to hold for $n = 0$ and for some $n^* > 0$. There cannot be another value of w, with $w < w^*$, that also satisfies (6) and (7) for some $n > 0$, $n^* = 0$, and the same w^*. For if (7) is to continue to hold for the same w^*, L_W^* must be unchanged so that the new value of n must be larger than the old value of n^*. But this will cause L_W to fall in equation (6), so that w will rise rather than fall; that is, $w < w^*$ is not possible. Similar arguments applied to the other possible cases establish that the LE curve is uniquely defined. Note that the curve will coincide with the 45° line for a range of values of $w = w^*$ allowing (6) and (7) to hold for nonnegative n and n^*.

International equilibrium is of course determined by the intersection of the Labor Equilibrium curve with the Manufacturing Equilibrium envelope. If that intersection is below the 45° line, all research and upstream production takes place at home; for intersections above the 45° line, they take place abroad. But the fact that the LE curve will in general coincide with the 45° line for part of its length implies that an intersection exactly on that line (that is, at point C in the panels of figure 2) cannot be dismissed as a fluke. Point E in figure 1 depicts an equilibrium where $w < w^*$. The earlier analysis then shows how these wages determine n, R, Q_L, and Q_H. The fact that (2) holds with equality for each variety implies balanced trade, ex post as well as ex ante.

4 Information and Industrial Structure

The previous section described equilibrium under a particular assumption about industrial structure. I now wish to examine how the informational considerations previously raised can be alternatively reflected in the structure of the model, and how these alternatives influence conclusions about the model's behavior and about the industrial structure to which it corresponds. The manufacturing sector contains four separate operations for each variety, so a substantial number of different types of integration could be considered. To limit the size of this paper, I consider only the possible integration of upstream production with both downstream activities and leave to the reader consideration of other possibilities. In particular, I assume throughout that research and upstream production are integrated within a firm, and that no integration across varieties is considered. As foreign downstream production is the only activity not performed at home, the integration decisions that I consider include whether to become a multinational enterprise. They also involve both horizontal and vertical integration.[15]

Consider the behavior of the internationally integrated firm as described in the previous section. In principle, this behavior could be duplicated by an arm's-length contract[16] between the home research and production firm and two independent downstream firms, with the contract calling for exactly the same behavior as described above. That is, the contract would commit the upstream firm to the same (R, Q_L, Q_H) as above and would call for the downstream firms to make some payment P per unit of output to the upstream firm. (Assuming free entry into the downstream activity in each country, P would simply equal that value that causes expected downstream profit to equal zero.) When is such a contract feasible?

The Public Good Nature of Information

The first point to notice is that the contract is conditional upon the results of the research undertaken by the home firm. But these results are proprietary to that firm, which presumably has an interest in keeping them secret. Thus, there is an inherent informational asymmetry. This need not render the contract infeasible: if the foreign distributor can be confident that the home firm will have no incentive to lie about the success, or the extent, of its research effort, then the two can agree that the home firm will declare, without outside verification, how successful its research has been.[17]

Since the home firm is risk neutral, it would not care if the state-invariant payment of P were replaced by a state-contingent payment schedule with the same expected value, that is, if the foreign distributor agreed to the price P_L when the home firm claimed $a = a_L$ and to the price P_H otherwise, where

$$P = p(R)P_L + [1 - p(R)]P_H. \tag{8}$$

It is possible to find an incentive-compatible, arm's-length contract that relieves the foreign firm from all risk. Consider the contract that calls for $Q_L = Q_1$ and $Q_H = 0$. If the foreign distributor is to bear no risk, P_H and P_L must be set so that $Q_1 - P_L - qw^* = 0 - P_H - qw^*$, or so that $Q_1 = P_L - P_H$. Substituting this into (8) reveals that $P_H = P - p(R)Q_1$ and $P_L = P + [1 - p(R)]Q_1$. This is incentive-compatible.[18] Verifying that the contracted amount of research is actually done is subject to the same informational problem. However, the contracted R will also be made incentive-compatible by the above state-contingent payment schedule. To see this, suppose that a contract (P_L, P_H, R, Q_L, Q_H) has been negotiated, and consider what level of R it is now in the firm's interest actually to undertake. Suppose that $w > 1/a_H$, so that $Q_L = Q_1$, $Q_H = 0$, and the contracted $R = R_2$ in equation (3). Then it will be in the home firm's interest actually to undertake the volume R of research that maximizes

$$p(R)[\mu Q_1 + (1 - \mu)P_L - a_L Q_1 w] + [1 - p(R)](1 - \mu)P_H - Rw - \mu qw.$$

Setting the derivative of this expression equal to zero yields the formula

$$p'(R) = \frac{w}{Q_1(\mu - a_L w) + (1 - \mu)(P_L - P_H)}.$$

The R that solves this expression will equal the contracted amount R_2, as given by equation (3), if $P_L - P_H = Q_1$. This is just our state-contingent payment schedule.

This escape works because the home firm is risk neutral. How valid is this assumption? It is justified if the owners of the firms can diversify away risk, and in this model domestic capitalists can eliminate risk by buying shares of all home manufacturing firms. Note that purely national capital markets suffice. But the lack of such markets is sometimes associated with the formation of multinational firms.

If instead both firms are risk averse, it could well be that the requirement that an arm's length contract be incentive-compatible would prove costly, so that there would be a motive for integration. By introducing a countervailing cost to administering integrated units, this could serve in a straightforward way as the basis for a theory of the multinational firm. Analysis of this would bring us to the issues treated in depth by the literature on labor contracts with asymmetric information.[19] But this is not the route of the present paper. Instead I return now to the assumption of home risk neutrality.

To summarize, the public good nature of information produces an informational asymmetry between the home and foreign firms, preventing the latter from directly verifying either the actual research effort of the former or the results of that effort. It will nevertheless be possible for the two firms to design an optimal incentive-compatible contract *if* at least one of the firms is risk neutral and *if* it is feasible for the contract to call for the payment schedule of the foreign firm to vary across all conceivable states of nature. Both requirements are demanding, and in particular the latter would require in practice extremely detailed and complex contracts. This brings us to our second informational issue.

The Multivariate Nature of Quality

The contract calls for delivery of goods of a certain quality. The model assumes that quality can be indicated by a single number, but of course it is almost always much more than that. This suggests the difficulty of including quality specification in an enforceable contract.[20] This problem is minimized for simple standardized goods whose quality can be objectively measured. The problem could be minimized also if the contract is simple enough. For example, if the required quality is state invariant, the partners to the contract might well allow the precise definition of quality to remain implicit and to rely on mutual goodwill to determine whether the goods in fact come up to snuff. (I would find it difficult to describe a McDonald's precisely, but I know one when I see it because they are always supposed to be the same.) This will be especially true if the model's equilibrium is interpreted as one that will be repeated over time. By contrast, the need for precision in defining quality becomes acute when the contract calls for quality to vary significantly across states. If there are countless aspects to quality, involving diverse facets of the good's preparation, design, delivery, and use, an enforceable contract involving state-dependent quality would necessarily be a very complex matter indeed. Perhaps so much so that its use would in truth constitute economic integration, de facto if not de jure.[21]

Modeling Internalization

These considerations strongly suggest how to distinguish between arm's-length transactions and internalization. I assume that if the home and downstream firms are to implement a state-dependent contract, they must first become one firm, so that the transaction is internalized, and act so as to maximize joint profit. If the firms remain at arm's length, the contract they negotiate is constrained to call for state-invariant quality. This constraint responds to both of the informational problems raised in this section. A contract featuring state-invariant quality will necessarily be incentive-compatible, and as just pointed out, it will minimize the difficulties due to the multivariate nature of quality.[22]

The basic idea, then, is that it is infeasible to write contracts with a huge number of contingencies but feasible to do so if the number is more modest. In this model two is "too many," while one is "enough." There would of course be no problem if "quality" were always in fact an observable scaler, as modeled here, rather than an indefinite number of characteristics admitting of no ex ante summary measure. I shall not apologize for reducing the complex reality to such a simple formal representation: this use of low dimensionality is basic to the simple trade models this paper attempts to emulate.

Equilibrium with National and Multinational Firms

Suppose first that $w < w^*$ and that the home upstream firm maintains an arm's-length relation with the downstream firms so that their contracts are constrained to call for state-invariant quality. Recall from the preceding section that the home firm would actually prefer such a contract if $w < 1/a_H$, and that it would decline to enter if $w > 1/a_L$. Thus, the constraint will matter only when $1/a_L > w > 1/a_H$. In this case the home firm's optimization problem is to choose Q and R to maximize

$$Q[1 - a^0(R)w] - [wR + w^0 q],$$

where $a^0(R) = p(R)a_L + [1 - p(R)]a_H$. Now in equilibrium w must be such as to make this profit zero, so that $1 > a^0(R)w$. But then the optimizing choice of Q is the largest one feasible: $Q = Q_1$. If the research effort is being carried to the point where an additional dollar offers a zero net benefit, it must be the case that $p'(R) = 1/Q_1(a_H - a_L)$. Thus, the firm behaves the same when $1/a_L > w > 1/a_H$ as when $1/a_H > w$. The Manufacturing Equilibrium schedule is thus now the graph of (5) for all values of w, and so, in figure 1, ME now becomes the straight line ABC.

It follows from this analysis that the Labor Equilibrium schedule in figure 1 is the same as before for $w < 1/a_H$, but is depicted by FD when $w > 1/a_H$.

The arm's-length equilibrium is now given by the intersection of the amended ME and LE schedules. The multinational equilibrium is of course just that analyzed earlier for the case of the internationally integrated firm.

The Emergence of Multinationals

If the amended ME and LE schedules in figure 1 intersect sufficiently low so that in equilibrium $w < 1/a_H$, as is the case the way the figure is drawn, the arm's-length equilibrium will be identical to the one with multinational firms. All firms will feel unconstrained by the need to deal in state-invariant contracts. Thus, there will be no reason for individual firms to form multinational enterprises, and no social consequences if they are not allowed to do so.

If the arm's-length equilibrium calls for $w > 1/a_H$, the two equilibria will clearly differ. In this case, with an initial arm's-length arrangement, firms would perceive it to be in their interest to form multinationals. If they are allowed to do so, it is therefore the equilibrium given by the original ME and LE schedules that is relevant.[23]

5 Patterns of Trade and Direct Investment

What is the influence of relative factor endowments? It should be apparent that they affect only the Labor Equilibrium schedule and are irrelevant to the Manufacturing Equilibrium envelope. For example, an increase in the stock of wheat-specific land must, at given L_W, increase the marginal productivity of labor in wheat production. It then follows from (6) and (7) that a rise in T^*, the foreign stock of land, or a fall in T will shift the LE schedule toward the right. A similar effect will be produced by a rise in L or reduction in L^*. Any combination of such changes will therefore raise w^* and lower w.

We have seen that since the LE schedule may coincide with the 45° line for a portion of its length, an equilibrium with $w = w^*$ is not necessarily unlikely. Consider the relation of such equilibria to factor endowments.

International Wage Equalization

As figure 2 makes clear, point C will be the intersection of the linear parts of ME and ME^* if the dispersion is small enough and of the nonlinear parts for a sufficiently large dispersion. I discuss only the former case: the latter leads to similar conclusions. It follows from equation (5) that, at such a point C, the common value of w and w^* is given by

$$w_c = \frac{Q_1}{Q_1 a(w) + R_1 + q}. \tag{9}$$

Setting the right-hand sides of (6) and (7) equal to this value enables one to solve those equations for n and n^* as functions of the factor endowments of the two countries. In order to study the role of these endowments, I shall hold fixed the world stocks of the two factors ($\bar{L} = L + L^*$ and $\bar{T} = T + T^*$) and see how international equilibrium responds to redistributions of these stocks between the two countries. Now equations (6) and (7) determine equilibrium wheat labor-land ratios in the two countries ($t = L_W/T$ and $t^* = L_W^*/T^*$):

$$w_c = F_L(t, 1) = F_L^*(t^*, 1).$$

Note that

$$L_M = L - tT \quad \text{and} \quad L_M^* = L^* - t^*T^*. \tag{10}$$

The world endowment ratio $\bar{L}/\bar{T}$ consequently must exceed at least one of t and t^* for both countries to undertake research and production. Otherwise at most one

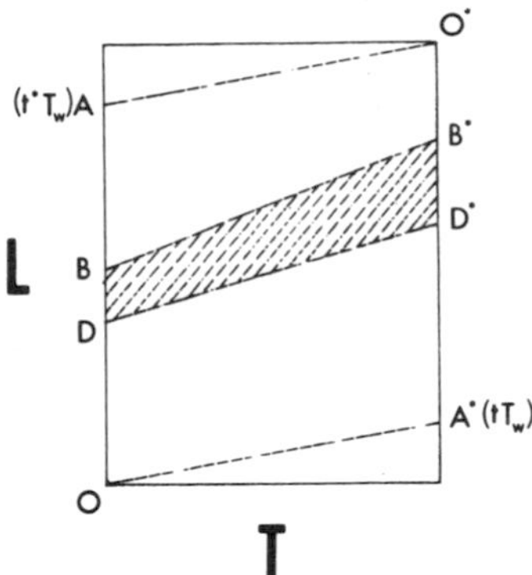

Figure 3

country will do so (endowments could be such that both countries produce only wheat in equilibrium). Figure 3 depicts the case where the world endowment ratio exceeds both t and t^*. The dimensions of the box equal L_W and T_W, respectively, with labor measured on the vertical axis and land on the horizontal, so that each point within the box represents one possible allocation of the world's factors. The home endowment is measured relative to the southwest corner of the box and the foreign endowment relative to the northeast corner. The slopes of the rays OA^* and O^*A, respectively, reflect t and t^*. Thus, the area between these two rays contains all allocations that are consistent with both $L_M > 0$ and $L_M^* > 0$. But this is only a necessary condition for n and n^* to be both positive, not a sufficient condition. The reason is that a country will provide downstream services even if it conducts no research or production. For both countries to do the latter, it is necessary for L_M and L_M^* to be such that equations (11) and (12) are solved for positive values of n and n^*:

$$n[a(w)Q_1 + R_1 + \mu q] + n^*\mu q = L_M \tag{11}$$

and

$$n(1-\mu)q + n^*[a(w)Q_1 + R_1 + (1-\mu)q] = L_M^*. \tag{12}$$

This will be the case when $b > (L_M/L_M^*) > d$, where

$$b = \frac{a(w)Q_1 + R_1 + \mu q}{(1-\mu)q}$$

and

$$d = \frac{\mu q}{a(w)Q_1 + R_1 + (1-\mu)q}.$$

In figure 3 the BB^* line shows endowment allocations for which $L_M/L_M^* = b$, and DD^* shows allocations where $L_M/L_M^* = d$. The "wage equalization region" is therefore DBB^*D^*. Allocations within this region result in an international equilibrium at point

C in figure 2. Both countries have firms conducting research and production, and they have a common wage w_c.[24] Allocations above the region imply an international equilibrium in which all research and production takes place at home, and all such activity takes place abroad with an allocation below the region. This is superficially similar to factor-price equalization in the familiar Heckscher-Ohlin-Samuelson model. It is worth pointing out, therefore, that wage equalization does not require identical production functions across countries and does not imply equalization of the returns to land.

The Influence of Factor Endowments

It is now possible to indicate how relative factor endowments and the size of the dispersion interact to determine the industrial structure, the volume and type (interindustry, intraindustry, or intrafirm) of international trade, the volume and type of direct investment (unidirectional or two-way), and the international pattern of factor prices. In the following discussion I call the relatively labor-abundant country the home one.

Suppose first that relative factor endowments differ greatly between the two countries. Then international equilibrium will take place on the linear part of the Manufacturing Equilibrium envelope below point C in figure 2. Then home wages are less than foreign wages, all research and production takes place at home, there is no direct investment,[25] and all trade is interindustry (and interfirm), with the home country exporting unfinished manufactures in exchange for wheat. As relative factor endowments become more nearly equal, home wages rise (and home rents fall), foreign wages fall, and the volume of (interindustry) trade declines. If the dispersion is large enough so that $w_c > (1/a_H)$, sufficiently similar relative factor endowments will cause the home manufacturing firms to undertake direct investment. Trade and direct investment now appear to be substitutes, as the former contracts while the latter expands. But there is no causal relation between the two developments: they are both due to the assumed convergence of relative endowments across countries. International trade will consist of the interindustry exchange of wheat for unfinished manufactures, but the export of the latter will now be intrafirm trade.

If relative endowments become still more similar, equilibrium will take place at point C in panel (b) of figure 2. The foreign economy will now undertake some research and production, with these foreign activities conducted by multinational firms. Direct investment is now two-way, and international trade consists of both interindustry trade and intraindustry trade, with each country exporting unfinished manufactures. The latter constitutes two-way intrafirm trade. Wages will also be equalized across countries. If endowments become still more similar, factor prices will not change further, but intraindustry (and intrafirm) trade will continue to displace interindustry trade. Note that now direct investment and trade (intraindustry) appear to be complements. If the dispersion is instead small enough so that $w_c < (1/a_H)$, direct investment will never take place, and therefore, there will never be any intrafirm trade. But the above description of the effects of changes in relative-factor endowments still applies to factor prices and to the respective roles of interindustry and intraindustry trade.

All this differs dramatically from the Markusen-Helpman model. There the formation of multinationals is associated with *differences* in relative factor endowments rather than similarities: multinationals cannot emerge at all if trade in goods would itself equalize factor prices (in that model both sectors use both factors and technology is identical across countries), though the presence of multinationals can produce factor-price equalization in some cases where trade alone cannot do so. Furthermore, two-way direct investment cannot take place at all without impediments to international exchange.[26]

Degree of Technological Dispersion

Now consider the effect of changes in the degree of dispersion, $a_H - a_L$. (I shall examine only equilibria where $w < w^*$ and leave other possibilities to the reader.) Start with the case $a_H = a_L$, and ask what happens to the equilibria as a_H is gradually increased. Panels (a)–(d) of figure 4 illustrate the result with snapshots taken along the way. In each case the arm's-length equilibrium is indicated by A and the multinational one by M. Small deviations of a_H above a_L of course give no benefit to integration. A range of larger dispersions results in $w = 1/a_H$; within this range, the larger the dispersion the larger is the number n of varieties, and the lower is the quality of those varieties for which $a = a_H$. Finally, very large dispersions introduce the possibility that

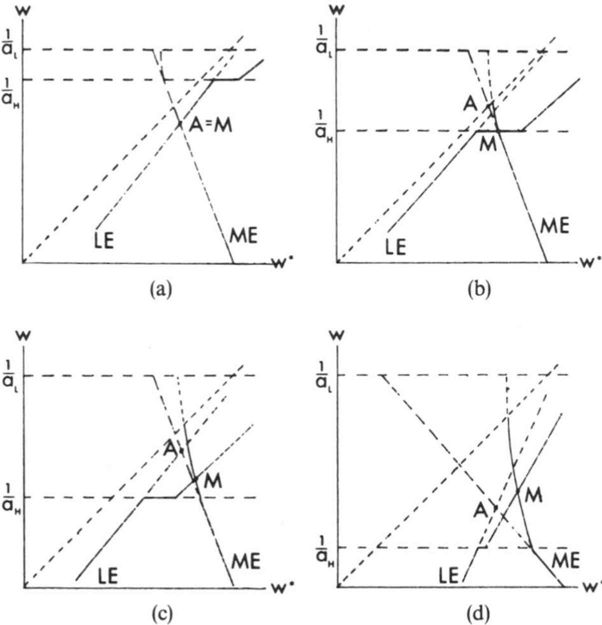

Figure 4

the home wage is larger in an equilibrium with multinationals than in one with arm's-length transactions.

In case (a), point A features $w < 1/a_H$, so $A = M$, and there is no incentive to form multinationals. In the other three cases $w > 1/a_H$ at A, so $A \neq M$. Because of the steplike shape of the amended LE schedule, it is not unlikely that $w = 1/a_H$ at point M, as shown in panel (b). In this case, with an integrated equilibrium, firms are indifferent about the quality of goods that they provide when $a = a_H$. Thus, they do not perceive that they derive any advantage from being multinational. However, if they were to respond by dismembering themselves, the now independent manufacturing firms would all have to offer Q_1 quality goods when $a = a_H$, which would cause w to rise. At the higher wage, the (now arm's-length) firms wish to integrate.

In all cases where integration is beneficial, the multinational equilibrium features a higher foreign wage w^* than does the arm's-length equilibrium. Therefore, land's rent is lower: the formation of multinationals redistributes income in the host country to the factor employed intensively in the multinational sector and away from the other factor. This is just the reverse of what happens in the Markusen-Helpman model. Panels (b) and (c) imply the opposite redistribution in the source country, but, as panel (d) demonstrates, it is possible for the establishment of multinationals to benefit labor worldwide at the expense of land. These possibilities also are at odds with the Markusen-Helpman model (and the latter case is quite different from the implications of international factor mobility in a factor-endowments trade model). Also, from (7) multinationalization increases n: there is a greater variety of goods with multinationals than without. When $a = a_L$, goods are produced at quality Q_1 with either form of industrial organization, the difference being the greater potential variety offered by multinationals. When $a = a_H$, arm's-length firms would still offer goods of quality Q_1, but multinationals would not produce, except possibly in the case of panel (b). Thus, in equilibrium the number of goods actually offered for sale by the multinationals, $[1 - p(R)]n$, may be either greater or less than in an arm's-length equilibrium.

Since the domestic wage may be either lower or higher with the multinational structure than with the arm's-length one, it follows from (3)—and also from the description of the properties of $R_2(w)$ immediately following (3)—that research may be either greater or less. Thus, $p(R)$, which, socially, equals the fraction of varieties for which $a = a_L$, may be either greater or less.

6 Concluding Remarks

This paper has developed a simple general equilibrium model of international trade offering an explanation for the emergence of multinational enterprises, within the general spirit of what Dunning calls the "eclectic theory," or the OLI framework. The paper first argues that the question critical for understanding direct investment in the context of trade theory is the nature of internalization, and that the essential aspect of the latter usually involves the exchange of information between agents. The central informational issues are the public good nature of information and the size and diversity of the information flows with which agents must contend.

A model was constructed to examine and reflect these concerns. The model contained two variables, research effort and product quality, respectively, associated with the two central informational issues. The basic parameters of the model were relative factor endowments and the dispersion (or degree of intrinsic uncertainty facing agents).

The role of multinational activity was discussed and related to the basic parameters. The presence of multinational firms is positively related to the size of the dispersion. Also, similarity in relative factor endowments makes direct investment more likely, and also provides a basis for intraindustry trade and causes wages to be more nearly equal internationally. Sufficient endowment similarity (and the presence of a large enough dispersion) cause international wage equalization and two-way direct investment, making intraindustry trade and intrafirm trade large relative to interindustry trade.

These implications are dramatically different from those of the Markusen-Helpman model, which took internalization for granted. It would be premature, I believe, to interpret this difference in results as a picture of the significance of internalization, since it is unclear how robust either set of results is. What has been established is the inherent importance of explicitly modeling the internalization decision.

Notes

An early version of this paper was written at the Institute for International Economic Studies in Stockholm and presented to the 1984 Annual Conference of the International Economics Study Group, held at the University of Sussex Conference Center, September 7–9, 1984. I am grateful to Lorraine Eden, Gene Grossman, Henrik Horn, and James Markusen for helpful suggestions. I have also received useful comments during seminars at the Universities of Maryland, Michigan, Pittsburgh, Southern California, and Virginia; at Queen's, Princeton, Howard, Harvard, Erasmus, and Duke Universities; the University of California at Berkeley and at the University of Western Ontario International Trade Conference of March 1985.

1. This approach to the theory of the firm derives from Coase (1937) and many followers. Important contributions with respect to the multinational corporation include Hymer (1960), Kindleberger (1969), Caves (1971, 1974), Buckley and Casson (1976), Dunning (1977, 1981), Casson (1979), and Rugman (1981), among others.

2. The literature on direct investment is vast and has been surveyed many times. (A survey article of the surveys would not be out of order.) Useful guides and collections include Kindleberger (1970), Dunning (1971, 1973, 1977), Stevens (1974), Hufbauer (1975), Vernon (1977), Lall and Streeten (1977), Hood and Young (1979), Agarwal (1980), Caves (1982), and Kindleberger and Audretsch (1983).

3. See, for example, Ethier (1983, ch. 7).

4. See Markusen (1984), Horstmann and Markusen (1987), Helpman (1983a, 1983b, 1984) and Helpman and Krugman (1985). An interesting alternative is provided by Cherkes (1984), who analyzes how historically sunk fixed costs can generate multinational firm activity.

5. Markusen and Helpman are both primarily concerned, however, to link their treatments of direct investment to the theory of international trade, not to the OLI framework.

6. Indeed this is basically what happens in the Markusen-Helpman model.

7. This view of internalization is forcefully espoused by Grossman and Hart (1984).

8. Magee (1977a, b) gives a very useful treatment of what is called "appropriability." See also Casson (1979).

9. In the terminology of Shaked and Sutton (1983, 1984), the manufacturing sector is characterized by both "horizontal" and "vertical" product differentiation.

10. See, for example, Ethier (1979, 1982), Helpman (1981), Krugman (1979, 1981), and Lancaster (1980).

11. However, I do conjecture that relaxations of my assumptions about functional forms would either leave the main results of this paper unchanged or alter them in ways that are obvious (at least to readers of Markusen 1984 and Helpman 1984). A more significant question—also beyond the scope of this paper—is the sensitivity of my conclusions to the assumption about industrial structure that will be made in section 4 below.

12. This is for expositional convenience. Nothing changes if each firm produces an assortment of varieties, as long as there are many firms and potential firms.

13. Implicit differentiation of (4)—with equality—confirms that it defines a relation between w and w^* that is strictly convex to the origin, when the optimality condition (3) is satisfied.

14. I assume the existence of a unique equilibrium in which each country consumes all (produced) goods in positive amounts.

15. These three decisions (horizontal integration, vertical integration, and going multinational) could be disentangled by allowing q to differ across countries and to be sensitive to whether the downstream activity occurred in the same country as the research and manufacturing. I resist the temptation to perform the exercise.

16. In what follows, an "arm's-length" arrangement can be interpreted as either simple exporting or licensing. For a recent treatment where the two are distinct, see Horstmann and Markusen (1986).

17. The following argument applies ideas from the literature on contracting in the presence of asymmetric information. See D'Aspremont and Gerard-Varet (1979), for example.

18. Suppose, for example, that $a = a_L$. If the home firm tells the truth, it will earn $Q_1(1 - a_L w) + (1 - \mu)[P - p(R)Q_1] - [R + \mu q]w$. If instead the home firm claims that $a = a_H$, it will earn $(1 - \mu)[P - p(R)Q_1] - [R + \mu q]w$, which is less by the amount $Q_1(1 - a_L w)$.

19. See Hart (1983) for a recent survey.

20. Or, to put it another way, that we use the variable Q to represent relevent considerations, of whatever sort, that cannot be contracted.

21. For a more detailed discussion of related issues, see Williamson (1975).

22. Of course, this is just one of the conceivable ways of characterizing the motive for internalization, and it would be interesting to contrast its implications with those of some of the alternatives. But in order to limit the length of this paper, I consider only the case that I find most appealing.

23. The firms may or may not find it to their advantage to shift from an arm's-length to a multinational arrangement, but they will never perceive it to be actually disadvantageous to do so. Much of the less formal literature has assumed or asserted that multinational operation is inherently costly. See also Ethier and Horn (1985). The most natural way to introduce such considerations here would be to assume that the per-unit downstream cost q is higher for an integrated firm. As the analysis is straightforward, it is omitted. The principal consequence would be to add a range of cases where a change from an arm's-length arrangement to an integrated one would be costly. If, in addition, internalization raises foreign q more than it would raise home q (as it would if integration is more costly when it involves operating across national and cultural barriers), there will be a range of cases where it would be advantageous for the upstream manufacturer to integrate with the home downstream firm but not with the foreign one.

24. More precisely, the international wage differential just equals the productivity differential of labor in the manufacturing sector (recall that foreign labor is measured in efficiency units).

25. More precisely, there is no reason why any direct investment should take place.

26. All this is quite clear in Helpman (1984), but Markusen (1984) appears to have reached different conclusions. However, this disparity simply reflects the one significant respect in which Markusen's model differs from Helpman's: the former assumes that there is only one variety of manufacture, so that with a multinational equilibrium that sector contains but a single monopolistic firm. If the two countries have identical endowments, so that manufacturing activity occurs in both, that monopolist must ipso facto be a multinational. If, in addition, it pays to concentrate the public activity (analogous to my R) in one country, factor prices and resource allocation must differ in the two countries. But if there were instead many varieties, they could be divided among the two countries, allowing each variety to be produced entirely in one country and eliminating the need for multinationals. Thus, this model produces the same conclusions

as Helpman's, once additional varieties are introduced, which is necessary to compare its implications with those of the present paper.

References

Agarwal, J. P. 1980. Determinants of foreign direct investment: A survey. *Weltwirtschaftliches Archiv* 116:739–773.

Buckley, P. J., and M. Casson. 1976. *The Future of the Multinational Enterprise*. London: Macmillan.

Casson, M. 1979. *Alternatives to the Multinational Enterprise*. London: Macmillan.

Caves, R. E. 1971. International corporations: The industrial economics of foreign investment. *Economica* 38:1–27.

Caves, R. E. 1974. International trade, international investment, and imperfect markets. *Special Papers in International Economics* no. 10. Princeton: International Finance Section, Princeton University.

Caves, R. E. 1982. *Multinational Enterprise and Economic Analysis*. Cambridge: Cambridge University Press.

Cherkes, M. 1984. The theory of multinational enterprise in manufacturing industries. Ph.D. diss., University of Pennsylvania.

Coase, R. H. 1937. The theory of the firm. *Economica* 4:386–405.

D'Aspremont, C., and L. Gerard-Varet. 1979. Incentives and incomplete information. *Journal of Public Economics* 11:25–45.

Dunning, J. H. 1973. The determinants of international production. *Oxford Economic Papers* 25:289–336.

Dunning, J. H. 1977. Trade, location of economic activity and MNE: A search for an eclectic approach. In B. Ohlin, P.-O. Hesselborn, and P. M. Wijkman (eds.), *The International Allocation of Economic Activity*. London: Macmillan.

Dunning, J. H. 1981. Explaining the international direct investment position of countries; Towards a dynamic or developmental approach. *Weltwirtschaftliches Archiv* 117:30–64.

Dunning, J. H. (ed.). 1971. *The Multinational Corporation*. London: Allen and Unwin.

Ethier, W. J. 1979. Internationally decreasing costs and world trade. *Journal of International Economics* 9:1–24.

Ethier, W. J. 1982. National and international returns to scale in the modern theory of international trade. *American Economic Review* 72:389–405.

Ethier, W. J. 1983. *Modern International Economics*. New York: Norton.

Ethier, W. J., and H. Horn. 1985. Multinational firms: The cost side. Unpublished manuscript.

Grossman, S. J., and O. Hart. 1984. The costs and benefits of ownership: A theory of vertical integration. Unpublished manuscript.

Hart, O. D. 1983. Optimal labour contracts under asymmetric information: An introduction. *Review of Economic Studies* 50:3–35.

Helpman, E. 1981. International trade in the presence of product differentiation, economies of scale and monopolistic competition. *Journal of International Economics* 11:305–340.

Helpman, E. 1983a. A theory of multinational corporations and the structure of foreign trade. Unpublished manuscript.

Helpman, E. 1983b. A theory of multinational corporations and the structure of foreign trade—Part II: Vertical integration. Unpublished manuscript.

Helpman, E. 1984. A simple theory of international trade with multinational corporations. *Journal of Political Economy* 92:451–471.

Helpman, E., and P. R. Krugman. 1985. *Market Structure and Foreign Trade*. Cambridge, Mass.: MIT Press.

Hood, N., and S. Young. 1979. *The Economics of Multinational Enterprise*. London: Longman.

Horstmann, I., and J. Markusen. 1986. Licensing versus direct investment: A model of internalization by the multinational enterprise. Unpublished manuscript.

Horstmann, I., and J. Markusen. 1987. Strategic investments and the development of multinationals. *International Economic Review* 28:109–121.

Hufbauer, G. C. 1975. The multinational corporation and direct investment. In P. B. Kenen (ed.), *International Trade and Finance*. Cambridge: Cambridge University Press.

Hymer, S. 1960. The international operations of national firms. Ph.D. diss., Massachusetts Institute of Technology.

Kindleberger, C. P. 1969. *American Business Abroad: Six Lectures on Direct Investment*. New Haven: Yale University Press.

Kindleberger, C. P. (ed.). 1970. *The International Corporation*. Cambridge, Mass.: MIT Press.

Kindleberger, C. P., and D. B. Audretsch (eds.). 1983. *The Multinational Corporation in the 1980s*. Cambridge, Mass.: MIT Press.

Krugman, P. 1979. Increasing returns, monopolistic competition, and international trade. *Journal of International Economics* 9:469–480.

Krugman, P. 1981. Intraindustry specialization and the gains from trade. *Journal of Political Economy* 89:959–973.

Lall, S., and P. Streeten. 1977. *Foreign Investment, Transnationals and Developing Countries*. London: Macmillan.

Lancaster, K. 1980. Intra-industry trade under perfect monopolistic competition. *Journal of International Economics* 10:151–176.

McCulloch, R. 1984. U.S. direct foreign investment and trade: Theories, trends, and public policy issues. In A. Erdilek (ed.), *Multinationals as Mutual Invaders: Intraindustry Direct Foreign Investment*. Beckenham, England: Croom Helm.

Magee, S. P. 1977a. Information and the multinational corporation: An appropriability theory of direct foreign investment. In J. N. Bhagwati (ed.), *The New International Economic Order: The North-South Debate*. Cambridge, Mass.: MIT Press.

Magee, S. P. 1977b. Multinational corporations, the industry technology cycle and development. *Journal of World Trade Law* 11:297–321.

Markusen, J. R. 1984. Multinationals, multi-plant economies, and the gains from trade. *Journal of International Economics* 16:205–226.

Rugman, A. M. 1980. Internalization as a general theory of foreign direct investment: A re-appraisal of the literature. *Weltwirtschaftliches Archiv* 116:365–379.

Shaked, A., and J. Sutton. 1983. Natural oligopolies. *Econometrica* 51:1469–1484.

Shaked, A., and J. Sutton. 1984. Natural oligopolies and international trade. In H. Kierzkowski (ed.), *Monopolistic Competition and International Trade*. Oxford: Oxford University Press.

Stevens, G. V. G. 1974. The determinants of investment. In J. H. Dunning (ed.), *Economic Analysis and the Multinational Enterprise*. London: Allen and Unwin.

Vernon, R. 1977. *Storm over the Multinationals: The Real Issues*. London: Macmillan.

Williamson, O. E. 1975. *Markets and Hierarchies: Analysis and Antitrust Implications: A Study in the Economics of Internal Organization*. New York: Free Press.

V TECHNOLOGY AND TRADE

17 Product Development and International Trade

Gene M. Grossman and Elhanan Helpman

1 Introduction

International economists have long used static models of comparative advantage and (more recently) scale economies to great advantage in studying the pattern of international trade and the normative properties of trading equilibria. But increasingly, issues of concern to theorists and casual observers alike are inherently *dynamic* in nature. Attention has focused recently on the creation of comparative advantage by technological innovation, the relationship between trade policy and economic growth, and the dynamic evolution of the volume and pattern of world trade. The static analysis of international trade must be extended if we are to deal with these new concerns.

In this paper, we develop a multicountry, dynamic, general equilibrium model of product innovation and international trade to study the creation of comparative advantage through research and development (R&D) and the evolution of world trade over time. We build on the static analyses of trade in differentiated products by Krugman (1979a, 1981), Dixit and Norman (1980), and Feenstra and Judd (1982), and also on Judd's 1985 investigation of product development in a closed economy.

In our model, firms incur resource costs to introduce new products. Forward-looking potential producers conduct R&D and enter the product market whenever profit opportunities exist. New products substitute imperfectly for old, and prices, interest rates, and the pattern of trade evolve over time as more commodities become available for purchase. Trade has both intraindustry and interindustry components, with the former governed by R&D expenditures and the latter by resource endowments. International capital flows take place to finance R&D, and in some circumstances multinational corporations may emerge.

The approach adopted here differs in important respects from several recent studies of the dynamics of trade with product innovation, such as Krugman (1979b), Dollar (1986), Jensen and Thursby (1987), and Segerstrom, Anant, and Dinopoulos (1987). These papers have provided useful insights into the steady-state properties of trading equilibria when products are initially developed in the North and later imitated by the South. But all except perhaps the last have been incomplete in important ways, because of a failure to incorporate all general equilibrium interactions, the lack of consideration of the economic factors that drive the rate of product innovation, or other features.[1] Our framework is distinguished by its explicit treatment of both the private incentive for investment in R&D and the resource requirements of this activity.

In order to focus sharply on the dynamics of product development and the creation of comparative advantage by R&D, in this study we abstract from all forms of factor accumulation. This abstraction helps us to bring out the novel features introduced by endogenous innovation and renders the exercise more tractable. Future research

Originally published in the *Journal of Political Economy* 97 (December 1989): 1261–1283.

might gainfully consider the interaction between the evolution of the pattern of trade that is dictated by technological progress and the more familiar dynamics emanating from resource expansion.

The organization of the paper and some of the major results are as follows. In section 2, we develop the model and derive the world equilibrium that would result in the absence of any international borders. Section 3 presents our investigation of the pattern of trade in a two-country, two-factor world, with the factors interpreted to be unskilled labor and human capital. If both R&D and the production of differentiated goods are more human capital–intensive activities than is the production of a traditional good and if all activities bear Leontief production technologies, then the human capital–rich country will be a net exporter of differentiated products and an importer of the traditional good *at every moment in time*. This is true despite the fact that the human capital–rich country initially devotes more of its resources to R&D (as opposed to production) and despite the fact that trade is not balanced along the equilibrium path. The model predicts a rising share of trade in world gross national product (GNP), at least when R&D is the most human capital intensive of the three activities. Concerning intertemporal trade, we show that the human capital–rich country has both a greater incentive to invest and a greater incentive to save (per capita), the latter because of its declining relative factor income. Consequently, it appears that this country may run either a surplus or a deficit on current account in the dynamic equilibrium.

In section 4, we introduce the possibility of multinational corporations in the manner of Helpman (1984). We assume that headquarter services can be separated geographically from production activities and that only the former must take place in the country in which a differentiated product has been developed. If headquarter services are more human capital intensive than production, then the possibility of multinational activity expands the set of distributions of the world's factor endowment for which international exchange can reproduce the integrated world equilibrium. For certain compositions of factor endowments, we predict that multinational enterprises will emerge at a particular point in time and remain active ever after. The extent of multinationality, as measured by output, employment of subsidiaries, or the number of multinational firms, expands over time, at least initially and as the world economy approaches the steady state.

2 A Dynamic Model of R&D

We consider a world economy with three activities: the production of a "traditional" commodity under competitive conditions, the production of a continuum of varieties of a "modern" industrial product, and research and development that leads to the acquisition of the know-how needed to produce new brands of the industrial good. Our modern goods are horizontally differentiated, so that newly invented products do not displace older varieties. We leave for future research the issue of trade dynamics in a world of vertically differentiated products, in which products become obsolete after a time.[2]

At every point in time there exists a given (measure of the) number of varieties that were developed in the past. Producers of these varieties engage in oligopolistic competition by setting prices. Given demands and costs, this process determines prices, outputs, and current operating profits. An entrepreneur who contemplates developing a new brand can calculate the future stream of potential operating profits. He or she chooses to develop the brand only if the present value of this stream is at least as large as the cost of R&D. The competitive entry process leads to aggregate investment in R&D such that a brand's development cost is just equal to the present value of its future profits (unless no further products are developed).

As in Helpman and Krugman (1985), it proves convenient to solve for the "integrated world equilibrium," that is, the equilibrium that would obtain in the absence of any international borders. Under conditions that give rise to factor-price equalization, a world trading equilibrium reproduces the integrated equilibrium in its essential details. So properties of the latter equilibrium can be applied to the analysis of the former. For this reason the following discussion deals first with the integrated economy.

Consumers

Infinitely lived consumers maximize total lifetime utility. The representative consumer has a time-separable intertemporal utility function

$$U = \int_0^\infty e^{-\rho t} \log u(\cdot)\, dt, \tag{1}$$

where ρ is the constant subjective discount rate and $u(\cdot)$ is an instantaneous subutility function. We adopt a particular form for $u(\cdot)$,

$$u = \left[\int_0^n c_x(i)^\alpha \, di\right]^{s_x/\alpha} c_y^{1-s_x}, \qquad \alpha, s_x \in (0, 1), \tag{2}$$

where $c_x(i)$ is consumption of differentiated product i, c_y is consumption of the traditional good, and n is the (measure of the) number of available varieties. We note that this form implies constant expenditure shares s_x and $1 - s_x$ on commodity classes x and y, and a constant elasticity of substitution between any two differentiated products of $\sigma = 1/(1 - \alpha) > 1$.

The consumer's maximization problem can be solved in two stages. First we find $\{c_x(i)\}$ and c_y to maximize $u(\cdot)$ given total expenditure at time t, $E(t)$, prices, and the available brands. Then we solve for the time pattern of expenditures that maximizes U. The solution to the first stage gives instantaneous demand functions[3]

$$c_x(i) = s_x E \frac{p(i)^{-\sigma}}{\int_0^{n(t)} p(j)^{1-\sigma}\, dj} \tag{3}$$

and $c_y = (1 - s_x)E/p_y$, where $p(i)$ is the price of differentiated product i and p_y is the price of the traditional good.

In maximizing U, the consumer must satisfy an intertemporal budget constraint. We assume that the consumer can borrow or lend freely on a capital market with instantaneous rate of interest $\dot{R}(\tau)$. The budget constraint is

$$\int_t^\infty e^{-[R(\tau)-R(t)]}E(\tau)\,d\tau = \int_t^\infty e^{-[R(\tau)-R(t)]}I(\tau)\,d\tau + A(t), \tag{4}$$

where $I(\tau)$ is the consumer's factor income in period τ, $A(t)$ is the value of his accumulated assets at t, with $A(0) = 0$, and $R(\tau)$ is the cumulative interest factor through time τ. Then if we substitute (3) into (2) and the result into (1), the first-order condition for maximizing U subject to (4) at $t = 0$ implies[4]

$$\frac{\dot{E}}{E} = \dot{R} - \rho. \tag{5}$$

Producers

Costs of manufacturing industrial products comprise two parts, fixed development costs and variable production costs. Production takes place under constant returns to scale, and the input requirements for R&D do not vary with the number of innovating firms. Let $\phi_x(\mathbf{w}_f)$ be the unit cost in production and $\phi_n(\mathbf{w}_f)$ the cost of developing a brand, where $\mathbf{w}_f$ is a vector of input prices.[5] These costs are the same for all brands, regardless of whether or not the variety has previously been introduced by another entrepreneur. Then $\phi_n(\cdot)$ is the fixed cost and $\phi_x(\cdot)$ is the average and marginal variable cost for all firms in this sector.

The number of potential products is infinite. Therefore, it will never be rational for an entrepreneur to develop an already existing brand, and each innovator enjoys monopoly power in the production of his particular variety for the indefinite future.

A producer of an existing brand faces at time t a measure $n(t)$ of competitors who have developed products in the past. He takes as given the aggregate expenditure level $E(t)$ and the pricing policy of the competitors and sets the price of his brand so as to maximize operating profits, namely, revenue minus production costs, using the demand function given in (3). As is well known, this results in fixed-markup pricing over unit production costs. Since all producers are similar, we consider the symmetric equilibrium. In this equilibrium, output per variety $x(i) = x$ and prices $p(i) = p$ for all $i \in [0, n(t)]$ satisfy

$$x = s_x \frac{E}{pn} \tag{6}$$

and

$$\alpha p = \phi_x(\mathbf{w}_f). \tag{7}$$

The resulting operating profits per variety are

$$\pi = (1 - \alpha)s_x \frac{E}{n}. \tag{8}$$

An entrepreneur has perfect foresight regarding the evolution of spending E and the number of firms n. Therefore, using (8), he has perfect foresight regarding profits per variety. In an equilibrium the present value of these profits cannot exceed current R&D costs. Hence, if at time t there is positive but finite investment in product development, each new variety breaks even, that is,

$$\int_t^\infty e^{-[R(\tau)-R(t)]}\pi(\tau)\,d\tau = \phi_n[\mathbf{w}_f(t)]. \tag{9}$$

We normalize nominal prices so that

$$1 = \phi_n[\mathbf{w}_f(t)] \qquad \text{for all } t. \tag{10}$$

With this choice of numeraire, (9) implies that the instantaneous interest rate is equal to the flow of operating profits, that is,

$$\pi(t) = \dot{R}(t). \tag{11}$$

The traditional good also is produced subject to constant returns to scale. Its unit cost function is $\phi_y(\mathbf{w}_f)$. Its price, which equals marginal cost, satisfies

$$p_y = \phi_y(\mathbf{w}_f). \tag{12}$$

Equations (7), (10), and (12) describe the equilibrium relationships between product and factor prices.

Integrated Equilibrium

First, substitute (8) and (11) into (5) to obtain

$$\frac{\dot{E}}{E} = (1 - \alpha)s_x \frac{E}{n} - \rho. \tag{13}$$

This is the first differential equation that will be used to describe the evolution of the integrated economy over time. It shows the rate of change of spending as a function of spending and the number of available varieties. The next step is to derive a differential equation for changes in the number of available brands, that is, an investment equation.

Let $\mathbf{a}_z(\mathbf{w}_f)$ be the (column vector) gradient of the unit cost function $\phi_z(\mathbf{w}_f)$, $z = n, x, y$. Then $\mathbf{a}_z(\mathbf{w}_f)$ represents the employment vector per unit output at factor prices $\mathbf{w}_f$, and the factor market–clearing conditions are

$$\mathbf{a}_n(\mathbf{w}_f)\dot{n} + \mathbf{a}_x(\mathbf{w}_f)X + \mathbf{a}_y(\mathbf{w}_f)Y = \mathbf{V}, \tag{14}$$

where

$$X = nx \tag{15}$$

is the aggregate output of industrial products, Y is output of the traditional goods, and $\mathbf{V}$ is the vector of available inputs. Using (7), (10), (12), and (14), together with the goods market–clearing conditions

$$s_x \frac{E}{p} = X \tag{16}$$

and

$$(1 - s_x)\frac{E}{p_y} = Y, \tag{17}$$

we can solve for equilibrium commodity and factor prices and sectoral output levels all as a function of the level of spending, E. We denote these functional relationships by $\mathbf{w}_f(E)$, $p(E)$, $p_y(E)$, $X(E)$, $Y(E)$, and

$$\dot{n} = v(E). \tag{18}$$

Equations (13) and (18) constitute an autonomous system of differential equations. They apply whenever the implied rate of product development is nonnegative. Global stability requires the function $v(\cdot)$ to be declining in E whenever $v(E) > 0$. For now, we simply assume that this condition is satisfied.[6]

The phase diagram for the system is depicted in figure 1. From (13), we see that the $\dot{E} = 0$ schedule is an upward-sloping line in (E, n) space with slope given by $\rho/(1 - \alpha)s_x$. Equation (18) implies that $\dot{n} = 0$ for some particular value of E, which we denote by $\bar{E}$. The horizontal line in the figure depicts points at which there is no product development. Note that there can be no equilibrium of the economy above this line because this would require negative product development, which of course is not feasible.[7] The relevant regions in the figure are those on or below the horizontal line.

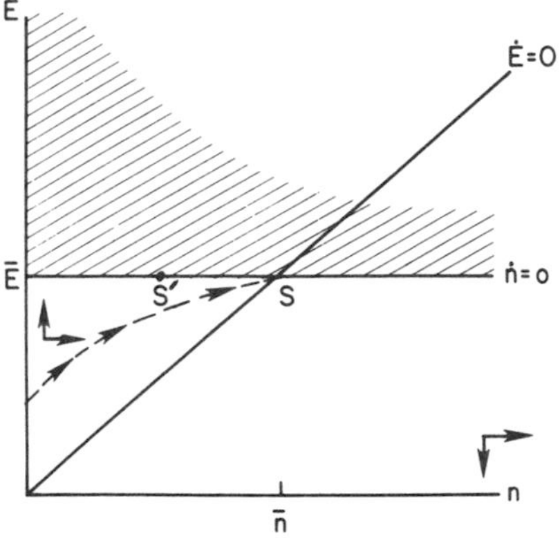

Figure 1

Point S in the figure represents the steady state. For $n(0) < \bar{n}$, there is a single trajectory that leads to point S, represented by the dashed path. This is, in fact, the unique *equilibrium* trajectory for $n(0) < \bar{n}$. For initial points below this trajectory, expenditure approaches zero as time progresses, which violates the conditions for consumer optimization. For initial points above the path, the conditions for profit maximization ultimately are violated. To see this, note that any such trajectory hits the horizontal line along which $\dot{n} = 0$ at a point such as S' to the left of S. With $E = \bar{E}$, it remains there ever after. But the constancy of expenditure implies, from (5), that $\dot{R} = \rho$. Since S' is above the upward-sloping ray, operating profits $\pi = (1 - \alpha) \cdot s_x \bar{E}/n$ are larger than ρ and hence the interest rate. This means that the present value of operating profits exceeds the cost of R&D, making it profitable to develop new products at S'. Therefore, trajectories that hit the horizontal line to the left of S are not consistent with long-run equilibrium.[8]

Special Case

We now consider a special case that will be used to discuss trade issues. There are only two factors of production—unskilled and skilled labor—and there are fixed input-output coefficients.[9] Hence,

$$\mathbf{V} = \begin{bmatrix} L \\ H \end{bmatrix}, \quad \mathbf{w}_f = \begin{bmatrix} w \\ r \end{bmatrix}, \quad \mathbf{a}_z(\mathbf{w}_f) = \begin{bmatrix} a_{Lz} \\ a_{Hz} \end{bmatrix} \qquad \text{for z} = n, x, y,$$

where L stands for unskilled labor and H stands for human capital, which is our measure of skilled labor. We assume that the traditional sector is the least human capital intensive and that the overall human capital to labor ratio satisfies $a_{Hy}/a_{Ly} < H/L < a_{Hj}/a_{Lj}$ for $j = x$, n. The latter assumption is needed to ensure full employment.

The comparative statics analysis of (7), (10), (12), (14), (16), and (17) that is executed in the appendix shows that the function $v(E)$ is declining for this case. Therefore, the dynamic path is as described in figure 1; the number of available brands and expenditure are increasing over time. This in turn implies that the level of R&D activity is declining through time, as well as the following price and quantity dynamics (see the appendix for a proof).[10]

PROPOSITION 1 (a) $\dot{w}/w > \dot{p}_y/p_y > \dot{p}/p > \dot{r}/r$; (b) $\dot{p}_y > 0$; (c) $\dot{r} < 0$; (d) $\dot{p} > 0$ if and only if $a_{Hn}/a_{Ln} > a_{Hx}/a_{Lx}$; (e) $\partial\dot{n}/\partial t < 0$; (f) $\dot{X} > 0$; (g) $\dot{Y} < 0$; if and only if $a_{Hn}/a_{Ln} > a_{Hx}/a_{Lx}$; and (h) $\dot{E} > 0$.

We see that the real wage (of unskilled labor) is rising and the real reward to human capital is falling through time. This statement refers, however, only to the standard method of measuring real incomes. Since in this type of an environment variety is valued per se (see Helpman and Krugman 1985, ch. 6) and the available variety increases over time, real incomes of unskilled workers necessarily increase but real incomes of skilled workers need not decline.[11] The product development sector contracts while the production of industrial goods expands. The decline in R&D can be understood intuitively as follows. At least in the neighborhood of the steady state, demand for each individual variety and hence profitability in the industrial sector decline over time (see sec. 4). As the profit rate falls, the (real) interest rate must fall as well if entrepreneurs are to be willing to invest in innovation. But as long as the interest rate remains above the discount rate, spending is rising, and resources must be released from the R&D sector to satisfy the increased consumer demand. The process stops when the profit rate has fallen to the level of the discount rate, at which time spending ceases to grow, but then consumers spend all their income and no savings exist to finance further innovation.

3 The Pattern of Trade in a Two-Country World

We suppose now that the world consists of two countries, labeled A and B. The two countries share common tastes and technologies identical to those specified for the integrated economy. We allow for the existence of integrated world commodity and financial markets but assume that factor services and "blueprints" are not tradable. In this section we assume as well that an entrepreneur cannot establish production facilities offshore; we relax this assumption in the next section to allow for the emergence of multinational corporations. We ask first whether, with trade, the world equilibrium replicates that of the integrated economy, as described in section 2. In other words, we consider the conditions under which factor-price equalization characterizes the trade equilibrium. Then, for those cross-country divisions of H and L that indeed are consistent with factor-price equalization everywhere along the equilibrium path, we describe the evolution of world trade.

Consider figure 2. The dimensions of the rectangle in the figure represent worldwide factor endowments, with the division of these endowments between countries represented by a point such as E in the interior of the rectangle. For concreteness,

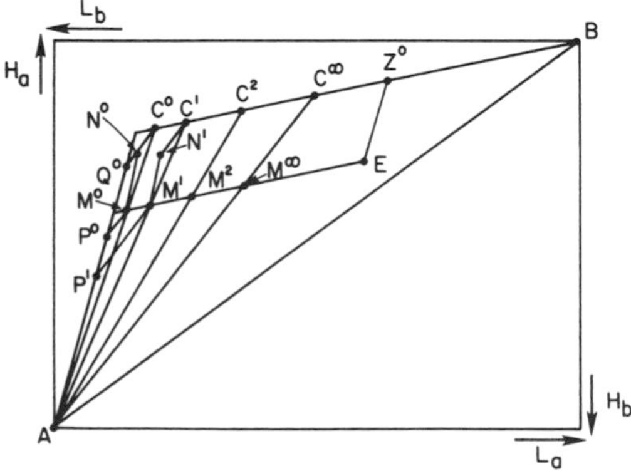

Figure 2

we suppose that country A is the relatively human capital–rich country, that is, $H_a/L_a > H_b/L_b$.

At time $t = 0$, the resource allocation of the integrated equilibrium is found by substituting $E(0)$ and $n(0) = 0$ from the equilibrium trajectory into (7), (10), (12), (14), (16), (17), and (18) and solving for $\dot{n}(0)$, $X(0)$, and $Y(0)$.[12] Let points Q^0 and C^0 in the figure represent this allocation, where vector AQ^0 is employed in R&D, Q^0C^0 is employed in the modern sector, and C^0B is employed in the traditional sector (and the slopes of these vectors correspond to the factor proportions required in each of these activities). The allocation of the integrated equilibrium can be achieved in a two-country world as long as it is possible to decompose the industry employment vectors into nonnegative components for each country that exhaust their separate endowments. In the figure, this is accomplished with employment vectors $AM^0(= AP^0 + P^0M^0)$ and M^0E in country A and vectors EZ^0 $(=M^0N^0 + N^0C^0)$ and Z^0B in country B. Evidently, the feasibility of such a decomposition requires that point E be in the interior of the triangle AC^0B. A sufficient condition for this is $a_{Hn}/a_{Ln} > H_a/L_a > H_bL_b > a_{Hy}/a_{Ly}$.

In the steady state, R&D ceases, and all resources are devoted to production. Let point C^∞ represent the allocation of resources to the two productive sectors in the steady-state equilibrium of the integrated economy. In the diagram, we depict the case in which R&D is more human capital intensive than production of the differentiated products. In any event, the allocation at point C^∞ can be decomposed into feasible allocations for the two countries provided that $a_{Hx}/a_{Lx} > H_a/L_a > H_b/L_b > a_{Hy}/a_{Ly}$. In the figure, this decomposition is achieved by allocating in country A the vector of factors AM^∞ to the production of modern goods and the vector $M^\infty E$ to the production of y.[13] Finally, consider allocations at times between $t = 0$ and $t = \infty$. Points C^1 and C^2 represent sectoral allocations for the equilibrium of the integrated economy. Each such point can be viewed as an allocation of some factors to industry y and some factors to the combined activity of development and production of modern goods. The latter composite activity requires factors in proportions intermediate to the requirements for the two component activities. It follows that if it is feasible to decompose the employment vectors of the integrated economy corresponding to the initial allocation and the steady-state allocation, then it will also be possible to do so for all times between these extremes. A sufficient condition for factor-price equalization to obtain all along the path of the trade equilibrium is that the human capital to labor ratios of the two countries be bounded by the factor intensities of (1) the less human capital–intensive activity among R&D and production of differentiated products, and (2) the production of good y. For the remainder of this section, we shall assume that this condition is satisfied.

At an arbitrary point in time, the full employment conditions for a single country can be represented with the help of (14)–(17) as

$$L_i = a_{Ly}Y_i + a_{Lx}\frac{s_xE}{np}n_i + a_{Ln}\dot{n}_i \tag{19}$$

and

$$H_i = a_{Hy} Y_i + a_{Hx} \frac{s_x E}{np} n_i + a_{Hn} \dot{n}_i, \tag{20}$$

for $i = a, b$. Combining these two equations and eliminating Y_i, we have

$$\dot{n}_i + b(t) n_i = k_i,$$

where

$$k_i = \frac{L_i[(H_i/L_i) - (a_{Hy}/a_{Ly})]}{a_{Ln}[(a_{Hn}/a_{Ln}) - (a_{Hy}/a_{Ly})]}, \qquad \text{for } i = a, b,$$

$$b(t) = \frac{a_{Lx}[(a_{Hx}/a_{Lx}) - (a_{Hy}/a_{Ly})]}{a_{Ln}[(a_{Hn}/a_{Ln}) - (a_{Hy}/a_{Ly})]} \frac{s_x E(t)}{n(t)p(t)},$$

and the functions $E(t)$, $p(t)$, and $n(t)$ are taken from the integrated world equilibrium. This differential equation can be solved explicitly, which gives

$$n_i(t) = k_i \int_0^t e^{-\int_z^t b(\tau)\, d\tau}\, dz. \tag{21}$$

In writing (21), we have set $n_i(0) = 0$.

An important conclusion emerges from equation (21): the ratio of the numbers of differentiated goods produced in either country is constant for all t. We see that $n_a(t)/n_b(t) = k_a/k_b$. Then the ratio of R&D activity in the two countries, $\dot{n}_a/\dot{n}_b$, is also constant and equal to k_a/k_b, as is the ratio of the total outputs of modern goods, X_a/X_b.[14]

These features of the trade equilibrium can also be seen from figure 2. Recall that the points M^0, M^1, M^2, and M^∞ represent allocations of factors in country A to the composite activity of R&D and the production of differentiated goods in the two-country equilibrium. These points all lie on a straight line through E with slope a_{Hy}/a_{Ly}. We can further decompose these allocations into vectors of factors employed in the component industries. For example, at time 1 (corresponding to global allocation C^1), country A employs the vector of factors AP^1 in R&D and the vector P^1M^1 in the production of differentiated products, while country B employs M^1N^1 in R&D and N^1C^1 in producing modern goods. The corresponding points for time 2 are shown in figure 3, where we have enlarged the relevant portion of figure 2. In figure 3, the triangles AP^1M^1 and $M^1N^1C^1$ are similar triangles, as are the triangles AP^2M^2 and $M^2N^2C^2$. Thus, at each moment in time, the ratio of investments in R&D in the two countries equals the ratio of their total outputs of differentiated products. Finally, because M^1M^2 is parallel to C^1C^2, both of these ratios must remain constant through time.

We are now prepared to investigate the evolution of the pattern of trade. Consider first the direction of trade in traditional goods at some arbitrary time t. From equations (19) and (20) we can solve for the ratio of outputs, which is given by

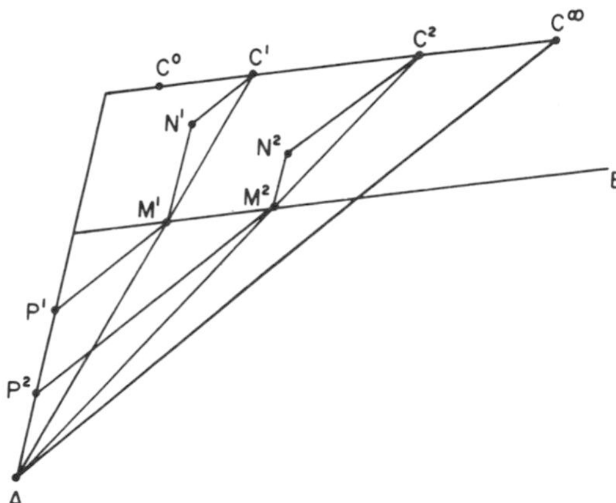

Figure 3

$$\frac{Y_a(t)}{Y_b(t)} = \frac{L_a[h_c(t) - (H_a/L_a)]}{L_b[h_c(t) - (H_b/L_b)]},$$

where $h_c(t)$ is the human capital to labor ratio in the composite activity of R&D and production of the modern goods. Since h_c is a weighted average of the human capital intensities of the two component activities, it is bounded by $h_n \equiv a_{Hn}/a_{Ln}$ and $h_x \equiv a_{Hx}/a_{Lx}$. But each of these exceeds $h_i \equiv H_i/L_i$ under the conditions needed for factor-price equalization, so $h_c(t) - (H_b/L_b) > h_c(t) - (H_a/L_a) > 0$. It follows that $Y_a(t)/Y_b(t) < L_a/L_b$.

Next we calculate the ratio of demands for the traditional good. In each country, expenditure on good y is a constant fraction of total expenditure. Since consumers in both countries face the same price for the good, the ratio of aggregate demands is equal to the ratio of total expenditures. Now, from (5), $E_i(t) = E_i(0)e^{R(t)-\rho t}$, so $E_a(t)/E_b(t) = E_a(0)/E_b(0)$. This ratio is, in turn, equal to the ratio of initial wealth levels, that is,

$$\frac{E_a(0)}{E_b(0)} = \frac{L_a \int_0^\infty e^{-R(t)}[w(t) + r(t)h_a]\,dt}{L_b \int_0^\infty e^{-R(t)}[w(t) + r(t)h_b]\,dt}. \tag{22}$$

Note that the ratio of initial wealth levels on the right-hand side of (22) includes only factor incomes because initial asset holdings are zero and assets acquired along the path earn no excess returns.

Equation (22) and $h_a/h_b > 1$ together imply $E_a(0)/E_b(0) > L_a/L_b$. Thus the ratio of demands for good y, $c_{ya}(t)/c_{yb}(t)$, also exceeds L_a/L_b. Since $Y_a(t)/Y_b(t) < L_a/L_b$, it follows immediately that $c_{ya}(t)/c_{yb}(t) > Y_a(t)/Y_b(t)$. But $c_{ya}(t) + c_{yb}(t) = Y_a(t) + Y_b(t)$ by market clearing, implying $c_{ya}(t) > Y_a(t)$, as stated in the following proposition.

PROPOSITION 2 The human capital–rich country imports the labor-intensive, traditional good at every moment in time.

It is not surprising, of course, that factor endowments should play a major role in determining the direction of trade in traditional goods. What is surprising, perhaps, is that neither the diversion of resources to R&D nor the existence of aggregate trade imbalances can upset the strong prediction of the Heckscher-Ohlin theorem at any point along the equilibrium path.

We establish a similar result for trade in differentiated products. Each differentiated product is manufactured in only one country, yet each is consumed worldwide, so the direction of trade in the individual products is clear-cut. The existence of such intra-industry trade features prominently in the static models of trade with increasing returns to scale. We focus here on the aggregate pattern of trade for the sector as a whole. We have already shown that X_a/X_b is constant over time. So too is C_{xa}/C_{xb}, where $C_{xi} \equiv nc_{xi}$. This ratio, like that for consumption of good y, equals the ratio of initial wealth levels in the two countries. Now if $C_{xa}/C_{xb} > X_a/X_b$, this would imply that country A imports both goods *for all t*. But such an outcome would violate the (aggregate) intertemporal budget constraint (4). We conclude, therefore, that $C_{xa}/C_{xb} < X_a/X_b$, as recorded in the following proposition.

PROPOSITION 3 The human capital–rich country is a net exporter of differentiated products at every moment in time.

Next we consider the volume of trade, which is defined as the sum of exports across countries and industries. In our case, it is given by

$$VT = p_y(Y_b - s_b Y) + s_a p X_b + s_b p X_a$$

where $s_i (i = a, b)$ is the share of country i in spending, and $X_i = n_i x$ is country i's output of manufactures. Dividing by world spending and rearranging, we obtain

$$\frac{VT}{E} = (1 - s_x)\left(\frac{Y_b}{Y} - s_b\right) + s_x\left(s_a \frac{X_b}{X} + s_b \frac{X_a}{X}\right), \tag{23}$$

where X and Y are the aggregate output levels for the world economy. The second term on the right-hand side is constant on the dynamic trajectory. The first term changes as a result of shifts in country B's share of output of traditional goods. When R&D is human capital intensive relative to production of differentiated products, Y_b/Y rises through time and the volume of trade rises faster than spending. In addition, because of declining investment, the ratio of world spending to world GNP increases over time. Hence, we have established the following proposition.

PROPOSITION 4 If product development is human capital intensive relative to production of differentiated products, the volume of world trade grows faster than world spending and GNP.

Finally, we consider the pattern of intertemporal trade. Aggregate national savings (the difference between GNP and total expenditure) are used to accumulate foreign assets. We may think of these assets as ownership shares in firms, in which case current account imbalances give rise to foreign equity ownership. Or we may think instead that international trade takes place in short-term bonds, with all firms owned by local residents. The two forms of portfolio trade are equivalent here, as is clear from the fact that the profit rate equals the instantaneous interest rate (see [11]).

There are two offsetting influences at work in determining the current account. On the one hand, the human capital–rich country undertakes relatively more investment in product development than would be predicted on the basis of its relative size alone. This excess of investment demand tends to create a current account deficit for this country. On the other hand, the reward to human capital is falling over time, while the wage rate of unskilled workers is rising, so that the human capital–rich country experiences a decline in its relative factor income. This effect alone should lead country A to save a relatively greater share of its income, at least early on. For these reasons, it seems possible that the human capital–rich country may be running either a deficit or a surplus on its current account. We have not been able to establish any analytical results that prove otherwise.

4 Multinational Corporations

Our analysis to this point has maintained an assumption that every brand must be produced in the country in which it was originally developed. This requirement excludes the possibilities of international licensing and multinational investment. Naturally, under the conditions of the previous section, entrepreneurs have no incentive to license and firms have no incentive to become multinational. Suppose, however, that R&D requires more human capital per unskilled labor than production of industrial goods and that country A's human capital to unskilled labor ratio is larger than factor proportions observed in the industrial sector. In terms of figure 2, this means that point E lies above the ray AC^{∞}. Then the integrated equilibrium cannot be replicated by commodity trade without either licensing or the emergence of multinational corporations. In what follows we explore the latter possibility.

Following Helpman (1984), we assume that production of a variety comprises two distinct activities that can be decomposed, so that headquarter services can be located in one country while actual manufacturing takes place in another. For simplicity we assume that headquarter services are produced with human capital and that production plants use these services and unskilled labor only.[15] Suppose also that headquarter services must be provided in the country in which a brand was developed. Then the integrated equilibrium can be reproduced even when the endowment point E is above AC^{∞} in figure 2. The resulting allocation patterns are shown in figure 4 for the case in which the extent of multinationality is minimal (see Helpman 1984 for a discussion of this assumption).

It is clear from the figure that up to time T_m, at which C^{T_m} represents resource allocation in the integrated equilibrium, there is no pressure for the formation of multinational corporations. However, immediately after this point in time, equality of

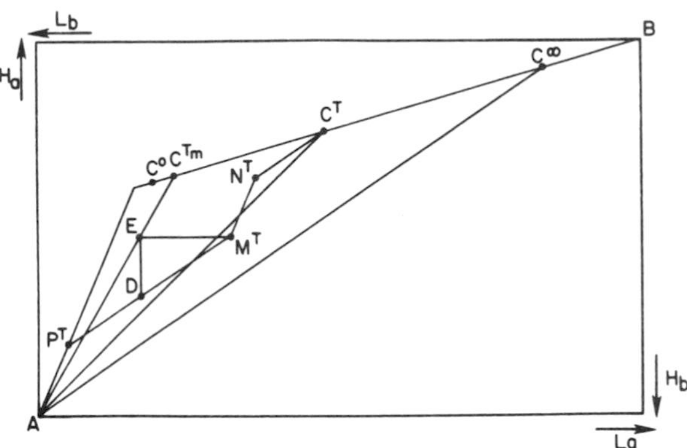

Figure 4

factor rewards cannot be maintained if both activities of industrial firms are concentrated in the same country. This exerts pressure for their separation, with the tendency to locate manufacturing operations in the potentially unskilled labor–cheap country (i.e., country B). At time T the allocation of the integrated equilibrium is described by point C^T in the figure. Its aggregate variables are reproduced by the following allocation in the equilibrium. Country A does not produce the traditional good. It devotes resources AP^{T} to R&D, $P^{\mathrm{T}}D$ to production of industrial products by firms that are not multinational, and DE to the production of headquarter services by its multinationals. Country B devotes resources BC^T to the production of y-goods, $C^{\mathrm{T}}N^{\mathrm{T}}$ to the production of industrial products by domestic firms (which are not multinational), $N^{\mathrm{T}}M^{\mathrm{T}}$ to R&D, and $M^{\mathrm{T}}E$ to production of modern goods in plants owned by country A's multinational corporations.

It is clear from this description that, starting with $t = T_m$, the extent of multinationality—as measured by employment in subsidiaries or their output volume—is increasing at least initially; we have not been able to prove that it is increasing throughout. We can show, however, that the extent of multinationality also increases during the final approach to the steady state. The latter point is seen as follows. The condition of minimal foreign involvement implies that from time T_m, country A does not produce the traditional good. Therefore, after that point in time, its factor market–clearing conditions read as (compare with the discussion of fig. 4)

$$a_{Ln}\dot{n}_a + a_{Lx}(n_a - m)x = L_a, \tag{24}$$

$$a_{Hn}\dot{n}_a + a_{Hx}n_a x = H_a, \tag{25}$$

where m is the number of products produced in foreign subsidiaries and x is output per firm, taken from the integrated world equilibrium.

From (25) we observe that output of modern products is increasing in country A if and only if R&D is declining. Since R&D approaches zero when the steady state is approached, $n_a x$ must be increasing close to the steady state. However, from (24) and

(25) we obtain

$$mx = \frac{L_a}{a_{Lx}h_n}(h_a - h_n) + \frac{1}{h_n}(h_n - h_x)n_a x,$$

which together with the previous result implies that the degree of multinationality increases close to the steady state (recall that $h_n > h_x$ is assumed in this section).

We have shown that the degree of multinationality—as measured by the volume of output or employment in subsidiaries—is increasing when the multinationals start to form and when the economy approaches a steady state. These results can be extended to cover a third definition of the extent of multinationality: the number of varieties produced by subsidiaries. This number obviously is rising initially when the multinationals start to form. That it is also rising close to the steady state we show by proving that x is declining close to the steady state. Since we have already shown that mx is rising, a declining x implies a rising m, that is, an increasing number of varieties produced by subsidiaries.

The proof proceeds as follows. Since the dashed path in figure 1 is above the $\dot{E} = 0$ line, the ratio E/n is declining when the trajectory approaches point $(\bar{n}, \bar{E})$. On the other hand, from part (d) of proposition 1 we know that p is increasing as this point is approached because in this section we require R&D to be more human capital intensive than x. Therefore, $x = s_x E/pn$ is declining close to the steady state. Hence, we have the following proposition.

PROPOSITION 5 If differences in factor composition are wide enough and product development is human capital intensive relative to production of differentiated products, then there exists a time at which multinational corporations emerge. The degree of multinationality—as measured by the number of products produced by subsidiaries, their volume of output, or employment—is rising initially and when the world economy approaches the steady state.

In closing this section we note that the pattern of trade described in the previous section need not hold in the presence of multinationals. It is clear that the direction of trade in traditional goods must be the same as before. However, the pattern of trade in modern goods might change over time. Country A, which begins as a net exporter of differentiated products prior to the emergence of multinationals, may evolve into a net importer of these goods if it ultimately exports a sufficient quantity of headquarter services.

5 Concluding Remarks

We have extended a number of important results in international trade theory to a dynamic environment in which comparative advantage must be developed over time via the allocation of resources to research and development. In our specification, R&D must take place prior to the production of any new variety of a differentiated product.

This R&D is motivated by the stream of profits that accrues to the producer of a differentiated good and is financed by savings that are endogenously determined. When R&D, production of differentiated products, and production of a homogeneous good all require fixed input proportions of two primary factors, then the Heckscher-Ohlin pattern of trade is preserved all along the dynamic path of the trading equilibrium. This is true despite the fact that trade is not balanced along this path. We also established that if product development is human capital intensive relative to production of differentiated products, the volume of trade as a fraction of world GNP or world expenditure grows over time. Finally, for certain factor endowments, we have predicted the emergence of multinational corporations and shown that in these circumstances the extent of multinational activity generally rises over time.

The framework that we have developed here is suitable for the study of additional issues. Our analysis has excluded factor accumulation and has restricted attention to horizontal product differentiation. We plan in future work to consider the interaction between capital investment and technological progress in determining trade dynamics and to study the evolution of trade patterns with vertically differentiated goods and hence endogenous product obsolescence. Perhaps more fundamentally, after slight adaptation of our framework, it becomes possible to study the links between the trade environment (including policy) and long-run rates of growth. We present our initial efforts to understand the relationship between aspects of the international economy and long-run economic performance when product innovation drives growth in Grossman and Helpman (1988).

Appendix

We provide in this appendix a proof of proposition 1 by explicitly calculating expressions for the comovement of six variables with expenditure E. By substituting (16) and (17) into (14) and using the result together with (7), (10), and (12) for the special case considered in section 2—namely, two factors of production and constant coefficients—we obtain the following system:

$$1 = a_{Ln}w + a_{Hn}r, \tag{A1}$$

$$\alpha p = a_{Lx}w + a_{Hx}r, \tag{A2}$$

$$p_y = a_{Ly}w + a_{Hy}r, \tag{A3}$$

$$L = a_{Ln}\dot{n} + a_{Lx}s_x\frac{E}{p} + a_{Ly}(1 - s_x)\frac{E}{p_y}, \tag{A4}$$

$$H = a_{Hn}\dot{n} + a_{Hx}s_x\frac{E}{p} + a_{Hy}(1 - s_x)\frac{E}{p_y}, \tag{A5}$$

where w is the reward to unskilled labor and r is the reward to human capital. This system enables us to solve $(w, r, p, p_y, \dot{n})$ as functions of E. In what follows, we calculate the proportional rate of change of each one of these variables in response to a proportional change in expenditure of $\hat{E} \equiv dE/E = 1$; a circumflex over a variable indicates a proportional rate of change. The following expressions use the standard notation; that is, θ_{ij} is the share of input i in the cost of activity j and λ_{ij} is the share of factor i employed in activity j:

$$\hat{w} = \frac{1}{\Delta}\theta_{Hn}(\lambda_{Hn} - \lambda_{Ln}), \tag{A6}$$

$$\hat{r} = \frac{1}{\Delta}\theta_{Ln}(\lambda_{Ln} - \lambda_{Hn}), \tag{A7}$$

$$\hat{p} = \frac{1}{\Delta}(\theta_{Lx} - \theta_{Ln})(\lambda_{Hn} - \lambda_{Ln}), \tag{A8}$$

$$\hat{p}_y = \frac{1}{\Delta}(\theta_{Ly} - \theta_{Ln})(\lambda_{Hn} - \lambda_{Ln}), \tag{A9}$$

$$\hat{n} = \frac{1}{\Delta}(\theta_{Ly} - \theta_{Lx})(\lambda_{Lx}\lambda_{Hy} - \lambda_{Ly}\lambda_{Hx}), \tag{A10}$$

where

$$\begin{aligned}\Delta = {} & (\theta_{Lx} - \theta_{Ln})(\lambda_{Lx}\lambda_{Hn} - \lambda_{Ln}\lambda_{Hx}) \\ & + (\theta_{Ly} - \theta_{Ln})(\lambda_{Ly}\lambda_{Hn} - \lambda_{Ln}\lambda_{Hy}).\end{aligned} \tag{A11}$$

From the definition of Δ, we have $\Delta > 0$ because $(\theta_{Li} - \theta_{Lj})$ is of the same sign as $(\lambda_{Li}\lambda_{Hj} - \lambda_{Lj}\lambda_{Hi})$, being positive when i is labor intensive relative to j and negative when i is human capital intensive relative to j. We have assumed that $a_{Hy}/a_{Ly} < H/L < a_{Hi}/a_{Li}$, $i = x, n$, which implies

$$\lambda_{Hy} - \lambda_{Ly} < 0, \tag{A12a}$$

$$\lambda_{Hi} - \lambda_{Li} > 0 \qquad \text{for } i = x, n. \tag{A12b}$$

Condition (A12b) proves parts (b) and (c) of proposition 1, given part (h), which is proved in the text. From (A6) and (A9), we obtain

$$\hat{w} - \hat{p}_y = \frac{1}{\Delta}\theta_{Hy}(\lambda_{Hn} - \lambda_{Ln}); \tag{A13}$$

from (A8) and (A9), we obtain

$$\hat{p}_y - \hat{p} = \frac{1}{\Delta}(\theta_{Ly} - \theta_{Lx})(\lambda_{Hn} - \lambda_{Ln}); \tag{A14}$$

and from (A7) and (A8), we obtain

$$\hat{p} - \hat{r} = \frac{1}{\Delta}\theta_{Lx}(\lambda_{Hn} - \lambda_{Ln}). \tag{A15}$$

Equations (A13)–(A15) together with (A12b), part (*h*), and the assumption that y is labor intensive relative to x—which implies $\theta_{Ly} > \theta_{Lx}$—prove part (a) of the proposition. Part (d) is a direct consequence of part (h), (A8), and (A12b). Part (e) is a direct consequence of (A10) and part (h). Moreover, (A10) proves that the function $v(E)$ is declining because the right-hand side of (A10) is negative.

From (16) and (17) we have $\hat{X} = \hat{E} - \hat{p}$ and $\hat{Y} = \hat{E} - \hat{p}_y$. Using these expressions, $\hat{E} = 1$, as well as (A8), (A9), and (A11), we obtain

$$\hat{X} = \frac{1}{\Delta}(\theta_{Ly} - \theta_{Lx})(\lambda_{Ly}\lambda_{Hn} - \lambda_{Ln}\lambda_{Hy}) \tag{A16}$$

and

$$\hat{Y} = \frac{1}{\Delta}(\theta_{Ly} - \theta_{Lx})(\lambda_{Ln}\lambda_{Hx} - \lambda_{Lx}\lambda_{Hn}). \tag{A17}$$

Equations (A12a) and (A12b), together with the assumption that y is labor intensive relative to x, imply that the right-hand side of (A16) is positive. This together with part (h) proves part (f) of the proposition. From (A17), it is evident that, given that y is labor intensive relative to x, the right-hand side is positive if and only if n is labor intensive relative to x, which together with part (h) proves part (g).

Notes

Grossman's research was supported by the Alfred P. Sloan Foundation and the National Science Foundation under grant SES-8606336. Helpman's research was supported by the Bank of Sweden Tercentenary Foundation. He thanks the Department of Economics at the Massachusetts Institute of Technology for providing a hospitable research environment. We are grateful to Itzhak Zilcha for helpful discussions and to Avinash Dixit and Carl Shapiro for comments on an earlier draft.

1. More specifically, Krugman posits exogenous rates of product innovation and imitation to study the determinants of steady-state wages and welfare in a one-sector model of the product cycle. Dollar improves on Krugman's work by allowing the rate of imitation to depend on manufacturing cost differentials. His relationship is essentially ad hoc, and he maintains Krugman's assumption that the rate of product innovation is exogenous. These authors do not consider the resource costs of innovation and imitation, nor do they allow for intertemporal profitability considerations. Jensen and Thursby do allow R&D to be determined by intertemporal profit maximization, but they assume that there is a single, monopolistic developer and that the interest rate is exogenous and constant. None of these studies, or any other with which we are familiar, devotes much attention to the evolution of the pattern of trade along the path to a steady state, which is our primary concern here.

2. The model studied by Segerstrom, Anant, and Dinopoulos (1987) does have the feature that improved products cause older variants to disappear, but the analysis focuses only on the steady-state properties of the equilibrium.

3. See Helpman and Krugman (1985, ch. 6) for more details.

4. This can be seen as follows. The indirect utility function derived from (2) has the form $v[p(t), E(t)] = E(t)f(p(t))$. Then $\log v(\cdot) = \log E(t) + \log f(p(t))$, and the first-order condition for maximization of (1) implies $e^{-\rho t}/E(t) = \zeta e^{-R(t)}$, where ζ is the time-independent Lagrange multiplier associated with the budget constraint in (4).

5. An implicit assumption here is that product development does not require finite time. We could relax this assumption without substantially affecting the structure of the model.

6. For the special case that we consider in the next subsection, we establish that the stability condition is always satisfied.

7. Suppose that $\dot{n} = 0$, and consider the system of equilibrium conditions comprising (7), (10), (12), (14), (16), and (17). These are $5 + k$ equations in $5 + k$ unknowns, where k is the number of factors of production. The unknowns in this system are the k factor rewards, two prices for final consumer goods, two aggregate output levels for the final-goods sectors, and the expenditure level. Naturally, the solution for the expenditure level in this system is $\bar{E}$. Thus $\dot{n} = 0$ in equilibrium implies $E = \bar{E}$, and the system can be only on or below the horizontal line in the figure.

8. If the initial number of products exceeds $\bar{n}$, the economy settles immediately at a stationary state, with the number of varieties and all real magnitudes forever constant. In what follows, attention is focused on the case in which the initial number of products is smaller than $\bar{n}$.

9. While our approach remains valid for more general production functions than the Leontief technology, the dynamics that result are considerably more complicated than here. We have so far been unable to derive interesting results about trade dynamics for the general case.

10. In deriving our comparative statics results, we have assumed that full employment of both factors obtains all along the equilibrium trajectory. As is well known, even in static models, full employment is not guaranteed for fixed-coefficient production functions. In the steady state of our dynamic system we have an essentially static two-sector model (because R&D is zero) with a piecewise-linear, kinked transformation curve. Full employment then requires restrictions on the parameters of the utility function so that the slope of the indifference curve at the kink, adjusted for the degree of monopoly power $1/\alpha$, falls between the slopes of the flat portions of the transformation curve. Put differently, full employment obtains in the steady state if, for $E = \bar{E}$, the solution to the system of equations (7), (10), (12), (14), (16), (17), and (18) yields nonnegative factor rewards. We also require nonnegative values of the factor rewards when the system is solved with $E = E(0)$. These two conditions at the endpoints ensure full employment and nonnegative factor rewards along the entire equilibrium trajectory since the wage rate is rising and the reward to human capital is falling whenever there is full employment (see parts (a), (b), and (c) of proposition 1). If these conditions are not met, however, there may be unemployment of unskilled labor during an initial phase of the dynamic equilibrium, unemployment of human capital during an ultimate stage, or both.

11. The temporal indirect utility function of a representative agent is calculated to be

$$\text{constant} + s_x(\alpha^{-1} - 1)\log n + \log I - [s_x \log p + (1 - s_x)\log p_y],$$

where I is his income. The last two terms represent the usual real income component, where the last term represents the deflator. It is clear from part (a) of proposition 1 that this real income component is rising for unskilled workers and falling for skilled workers. However, apart from this component, there exists the term with n, which represents the love-of-variety effect. This real income component is rising as a result of expanding variety.

12. The system of equations that determines resource allocations, commodity prices, and factor rewards yields a solution for $X(0)$ that is strictly positive when $E = E(0)$, despite the fact that $n(0) = 0$. Strictly positive consumption of both classes of goods is dictated by the Cobb-Douglas form of the subutility function. It requires, of course, that $x(t) \to \infty$ as $t \to 0$ from above. Although our model breaks down at $t = 0$, it is well behaved in the limit as $t \to 0$ from above. Therefore, we feel justified in ignoring the technical problems that arise at time 0.

13. We must show further that this proposed allocation of resources to the production of industrial goods in each country is consistent with the number of products previously developed there since outputs of all varieties are equal in the integrated equilibrium. We establish below that this condition is indeed satisfied for the proposed decomposition.

14. We note that $x(t)$ is common to goods produced in both countries because factor-price equalization implies equal prices of the different differentiated goods, and thus equal amounts of these goods are demanded by consumers. Since $X_i(t) = n_i(t)x(t)$, the last statement follows.

15. It is easy to see how the analysis is modified when both activities require human capital and unskilled labor, as in Helpman and Krugman (1985, ch. 12).

References

Dixit, Avinash K., and Victor D. Norman. 1980. *Theory of International Trade: A Dual, General Equilibrium Approach.* Cambridge: Cambridge University Press.

Dollar, David. 1986. Technological innovation, capital mobility, and the product cycle in the North-South trade. *American Economic Review* 76:177–190.

Feenstra, Robert C., and Kenneth L. Judd. 1982. Tariffs, technology transfer, and welfare. *Journal of Political Economy* 90:1142–1165.

Grossman, Gene M., and Elhanan Helpman. 1988. Comparative advantage and long-run growth. Discussion Paper in Economics no. 142. Princeton, N.J.: Princeton University, Woodrow Wilson School.

Helpman, Elhanan. 1984. A simple theory of international trade with multinational corporations. *Journal of Political Economy* 92:451–471.

Helpman, Elhanan, and Paul R. Krugman. 1985. *Market Structure and Foreign Trade: Increasing Returns, Imperfect Competition, and the International Economy*. Cambridge, Mass.: MIT Press.

Jensen, Richard, and Marie A. Thursby. 1987. Decision theoretical model of innovation, technology transfer, and trade. *Review of Economic Studies* 54:631–647.

Judd, Kenneth L. 1985. On the performance of patents. *Econometrica* 53:567–585.

Krugman, Paul R. 1979a. Increasing returns, monopolistic competition, and international trade. *Journal of International Economics* 9:469–479.

Krugman, Paul R. 1979b. A model of innovation, technology transfer, and the world distribution of income. *Journal of Political Economy* 87:253–266.

Krugman, Paul R. 1981. Intraindustry specialization and the gains from trade. *Journal of Political Economy* 89:959–973.

Segerstrom, Paul, S., T. C. A. Anant, and Elias Dinopoulos. 1987. A Schumpeterian model of the product life cycle. Econometrics and Economic Theory paper no. 8606. East Lansing: Michigan State University.

18 Economic Integration and Endogenous Growth

Luis A. Rivera-Batiz and Paul M. Romer

1 Introduction

Many economists believe that increased economic integration between the developed economies of the world has tended to increase the long-run rate of economic growth. If they were asked to make an intuitive prediction, they would suggest that prospects for growth would be permanently diminished if a barrier were erected that impeded the flow of all goods, ideas, and people between Asia, Europe, and North America. Yet it would be difficult for any of us to offer a rigorous model that has been (or even could be) calibrated to data and that could justify this belief.

We know what some of the basic elements of such a growth model would be. Historical analysis (e.g., Rosenberg 1980) shows that the creation and transmission of ideas has been extremely important in the development of modern standards of living. Theoretical arguments dating from Adam Smith's analysis of the pin factory have emphasized the potential importance of fixed costs and the extent of the market. There is a long tradition in trade theory of using models with Marshallian external effects to approach questions about increasing returns. More recently, static models with fixed costs and international specialization have been proposed that come closer to Smith's description of the sources of the gains from trade (Dixit and Norman 1980; Ethier 1982; Krugman 1979, 1981; Lancaster 1980). There are also dynamic models with fixed costs and differentiated products in which output grows toward a fixed steady state level (Grossman and Helpman, 1989a).

Recent models of endogenous growth have used these ideas to study the effects that trade can have on the long-run rate of growth. (See, for example, the theoretical papers by Dinopoulos, Oehmke, and Segerstrom 1990; Feenstra 1990; Grossman and Helpman 1989b, 1989c, 1989d, 1989e, 1990; Krugman 1990, ch. 11; Lucas 1988; Romer 1990; Segerstrom, Anant, and Dinopoulos 1990; and Young 1991. Backus, Kehoe, and Kehoe 1991 present both theoretical models and cross-country empirical evidence that bears on their models.) These models permit a distinction between a one-shot gain (i.e., a level effect) and a permanent change in the growth rate (i.e., a growth effect) that is extremely important in making an order of magnitude estimate of the benefits of economic integration. Conventional attempts to quantify the effects of integration using the neoclassical growth model often suggest that the gains from integration are small. If these estimates were calculated in the context of an endogenous growth model, integration might be found to be much more important.

The papers written so far have already demonstrated, however, that the growth effects of trade restrictions are very complicated in the most general case. Grossman and Helpman (1989b, 1989c, 1989e, 1990) have been particularly explicit about the fact

Originally published in the *Quarterly Journal of Economics* 106 (May 1991): 531–556.

that no universally applicable conclusions can be drawn. There are some models in which trade restrictions can slow down the worldwide rate of growth. There are others in which they can speed up the worldwide rate of growth.

To provide some intuition for the conjecture described in the first paragraph, that trade between the advanced countries does foster growth, we narrow the focus in this paper. We do not consider the general case of trade between countries with different endowments and technologies. Instead, we focus on the pure scale effects of integration. To set aside the other "comparative advantage" effects that trade induces in multisector trade models, we consider integration only between countries or regions that are similar. Therefore, we do not address the kinds of questions that are relevant for modeling the effects that trade between a poor LDC and a developed country can have on the worldwide rate of growth.

In the early stages of our analysis of integration and growth, it became clear that the theoretical treatment of ideas has a decisive effect on the conclusions one draws. In many of the existing models, flows of ideas cannot be separated from flows of goods. In others, flows of ideas are exogenously limited by national boundaries regardless of the trade regime. In either of these cases, economic integration can refer only to flows of goods along cargo networks. We consider a broader notion of integration, one that assigns an effect to flows of ideas along communication networks.

Flows of ideas deserve attention comparable to that devoted to flows of goods, for public policy can influence international communications and information flows to the same extent that it influences goods flows. Governments often subsidize language training and study abroad. Tax policies directly affect the incentive to station company employees in foreign nations. Immigration and visa policies directly limit the movement of people. Telecommunications networks are either run by government agencies or controlled by regulators. Some governments restrict direct foreign investment, which presumably is important in the international transmission of ideas. Others have made the acquisition of commercial and technical information a high-priority task for their intelligence agencies.

Although these are the only ones we consider, it should be clear that flows of goods and flows of ideas are not the only elements in economic integration. Under some assumptions about nominal variables and the operation of financial markets, economic integration will also depend on monetary and institutional arrangements. The growth models we consider are too simple to consider these effects. It should also be clear that economic integration is not synonymous with political integration. Firms in Windsor, Ontario, may be more closely integrated into markets in the United States than they are to markets in the neighboring province of Quebec. Moreover, the notion of full economic integration does not entail the abolition of citizenship distinctions that has taken place in Germany's reunification.

The structure of the paper is as follows. Section 2 lays out the basic features of the production structure on which all arguments rely. It describes preferences, endowments, and the nature of equilibrium under the two specifications of R&D. Section 3 describes the equilibrium for both models in the closed economy and complete integration cases, and illustrates the scale effects that are present. Section 4 presents the three main thought experiments concerning partial integration. Sections 5 and 6 describe the general lessons that can be learned about the relation between the scale of the market and growth and discuss limitations of the models, extensions, and the relation to other models of endogenous growth.

2 Specification of the Models

Functional Forms and Decentralization in the Manufacturing Sector

The specification of the production technology for the manufacturing sector is taken from Romer (1990). Manufacturing output is a function of human capital H, labor L, and a set $x(i)$ of capital goods indexed by the variable i. To avoid complications arising from integer constraints, the index i is modeled as a continuous variable. Technological progress is represented by the invention of new types of capital goods.

There are two types of manufacturing activities: production of consumption goods and production of the physical units of the types of capital goods that have already been invented. A third activity, research and development (R&D), creates designs for new types of capital goods. This activity is discussed in the next section.

Both manufacturing activities use the same production function. Let $x(i)$ denote the stock of capital of type i that is used in production, and let A be the index of the most recently invented good. By the definition of A, $x(i) = 0$ for all $i > A$. Output Y is assumed to take the form

$$Y(H, L, x(\cdot)) = H^{\alpha} L^{\beta} \int_{0}^{A} x(i)^{1-\alpha-\beta}\, di. \tag{1}$$

Since the production function for manufacturing consumption goods is the same as that for manufacturing units of any type of existing capital, the relative prices of consumption goods and all types of existing capital goods are fixed by the technology. For simplicity, we choose units so that all of these relative prices are one. Fixed prices imply that the aggregate capital stock $K = \int_0^A x(i)\, di$ is well defined, as is aggregate output Y.

In this specification one unit of any capital good can be produced if one unit of consumption goods is forgone. This does not mean that consumption goods are directly converted into capital goods. Rather, the inputs needed to produce one unit of consumption are shifted from the production of consumption goods into the production of a capital good. Since inputs are used in the same proportions, it is easy to infer the allocation of inputs between the different production activities from the level of output of those activities. Because all the outputs here have the same production function, the consumption sector and all of the sectors producing the different capital goods can be collapsed into a single sector. We can therefore represent total manufacturing output as a function of the total stock of inputs used in the combined manufacturing sectors and can describe the division of inputs between sectors by the constraint $Y = C + K$. For one of the models of R&D described in the next section, we can use this same observation to combine the research sector and the aggregate manufacturing sector into a single sector describing all output in the economy. In the other model the R&D and manufacturing sectors must be kept separate.

There are many equivalent institutional structures that can support a decentralized equilibrium in manufacturing. For instance, the holder of a patent on good j could become a manufacturer, producing and selling good j. Alternatively, the patent holder could license the design to other manufacturers for a fee. Formally, it is useful to separate the manufacturing decision from the monopoly pricing decision of the patent holder, so we assume that patent holders contract out manufacturing to separate firms. It is also easier to assume that the patent holder collects rent on its capital goods rather than selling them. For analytical convenience, we therefore describe the institutional arrangements in the following, slightly artificial way. First, there are many firms that rent capital goods $x(i)$ from the patent holders, hire unskilled labor L, and employ skilled human capital H to produce manufactured goods. Each of these firms can produce consumption goods for sale to consumers. It can also produce one of the capital goods on contract for the holder of the patent. All of the manufacturing firms have the production function given in equation (1), which is homogeneous of degree one. They are price takers and earn zero profit. Manufacturing output is taken as the numeraire.

The firm that holds the patent on good j bids out the production of the actual capital goods to a specific manufacturer. It purchases physical units of the good for the competitive price, by normalization equal to one. The patent holder then rents out the units to all manufacturing firms at the profit-maximizing monopoly rental rate. It can do this because patent law prohibits any firm from manufacturing a capital good without the consent of the patent holder. The patent is a tradable asset with a price of P_A that is equal to the present discounted value of the stream of monopoly rent minus the cost of the machines. It is easy to verify that this set of institutional arrangements is equivalent to other arrangements. For example, the equivalent licensing fee for each unit of capital sold by a licensee is the present value of the stream of monopoly rent on one machine minus the unit cost of manufacturing it.

Functional Forms and Decentralization in R&D

We consider two specifications of the technology of R&D that permit easy analytic solutions. Each specification captures different features of the world, and neither alone gives a complete description of R&D. We use both of them because they help us isolate the exact sense in which economic integration can influence long-run growth. As the example in the next section shows, it would be easy to come to misleading conclusions about integration and growth if one generalized from a single example.

The first specification of the technology for producing designs for new capital goods assumes that human capital and knowledge are the only inputs that influence the output of designs:

$$\dot{A} = \delta H A, \tag{2}$$

where H denotes the stock of human capital used in research. The stock of existing designs A is a measure of general scientific and engineering knowledge as well as practical know-how that accumulated as previous design problems were solved. (See Romer 1990 for additional discussion of this specification.) New designs build on this knowledge, so we refer to this type of R&D process as the knowledge-driven specification of R&D. This specification imposes a sharp factor-intensity difference between R&D and manufacturing. Neither unskilled labor nor physical capital has any value in R&D. Because of this difference, the resulting model must be analyzed using a two-sector framework.

A useful polar case is a technology for R&D that uses the same inputs as the manufacturing technology, in the same proportions. If H, L, and x_i denote inputs used in R&D and B denotes a constant scale factor, output of designs can be written as

$$\dot{A} = BH^{\alpha}L^{\beta}\int_0^A x(i)^{1-\alpha-\beta}\,di. \tag{3}$$

This specification says that human capital, unskilled labor, and capital goods (such as personal computers or oscilloscopes) are productive in research. But in contrast to the previous specification, knowledge per se has no productive value. Access to the designs for all previous goods, and familiarity with the ideas and know-how that they represent, does not aid the creation of new designs. We refer to this as the lab equipment specification of R&D.

As noted above, the growth model with the knowledge-driven specification for R&D has an unavoidable two-sector structure. The production possibility frontier in the space of designs and manufactured goods takes on the usual curved shape. In the lab equipment model the production functions of the goods and R&D sectors are the same, so the production possibility frontier is a straight line. If the output of goods is reduced by one unit and the inputs released are transferred to the R&D sector, they yield B patents. Thus, the price P_A of a patent in terms of goods is determined on the technology side as $P_A = 1/\mathrm{B}$. Since capital goods and consumption goods have the same production technology, we integrated them into a single manufacturing sector in the last section. In the lab equipment model we can go farther and aggregate manufacturing and research into a single sector. Let H, L, and $x(i)$ denote the entire stock of inputs available in the economy at date t. Then we can express the value of total output $C + \dot{K} + \dot{A}/B$ in terms of the total stock of inputs,

$$C + \dot{K} + \frac{\dot{A}}{B} = H^{\alpha}L^{\beta}\int_0^A x(i)^{1-\alpha-\beta}\,di. \tag{4}$$

The model's symmetry implies that $x(i) = x(j)$ for all i and j less than A. We can therefore substitute $K/A = x(i)$ in equation (4) to obtain a reduced-form expression for total output in terms of H, K, L, and A:

$$C + \dot{K} + \frac{\dot{A}}{B} = H^{\alpha}L^{\beta}A\left(\frac{K}{A}\right)^{1-\alpha-\beta}$$

$$= H^{\alpha}L^{\beta}K^{1-\alpha-\beta}A^{\alpha+\beta}. \quad (5)$$

The knowledge-driven and lab equipment specifications of the R&D sector lead to different assumptions about how equilibrium in the R&D sector is decentralized. In the knowledge-driven model, output of designs is homogeneous of degree two. By Euler's theorem it is not possible for both of the inputs A and H to be paid their marginal product. We make the assumption that A receives no compensation. Holders of patents on previous designs have no technological or legal means of preventing designers of new goods from using the ideas implicit in the existing designs. The stock of A that can be put to use, with no compensation, by any individual researcher is therefore the entire stock of knowledge about previous designs, provided that there exists a communication network that makes this information available. The equilibrium is one with knowledge spillovers or external effects in the R&D sector (but not in the manufacturing sector). In this case, we can describe research as if it were done by independent researchers who use their human capital to produce designs, which they subsequently sell.

In the lab equipment model, output of designs is the same, homogeneous-of-degree-one production function as in the manufacturing sector. As is the case for the manufacturing sector, the equilibrium is one in which patents convey market power but in which there are no other entry restrictions. There are no external effects and no knowledge spillovers. There is free entry into both R&D and manufacturing. The only restriction is that no one can manufacture capital of type i without the consent of the holder of the patent on good i. In this case we conceive of R&D as being undertaken by separate firms that hire inputs, produce patentable designs, and sell them for a price P_A.

3 Balanced Growth and Integration

The description of the technology given so far represents output as a function of the inputs H, L, K, and A, and specifies the evolution equations for K and A. To facilitate the simple balanced growth analysis that we undertake, the stocks of L and H are each taken as given. Increases in either L or H could be accommodated if we undertook the more complicated task of solving a nonlinear system of differential equations with growth rates that vary over time.

The calculation of a balanced growth equilibrium for each of the two specifications of the R&D technology can be summarized in terms of two linear relations between the rate of growth and the interest rate that hold along a balanced growth path. One relation comes from the conditions of equilibrium in production and the other from preferences.

As shown in the Appendix and as illustrated in figure 1, the interest rate implied by equilibrium in the production sector is decreasing in the rate of growth of output for

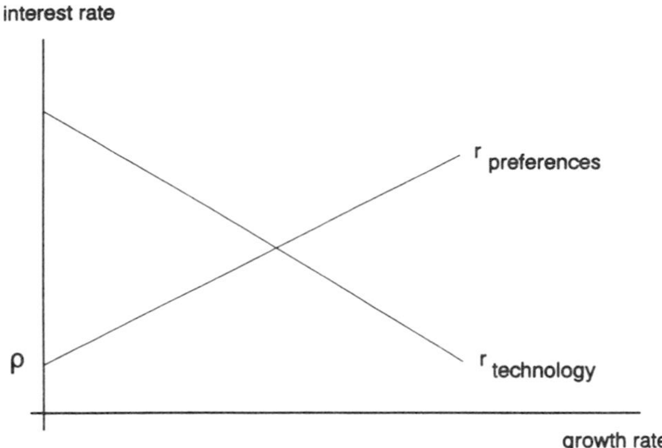

Figure 1
The balanced growth equilibrium in the knowledge-driven model

the knowledge-driven model:

$$r_{\text{technology}} = \frac{\delta H - g}{\Lambda}. \tag{6}$$

The term in the denominator depends only on the production function parameters, $\Lambda = \alpha(\alpha + \beta)^{-1}(1 - \alpha - \beta)^{-1}$.

The corresponding expression for the interest rate from the lab equipment model is shown in the Appendix to be a function of the production parameters and the stock of H and L. It does not, however, depend on the rate of growth:

$$r_{\text{technology}} = \Gamma H^{\alpha} L^{\beta}, \tag{7}$$

where Γ is defined by $\Gamma = B^{\alpha+\beta}(\alpha + \beta)^{\alpha+\beta}(1 - \alpha - \beta)^{2-\alpha-\beta}$.

In the knowledge-driven specification the negative relation between the interest rate and the growth rate arises because an increase in the interest rate reduces the demand for capital goods. The calculations in the Appendix show that an increase in the interest rate reduces the number of units of each capital good that are rented, and thereby reduces the value of a patent. According to the curved production possibility frontier between designs and manufactured goods, the reduction in the price of the patented design causes a shift in human capital out of the production of new designs and into the production of manufactured goods. This shift slows down the creation of technology and thereby slows growth. In the lab equipment model only a single value of the interest rate is consistent with production of both goods and designs. The relative price of patents and final goods is fixed, so the interest rate is technologically determined (see figure 2).

It remains to specify the preferences that provide the other balanced growth relation between the interest rate and the rate of growth. The simplest formulation to work with is Ramsey preferences with constant elasticity utility,

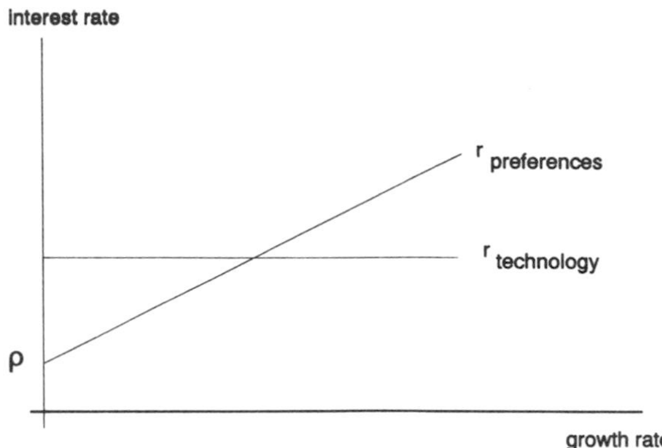

Figure 2
The balanced growth equilibrium in the lab equipment model

$$U = \int_0^\infty \frac{C^{1-\sigma}}{1-\sigma} e^{-\rho t}\, dt, \qquad \sigma \in [0, \infty).$$

Under balanced growth the rate of growth of consumption must be equal to the rate of growth of output. Thus, for any fixed rate of growth $g = \dot{C}/C$, we can calculate the implied interest rate from the consumer's first-order conditions for intertemporal optimization:

$$r_{\text{preferences}} = \rho + \sigma g. \tag{8}$$

These preferences yield a positive relation between the interest rate and the growth rate because when consumption is growing more rapidly, current consumption is more valuable compared with future consumption, so the marginal rate of substitution between present and future consumption is higher. Consumers would therefore be willing to borrow at higher interest rates.

There is a parameter restriction that is necessary to ensure that the growth rate is not larger than the interest rate. If it is, present values will not be finite, and the integral that defines utility will diverge. In terms of figures 1 and 2, the restriction is that the intersection of the two curves must lie above the 45 degree line. This will always be true if σ is greater than or equal to one, since in this case, the $r_{\text{preferences}}$ curve always lies above the 45 degree line. If σ is less than one, the $r_{\text{technology}}$ curve must not lie too far up and to the right.

Because the rate of growth under each specification is determined by the intersection of two straight lines, it can be calculated directly from the relation between r and g determined on the preference side, equation (8), and the relation between r and g determined by the technology, either equation (6) or (7). The balanced rate of growth for a closed economy under the knowledge-driven model of the research sector is

$$g = \frac{\delta H - \Lambda\rho}{\Lambda\sigma + 1}. \tag{9}$$

The balanced rate of growth for the lab equipment model is

$$g = \frac{\Gamma H^{\alpha} L^{\beta} - \rho}{\sigma}. \tag{10}$$

Both of these models have a dependence on scale that is crucial to the analysis of the effects of trade. To see this, consider two economies that have identical endowments of H and L. In the long run these economies will have the same stocks of accumulated inputs as well, so that scale effects offer the only lasting source of gains from trade and economic integration.

Suppose that the two economies are physically contiguous, yet are totally isolated from each other by an impenetrable barrier that impedes the flow of goods, people, and ideas. If these economies evolve under isolation, the balanced rate of growth in each is characterized by figures 1 and 2 and calculated in equations (9) and (10). Now suppose that the barrier is removed, so that the economies are completely integrated into a single economy. The change from two economies with endowments H and L to one economy with stocks $2H$ and $2L$ causes an upward shift in the $r_{\text{technology}}$ curve in both figures. Both the rate of growth and the interest rate increase after complete economic integration takes place, regardless of the specification of the technology for R&D. In both models (even the knowledge-driven model with no knowledge spillovers) the rate of growth is too low compared with the rate that would be selected by a social planner.[1] As a result, one would expect integration to be welfare improving. A full welfare analysis, however, would require explicit consideration of the dynamics along the transition path.

With this discussion as background the examples in the next section are designed to address three questions. First, can free trade in goods between countries induce the same increase in the balanced growth rate as complete integration into a single economy? If not, can the free movement of goods, combined with the free movement of ideas, reproduce the rate of growth under full integration? And finally, what is the underlying explanation for the dependence of the growth rate on the extent of the market?

4 Trade in Goods and Flows of Ideas

In this section we conduct a series of thought experiments about partial integration. In the first two experiments we focus on the knowledge-driven specification for R&D because it permits a sharp distinction between flows of goods and flows of ideas. In the third we consider the lab equipment specification in which ideas have no direct effect on production.

In the analysis of the knowledge-driven specification, we start with two identical, completely isolated economies that are growing at the balanced growth rate. We first allow for trade in goods, but continue to restrict the flow of ideas. To emphasize the distinction between goods and ideas, we assume that trade in goods does not induce any transmission of ideas. For example, we assume that it is impossible to reverse-engineer an imported good to learn the secrets of its design. Under these assumptions we show that trade in goods has no effect on the long-run rate of growth. Then in the second experiment we calculate the additional effect of opening communications networks and permitting flows of ideas. We show that allowing flows of ideas results in a permanently higher growth rate.

In the third experiment we consider the effects of opening trade in goods under the lab equipment specification. In this case trade in goods alone causes the same permanent increase in the rate of growth as complete integration. Since ideas per se have no effect on production, the creation of communications networks has no additional effect.

Flows of Goods with No Flows of Ideas in the Knowledge-Driven Model

In all of the experiments considered here, the form of trade between the two countries is very simple. By symmetry there are no opportunities for intertemporal trade along a balanced growth path, hence no international lending. Because there is only a single final consumption good, the only trades that take place are exchanges of capital goods produced in one country for capital goods produced in the other.

With the knowledge-driven model of research, it is straightforward to show that opening trade in goods has no permanent effect on the rate of growth. In balanced growth the rate of growth of output is equal to the rate of growth of A, $\dot{A}/A = \delta H_A$, which is determined by the split of human capital $H = H_Y + H_A$ between the manufacturing sector and the research sector. Opening trade in goods has two offsetting effects on wages for human capital in these two sectors. Before trade is opened, the number of different types of machines that are used in the manufacturing sector must equal the number that has been designed and produced domestically. Along the new balanced growth path after trade is opened, the number of types of machines used in each country approaches twice the number that has been produced and designed domestically. In their pursuit of monopoly rents, researchers in the two countries will specialize in the production of different types of designs and avoid redundancy, so the worldwide stock of designs will ultimately be twice as large as the stock that has been produced in either country.

With trade in the specialized capital goods, domestic manufacturers can take advantage of foreign designs and vice versa. Ultimately, the level $\bar{x}$ at which each durable is used in each country will return to the level that obtained under isolation. From equation (1) it follows that the increase in A doubles the marginal product of human capital in the manufacturing sector, increasing it from $\partial Y/\partial H = \alpha H_A^{\alpha-1} L^{\beta} \bar{x}^{1-\alpha-\beta} A$ to $\partial Y/\partial H = \alpha H_A^{\alpha-1} L^{\beta} \bar{x}^{1-\alpha-\beta}(A + A^*)$, where A^* is the set of durables available from abroad.

For the research sector, opening of trade implies that the market for any newly designed good is twice as large as it was in the absence of trade. This doubles the price of the patents and raises the return to investing human capital in research from $P_A \delta A$ to $2P_A \delta A$. The knowledge represented by A^* is not available for use in research because flows of ideas are not permitted. Since the return to human capital doubles in both of the competing sectors, free trade in goods does not affect the split of human capital between manufacturing and research. Hence, it does not change the balanced rate of economic growth or the interest rate. In terms of figure 1, opening trade in goods does not change the position of either the $r_{\text{preferences}}$ locus or the $r_{\text{technology}}$ locus.

This result does not imply that free trade in goods has no effect on output or welfare. Consider, for example, the extreme case in which two isolated economies start from completely nonintersecting sets of capital goods A and A^* that have the same measure. Before trade in goods, the home country will use capital at the level $\bar{x}$ for A types of capital goods and the foreign country will use capital at the same level $\bar{x}$ for A^* different types of capital goods. If existing capital is freely mobile, each country will immediately exchange half of its capital stock for half of the capital stock of the other country when trade in capital goods is allowed. Each will then be using capital at the level $\bar{x}/2$ on a set of capital goods of measure $A + A^*$. (Over time, the level of usage will climb back to $\bar{x}$ as capital accumulation takes place because the level of x is determined by r and g, and on the new balanced growth path these are the same as before.) From the form of production in manufacturing given in equation (1), it follows that immediately after trade is opened output in each country jumps by a factor of $2^{\alpha+\beta}$. This is analogous to the kind of level effect one encounters in the neoclassical model and in static models of trade with differentiated inputs in production (e.g., Ethier 1982). In the specific model outlined here, free trade in goods can affect the level of output and can therefore affect welfare, but it does not affect long-run growth rates.

If the two different economies start from a position with exactly overlapping sets of goods prior to the opening of trade, the timing of the effect on output is different, but the ultimate effect is the same. The level of output at future dates will differ from what it would have been without trade in goods and will generally be higher. But once the transitory effects have died out, the underlying growth rate will be the same as it was prior to the opening of trade in the capital goods.

Flows of Information in the Knowledge-Driven Model of Research

This second example shows that greater flows of ideas can permanently increase the rate of growth in the knowledge-driven model of research. Once we allow for flows of information, we must make some assumption about international protection of intellectual property rights. In each country we have assumed that patents protect any designs produced domestically. Once ideas and designs created abroad become available, the government could try to expropriate the monopoly rents that would accrue to the foreigners by refusing to uphold their patents. To simplify the discussion here, we assume that neither government engages in this practice. A patent in one country is fully respected in the other. (For a discussion of incomplete protection of intellectual property rights, see Rivera-Batiz and Romer 1991.)

Consider the two identical economies with the knowledge-driven specification of the research sector described in the first experiment. Trade in goods has already been allowed, and this creates the incentive for researchers to specialize in different designs.

Over time the sets of designs that are in use in the two countries will be almost entirely distinct, so the worldwide stock of knowledge approaches twice the stock of designs in either country. In the absence of communications links, this means that researchers in each country will ultimately be using only one half of the worldwide stock of knowledge. In the domestic country the rate of growth of A is given by $\dot{A} = \delta H_A A$. In the foreign country it is given by $\dot{A}^* = \delta H_A^* A^*$.

Now suppose that flows of ideas between the two countries are permitted. Research in each country now depends on the total worldwide stock of ideas as contained in the union of A and A^*. If the ideas in each country are completely nonintersecting, the effective stock of knowledge that could be used in research after communication opens would be twice as large as it was before: $\dot{A} = \dot{A}^* = \delta H_A(A + A^*) = 2\delta H_A A$. Even if the allocation of $H = H_Y + H_A$ between manufacturing and research did not change, the rate of growth of A would double. But the increase in the set of ideas available for use in research increases the productivity of human capital in research and has no effect on its productivity in manufacturing. This change in relative productivity induces a shift of human capital out of manufacturing and into research. For two reasons communication of ideas speeds up growth.

Increasing the flow of ideas has the effect of doubling the productivity of research in each country. Compared with the closed economy model, the formal effect is the same as a doubling of the research productivity parameter δ. This would shift the $r_{\text{technology}}$ curve in figure 1 upward and lead to a higher equilibrium growth rate and interest rate. The algebraic solution for the balanced growth rate of A (and therefore also of Y, C, and K) can be determined by replacing δ with 2δ in equation (9) to obtain $g = (2\delta H - \Lambda\rho)/(\sigma\Lambda + 1)$.

Doubling the value of the productivity parameter δ has exactly the same effect on the rate of growth of output and designs as a doubling of H. And according to the discussion in section 2, doubling H has the same effect on growth as complete integration of the two economies into a single economy. Flows of ideas and goods together have the same effect on the growth rate as does complete integration. Complete integration would permit permanent migration as well, but since ideas and goods are already mobile and because the ratio of H to L was assumed to be the same in the two countries, migration is not necessary to achieve productive efficiency. For symmetric economies, allowing both trade in goods and free flows of ideas is enough to reproduce the resource allocation under complete integration.

So far, we have considered the additional effect that free flows of information would have if free trade in goods were already permitted. It is useful to consider the alternative case in which flows of information are permitted but flows of goods are not. In this case the results hinge on the degree of overlap between the set of ideas that are produced in each country.

In the absence of trade in goods, there would be no incentive for researchers in different countries to specialize in different designs either before or after flows of information are permitted. Moreover, after flows of information are opened, there would be a positive incentive for researchers in one country to copy designs from the other, and little offsetting incentives to enforce property rights. If the firm that owns the patent on good j is not permitted to sell the good in a foreign country, it has no economic stake in the decision by a foreign firm to copy good j and sell it in the foreign market. (The domestic firm would, of course, have both the incentive and the legal power to stop exports of the copies from the foreign country.) In the extreme case in which identical knowledge is created in each country, opening flows of information has no effect at all on production.

Alternatively, one could imagine that discovery is a random process with a high variance so that truly independent discoveries would take place in the different isolated countries. In this case, permitting the international transmission of ideas would speed up worldwide growth rates to some extent, even in the absence of trade in goods. With free communication each researcher would be working with a larger stock of ideas than would otherwise have been the case. For example, when the first overland routes to China were opened in the Middle Ages, transportation of goods was so expensive that the economic effects of trade in goods was small. But the economic consequences of the ideas that travelers brought back (e.g., the principle behind the magnetic compass and the formula for gunpowder) were large.

Flows of Goods in the Lab Equipment Model of Research

The two previous examples show that there is sometimes a separation between growth effects and level effects. In the first experiment, opening trade in goods had level effects but no growth effects. In the second experiment, opening flows of ideas had both a growth effect and a level effect. (Manufacturing output goes down when H shifts into research, and research output goes up.)

From the first two examples it is tempting to conclude that flows of goods will generally have level effects of the type that are familiar from neoclassical analysis and that it is only flows of ideas that have growth effects. The third example considered shows that this conclusion is wrong. The lab equipment model is constructed so that ideas per se have no effect on production. Hence, permitting international flows of ideas can have no economic effect. Yet we know from the discussion in section 3 that complete integration causes a permanent increase in the rate of growth. The experiment considered in this example shows that trade in goods is all that is needed to achieve this result.

Recall that, when trade in goods is permitted in the knowledge-driven model, this increases the profits that the holder of each patent can extract because it increases the market for the good. By itself this increase in the return to producing designs would tend to increase the production of designs, but in the knowledge-driven specification this effect is exactly offset by the increase in the marginal productivity of human capital in manufacturing.

In the lab equipment specification, opening trade in goods would cause the same kind of increase in the profit earned at each date by the holder of a patent if the interest rate remained constant. But as was noted in section 2, the price of the patent $P_A = 1/B$ is determined by the technology. The only way that the larger market can be reconciled with a fixed price for the patent is if the interest rate increases. A higher interest rate reduces the demand for capital goods, thereby lowering the profit earned by the monopolist at each date. The calculation in the Appendix shows that the required increase in the interest rate is by a factor of $2^{\alpha+\beta}$. When two identical economies are integrated and $2H$ is substituted for H and $2L$ is substituted for L in equation (7), the same increase in r obtains. In each case the higher interest rate leads to higher savings. From figure 2 or from equation (10), it follows that this increase in the interest rate leads to the same faster rate of growth as complete integration.

5 Scale Effects and Growth

In the last example we noted one incorrect conjecture about why tighter economic integration leads to faster growth. From the knowledge-driven model one might conclude that flows of ideas are crucial to the finding that economic integration can speed up growth. But the lab equipment model shows that closer integration can speed up growth even in a model in which flows of ideas have no effect on production. A related conjecture is that knowledge spillovers are fundamental and that increasing the extent of the spillovers is how integration speeds up growth. The lab equipment model shows that this too is incorrect, for it has no knowledge spillovers.

Finally, one might conclude that it is the increasing returns to scale in the production function for designs, $\dot{A} = \delta H_A A$, that causes integration to have a growth effect in the knowledge-driven model. This conjecture seems to us to come closest to the mark, but it needs to be interpreted carefully. To see why, recall that the production function for designs in the lab equipment model, $\dot{A} = BH_A^\alpha L_A^\beta \int_0^A x_A(i)^{1-\alpha-\beta}\,di$, exhibits constant returns to scale as a function of H, L, and the capital goods $x(i)$. There is, nonetheless, a form of increasing returns that is present in this model. It comes from the fixed cost that must be incurred to design a new good. With integration this fixed cost need be incurred only once. Under isolation it must be incurred twice, once in each country.

To bring out the underlying form of increasing returns, recall from equation (5) that we can substitute $x = K_A/A$ into the expression for $\dot{A}$ and write it as a function of H, L, K, and A that is homogeneous of degree $1 + \alpha + \beta$: $\dot{A} = BH_A^\alpha L_A^\beta K_A^{1-\alpha-\beta} A^{\alpha+\beta}$. Interpreted as a statement about this kind of reduced-form expression, it is correct to say that both models exhibit increasing returns to scale in the production of new designs as a function of the stocks of basic inputs. Consequently, operating two research sectors in isolation is not as efficient as operating a single integrated research sector. To operate an integrated research sector in the knowledge-driven model, two things are required. First, one must avoid redundant effort, that is, devoting resources in one economy to rediscovering a design that already exists in the other. Trade in goods provides the incentive to avoid redundancy. Second, one must make sure that ideas discovered in one country are available for use in research in both countries. Flows of ideas along communications networks serve this function.

In the lab equipment model, trade in goods once again provides the incentive to avoid redundant effort. Beyond this, all that is needed to create a single worldwide research sector is to ensure that all types of capital equipment available worldwide are used in all research activities undertaken anywhere in the world. Since ideas do not matter in research, trade in the capital goods is all that is needed.

There is one final point worth emphasizing. Rebelo (1991) offers a general observation about multisector models that is relevant for the experiments considered here. Consider a single-sector model of the form, $C + \dot{K} + \dot{A} = B_0 F_0(K, A)$, where $F_0(\cdot)$ is a homogeneous of degree one function. In this example, K and A can denote any two arbitrary capital goods. If the productivity parameter B_0 increases, the balanced growth rate increases. Consider next a two-sector model in which there is an essential fixed factor L that enters as an input in the homogeneous of degree one production function for consumption and capital of type K: $C + \dot{K} = B_1 F_1(K_1, A_1, L)$. The capital good A, however, is produced by a homogeneous of degree one function $F_2(\cdot)$ of K and A alone: $\dot{A} = B_2 F_2(K_2, A_2)$. In this case a change in the productivity parameter B_1 has no effect on the balanced rate of growth. It has only level effects. In contrast, an increase in B_2 increases the balanced rate of growth.

The connection between Rebelo's observation and our results is as follows. We do not consider changes in technology parameters like B_1 and B_2, but we do induce changes in scale for functions that are homogeneous of some degree greater than one. Increases in scale are analogous to increases in the productivity parameters. In the knowledge-driven model trade in goods exploits increasing returns in the sector that produces C and K, but not in the sector that produces A. It is like an increase in B_1 in Rebelo's two-sector model and induces only level effects. In contrast, flows of ideas increase the productivity in the research sector that produces A, and are analogous to an increase in Rebelo's coefficient B_2. Finally, trade in goods in the lab equipment model induces a scale effect that is like an increase in B_0 in Rebelo's one-sector model.

6 Limitations of the Models and Extensions

As noted in the introduction, the analysis carried out in this paper takes the form of thought experiments for idealized cases. These experiments reveal the following general insight about the connection between economic integration and the rate of economic growth. In a model of endogenous growth, if economic integration lets two economies exploit increasing returns to scale in the equation that represents the engine of growth, integration will raise the long-run rate of growth purely because it increases the extent of the market. Depending on the form of the model, this integration could take the form of trade in goods, flows of ideas, or both.

This conclusion must be tempered by a large number of qualifications. First, there is no consensus yet about whether the equation that is the engine of growth is homogeneous of some degree that is greater than one in the basic inputs (as it is in both of the models considered here) or instead is homogeneous of degree one (as it is, for example, in the papers by Rebelo 1991 and Lucas 1988).

Second, as noted in the introduction, we have focused on trade between economies with identical endowments and technologies to highlight the scale effects induced by economic integration. In a general two-sector framework, trade between economies that have different endowments or technologies will induce allocation effects that shift resources between the two sectors in each country. For example, Grossman and Helpman (1990) show that trade between countries that have different endowments or technologies will induce shifts between the manufacturing sector and the R&D sector that can either speed up or slow down worldwide growth. If one wants to take the optimistic conclusions reached in this paper literally, they are most likely to apply to integration between similar developed regions of the world, for example, between North America, Europe, and Japan.

There are many details of R&D at the micro level that have been ignored in all of the analysis. We have assumed that giving participants in the economy an incentive to avoid redundancy in research is sufficient to ensure that no redundancy takes place. We have also assumed that patents are infinitely lived and, implicitly, that the institutional structure avoids patent races. We have not considered the role of secrecy in preserving economic value for ideas. All of these restrictions are very strong. Grossman and Helpman (1989d) show how one element of the microeconomic literature on patents, the destruction of monopoly profits by new discoveries, can be included in an aggregate growth model. Other extensions will no doubt follow.

The functional forms used here cannot be literally correct. For example, in both of our models the output of patents at any date increases in proportion to the resources devoted to R&D. This permits the solution for balanced growth paths using linear equations, but it cannot be a good description of actual research opportunities. We would expect that a doubling of research effort would lead to a less than two-fold increase in R&D output, in large part because of the coordination and redundancy problems at the micro level that we have ignored. Addressing these issues would help reconcile a model in which growth rates increase linearly in H in one case, or as a power of H and L in the second, with a historical record showing that growth rates have indeed increased over time, but not nearly as much as the functional forms used here would suggest. More precision in the definition of the input H that is most important for research would also be helpful in this regard. In terms of their effects on research output, one presumably does not literally want to equate two people holding high school degrees with one person holding a Ph.D. degree.

Perhaps the most interesting limitation of the model considered here is one that it shares with many other models: there is no description of how ideas or information affect the production of goods. Once one admits that ideas per se can influence research output, it is apparent that they can influence the output of goods as well. Presumably this is what learning-by-doing models try to capture with the assumption that some production parameter increases with cumulative experience: producing goods yields both goods and ideas, and the ideas raise the productivity of the other inputs. Formal models in the tradition of Arrow (1962) have not yet addressed the importance of communication networks and information flows. When the learning-by-doing models are used in international trade, it is implicitly assumed that there is a communication network that extends throughout one national economy, yet does not cross national boundaries. Little theoretical attention has been given to the analysis of policy choices that can affect the efficiency of international communication networks and to explaining historical episodes (e.g., the emergence of the textile industry in the United States and of the automobile industry in Japan) that reflect large flows of information from developed industries in one country to developing industries in another.

Given these limitations and qualifications, our only claim is to have formalized, and we hope illuminated, an effect that is potentially important. If the discovery of new ideas is central to economic growth, one should expect that increasing returns associated with the opportunity to reuse existing ideas will be present. If the increasing returns extend to the sector of the economy that generates growth, economic integration will induce scale effects that will raise the long-run rate of growth. And because of the remarkable growth of the exponential function, policies that affect long-run rates of growth can have very large cumulative effects on economic welfare. Many other effects may be present as well, but in future theoretical and empirical work, we argue that scale effects on growth that are induced by economic integration are worth watching out for.

Appendix

Derivation of Equation (7)

In the lab equipment model the value of total production in manufacturing and research depends only on the aggregate stocks of inputs, not on their allocation between the two sectors:

$$Y + \frac{\dot{A}}{B} = H^{\alpha}L^{\beta}\int_0^A x(i)^{1-\alpha-\beta}\,di.$$

Taking its supply of H and L as given, each representative firm in the manufacturing sector chooses levels of $x(i)$ to maximize profits. Consequently, the first-order condition for the problem of maximizing $Y + \dot{A}/B$ minus total input cost $\int p(i)x(i)\,di$ with respect to the use of input i yields the economywide inverse demand curve for good i. The rental rate p that results when x units of the capital good are supplied is

$$p = (1-\alpha-\beta)H^{\alpha}L^{\beta}x^{-(\alpha+\beta)}. \tag{A1}$$

Input producers choose x to maximize the present value of monopoly rent minus x times the unit cost of each piece of capital, $P_A = \max(px/r) - x$. Using equation (A1), the first-order condition that determines the number of machines $\bar{x}$ that the holder of the patent on good i rents to manufacturing firms is

$$(1-\alpha-\beta)^2 H^\alpha L^\beta \bar{x}^{-(\alpha+\beta)} r^{-1} - 1 = 0, \tag{A2}$$

which implies that $p/r = (1-\alpha-\beta)^{-1}$. The present discounted value of profit collected by the holder of the patent can then be simplified to

$$P_A = \left(\frac{p\bar{x}}{r}\right) - \bar{x} = \frac{\alpha+\beta}{1-\alpha-\beta}\bar{x}. \tag{A3}$$

Since $P_A = 1/B$, this implies that $\bar{x} = (1-\alpha-\beta)/B(\alpha+\beta)$. Substituting this expression into equation (A2) yields equation (7) in the text:

$$r_{\text{technology}} = B^{\alpha+\beta}(\alpha+\beta)^{\alpha+\beta}(1-\alpha-\beta)^{2-\alpha-\beta} H^\alpha L^\beta.$$

Derivation of Equation (6)

The demand for the capital goods in this model has exactly the same form as in the lab equipment model, with the qualification that since all of the demand comes from the manufacturing sector, H must be replaced by H_Y. If we use equation (A1) with this replacement to substitute for p in the expression for P_A, we have

$$P_A = (\alpha+\beta)\frac{p\bar{x}}{r} = \frac{\alpha+\beta}{r}(1-\alpha-\beta)H_Y^\alpha L^\beta \bar{x}^{1-\alpha-\beta}.$$

Equating the wages of human capital in manufacturing and research yields $P_A \delta A = \alpha H_Y^{\alpha-1} L^\beta A \bar{x}^{1-\alpha-\beta}$. Combining these expressions and solving for H_Y gives $H_Y = (1/\delta)\cdot \alpha(\alpha+\beta)^{-1}(1-\alpha-\beta)^{-1} r = (\Lambda/\delta)r$. Hence, $g = \delta H_A = \delta H - \delta H_Y = \delta H - \Lambda r$.

Trade in Goods in Lab Equipment Model Is Equivalent to Complete Integration

If the interest rate remained constant, the value of a patent $P_A = \pi/r$ would double when trade in goods between two identical markets is introduced in this model. The monopolist that sells in two identical markets and faces constant marginal costs of production will maximize profits in each market independently and earn twice the flow of profits that would accrue from one market alone. Since the value of the patent must remain fixed at $1/B$ by the specification of the technology for producing patents, the interest rate must increase to restore equilibrium.

As shown above, maximization of profit by the monopolist implies that p/r is constant, so profit is proportional to $\bar{x}$. To offset the doubling of profit that the opening of trade would otherwise induce, r must increase by enough to make the number of units of capital supplied by the monopolist in each country fall by one half. From equation (A2) this will happen if r increases by a factor of $2^{\alpha+\beta}$. This is the same as the increase in r that results from doubling H and L when the two countries are combined.

Notes

Conversations with Robert Barro, Gene Grossman, Elhanan Helpman, and Danyang Xie about their work on related issues have been very helpful, as were comments by Ray Riezman and Robert Staiger on earlier versions of this paper. The work of the second author was supported by NSF grant #SES88-22052, by a Sloan Foundation Fellowship, and by the Center for Advanced Studies in the Behavioral Sciences, which received support from NSF grant #BNS87-00864.

1. For the knowledge driven model, this is shown in Romer (1990). For an early version of the lab equipment model, this is shown in Romer (1987). See Barro and Sala i Martin (1990) for a discussion of the optimality of the no-intervention equilibrium and of tax and subsidy policies that can achieve the socially optimal balanced rate of growth in a variety of endogenous growth models.

References

Arrow, Kenneth J. 1962. The economic implications of learning by doing. *Review of Economic Studies* 29:155–173.

Backus, David, Patrick Kehoe, and Timothy Kehoe. 1991. In search of scale effects in trade and growth. Working Paper no. 451, Federal Reserve Bank of Minneapolis.

Barro, Robert, and Xavier Sala i Martin. 1990. Public finance in models of economic growth. National Bureau of Economic Research, working paper no. 3362.

Dinopoulos, Elias, James Oehmke, and Paul Segerstrom. 1990. High technology industry trade and investment: The role of factor endowments. University of Florida working paper.

Dixit, Avinash, and V. Norman. 1980. *Theory of International Trade*. Cambridge: Cambridge University Press.

Ethier, Wilfred J. 1982. National and international returns to scale in the modern theory of international trade. *American Economic Review* 72:389–405.

Feenstra, Robert. 1990. Trade and uneven growth. National Bureau of Economic Research, working paper no. 3276.

Grossman, Gene, and Elhanan Helpman. 1989a. Product development and international trade. *Journal of Political Economy* 97:1261–1283.

Grossman, Gene, and Elhanan Helpman. 1989b. Endogeneous product cycles. National Bureau of Economic Research, working paper no. 2113.

Grossman, Gene, and Elhanan Helpman. 1989c. Growth and welfare in a small open economy. National Bureau of Economic Research, working paper no. 2809.

Grossman, Gene, and Elhanan Helpman. 1989d. Quality ladders in the theory of growth. National Bureau of Economic Research, working paper no. 3099.

Grossman, Gene, and Elhanan Helpman. 1990. Comparative advantage and long-run growth. *American Economic Review* 80:796–815.

Grossman, Gene, and Elhanan Helpman. 1991. Quality ladders and product cycles. *Quarterly Journal of Economics* 106:557–586.

Krugman, Paul. 1979. Increasing returns, monopolistic competition, and international trade. *Journal of International Economics* 9:469–479.

Krugman, Paul. 1981. Intraindustry specialization and the gains from trade. *Journal of Political Economy* 89:959–973.

Krugman, Paul. 1990. *Rethinking International Trade*. Cambridge, Mass.: MIT Press.

Lancaster, Kelvin. 1980. Intraindustry trade under perfect monopolistic competition. *Journal of International Economics* 10:151–175.

Lucas, Robert E., Jr. 1988. On the mechanics of economic development. *Journal of Monetary Economics* 22:3–42.

Rebelo, Sergio. 1991. Long-run policy analysis and long-run growth. *Journal of Political Economy* 99:500–521.

Rivera-Batiz, Luis A., and Paul M. Romer. 1991. International trade with endogenous technological change. *European Economic Review* 35:971–1001.

Romer, Paul M. 1987. Growth based on increasing returns due to specialization. *American Economic Review* 77:56–62.

Romer, Paul M. 1990. Endogeneous technological change. *Journal of Political Economy* 98:S71–S102.

Rosenberg, Nathan. 1980. *Inside the Black Box*. Cambridge: Cambridge University Press.

Segerstrom, Paul, T. C. A. Anant, and Elias Dinopoulos. 1990. A Schumpeterian model of the product life cycle. *American Economic Review* 80:1077–1091.

Young, Alwyn. 1991. Learning by doing and the dynamic effects of international trade. *Quarterly Journal of Economics* 106:369–405.

19 A Model of Quality Competition and Dynamic Comparative Advantage

Gene M. Grossman

The reprinted sections present and analyze a two-country model of dynamic comparative advantage based on endogeneous technological innovation. In the model, firms employ two primary factors in a research activity and in two manufacturing sectors. Resources devoted to R&D are used to improve the quality of a set of high-technology products. The model is used to study the structural and policy determinants of the long-run pattern of trade and the long-run rates of innovation in each of the trading countries. The omitted sections of the original article relate the model to the recent growth and trade experience of the Japanese economy.

In the light of the previous discussion, it seems that a minimal model of innovation and trade ought to include the following: (1) two sectors, one comprising high-technology goods and one in which competitive advantage is determined by more static considerations; (2) two factors, human capital and natural resources; (3) competitiveness in the high-technology sector that is determined as much by the quality of the goods as by their price; and (4) industrial R&D efforts aimed at raising product quality. I present a model with these features in the current section and study its properties in the sections that follow.[1]

The high-technology sector comprises a continuum of industries indexed by $\omega \in [0, 1]$. The product of each industry potentially can be improved an unlimited number of times. Each improvement raises the quality of the state-of-the-art product (i.e., the best existing variety) by a fixed percentage, to a level $\lambda > 1$ times as great as before. Quality improvements occur stochastically when firms devote resources to industrial research. I shall defer until later the specification of the R&D technology.

Consumers worldwide maximize an additively separable intertemporal utility function of the form

$$U = \int_0^\infty e^{-\rho t} \log u(t)\, dt, \tag{1}$$

where ρ is the common subjective discount rate and

$$\log u(t) = s_x \int_0^1 \log\left[\sum_m q_m(\omega)\, d_{mt}(\omega)\right] d\omega + (1 - s_x) \log d_{yt} \tag{2}$$

represents instantaneous utility at time t. In (2), $q_m(\omega) = \lambda^m$ is the measure of the quality of high-tech product ω after m improvements, with $q_0 = 1$ by choice of units; $d_{mt}(\omega)$ denotes consumption of quality m of product type ω at time t; and d_{yt} denotes consumption of a homogeneous good.

Excerpted from "Explaining Japan's Innovation and Trade: A Model of Quality Competition and Dynamic Comparative Advantage," appearing in *Bank of Japan Monetary and Economic Studies* 8 (September 1990): 75–100. This chapter reprints sections 3–6.

The representative consumer maximizes utility by choosing an optimal time pattern for spending and by allocating spending optimally at each point in time. Given prices $p_{mt}(\omega)$ for the high-technology goods and p_{yt} for the homogeneous good, and given expenditure $E(t) = \int_0^1 [\sum_m p_{mt}(\omega)\, d_{mt}(\omega)]\, d\omega + p_{yt} d_{yt}$, the consumer maximizes (2) by allocating a share s_x of spending to high-tech goods and spreading this evenly across the product types. For each ω, the consumer should choose the single variety that offers the lowest quality-adjusted price, $p_{mt}(\omega)/q_m(\omega)$. We shall find that in equilibrium it is always the highest available quality that provides the lowest quality-adjusted price. Substituting the optimal, static allocation of spending into (2), and the result into (1), we obtain the indirect utility function

$$U = \int_0^\infty e^{-\rho t} \left\{ \log E(t) - s_x \int_0^1 \log \left[\frac{p_t(\omega)}{q_t(\omega)} \right] d\omega - (1 - s_x) \log p_{yt} \right\} dt, \tag{3}$$

where $q_t(\omega)$ denotes the quality of the state-of-the-art variety of product ω at time t, and $p_t(\omega)$ denotes its price.

Consumers can borrow or lend freely on an international capital market with instantaneous (and riskless) rate of interest r.[2] They take this interest rate as given, though its value will be determined in the general equilibrium. The optimal time profile for nominal spending maximizes (3), subject to an intertemporal budget constraint limiting the present value of expenditures to the present value of income plus the value of initial asset holdings. The solution to this problem yields the following differential equation for spending:

$$\frac{\dot{E}}{E} = r - \rho. \tag{4}$$

The consumer-investor also must solve a portfolio allocation problem. He may choose among shares in a variety of domestic or foreign profit-making firms and among interest-bearing bonds. Claims on particular firms bear risk, as we shall see. However, the risk attached to each equity is idiosyncratic, so the investor can earn a sure rate of return by holding a diversified portfolio of shares. It follows that, in equilibrium, all assets must earn the same expected rate of return.

Consider the value of equity shares in a firm that earns a profit stream $\pi(\tau)$ for $\tau \geq t$. Below we will find that profits accrue only to firms that are able to manufacture a state-of-the-art product. The stream of profits of such a producer continues until the time that another firm succeeds in bettering its product. Then the value of shares in the displaced leader falls to zero. Recognizing this risk of total capital loss, we can calculate the expected return to any equity as follows. If $v(t)$ is the value of a firm at time t, $(\pi/v)\, dt$ is the dividend rate in a time interval of length dt and $(\dot{v}/v)\, dt$ is the rate of capital gain. With probability $f dt$ the shareholders will suffer a capital loss of v at the end of the interval. Summing these components of the expected return and equating the result to the sure rate of return on bonds, we have

$$\frac{\pi}{v} + \frac{\dot{v}}{v} - f = r. \tag{5}$$

This equation implicitly determines the value of any firm as a function of its profit rate, the interest rate, the rate of capital gain, and the relevant value for f. In what follows, I shall link f to the activities that competitors undertake in order to supplant the industry leaders.

Let us turn now to the production side of the economy. The homogeneous good can be produced in either country A or country B by a constant-returns-to-scale technology that does not change over time. The market structure in this sector is that of perfect competition. Let $c^Y(w^i, z^i)$ be the cost of producing this good in country i, $i = A, B$, where w^i is the wage of skilled labor in country i and z^i is the local factor payment to a nontraded resource (e.g., land). If production of this good takes place in both countries, then we must have

$$p^Y = c^Y(w^i, z^i), \qquad i = A, B. \tag{6}$$

I assume that all high-technology goods can be manufactured according to a common, constant-returns-to-scale production function, regardless of their type ω or quality q. Let $c^X(w^i, z^i)$ denote the cost of producing a unit of any one of these goods in country i. Of course, high-technology goods cannot be produced by any firm unless its research laboratory has succeeded in developing the requisite prototype.

Producers in the same industry ω compete as Bertrand (price-setting) oligopolists. Competition in the high-technology sector takes place, therefore, in both price and quality dimensions. Consider a firm that has succeeded in its efforts to improve upon the state-of-the-art variety of some product ω, and so is able to produce a good that is better than that of any of its rivals. Suppose, as will be the case in the equilibrium below, that the product is exactly one quality increment better than that offered by the nearest rival. Then the industry leader maximizes profits by setting a price that is λ times the cost of production of that nearest competitor. By so doing, the leader captures the entire market for product ω. Higher prices would allow the competitor to profitably undercut, while lower prices are not optimal given the unit elastic demand for product group ω. With this optimal pricing strategy, an industry leader located in country i facing a nearest competitor in country j makes sales $x^{ij}(\omega) = s_x E/\lambda c^X(w^j, z^j)$ and earns profits

$$\pi^{ij}(\omega) = s_x E\left[1 - \frac{c^X(w^i, z^i)}{\lambda c^X(w^j, z^j)}\right]. \tag{7}$$

Two things are apparent from (7). First, profits do not depend upon ω or the quality level that has been achieved in that industry. Second, all firms earn higher profits when their nearest competitor resides in a high-cost country. This latter fact implies that all researchers, no matter what their national origin, prefer to improve upon products that are at the moment being produced in a high-cost country. If one country indeed were to exhibit a higher cost of production for high-tech products, then over time it would lose competitiveness in all such products. This is because all research efforts worldwide would be targeted at improving that country's products, and each success abroad would mean the loss of a product that would never be recaptured. Such a situation cannot be consistent with a steady state in which high-tech products are manufactured in both countries. As a condition of steady-state equilibrium with incomplete specialization, we have

$$c^X(w^i, z^i) = c^X(w^j, z^j). \tag{8}$$

Equation (8) implies $\pi^{ij}(\omega) = (1 - \delta)s_x E$ for all i, j, and ω, where $\delta \equiv 1/\lambda$.

I allow free entry into the R&D activity. Any entrepreneur can open a research lab and attempt to improve upon the best available variety in some industry ω.[3] If successful, the entrepreneur will become an industry leader and so earn profits until the next improvement comes along. This specification captures a public good aspect of technology, inasmuch as newcomers can learn from observing the state-of-the-art product even if they are unable to produce it (see Grossman and Helpman 1989a for further discussion of this point).

The technology for industrial research is as follows. A firm that targets some product ω for improvement and undertakes R&D at intensity ι for a time interval of length dt will succeed in its efforts to develop the next generation product with probability ιdt. Thus, research entails uncertainty, and successes follow a Poisson process, as in Lee and Wilde (1980). The flow cost of undertaking research at intensity ι is $c^\iota(w^i, z^i)\iota$ in country i.

Let v^i be the value of a firm in country i that holds the technological lead in some industry ω. Entrepreneurs in country i can attain stock market value v^i with probability ιdt by undertaking research at intensity ι for a time interval of length dt. The cost of such research is $c^\iota(w^i, z^i)\iota dt$. Maximization of stock market value requires infinite research effort whenever $v^i > c^\iota(w^i, z^i)$, and zero effort whenever $v^i < c^\iota(w^i, z^i)$. Accordingly, in an equilibrium with active R&D sectors in both countries, we must have

$$v^i = c^\iota(w^i, z^i) \qquad \text{for } i = A, B. \tag{9}$$

In a steady-state equilibrium industry leaders undertake no research. This is because the *incremental* profits that a leader stands to gain from a research success are strictly less than the profits that nonleaders can obtain by innovating. A leader who further improves a high-tech product would find itself two steps ahead of its nearest rival on the quality ladder. It would then be able to charge a price equal to $\lambda^2 c^X(\cdot)$. With this price, the firm would earn *extra* profits equal to δ times its original profits. But $\delta < 1$, so the nonleaders always have greater incentive to undertake R&D than do the leaders.[4] This justifies my supposition that leaders always are exactly one quality increment ahead of their nearest competitors.

In a steady state, all nominal variables grow at a common rate. This implies, for instance, that $\dot{v}^i/v^i = \dot{E}/E$ for $i = A, B$. I choose $E = 1$ as numeraire. This implies $\dot{E} = 0$. Then $\dot{v}^i = 0$ in a steady state. Let ι^i, $i = A, B$, denote the aggregate intensity of global research effort targeted at a typical product currently being manufactured in country i. Using (4), (9), the no-arbitrage condition (5), and the fact that $\dot{v}^i = 0$ in a steady state, we have

$$\frac{(1-\delta)s_x}{c^i(w^i, z^i)} = \rho + \iota^i \qquad \text{for } i = A, B. \tag{10}$$

In writing (10), I have made use of the fact that the probability of catastrophic loss for an industry leader, $f dt$ in (5), is just the aggregate probability of a research breakthrough by a would-be successor, $\iota^i dt$.

Next we have the factor market–clearing conditions. In country i, employment of skilled labor in R&D is $(\iota^{ii}n^i + \iota^{ji}n^j)c^\iota_w(w^i, z^i)$, where ι^{ji} is the aggregate intensity of research targeted at each good manufactured in country j by firms located in country i, n^i is the number of high-tech goods produced in country i, and thus $\iota^{ii}n^i + \iota^{ji}n^j$ is the aggregate level of research activity undertaken in country i. Similarly, the input of natural resources to R&D is $(\iota^{ii}n^i + \iota^{ji}n^j)c^\iota_z(w^i, z^i)$. Aggregate output of high-tech goods is $n^i\delta s_x/c^X(w^i, z^i)$ in country i. Each unit of output is produced with $c^X_w(w^i, z^i)$ units of skilled labor and $c^X_z(w^i, z^i)$ units of the natural resource. Finally, country i produces Y^i units of the homogeneous good, each with $c^Y_w(w^i, z^i)$ units of skilled labor and $c^Y_z(w^i, z^i)$ units of the resource. Equating factor supplies to factor demands in each country, we have

$$(\iota^{ii}n^i + \iota^{ji}n^j)c^\iota_w(w^i, z^i) + \frac{n^i\delta s_x c^X_w(w^i, z^i)}{c^X(w^i, z^i)} + Y^i c^Y_w(w^i, z^i) = H^i, \qquad i = A, B, \tag{11}$$

$$(\iota^{ii}n^i + \iota^{ji}n^j)c^\iota_z(w^i, z^i) + \frac{n^i\delta s_x c^X_z(w^i, z^i)}{c^X(w^i, z^i)} + Y^i c^Y_z(w^i, z^i) = R^i, \qquad i = A, B, \tag{12}$$

where H^i is the (fixed) stock of skilled labor in country i, and R^i is the (fixed) stock of resources there.

The world market for the homogeneous good must clear as well.[5] Aggregate spending on this good is $1 - s_x$. (Recall that $E = 1$.) The value of world output is $p^Y(Y^A + Y^B)$. Therefore, in equilibrium,

$$1 - s_x = p^Y(Y^A + Y^B). \tag{13}$$

Finally, we have a steady-state condition that ensures that the number of high-tech goods produced in each country remains constant over time. At every instant country A researchers will successfully improve upon a fraction ι^{BA} of the n^B high-tech products that country B manufactured the moment before. Similarly, country B acquires leadership position in $\iota^{AB}n^A$ goods formerly produced in country A. In a steady state, these flows balance, or

$$\iota^{BA}n^B = \iota^{AB}n^A. \tag{14}$$

Using (14), we may rewrite the factor market–clearing conditions as follows:

$$\iota^i n^i c_w^I(w^i, z^i) + \frac{n^i \delta s_x c_w^X(w^i, z^i)}{c^X(w^i, z^i)} + Y^i c_w^Y(w^i, z^i) = H^i, \qquad i = A, B, \tag{15}$$

$$\iota^i n^i c_z^I(w^i, z^i) + \frac{n^i \delta s_x c_z^X(w^i, z^i)}{c^X(w^i, z^i)} + Y^i c_z^Y(w^i, z^i) = R^i, \qquad i = A, B, \tag{16}$$

Equations (6), (8), (10), (13), (15), and (16) constitute ten independent relationships that determine the steady-state values of n^A, p^Y, and ι^i, w^i, z^i, Y^i, for $i = A, B$, where we recall that $n^B = 1 - n^A$. These equations apply provided that the solution yields nonnegative values for all outputs, factor prices, and R&D intensities. If no such solution exists, then a steady-state equilibrium with incomplete specialization is impossible.

Before proceeding, it is worthwhile to review the qualitative nature of the equilibrium that we have described. At every moment in time, each country enjoys technological leadership in some subset of high-technology goods. Industry leaders export their state-of-the-art products and also sell them at home. Thus, intraindustry trade takes place. Competitiveness in particular high-tech products evolves dynamically over time as firms in each country race to bring out the next generation of products. When a research effort succeeds, a new firm takes over the market for the targeted good. The intensity of R&D and the number of high-technology goods produced in each country are determined in the general equilibrium. So is the pattern of interindustry trade, to which we now turn.

1 The Pattern of Specialization and Trade

Our first task will be to analyze the long-run pattern of specialization and trade. I focus on steady-state equilibria characterized by incomplete specialization in both countries. With incomplete specialization, equations (6) and (8) imply factor-price equalization, namely, $w^A = w^B$ and $z^A = z^B$. Then (10) implies that the intensities with which goods manufactured in each country are targeted for improvement are equal, namely, $\iota^A = \iota^B$. In this case, free commodity trade is sufficient to reproduce the long-run equilibrium that would obtain in a hypothetical "integrated world economy" —one in which no international borders exist to limit factor movements.

The pattern of global specialization in a free trade equilibrium with factor-price equalization can be described with the aid of figure 1. In the figure I have drawn a rectangle with dimensions that represent global factor endowments, $H^A + H^B$ and $R^A + R^B$. Let the line segment $O^A M$ in the figure represent the vector of resources that would be deployed in R&D in a hypothetical long-run equilibrium of an integrated world economy. Similarly, let MN represent those that would be used in manufacturing high-technology goods, and NO^B those that would be used in producing homogeneous goods, in such an equilibrium. Notice that the relative slopes of these segments imply that R&D is the most human capital-intensive activity and that production of

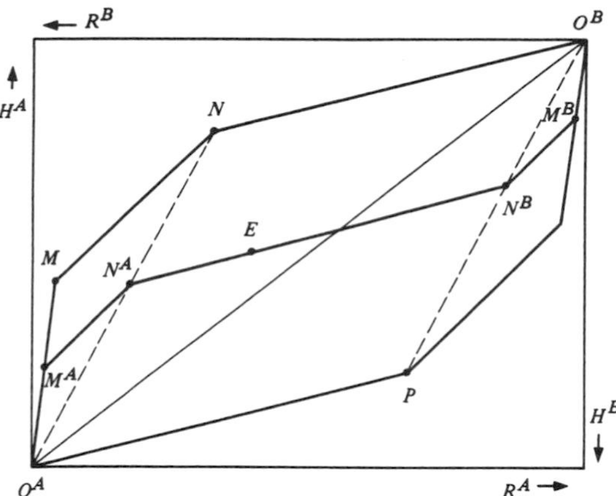

Figure 1

the homogeneous good is the most resource-intensive activity. I shall maintain this ranking throughout.

Let a point such as E represent the factor endowments of the two trading countries; that is, the vector O^AE (not drawn) is the endowment bundle of country A and the vector EO^B is that of country B. Since point E lies above the diagonal, country A is relatively well endowed with skilled labor.[6] We use now the facts that factor prices are equalized, that the trade equilibrium reproduces the aggregate outputs of the integrated equilibrium, and that factor markets must clear separately in each country. Consider the following allocation of resources. Country A devotes inputs O^AM^A to R&D, M^AN^A to the production of high-technology goods (where N^A lies along the line segment joining O^A and N), and N^AE to the production of the homogeneous good. Country B devotes O^BM^B to R&D, M^BN^B to the manufacture of high-technology goods, and N^BE to the production of the homogeneous good, where O^BM^B is parallel to O^AM^A, M^BN^B is parallel to M^AN^A and N^BE is parallel to N^AE. I shall argue that this allocation satisfies all of the conditions for a long-run equilibrium.

The fact that corresponding input vectors are parallel implies that techniques of production are the same in the two countries, as must be the case with factor prices equalized. Notice too that the techniques are the same as those for the integrated equilibrium. This, together with the fact that the aggregate inputs to the three activities are the same as in the integrated equilibrium implies that aggregate outputs are equal to those of the integrated equilibrium. All activities earn zero excess profits in the integrated equilibrium. This must be so in the proposed free trade equilibrium as well, since factor prices are the same. Also, the no-arbitrage condition (10) must be satisfied for both countries in the proposed free trade equilibrium, since it is so for the integrated equilibrium and we have already seen that factor-price equalization implies $\iota^A = \iota^B$.

It remains to be shown only that product markets clear in the proposed equilibrium, and that the R&D undertaken in each country and so the extent of each country's competitiveness in high-technology goods are consistent with the designated quantities of production of these goods in each country. The fact that factor prices are the same in the proposed free trade equilibrium as in the integrated equilibrium means that commodity prices are the same as in that equilibrium, and so is aggregate world income. But then, since preferences in (1) and (2) are homothetic, aggregate world demands must be the same. We have seen that aggregate supplies are the same, so commodity markets must clear under the proposed allocation. Finally, it can be seen from (15) and (16) that, with factor-price equalization and $\iota^A = \iota^B$, the ratios of the use of either factor in R&D to the use of that same factor in the production of high-technology goods must be identical for the two countries. This requirement indeed is satisfied in the proposed allocation, as can be verified by noting the similarity of triangles $O^A M^A N^A$ and $O^B M^B N^B$.

As is evident from the figure, in a free trade equilibrium, the skilled labor–rich country specializes relatively in both R&D and in production of high-technology goods. The resource-rich country specializes relatively in the production of the homogeneous good. We have then a prediction about the pattern of world specialization that is reminiscent of that from static theories of factor-endowment based trade, but one that has been derived from a dynamic model in which innovation is endogenous and competitiveness must be created in the industrial research laboratory. Our model predicts, for example, that Japan—with its abundance of skilled labor and its paucity of natural resources—ought to be found specializing in high-technology sectors, not because of any superiority in the Japanese system or due to the influences of industrial policy (other than perhaps policies aimed at the accumulation of human capital), but because the forces of long-run equilibrium in world factor and commodity markets dictate this pattern of production.

What then is the pattern of trade in the long-run equilibrium? Since I have assumed that financial assets can be traded internationally, there is no guarantee that commodity trade will balance in the long run. A country might, for example, finance a steady-state deficit on trade account by a surplus on service account. It might even happen, then, that in the steady state one country imports both the homogeneous product and (on net) high-technology goods. If this does not occur, then only one pattern of trade is possible.[7] With homothetic preferences, the composition of aggregate demands is the same in the two countries. But we have seen that the composition of outputs differs systematically. Thus, if one country imports the homogeneous good and exports (on net) the high-tech goods, it must be the country that is relatively better endowed with skilled labor.

I summarize the findings in

PROPOSITION 1 In a long-run, free trade equilibrium with incomplete specialization, the skilled labor–abundant country specializes relatively in R&D and the production of high-technology goods. It imports the resource-intensive good and exports (on net) high-technology products, unless its long-run trade account is highly imbalanced.

2 Factor Accumulation

The remainder of this paper is devoted to analyzing the long-run comparative static effects of endowment and policy changes. To simplify the calculations and exposition, I shall specialize the production technology somewhat further. I assume henceforth that R&D requires only skilled labor as an input, with unit input coefficient α, and that the manufacture of high-technology goods and homogeneous goods use skilled labor and natural resources in fixed proportions. I denote the unit input coefficients in the latter two activities by a_{ij}, $i = H, R$ and $j = X, Y$.

With these assumptions, the steady-state equilibrium can be expressed in a simple reduced form that will facilitate a diagrammatic analysis. First use (16) applied for $i = A, B$ to solve for Y^A and Y^B. Substitute these solutions into (15). Then sum the equations for the two countries and recall that $p^X = \lambda c^X$ to derive

$$\alpha g + \frac{n^A s_x D}{p^X a_{RY}} = H^A + H^B - \frac{a_{HY}}{a_{RY}}(R^A + R^B), \tag{17}$$

where $D \equiv a_{HX}a_{RY} - a_{RX}a_{HY} > 0$ and $g \equiv \iota^A n^A + \iota^B(1 - n^A)$ is the aggregate rate of innovation for the world as a whole. I plot this curve as HH in panel (a) of figure 2. The curve represents combinations of g and p^X that are consistent with equilibrium in the two markets for skilled labor. Its slope can be understood as follows. An increase in g increases employment of skilled labor in R&D. Then p^X must rise to alleviate demand for high-technology goods and so release skilled labor from the manufacturing sectors.

Next, solve for p^Y in terms of p^X and ι^A using (6) and (10). Then compute $Y^A + Y^B$ from (16). Substitute these expressions into (13), noting that $\iota^A = \iota^B$ implies $g = \iota^A$, and rearrange to find

$$\left(R^A + R^B - \frac{s_x a_{RX}}{p^X}\right)\left[a_{RY}\delta p^X - \frac{D(1-\delta)s_x}{\alpha(\rho + g)}\right] = a_{RY}a_{RY}(1 - s_x). \tag{18}$$

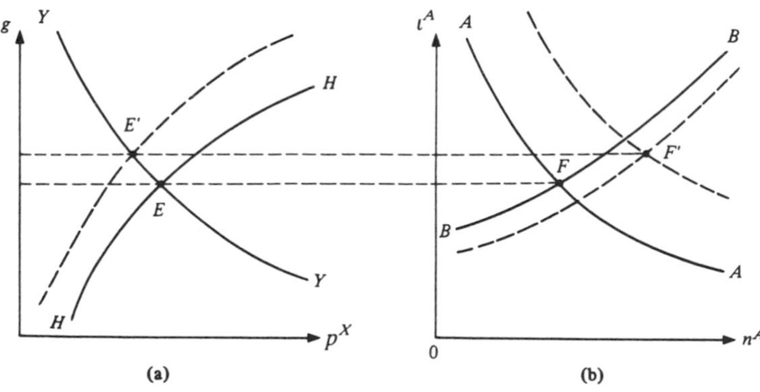

Figure 2

This equation, shown as YY in the figure, expresses equilibrium in the world market for the homogeneous good. When g rises, w must fall to maintain the no-arbitrage condition. Then p^Y rises, which chokes off demand for the homogeneous good and creates a situation of excess supply. The price of high-technology goods must fall, which reduces supply of the homogeneous good and, because p^Y falls with p^X, raises demand.

The long-run equilibrium values of p^X and g can be found at the intersection of these two curves (at point E). Panel (b) of the figure can now be used to decompose g into component parts that reflect the number of high-technology goods manufactured in each country and the intensity of research effort targeted at each country's products. The curve AA in the figure represents combinations of ι^A and n^A that enable the market for skilled labor in country A to clear. The equation for this curve is found using (15) and (16), and is given by

$$\alpha \iota^A n^A + \frac{n^A s_x D}{p^X a_{RY}} = H^A - \frac{a_{HY}}{a_{RY}} R^A. \tag{19}$$

The curve is drawn for the particular value of p^X that satisfies (17) and (18). It slopes upward, because an increase in ι^A raises employment of skilled labor in R&D in country A (employment equals $\alpha \iota^A n^A$), and so n^A must fall to reduce demand for skilled labor in both R&D and the production of high-technology goods. The curve BB expresses the analogous relationship for the skilled labor market in country B. The equation for the curve is

$$\alpha \iota^A (1 - n^A) + \frac{(1 - n^A) s_x D}{p^X a_{RY}} = H^B - \frac{a_{HY}}{a_{RY}} R^B, \tag{20}$$

where I have used the fact that $\iota^A = \iota^B$ in writing the first term of (20). The curve slopes downward, because employment of skilled labor in R&D and the production of high-tech goods in country B are proportional to $n^B = 1 - n^A$. The intersection of AA and BB at F gives us the equilibrium values of n^A and ι^A.

We use the figure to explore the consequences of a buildup of human capital, such as has occurred in Japan over the last twenty-five years. An increase in H^A shifts the HH curve to the left. The new equilibrium at E' has a faster aggregate rate of innovation in the world economy and a lower relative price of high-technology goods (measured in units of expenditure). Turning to panel (b), the BB curve shifts down due to the fall in p^X, while the AA curve also shifts down for this reason but shifts up due to the direct effect of the increase in skilled labor supply there. The net movement must be upward, since we know that ι^A $(=g)$ must rise.

At F', both ι^A and n^A are larger than at F. Thus, accumulation of human capital causes the R&D sector in country A to expand (its size is proportional to $\iota^A n^A$) and the range of high-technology goods produced there to grow. This finding accords well with intuition, and also with the evidence concerning the transformation of the Japanese economy discussed above.

We can also derive the consequences of this buildup of human capital for the structure of production in the trade partner country. There, ι^B rises, but $n^B = 1 - n^A$ falls. It is possible to show, however, that the former response is proportionately larger, so that innovation abroad, which is the product of these two, must accelerate.[8] The foreign country conducts more R&D, but the range of high-technology goods that it produces in the long-run equilibrium contracts. I summarize in

PROPOSITION 2 An increase in the supply of skilled labor in one country expands the number of high-technology goods produced there and accelerates steady-state innovation in both countries.

For completeness, let us consider also the implications of growth in the stock of natural resources, R^A. This analysis makes use of the two panels of figure 3. In panel (a), both the HH and YY curves shift downward when R^A expands. The aggregate rate of innovation in the world economy must decline, but p^X may rise or fall. If it rises (case not drawn), then BB shifts up, while AA shifts up for this reason but down in response to the resource expansion. The net movement is downward, so both n^A and ι^A decline. If, on the other hand, p^X falls in the adjustment to the new long-run equilibrium, then we have the case depicted in figure 3. Both the AA and the BB curves shift downward, but the former shifts by more (for given n^A). This is because the decline in p^X causes both curves to shift down by the same amount, but AA shifts down by an additional amount due to the rise in R^A. It follows that, in this case as well, both ι^A and n^A decline in response to an increase in R^A.

Clearly, the rate of innovation falls in country A. It can also be established that the rate of innovation declines in country B, as ι^A falls by proportionately more than n^A rises. We have then

PROPOSITION 3 An expansion in the stock of natural resources in one country reduces the number of high-technology goods produced there and slows steady-state innovation in both countries.

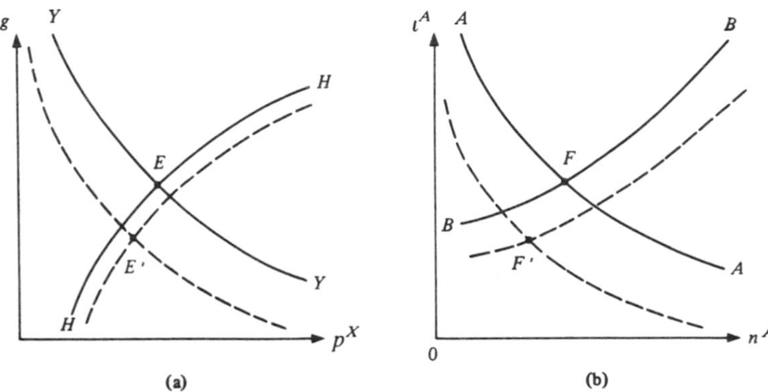

Figure 3

Taken together the two propositions imply that the long-run rate of innovation in the world economy responds positively to accumulation of the factor used intensively in R&D, and negatively to accumulation of the remaining factor. When one trade partner accumulates human capital faster than the other, its comparative advantage in high-technology goods expands. Thus, our model can account for at least part of Japan's recent success in the high-technology industries without any reference to industrial policy. Nonetheless, the model provides a useful tool for exploring the long-run effects on innovation and trade patterns of a variety of policy measures. I turn to these matters in the section that follows.

3 Industrial and Trade Policies

I study first the effects of a subsidy to R&D in country A. I assume that the payments are financed by lump-sum taxes that keep the government's budget intertemporally balanced. Let σ be the share of private R&D costs that the government finances. With this policy in place, the no-arbitrage condition (10) relevant for firms in country A must be modified to

$$\frac{(1-\delta)s_x}{(1-\sigma)\alpha w^A} = \rho + \iota^A. \tag{21}$$

The other equilibrium conditions remain as before. Notice that (6) and (8) continue to imply factor-price equalization in an equilibrium with incomplete specialization, but (10) and (21) now imply $\iota^A > \iota^B$. That is, in long-run equilibrium, researchers target high-technology goods manufactured in country A for improvement to a greater extent than they do those manufactured in country B. This means, of course, that the stream of monopoly profits that accrues to an industry leader in country A lasts on average for a shorter period of time. The lower private cost of research in country A is matched in equilibrium by a lower expected return to success, and so the rate of return on equities in country A firms remains "normal."

When we solve for the new reduced form using (21), we find two modifications of the system. First, since $\iota^B = (1-\sigma)(\rho + \iota^A) - \rho$, the first term in (20) becomes $\alpha(1-n^A)\cdot[(1-\sigma)(\rho+\iota^A)-\rho]$. Second, since (10) and (21) imply $\alpha w^A = (1-\delta)s_x[1+\sigma n^A/(1-\sigma)]/\alpha(\rho+g)$, the term in square brackets in (18) becomes

$$a_{RY}\delta p^X - \frac{D(1-\delta)s_x}{\alpha(\rho+\iota^A)}\left(1+\frac{\sigma}{1-\sigma}n^A\right).$$

Accordingly, the introduction of a subsidy to R&D shifts the YY curve in figure 4 upward and leads to a rise in both g and p^X. The rise in p^X causes both the AA and the BB curve in the right-hand panel to shift upward by equal amounts. The BB curve shifts up by an additional amount due to the direct effect of σ in (20). The figure shows a rise in ι^A and a decline in n^A.

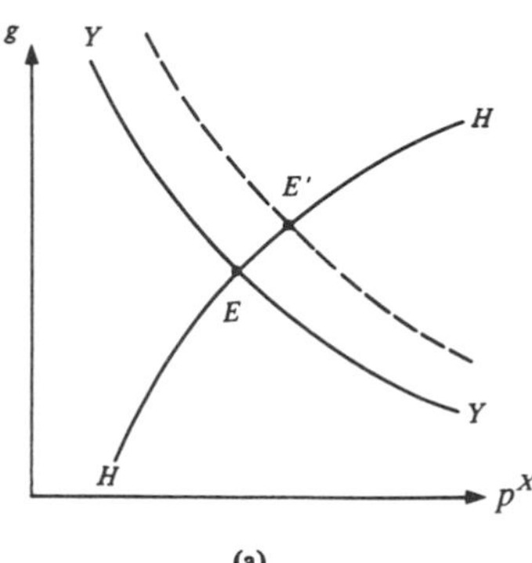

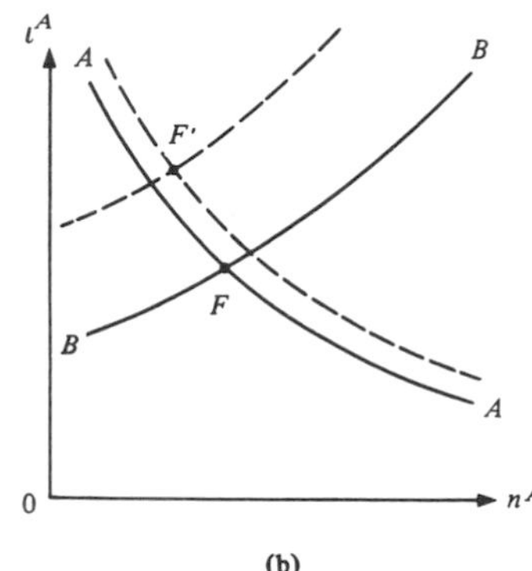

Figure 4

What then are the effects of the subsidy? The aggregate rate of technological progress increases, as does the rate of innovation in the subsidizing country. The latter claim can be seen from equation (19). We have seen that n^A falls and p^X rises, so the second term on the left-hand side must shrink. Then the first term must grow, and so $\iota^A n^A$ rises. It is also possible to show that the rate of innovation in the trade partner country (without any subsidy) declines. But the fact that n^A falls means that, in the long run, the country that subsidizes R&D will enjoy comparative advantage in a *smaller* range of high-technology products than before. This counterintuitive result can be understood as follows. Although country A undertakes more R&D with the subsidy than without, and country B less, researchers worldwide devote more attention to improving the products of country A than those of country B. On net, country A loses products in this process. Put differently, country A uses more of its skilled labor in the research lab when R&D is subsidized, and so less is available for manufacturing high-technology goods. At the same time, skilled labor in the trade partner country is released by the R&D sector, and so becomes available for production.[9]

This finding is particularly interesting in the light of the evidence that the Japanese government finances a much smaller fraction of private R&D than is typical for the advanced, industrial countries. My analysis suggests that this policy asymmetry contributes to an *expansion* in the size of the Japanese high-technology sector (or, at least, that part of it engaged in production). I record

PROPOSITION 4 An R&D subsidy raises the rate of innovation in the policy-active country, lowers the rate of innovation in the trade partner country, and raises the global rate of technological progress. The number of high-technology goods produced in the policy-active country declines.

Next I shall consider subsidies to production. It is sometimes alleged that Japan implicitly subsidizes the production of high-technology goods via the government's procurement practices. Other governments seemingly do likewise, especially where products with defense applications are concerned.

Let β be the ad valorem rate of subsidy to manufacturers of high-technology products in country A, again financed by lump-sum taxation. The introduction of such a subsidy modifies the equilibrium relationships in two ways. First, manufacturing costs in country A must exceed those in country B. Otherwise, researchers will prefer to target country B products for improvement, since the unsubsidized producers would be less formidable rivals when a research success is achieved. In place of (8), we have now

$$w^A a_{HX} + z^A a_{RX} = (1 + \beta)(w^B a_{HX} + z^B a_{RX}). \tag{22}$$

Second, the subsidy raises the profit rate for producers of high-tech products in country A, so that (10) becomes

$$\frac{(1 + \beta)(1 - \delta)s_y}{\alpha w^A} = \rho + \iota^A. \tag{23}$$

With these changes in the equilibrium system, there are again two modifications of the reduced form. In (20), the first term becomes $\alpha(1 - n^A)[(\rho + \iota^A)\gamma - \rho]$, where

$$\gamma = \left[1 + \beta - \frac{\beta\alpha a_{RY}\delta p^X(\rho + \iota^A)}{D(1 - \delta)s_x}\right]^{-1},$$

and p^X represents now the price paid by consumers for high-technology goods. Also, in (18), the term in the square brackets is replaced by

$$\left[a_{RY}\delta p^X - \frac{D(1 - \delta)s_x}{\alpha(\rho + g)}\right]\left(1 + \frac{1 - \gamma}{\gamma}n^A\right).$$

After some inspection, it becomes clear that the reduced form system with a production subsidy in place mirrors that for an R&D subsidy, but with $1 - \sigma$ replaced by γ. Since γ is an increasing function of β, it follows that the long-run effects of a subsidy to production of high-technology goods are just the *opposite* of those of a subsidy to research. Namely, we have

PROPOSITION 5 A production subsidy for high-technology goods reduces the rate of innovation in the policy active country, increases the rate of innovation in the trade partner country, and slows the global rate of technological progress. The number of high-technology goods manufactured in the policy-active country increases.

Intuitively, the subsidy has offsetting effects on the incentives for innovation. On the one hand, the higher prices received by producers of high-technology goods raise the profitability of quality improvements. On the other hand, the increased wage of skilled workers caused by the expansion of demand for these individuals in the manufacturing sector raises the cost of R&D. Evidently, the latter effect dominates.

We are interested, finally, in the long-run effects of trade policy. Recognizing that trade policies combine elements of a production subsidy and a consumption tax, it

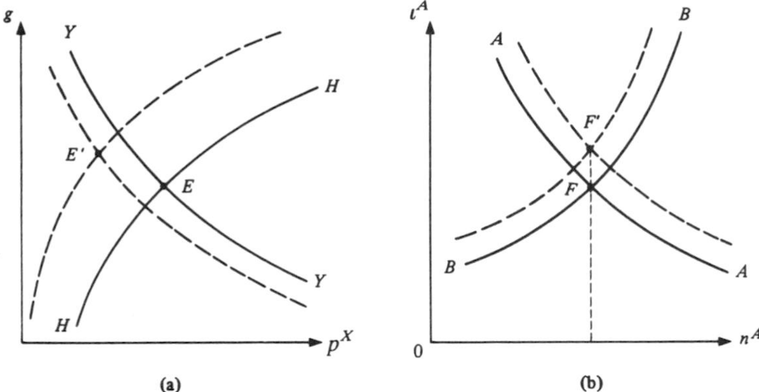

Figure 5

proves useful to consider first the effects of a consumption tax alone. This policy raises the price paid by consumers in country A for high-technology products. Let t be the rate of ad valorem taxation and let p^X represent now the price received by producers. Then consumers in country A pay $p^X(1 + t)$. Sales of each high-technology good are given now by $s_x[1 - tE^A/(1 + t)]/p^X$, where E^i is steady-state expenditure in country i, and $E^A + E^B = 1$ as before. This change affects (10), (15) and (16). In the reduced form we find all occurrences of s_x replaced by $s_x[1 - tE^A/(1 + t)]$, with the exception of the term $(1 - s_x)$ on the right-hand side of (18).

The effects of a small tax on consumption of high-technology goods from an initial position of laissez-faire are shown in figure 5. In panel (a), the HH and YY curves both shift leftward. However, for given g, the former curve shifts by more.[10] Thus, the tax causes the rate of innovation to rise and the relative price of high-technology goods to fall. Both the tax and the adjustment of p^X shift the AA and BB curves in panel (b) by equal (vertical) distances. It follows that a small tax on consumption of high-technology products increases the rate of innovation in both countries, while leaving the number of high-tech goods produced by each unchanged.

Turning to trade policy, I consider a small tariff on imports of all high-technology goods coupled with a small export subsidy for these goods at an equal ad valorem rate. This corresponds to a subsidy to production of high-technology products and an equal rate tax on consumption. The production subsidy expands the number of high-technology goods produced in the policy-active country, whereas the consumption tax has no effect on n^A. Accordingly, an import tariff cum export subsidy causes n^A to rise. The two policies have, as we have seen, offsetting effects on the rate of innovation. It turns out that, where domestic innovation is concerned, the effect of the production subsidy wins out: an import tariff cum export subsidy on high-technology products reduces the size of the local R&D sector. For the world as a whole, the effect of the consumption tax varies directly with the level of local consumption of high-technology goods, whereas the effect of the production subsidy varies with the scale of local production. By direct calculation we can prove that trade intervention increases the rate of global technological progress if and only if the policy-active country is a net importer of high-technology goods. The following proposition summarizes these findings.

PROPOSITION 6 A small tariff on imports of high-technology goods coupled with a small subsidy to exports of these goods at equal ad valorem rate expands the number of high-technology goods manufactured and exported by the policy-active country. The rate of technological progress falls in the policy-active country. It rises for the world as a whole if and only if this country imports high-technology products on net.

Notes

This paper was written while the author was a Visiting Scholar at the Institute for Monetary and Economic Studies, Bank of Japan. The theoretical model in this paper draws heavily on the author's ongoing collaboration with Elhanan Helpman of Tel Aviv University. The paper would not have been possible without his considerable input. The author is grateful to Hirochika Nishikawa for research assistance and to the National Science Foundation for partial financial support.

1. The basis for the model presented here is developed in Grossman and Helpman (1989a). It draws several building blocks from earlier work by Segerstrom, Anant, and Dinopoulos (1988), and Aghion and Howitt (1990).

2. The allocation of resources in the steady-state equilibrium does not depend upon whether capital is internationally mobile or not. For expositional convenience I present the model under the assumption that capital is mobile.

3. I do not allow for imitation here. In an equilibrium with factor-price equalization, such as that which arises below in a regime of free trade, costly imitation would never be undertaken. This is because, even if successful, an imitator stands to earn no profits in the resulting Bertrand equilibrium. We study imitation in a model of North-South trade in Grossman and Helpman (1989b).

4. In Grossman and Helpman (1989b) we provide industry leaders with a cost advantage in developing the next generation product. Then we may find active research departments in both leading and following firms in equilibrium.

5. We have already ensured that the market for each high-technology good clears by writing the quantity of output as $\delta s_x/c^X(w^i, z^i)$, which we know to be the demand for that product.

6. Point E must lie in the interior of the parallelogram O^ANO^BP, or else a steady-state equilibrium with incomplete specialization does not exist. This corresponds to a familiar proposition from static theories of trade, namely that factor-price equalization requires that countries' relative factor endowments not be "too" different.

7. In the absence of international capital mobility, the trade account must always balance. Then the trade pattern must be as described below.

8. This and other claims not explicitly proved in the text can be established by differentiating the complete system of equilibrium conditions. These calculations have been collected in an appendix that is available from the author.

9. It is possible to show, moreover, that these effects hold not only for the introduction of an R&D subsidy from an initial situation with $\sigma = 0$, but also for any increase in σ from an arbitrary initial value. Such an increase causes YY to shift up for given n^A, but the decline in n^A has an offsetting influence. Suppose that the latter dominated. Then p^X would fall, which would require a fall in w^B hence a rise in ι^B. But then (20) could not be satisfied, because all terms on the left-hand side would have increased. It follows that any increase in σ causes g and p^X to rise. The other implications follow then by the same arguments as in the text.

10. The HH curve shifts to the left by $E^Ap^X\,dt$. This fall in p^X leaves $s_x[1 - tE^A/(1 + t)]/p^X$ unchanged. It therefore causes the left-hand side of (18) to decline. It follows that the leftward shift of YY is smaller.

References

Aghion, Philippe, and Peter Howitt. 1990. A model of growth through creative destruction. National Bureau of Economic Research, working paper no. 3223.

Grossman, Gene M., and Elhanan Helpman. 1989a. Quality ladders in the theory of growth. Discussion Paper in Economics no. 148, Woodrow Wilson School of Public and International Affairs, Princeton University.

Grossman, Gene M., and Elhanan Helpman. 1989b. Quality ladders and product cycles. Discussion Paper in Economics no. 152, Woodrow Wilson School of Public and International Affairs, Princeton University.

Lee, Tom, and Louis L. Wilde. 1980. Market structure and innovation: A reformulation. *Quarterly Journal of Economics* 94:429–436.

Segerstrom, Paul S., T. C. A. Anant, and Elias Dinopoulos. 1988. A Schumpeterian model of the product life cycle. Mimeo, Michigan State University.

Name Index